ART AND THE REFORMATION

Frontispiece.]

THE CATHEDRAL OF CHARTRES FROM THE AIR.

ART AND THE
REFORMATION

By

G. George G. COULTON

ARCHON BOOKS
1969

TO

M. R. C.

First published 1928
Reprinted 1969 with permission of Cambridge University Press
in an unaltered and and unabridged edition

SBN: 208 00738 5
Library of Congress Catalog Card Number: 69-15789
Printed in the United States of America

PREFACE

THIS volume has grown out of Lowell Lectures delivered at Boston, Massachusetts, in the spring of 1923. It is now dedicated, with hearty gratitude, to those who did so much to lighten my burden of work in America, and to send me home with a still firmer belief in the future of that country. They will accept the book, I hope, as an honest attempt to get at ancient realities which are separated from us by a wider and deeper gulf than the Atlantic, but which can be grasped in their essence, even as transatlantic friendship can be reached, by good-will and patience and hard work.

> These things seem small and undistinguishable,
> Like far-off mountains turnèd into clouds,

and one man may guess aright, while another guesses wrong; but all have it in their power to pass, if they will, beyond the stage of merest guess-work.

In England, the book owes most of all to Professor W. R. Lethaby, who has not only taken the trouble of looking through my proofs, but has also helped me with invaluable advice and encouragement. I must further record my sincere gratitude, for very generous help towards the illustrations, to Mr. C. Symonds of Over and my elder daughter; to Mr. S. Smith of Lincoln, Mr. E. M. Beloe, Mr. A. Thomas Loyd, Mr. A. Gardner, Professors S. H. Reynolds and Theodore

Spencer, the Professor of Fine Art at Breslau, Mr. H. H. Brindley, and the King's Lynn Publicity Committee.

Here, as in the *Cambridge Studies in Medieval Life and Thought*, I shall be glad to publish in due time, on an errata-slip, all errors of actual fact which may be brought to my notice.

St. John's College, Cambridge.
  December, 1927.

CONTENTS

CONTENTS

APPENDIXES

LIST OF ILLUSTRATIONS

PLATES

xi

TEXT-FIGURES

PAGE

b

The reproduction of the Gokstad Ship is from " Britain's Sea Story "
(Oxford University Press), and the " Serpent beguiling Eve " comes
from Messrs. Cook and Wedderburn's edition of the " Works of
Ruskin " (Messrs. George Allen and Unwin). They appear here by
kind permission of the publishers.

AUTHORITIES

This list is not in any sense exhaustive, nor is it a bibliography. It is compiled merely for facilitating reference to books which are quoted, but not fully described in the footnotes.

Adderbury " Rectoria "—Oxfordshire Record Soc. vol. VIII, 1926, edited by T. F. Hobson.

A. L. K. G.—*Archiv f. Litt.—u. Kirchengesch. d. Mittelalters.* ed. Denifle & Ehrle, 1885– .

Aube—*Mémoires de la Société académique du département de l'Aube.* Troyes, v.d.

Baldwin Brown—G. Baldwin Brown, *Arts in Early England,* 1903.

Brutails—J. A. Brutails, *Deux chantiers bordelais* (1486–1521) (Extrait du *Moyen Âge* 1899–1901).

Burbure—*Notice sur les auteurs de l'ancien jubé à Bourbourg,* par Léon de Burbure. Lille 1864 (Extrait du *Bulletin du Comité flamand de France,* tome III.).

Cennino—*The Book of the Art of Cennino Cennini,* Christina H. I. Herringham, 1899.

Chapman *Sacrist Rolls*—F. R. Chapman. *Sacrist Rolls of Ely.* Privately printed, 1907.

Cooke-Baker—Brit. Mus. MS. Add. 23,198, probably dating from about 1480, printed by M. Cooke in *History and Articles of Masonry,* 1861.

Crouch—Joseph Crouch, *Puritanism and Art,* 1910.

Cunningham—*Notes on the Organisation of the Mason's Craft in England,* by W. Cunningham, F.B.A. (Pub. Brit. Acad. vol. VI.).

Dejob—Ch. Dejob, *De l'influence du Concile de Trente sur la littérature et les beaux-arts chez les peuples catholiques.*

Didron. *Annales.*—A. N. Didron, *Annales archéologiques.* Paris, 1844.

Didron. *Icon.*—A. N. Didron, *Christian Iconography*, E. H. J. Millington (Bohn's Libraries, 1886).

Edelmaier—*Das Kloster Schönau*, by R. Edelmaier, Heidelberg, 1915.

Gould—R. F. Gould, *History of Freemasonry*, 1883.

Halliwell—J. O. Halliwell, *Early Hist. of Freemasonry in England*, 1844.

Heideloff—Carl Heideloff, *Die Bauhütte des Mittelalters in Deutschland*, Nürnberg, 1844.

Hirn—Yrjö Hirn, *The Sacred Shrine*, Macmillan, 1912.

Janner—F. Janner, *Die Bauhütten d. Mittelalters*, Leipzig, 1876.

Jarrett—Bede Jarrett, O.P., *Social Theories of the M. Ages* (Benn, 1926).

Kendon—Frank Kendon, *Mural Paintings in English Churches during the Middle Ages* (John Lane, 1923).

Kirby Muxloe—A. Hamilton Thompson, *The Building Accts. of K. M. Castle*, in *Trans. Leics. Arch. Soc.* vol. XI., p. 193.

K. K.=Werner Sombart, *Krieg und Kapitalismus*, Leipzig, 1913.

Landucci—*A Florentine Diary*, by Luca Landucci, tr. A. D. Jervis, 1927.

Lefèvre-Pontalis—*Répertoire des architectes &c.*, par E. Lefèvre-Pontalis, Caen, 1912.

Lenoir. *Arch. Mon.*—A. Lenoir, *Architecture monastique*, 1852.

Lethaby. *Craftsmen*—W. R. Lethaby, *Westminster Abbey and the King's Craftsmen*, 1906.

Lethaby. *Med. Art*—W. R. Lethaby, *Medieval Art*, 1904.

Lethaby. *Westminster I*—W. R. Lethaby, *Westminster Abbey and the King's Craftsmen*, 1906.

Lethaby. *Westminster II*—W. R. Lethaby, *Westminster Abbey Re-examined*, 1925.

Life in Medieval Europe—G. G. Coulton, *Life in Medieval Europe*, a reprint of the *Medieval Garner* rëarranged in separate volumes by the Camb. Univ. Press.

L. K.=Werner Sombart, *Luxus und Kapitalismus*, Leipzig, 1913.

Mâle I—Émile Mâle. *L'art religieux du XIIe siècle en France*, Paris, 1922.

Mâle II—Émile Mâle. *L'art religieux du XIIIe siècle en France*, Paris, 1898.

Mâle III—Émile Mâle. *L'art religieux de la fin du moyen âge en France*, Paris, 1908.

Med. Build. Doc.—A. Hamilton Thompson, *Medieval Building Documents* (Presidential Address, in *Proc. Somerset Arch. Soc.* vol. LXVI., 1920).

Medieval Garner—G. G. Coulton, *A Medieval Garner*, 1908.

Merrifield—*Original Treatises on the Arts of Painting*, by Mrs. Merrifield, 1849.

M. K.=Werner Sombart, *Der Moderne Kapitalismus*, vol. II., pt. ii., Munich and Leipzig, 1919.

Molanus—Joannes Molanus, *De Historia SS. Imaginum et Picturarum*, ed. J. N. Paquot, Louvain, 1721.

Mortet—V. Mortet, *Recueil de textes relatifs à l'hist. de l'architecture, &c.*, 1911.

Müntz—E. Müntz, *Les arts à la cour des papes*. This came out in four instalments ; the first three were published in *Bib. des écoles françaises d'Athènes et de Rome*, in 1878, 1879, and 1882 respectively ; the last by Leroux in 1898. I quote the volumes by their respective dates.

Quicherat—*Mélanges d'archéologie et d'histoire*, par Jules Quicherat. Série II, 1886.

Renan and Leclerc—*Discours sur l'état des lettres. . . . Discours sur l'état des beaux-arts . . . au 14e siècle* (reprinted from *Hist. litt. de la France*, second ed. 1865).

Riley—H. T. Riley, *Memorials of London, &c.*, 1868.

Schlosser, Beiträge—Julius v. Schlosser, *Beiträge zur Kunstgeschichte, u.s.w.*, in *Sitzungsberichte d. phil. hist. Classe d. K. Akad. in Wien*, vol. 123, 1891.

Schlosser, Quellenbuch—J. v. Schlosser, *Quellenbuch z. Kunstgeschichte, u.s.w.*, Vienna, Graeser, 1896.

Schnaase—K. J. F. Schnaase, *Gesch. d. bild. Künste*, 1843–

Social Life in Britain—G. G. Coulton, *Social Life in Britain from the Conquest to the Reformation*, Camb. Univ. Press, 1918.

Test Eborac.=*Testamenta Eboracensia*, Surtees. Soc., 1836–69.

Westlake, *Last Days*—H. F. Westlake, *Westminster Abbey, the Last Days of the Monastery*, 1921.

Willis and Clark—R. Willis and J. W. Clark, *Architectural History of the University of Cambridge*, 1886.

Wulf—M. de Wulf, *Philosophy and Civilization in the Middle Ages* (1922).

ERRATA AND ADDITIONS

Page	*for*	*read*
4, line 4 from end	this	the
41, line 10	what	which
81, note 1	later	lower
83, note 4	tib	tit
87, line 8	Swynnow	Swynow
104, line 13	commence	conmence
171, note 1	Avignon	Aix
203, note 1	Josas	Visites de Josas
207, note 2	tib	tit
249, note 2	Abbeilley	Abbeville
265, line 24	Fungar	Fungai
292, line 11	Annunciation	Salutation
353, line 3 from end	ptoj	pro j
360, line 12	quodcwmque	quodcumque
385, line 5	anathemana	anathema
457, note 4	E.G.T.S.	E.E.T.S.
470, line 1	statues	statutes
501, line 21	Attila's	Alarick's

For an important reference to Chapter II, which to some extent should modify my conclusions, I am indebted to Mr. C. H. Smyth. He refers me to Bp. Barlowe's *Dialogue on the Lutheran Factions* (1531), pp. 87–8 of Lunn's reprint (1897).

Page 117, line 11 : By an oversight, my copyist here omitted the following passage from Cennino :

" Chap. 28.—*How, more than from Masters, you should draw continually from nature.*

Remember that the most perfect guide that you can

have and the best course (helm), is the triumphal gateway of drawing from nature : it is before all other examples, and with a bold heart you may always trust to it, especially when you begin to have some judgment in design. And continue always, and without fail, to draw something every day, not too little to be enough, and it will do you excellent service."

Pages 152–3 : I am now convinced, by comparison with other examples in Burgundy and Switzerland, that these are not personal-marks but position-marks, indicating the thickness of the stone and therefore the course into which it may be laid.

Page 166 : A later and longer study of Melrose has convinced me reluctantly that this survey is too imperfect, taking no account of the height from the ground at which the marks occur ; yet that is an essential point for correct calculations.

Page 247 : Professor Baldwin Brown points out that this quotation from Venantius Fortunatus really goes back two centuries farther, to Paulinus of Nola.

Page 279 : These toothache caricatures occur also at Snettisham (Norf.) as a gargoyle, and on a miserere at Sherborne Minster.

Page 337 : Professor Baldwin Brown writes : " The story is in itself perfectly true and attested by contemporary records ; but it was played not at Florence but at Siena, and the painter was the Sienese Duccio. the picture his great altarpiece for the Duomo."

Page 485, line 3 : Honorius's actual words are here accidentally omitted : they run : " Almost all [of the various classes of artificers] are damned ; for whatsoever they do, they do with the greatest fraud " (Migne, *P.L.*, vol. 172, col. 1148, c).

ART AND THE REFORMATION

CHAPTER I

INTRODUCTORY

MY object in this volume is to trace very briefly the rise and decay of Medieval Art, and thence to argue first that its origin was less definitely religious than is commonly supposed; secondly, that its decay was gradual—a logical and natural consequence of its evolution—and lastly, that its deathblow came not so much from the Reformation as from that general transformation of the western intellect which we call the Renaissance. The majority of disputes and misunderstandings arise from confusion of thought on one side or the other, or on both. Let me clearly state, therefore, that in this book, when I use the word Art, I confine myself mainly to architecture and its subsidiary arts during the Middle Ages and the early Reformation period. Music no doubt has a real importance of its own; but I do not think it would materially affect the problem, and I cannot speak of it with knowledge. By art, therefore, except where otherwise defined, I mean Romanesque and Gothic Art. *Religion*, again, I shall use in a similarly restricted sense, confining myself to the Christian religion as conceived (to take two rough dates) between A.D. 1000 and 1600. And I must beg my readers to keep these two ideas of Art and Christianity consistently apart in their own minds, except where facts compel us to deal with both together. Further, and most especially, I beg them to remember that all full religion is intellectual as well as emotional: only in this completeness of emotional and intellectual assent can it get anything

like a complete and permanent hold on any society.
That has been too much forgotten, I think, by some of
the most ambitious writers on this subject, who write
temperamentally as partisans, and seem to forget that the
average man cannot altogether stifle his intellect.

It is more than forty years since one of the ablest
of English churchmen—C. J. Vaughan, whose memory
many men have reason to bless—put into my hands
a little book by one whom he described as the greatest
living preacher in the English language—Bishop
Phillips Brooks of Boston.[1] There I found a story which
has stuck in my memory ever since. " I remember "
(writes Phillips Brooks) " going years ago with an intelligent friend to hear a great orator lecture. The discourse
was rich, thoughtful, glowing, and delightful. As we
came away, my companion seemed meditative. By and
by he said, ' Did you see where his power lay ? ' I felt
unable to analyse and epitomize in an instant such a
complex result, and meekly I said, ' No; did you ? '
' Yes,' he replied briskly; ' I watched him, and it is in
the double motion of his hand. When he wanted to
solemnize and calm and subdue us, he turned the palm
of his hand down; when he wanted to elevate and
inspire us, he turned the palm of his hand up. That
was it.' . . . He was no fool, but he was an imitator.
He was looking for a single secret for a multifarious
effect." So there is a whole school of writers at the
present day who attribute to medieval religion practically
all that is of value in medieval art. Epigrammatic
utterances of Goethe and Victor Hugo and Ruskin—
epigrams with that strong alloy of exaggeration, and
therefore of falsehood, which is often necessary for
making a brief generalization into current coin—have
been repeated and still further exaggerated from mouth
to mouth in our generation, to the neglect of the actual
records of the Middle Ages. It is time that this should

---

[1] *Lectures on Preaching* (Macmillans). In the 1903 edition this quotation occurs on p. 167.

cease, and that we should emphasize what contemporary writers of the Middle Ages have actually to tell us on the subject of medieval religion and art in their mutual relations. Religion and art are indeed natural concomitants; they do indeed owe much to common sources, and are constantly acting and reacting upon each other. It is true that Roman Catholic religion and Gothic art were at their zenith in the thirteenth century; it is true that in the sixteenth century the dominant religion received a staggering blow and Gothic art was almost killed. But we must not here take the line of least intellectual resistance, and assume that we can find a single secret for the complicated process of Gothic decay; and it is the object of this book, not indeed to explain away the connexion between the outward aspect of a Gothic cathedral and the soul of the men who built it or who worshipped in it, but to disentangle the truth from the mass of writings which confuse between religion and art. For I am convinced that this confusion does honour neither to art nor to religion. All that was best in medieval religion was too good to need extraneous (and perhaps incongruous) adornment. If the faith of St. Bernard and St. Francis does not convince by its own merits, we shall get no converts worth having by advertising these men (so to speak) under the name of another firm.

Art implies a certain equilibrium between economic requirements and the farther refinements of a leisured life. Useful things are ugly at first, because the eye is distressed by their want of completeness and proportion: they will be improved upon to-morrow, and altered again next day; and we recognize instinctively that they are in a state of transition, and therefore the eye has no abiding satisfaction in contemplating them; they look clumsy and untidy. The first plough was just a ragged branch torn from a tree—as untidy as those which the children tear off from the trees in a park and leave lying about. Yet, many centuries ago, the plough had reached an equilibrium; the medieval plough had become as exactly adapted to overcoming the resistance of the earth as any merely wooden instrument could be; here is a Norfolk plough, practically medieval, seen in its field by John Sell Cotman a century ago, and seized upon for its picturesque qualities as a subject for one of his soft-ground etchings. Again, the primitive dug-out canoes, as made by the lowest savages, were just clumsy and ugly—

A NORFOLK PLOUGH.

almost as untidy-looking as these heaps of derelict tin cans which lie about in neglected corners of our cities. But when, after we know not how many centuries, the lines of ships had been gradually fashioned so as to reach something like the maximum of utility—so as to present the least possible resistance to the waves—then they became supremely beautiful; whether we consider this Greek ship on a vase of 500 B.C., or the Gokstad Viking ship of A.D. 900. And beauty of line, once learnt, is never forgotten. The same men who shaped that

Viking ship to rule the waves, fashioned even the details of it with the same commanding grace ; here, from that same boat, are the horses' heads that form the ends of

A GOKSTAD SHIP.

the captain's seat ; we may compare them with the heads on the couch of Tut-ankhamen. Our present Cunarders and White Star liners are, under water, as beautiful as the Greek ship ; it is only the floating hotel above water that is ugly, because it is hesitating and imperfect ; and, at its present stage, it is inspired as much by snobbery as by utility ; men have not yet learnt to get the maximum of house comfort and of balance, together with the minimum resistance to wind and weather. Some day, when those problems have been worked out to the extreme of perfection which

BENCH ENDS FROM GOKSTAD SHIP.

steel permits, then even the upper part of a Cunarder will be made beautiful, or we shall have flying-machines comparable in grace to birds.

Gothic art, then, attained such an equilibrium as this ; in its own way it is almost perfect, like Greek art of the time of Pericles, and Japanese art of the best period. The thirteenth century attained to what seemed for a moment, to most people, a stable equilibrium in faith ; that is the moment in the history of Europe when most people were willing to accept the same religious dogmas without too great sense of incongruity. Not as a direct consequence of this faith, but by a similar evolution of society, architecture reached about the same time its completest conformity to the needs of its environment. Great churches were wanted, and (what is too often forgotten) great castles also ;[1] and masons and carpenters had gradually risen to this greatness. It was a time of equilibrium, but not of immobility ; a time of constant vibration, pulsation, and motion ; but the changes as yet were gradual, not catastrophic. The workmen had gradually evolved buildings which were beautiful in their supreme conformity to the evident needs of their environment ; that was unconscious art. Thence they now proceeded to conscious art, conscious ornament, the leisurely shaping of details. But this thirteenth century had not in fact reached quite such an equilibrium as it coveted. There was a great deal more scepticism in that century than is generally realized by modern historians ; material and economic requirements were changing also ; and the change became still more marked in succeeding centuries. The same causes which affected men's material and spiritual needs worked upon their art ; therefore, already before 1350, before that Black Death which is too often invoked to excuse the changes in later medieval society, Gothic art was on the downward grade. The thirteenth

---

[1] This is very fully recognized by Prof. G. Baldwin Brown, whose command of medieval documents, and general accuracy in their use, give great value to all he writes.

century was a time which could neither be retained nor recalled; its very greatness lies rather in its struggles than in its immobility. It was like that wonderful moment in a summer dawn, when the first light of day grows and broadens upon a world still fresh with all the dews of night; no power on earth could have kept it in that same freshness until noonday; and no power in heaven would wish to keep it so; God wants the world to move on and on.

The roots of Gothic art are in Byzantine, and especially in Justinian's great buildings at Constantinople from about A.D. 530 onwards.[1] From Byzantine, architectural traditions spread along the trade routes; the so-called " Lombardic " of Italy, the " Romanesque " of Germany and France, the " Norman " of England, all derive more or less directly from this Byzantine source. It is significant that, to the end of the Middle Ages, one of the commonest words for a mason was the Greek *lathomus* or *latomus* (λατόμος). But these less skilled masons of the comparatively barbarous West, with their more primitive methods and their rougher materials, had a great deal to learn by bitter experience. When, in the eleventh century, a great building era set in—the era of that " white robe of churches " which began to cover the whole West, especially under the influence of the Cluniac revival in monastic life—then the engineering problems involved in the construction of these great monastic churches taxed the builders' resources to the utmost, and, often, even beyond. As Bishop Creighton put it with characteristic incisiveness, whenever we are shown over an English cathedral, we should begin by asking our guide when it was that the central tower fell; for nearly all have fallen, at one time or another. An imperfectly civilized people was gradually learning, by a path of gropings and failures and half-successes, to rival in architecture the achievements of Graeco-Roman

[1] See especially Prof. W. R. Lethaby's article in the third volume of the *Cambridge Medieval History*, and pp. 80 ff. of his *Medieval Art*.

civilization; just as they were gradually struggling upwards from creeds of nature-worship and the practice of infanticide and private vendettas into something like the order of modern society. Both processes, naturally enough, ran on roughly parallel lines, growing side by side and culminating very nearly in the same age; for each marked a different side of what was in effect the same social-religious movement. In proportion as Christianity won ground over heathenism, the Christian priesthood and the Christian temples became richer and more commanding; again, just as pre-Christian ideas clung stubbornly to men's minds and remained to leaven the conquering religion, so also many pre-Christian motives leavened Christian art. In religious thought, as in art, there was a long period of accumulation and tentative experience. The first great book of systematization, Gratian's volume, which became the foundation of Church Law, was called by its author *The Concordance of Discordant Canons*; it attempted to arrange and cement the disorderly mass of traditional material into one complete and sufficiently harmonious structure. It is as rude and primitive as an early Romanesque church, but essentially as solid for its own purpose; like many Romanesque churches, it has stood to the present day.[1] Abailard a few years before Gratian, and Abailard's pupil Peter Lombard a few years later, set themselves to the task of systematizing the scattered and disparate biblical and patristic texts upon which the main Christian dogmas had been founded. Peter Lombard's *Sentences* became such a standard and popular work in the theological schools that later university scholars complained of it as having ousted the direct study of the Bible. Then a great constructive genius realized how this intellectual engineering could be carried a whole step farther. St. Thomas Aquinas brought to the problem a profound study not only of the Bible and the Fathers, but of

[1] Or, at least, till yesterday; the recent codification of Canon Law by a Papal Commission may be said to have rendered Gratian obsolete.

Aristotle also ; and this gave him an advance not merely in arithmetical but in geometrical progression.[1] It is this complete grasp of all the existing metaphysical material and exploitation of all its possibilities, which puts his *Summa Theologica* as far in advance of Peter Lombard, or even of Alexander of Hales and Albert the Great, as Gothic architecture was beyond the Romanesque or the transitional phase. Medieval thought in Aquinas reaches something like an equilibrium,[2] just as architecture does in the almost contemporary structures of Amiens and Reims.[3]

For, though medieval architecture blossomed out to its full as suddenly as scholastic philosophy, and even earlier, yet this was the climax of an equally slow development. Just as sixteenth-century England, until then so backward, suddenly assimilated its inheritance in the Bible and in classical antiquity, and burst out into the richest drama in Europe, so also, in medieval France, the most backward of the provinces came suddenly into the heritage of others' experience ; thus freshness of outlook combined with rich tradition to produce a most

[1] Cf. Browning's "Abt Vogler : "

> And I know not if, save in this, such gift be allowed to man
> That out of three sounds he frame, not a fourth sound, but
> a star.

[2] For the purely literary side of this equilibrium, see pp. 19 ff. and 48 ff. of Prof. H. J. C. Grierson's Leslie Stephen Lecture, *Classical and Romantic* (Camb. Univ. Press, 1923). The philosophic side is treated in Prof. M. de Wulf's *Philosophy and Civilization in the Middle Ages* (1922, pp.18, 268 ; a book to be read with caution whenever the author is not on purely philosophical ground).

[3] St. Thomas was working at the *Summa* until his death in 1274. Laon is generally cited as the first complete cathedral in definitely Gothic style ; it was probably begun about 1160 and the west front finished by 1200. " Reims opens the period of perfect maturity " (Lethaby) ; it was begun in 1211, the choir was finished in 1241, and the great porches about 10 years later. The west front of Amiens was finished by about 1240, and the whole building was practically finished in 1269. It had been begun in 1218 ; and we must bear in mind that the design of a cathedral dates mainly from its commencement and not from its completion.

abundant harvest.[1] The greatest Romanesque buildings had been predominantly monastic, expressing the wealth and influence of the monastic corporations. In the twelfth century there was a great movement towards civic freedom, corresponding to the increase of wealth and ambition among the trading classes : the bishops could now appeal to the citizen for as much money as the monks had commanded, or even for more ; the cathedrals rivalled or outdid the monastic churches. We must not exaggerate this natural rivalry, but we cannot overlook it altogether ; Viollet-le-Duc is right, in the main, when he insists upon the non-monastic spirit in which the great French cathedrals were built. For a time, at least, the populations were kindled to an almost boundless enthusiasm for these great buildings which appealed equally to religious faith and to human pride ; [2] the buildings done between 1150 and 1250 were quite comparable in cubic mass to the Cluniac " white robe of churches," and incomparably superior in artistic value. Especially remarkable was the progress of the Île de France. This province, though the nucleus of the French Kingdom, was comparatively unimportant until the time of Philip Augustus, who, during his long reign, made territorial acquisitions which enormously increased the political importance and the economic prosperity of his hereditary dominion. The Île de France was now one of the most prosperous provinces in Europe ; Paris was the most important of European capitals with the possible exception of Rome ; and in living thought it far surpassed Rome ; its university was incontestably supreme in theology and philosophy. It was poor in churches ; all its cathedrals were ripe for rebuilding ; it had the ambition, the energy, and the material resources for an effort

---

[1] I follow here what seems the soundest theory as to the causes of this sudden efflorescence. But my main argument is independent of this theory ; concerning the efflorescence itself, and its main lines of evolution, no doubt seems possible.

[2] See ch. xvii here below.

that should outdo all previous efforts ; and, whether by fortunate chance or in obedience to the law of supply and demand, the architects showed a living originality worthy of the university itself. Villard de Honnecourt's notebook shows that these men discussed their own technical problems as keenly as any scholastic disputant.[1] The reigns of Philip and his two successors show a quite unrivalled series of Gothic edifices, not only in great cities but sometimes in small villages, scattered over the Île de France proper and the adjoining territories. The characteristics distinguishing this matured style from its predecessors have been variously reckoned by different writers, as we might find many different enumerations of the features which differentiate one animal species from another ; yet the typical Romanesque church and the typical Gothic are as unmistakably different as the horse is from the cow. Perhaps the most satisfactory description is Enlart's [2] : " The Gothic style has three characteristic elements—the pointed vault, the flying buttress, and an entirely new system of ornament, drawn not from tradition but from direct study of nature. These elements need not all be there ; some schools of Gothic have no flying buttresses, and many buildings have no vaulted roof." Upon this Prof. Lethaby comments : " This is a *Cathedral* definition, not a *Castle* one ; a vast building one, not a small. Vaults and buttresses were in a way accidental. An ivory carving is as ' Gothic ' as a cathedral." But Gothic is the style which, for the first time, mastered the problem of the vault by introducing the flying buttress as a mechanical device, and by turning it to artistic purposes. This, in fact, is characteristic of all the best Gothic, that its ornamentation is mainly structural. The main effect comes from the right proportions and dispositions of such essential and necessary features as doors, windows, arches, pillars with their capitals, and buttresses ; if every statue were torn down from Notre-

---

[1] See ch. vi here below.

[2] *Manuel d'archéologie française*, vol. i (1902), pp. 434-5.

Dame, and every leaf and flower of its carvings defaced, it would still be a very noble building. We can thus trace a great and inspiring stream of cultural progress, as Europe gradually emerged from the welter of feudalism and private wars into greater states, greater general conceptions; greater wars, it is true, at intervals, but on the whole far less human slaughter and oppression; far more peace and prosperity both for rich and poor; comparative security for traders and writers and artists; growing population and increasing wealth. Greater and greater churches and castles were needed; masons and carpenters rose to those more insistent demands, until they had reached the limits of possibility in their own day; until they were prepared to do all that could be done with the ordinary stone, the ordinary timber, the ordinary numbers of workmen and the ordinary wooden machinery of an age in which capitalism was only beginning. Thus that earlier half-conscious art which, starting from utilitarian necessities, had gradually produced buildings exactly conformable with the needs of the time, grew into a fully-conscious art which set itself at leisure to shape every detail of these massive buildings into forms pleasing to the eye and suggestive of the highest human aspirations. The ornamentation was still essentially structural. Here there is substantial unanimity among writers who differ widely on other points; Gothic art began to decline as soon as ornamentation became superficial rather than structural; rather a veneer than an essential constituent of the building itself. This is recognised in detail even by those who forget it in the course of their general argument, and who ignore the fact that decadence in art set in long before those religious changes to which they attribute it. When we look at the actual dates, we cannot even invoke the easy fallacy of *post hoc, ergo propter hoc*, in justification of a theory which imports religious controversies into art history. The Gothic style was definitely past its best even before Wyclif appeared; and that traffic in indulgences which brought Luther forward

OPEN-WORK VAULTING AT BRISTOL.

OPEN-WORK VAULTING AT BRISTOL

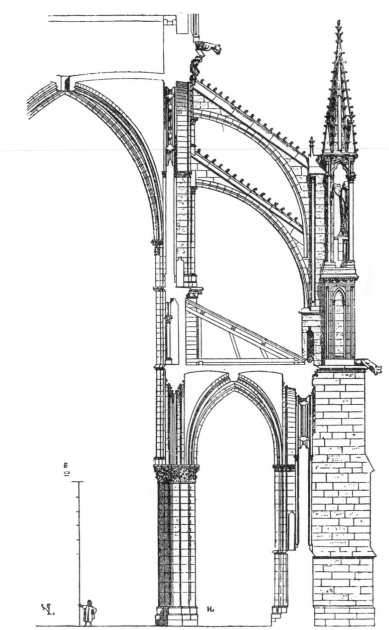

SECTION OF THE CATHEDRAL OF REIMS.
Showing how its mechanism is turned to ornament.

was in favour not of a Gothic building, but of that new
Classical architecture which was sweeping the old Gothic
away as fast as popes and princes and nobles could raise
money for rebuilding those out-of-date piles which had
satisfied their medieval ancestors.

It is very generally admitted, then, that Gothic art
was at its best between 1180 and 1280, to choose a single
century in round numbers. The transition from this
age, in which the ornament was structural, to an age in
which it was superficial, is even more notable in England
than in France; most marked of all, perhaps, in Italy,
where the Franciscan revival turned many of the churches
into great preaching-halls with little elaboration of door
or of window-tracery, but with vast flat spaces of interior
wall for the painter to work upon. In England, even at
the best time, the west front of Wells may be condemned,
in comparison with the great French façades, as being
scarcely more than a flat screen for the exhibition of the
statues. At Lichfield (about 1275) this is far more
marked; here, even the deep buttresses of Wells have
almost disappeared. And if, with Ruskin, we are obliged
to criticize Strassburg as "stiff and ironworky," what
must we say to the west front of Winchester? Of all
the qualities which are rightly claimed as giving glory to
Gothic, is there not less in this Winchester façade than
in an average good façade of the Renaissance? Is there
not a wider gulf, here, between Notre-Dame and Winchester than between Winchester and St. Paul's, even if
we judge on the most orthodox Gothic principles?[1]
How, then, did this come about?

So far as England is concerned, this is one of the
romances of art-history. While France and other
countries still confined themselves almost entirely to

[1] Here Prof. Lethaby writes: "No, one is still *custom*, the other is
learning," and I dare not let my text stand without registering this
criticism, together with the fact that he feels I do not do full justice
to the west front of Winchester. Yet, on the other hand, I feel bound
to register my personal impression.

geometrical tracery for window decoration, that is, to permutations and combinations of two main elements, the circle and the pointed arch, England evolved from this, in the early fourteenth century, a system of flowing tracery, of delicate labyrinthine sinuous lace-work in

THE BISHOP'S EYE, LINCOLN.

stone. Here, at its best, we find something of the inexhaustible interest that there always is in the swirls and eddies of a rapid river; the eye wanders from curve to curve with the same pleasure that the hand feels in stroking a piece of velvet or a cat's back; we have here the fulfilment of Goethe's " sehe mit fühlendem Blick ";

and even the unmusical soul may catch something of Milton's musical inspiration—

> Many a winding bout
> Of linked sweetness long drawn out ;
> With wanton heed and giddy cunning
> The melting *line* through mazes running,
> Untwisting all the chains that tie
> The hidden soul of harmony.

At the same time, there was a great exuberance of leaf and flower work, closely copied from nature. But all this ornament was already superficial in comparison with the best that had preceded it ; it may be said that the sculptor of the leafage at Southwell was thinking in one plane, while his predecessor in the best work of Lincoln or of Westminster triforium had thought in two. Moreover, the cliché began to come in, as we shall see in the case of Bristol (Chapter XI). Before the Black Death, which is too often invoked as the cause of movements which, at most, it only hastened, there was a marked tendency to substitute elaboration of surface ornament for grandeur of design ; and then a sudden and dramatic political revolution brought with it, incidentally, an equally dramatic change in the masons' lodge.

Edward II was murdered at Berkeley Castle in 1327. His private and public life had been far from exemplary ; but many people had political reasons for regretting him, and still stronger reasons for disliking his enemies, the Queen and Mortimer. In the Middle Ages, popular opinion often found a characteristic expression under such circumstances as these ; the dead man was worshipped as a saint, and miracles duly followed at his tomb. Thomas, Earl of Lancaster, Edward's great enemy, had been a mere self-seeking politician ; but, when Edward caught and beheaded him, then the anti-royal party worshipped at Thomas's tomb.[1] They were now

---

[1] For these popular canonizations by political parties, see p. 311 of my *Chaucer and his England*, and p. 201 of *Social Life in Britain from the Conquest to the Reformation*.

WINCHESTER CATHEDRAL, WEST FRONT.

victorious; it was Edward who was now the political
martyr; Edward's tomb became a pilgrimage shrine far
more popular than Lancaster's had ever been; and this
new cult, as chance would have it, gave birth to a new
architectural style. This will be best understood from
a few quotations from the Chronicle of Gloucester Abbey.[1]
" In the time of this abbot [John Thoky], King Edward II
came to Gloucester and was honourably entertained by
the abbot and convent. As he sat at table in the abbot's
hall, and noted how the Kings his predecessors were
painted there, he asked the abbot in jest whether his own
portrait should be added to theirs, or no. To whom the
abbot replied, rather in the spirit of prophecy than in
that of jest, that he hoped he would have King Edward II
in a more honourable place than this; as indeed it came
to pass. For, after the King's death, his venerable body
was refused by certain monasteries hard by; to wit,
St. Augustine's at Bristol, St. Mary's at Kingswood, and
St. Aldhelm's at Malmesbury, for fear of Roger de
Mortimer and Queen Isabella and their accomplices.
Yet abbot Thoky fetched him from Berkeley Castle in
his own chariot, sumptuously adorned and painted with
the arms of our monastery, and brought him to Gloucester,
where the abbot and all the convent received him honourably in their solemn robes, with a procession of the whole
city, and buried him in our church, in the north aisle,
hard by the high altar." Thoky's successor, John Wigmore, was not only an art lover but an artist, " who took
much delight in divers arts, so that he himself very often
wrought in them, and surpassed many different workmen
in divers arts, not only in mechanical work but in weaving.[2]
In his reign [1329-1337] began the offerings of the faithful
and the abbot's devotion to King Edward, buried in our

[1] Published in the Rolls Series, 1863. The extracts given here are
from pp. 44-48.

[2] " Tam in opere mechanico quam in textura." It is just possible
that this may mean " not only in actual execution of detail, but also in
designing."

C

church; so that, within a few years, so great was the
concourse of people that our city of Gloucester could
scarce contain the multitudes which flocked thither from
divers cities, towns, and villages of England; so that the
abbot completed St. Andrew's aisle,[1] from top to bottom,
within the six years of his prelacy, from the offerings at
that tomb." Wigmore was succeeded by Adam de
Staunton, " in whose time the great vault of the choir
was built, at great and sumptuous expense, with it stalls
on the prior's side, from the offerings of the faithful who
flocked to the tomb; for common opinion hath it that,
if all the oblations there made were spent upon the
church, it might easily have been rebuilt anew; so great
in those days were the offerings of great and rich men, in
the shape of gold brocade and other things of price,[2]
that a hundred silk and gold brocades were sold at a small
price, both of best quality and of such as had been well
worn. In those same days King Edward III, son of the
dead King, having been tossed well-nigh unto shipwreck
at sea, and having been saved by his prayers to his dead
father, offered a ship of gold; and another which he had
vowed in his devotion was redeemed, at the prayer of the
abbot and convent, at the price of a hundred pounds.[3]
The other jewels which hang there by the ship were given
by others; his firstborn, Edward Prince of Wales, gave a
gold cross of great price, wherein was enclosed a particle
of the True Cross; and the brooch with that precious
stone called *ruby* was given by the King's sister, Queen of
Scotland, and daughter to the dead King of our tomb;
and the golden heart and ear were given by Queen

[1] I.e. the south transept. St. Paul's aisle was the north transept.

[2] *Jocalibus*, a word which includes not only jewels but plate and valuables
of all kinds in small bulk.

[3] A sum which would have defrayed the wages of forty masons for two
years; see J. E. T. Roger's *Hist. Agric. and Prices*, vol. 1, p. 317. The
storm here referred to is told by Walsingham (*Hist. Ang.* R.S. vol. i,
p. 253) under the year 1341: " On his return from Brittany he suffered
vast discomfort from a tempest at sea, which was said to have been conjured
up by the necromancers of the French king."

Philippa; and divers other lords and ladies offered divers other oblations, whether in silver or in silver-gilt." The north transept alone, as the chronicler tells us on a later page, cost altogether £781 os. 2d., " as appeareth in the account-rolls of the aforesaid work."

One sentence here is most significant; it tells us that the money actually spent was not, in fact, sufficient to " rebuild the church anew." But it was sufficient to alter its whole outward appearance; to drape (so to speak) this old Norman building in a new mantle of outward ornament. There was already in this west country a school of clever and rather eccentric artists, who were playing tricks in stone, and especially imitating methods which belong more properly to woodwork, with its long and comparatively rectilinear grain. They had vaulted, or were vaulting, parts of what is now Bristol Cathedral with filagree arches in imitation of open wooden roof-work; a triumph of technical skill at the expense of artistic propriety. Similar approximations of stonework to open woodwork may be seen in the tomb-canopies at Gloucester and at Tewkesbury. Such a mason (it may be surmised with something like certainty) was called in to advise at Gloucester; he undertook to reduce the existing church to its elementary structural framework, and to cover this throughout with a veneer of fretwork panelling. It was obviously impossible to undertake this on any scale which might involve fresh and independent thought for each square yard of ornament; the thing must be done in gross, with constant repetition of detail, like a modern wallpaper; the designer must take the line of least resistance. He evolved, therefore, a scheme of intersecting straight lines, the vertical at regular intervals, and the horizontal somewhat varied. Sometimes these came close enough to form exact squares, which were made into quatrefoils; more often the panels were elongated, and terminated in elaborately cusped arches. Even the former curvilinear character of the window-tracery was modified in this same direction; the whole scheme of ornament became predominantly rectilinear; the so-called Perpendicular style was born. It was not fashioned in heresy, but in high-and-dry orthodoxy; conceived in miracle, born within the claustral precincts, and nursed on the knees of the Gloucester monks. The Black Death, as yet, lurked twelve years distant in the future. This new style spread with extraordinary rapidity; it replaced more than half of the older buildings in England, and lasted far longer than any previous style since the Norman Conquest; indeed, it lasted longer than all the rest put together. Between 1066 and 1337, Norman, Transitional, Early English and Decorated came and went; except so far as Decorated lingered here and there, especially in the eastern counties, after the rise of the new work at Gloucester. Between 1337 and 1537, 90 per cent. of English building was in this single Perpendicular style; and men were still employing it here and there in 1637, especially at the two universities.

THE RECONSTRUCTION OF GLOUCESTER CATHEDRAL.

For everybody realized, as the monks and their technical advisers had realized, that this was how the maximum of effect could be obtained at the minimum of cost in thought, in labour and in money. Monastery buildings were in many places out of repair; some were growing quite ruinous; so also with a good many of the village churches. A Devonshire visitation of 1342, which has been printed in full (*English Historical Review*, January 1911, pp. 108 ff.) shows how many were denounced to the authorities as "too small" and "too dark," in other words, they were still the original Norman or Early English structures, with narrow single windows. The medieval mind did not cultivate artificial gloom, as an excuse for a multiplicity of candles on the altar, so willingly as it has sometimes been cultivated in modern times; people contrasted these dark old-fashioned little churches unfavourably with the new fashionable style. Fortunately, money was not easily found in every parish, or very little of the earlier work would have survived. At the Devon village of Ringmore, for instance, we have still a very delightful little church of about A.D. 1200; but it was condemned in 1342. In the eastern counties, however, people had much more money, and much more Perpendicular was built. The citizens were growing richer and richer; the Black Death hardly checked for a single decade the rapid growth of our towns; and citizens liked showy value for their money. The Friars wanted their churches to be great preaching-halls for large congregations; in Italy, Franciscan and Dominican churches were evidently designed for a maximum of cubic space at a minimum of cost; so also (after a somewhat different type) in Germany and France; and the few English survivals (e.g. St. Andrew's Hall at Norwich) suggest the same. Finally, the Black Death itself may have hastened the movement, though it had nothing to do with its origin.[1] Masons, like other people, died in great numbers; there, as in all other crafts, the survivors naturally tried to sell their labour dear, and were tempted to lighten the work even where they could not raise the pay. Again, we may surmise among them what we know among the clergy, that men were often hurried through their apprenticeship in order to meet demands for work which brooked no delay; in many other ways also the new generation must have taken the line of least resistance, which they found in this new style. Flowers and leaves were conventionalized into easy shallow patterns which a workman could repeat almost with his eyes shut;

[1] See Appendix 1.

in spite of real development in towers and vaulting and some other ways, the last two centuries before the Reformation were an age of shop-work, as compared with the real originality of the twelfth and thirteenth centuries.

Therefore, though it is true that Art and Religion, from A.D. 1000 to 1600 and later, went through a very similar evolution, yet it was not entirely the course of Religion which dominated that of Art; we have no real excuse for talking of Religion as the bed through which the stream of Art flowed. Each evolved in accordance with wider social influences; and I must try to bring this out in subsequent chapters. In those chapters it will be my aim to avoid disputable questions of taste and of religion as much as possible. Here and there I must so far trespass upon what may be called the field of religious politics as to answer some of the arguments which have been, and are still very frequently, put forward from that point of view. But in one sense at least I aim at impartiality; I have tried to advance no single argument which would depend upon our moral judgment of that religious revolution which even Roman Catholics are willing, under protest, to call the Reformation, just as even Protestants, under protest, grant to the Roman Church that term Catholic, whose full logical implications they would deny. I have my own opinion of the Reformation, which I need not attempt to disguise; but here I do attempt to confine myself to facts and arguments whose logical cogency is the same, or nearly the same, to one man who looks upon the Reformation as a blessing, and to another who regards it as a curse. If one factor must be put first in religion, I willingly grant that it should be the emotional; but I do protest against stopping short at emotion; for this, I am convinced, is the main fallacy here. It sometimes tempted Ruskin and Morris into exaggerations; it has tempted their followers into farther exaggerations which Ruskin and Morris were wise enough to avoid; and these exaggerations have now become so general and so habitual that, in my opinion, the fashionable doctrine of the present day as to the relations of medieval art and medieval religion is not only far from the truth, but very mischievously remote, resting upon a superficial confusion of two things which are, indeed, often found in actual combination but which must be kept strictly apart in logical thought. One remedy here, as in other fields of history, is to take a little more trouble about our facts, and to avoid generalizations except so far as these can be justified by documentary evidence. Nobody is better qualified to pronounce on this point than Julius v. Schlosser, who, in Austria, has promoted the publication of a shelf-full of original sources for art history, while we, in England, are still lagging behind. In 1891, at a sitting of the Viennese Academy, he quoted with approval the words of Ramé : " We have had, in these last centuries, an erudite archæology which knew the texts and ignored the actual monuments ; at present, we have an intuitive archæology which is familiar with the monuments and ignores the texts. It is time now to avoid excesses on either side, developing textual and monumental study side by side. We might at least try whether the control which one study thus exercises upon the other would not throw some new light upon the progress and development of art."[1]

Here, then, is an attempt to supply a source-book, far from exhaustive, and even less systematic than it might have been made with a little more leisure. I have not had time to incorporate half my own notes, which, of course, do not represent one-fiftieth part of the available printed material, quite apart from the mass which is still buried in manuscript. But the volume does aim at supplying, for the time, documentary facts arranged on some sort of system, and with attempts, however summary, to grapple with the emergent problems. The author's interest, and, it may be hoped, that of his readers, fastens even more upon the men than upon their

[1] *Sitzungsberichte d. k. Acad.*, phil.-hist., vol. cxxiii (1891).

work. The concluding chapter will attempt to focus this personal interest more exactly ; meanwhile let us strive to look through the written records and the building-stones and the paintings into the men's minds that made them. Their creative instincts expanded along the bed of a great current of human endeavour ; the work they have left us testifies to the unconquerable human soul ; to man's strength both in patient routine and in far-flung adventure. Morris's emotion was a workman's emotion, as deeply rooted in the human heart as even the emotion of motherhood ; the artist when he is in travail hath sorrow ; but as soon as the work is done, all is swallowed up in the joy that this is born into the world. And that can be truly said of all times and of all arts ; it comes out as strongly in the healthy man's search for truth as in his search for beauty. A great Cambridge teacher, addressing a body of younger inquirers not many years ago, took as his text the official motto of the University of New Zealand : *Sapere aude*—" dare to be wise."[1] And he ended with an admonition, as healthily encouraging as every true and wise warning must be, upon the text of William Morris's *Love is Enough*. " The reward of the search—are we sure that it will be anything but the search ? Can we give any other bidding than that which was once given to a search yet more sacred ?

> Come—pain ye shall have, and be blind to the ending !
> Come—fear ye shall have, mid the sky's overcasting !
> Come—change ye shall have, for far are ye wending !
> Come—no crown ye shall have for your thirst and your fasting,
> But——

And here we must stop, before the promise that follows. The crown of our thirst and our fasting may be the opened heavens and the Beatific Vision. It may be nothing but the thirst and the fasting itself. No great inducement, perhaps, all this ? And no inducement is needed. There are those who long for truth with a

[1] J. M. E. McTaggart, *Dare to be Wise*, London. Watts & Co. 1909. 3d.

longing as simple, as ultimate, as powerful as the drunkard's longing for his wine and the lover's longing for his beloved. They will search, because they must. Our search has begun."

CHAPTER II

MONASTIC ARTISTS (1)

WE come, in this chapter, to a class of people who have been extravagantly over-praised on one side, and over-blamed on the other. Within the last half century and more, by a generous reaction, the party of praise has predominated. By all means let us err on the side of over-generosity if we must err at all ; but let us try not to err on either side ; let us try to get at the actual facts. What does the art of the Middle Ages really owe to the monks ? My own conviction is that it owes far less than is generally supposed, or than is taken for granted by most modern writers on art. In fact, I know only two authors, though there are doubtless others, who go into the question with some fulness and treat it seriously, as it deserves, from the historical point of view. The first is Mr. A. Kingsley Porter, in the second volume of his *Medieval Architecture*.[1] " Who," he asks very pertinently, " constructed the small county churches of the Île de France where most of the great architectural discoveries of the twelfth century originated ? " And, though he still seems to grant to Alan of Walsingham, at Ely Cathedral, a more definitely professional rôle as architect than the best authorities would now grant, his general conclusions accord very nearly with those which will be found in the three chapters which I am here devoting to this subject. The second is Prof. A. Hamilton Thompson, in his Presidential Address

[1] Batsford, 1909, pp. 181 ff. But neither author utilizes the strongest evidence, the complete silence of medieval monastic apologists.

to the Somersetshire Archæological Society, who brings
still more evidence from a wide archæological experience.[1]
But we still have the weight of modern tradition
against us ; and since, in combating any current
doctrine, it is well to take the line not of least but
of greatest resistance, I will take my texts here from
Prof. C. H. Moore's excellent book on *Gothic Architecture*, and from the lectures on Medieval Philosophy
and Civilization, delivered recently before Princeton
University by Maurice de Wulf, a distinguished
professor of philosophy at the University of Louvain.
Here is what Prof. Moore says : " The monastic
buildings were not only planned, and the works on
them directed, by the monks but they were also largely,
if not entirely, constructed with their own hands.
Cf. Lenoir, *Architecture Monastique*, p. 36 et seq., and
Montalembert, *Les Moines d'Occident*, vol. vi, p. 242 et
seq." [2] Prof. de Wulf says (p. 36) : " Artist monks were
trained in sculpturing columns and statues, and they
travelled from one workshop to another ; while yet
others opened schools of painting, as in St.-Savin near
Poitiers, where the twelfth century frescoes still retain
their bright colouring." Here, the reader should specially
notice how Prof. de Wulf bases his assertion on a reference
to the wonderful mural paintings of St.-Savin, and how
Prof. Moore claims the authority of Lenoir and Montalembert. For the fact is that these three apparently independent references are reducible to a single one ; it is
with Montalembert's sole authority that these confident
assertions of Moore and de Wulf and Lenoir really stand
or fall. For Lenoir, in his three quarto volumes, writes
mainly as a student of art ; he was no historian in any

[1] Printed in the Society's *Proceedings*, vol. lxvi (1920). This is bearing
fruit ; we may read now in the late Mr. S. D. Le Couteur's *English Med.
Painted Glass*, 1926, p. 22 : " There seems to be a popular and widespread belief that the craftsmen who produced much of this glass-painting
were monks. In reality this was very far from being the case."

[2] *Gothic Architecture.* Macmillan Co. 1899. p. 27.

special sense ; nearly all of what he says on this point is
taken textually from Montalembert's *Monks of the West*.
In that very bulky work Montalembert undertakes to
write the history of western monasticism from St. Benedict
to St. Bernard ; the book has obtained a general acceptance
far beyond its deserts ; for it is indeed nothing but an
elaborate party pamphlet, written by an eloquent states-
man who, like Gladstone, would have been a great scholar
if he had given his life to scholarship, but who, in fact,
wrote these seven volumes in the intervals of politics, for
a political object, and with so little fundamental seriousness that, when his own daughter took him at his word
and insisted on retiring into a convent, he was very much
distressed at her choice.[1] Lord Acton, by far the greatest
historical scholar who has ever arisen among English-
speaking Roman Catholics, says truly of this *Monks of the
West* that it is " a book with a tendency, not written for
learning's sake, but for an external political momentary
purpose, therefore without the dignity of real history in
its design, though very good in great part of the execution."[2]   Another distinguished scholar of the Roman
communion, Abbot Cabrol, notes truly that most of what
is historically valuable in Montalembert's book is taken
from the collections of the great Benedictine scholar of
the seventeenth century, Jean Mabillon.[3]   Here and there
Montalembert strays beyond Mabillon, and pauses to
generalize on the monks' services to civilization, in a tone
of exaggeration in which Mabillon never did write and
never would have written, devoted though he was to his
Order.   In this way Montalembert fills twenty pages of
his sixth volume with a detailed description of the monk
as artist ; and those twenty pages form practically the
basis of all that has been written on that subject for the
last sixty years ; for writers on art are not likely to find
time (even if they have the linguistic equipment and the

[1] B. Holland, *Memoir of Kenelm Digby*, 1919, pp. 163 ff.

[2] *Lord Acton and his Circle*, p. 198.

[3] *Mélanges Mabillon*, introd., p. 14.

necessary access to a great library) to verify the numerous references by means of which this great French politician seems so clearly to establish his case. When a man with a world-wide reputation writes at a favourable time and place, and when he is what James Russell Lowell once called " an inaccurate man with an accurate manner," then there is scarcely any limit to the misconceptions which he can set afloat for a very long time.

I had long known the extreme weakness of Montalembert's case ; but, for the purpose of this present volume, it was necessary to go systematically through his references. It took me nearly a week to verify them, with the necessary consideration of their context ; and even then I was obliged to leave three unverified, of which two were to publications not found in the Cambridge University Library. The remaining fifty cases which he quotes in support of his thesis can be divided roughly as follows :—

In twenty-one cases either he gives no proper reference, or, when you have run his reference down, you find that there is no real proof that the artists there mentioned were monks at all ; the most that his documents prove is that the work was done *for* some monastery or *in* some monastery—a very different thing.[1]

In six cases the document not only does not prove that we are dealing with monastic artists, but actually proves or implies that they were non-monastic : they actually upset Montalembert's contention.

In fifteen cases we do really find monastic artists, but in every one of these the context shows the phenomenon to be not normal, but exceptional—for instance, cases where monks under missionary conditions worked at their own buildings, just as a modern missionary will build a brick-kiln and bake bricks for his mission-room in equatorial Africa (I quote an actual example of to-day)—

[1] See Appendix 2. I am more and more inclined to suspect that a great deal of Montalembert's work was " devilled " for him, and that he himself had often not read the books from which he quotes.

or, again, monks working themselves because they were
too poor to hire workmen—or, finally, monks of whom
it is quoted, in proof of their special sanctity or humility,
that they actually deigned to work with the labourers.

We have thus a residuum of only eight cases—16 per
cent.—which Montalembert has legitimately quoted in
support of his thesis : 84 per cent. of his own chosen
witnesses either break down or turn definitely against him.
I will give one concrete instance—one of the worst, it is
true—in support of this present criticism. Among the
glories which we owe to monastic artists, Montalembert
quotes those paintings at St.-Savin near Poitiers ; and
this instance seems so striking to Prof. de Wulf (who is a
good philosopher, but a very poor historian) that he
quotes it as clinching the whole case. Montalembert, for
this argument, refers us to Prosper Mérimée's great monograph on the St.-Savin paintings, but without even troubling to indicate the page of Mérimée on which he rests
his theory. You will have to work through fifty-six pages
of this exceptionally large folio, inaccessible except in the
most privileged libraries, before you discover that
Mérimée says the very opposite of what Montalembert
leads you to expect, pronouncing these artists of St.-Savin
to have been not the monks themselves, but Greek
painters brought in for the purpose ! Nor is it only on
this question of monastic art that Montalembert is thus
inaccurate ; I have shown the same for monastic field-
labour,[1] and am prepared to show that nearly all his
most brilliant generalizations—which are naturally quoted
from writer to writer without suspicion, so that a whole
monastic legend has grown up on this foundation—
that nearly all these generalizations, under reference
to the actual documents—crumble to pieces in the
same way.[2]

Let me quote here, then, the half-dozen sentences in

[1] *The Medieval Village*, 1925, pp. 149, 197, 218, and Appendix 4.
[2] Even Lefèvre-Pontalis generalizes rashly here; see Appendix 2 to this
present volume.

which he himself sums up his own thesis :[1] " When we say that the innumerable monastic churches scattered over the whole face of Europe were built by the monks, this assertion must be taken in its literal sense. They were, in fact, not only the architects but also the masons of their buildings ; after having drawn up their plans, whose noble and scientific character still excites our admiration, they worked them out with their own hands, in general, without the help of outside workmen. They chanted psalms as they worked, and laid down their tools only to go to the altar or the choir.[2] . . . While simple monks were often the chief architects of these buildings, abbots gladly condescended to play the part of common workmen." Assertions so confident as this, from a man of such reputation, have very naturally been taken at their face value by even the best writers who have had no time for direct research on this special point. The story of Heckington in Lincolnshire illustrates this very clearly. It became a universally-accepted legend that, since this extraordinarily beautiful village church was appropriated to Bardney Abbey, therefore it was the monks who had built it, and perhaps with their own hands. But, as Prof. A. Hamilton Thompson has shown, the church was built before the parish came into the hands of the monks, and probably by a rector who was a well-to-do clerk in the king's service.[3] Therefore, to Montalembert's words,

[1] *Moines d'Occident*, Nouvelle Édition (1882), vol. vi, p. 248, liv. xviii, chap. 4.

[2] It is characteristic of Montalembert that this sentence is directly contradicted by Trithemius, the best of the authorities whom he tries to enlist into his theories. Trithemius, writing of these buildings at Hirschau, says that, outside service-time, there was no sound in the whole monastery "except the sound of the tools of the artisans who were working." (*Ann. Hirsaug*, vol. i, p. 230).

[3] *Parish History and its Records*, pp. 54 ff. (Hist. Assn. Leaflet No. 66), G. Bell & Sons, 1926 ; a monograph of which the value is out of all proportion to its small size and price. Cf. also the same author's *Med. Build. Doc.*, p. 20. Prof. Thompson has since noted that the two ecclesiastics described as monks on p. 24 were in fact secular clerics. For Heckington, see Appendix 3.

I will now venture to oppose the following counter-generalization. The monks who did any kind of artistic work, at the most favourable times and places, were a small minority in the community ; and, if we take all times and places together, the monastic artist was quite an exception. As to monastic workman-builders, we have evidence for them only under still more exceptional circumstances. And, in order to meet Montalembert on the ground where he emphatically claims to be strongest, let us take hold of that chronicler whom he himself singles out as proving beyond question his assertion that the monks generally built their monasteries without the help of outside workmen. This chronicler is the celebrated Trithemius, or Abbot Johann v. Trittenheim, one of the most learned men in fifteenth century Germany, who has left us a very valuable chronicle of the monastery of Hirschau. He is recording the achievements of an early abbot, St. William, who began to rebuild the abbey in 1070 ; he expatiates on St. William's extraordinary magnetic force and powers of organization ; and on the healthy activities which he fostered among the monks proper, the choir-monks. " These monks," writes Trithemius, " were always given up to the praise of God, and continually intent upon prayer, meditation, and the reading of Holy Scriptures. Those who seemed less suited for the contemplation of heavenly things were deputed to necessary manual labour, that none of their time might be passed in idleness. . . . He appointed the twelve fittest of his [150 monks] as writers . . . beyond whom were other writers also, without definite number, who busied themselves with equal diligence in transcribing books. Over all these writers one monk was set, most learned in all kinds of knowledge, who appointed to each [of them] some good work to transcribe, and corrected the errors made by those who wrote more negligently. . . . Beyond the above-mentioned number of 150 monks, St. William had also other bearded brethren, very many in number, men outside the clerical order, who are also called

GLOUCESTER CATHEDRAL.
COMPARTMENTS S. SIDE OF CHOIR.

THREE BAYS OF GLOUCESTER CATHEDRAL.

lay-brethren. These lay-brethren's business was to devote themselves to manual work and temporal affairs, under command of their superiors, and to provide the necessaries of life for the monks, who were given up to contemplation. Among these lay-brethren were most skilful workers in all mechanical arts which it seemed needful to practise in the abbey; and these completed all the buildings of the whole abbey, with the utmost diligence, by the work of their own hands. For there were excellent carpenters and smiths, stone-hewers and masons, who constructed both the monastery and its whole church (as may be seen to this day in the carving of the towers) according to an excellent design. There were also tailors, leather-dressers, shoemakers, and artisans of all that was needed by the monks [*ad usum claustralium*]; these were not worldly folk or mercenaries or hirelings, but all are recorded to have been lay-brethren, or [as they are also called] bearded monks. Now this St. William was the first abbot to institute this order of lay-brethren in Germany; and it was by the help of their labours that he founded so many [as eight] monasteries, and laudably fulfilled all the needs of the monks." Trithemius then goes on to describe the manner of life which St. William prescribed to these lay-brethren; one of the rules being that " because the lay-brethren were wearied with long handiwork, lest the long vigils should tax them beyond their strength, they had shorter matins to sing." Moreover, St. William instituted yet a third order, whom he called *Oblates*; men who did not live in the monastery at all, but did a great deal of the unskilled work, such as carting stones and sand, burning lime, and so on. There were sixty lay-brethren and forty oblates to the 150 monks proper.[1]

The whole of St. William's building work took ten years; and Trithemius returns to the subject about thirty pages later in his chronicle (p. 255). Here he says (and we must carefully note his words) : " Now the artificers of this building, as we have said above, were for the most

[1] *Ann. Hirsaug*, vol. i, pp. 227 ff.

D

part[1] bearded monks, or lay brethren, and oblates . . .
among whom were masons, carpenters, smiths, and
masters certainly most skilled in all architectural knowledge, who planned and executed the whole work, with
fair stone arcading, as we still see in the building of the
church itself."

I do not wish to insist too much—though I do not
think we can neglect it altogether—upon the discrepancy
between these two accounts; upon the casual way in
which Trithemius uses *wholly* and *for the most part* as
interchangeable terms. My own belief is that, under
cross-examination, he would have held only to his *for the
most part*, and would have admitted the *wholly* to be a
rhetorical exaggeration; for we must remember that he
is here writing the panegyric of a sainted fellow-abbot,
after a lapse of four centuries. But we must not insist
upon this; let us take his *wholly* in the strictest sense,
and see what his evidence really amounts to.

In the first place, he is describing a most exceptional
man and a most exceptional movement. In all those
twelve and a half centuries of Benedictine history, from
the sixth century to the French Revolution, it is doubtful
whether twelve greater reformers and organizers can be
found than St. William of Hirschau: William was, literally, a man in fifty thousand. Trithemius himself writes
as one who fully realizes the exceptional nature of what
he is describing; and indeed I know only two complete
parallels to this Hirschau incident, one on a large scale
and one on a smaller.

The first is recorded in the life of St. Bernard of Tiron,[2]
who lived at the same period of exceptional monastic
reform as St. William of Hirschau. He also founded a
whole congregation of monasteries; and of him it is
recorded that, when he was founding a new settlement
near Chartres, he invited all his disciples to continue the

---

[1] Or perhaps only " in great part "—*pro magna parte.*

[2] To be carefully distinguished from his greater contemporary, St.
Bernard of Clairvaux.

practice of the arts to which they were accustomed.
" As a consequence there gathered about him freely
craftsmen both in wood and iron, carvers and goldsmiths,
painters and stonemasons, vinedressers and husbandmen,
and others skilled in all manner of cunning work." [1]

Here, again, is an obviously exceptional case ; St.
Bernard of Tiron was a fervid mission-preacher who
made an unusual number of converts, and wisely set
them, as far as possible, to continue their worldly occupations in the new monasteries which had to be built for
them. On the other hand, an almost equally zealous
contemporary abbot, St. Stephen of Obazine, had his
monastery built mainly not by monks but by hired workmen, as we shall see in a later chapter.

Let us now come to less exceptional cases, even while
we still keep on the side of unusual efficiency. There are
many descriptions of model monasteries in different
generations, by contemporary chroniclers ; yet in these
very little is said—if indeed anything is said at all—
about the practice of art by monks. The reader will
probably have noticed already that even St. William of
Hirschau looked upon art only as a *pis-aller* for the monks
who had nothing better to do ; and there is not a word
in Trithemius to imply that any one of William's 150
monks proper—the choir-monks—took any part in that
great ten years' building work ; on the contrary, he tells
us this was wholly done by the lay brethren and oblates.
The manual labour of the choir-monks to which he
alludes, in so far as it was not writing work, was done
probably in the kitchen and scullery and the domestic
offices, as we know to have been the custom in other
monastic reforms. His words do not indeed actually
exclude the possibility of an artist here and there among
these 150 ; but, taken as they actually stand, they cannot possibly be enlisted into the service of Montalembert's
theory that monks were normally the builders of their
own monasteries.

[1] Ordericus Vitalis, *Hist. Eccl.*, lib. viii, c. 26.

There is, however, another very interesting case from that same age of fervid reform. The Cistercian monastery of Schönau, not far from Heidelberg, was founded in 1142, and furnished with extemporized buildings, probably of wood. A few years later, stone buildings were erected.[1] The Germanisches Museum at Nuremberg possesses a series

BEARDED BRETHREN AT WORK.

of cartoons for wall - paintings or, more probably, glass-paintings, illustrating two episodes in the history of Schönau which have become famous; namely, the life of St. Hildegund, who lived as a man for a whole year in the monastery, dying at the end of her noviciate,[2] and the rebellion of the lay brethren, who refused to wear the priests' old boots, and organized a strike in order to get new boots of their own.[3] These cartoons date from the first half of the sixteenth century, more than 350 years later than the events which they commemorate;

[1] See Huffschmid in *Zeitschrift f. d. Gesch. d. Oberrheins*, vol. xlv, 1891, p. 427, and R. Edelmaier, *Das Kloster Schönau*, Heidelberg, 1915.

[2] Told by Cæsarius of Heisterbach, in his *Dialogus Miraculorum*, Dist. I, c. 40.

[3] Told in *Exordium Magnum Cisterciense*, Migne P. L., vol. 185, col. 1140. Huffschmid has not quite understood this story, though the picture corroborates the *Exordium*.

and in some respects they do not correspond exactly with what we know of the facts. But at least they testify to the tradition in the monastery ; and, while one picture represents St. Hildegund labouring at the building of the dormitory, another shows the lay brethren busied in the construction of the church. Including shovellers, quarrymen and carters, there are only nineteen of them ; and this would answer very closely to the probable number, since this new foundation started with only the regulation number of thirteen choir-brethren. It would fit in with the fact that the church was not finished until a little before 1215, although rich gifts had been made in 1167 and [1190] for the building of church and chapter house ; a fact which seems to imply hired labour also, since the monks had apparently their own quarry. The original drawing is of extreme interest, not only from its artistic merit, but as illustrating the artist's conception of such activities as we know for certain in the Hirschau case. And it is quite in accordance with that precedent that we see no choir-monk directing the lay brethren ; all are alike *barbati*, from those who are doing the roughest work to him who is taking a well-earned draught from the wine-flask. The legend under the picture runs : " Lay brethren built the monastery of Schönau, led by devout love of religion." [1]

We shall be better able now to estimate the significance of the Hirschau operations as described by Trithemius, and those at Schönau as conceived by the sixteenth-century artist, if we compare them with parallel cases of a later date. At the very end of the fourteenth century there came another considerable wave of monastic or semi-monastic reform in Northern Germany. This movement was inaugurated by Gerhard Groot, whose Brethren of the Common Life were not monks in the strict sense, but who, in his last years, helped towards a definitely monastic foundation. The convent of Mount St. Agnes,

[1] Construxere domum Conversi Schönaviensem quos pius induxit religionis amor.

founded by his immediate disciples, produced Thomas à
Kempis ; and a new congregation soon arose of which the
head house was Windesheim. This Windesheim reform
has found a worthy chronicler in Johann Busch, himself
one of the most active and successful of monastic disciplinarians, who took the vows at Windesheim at a time
when some of the heroes of that first foundation were
still alive. Busch describes how the monastery was built ;
he writes : [1] " All these buildings could not be completed
by the labours of our lay-brethren and our hired workmen
without the busy manual assistance of the monks themselves [*fratrum conventualium*], since these latter often
suffered no little default in their efforts to collect the
money that was needed to pay the workmen. Therefore
the choir-brethren themselves [*fratres chorales*] shrank from
no labour, however humble and despised, even sometimes
beyond their bodily strength. . . . For, of their own
accord, they undertook many manual works, of a highly
technical kind [*satis artificiosa*] and unusual for clerics,
in order to hasten the building and to spare expense.
The first head of the monastery, brother Henry of Höxter,
learned how to chisel stones for the framework of doors
and windows, and to form them and square them perfectly
according to their proper pattern. So also, even to the
end of his life, he ceased not to do carpenter's work,
smoothing and shaping beams and boards and the like,
with axe or with adze, to the great profit and use of the
brethren ; and sometimes he worked so vigorously that
I could see sweat dropping from every limb of his body.
I have seen other brethren of the monastery also—three
or four or five or six of the most active and strongest—
wielding the trowel and laying stones and mortar. . . .
others, again, mixing sand and lime and water, and making
mortar in due course with great labour ; others nimbly
bearing stones or mortar on their backs or in their hands ;
others most faithfully labouring at divers works for the
rapid completion of the buildings, while the weaker

[1] *Chron. Windesh.*, cap. vii (ed. K. Grube, p. 21).

brethren, whose bodily strength failed them, vied with
the rest, by laying stones on the barrows, filling the
bearers' baskets here and there, or gathering laths under
the carpenters' orders."

Busch goes on to describe how others of the conventual
brethren " very often undertook other humble and rustic
works for the sake of necessity or of exercise," as, for
instance, cleaning dishes in the scullery, washing clothes,
working in the bakery, the brewhouse or the harvest-
field. And he adds that, " although our brethren were
compelled to labour in many external and rustic works
for the construction of the monastery and the full completion of its several buildings," yet they did not neglect
their more strictly monastic duties of prayer and of
writing.

Here, then, we have the same point of view as that of
St. William and of Trithemius ; next to divine service,
the monk's most natural work is that of writing ; other
occupations need scarcely be mentioned in comparison
with these ; but exceptionally, under stress of necessity,
such others may be undertaken. Therefore he tells how
one single monk, at this time of extreme stress, qualified
as a fairly expert mason and carpenter ; the rest did less
skilled work.

This comes out even more clearly, perhaps, in Busch's
description of the houses which he himself reformed in
later days, and which he holds up to us for models of
healthy monastic activities, as indeed they were. Here,
for instance, is what he says of Dalem (p. 494 : lib. ii,
c. 34) : " The prior has built a great new church, long
and broad, on the hill-top within the monastery precincts,
of hewn and squared stones quarried from the hill itself
. . . for he wishes to transfer to that hill-top the whole
monastery, with new dormitory and refectory and kitchen
and other suchlike buildings, and to leave the lay-brethren
at the bottom of the hill, with their own offices and their
herds and their workshops. For he hath many lay-
brethren, almost a hundred, who work continually in the

kitchen and cellar and brewhouse and bakery and farm
and house, and exercise their mechanical arts in the other
workshops for the common good." It will be noted that,
though all this building was either done or contemplated
at Dalem, there is no mention even of lay-brethren
among the masons, still less of monks proper. This is
still more striking in his description of Bodike, the
monastery which had served as model for the rest of these
reforms. There, again, Busch tells us of a fine vaulted
church, with other buildings; but here is the list of
trades which he describes among the lay-brethren:
" Cobblers, tailors, smiths, carpenters, land-labourers,
milkmen, bakers, brewers, shepherds, swineherds, cooks,
butchers, barbers for shaving and for bleeding; and other
necessary workmen." A third model monastery, Molen-
beke, is described equally fully. The list there is verbally
identical, with only the omission of butchers and the
addition of a corn-mill and a saw-mill for timber. Therefore the inference is that these three monasteries, being
old and well-endowed, managed their constructions, as
other people did, through the regular building-trade of
the day.

CHAPTER III

MONASTIC ARTISTS (2)

BUT, it may be asked, what is the value of such negative references in the face of the positive testimony, repeated from writer to writer, in favour of actual monastic artists ? We shall find, I think, that nearly all these writers rely, like Montalembert, on a few stock instances of individual artists, which have not always even the merit of accuracy within their own narrow limits. For instance, Alan of Walsingham, sub-prior of Ely, is generally quoted as the architect of the central tower there ; yet the *Historia Eliensis*, from what we know of Alan's work, says no such thing.[1] It does not even assert plainly that Alan himself measured and marked the position of the eight pillars upon which it was to rest, although the words are capable of that interpretation among others. All that we know for certain is, that he caused the workmen to make specially secure foundations at those eight spots, and that he directed the rest of the work, in the sense in which Chaucer directed architectural works, i.e. as paymaster and general superintendent. We may believe Alan to have been an artist if we choose ; but we have no documentary evidence for it ; and this is generally admitted now by careful writers upon art.

But, apart from such individual cases, which cannot carry us very far even where they will bear separate examination, the theory of regular monastic art-work is mainly based upon two instances which are quoted every-

[1] Wharton, *Anglia Sacra*, vol. i (1691), p. 644.

where as typical, and therefore as supplying a sound basis for sweeping generalizations; the case of St. Gall, and

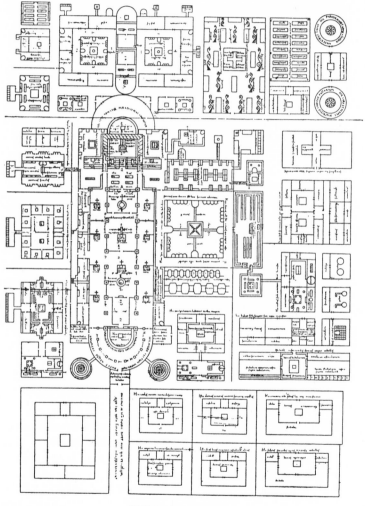

THE ST. GALL PLAN.

the case of Farfa. Yet, on analysis, it will be found not only that both are far from typical, but that neither can be used to prove even the exceptional existence of those monastic artists who have often been inferred from it.

The famous plan of St. Gall, which is perhaps as early as the eighth century, was engraved by Mabillon for the second volume of his *Annales Benedictini*, and has often since been published in facsimile. But it is now admitted on all hands that this does not represent any actual building ; it is an imaginative plan of a perfect monastery, such as the designer would have built if he had had unlimited men and money, and had been able to complete this vast monastic house—it may almost be said, this monastic village—in uninterrupted pursuance of an ideal design.[1] Fancy often works most freely in the early days when realization is frankly impossible, and when the speculator commits himself to no practical consequences ; a similar semi-legendary palace of magnificent size and ideal completeness of proportion hovered in the imagination of these same centuries.[2] Moreover, even though it were possible still to believe, with Mabillon and other early pioneers, that the plan represented the actual building of St. Gall in Carolingian times, yet this would be far from proving what it has often been taken to prove. There is, indeed, an imposing square block of building in which a room is marked for the goldsmiths— *aurifices*. But the whole context forbids our applying this to a group of tonsured artists. Another room is devoted to the " cleaners and polishers of swords," *emundatores et politores gladiorum* ; another to the *scutarii*. Lenoir (II, 427) would translate these as " shield-makers " ; thence he infers a system of manufacture of weapons for sale outside the monastery. But

---

[1] See the article by Julius Schlosser in *Sitzungsberichte d. k. Akad. in Wien*, vol. 123 (1891), p. 31. This ground-plan " is a theoretical conception, the invention of a learned monk who knew his Vitruvius." Compare Th. Sommerlad, *Die wirtschaftliche Tätigkeit d. Kirche in Deutschland*, Leipzig, 1900–5, vol. ii, p. 151, and note 6.

[2] E.g. Julius Schlosser *l. c.*, pp. 41 ff. ; cf. p. 32. It is perhaps no mere chance that this tradition of a palace in the air is closely connected with the monastery of Farfa.

scutarius is rare in this sense, while it is very common in the sense of armed retainer (*Fr.* écuyer, *Eng.* squire).

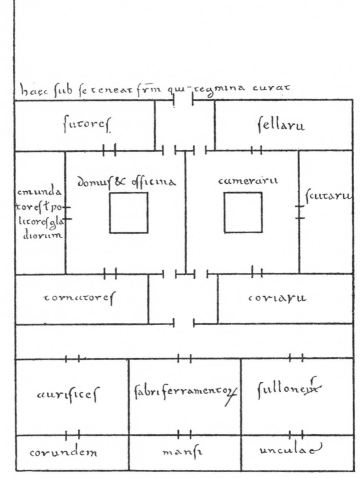

THE WORKMEN'S QUARTERS AT ST. GALL.

Monastic records are full of these *scutarii, scutiferi, armigeri*, who in early times answered strictly to their name, being armed tenants whose fighting qualities were of great importance for the protection of the monks' persons and property. St. Gall, especially, had a large number of such dependents, some of whom, in the eleventh and succeeding centuries, became squires in the modern sense, and gave the abbey more trouble than help. Still, these *scutarii* may be shield-makers; but there is not the least indication that they were monks. The other rooms of this block are labelled *tornatores* (turners), *sutores* (shoemakers), *sellarii* (saddlers), *coriarii* (curriers), *fullones* (fullers), and *fabri ferramentorum* (blacksmiths). There is no hint of masons, carpenters, glaziers or painters. On the very face of it, this block seems destined for the professional artisans, regular servants of the monastery, of the kind to which there is reference in the Rule and in other monastic records. And, to strengthen this first presumption, we find on inspection that all one side of this artisans' block was occupied by lodgings for those who worked in it—*eorundem mansiunculæ*—just as the *mansio pullorum custodis* (fowl-keeper's lodging), in another part of the plan adjoins the great fowl-house. The monks, as it is hardly necessary to remind the reader, lodged in their own cloister and dormitory. Therefore, while there is nothing to exclude the supposition of occasional monks working among the goldsmiths, yet this supposition cannot claim more than conjectural validity; true, this famous ground-plan suggests nothing against it, but, again, nothing in its favour.

Almost equally inconclusive is that description of an abbey-studio—unique, I think, of its kind—which is misleadingly quoted as typical. Sir T. G. Jackson, in a recent valuable article, writes : " A great number [of the monks] were artisans. . . . In every convent were workshops, the specification sent from Cluny for the buildings at Farfa provides a building 125 feet by 25 for the work of the glaziers, jewellers and goldsmiths." [1] Cluny was

---

[1] *Medieval France*, edited by Arthur Tilley (Camb. Univ. Press, 1922), p. 343. No reference is given, but the original document may be found in *M.G.H. Scriptt*, vol. xi, p. 546; M. Herrgott, *Vetus Disciplina Monastica*, 1726, p. 87 ; and Mabillon, *Ann. Bened.*, vol. iv, lib. liii, s. 19.

the greatest monastery in the world, and Farfa at that date (c. 1030) one of the three greatest and most prosperous in Italy, if not at the very head of the three. Abbot Hugh did what he could to introduce the Cluniac customs to Farfa, and his emissary added to them, probably after inspection of the vast Cluny buildings and consultation with the authorities there, a specification of the edifices that would be proper for Farfa. This list of buildings begins in the present indicative and so continues till nearly halfway—*habent, sunt,* etc. But, then passing on to describe the infirmary, the writer begins changing to the subjunctive and the future—*sit, sit, debet esse*—" let there be," " there ought to be." This change from actuality to potentiality continues through the second half of the document, which ends " Next to [the novice-room] let another room be placed, where the goldsmiths or enamellers or masters in glasswork [1] may come together to practise their art." This is the whole foundation upon which Jackson and others have built. It proves, indeed, that such a group of workshops was part of the Cluniac ideal for a very large and rich monastery; and we have other evidence for believing that at Cluny itself there was some such organization; this was the head of a vast congregation, as big as a small town, with a church of greater cubic content than any even in Rome, and an abbot who was in effect the greatest ecclesiastical potentate after the pope, and a host of dependent monasteries which took many of their ideas in art and in literature from the parent house. But we cannot assume that this Cluniac ideal was actually fulfilled even in the great abbey of Farfa; nor, if we assume that, have we the least hint that these artists were intended to be actual monks. On the contrary, they are called *magistri*, masters; and I think it will be found that a monk is seldom or never called *magister* unless he had either gained this title before taking the vows, or (much more rarely), gained it by teaching outside the cloister.

[1] *Inclusores seu vitrei magistri.*

Therefore, although Jackson rightly continues : " In these hives of industry traditions of art would insensibly grow up, schools of design would naturally be formed," yet the truth of this latter generalization is entirely independent of the document upon which it is proposedly based. There is no proof, either in the St. Gall plan or in the Farfa customal, of monastic workmen ; the implication, in so far as either document helps us at all, is rather to the contrary. This is greatly strengthened, also, by the remarkable *Dialogue of a Cistercian and a Cluniac*, written between 1135 and 1175. The pertinent passage runs thus :—

" *Clun.*—Although we labour neither in the garden nor in the field, yet we are not utterly idle. Some read, some work with their hands.

Cist.—I know those idle works of yours.

Clun.—Why do you call them idle ?

Cist.—Even as those words which do not edify are idle, so those works which pertain not to necessary uses are rightly called idle. I will say no more of the others, but will ask, Is it not useless and idle work to grind gold to powder, and therewith to paint great capital letters ? . . . .

Clun.—You reproach us with our handiwork, calling it idle and useless, as if your own were very laborious and very useful.

Cist.—We devote ourselves to the field-work which God created ; we all work together, we [choir-monks] and our [lay] brethren and our hirelings, each according to his ability ; and all in common we live on our labour." [1]

This passage shows clearly, first, that only some monks practised even illumination, and the Cluniac disputant cannot claim any other art-work as a regular factor in monastic life. Secondly, the Cistercian repudiates even that small practice of art ; for him, work is either garden or field work. It is legitimate, in both these cases, to argue thus

[1] Martène, *Thesaurus*, vol. v, col. 1623.

strongly, if not absolutely, from silence, since the whole
purpose of the *Dialogue*, from beginning to end, is to
show what criticisms were ordinarily passed upon both
the Orders, and how far these could be fairly and truly
met. The author, it is true, is a Cistercian, and we see
his bias; but that bias would not tempt him astray in
this case; if many Cluniacs had been devoted to other
forms of art, he would have lost nothing by rehearsing
these also, and condemning them, like the illuminations,
as idle vanities.

But, apart from this question of *personnel* in art-work,
even though the paintings and carvings and stone-
dressing in monastic buildings was done in the ordinary
way by hired laymen, yet it is perfectly true that great
monasteries on a great scale, and the smaller on a lesser
scale, formed schools of art. Professor Kingsley Porter has
said very truly that the one real school of architecture is
the construction of a great building; and the monks did
unquestionably commission, pay for either directly or
indirectly, and sometimes even superintend, some of the
greatest constructions of the Middle Ages.

We must return, however, to this question of *personnel*,
since it is here that the neglect of actual documents has
been most fatal. The weakness of the traditional case is
betrayed by the constant quotation of these two examples
from St. Gall and Farfa as conclusive.

The evidence of monastic customals, on the whole, is
distinctly unfavourable. Although there is frequent
mention of the scriptorium, has any customal ever been
quoted for evidence of a room or rooms devoted to the
monastic artist? Again, the prescriptions for monastic
labour (though monastic labour of any kind was practically dead, except here and there, before 1300) not only
do not imply art-work, but seem irreconcilable with it in
any but an exceptional sense. The ideal monks, for
instance, chanted psalms in chorus as they worked, or
listened to edifying reading, in a fashion which would be
possible as they hoed the furrows or trimmed the vines,

but not while they hewed stone or sawed timber. And, when an exception is made in the customal, and it is recognised that some kinds of labour are incompatible with this simultaneous worship or edification, it is not art-work that the legislator specifies, but the strenuous labour of the kneading-trough in the bake-house.[1]

These inferences are greatly strengthened when we make use of one or two very valuable sidelights, which, so far as I know, have been altogether neglected.

All students of monastic history, even those who disagree on other points, would concur in that which I have pointed out as implied in Busch's words—that, of all manual occupations, writing was the most natural and general among the monks proper as distinguished from the lay brethren ; and it must be remembered that, during the five centuries and more which we are now considering, the lay brethren formed, on the whole, a very small fraction of the total monastic population ; certainly not one in ten, and probably not one in fifty. *A priori*, therefore, it is most improbable that monks should have practised art-work to the same extent as copying. Yet even the monastic copyist himself, directly we look into the real evidence, appears not as a regular phenomenon, but as an exception.[2] From many different sources, we can get at statistics which mark very clearly the limits of monastic writing ; for we possess a number of catalogues showing how many volumes the monks owned at different times. I think it will be found, if we take even the most favourable of these catalogues, and work out how much time it would have taken to produce the books there

[1] Herrgott, *Vetus Disciplina*, p. 283 (Cluniac constitutions of about 1080)·

[2] I hope to discuss this question fully in the third volume of *Five Centuries of Religion*. The scriptorium, at best, played a very small part in the total life of an average monastery ; as Dr. M. R. James writes : " There was not always a separate building for the library ; the books were often kept in presses in the cloister . . . and it is doubtful if in any of our monasteries the site of the *scriptorium*, or writing-room, can be pointed out." (*Royal Commission on Historical Monuments* : London, *I*, *Westminster Abbey*, 1924, p. 11).

E

recorded; and if, again, we count the monk's rate of
production, busy as he was with other things, at only
half the rate of a professional scribe, which we have
plenty of data for estimating—we shall then find, I think,
even in the most favourable cases, that no more books
were produced than would have been written by the
labours of one monk out of every forty or fifty spending
his leisure steadily on this work; and in many cases,
especially in the later Middle Ages, we might divide even
this small proportion of monastic writers by ten. At the
great cathedral monastery of Worcester, for instance,
among at least forty or fifty monks, a book was in hand
thirteen years, which a single hired scribe would almost
have finished in as many weeks. In 1450, Thos. Gascoigne,
the great Chancellor of Oxford University, asserted
roundly that the monks were destroying more books
than they were making.[1] If it can be proved, then, that
very little work was done in the scriptorium, the burden
of proof certainly lies upon those who would argue that
the men who did so little for writing were doing so much
for art. Has any modern author ever attempted to
shoulder that burden? Certainly the ordinary treatment of the subject, even by writers in other ways admirable, seems to suggest that they scarcely realize the nature
of their task. They take the monastic artist for granted;
Montalembert (they seem to assume) has proved once for
all that this man was the rule and not the exception;
therefore, all that is now expected of us is to quote one
or two concrete instances in illustration of such a well-
known rule.[2] But the present problem, by its very nature,
is not soluble by the mere production of individual cases
—even though the believer in monastic artistry took

---

[1] *Loci e Libro Veritatum*, ed. J. E. T. Rogers, p. 73.

[2] We must also take account of the fact, admitted now by the best
writers of all schools, that earlier students of this subject were often misled
by the word *fecit*. The context frequently shows that this word, used
of an abbot or prelate, does not imply work with his own hands, but
simply work that he ordered and paid for.

pains to discuss such cases in detail, and to show us why
we must regard them as typical and not as exceptional;
which, so far as my experience goes, he never does. The
total monastic population of the West, if we take all who
lived and died between St. Benedict and the Reformation,
cannot have been less than half a million, and probably
far exceeded that figure. Among half a million persons,
we may easily find records of a few dozen examples of
anything that we want to prove, so long as we content
ourselves with mere indiscriminate counting of heads. It
is quite possible that, if it were worth while, a student
could pick out of the existing records as many concrete
examples of monastic felons as of monastic artists; and
yet nobody would be prejudiced enough to argue that
the average monk was a murderer or a thief. The first
step, if this problem is ever to be solved satisfactorily, is
to abandon Montalembert's easy system of counting a
few heads at random. The individual cases recorded
must be considered in the light of their attendant circumstances; and we must control by reflection the merely
superficial impressions produced by a list of artists which,
in the nature of the case, must be ludicrously insufficient
to prove, by its bare rehearsal, the wide general proposi-
tion.[1] Individual cases may be of the greatest value as
illustrations; but we cannot possibly generalize from the
comparatively brief lists which are the most that have
ever been produced. For a great many years I have
noted cases of monastic or non-monastic artists in monasteries, wherever the context gave any indication which
permits us to infer a distinction. Time has always failed

[1] I may be permitted to illustrate this by an example from my own
experience. In my boyhood an American friend sent my father a scrap-
book, full of brilliant crimson and yellow leaves, to exemplify an
autumn in New England. We ourselves set to work, and had no difficulty
in finding an equal number of leaves, almost or quite as brilliant, in our
own hedges. If we had wanted to boast our English autumn tints against
theirs, we could easily have produced, under the guise of typical instances,
so many hundred exceptions that we could have given a very false idea
of the real facts.

me to marshal these instances exhaustively according to time and place; but I have no hesitation in saying that, so far as these documents go, there is overwhelmingly more evidence for the lay than for the monastic artist.

For the moment we test Montalembert's references seriously, we constantly find that examples which are quoted in favour of his thesis prove, on examination, to tell against it. For instance, medieval writers have sometimes left us admiring descriptions of the amount of work done by some particular man or at some particular monastery. These, so far as I know them, never suggest anything like the amount of work that would have been done in one-tenth of the time by a professional artist; and yet they move the monastic writer to an enthusiasm which clearly marks the case as exceptional.[1]

The monk of Canterbury Cathedral who has left us a list of all his brethren from A.D. 1207 to 1540, often appends some note of distinction to the bare name; a few of the brethren are thus distinguished as students, teachers or writers; three are lauded for their musical skill; but there is no hint of monastic artists.[2]

In Vasari's *Lives of the Painters*, again, it is far more frequent to find the painting in a monastery done by a hired lay artist than by a monk.

Again, medieval apologists constantly found themselves called upon to refute the charges of idleness brought against the monks by their medieval critics. These

---

[1] This comes out very plainly also in modern monographs, directly we look into the actual evidence which they afford on both sides. For instance, Fr. Jacob Wichner published at Vienna, in 1888, a book of 239 pages on "The Monastery of Admont and its Relations to Art, from Documentary Sources." Admont was one of the greatest and richest houses in Austria; yet anyone who troubles to follow up the positive evidence alleged by Fr. Wichner, and the negative evidence which he does not so much emphasize, will, I think, feel the strength of my objections here. The relevant pages are, for non-monastic artists about the place, 65, 67–8, 70–3, 98–101, 115, 133, 143–5, 148, 150–2, 185, 187, 193, 196; for monastic artists 66 ?, 115, 133, 143 ?, 222 ?.

[2] W. G. Searle: *Christ Church, Canterbury* (1902), pp. 172 ff.

apologists naturally plead all that can be said in favour of their clients; yet never once, among all that I have read, is there any claim of their services to art. It is only modern apologists who have invented this plea.

When St. Bernard, again, wrote his famous letter against what he looked upon as the extravagances of early twelfth-century monastic art, there is not a word in that letter, I believe, which can be construed into an implication that these monks were themselves artists. On the contrary, when he speaks of waste, it is not for wasted time that he blames the monks of great abbeys (as would have been the case if they had done the carvings and paintings themselves) but for wasted money.

And, as a last argument in this direction, we may ask how it is that the monks after the Reformation, in France and Austria and Italy and Spain, where they were left in full freedom of action, did practically nothing as artists?

CHAPTER IV

MONASTIC ARTISTS (3)

NOR are all these testimonies merely accidental, against the theory of regular artistic work done by monks ; on the contrary, they are in accordance with the fundamental postulates of the Religious life. It was not easy for a medieval monk to become a real all-round artist (except under comparatively infrequent missionary conditions), and yet to remain faithful to his Rule. St. Benedict does, indeed, legislate for *artifices* in the monastery ; but this word means *artisan* rather than *artist*, in so far as the two ideas were ever distinguished in the Middle Ages. The catalogues in Trithemius and Busch are significant in this connexion. Moreover, in St. Benedict's time the choir-services were far shorter, nor had the idea yet grown up (though we find it very soon after his death) that the monk's business was so predominantly one of psalmody and brain-work as to render hard manual work incongruous. Those later developments worked so wide a separation between the choir-monk's and the artist's ideal as to make it difficult for any one man to combine both ; therefore, of the individual cases of monastic artists, an ominous proportion were unmonastic in their lives, for the Rule prescribes that the monk shall, if possible, never leave the precincts of the monastery. Therefore, his carving or painting or metalwork must normally be done for home consumption. We have the most abundant evidence of monks as traders in corn and wine and wool, but only the rarest and most exceptional notice of their making objects of art for sale.

54

Nuns, in fact, were often expressly forbidden to do so, except in the case of ecclesiastical vestments.[1] Very soon after a monastery had been well founded, the monks' own crying need for these things had nearly always been satisfied; in a few cases, the monks themselves had fashioned all the necessary church ornaments; in others the stuff had been bought or given, as the chronicles themselves record, by wealthy donors; then we do sometimes find monasteries selling their superfluous plate or vestments, but without any hint that those had been made on the premises. The monastic artist, there-fore, when he existed, was often tempted to wander outside his monastery; and all medieval moralists con-demn this as ruinous to the soul. Tuotilo of St. Gall is indeed represented as having worked thus outside his own monastery, in the early tenth century. The chronicler, Ekkehard IV, who wrote more than a century later,[2] tells us how, " While Tuotilo was working at his sculpture in Metz, two pilgrims came to him as he carved a statue of the Blessed Virgin, and begged for alms. He slipped some money into their hands; and, as they moved away, they said unto a cleric who stood by, ' God bless that man who hath been so merciful to us to-day; but is that his sister ?—that lady of wondrous beauty who is so serviceable to hand him his chisels and teach him how to use them ? ' The cleric marvelled at their words; for he had but lately parted from Tuotilo and had seen no such lady; wherefore he went back;

[1] Nuns were generally on a very different financial footing from that of the monks; this comes out very plainly in visitatorial injunctions. One of their great temptations was to eke out their scanty means, or to get a little forbidden private pocket-money, by working purses, girdles, etc., for sale.

[2] Schlosser rightly emphasizes the fact that Ekkehard is demonstrably mistaken in important particulars when he describes this heroic group of a century ago under Abbot Solomon—Iso, Karl, Notker Balbulus, Tuotilo, and Ratpert—*Reipublicae nostrae senatores*. Tuotilo especially, he shows, had by this time become a legendary figure (*Quellenbuch*, xix, pp. 152).

and for one bare moment, in the twinkling of an eye, he saw what they had described. Wherefore he and the pilgrims said unto Tuotilo, ' Father, Blessed art thou of the Lord, who hast so great a lady to instruct thee in thy work ! ' Tuotilo replied that he knew not what they said ; and he forbade them most strictly to say any such thing. On the morrow, hearing many folk report this glorious thing concerning himself, he withdrew himself from them and departed, nor would he ever thence-forward continue his work in that city. But, on the gilded [nimbus], where he left a plain flat surface, some other hand (I know not whose) has since carved these letters 'This holy object was carved by the Holy Mary herself.' The image itself, seated, and seeming as though it were living, is an object of veneration to all beholders even unto this day."[1] Such work might safely be committed to such a man as Ekkehard has described to us a few chapters earlier : "Tuotilo was very different [from Notker, whose fervent spirit burned in a frail body].[2] He was a good and vigorous man in his arms and in all his limbs, such as Favius teaches us to choose for athletes.[3] He was eloquent, clear of voice, an elegant workman in carving and painting ; musical, even as his companions were, but surpassing all in every kind of cithern and pipe ; for he taught the cithern also to the sons of the nobles in the building which the abbot set apart for them. He was a cunning messenger, for far or near, efficient in building and other arts of his own, endowed by nature with a strong and ready command of both languages [Latin and German], entertaining both in the grave and in the jocund vein, so that our fellow-monk Karl once said,

[1] M. G. H. *Scriptt*, vol. ii, p. 100.

[2] As critics have sometimes blamed me for using old editions, it may be noted that the Goldast-Senckenberg edition of Ekkehard (Frankfort a/M, 1730) has here a punctuation obviously more suited to the context than the modern M. G. H. edition, which is seriously misleading as to the sense of Ekkehard's words.

[3] Quintilian, *Inst. Orat.*, x, i, 333.

' Curses on the man who made a fellow of this kind into a monk ! ' But, with all these qualities, he had one more excellent ; in secret prayer he had the gift of tears ; he was a most ready composer of verses and melodies ; he was chaste, as a disciple of [the famous conventual schoolmaster] Marcellus [of St. Gall], who shut his eyes against women." [1]

Side by side with Tuotilo, we may fairly put a brief notice of a monastic artist from the pen of Tuotilo's own contemporary, Notker Balbulus.[2] Notker is telling of Charles the Great's palace at Aachen, and he adds : " There was in that city another artist [*opifex*], most excellent in all copper work and glass work," who, he goes on to say, cast a bell in rivalry with one cast by " Tancho, formerly monk of St. Gall," and cheated the Emperor out of a hundred pounds of silver. While, on the one hand, this gives us one more name of a monastic artist, on the other hand it shows what dangers art had for monasticism ; the clear implication is that Tancho had drifted out into the world, and had abandoned the monastic life. Tuotilo, indeed, is admirable in his harmony of art with religion in their early stages. Here we have both sides of the ideal embodied in actual life. the *Mirror of Monks* tells the cloisterer that he must live like Melchizedek, without father or mother or kindred ; the great Franciscan David of Augsburg insists that, except where edification is concerned, he must take no more interest in his fellow-men than in so many sheep. That puritanical theory could still be reconciled with an art like Tuotilo's (if the surviving ivory tablet ascribed to him be indeed his) and with all the art of his time. He might refuse ever to open his eyes upon a living

[1] Or, possibly, " For he [Tuotilo], shut," etc., M. G. H., vol. ii, p. 94.

[2] *The Monk of St. Gall*, in Jaffé, Bib. Rer. Germ. iv, 660, and M. G. H., vol. ii, p. 744, §29. Goldast, long ago, identified this nameless chronicler with Notker, and K. Zeumer seems to have put this beyond reasonable doubt (*Hist. Aufsätze G. Waitz gewidmet*, 1886, pp. 97 ff). Professor A. J. Grant's translation, in *The King's Classics* (p. 94), identifies the monk with the fraudulent artist.

woman, and yet carve or paint with perfect success
those Byzantine Madonnas and saints, conventionally
featured, conventionally clad, conventionally coloured,
which are so definitely characteristic of western art in
its cradle. But, when it began to take more definite
inspiration from human life, the full-blooded artist could
scarcely continue to ignore one half of the human race.
Quite as truly as Tuotilo typifies one class of monastic
artist in A.D. 900, the penitent of Montier-en-Der
typifies another class a century and a half later, when
cathedrals were beginning to rival or outdo the great
monastic churches, and a great public was forming
which was enthusiastically appreciative of the craftsman's performance in his craft, and comparatively indifferent to the facts of his private life. Even a great and
pious bishop like Hildebert of Le Mans might be tempted
to think more of a monk's artistic value than of his soul.
Geoffrey of Vendôme was one of the greatest French
churchmen of about A.D. 1100; five of his letters to
Hildebert deal with one insistent problem.[1] He had
lent "John the Mason, our monk" to the Bishop,
evidently for the work of the cathedral, and he now
writes, "Know that we have certainly excommunicated
this man because of his iniquity." His next letter runs,
"You have signified to me that John the monk has
come back from [his pilgrimage to] Jerusalem. It would
have been far better for him to have lived well in his own
monastery; not all who have seen the earthly Jerusalem
have earned the heavenly Jerusalem, but those who have
done well . . . You desire that he may live with you by
our leave; this is not to consider his soul, but rather
to harm it. [I therefore demand his return, and] if he
despises the bowels of mercy of his mother [monastery], I excommunicate him as a sacrilegious man." The next letter
is still more emphatic; "He has left us in disobedience,
yet you have long kept him, and keep him still, contrary
to his solemn vow and to our will; wherein you would

[1] Nos. 16, 24, 25, 29, 30; Mortet, p. 292.

seem to despise the safety of his soul and to forget your own promise." In the next letter, " we have oftentimes summoned him to return ; he has oftentimes promised, yet he cometh not ; if he does not come by Thursday next (short of grievous bodily infirmity), then we must proceed to extremities." And, in the last : " Know that we have excommunicated him and cut him off from the body of Holy Church . . . wherefore we beseech all Christian believers in that Christ who knoweth no man outside the unity of the Catholic and Apostolic Church to abstain from all association with this excommunicate person, lest (which God forbid !) they be infected by this foul and filthy communication and go to perdition." We therefore beg the bishop of Le Mans not only to abstain from the man's society but to fulfil his own promise and send him back. That letter was probably effectual ; for we hear no more of John the Mason, and Geoffrey was a pertinacious man where he felt that any principle was at stake.

A still more interesting story, supplying much that we can only guess at in this Vendôme case, is narrated in a collection of miracles of St.-Berchaire, compiled by a monk at the bidding of Abbot Berno or Bruno, who was present at the Council of Reims in 1049.[1] He writes : " Brother Hugh was offered to God, as a boy, at the monastery of [*illegible in MS.*]. The discipline of the place kept him long within bounds ; the monks taught him well in different branches of art and compelled him to follow their own regular course of life. But, as he grew up to manhood, he longed, as youth naturally does, to live his own irregular life as his fancy might dictate. The monastery rendered this impossible, so, hating what he should have loved, he deserted the community which had brought him up, and fled to Châlons. The then bishop of Châlons, Gibuin, recognised his talents and kept him at his court, stimulating him to work upon the new cathedral which he was building, and helping

[1] Printed by Mabillon, in *AA. SS. O. S. B.* Saec. II, pp. 835 ff.

him liberally with money. [This cathedral was finished in 1147.] But the young man, enjoying now so freely the glory of his mortal life, began to lapse into utter forgetfulness of the life to come. Yet that most loving Lord who would that all men should not perish, but be saved, caught him in the cords of His most merciful pity and recalled him marvellously from the snares of death. For this bishop of Châlons, whose patronage this young Hugh enjoyed, came to consecrate the abbey church of Montier-en-Der, where St.-Berchaire is buried ; and, by God's providence, he took Hugh with him. There the honourable Abbot Bérenger, and his monks, hearing from the Bishop how expert this Hugh was in art, besought him so urgently to leave the young man behind in the monastery that the Bishop at last consented. So the prelate returned to his own cathedral, and the monks with their abbot prepared a lodging for the guest so graciously left to their care ; a lodging (I say) apart from the rest, where he had not only all that he needed, but, sad to relate, even all sorts of superfluities at his own desire. Here they set him to fashion a beautiful crucifix, after the form in which they knew him to be skilled. But the Saviour of the World, who washed away the sins of mankind, did not suffer patiently that His face should be fashioned by the neglected hands of this man whom His long-suffering tolerance had long expected. For, while the artist was carving this crucifix, and was carving in shapely fashion this image of the Redeemer who suffered for the salvation of all men, he was seized with a sharp sickness and lay hard at death's door. Then, oppressed with almost intolerable anguish, he began to implore the help of the brethren with tears and supplications ; ' O ! ' cried he, ' hasten to make a new man of me by clothing me in that monastic cowl wherein, I confess, I lived fraudulently as a wolf in sheep's clothing.' So the brethren, pitying his vehement anguish, filled the private chamber wherein the sick man lay, and, with tears and fervent charity, granted his petition according to the Rule. But the

devil, who lieth in wait for souls and envieth all that
is good, seeing that the poor wretch was now reformed,
and clad in the habit that he had so long and foolishly
despised—the devil (I say), who had long grudged at
this Holy Order of monks, hating it for the harm that
they had done him, turned all his wrath upon this
artist, renewing his manifold and crafty devices with
many turns of guile.   Soon, therefore, a vast host of
demons burst upon him, led by two more grisly than the
rest, who rushed with savage violence into the sick man's
chamber and strove with all their power to tear his
wretched soul from his body.   Yet, by God's merciful
protection, there came a pause in their onslaught, wherein
one of the demons reproached his fellow for his delay
in bearing off this soul which they had come to snatch.
The other answered that he was powerless against the
protection of the most renowned martyr St.-Berchaire,
whose holy bones were there buried and worshipped;
'Yea,' said the first, 'and I can do nothing because
I see him fortified with the Last Communion of the
Body of Christ, and defended by the prayers of St.-
Berchaire's monks.'   Thus their dispute dragged on,
while the poor wretch shuddered at the horrible tumult;
when, suddenly and marvellously, while the sick man
lay a helpless spectator of all these things, there appeared
a single Hand, which in its unspeakable mercy scattered
the demons and put them to flight, thus, by God's
commanding power, supplying the patient's weakness.
For that blessed and truly blessed Mother of God, who
is glorious with all mercy, listening with her most pitiful
ears to the complaints of the brethren whose prayers
warned her of the sick man's approaching departure,
hastened to send her protection to bear up the failing
forces of this single sufferer.   And, not long afterwards,
this Mistress of the Archangels came in her own person,
intending in her kindly compassion to see with her own
eyes the sufferer's palsied limbs, lest the Evil One should
bear away him whom her Son Jesus Christ had redeemed

with His sacred blood. For, suddenly, on the label of the crucifix[1] which stood at the foot of the prostrate artist, there burst forth to his sight an ethereal globe surrounded with milk-white circles and adorned at certain marked points with shining stars.[2] Here, by God's grace, the globe was seen to cleave in twain, and there shone in the midst of this division a heavenly queen, clad in fine-spun robes of so ineffable beauty that none could doubt her to be the Mother of God. Her sacred head shone with glory and bliss ; and she moved downwards along the cross, gliding from top to bottom as on a track of beaten gold, and taking her seat as Mistress in the Throne of Her Son. Then this most pitiful Virgin deigned to comfort this monk, broken in body by the grievous torments of his sickness and in soul by the devices of these demons : ' Poor wretch ! ' she said, ' Lo ! my Son hath been moved to mercy by my prayers and by those of His servant St.-Berchaire. He hath now granted thee a respite for repentance, that thou mayest return into the place wherein thou wast offered to God and to His saints, and mayest henceforth amend thy life as He would have it.' With these words she stretched out the hand of mercy in the face of the dismayed crowd of devils, raised him from his couch, and left him in good health, eager to tell the bystanders the lamentable story of all that he had suffered and seen."

Here we see, through the embarrassed periods of the good monk's rudimentary Latinity, the delirium of a real artist. Unfortunately, he is concerned only with the miracle ; we may feel the keenest curiosity as to the young man's later life and final fate, but of that the chronicler tells us nothing. Almost equally romantic, though in a different way, is what Salimbene tells us concerning a musical friend of his own, in the middle of

[1] *In titulo crucis.*

[2] According to the medieval conception of the earth as placed in the midst of a series of concentric hollow spheres, in each of which a planet was set.

the thirteenth century. This was Brother Vita, of Lucca, "the best singer in the world of his own time in both kinds, namely in harmony and in plain-song," who often left the Franciscan Order for the milder Rule of St. Benedict, but "when he wished to return, Pope Gregory IX was ever indulgent to him, both for St. Francis's sake and for the sweetness of his song. For once he sang so enchantingly that a certain nun, hearing his song, cast herself down from a window to follow him; but this might not be, for she broke her leg with the fall. This was no such hearkening as is written in the last chapter of the Song of Solomon : ' Thou that dwellest in the gardens, the friends hearken, make me hear Thy voice.' " [1]

When we come to the Renaissance, with its quickened sense of artistic individualism and its laxer monastic discipline, instances of this kind become more common. Side by side with Fra Angelico, as real a Dominican as Tuotilo was Benedictine, yet working often under Popes and great churchmen outside his own monastery,[2] we get a friar like Lippo Lippi, who cast the frock to the nettles and married a nun. Of another, Müntz writes with perfect truth : " This brother Giuliano di Amadeo is better known for his maladministration of the monastery of which he was prior than for his artistic talent." [3] And, counting the bad with the good, we find only a small proportion of monastic artists in Vasari's *Lives*.

If this be so in the comparatively easy work of painting, we need not wonder that monks were even less anxious to monopolize the harder work of stone-carving, or the really laborious task of dressing freestone and great oaken beams. The very emphasis which writers find themselves forced to lay upon a few instances, repeated

[1] *From St. Francis to Dante*, 2nd ed., p. 99.

[2] It must be remembered that the Dominicans had nothing like the 66th chapter of the Benedictine Rule, which prescribes strict claustration within the monastic precincts.

[3] *Les arts à la cour des papes*, vol. ii (1879), p. 31.

regularly from book to book, is in itself suggestive. We have already seen monks working occasionally at their own buildings in the exceptional fervour of some great reform; and there is an often-quoted passage in the Gloucester chronicle: " In the year of our Lord 1242, the new vault over the nave of our church was finished not by the help of artisans, as before, but by the spirit and vigour of monks dwelling there in the said monastery."[1] But Prof. Willis suggested poverty as the cause of this exceptional proceeding; and Miss Rose Graham shows that there is documentary evidence of debt and mismanagement at the monastery during these very years.[2] In any case, this amateur work " was not an artistic success. They cut and maimed the features of the fine old Norman clerestory, and placed their weak work too low . . . there, in this first pointed vaulting, was a grievous and irreparable injury."[3]

This story has come down to us only in one brief sentence; but two far more significant episodes are recorded at nearly five hundred years' interval.

Bede shows us the lay workman attached to, and domiciled within, the monastery. The whole context implies that this was an ordinary arrangement, and emphasizes the rashness of those who, like Montalembert, take every case of a workman labouring in the precincts as proof of artwork done by the monks themselves.

Bede writes (*Ecclesiastical History*, Book V, Chap. XIV, A.D. 704): " I knew a brother myself—would to God I had not known him—whose name I could mention if it were necessary, and who resided in a noble monastery, but lived himself ignobly. He was frequently reproved by the brethren and elders of the place, and admonished to adopt a more regular life; and though he would not give ear to them, he was long patiently borne with by them, on account of his usefulness in temporal works, for

[1] *Chron. et Cart. Glouc.*, R. S., vol. i, p. 29.

[2] V. C. H. *Gloucs.*, vol. ii, p. 55.

[3] Gambier Parry, quoted in Bell's Cath. Series, *Gloucester*, p. 32.

he was an excellent carpenter; he was much addicted to drunkenness, and other enticements of a lawless life, and was more accustomed to stop in his workhouse day and night, than to go to church to sing and pray, and hear the word of life with the brethren. For which reason it happened to him according to the saying, that he who will not willingly and humbly enter the gate of the church, will certainly be damned, and enter the gate of hell whether he will or no. For he falling sick, and being reduced to extremity, called the brethren, and with much lamentation, and like unto one damned, began to tell them, that he saw hell open, and Satan at the bottom thereof; as also Caiaphas, with the others that slew our Lord, by Satan's side, and delivered up to avenging flames. 'In whose neighbourhood,' said he, 'I see a place of eternal perdition provided for me, miserable wretch that I am.' The brothers, hearing these words, began seriously to exhort him, that he should repent even then whilst he was in the flesh. He answered in despair, 'It is now no longer time to change my course of life, when I have myself seen my judgment passed.' Whilst uttering these words, he died without having received the last Communion, and his body was buried in the remotest parts of the monastery, nor did any one dare either to say masses or sing psalms, or even to pray for him.' " [1]

The second story is recorded in the contemporary *Life* of St. Stephen, Abbot of Obazine near Limoges, who flourished in 1150.[2] When he built his abbey-church, although the brethren laboured at the work (for this was a new and reformed community), yet they were insufficient to complete it themselves, and a band of lay masons was engaged. The biographer, in his eagerness to prove St. Stephen's miraculous powers, shows us

---

[1] The story is quoted from Bede, without comment, by a Franciscan of about 1270 (A. G. Little, *Liber Exemplorum*, 1908, p. 94).

[2] I have translated this whole episode at length in *Medieval Garner* (1st ed., p. 86; 2nd ed., vol. ii).

F

incidentally how sadly the monks lacked masonic skill, and the skilled masons lacked monastic self-denial. St. Stephen laid so great stress on the Benedictine prohibition of a flesh diet, that he would suffer no butcher's meat upon the premises, even for the use of these unfortunate hirelings, who were guiltless of Benedictine vows. He evidently reasoned, " Who builds good churches must himself be good "—a sophism which Dr. Johnson had not yet arisen to explode. The workmen, loathing the daily round of herbs and pulse, secretly bought a pig and cooked it in the forest, bringing back the unconsumed remnants to hide at home. A little bird brought the news to St. Stephen, who came round with several of his seniors, and discovered the abomination hidden betwixt two barrels in the masons' lodge. What should be done with this unclean flesh ? The seniors counselled moderation, but the saint knew no compromise in such a matter ; he cast the pork solemnly upon the dunghill, with every attendant circumstance of ignominy. The workmen, learning this, threw down their tools and proclaimed a general strike. St. Stephen, after vainly arguing the question on moral grounds, fell back upon the employer's last resource in all ages, and assured them that he could get plenty of better men in their stead. No doubt the capitalist had a distinctly more favourable position, as against the striking operative, in the twelfth century than he has now ; but we may infer from other authentic evidence that St. Stephen was one of those men whose real piety and charity is bound up with so plain a resolve to have their own way in the long run, that men find it cheaper to grant it them at once. However this may be, the masons were presently " pricked to the heart," and " resumed the work, to their own profit and that of their souls." It is difficult to conceive how St. Stephen could have faced these difficulties and risks involved in the employment of a considerable band of laymen on the monastic premises, unless real manual work in building had been far from the

average monk's ordinary vocation, even in this new and
enthusiastic community at the high tide of the great
twelfth century reform. We shall come, in a later
chapter, to one undoubted monastic artist, whose book
also implies a school of monastic pupils in his own
monastery, the so-called Monk Theophilus, at the end
of the eleventh century. He wrote an admirable handbook for the practice of all arts, compiled from previously-
existing sources, which may be traced back to Greece, and
ultimately to Egypt.[1] But we cannot infer from these
surviving handbooks, which are generally rather assumed
than proved to be monastic, anything more than what
we know from other sources ; that art was often practised
within the monastic precincts, and sometimes by the monks
themselves.

I feel, then, that the story of the monastic artist (even
in the more moderate forms in which it is presented by
such able writers as Professors Moore and Baldwin Brown
and Sir T. G. Jackson) is to a great extent legendary ;
and, if so, then it is a mischievous legend, since it tends
to falsify the real perspective of medieval art history, and
to misdirect our aspirations for the future. But, lest
I should seem to exaggerate in the other direction, let
me conclude with a brief summary of the facts as I conceive them.

Art is no essential part of the monk's vocation in the
Benedictine or any other Rule ; it may almost be said
that some of the best-known Rules, such as the Cistercian
and Carthusian, practically exclude it altogether. It is
true, St. Benedict speaks of *artifices*, but the natural
sense of this word is *artisans ;* or rather, nobody then
clearly differentiated between the two ideas. Lenoir, when
he explains it otherwise, deserts the paths of ordinary history and follows blindly after Montalembert's imagina-

---

[1] The earliest is a papyrus found in a tomb at Thebes, dating from
the third or early fourth century A.D. *Cennino,* p. xxii. These few
pages of Mrs. Herringham's introduction give a useful conspectus of
the subject.

tion.[1] We have therefore no right to go here beyond the
fact that St. Benedict, and practically all other monastic
law-givers, insisted on a certain amount of manual work,
which in the nature of the case was generally the rough
work needed in house or field. Even that prescription of
manual work was very early neglected; this transpires
from a hundred little indications; for instance, St.
Benedict's own disciple, St. Maur, saw no reason why
the monks should labour in the fields now that they were
well enough endowed to hire workmen; and Peter the
Venerable, in about 1130, is most apologetic to his subjects
of the great reformed Cluniac Order when he explains
why he has tried to recall them to some slight imitation
of the Benedictine precept of manual work.[2] The best
monks were inclined to exaggerate their ideal of other-
worldliness, and to assume that, as against their main
duties of prayer and contemplation, all other activities
weighed as mere dust in the balance. Less fervent
monks, on the other hand, would not naturally spend their
spare time in labouring for the adornment of a church
and cloister where they could afford to employ professionals who, in at least nine cases out of ten, would do
the work far better for the hire of a day labourer. I do
not mean that we can pigeon-hole men's motives exactly
like this; but I do hold that neither religious reasons
nor worldly reasons would, in the large majority of cases,
turn the monk into an artist. Moreover, it must be
remembered that, in many places and at many times,
only a minority of the monks were men with a real
monastic vocation; pious and orthodox contemporaries
assure us over and over again that the majority had

[1] Lenoir, *Arch. Mon.*, vol. i, p. 34 : " Bientôt saint Benoît établit dans sa
règle que l'architecture, la peinture, la mosaïque, la sculpture et toutes les
branches de l'art seraient étudiées dans les monastères ; aussi le premier
devoir des abbés, des prieurs, des doyens, était-il de tracer le plan des
églises et des constructions secondaires des communautés qu'ils étaient
appelés à diriger."

[2] I hope to give full evidence on this point in the third volume of
Five Centuries of Religion.

drifted into the cloister as a place where they would be better off, on the whole, than they were likely to be in the world.[1] That, I think, is the main explanation of the admitted barrenness of post-reformation monasteries in matters of art.

But, in the quite early age, things were different. For about three centuries—let us say, roughly, from A.D. 500 to 800—Western civilization was under such an eclipse as we see at this moment in Russia. In those wild times not much of art or letters could survive except within the walls of a monastery; and therefore the majority of artists were either monks or lay workmen living under shelter of a monastery.[2] The same may be said again, though rather less emphatically, of at least another century from about A.D. 900 to 1000. Then, with a strong wave of comparative peace and material prosperity all over Europe, came a great monastic revival and a great era of church-building; and, in that sense, Romanesque architecture is rightly called a monastic art. But, even at this time of exceptional fervour and prosperity, there is no real evidence that any but a very small minority of the monks worked themselves, either as designers or as craftsmen.[3] The lay brethren, of course, did so more frequently; but the system of lay brethren had practically died out even in the most fervent Orders before the end of the Middle Ages, and among the Benedictines and Austin Canons—that is, at least two-

[1] This has lately been brought out with great force by Dom Berlière, in his paper read before the Royal Academy of Belgium (Oct. 8, 1923).

[2] Even the master-mason, it will be seen, was sometimes a bondman.

[3] One of the most valuable source-books for the student is the late Victor Mortet's *Recueil de textes relatifs à l'histoire de l'architecture, etc.* published in 1911. This collection of more than 400 octavo pages covers the years 1000–1200, and on pp. 44 ff. Mortet brings together the texts relating to " the personal contribution of monks and abbots to the works, materials (masonry, or carriage of stones) in different monasteries [between 1005 and 1077]." These are only three in number, and fill only three pages, though the period is one of exceptional monastic activity. There is, however, an interesting monastic artist in Cæsarius of Heisterbach, *Dialogus Miraculorum*, bk. viii, ch. 24.

thirds of monasticism as a whole—it had never been
strong at any time. Moreover, the buildings themselves,
where they remain, frequently suggest that they were
done by hired workmen; for they are covered with
masons' marks, a fact which, as I hope to show in a later
chapter, implies business and not merely friendly relations
between employers and employed. This may be verified,
for instance, at Fountains Abbey, at Fontenay in Burgundy
and at the ruins of Dammartin in the Pas de Calais.

Then, roughly from 1150 onwards, the great towns
wished to have cathedrals which should not only rival
but outdo the great monastic churches. To that movement I come in Chapter XVII.; here it is only sufficient
to say that all the best authorities, from Viollet-le-Duc
onwards, recognize that the builders of these cathedrals
were laymen, and that though earlier art had been in a
sense monastic, this could no longer be said with truth of
Gothic art. Even in metal-work and miniatures, the two
arts in which monks had most excelled, the best work,
and the vast majority of the work, is henceforward done
by professionals. When we do get some casual notice
connecting a Religious with art, it is remarkable how often
the notice itself implies that the case is in some way
exceptional. " Giovanni de Rossi had a son named
Antonio who became a Dominican in the Convent of
Sta. Maria Novella, at Florence, and who being afflicted
with a tedious and incurable malady which rendered him
unfit for other studies, occupied himself entirely in writing
and illuminating the choral books of the convent. He
died of plague in 1495." [1] The *Opus Anglicanum*, that
beautiful ecclesiastical embroidery for which medieval
England was famed on the Continent, has been confidently ascribed to the nuns, but on insufficient authority.

---

[1] Merrifield, vol. i, p. 12. Illuminating and glass-painting, however,
seem to have been much more commonly practised by Religious in
Renaissance Italy than during the Middle Ages proper; ibid., introd.,
pp. xxxi–lxxv. This was a place and a time at which conventual discipline
was much relaxed.

The nuns are frequently blamed by strict disciplinarians for embroidering small things for the sake of forbidden pocket-money; but no evidence has been produced to prove their work on a great scale. Indeed, Professor Lethaby has recently expressed himself strongly to the contrary. " He had long held the view that the famous works of Opus Anglicanum embroidery were produced by highly-trained experts in London shops, and therefore designed by London artists. Master Walter, the King's painter, they might hardly doubt, was one of these." [1]

We cannot assume manual skill, though it may be implied, in such a casual notice as we find in Bishop Alnwick's visitation of Daventry Priory in 1442: " Brother William Watforde, the sub-prior, says that the prior is of no account in matters temporal; therefore all things are like to go to naught; albeit he has some degree of experience in the craft of the stone-mason and the carpenter." [2] The most we can certainly infer is that William, though unequal to the financial management of a good-sized monastery, had real capacity for supervising the building work. However, the true monastic artist survives here and there, even to the end of the Middle Ages, as an exception. The beautiful Sherborne Missal, for instance, was written for an abbot of Sherborne in the later fourteenth century by a monk of that Benedictine house, and was illuminated by a Dominican friar.[3] Dr. M. R. James seems rather inclined to look upon the sketch-book in the Pepys library, which was begun about this same time, as the product of a monastic atelier; but he warns us that he does not plead his reasons as decisive; and, in any case, the product of a monastic atelier cannot safely be assumed, without further evidence, as the handiwork of an actual monk.[4]

[1] *The Times*, June 16, 1927, p. 9 (a paper read before the British Academy).
[2] Lincoln Record Soc., vol. 14 (1918), p. 61.
[3] See the Roxburghe Club volume for 1920, and Mr. Herbert's introduction, p. 15.
[4] Walpole Society, vol. xiii, p. 16.

Gothic art, therefore, is not in any real sense a monastic art, although monks were certainly among its most liberal patrons, being able to spend far more money upon building than most other people, and struggling with a natural and healthy rivalry to outdo the bishops, as the bishops strove to outdo the monks. The monasteries, then, produced in the Gothic period patrons rather than artists ; the very Rule of the monk would have made it almost impossible for him to arrive at anything like that artistic proficiency on so large a scale which we see in the great Gothic churches. Moreover, we must beware of connecting Gothic art too closely, in any direction, with the real religious spirit. Many of the medieval saints had less sympathy with the sculpture of their own day than Milton had, looking back upon the great monuments of the past. It would be difficult to find, in any of the saints or theologians or poets of the Middle Ages, a parallel to those dozen lines from *Il Penseroso* :—

> " But let my due feet never fail
> To walk the studious cloister's pale
> And love the high imbowëd roof,
> With antique pillars massy proof,
> And storied windows richly dight
> Casting a dim religious light.
> There let the pealing organ blow
> To the full-voiced quire below,
> In service high, and anthems clear,
> As may with sweetness, through mine ear
> Dissolve me into ecstasies
> And bring all Heaven before mine eyes.

The monk " Theophilus " himself, in the famous rhapsody which celebrates the glories of his art, scarcely rises to higher enthusiasm than this.

CHAPTER V

THE LAY ARTIST

THE story of St. Stephen of Obazine illustrates the shifting of gravity from the cloister to the world outside. It shows how, at least as late as 1150, when the west front of Chartres was being built, and when general enthusiasm for building was about at its highest, it was natural for the layman even to invade the monastic precincts. This new community of Obazine, comparatively poor, and exceptionally earnest under its saintly abbot, might indeed give some help to the hired masons; but only in the last resort, if at all, could it do without them. From this century onward the monastic artist is negligible almost everywhere, as for some time past he had grown more and more exceptional. We shall come back to him for a while in Chapter XVII; meanwhile it is the layman with whom we are concerned, and a layman who differed little in temperament and training from the modern artist. In 1259 Henry III is still speaking of a monk of Westminster as " our beloved painter "; in 1290, Edward I had a monk of Bury for his painter; but, as early as 1238, Grosseteste had fulminated against artists who ground their colours on the altars of the churches[1]; and Edward II's court painter had no

---

[1] *Epistolæ*, R. S., p. 156, a prohibition which is more than once repeated by English diocesan synods or provincial councils. A marble slab for grinding colours was an indispensable article to the painter, but it was costly and heavy to carry; hence the temptation to use the altar-slab for these profane purposes. A cathedral painter at York left his two grinding-slabs as valuable legacies (*York Fabric Rolls*, p. 207). Cennini (ch. 36) does not expect the painter to be able to afford a stone of more than one foot square.

more tincture of ecclesiastical dignity than his cook. We find, among that king's wardrobe accounts : "*Item*, paid to Jak de Seint Albon, Painter Royal, who danced on a table before the king and made him laugh beyond measure, by way of gift through the king's own hands, to help himself, his wife, and his children, 50 shillings. . . . *Item*, paid at Wolmer Lodge, where the king chased the stag, to Morris Cook, of the kitchen, because he rode there before the king and fell oftentimes from his horse, whereat the king laughed heartily, in manner of gift by royal command, 20 shillings."[1]

Even in the "monastic" period of architecture, the greatest buildings were often raised by hordes of comparatively unskilled labourers, free or unfree, whose numbers compensated in some measure for their want of technical skill. The masons' marks scrawled on the piers of Ely nave, in their careless haste and their inequality, tell as plain a tale as the rough axe-hewn stones, and the wide ill-fitting joints. One type of miracle is very common in the lives of saints about this time ; during the building of some church, a portion of the fabric collapsed, or the scaffolding fell, or some other similar accident ; yet, through the merits of the particular saint concerned, nobody was hurt ; or, at least, the damage was less than might reasonably be expected. The master-mason of those days—that is, the architect— might even be a serf ; William, the Second Earl of Warrenne, who was the virtual founder of Castleacre Priory in about 1100, gave to the monks, among other lands and perquisites, "Wolmar the mason, with his holding of 15 acres, and a garden worth twelve shillings." [2] The cathedral of Freising, about A.D. 750, possessed a serf who was a skilled metal-worker (*artifex malleator*), and Schlosser has found two other similar examples about the same time.[3] Two serf-artists are mentioned in

[1] F. Peck, *Antiq. Repertory*, vol. ii, p. 407.
[2] Dugdale-Caley, vol. v, p. 50.
[3] Schlosser, *Beiträge*, p. 179.

different contexts in the life of St. Eloi.[1] About 1090, the abbot of St.-Aubin d'Angers gave to Fulk, a serf, the privilege of fraternity, and an acre of vineyard and a house, on condition that he would paint and glaze the abbey church. Land and house were to return to the abbey at his death, " unless he have a son skilled in his father's art and willing to use it in St.-Aubin's service." (Mortet, p. 264.) But Mortet is mistaken in describing Fulk as a lay-brother ; in that case, there could be no question of his having a son later on. Again Eugenius III, in 1146, confirmed to the monks of Peterborough, among other gifts of land, etc., " the services of Aluric the mason, Egelred the cordwainer . . ., Lefwin the carpenter . . ., Alberic Norman the secretary," whom some benefactor had given to the abbey.[2] In 1304 we find that an English mason's wife is a bond-woman, and probably he himself a bondman.[3] As late as 1475, the Margrave of Baden had a bondman-mason ; as his status allowed him no seal others had to seal a contract for him.[4] But the earliest English masonic statutes, of the early fifteenth century, expressly exclude serfs from the gild ; since, if their lords came to claim them, this would provoke a fight in the lodge.[5]

Naturally, therefore, even when the medieval artist grew rapidly in skill, he still occupied a low rank in the feudal system, in which " land was at the base of society ; and . . . a person's condition was far less definitely deter-mined by education, by merit, or even by birth, than by property." [6] The mason and the carpenter were

---

[1] Migne, P. L., vol. 87, col. 487 d. and 488 d.

[2] *Cal. Pap. Letters*, vol. i, p. 558.

[3] J. E. T. Rogers, *Ag. and Prices*, vol. ii, p. 610.

[4] Janner, p. 115.

[5] Halliwell, § 4. By § 5, it was equally forbidden to receive illegitimate sons, or men who were halt or lame. But we must make allowance for poetic exaggeration in all these articles, which claim that " by old time," the laws required " gentle kind," and that " great lords' sons " sometimes became masons.

[6] B. Guérard, *Cart. de St.-Père*, 1840, p. cxiii.

ordinarily brothers or sons of the agricultural labourer, the smith, the town artisan, or small tradesman ; and it was exceptional for these craftsmen-artists to rise perceptibly above their parents or their brethren. In the thirteenth century, we find them most frequently paid at 3*d.* a day, which would perhaps have the purchasing power of from £2 to £2 10*s.* a week in present-day currency. A large proportion received only 2½*d.* or 2*d.* a day ; on the other hand, we occasionally find even 4*d.*, 5*d.*, 5½*d.*, 6*d.* ; but certainly some of these, and probably all, were master-masons.[1] In the fourteenth century, and at great royal buildings like Westminster Abbey or Palace, we find the master-mason receiving 9*d.* a day (c. 1300) or 1*s.* (1332 and 1385), or even 1*s.* 6*d.* (1352, marble-carver at St. Stephen's Chapel). At these sometimes a few lower, but still high-grade masons received 6*d.* The master-carpenter sometimes had 1*s.* (1383, the construction of the wonderful roof of Westminster Hall).[2] It is very seldom that we find much difference in the payment of masons or carpenters or smiths as such ; and the most striking exception known to me is curious in more respects than one. At St. George's, Windsor, at the end of the fifteenth century, the master-smith was paid twice as much in money as the master-mason.[3] In

[1] J. E. T. Rogers, *Hist. Agric., and Prices*, vol. ii, *passim*.

[2] Lethaby, Westminster I, pp. 186, 189, 192 ; II, pp. 133, 139, 149–50, 153. I have omitted cases where it is pretty plain that the mason got his food and a clothing allowance into the bargain. At this time, St. Louis's master-mason was receiving 4 sols a day (=1*s.* sterling) +100 sols a year for robes, his food and keep for two horses at the palace. He would have many business journeys (Lethaby, *Med. Art*, p. 253). At St.-Gilles, about 1250, the master-mason had the equivalent of £3 15*s.* a year; at Girona in Spain (1320) he received £12 10*s.*, which Quicherat regards as a high wage (*Mélanges d'arch el d'hist.*, vol. ii, p. 180 ; cf. p. 210 for wages in 1384).

[3] W. St. J. Hope, *Windsor Castle*, pp. 378 (where £23 5*s.* comes by a slip for £24 5*s.*), 399, 403, 406. Sir William, who had not at first noted the significance of these figures, was quite inclined to agree with the explanation here offered. On one occasion, at least, the clerk and mason are recorded to have received robes, and not the smith, though robes are mentioned in his covenant.

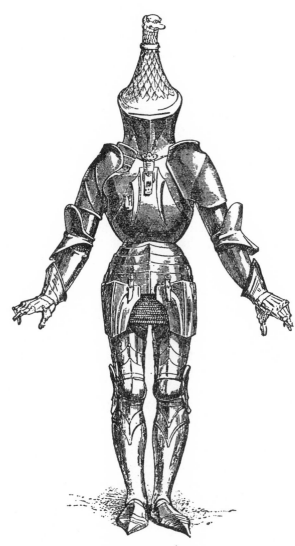

THE ARMOURER'S ART.

1477–78 the clerk of the works (business superintendent) got £10 a year, the master-mason £12, and the master-smith £24 5*s*. ; these wages remain exactly the same in two later years for which the rolls have survived. At the same time William Smyth, an ordinary workman kept to repair the masons' and carpenters' tools, received £4 per annum. The reason for this particular master-smith's higher wages—for definitely higher they must have been, however we suppose the master-mason to have had extras denied to the smith—was probably this ; that the smith was not only as fine an artist as any mason, but that he also added utility to beauty, and was an indispensable servant to the richest class in society. Nobles and knights needed armour ; the armour of that date was a marvel of delicate artistic curve combined with complicated mechanical adjustment ; and he who could thus combine the beautiful with the useful was worth, to the nobility, double the wage of a mere creator of beauty.[1]

That, however, is speculative ; the solid fact is that the artist was commonly paid as an artisan and reckoned as an artisan, and therefore art-work of all kinds was very cheap in comparison with modern prices. Chancels might be rebuilt for small parish churches, in 1342, at prices ranging from £10 to £172 ; the carving of the magnificent bishop's throne at Exeter Cathedral, a quarter of a century earlier, cost only about £12 10*s*. ; or, to estimate roughly in purchasing power at the present moment, from £250 to £400 at most.[2] In the later Middle Ages, we find the artist's wage and estimation rising, even in comparatively backward England. Henry de Yevele, Chaucer's contemporary and colleague, whom we have seen receiving 1*s*. a day, died in possession of two country

---

[1] For the armourer as artist see Viollet-le-Duc, *Dict. du Mobilier*, vol. v, p. 234.

[2] *E. H. R.*, 1911, pp. 110 ff. But these are only cases of rough rebuilding. See Appendix 4.

manors and several houses in London.[1] Thomas Draw-swerd, stone-carver of York, became sheriff of his native city, and finally represented it in Parliament (1512). Gibbon was not ashamed to trace his pedigree back to the marble-worker whom Edward III employed to build Queenborough Castle, and whom he rewarded with " an hereditary toll on the passage from Sandwich to Stonar." The family of Bertie, which has come in modern times to the two earldoms of Abingdon and Lindsey, is descended " from a mason who was employed in Winchester Cathedral, and afterwards built Calshot and other Solent castles, and whose father was a small copyhold farmer at Bersted early in the sixteenth century."[2] But these instances come from days when the modern capitalist system was rapidly developing; Yevele, for instance, earned part of his money by selling designs for other men to work out ; and this became fairly common ; at Bourges, in 1489, the citizens paid the equivalent of something like £50 modern " to Jacquet de Pigny, mason, for making a design for the Hotel de Ville."[3] It became common also for masons and carpenters to be paid for inspection of buildings. Sacchetti, writing in about Chaucer's time concerning Florence, shows us a painter of crucifixes who ordinarily had four or five or six in stock, all life-size ; he was trader as well as artist [4] ; so, again, at York, the master-mason who died in 1322 was a dealer in tombstones.[5]

But, even though the artist must generally content himself with an artisan's wages, did he not at least enjoy far higher estimation than his brother, the ploughman, or the yeoman farmer or the baron's retainer ? In exceptional

---

[1] His career may be traced through the indexes to Prof. Lethaby's *Westminster I* and *Westminster II*.

[2] *The Athenæum*, June 4, 1910, p. 668.

[3] Didron, *Annales archéologiques*, vol. i, p. 139. An instance of inspectors (A.D. 1521) on the same page.

[4] Novella 84.

[5] *York Fabric Rolls*, p. 207, note.

cases, this was certainly so. Professor Lethaby, writing of France, says : " These King's masons were, of course, held in high consideration, and were constantly in close contact with the king. The son of Raymond du Temple, king's mason, was godson of the king and a student at the University of Orleans." [1] But this was under Charles V, an exceptional patron of letters and arts ; and it would seem dangerous to press the inference very far. There is no more in the facts than we might possibly discover about any other artisan ; a royal huntsman's son then, like a gamekeeper's of to-day, might well be godson to royalty and university student. The general evidence seems to indicate an ordinary artisan's estimation for the mason or wood-carver or painter, correspondent with his artisan's pay. It is noticeable, to begin with, how inconspicuous he is in romance or poetry ; far less conspicuous than the modern artist.[2] And, in so far as he appears, he is seldom on the level of Raymond du Temple. There is sometimes the casual notice, when a great castle or church is mentioned in romance, that it had been built by a marvellous architect ; but this does not take us far beyond the baldest utilitarian relations between lord and artist. The monastic chronicler Ordericus Vitalis tells us, in quite a natural tone, about the castle of Ivry, that " famous, vast and most strongly fortified tower, built by Aubrée, wife of Ralph, Count of Bayeux, which Hugh, Bishop of Bayeux and brother to John, Archbishop of Rouen, held for a long time against the Norman dukes [his suzerains]. Men say that the countess aforesaid caused

[1] *Med. Art*, p, 256 ; cf. 258,

[2] L. Gautier, *La Chevalerie*, nouvelle éd., p. 468, note. " Il est très rare que nos chansous [de geste] donnent le nom de l'architecte d'un château. Dans la *Prise d'Orange*, on nomme celui qui a fait la tour de Gloriette, mais c'est un Sarrasin." Froissart, lover of art as he was, devotes six lines of praise to the greatest painter of his day north of the Alps, André Beaunepveu ; moreover, even these seem mainly due to the fact that André was a fellow-countryman ; and the notice is not brought in for its own sake, but as a side-light on the Duc de Berry's political manœuvres (ed. Buchon, vol. iii, p. 74).

the castle to be built by the architect Lanfred, whom she created Master of the Works after the building of the tower of Pithiviers, a man whose skill was praised far beyond that of all other artificers of his time in France. Then, when Lanfred had completed this castle of Ivry with much labour and at great cost, she caused him to be beheaded lest he should build another equal to it elsewhere."[1] In 1431 a distinguished notary at Paris, Jehan le Bègue, who was very much interested in art, made a collection of recipes and observations from all kinds of sources ; among these he relates, with no more apparent disgust than Ordericus, a much older story of the same kind :

" It is related that in the reign of Tiberius Cæsar a certain artist had discovered a way of making glass flexible and ductile. When he was admitted into Cæsar's presence, he handed a phial to him, which Cæsar indignantly threw on the ground, and it bent like a brazen vessel. The artist took up the phial from the pavement, and then taking a hammer out of his bosom he repaired the phial. Upon this Cæsar asked the artist whether any other person was acquainted with that method of making glass. When he affirmed with an oath that no other person knew the secret, Cæsar ordered him to be beheaded, lest, when this was known, gold and silver should be held dirt cheap, and the prices of all metals be reduced. And, indeed, if glass vessels did not break, they would be better than gold or silver."[2] Dante, it is true, brings Giotto and Cimabue into his epic, together with the illuminators, Oderisi and Franco, as instances of the fickleness of human fame ; but in Dante's Italy the Renaissance had already begun ; moreover, in this par-

---

[1] *Hist. Eccl.*, l. viii, c. 22. P. L., vol. 188, col. 628. The other instances briefly cited later down may be found in fuller detail in my *Social Life in Britain*, pp. 468 ff.

[2] Merrifield, vol. 1, p. 210. The story is also in *Gesta Romanorum* (ed. Swan, No. 44, p. 78). Here, however, there is a definite note of disapproval.

G

ticular matter, Dante was outstripping not only his contemporaries but even the ideas of two generations later. Benvenuto da Imola, professor at Bologna and contemporary of Chaucer, tells us how " some men " marvelled that the great poet should thus immortalize " men of unknown name and low occupation," *homines ignoti nominis et bassae artis*. But herein, thinks Benvenuto, Dante showed his genius, " for thereby he giveth silently to be understood how the love of glory doth so indifferently fasten upon all men, that even petty artisans—*parvi artifices*—are anxious to earn it, just as we see that painters append their names to their works." In short, we must read Dante here as we read Shakespeare in *Measure for Measure* :—

> The poor beetle, that we tread upon,
> In corporal sufferance finds a pang as great
> As when a giant dies.

That is, the mere artist may actually feel such pangs as the disappointed poet and the distinguished politician of whom Dante goes on to speak in his poem.

The novelist Sacchetti, a generation after Dante, represents an artist like Bonamico [Buffalmacco] as enjoying a great reputation in his meridian ; but he shows him badly sweated during his apprenticeship ; nor do any of the novelist's other stories of artists suggest anything like the consideration which men of the same class enjoyed in the full tide of the Renaissance ; though even that, as recent studies have shown, may easily be exaggerated.[1] The painter Calandrino, in Boccaccio's tale (*Dec.* VIII, 3) is easily duped by the sly companions who promise to show him a short way of cheating himself into a fortune ; for then, says he, " we can enrich ourselves in the twinkling of an eye, without having to drudge all day at daubing over the walls after the fashion

[1] Novella 191, see App. 5 ; the others dealing with artists are Nos. 84, 161, 169, 170–71, 192, 229. Boccaccio deals with them in Giorn. VI, 5 ; VIII, 3, 6, 9 ; IX, 3, 5. For Renaissance Italy, see Chapters XXIII–XXIV.

of a snail." And we get similar glimpses of the medieval scribe, who was just such an artisan-artist as the painter or the carver. Very frequent are the writer's expressions of relief at having finished his task: " The book is done, and the scribe dances with gladsome foot " ; " For such a price as this I will never write again " ; " Let the writer's pen, so full of labour, now find rest " ; " There is the very end ; for Christ's sake give me a drink ! " [1] At King's College Chapel, two of the overseers of the works received, by royal favour, a grant of arms, and were thenceforward within the exclusive gentleman-caste ; no such grant is recorded to any of the artists who laboured at King Henry VI's chapels, or indeed at any cathedral.[2]

It is interesting, also, to note what the great theologians and moralists say concerning the workers in " mechanical " arts ; a term which embraced artists and artisans, as distinguished from the " liberal " arts of theology, science and literature. The great mystic Hugh of St. Victor (c. 1120), writes that " these are called *mechanical,* that is, adulterine [from the Latin *mœchus,* adulterer] because they deal with the work of an artificer, which borrows its form from nature. So the other seven arts are called *liberal,* either because they demand liberty of mind (that is freedom of activity, seeing that they dispute subtly concerning the causes of the things) or because, of old, it was only freemen (that is, nobles) who were wont to study therein, while plebeians and the sons of ignoble folk practised the mechanical arts by reason of their skill in handiwork." [3] So, again writes St. Antonino of Florence, three centuries later.[4] " Now the mechanical arts are so called from the word *mœchor* [to commit adultery] ; for in them man's intellect is as it were adulterated, since it is created principally for the understanding of spiritual things, and

---

[1] For originals of these and others, see Appendix 6.
[2] See Willis and Clark, vol. i, p. 468.
[3] *Didascal,* l. II, c. 21 ; P. L., vol. 176, col. 760.
[4] *Summa Theologica,* pars. I, tib. i, cap. 3, §§ 3, 4 (ed. Verona, 1740, vol. i, col. 34).

in these mechanical arts it is occupied with material [*factibilia*] things. There are seven such arts : wool, construction [*armatura*], navigation, agriculture, hunting, medicine and the theatre. . . . Construction is divided into two branches, viz., architecture and metal-work. Architecture is divided into masoncraft and carpentry ; metal-work into those of the smithy and of the foundry. . . . And note that the inventors of the liberal and mechanical arts and philosophy, and authors of the books on those arts were commonly heathens and reprobate folk. . . . The fourth chapter of Genesis gives us to understand that it was the progeny of Cain who invented most of the mechanical arts ; and these men, in the matter of morals, commonly imitated their guilty father ; Cain it was who built the first city in this world, as though he would thereby signify that he had no lot in the heavenly city, Jerusalem." Bishop Rodrigo of Zamora dismisses the masons in one uncomplimentary sentence : " O how many false masonries and stones, how many false operations they work in carving or painting of wood ! " [1] Berthold of Regensburg, the great Franciscan mission-preacher, had said much the same a couple of centuries earlier ; between these two (about 1350) comes the mystic Rulman Merswin of Strassburg, who has a chapter uncomplimentary to " mechanical artists." [2] St. Bernardino of Siena (d. 1444) is no more favourable than St. Antonino. Among " necessary arts " he reckons " the art of architects, of shoemakers, of weavers and the like." But some folk abuse even these necessary arts ; " as to the superfluous and costly fabrication of hangings and coverlets and shirts, where the work costs ten times as much as the whole shirt, and dice, and backgammon-boards, and vain cards, and elaborate cages or bonnets for women's heads,

---

[1] *Speculum Humanæ Vitæ*, lib. 1, c. 26. The work was dedicated to Pope Paul II, to whose court Rodrigo was attached.

[2] *V. d. Neun Felsen* (1859), p. 41 ; Latinized by Surius in *Susonis Opera*, 1588, p. 377.

and women's face-paints and coronets of flowers, and
wanton pictures exciting to vanity or lust, and such-like
things, it is a most mortal sin to practise those arts, by
making or keeping or selling or giving such objects."
Plato, he thinks, was right, such folk should be extirpated
from the state ; nor are they excused from sin by pleading
that they are only following the example of the majority.
" Artificers of ornaments sin when they invent superfluous and curious things ; wherefore St. Chrysostom
saith (sup. Matt. hom. 49), 'we must cut much away
from the art of shoemakers and weavers,' " and all good
confessors will grope the artificer's conscience very
thoroughly on these points.[1] As to those who practise
elaborate church music, St. Bernardino quotes from
Canon Law : " such a singer-minister exasperates God
with his morals while he delights the people with his
voice." [2] The puritanism of Savonarola is well-known ;
but it is seldom realized that in this he did no more than
to push the teaching of orthodox disciplinarians to their
logical conclusion, and to interpret it fearlessly in action.[3]
Modern attempts to show that St. Thomas and other
scholastic philosophers were really interested in medieval
art, and worked out anything like a theoretical basis for
it, have not yet resulted in the production of any cogent
evidence.[4]

The question of anonymity in medieval art is thorny
and complicated. A saying has been ascribed to the great
palæographer, Léopold Delisle, to the effect that anonymity was practically imposed on fourteenth century
illuminators by the professional copyists and booksellers
who engaged them. But I have the assurance of his
successor in charge of the manuscripts at the Biblio-

[1] Opp., ed. de la Haye, vol. i, p. 161 (serm. 36). Compare the references which will be found in the index under ars, artifex, pictor, pictura,
pulcritudo, ornamenta.
[2] Ibid., vol. iii, p. 160, from Gratian, dist. xcii, c. 2.
[3] See farther in my later chapters.
[4] See later in Chapter XV and Appendix 23.

thèque Nationale, Monsieur Henri Omont, that Delisle
never committed himself to anything so strong ; and even
his milder verdicts on this subject have been disputed
recently by Monsieur F. de Mély.[1] But, much as we
owe to this writer's industry and minute observation, the
conclusion seems to be that those artists who signed at
all nearly always did so in very modest corners, and that
it is very exceptional to find a case where the man who
wrought the stone or limned the picture is granted anything like the prominence afforded to him who paid for
the work. It is significant, also, that the chief exceptions
are in Italy, Spain and the south of France, where the
great traditions of antiquity were most continuous, and
where we find least evidence for mason-serfs. Here and
there an English mason has incidentally recorded his
own share in the work ; but not with the splendid
formality of Constantin de Jarnac, whose *fecit hoc opus*
is quite as conspicuous as the epitaph of the bishop on
whose tomb he wrought. Compared with this, Andrew
Swinnow cuts a poor figure with his record casually
scratched on a pillar, or even Thomas Bate with his deep-
chiselled inscription on a capital. It is seldom that the
mason allows himself even the more modest signature of
a *rebus*, as when W. Hyndley carved a hind in the choir
of York Minster in memory of his work. Moreover, even
in Italy, and even when the current of the Renaissance
was running strongly, the artist was often kept strangely
in the background. The first great humanist pope,
Nicholas V (1447–1458), had no scruples of modesty for
himself ; but we know very little about his artists. " The
smallest tiles or bricks of St. Peter's and of the Vatican
palace were adorned with his arms ; he proudly opposed
his inscription of *Nic. PP. V.* to that of *Constantinus
Augustus.*" Yet, of the two chief artists whom he
employed, " nothing is more obscure than the biography

---

[1] *Revue archéologique*, Jan., 1911, p. 67 ff ; also in a large volume,
Signatures de Primitifs. Compare a much earlier article in *Annales archéologiques*, vol. i, pp. 78 ff.

of the Florentine sculptor and architect Bernardo Gamberelli," while Antonio of Florence has been at last

FROM COTON CHURCH, CAMBS.

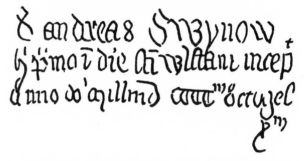

ANDREAS SWYNNOW HOC PRIMO IN DIE SANCTI WLSTANI INCEPIT ANNO DOMINI MILLESIMO CCCC^{mo} OCTOGESIMO PRIMO.

" Andrew Swynnow began this [pillar] first on St. Wulstan's Day, A.D. 1481."

FROM ROPSLEY CHURCH, LINCOLNSHIRE.

ista colūnna: facta : fuit: ad: fm̄: sti:

michit: anno: dm̄: iiĭ: q̊: lxxx̊: et:

nomē: factoris: thom̄s: bate: ðe: corby.

ISTA COLUMNA FACTA FUIT AD FESTUM SANCTI MICHAELIS ANNO DOMINI M°CCC°LXXX° ET NOMEN FACTORIS THOMAS BATE DE CORBY.

" This pillar was made on Michaelmas Day A.D. 1380, and the name of him who made it is Thomas Bate of Corby."

identified only in our own day, and nobody yet knows his family name.[1]

Here, again, is another indication from real life. Henri de Bruxelles was architect and mason of the great *jubé*,

[1] Müntz, 1878, pp. 77–83; so again for Pius II and his architects (p. 230); cf. 1879, pp. 13–14 (1464–1471).

or *pulpitum*, which divided nave from choir at the cathedral of Troyes. When he married, in 1384, the canons docked him of a day's pay, though they made up for this by a wedding present of twelve loaves and eight pints of wine, which would come to very much the same cost. And the negative side of this action was strictly according to the contract, which bound Henri and his companions " to work at the said *jubé* continually, summer and winter . . . and in case the said masons, or any one of them, shall cease to work upon any work-day, whether wilfully or for sickness or otherwise, he shall be docked and discounted for each day five shillings of Tours. . . . *Item*, the said masons have promised to continue their work between September 8th to Eastertide, from sunrise to sunset, without leaving the lodge except to dine competently once in the day. *Item*, during the said work, the Master of the Cathedral works shall provide them with coals for warming their lodge when it is necessary. And between Easter and September 8th the said masons shall continue the said work from a little after sunrise, after the fashion above rehearsed, until the hour when they may sup, at sunset." [1] At York Minster, in 1370, the masons swore to observe similar rules, under penalty of incurring " God's malison and St. Peter's," to whom the church was dedicated. Very similar were the conditions of the masons at Eton College in the fifteenth century, as we shall presently see.[2] Brutails (p. 49) notes the same concerning the master-mason's contract for building the great tower of St.-Michel de Bordeaux in 1464. " What strikes us most in Lebas's contract is the strictness of his engagement, and the close bond which ties him to his work. Not only does he promise to remain in the service of the building until death, but he further binds himself to live within the parish, without being able to leave it and visit his family at Saintes

[1] Quicherat, pp. 208 ff. See farther in Appendix 8.
[2] See here below, Chapter X: briefer extracts in Willis and Clark, *Architectural Hist. of the Univ. of Cambridge*, vol. i, p. 382.

TOMB OF BISHOP JEAN D'ASSIDE AT PÉRIGUEUX.

except once a year. In 1425, the chapter of Bordeaux Cathedral had gone farther still; it had imposed on its master of the works, Colin Trenchant, the obligation of living in the lodge, with the special proviso that he must sleep there." At St.-André-de-Bordeaux, in 1519, the clerk of the works paid " the wife of Master Mathelin, master-mason [of this church] for having cleared away the earth and other dirt [*ordures*] which lay in front of the mason's lodge as far as the Archbishop's palace" (*ibid.* 47). " Lebas and his assistants, so long as they do their duty, cannot be dismissed. If, through age or sickness, Lebas is too weak to work and to superintend the lodge, and is destitute, then the building-fund must in conscience provide his keep. . . . If, at his work, he contracts an illness which prevents his working, but not his superintending, he and his ' valets ' [two personal assistants] shall keep their wages for three weeks or a month. In 1448, Botarel had been more favoured; an article of his contract (not, it must be confessed, very definite) provided that his wages should be paid during his illnesses, unless these were due to his own fault. . . . A mason of St.-Michel having been killed by a stone, the treasurer paid a franc of Bordeaux (4fr. 50c. of pre-war value) for his burial. The registers of St. André mention two accidents also; but the victims were workmen hired by a contractor; one was ' a mason's labourer who had spoiled and broken his shoulders at the work of the said church '; they gave him 3 sols tournois (3 francs) ' for charity to the poor man.' The other was the lime-burner's servant who had fallen into the lime-pit; they gave him 3 francs of Bordeaux (13fr. 50c.) ' for love of God.' "[1] Among the working masons, the labourers [*manœuvres*] were less considered than the journeymen [*compagnons*]; they were not, like the latter, invited to the Ascension feast; they were sometimes hired in the market-place; they were paid by the day, and at a lower

---

[1] At Xanten, in 1375, the master bell-founder hurt his foot, and therefore received no wage for the week that he lost at his work (Beissel, I. 116).

rate; in short, the accounts treat them as nameless units; they are scarcely ever mentioned by name (*ibid.* p. 51).

This feast is described on p. 47. " The account-book of the works at St.-Michel gives glimpses of the cordial relations between employers and employed; the devotion of the latter and the benevolence of the former. It was usual for the fabric-fund to treat the workmen on Ascension Day, which is still the feast-day of journeymen masons; it sometimes invited ' the *messieurs* who employ the workmen.'[1] On October 25, 1492, when the scaffolding was taken down from the spire, the fabric-fund invited the master-mason, the master carpenter, the master-bell-founder, and the journeymen masons and carpenters. On this point also the documents of St. André leave a less favourable impression. The Chapter respects established custom; on Ascension Day it gives the masons a sheep, and even bread and wine, ' because it is their feast '; it pays for a drink to the workmen, either because they had a hard job or because they were beginning a work. But at these works there were too frequent difficulties; in 1517 the canons went to law with the master of the works; in 1511 a regular strike broke out among the labourers. It was in November, and they were digging a trench for the foundation of the pier of a flying buttress. The trench filled with water, and the labour was hard as well as dangerous. On the 10th, the workmen refused to continue at ordinary wages; on the 12th, the wages of the men who drew water by day and night were raised from 12 to 15 liards (75 c. modern to 1 fr. 12 c.). On the 23rd, the gang had to work for only part of the night; and for that day the treasurer lowered the wages. The dissatisfied workmen broke by night the machine that had been built to empty

---

[1] Apparently, to the senior masons and their assistants; the cost of the whole, with money given to the carpenters, was about 22 fr. 50 c. of pre-war French money. Similar " drink-money " was given at Xanten to celebrate the completion of important work (Beissel, I., pp. 102, 116).

the pit. Next day, the canons bought some trusses of straw for the workmen who spent the night there ; and they paid separately for this night-work. There was one workman to whom the canons were very kind, because they needed him ; that man was actually petted. He was a very skilful limeburner, Menjolet de Poey, ' qui bene scit calcem facere.'[1] They sent for him to his home ; they paid his expenses while he stayed at Bordeaux ; they paid for his journey home to fetch his tools and his son ; and they installed him at last at Verteuil with provisions " (*ibid.*, pp. 47–49).

Then, again, we must take account of the impressment system. Even popes resorted to the pressgang for their great buildings.[2] The English kings did so on a great scale ; the palace of Westminster, Windsor and other royal castles, Eton College and King's, Cambridge, were to a great extent built by pressed workmen. Here, for instance, are examples from five years taken at random from about the middle of Edward III's reign. In 1351, three commissioners were appointed to arrest 17 carpenters, specified by name, who had been "" taken by the Sheriff of Essex, pursuant to the king's writ, to make good defects in the castle of Hertford." [3] In six cases the men's domiciles are mentioned ; two of them are Cambridge and Haslingfield, well outside the Essex border ; the sheriff must have cast his net widely. A few months later, the clerk of the works at Windsor is commissioned to recover runaways. In 1351, " masons, carpenters and other workmen " are impressed for the king's works on the Tower and Westminster Palace. In 1352, two officers are commissioned "to take painters for the king's works in the Palace of Westminster, and to arrest and commit to prison all those whom they find contrariant or rebellious herein." In the same year, there is wholesale impressment of " carpenters, masons, reapers, mowers,

---

[1] ' Who knoweth well how to make lime.'
[2] Müntz, 1882, p. 69 ; A.D. 1481.
[3] *Calendar of Patent Rolls*, 1350–1354, pp. 80, 128, 134, 308, 336.

carters, tillers of the field and other labourers required by the king's manor of Henley by Guildford." In the five years covered by this volume, there are 30 entries of this kind in all. Workmen were even carried overseas ; in 1381 30 masons were taken and delivered " to William Lakenhethe, serjeant-at-arms, for service in Britanny with the king's uncle, Thomas, Earl of Buckingham." [1] The man who had to make these arrests was himself a mason, Chaucer's fellow-official, Henry de Yevele, who was frequently entrusted with these invidious commissions. The letters often make special exceptions for workmen " in the fee of the Church " ; yet these were not excused as a matter of course. The York Fabric Rolls, under the year 1479 (p. 84), record " the expenses of a servant of Master Henry Gillow, riding to commune with Master Gervase Clifton for the excusation of masons working at St. Peter's Minster, and requisitioned and taken by the officers of my lord king for his works at Nottingham [Castle]." The editor notes that " a similar occurrence took place about this time at Oxford, where the workmen employed upon the new schools were carried off to Windsor."

And, if kings and prelates protected their own masons, they also hampered their freedom. We see that plainly in the Troyes contract which Quicherat quotes ; it comes out in the York Fabric Rolls, which show a quasi-military discipline reigning in the lodge. Under the greatest royal art-patron of medieval France, Charles V, " express orders reserved for the king and his Exchequer the arrangement of even the minutest details of crown buildings, absolutely forbidding the carpenters and masons to work on these edifices except in case of imminent danger." [2] The mason was engineer as well as artist ;[3] he wore that double crown but supported also that

---

[1] Ibid., 1377–1381, p. 606.

[2] Leclerc and Renan, *Discours, etc.*, vol. ii, p. 181 ; cf. Willis and Clark, vol. i, pp. 366, 268.

[3] Cf. Renan in *Rev. d. d. mondes*, July, 1860, pp. 212, 216–218.

double burden. Popes set even distinguished sculptors
to make cannon-balls; for the artillery of those days
commonly carried stone, since marble *plus* the time of a
real artist came cheaper, in the long run, than cast-iron
shot. The account-rolls of Pius II bear an item for
Nov. 10, 1460: "To Master Paolo Mariani of Rome and
Master Isaiah of Pisa his partner, sculptors, 5 florins and
54 pence [bolovienses] for twenty days' work expended by
them in making the aforesaid cannon-balls and carrying
the same." "Yet Paolo was on the list of 'ministers
and officials' of Pius II; he fed (and was perhaps lodged)
at the pope's expense, ate at the first table and had the
right to bring a 'familiaris' with him." [1] Again, one of
the architects employed by Innocent VIII, about 1485,
is mainly engaged on making cannon or gun-carriages;
two stone-carvers this pope employed to make cannon-
balls; another architect was set to the job of erecting the
scaffolding on which a friar was to be publicly degraded. [2]
We find Paul II, about 1470, employing at his new palace
of San Marco a sculptor named Corso di Bastiano, but
specially "for the garden benches. Thus we see a master
who is known and esteemed at a town so fastidious in
matters of taste as Siena, a master who has carved statues
which are an ornament of the cathedral, yet at Rome he
consents to accept works of an absolutely inferior rank.
Here is one more of those many facts which prove the
intimate union of art and handicraft in the fifteenth
century." [3] "Another artist, Agostino Nicolai of
Piacenza, had the double function of architect, or rather
engineer, of the papal palace, and 'master of the bom-
bards,' or 'bombardier of the army of the Holy Roman
Church.' This name occurs often in the account rolls

[1] Müntz, 1878, p. 247. For Paolo see also p. 259. There is a large
collection of stone cannon-balls, for instance, at the castle of Les Clées
in the Swiss Jura; a study of these rough limestone shot will explain
why it would be well worth a pope's while, from the military and financial
points of view, to get them done by artists in marble.

[2] Müntz, 1898, pp. 47, 50, 57.

[3] Müntz, 1879, p. 28.

of Pius II, and even in that pope's *Commentaries*." [1]
The same pope, " in 1462, commissioned his favourite
sculptor [Paolo Romano] with a job which will not
seem strange if we think of the manners of that
day ; this was the fabrication of two lay-figures representing the pope's mortal enemy, Sigismondo Malatesta.
These figures were to be burned publicly in front of
St. Peter's. The pope, in his *Commentaries*, extols the
perfect resemblance of these two effigies." [2]   In most
medieval towns there was no painters' gild ; the painters
were a branch of the saddlers ; that was at first their
main job.   Even far later, down to the days of Charles
the Bold at least, "men drew no distinction in the painter's
work between the artist and the decorator.   The best
workmen of the time figure in the account-rolls of the
house of Burgundy for pennons, banners, streamers, and
for the painting of hearses.   But we must remember that
decorative painting was not then so commonplace as in
our day." [3]

[1] Müntz, 1878, p. 235.
[2] Ibid., 248.
[3] Leclerc and Renan, *Discours, etc.*, vol. ii, p. 256.

CHAPTER VI

FOUR SELF-CHARACTERIZATIONS

OMITTING Leonardo da Vinci, as a figure too exceptional and too modern to come in naturally here by way of illustration, we may find three medieval artists and one bred in that earlier world, though he worked in the later, who have left us sidelights on their own life and thought. These are the North-German monk " Theophilus " (d. circa 1120) ; the French master-mason Villard de Honnecourt (d. c. 1260) ; the Italian painter Cennino Cennini (d. c. 1420) ; and the South German Albrecht Dürer (1471–1528). It will be seen at a glance what variety of time and place we have here, and how much this must add to the significance of the separate indications.

The writer who called himself Theophilus has been pretty certainly identified with Roger, a monk of Helmershausen, in the diocese of Paderborn.[1] The revenues of this monastery were united to those of the see of Paderborn under Bishop Meinwerc, one of the most energetic builders among all German bishops, whose successors kept up this artistic tradition all through the eleventh century ; there was a great art school at this same time in connexion with the neighbouring cathedral of Hildesheim. Bishop Henry of Paderborn, in about 1100, paid for a costly portable altar, made by the monk Roger of Helmershausen, which is still preserved in the cathedral treasury ; and a twelfth century MS. of the book preserved at Vienna tells us that the author was Roger, a Benedictine monk.

It is called *Schedula Diversarum Artium*—" A Little Scroll of Divers Arts," and runs to 150 octavo pages of print, with a few extra chapters probably added later.

[1] Ilg, p. 43.

Most of the book is taken up with severely practical
recipes. These have a long pedigree. A Græco-
Egyptian papyrus, found in a tomb at Thebes, dates
from the third or early fourth century; a MS. in the
cathedral library at Lucca, compiled in the eighth century
by an Italian from Greek originals, contains several of the
recipes in the papyrus.[1] Then comes the *De Artibus
Romanorum*, by an otherwise unknown Eraclius; then our
Theophilus; thence others, at intervals, down to and
beyond Cennino, to whom we shall come later.[2] Of all
these, Theophilus is the fullest and most practical. He is

1.

Incipit prologus libri primi
Theophili qd Rvgervs, de diuisi artib'
eophilus humilis pbr seruus seruug
di. indigni nomine profefsione monachi
omib; meus desidia animeq; uagatio
ne utili manuu ocupatione delecta
bili nourtatu meditati one declina
re r calcare uolentib; retbuti one
celestis pmu.

"THEOPHILUS": FIRST LINES OF MS. WHICH GIVES THE NAME
RUGERUS.

accessible in a good serviceable English version with very
useful notes by R. Hendrie (Murray, 1847); but the best
and most recent text is that of A. Ilg (Vienna, 1874),
which I here adopt for page references.

His book assumes a continuity of tradition, a certainty
of income, and a variety of output such as would be
unlikely anywhere but in a rich monastery or under a
succession of art-loving bishops. The workshops, the
furnaces and kilns, the tools, must all be on an elaborate
scale, since almost everything must be made on the
premises.[3] They must make their own linseed oil for

[1] *Cennino Cennini*, ed. Herringham, pp. 22 ff.
[2] Many of these are printed in Merrifield's *Original Treatises*, etc.,
1849.
[3] See Appendix 2.B.

painting; though here Theophilus assumes the neighbourhood of an oil-press ordinarily used for olives or
walnuts or poppy-seed, which his artists may borrow
temporarily for their linseed (p. 45); he assumes also,
here and there, worldly tools, as the beading-plane and
the concave-plane used by coopers (39–41); he assumes
again that the necessary gums and chemicals can be
bought. Otherwise they must do all themselves, from
beginning to end; beat out their own gold-leaf (53);
make their own little mill and grind gold to powder for
paint (65, 73, 202, specially interesting descriptions);
make their own ink, and wire, and nails (91, 163, 169).
Most elaborate of all is the manufacture of glass, from
the first building of furnaces for plain glass and coloured,
through the painting and cutting and baking in home-
made kilns, down to the final fitting of the windows with
home-made strips of grooved lead (99–137). He advises
us to plunder ancient mosaics and melt down their
beautiful glass " even as the French collect them, who
are most skilful in this work " (113); let us imitate " all
the French love of precious variety in windows " (11).

Most enlightening, however, are the personal touches
which distinguish this book (I believe) from all other
early manuals. Roger addresses himself throughout to a
pupil, " my son," " my brother "; he is consciously
founding a school, and claims the highest inspiration for
his art. His preface strikes this note from the first
sentence onwards : " Theophilus, humble priest, servant
of the servants of God, unworthy of the name and
profession of a monk, wishes the guerdon of heavenly
reward to all who are willing to shun and tread under-
foot, by useful handiwork and delectable meditation of
novelties, all idleness and wandering of mind." Man was
made in God's likeness; the Devil deceived him and
deprived him of Paradise, yet not of this inborn capacity
to learn divers arts. These, in heathen times, he pursued
for his own pleasure or for gain; now, the devout may
turn them to God's service. Let not him who had

H

received this talent hide it in a napkin, thus incurring the stigma of an unprofitable servant ; " which sentence I fear to incur ; and therefore, however mean and of little reputation, I here offer, without money and without price, to all who would fain humbly learn, whatsoever hath been given to me by Him who giveth to all men abundantly and upbraideth not. . . . Thou therefore, beloved son, whosoever thou mayest be, into whose heart God hath set the yearning to explore fully that great and wide field of divers arts . . . dearest son, whom God hath enriched [through the tradition of other men's experience], whereby those things are offered freely unto thee which many others acquire by intolerable travail, cleaving the sea-waves with much peril of their lives, constrained by need and cold and hunger, yet oppressed by an overwhelming desire to learn ; do thou (I say) now greedily behold and covet this *Little Roll of Divers Arts*, read it through, hold it fast in memory, and embrace it with ardent desire. For, if thou study it with all diligence, thou wilt here find whatsoever Greece hath in divers kinds and mixtures of colours ; with all that Tuscany knows of laborious mosaic or of varied enamels ; with all that Arabia displays in casting or hammering or chasing of metal ; with whatsoever Italy adorns with gold, in various vessels or carvings in gems or in bone ; with all that France loves in precious variety of windows, or that industrious Germany approves in cunning work of gold, silver, copper or iron, timber or stone. When thou hast read this again and again, and laid it fast in thy memory, then shalt thou thus reward me for my teaching, that, whensoever thou makest good use of my labours, thou shalt commend me in prayer to the mercy of Almighty God, who knoweth that I have written the things here set forth neither for love of man's praise nor for covetousness of worldly reward, nor again have I enviously or jealously held back aught that is precious or rare, nor kept silence to reserve such things for myself alone ; nay, rather, for the increase of His honour and the glory of

His name have I succoured many men's needs and taken thought for their profit."

The Prologue to his Second Book strikes the moral note clearly again. His object is to save his pupil from indolence. "For it is clearer than daylight that whosoever spends his time in idleness and levity doth also busy himself with superfluous talk and jesting, curiosity, drink, drunkenness, quarrels, fightings, manslaughter, bribery, theft, sacrilege, perjury and other like faults which are hateful in the eyes of that God who looketh upon the humble and quiet man that worketh silently in God's name and in obedience to St. Paul's precept : *But rather let him labour, working with his hands the thing which is good, that he may have to give to him that needeth."*

But it is in the Prologue to his Third Book that Roger rises to his full height.[1] If David and Solomon were so solicitous to adorn God's house, how much more may the artist of our own day, when he serves the Church, feel himself inspired by the Sevenfold Spirit of God ? Thus animated, he will strive to " show forth to the beholders a vision of God's paradise, bright as springtide with flowers of every hue." The walls and the vaults will be as gay as a meadow or an embroidered mantle ; the glass will outshine them all. For deeper devotion, there will be Christ's passion, and the sufferings of the Saints, and their final reward of glory. " Work therefore now, good man, happy in this life before God's face and man's, and happier still in the life to come " ; for your daily work is a daily burnt-sacrifice to God. Nor need you ever lack employment, for infinite are the needs of the Church in greater or lesser ornaments.

Our second figure is Villard de Honnecourt—Vilars de Honecort—a name which survives in the modern French Huillard and the English Willard. He was a native of Honnecourt, near Cambrai, and all we know of him is his

---

[1] I have translated the greater part of this long preface in *Medieval Garner*, (1st ed., p. 166, 2nd ed., vol. iv.) and in *Social Life in Britain*, pp. 466 ff.

sketch book—or, rather, the thirty-three remaining sheets of a little skin-covered parchment volume which once contained forty-two.[1] From the brief notes in his book, from contemporary buildings still existing, and from records of those which have perished, it is possible to reconstruct a little of Villard's life. He was certainly working in 1250, sometimes in company with another mason called Pierre and hailing from Corbie in Villard's own Picardy. He was engaged as master or as assistant at several great churches; St. Faron and St. Étienne at Meaux, the cathedral of Cambrai (which he may have designed), and Kaschau in Hungary, of which he seems pretty certainly to have been master-mason. The work here certainly stopped abruptly about 1272, at the death of the Prince who had patronized it; and we may surmise that Villard then wandered back to France.

For this " Album " is, first of all, a wanderer's sketch-book; secondly, a technical manual; and, incidentally, a testimonial to the variety of a master-mason's jobs and to the active thought and discussion which went on in the lodge. It begins: " Villard de Honnecourt greets you, and prays all those who work at the artifices which will be found in this book to pray for his soul, and to bear him in mind. For in this book will be found good advice for the great power of masonry and of engines of carpentry. You will find likewise the power of portraiture and design, even as the art of geometry biddeth and teacheth." [2] The drawings are arranged roughly,

---

[1] There are three editions of Villard's " Album," (1) with lithographic facsimiles, translations and full comments, by J. B. A. Lassus, Paris, 1858 ; (2) a translation of this, with additional notes, by Prof. R. Willis (1859) ; and (3) photographic reproductions of the drawings, with introduction by H. Omont, published by the Bibliothèque Nationale. There is much valuable comment on it by E. Renan in *Rev. d. d. Mondes*, July, 1862, pp. 203 ff, and *Hist. Lit. de la France*, vol. xxv, pp. 1 ff ; see also J. Quicherat's essay in *Mélanges d'hist. et d'archéologie*, vol. ii.

[2] I have printed three pages of extracts, with illustrations, on pp. 476 ff. of *Social Life in Britain*.

but far from strictly, according to subjects ; and it seems probable that Villard, having made sketches up and down, from year to year, for his own use, on scattered pieces of paper or parchment, copied them now, or added sketches from memory, with notes for the assistance of colleagues, pupils, and successors.[1] There are sketches from Cambrai Cathedral and neighbouring Vaucelles, from Chartres, Laon, Lausanne, Reims and Meaux. Reims, which was then building, he had studied with especial care, down to the sections of the mouldings. This cathedral, he tells us, will be a model for that of Cambrai.

THE WHEEL WINDOW OF CHARTRES.
From Villard de Honnecourt's notebook.

[1] It is difficult to admit the cogency of Professor Willis's argument (p. 14) that the sketches were done from the first in this book, and without thought of didactic purpose, because so little space is left for the notes, which are squeezed in after a very rough fashion. It would seem natural enough for Villard to think almost entirely of the drawings, leaving the notes to fit in as best they could; and, on the other hand, it is not probable that the book would show so much subject-arrangement if these sketches, from so many different places and times, had all been made fresh on the spot. Prof. Lethaby adds : " The text shows a ' publishing ' purpose parallel to Theophilus. It was a *book*, not a ' sketchbook.' "

Many other details are sketched, evidently from buildings or carvings which had impressed him, though he too seldom tells us where. He draws, in rapid but sure strokes, one of the windows at Reims : " I was sent for to the land of Hungary when I drew this, because it pleased me best " ; as well it might, for these Reims windows served also as models for the architect of Westminster Abbey. Again : " I have been in many countries, as you may see by this book ; but never in any place did I see a tower like this of Laon." On another page he has imitated (not very accurately) the Greek inscription over a Crucifixion ; on another, we have a study of a figure clad in the Greek chlamys, probably drawn from an ancient statue.

I'ESTOIE UNE FOIS EN HONGRIE LA U JE MES MAINT JOR LA VI IO LE PAVEMENT D'UNE GLIZE DE SI FAITE MANIERE.

" I was once in Hungary, where I dwelt many days, and there I saw the pavement of a church made in this fashion."

Elsewhere, again : " Such was the fashion of the tomb of a Saracen that I once saw ; " and here we have a sketch, pretty evidently from memory, of a classical monument ; for all pagans, in medieval parlance, were " Saracens." Again : " I was once in Hungary, where I lived for many a day ; and there I saw a church pavement of this fashion " (five different patterns of inlaid pavement). A few others, though not thus inscribed by Villard, may be guessed at with some probability : a sketch of choir-stalls resembles those at Sankt Gereon at Cologne ; two naked wrestlers recall a subject in Lausanne Cathedral ; or, in this case, both Villard and the Lausanne carver may have taken their inspiration separately from those wrestling matches which are still among the favourite public shows of Switzerland.

There are also many studies from nature. Two at least are direct and original ; they are full-face and

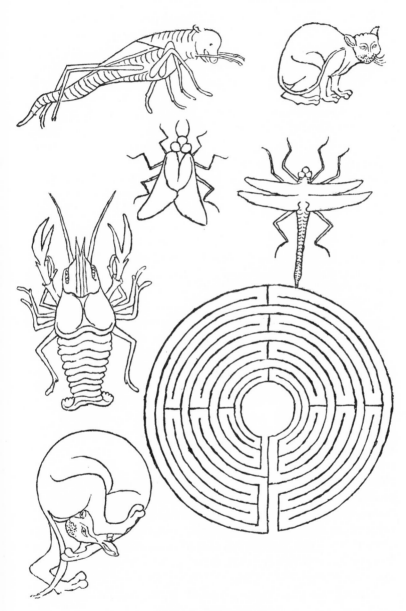

ANIMALS, AND A MAZE.

profile of a lion, and in both cases Villard writes with
pardonable pride: "Know well that this lion was
drawn from life." [1]   Others, as the wild boar, rabbit,
swan and bear, are natural and correct ; others, again,
are rather strongly conventionalized, whether because
our artist took them at second hand or because he habitually saw natural forms in terms of architectural ornament.   This will be evident, for instance, in the grass-
hopper, and in the geometrical circle which he has given
to his otherwise most natural dog.

But it comes out far more clearly in the four crowded
pages which, as he himself tells us, constitute a separate
section of his book: *Chi commence le mat[ie]re de la portraiture—Incipit materia portrature.*[2]   Here Villard shows
how characteristic attitudes of living creatures can be
stereotyped and borne in mind by a mnemonic system of
geometrical figures.   Of this Quicherat, the earliest and
in many ways the greatest of those who have studied the
book, remarks : " The *matière de portraiture* is, in truth,
a mere routine, and the drawings are a set of patterns
for a certain number of selected subjects.   But it is
remarkable that the peculiar attitudes and aspects produced by this method are precisely those which charac-
terize the works of the painters and the sculptors of the
thirteenth century."   For the " Madonna and Child "
at the top, this will be evident at once ; for the " King
on His Throne," let the reader compare the attitude of
the left arm resting upon his thigh with similar royal
attitudes on the west fronts of Wells or Exeter, for
instance.   But to say this, is to say that we have here
already the beginnings of shop-work ; a method far
removed from the inspired originality of a man like J. F.

[1] The drawing, with Villard's long description of lion-taming, may
be found on p. 336 of my *Medieval Garner* (first ed.).   He notes on his
drawing of the porcupine : " This is a little beast which shoots out its
quills when it is angry," but makes no claim of personal observation here.

[2] *Protrahere*, " to draw forward," is used already by Roger Theophilus
in the modern artistic sense of drawing ; so also is *designare* ; cf. French
dessiner.

ohi commence le mate de la portraiture

Incipit materia portratture

THE ART OF DESIGN.

Millet, who in his maturity never drew from the man or beast before him, but studied them until he knew them by heart, and could fetch them forth as living things from his memory. Much, of course, may be explained by the necessary subjection of all medieval sculpture to strict architectural requirements; but there remains a real truth in Renan's final judgment on Villard: "Here and there we are reminded of Leonardo da Vinci or Michael Angelo, when we note this ebullition of bold conceptions, this feverish anxiety to surpass other men, this naïve variety of objects which rouse the artist's curiosity. We might think ourselves here on the verge of a Renaissance; yet in fact we are on the eve of decay." In this later thirteenth century Gothic architecture was already going down hill. It was full of life; but, instead of arriving at the classic perfection of Greece, it was tempted away into other fields by the desire for novelty; the choir of Westminster was already old-fashioned, and the current was tending towards Henry VII's chapel. The fact itself can scarcely be denied even by those who least regret it, and who feel, not only in the face of later Gothic but of the Renaissance also, that God fulfils Himself in many ways.

But Villard and his friends were full of life; the sketch-book would convince us even if we had not known it already. The most precious sentences in the book, to my mind, are two chance references to craftsmen who worked and talked and sported with him, and wandered each his own way as his own star called him, and lie now under the cloister-pavement or the green turf in far-distant graves.[1] Villard gives the plan of a presbytery of a church, with alternate square and round chapels, and therefore with complicated vaulting problems; this he

---

[1] See the portraits of two contemporary masons in Lethaby's *Medieval Art*, pp. 246, 252. The former of these, who built St.-Nicaise de Reims, must almost certainly have met and discussed with Villard. Another, obviously a portrait, is on p. 254. Prof. Lethaby reproduces some of Villard's own sketches, pp. 172, 197, 238, 249.

explains in Latin as well as in French : " Here is a presbytery which Villard de Honnecourt and Pierre de Corbie
invented in discussion with each other "—*inter se dis-
putando*. And, again, under a full plate drawing of a
mechanical device, he begins thus : *Maint ior se sunt
maistre dispute*, " many a time have masters discussed "—
how to make a wheel turn of its own accord. The thing
can be done, thinks Villard, by providing the circum-
ference of the wheel with an *uneven* number of bags of
quicksilver, or of mallets moving on a pivot. Thus, at
any given moment, there will be more bags or mallets on
one side than on another ; e.g. the four in his sketch will
weigh down the three, until one of these three comes up
to the top, and, in its turn, falls down to the left, and
helps to outweigh its former brethren : we may thus get
perpetual motion.[1]

We have here two characteristics which run through
the whole book ; the universality of this artist's interests,
and his temptation to seek after the *tour de force* ; that
admiration of the trick for the trick's sake which we have
seen in the Bristol-Gloucester school and in the new-
born Perpendicular. It is not only that some of his
diagrams and recipes are for mere playthings. " By this
means we may place an egg exactly beneath a [ripe] pear
[on its tree], by [trigonometrical] measurement, so that
the pear may fall plumb upon the egg." . . . " Take
boiled quicklime and orpiment, and put them into boiling
water and oil. This makes a good ointment for removing
superfluous hairs." . . . " Thus may we make a crossbow that cannot miss its mark " ; the crossbow is fitted
with a sort of pinhole-sight. . . . " Thus may we make the
eagle [on the lectern] turn his head towards the deacon
when he reads the Gospel [at Mass]." Upon this we must
not lay too much stress ; let us say that these were the
amusements of his leisure hours ; but it is difficult to
imagine that the curious presbytery worked out with
Pierre de Corbie would have a beauty at all proportionate

[1] I have reproduced the sketch to face p. 476 of *Social Life in Britain*.

to its eccentricity. Again, Villard's project for a hanging arch (p. 145) is an anticipation of one of the least defensible tricks in the architecture of the fourteenth and fifteenth centuries.[1] Renan seems right in saying that architecture is already beginning to suffer from the disease of too much paper-work; that the period of perfect and simple proportions, clearly conceived and always present in the master-mind, is passing into a period of over-elaboration in detail. On the other hand, we must always admire the width of Villard's interests and knowledge. He shows the solution of difficult practical problems not in stone-cutting only, but in carpentry; he shows the working of a saw-mill, of a screw-jack, and how to cut a screw; how to make a machine for straightening timber houses that lean from the perpendicular, and the construction of a great mangonel for siege operations. He can take approximate measurements from a distance by rough-and-ready trigonometrical methods. He gives one careful study from the nude, in outline shaded with bistre; this looks less like an original drawing than a copy from a Greek medical book. And he ends with a recipe, the longest in the book, for a potion that is sovereign for all wounds : " drink not too much, for in an eggshell ye may have enough. . . . Whatsoever wound or sore ye may have, this will heal you." The mason's hammer-axe was as definite a part of his stock-in-trade as the square and compasses themselves, and scattered notices have floated down to us which suggest that peace did not always reign in the lodge; it is probable that this, Villard's concluding recipe, may have been more to the point than his instructions " how to trace the plan of a five-cornered tower," or " to draw three kinds of arches with one opening of the compasses." It is this width of interest, and the directly personal character of the book, bringing us at once into the presence of Villard and his

[1] The other similar tricks will be found on pp. 53, 130, 131, 161 of Willis's edition. But Prof. Lethaby's warning must be added here : " This is a little harsh on Villard. Only curiosity and joy, not decline."

fellows, that prompts Renan's encomium : " If we except Roger Bacon, there is perhaps no man of St.-Louis's day who was so near to ourselves as this obscure artificer ; and doubtless Villard was in no way superior to his fellows " ; for he simply inherits the teaching of a great school.[1] But we must here make the same allowances which we make for Roger Bacon ; apart from what strictly concerned his own art, we see rather his aspirations than his performances. Prof. Willis, than whom none had a better right to judge, was driven to conclude that Villard's elementary trigonometry, put to a practical test, " forms a very curious illustration of the extreme poverty of the art of measuring heights and distances in the thirteenth century " (p. 146).

Before leaving Villard altogether, it is worth noting that two collections have recently been published which, though lacking direct autobiographical value, do much to illustrate his methods. One is an illuminator's sketch-book of the late twelfth century, reproduced in *Beschreibendes Verzeichnis d. illum. MSS in Oesterreich*, VIII Bd., ii Theil, p. 352. The other forms the thirteenth volume of the Walpole Society publications, and is edited by Dr. M. R. James. It dates from the later fourteenth century ; this, again, is a painter's sketch-book, and it is specially strong in a field in which English medieval artists excelled, that of bird-life.

In Villard's time it was France that led the Western lands in art ; but, when our next figure comes forward, the palm has passed definitely to Italy. Cennino Cennini was born at Colle di Valdelsa, in Tuscany, between Florence and Siena, perhaps of peasant-farmer stock,[2]

[1] *Hist. Litt. France*, vol. xxv, p. 8.

[2] See *The Book of the Art of Cennino Cennini*, translated, with notes and introduction, by Christiana Herringham. (George Allen, 1899.) Though I have mainly translated from Ilg's German version (the original being inaccessible in Cambridge), I am much indebted to the notes and introduction of both editions. In connexion with Cennini, it is worth while to refer to an account of his contemporary Niccolo of Foligno, on pp. 327 ff. of *The Cornhill Magazine* for March, 1876.

or possibly his father also had been an artisan, as Ilg con-
jectures. He tells us that he studied twelve years with
Agnolo Gaddi, son of that Taddeo Gaddi who had been
Giotto's pupil and godson. Agnolo died in 1396, so that
Cennino can scarcely have been born later than 1372,
and probably rather earlier. Two legal records, which
have survived by chance, show that he was living in 1398
at Padua, that his wife was from neighbouring Citadella,
and that his brother was a trumpeter in the pay of the
Prince of Padua. At the end of one manuscript of his
book we read : " This book is finished ; let us give
thanks to Christ. In the year 1437, July 31, from the
Stinche." The Stinche was a debtor's prison at Florence,
and this *explicit* has suggested surmises unfavourable to
the artist ; yet it is practically certain that we have here
not the author's words, but only the usual disburdening
of a copyist's mind. It seems evident that Cennino
wrote his book at Padua, where, as we know, another of
Agnolo's pupils was then working, and where there was
plenty to be done. Vasari thus sums him up at the end
of his life of Agnolo Gaddi : " Cennino di Drea [i.e. son
of Andrew] Cennini, of Colle di Valdelsa, learned painting from this same Agnolo, and for love of his art he
wrote with his own hand on the methods of painting in
fresco, in tempera, in size, and in gum, and besides how
to paint in miniature, and how gold is laid on for all
these different kinds of painting, which book is in the
hands of Giuliano, a Sienese goldsmith, an excellent
master and a friend of these arts. At the beginning of
his book he treated of the nature of pigments, minerals,
and earths, as he had learned from Agnolo his master,
wishing, as perhaps he had not succeeded in learning to
paint perfectly, at least to know the way to use colours,
temperas, sizes, and how to make grounds ; and which
colours must be avoided in mixture as injurious to each
other, and in short many other matters, about which it
is not necessary to speak, all those things being well
known in our day which in those times they thought very

secret and uncommon. . . . Besides the works which he carried out in Florence with his master, there is by his own hand under the loggia of the hospital of Bonifazio Lupi, a Madonna with certain saints, coloured in such manner that it is very well preserved at the present day." This loggia was rebuilt in 1787; Cennino's picture was then detached, mounted on canvas, and transferred to the Academia delle Belle Arti; thence to a chamber in another hospital, where it seems to have perished altogether.

The technical matters of which Cennini mainly treats have not very much interest for us; not only were most of them already common property in Vasari's time, but many occur, in one form or another, in those earlier manuals which derive even from pre-Christian times. Their main interest lies in the evidence they afford of traditions handed down from workshop to workshop; preserved mainly in monasteries during those Dark Ages in which the Church alone could keep books with some sort of safety; then, as civilization spread, passing from master to master in the world. But here and there, among his technical recipes, Cennino gives glimpses of his own outlook on life, whether conventional or personal and original.

His prologue resembles that of Theophilus as closely as we could expect from a married Italian, earning his daily bread by his art, and not at all inclined to follow the Church teaching about holy days when it would interfere with this bread-work (ch. 104). The Devil, cheating our first parents of their repose in Paradise, forced Adam to invent the spade and Eve the distaff; thence mankind stepped on from art to art. One of these is " the art called painting, which requires both manual skill and imagination, not only to invent things which we have never seen, since they lurk within the husk of natural objects, but also to grasp them with the hand and to represent as a reality the thing which is not present before us. Therefore does painting deserve the next place after Science, and to be crowned by Poetry." Hence it follows that he who feels himself to possess anything of this talent must not hide it under a bushel. "Thus was I, Cennino di Drea Cennini, born at Colle di Valdelsa, taught twelve years here in Florence, as a humble working member of the painter's art, by my master Agnolo, son of Taddeo, from whom he had learned his art. This father of his was held by Giotto at the baptismal font, and worked for 24 years as his pupil. Giotto it was who transformed the painter's art from Greek to Italian, and brought it to its present state. In order to encourage all who would fain come to art, I here record that which has been shown me by my aforesaid master Agnolo, and also that which I have proved with mine own hand. Wherein I call first of all unto God Almighty, Father, Son and Holy Ghost, and next unto that most beloved advocate of all sinners, the Virgin Mary, and then upon St. Luke, the first Christian painter, and mine advocate St. Eustace and all the Saints of Paradise. Amen." A new section (ch. 67) begins with: "In the name of the Holy Trinity, I will now introduce you to the laying on of colours." Presently again (ch. 105): "When you begin to paint on panels in the name of the Holy Trinity, always invoking that name and that of the glorious Virgin Mary, begin first of all with the foundations of glue in their different kinds." And the whole book concludes with a prayer, "That the Most High God, our dear Lady, St. John, St. Luke, evangelist and painter, St. Eustachius, St. Francis and St. Antony of Padua may vouchsafe us grace and strength to sustain and suffer in peace the burdens and travail of this world; and also that they may help all who see this book to study and remember it well, that they may live in peace by their own labour, and support their families in this world, and be glorified at last with them in the world to come, for ever and everlasting. Amen." For the man who would support his family needed generally to work as hard in medieval Tuscany or Lombardy as in the modern world;

there was the same struggle between the material and the ideal. " There are some who follow the arts from poverty and necessity ; but those who pursue them from love of the art and true nobleness of mind are to be commended above all others " (2). Again, in his ninety-sixth chapter, he writes : " It is usual to adorn walls with gilded tin, because it is less expensive than gold. Nevertheless, I give you this advice, that you endeavour always to use fine gold and good colours, particularly in painting representations of our Lady. And if you say that a poor person cannot afford the expense, I answer, that if you work well (and give sufficient time to your works), and paint with good colours, you will acquire so much fame, that from a poor person you will become a rich one ; and your name will stand so high for using good colours, that if some masters receive a ducat for painting one figure, you will certainly be offered two, and your wishes will be fulfilled : according to the old proverb, Good work, good pay. And even should you not be well paid, God and our Lady will reward your soul and body for it."

There is only one monastic reference. Speaking of vermilion, he excuses himself for not describing its manufacture, because plenty of recipes could be collected, if it were worth while, from the " brethren "—i.e. monks or friars (ch. 40). But he takes his vocation very seriously ; if the monk is not an artist, the artist will be the better by imitating the monk's virtues. " Let thy manner of life be as though thou wert a student in Theology, Philosophy, or some other science. I mean, thou shalt be temperate in eating and drinking, taking two meals at most in the day, with light and nourishing food and little wine. Guard and spare thine hand, keeping away from all such strain as the casting of stones or iron bars or many other things that might make it less supple. There is another thing which may make thy hand so unsteady that it will tremble and flutter more than a leaf in the wind ; and that is, to frequent the ladies

I

too much. But now let us come back to our subject "
(ch. 29).

Cennino believes most of all, as Turner believed, in
"d——d hard work " (ch. 13—cf. 104—16, 30, 31, 32,
36, 47, 122, 138). The student, he says, must begin with
something like a year's practice with the lead pencil.
And again : " Know that you cannot learn to paint in
less time than that which I shall name to you. In the
first place, you must study drawing for at least one year ;
then you must remain with a master at the workshop for
the space of six years at least, that you may learn all the
parts and members of the art—to grind colours, to boil
down glues, to grind plaster, to acquire the practice of
laying grounds on pictures, to work in relief, and to
scrape or smooth the surface, and to gild ; afterwards to
practise colouring, to adorn with mordants, paint cloths
of gold, and paint on walls, for six more years—drawing
without intermission on holy days and workdays. And
by this means you will acquire great experience. If you
do otherwise, you will never attain perfection. There
are many who say that you may learn the art without the
assistance of a master. Do not believe them ; let this
book be an example to you, studying it day and night.
And if you do not study under some master, you will
never be fit for anything ; nor will you be able to show
your face among the masters." You cannot grind your
colours too patiently or too long ; if you were to grind
them for a year, so much the better ; for ten years,
better still. The truth may long elude you, but " you
must use your understanding." Do not hurry over your
shading ; a multiplicity of thin coats will give the softest
effect. " Practise as frequently as you can, for it is the
whole of your education." " When you have finished
drawing your figure (and especially if it be a picture of
great value from which you expect reward and honour),
then leave it alone for some days, in order to return to
it over and over again, and improve it where it may
need." " If you can afford the expense [of double-gilding

your backgrounds], it will be a glorious thing and an honour to yourself." Only once, I think, does he counsel what we might call scamping ; he will allow you to shade some of your stained glass with mere oil-paint (which of course will gradually weather away) instead of baking a vitreous pigment in (ch. 171). For we can hardly condemn his other anticipation that when we have to paint Our Lady's blue cloak—a considerable extent of colour— we should sometimes use "German blue," or oxidized copper ore, a far cheaper article than ultramarine.[1]

In Cennini's days, when Italian commerce is at its height, and Constantinople not yet taken by the Turks, far more can be bought than in the time of Theophilus ; we need no longer make the very simplest things for ourselves. True, we still make our own pens (ch. 14), tracing-paper (24–6), charcoal crayons (33), black paint of different kinds (37), dye from wild plums (54), paint-brushes, both of hair and of bristle (63–5), which we have a most ingenious way of protecting from moths (66). We make our own glues, sizes, and cements. We must also grind all the colours for ourselves, and invent means of keeping these ground colours until we need them for use (62). We mix them sometimes with the same strange but natural ingredients which play so conspicuous a part in medieval medicine (5, 44).[2] But, on the other hand, we can buy what we want from the goldsmiths (5), or the merchants (6), or the miniature-painters (12). We go to the shop for cotton paper (10) ; if it is too much trouble to make our own glue, we take it " as sold by the apothecaries," either fish-glue or strong glue (16). Trac-

---

[1] Ch. 83. For the expense of real ultramarine, see ch. 62 ; also the entertaining story which Vasari tells, in his life of Perugino, concerning the stingy Prior of the Gesuati. It is well known that Fra Angelico's great Crucifixion at San Marco has been robbed of its ultramarine background by later cupidity.

[2] For easily-accessible parallels here, see pp. 299, 301 of the *Liber de Coloribus*, a MS. of about 1400, published by Mr. D. V. Thompson in *Speculum*, Vol. I. Azure is to be tempered with goat's milk or woman's milk ; glass must be softened with the blood of a he-goat and a goose.

ing-paper also may apparently be bought (23). There is
even standardization, a sign of considerable development
in trade ; you may get not only an ordinary sheet of
paper, but a " royal sheet " (29)—that which, folded into
eight, forms the familiar modern " royal octavo." You
may sketch with " a certain black stone which comes
from Piedmont " (34), i.e. black lead ; and in Florence
you may buy a very fine white called after the local
saint, " St. John's White " (39). As for vermilion, don't
waste time over recipes for making it, but " get what
you want at the apothecary's and pay for it " (40). You
can even buy a sort of rudimentary anticipation of the
modern " dolly dyes " (12, 161). You buy your glass, of
any colour, just as you would buy it nowadays (171).
But measures are often primitive ; " the size of a bean,"
" less than the size of a bean," " less than the size of half
a bean " (20–22). And we catch interesting glimpses of
daily life. You make your own bone-dust for priming
panels : " Take the ribs or wing-bones of hares or capons.
The older, the better. Just as you find them under the
table, put them in the fire," etc. etc. (7). Your window
will probably be not of glass, but of oiled linen (172).
The Church is a sort of art-school ; you will probably
begin by copying in churches and chapels, and you will
find others doing the same, " and, the more intellectual
these companions are, the better it will be for you " (29).
Your profession lays you open to the solicitations of
" youthful ladies, especially those of Tuscany," for face-
paints and complexion-waters ; " but the Paduan women
do not use them "—Cennini wrote this among the
Paduans—" therefore, not to give them any cause for
blaming me, and because such things are not pleasing to
God and Our Lady, I will keep silence on this matter "
(180). There we have an interesting illustration of the
136th novel of Sacchetti, a generation before Cennino
Orcagna, Taddeo Gaddi and other painters " having
eaten well and filled themselves well with wine " at the
table of the abbot of San Miniato, discussed who was the

greatest painter that had ever lived, from Giotto onwards. When all had spoken, the sculptor Alberto Arnoldi gave his opinion ; no other painter is comparable with the ladies of Florence, who habitually improve upon the Almighty's own handiwork. Are we to believe that God never created a dark Florentine ? Yet who knows a lady whose face is not white ? The prize was unanimously adjudged to Alberto. But even in the Middle Ages, if we are to believe the preachers, these works of complexional art betrayed a painful lack of durability.

Cennino is emphatic as to the need of nature-study (27). " If there are many good masters in the place where you live, so much the better for you. But I advise you always to select the best and most celebrated ; and, if you daily imitate his manner, it is scarcely possible but that you will acquire it ; for if you copy to-day from this master and to-morrow from that, you will not acquire the manner of either ; and, as the different style of each master unsettles your mind, your own manner will become fantastic. If you will study this manner to-day and that to-morrow, you must of necessity copy neither perfectly ; but if you continually adopt the manner of one master, your intellect must be very dull indeed if you do not find something to nourish it. And it will happen that, if nature has bestowed on you any invention, you will acquire a manner of your own, which cannot be other than good, because your hand and your understanding, being always accustomed to gather the flowers, will always avoid the thorns." Yet we must not interpret this insistence upon nature-study, any more than his other excellent advice, too literally. It is true he shows a clearer knowledge of perspective than Villard, whose side-views of an arch are flattened where it ought to bulge, and bulge where it ought to flatten. But Cennino bids us paint our trunks of trees " with pure black " (86), and our mountains, apparently, in violation of the rules of aerial perspective (85). And, as for their forms, " If you would have a good model for mountains, so that they should appear natural, procure some large and broken pieces of rock, and draw from these, giving them lights and shades as you see them on the stones before you." He is much concerned again with the human figure (181–6)[1]; it is " most useful " to " take casts from life." He will teach his pupil how to " take a cast of the face of a man or woman, of whatever rank."[2] It is done, of course, with fine plaster; " and remember, that when you are taking a cast of a person of high rank, such as a lord, a king, a pope, an emperor, you should mix the plaster with lukewarm rose-water ; but for other persons it is sufficient to use any lukewarm water, from fountains, rivers or wells." Thus you may take a cast not only of a face but of a whole body, man or woman or animal, or from your own body, " like the many antique figures, of which so many remain." He will teach you artistic anatomy : " before I proceed further, I will make you acquainted with the proportions of a man ; I omit those of a woman, because there is not one of them perfectly proportioned."[3] A man's height is $8\frac{2}{3}$ times the length of his face ; also note that " he has on his left side one rib less than a woman. . . . A comely man should be dark, a woman fair, etc. [sic]. I shall not speak of irrational animals, because they appear to have no certain proportions. Draw them as frequently as you can from nature, and try for yourself. And this requires much practice " (ch. 70–71). We see at once that most of this paragraph was written less from experience than from hearsay, and in this Cennino is not yet emancipated from medieval tradition. Renan quotes from a MS. in the *Bibliothèque Nationale* : " The Dominican Bernard d'Auvergne, in a discourse on the text *Put on* [*clothes*], *therefore, as the elect of God*, enumerates all the reasons why body and spirit need clothing, and holds that the

---

[1] In Mrs. Merrifield's translation (1844) these chapters are numbered 164–8.

[2] Or, possibly, " of whatever character."

[3] Or, " because she has no regular proportions."

body needs clothes 'to add to its grace.' Just as all naked flesh (he says) is deformed to the sight, so a soul bare of clothing is detestable in God's sight. It has been asserted that St. Louis tore out the first page of his Bible, because the Bible story of the first tragedy of humanity was shown there in its naked truth." And he sums up, without too great exaggeration for an epigram : " Naked-ness was counted not only obscene, but unsightly : it was suffered only in the case of persons [who had to be represented as] ugly or accursed." [1]

Our fourth artist, Albrecht Dürer, is too well known to need many words. He was born at Nürnberg in 1471, of orthodox parents ; at his mother's death in 1514 he was still orthodox ; in 1520 we find him on Luther's side, and intending to engrave his portrait " for a lasting remembrance of a Christian man who helped me out of great distress, though he never took any formal step to break with the Church." [2] And, among his sketches and memoranda, there are utterances no less deeply religious than those of Theophilus. He took his stand upon the Bible : " All worldly rulers in these dangerous times should give good heed that they receive not human misguidance for the Word of God, for God will have nothing added to His Word nor taken away from it." And again : "Into whomsoever Christ comes he lives, and Himself lives in Christ. Therefore all things are in Christ good things. There is nothing good in us except it becomes good in Christ. Whosoever, therefore, will altogether justify himself is unjust. If we will what is good, Christ wills it in us. No human repentance is enough to equalise deadly sin and be fruitful." In this spirit he looks upon his art with Milton's eyes, as " that one talent which is death to hide." " I would gladly give everything I know

[1] Leclerc and Renan, *Discours*, etc., Nouv. ed., 1865, p. 253. Jean Beleth, however, was more liberal in his ideas ; see my later chapter on Symbolism.

[2] Crouch, p. 305 ; I am indebted to his book for all the following quotations.

to the light, for the good of cunning students who prize such art more highly than silver or gold. I further admonish all who have any knowledge in these matters that they write it down. Do it truly and plainly, not toilsomely and at great length, for the sake of those who seek and are glad to learn, to the great honour of God and your own praise. If I then set something burning, and ye all add to it with skilful furthering, a blaze may in time arise therefrom which shall shine throughout the whole world." Yet, with all this consciousness of good work in the past, and good work in the present, he measures himself against the greater future with Pauline humility : " not as though I had already attained, either were already perfect ; but I follow after. . . . This one thing I do, forgetting those things which are behind, and reaching forth unto those things which are before, I press towards the mark." For, writes Dürer, " Sure am I that many notable men will arise, all of whom will write both well and better about this art, and will teach it better than I. . . . Would to God it were possible for me to see the work and art of the mighty masters to come, who are yet unborn, for I know that I might be improved."

We may see here that the true artist, like the true mystic, is of all creeds. In proportion as he takes his art seriously, as a thing not only intensely interesting but most exacting in its demand upon the whole man, body and soul, in that proportion does it call out all that is best in him. Thus the most different manifestations find their source in one pure fount of light, only broken and diversified by refraction, according to the different texture of the minds through which they pass. And the sympathetic student of the plastic arts will there find his own higher moods interpreted, whether through a cathedral or a landscape or a child's dimpled fingers, just as Sir Thomas Browne tells us of his own transfiguration through music. " For even that vulgar and tavern musick which makes one man merry, another mad, strikes

in me a deep fit of devotion, and a profound contemplation of the first composer. There is something in it of
divinity more than the ear discovers: it is a micro-
physical and shadowed lesson of the whole world and
creatures of God—such a melody to the ear, as the whole
world, well understood, would afford the understanding.
In brief, it is a sensible fit of that harmony which intel-
lectually sounds in the ear of God."

CHAPTER VII

THE FREEMASONS

HALLAM complained, in 1818, that "the curious subject of freemasonry has unfortunately been treated only by panegyrists or calumniators, both equally mendacious." Here, however, is a field into which the last century of discussion has brought real light; and masonic writers agree now with non-masonic upon all points of primary interest.

When we first trace the western mason in any sort of association, the notice is extremely vague. The laws of the Lombard King Rothari (643) speak of *Magistri commacini*, "Commacine Masters," who are masons. The brief notice has given rise to many far-fetched suppositions. It is extremely improbable that the word has anything to do with Como. The most we can safely assume is that, in Northern Italy, there still survived from Imperial times some sort of organization among the masons, as also among some other crafts or trades. There was, for instance, a shipwrights' gild and a soap-makers' gild.[1] Beyond this, we get no real documentary evidence for masons' gilds, I think, until we come to the *Livre des Métiers*, which was drawn up for Paris by Étienne Boileau, whom St.-Louis put into office to reform the whole government of that city.[2] The 48th chapter

[1] For this, and other information on Italian conditions, I am indebted to Mr. C. W. Previté-Orton.

[2] Published in 1879 by R. de l'Espinasse, as a volume of the *Histoire générale de Paris*. The book was probably written in 1268. Didron quotes German authors who claim masonic gilds for their country in the twelfth century; but there seems to be no definite evidence.

(pp. 88 ff) deals with the Masons' Gild. There is nothing in this chapter which really differentiates the gild from the rest. We may be struck by an assertion of freedom in the first paragraph; but we shall presently find close analogies in the beer-sellers, goldsmiths, pewterers (great and small), ropemakers, and knife-handle makers; out of the 100 gilds, sixty-two have some such notice. Indeed, it is probable that *freemason* means *worker in freestone*, for *freestone* is mentioned in much earlier documents than *freemason*; and, again, building accounts distinguish between the freemason on one hand and the rough-mason or hard-hewer on the other, very much as our fathers distinguished between *whitesmith* and *blacksmith*, and as the Germans still call the latter *Grobschmied*, "rough-smith."[1] The painters in London and Paris were originally of the saddlers' gild, since saddles were often painted; at Florence, they were classed with the apothecaries.[2] The Paris masons are in a single gild with the mortar-makers and plasterers; the king appointed the chief master of their craft; but " beyond this, the regulations contain nothing unusual; nothing which contrasts with other professions. The ancient statutes of the masons' gild at Montpellier have lately been discovered, and here, again, we have proof that it was an ordinary confraternity."[3] Much has been made of the oath of secrecy; but this was the normal thing; all medieval gildmen swore not to betray the secrets of their association.

Several causes, however, contributed gradually to differentiate the building craftsmen from others. They

[1] Cunningham, p. 7, suggests that *freemason* came to mean " one who has the freedom of the town." Like every other suggestion of his, this deserves consideration; but his evidence seems very inconclusive. And there is no historical evidence, I believe, for Mr. Kingsley Porter's explanation, " ' free '—that is, no fee was demanded of those who entered the trade " (ii, 192). The Eton building accounts, by themselves, are sufficient to negative this conjecture.

[2] Leader Scott, *Donatello*, 1882, p. 52.

[3] Didron, *Annales*, vol. xi, p. 327, article by Schnaase.

often worked in far larger numbers ; at Westminster Abbey there were sometimes as many as 160 building craftsmen, with 176 labourers ; of masons alone, at King's College, Cambridge, 105 ; at Eton College, 77 ; and at York Minster, 50. [1] Again, the seventeen runaways from Hertford Castle must point to a far larger number of carpenters on the whole staff ; at Eton there were 45. At Coucy, the banker-marks of 100 simultaneous masons have been counted,[2] and 400 at Aigues-Mortes.[3] These latter would not all be working at the same time ; but at Peterborough there are at least 100 contemporary marks of about 1100–1120, and probably more ; at St. Nicholas' Chapel, Lynn, which we know to have been built between 1399 and 1418, there are 11. " There were no fewer than 346 artificers and workmen on the household establishment of Edward III." (Cunningham, p. 4, v. 5). In earlier days, e.g. at Ely and Peterborough, these men doubtless lived within the monastic precincts just as we have seen in the Obazine case, and were disciplined by their monastic employers, whose servants would at once eject without difficulty any workman reported for insubordination by the master-mason. But, when the work no longer went on within the monastic precincts, then came real problems of self-government and discipline. There was no town in Western Europe where large numbers of saddlers or tailors or shoemakers were congregated in a single workshop ; nothing, therefore, in those gilds, answering on this point to the conditions in the masons' lodge. It was natural that these more difficult conditions should be met by stricter and more elaborate organization.[4] Clothworkers, it is true, did exist in very large numbers here and there, as in the Low Countries and in Northern Italy ; and this accounts

---

[1] G. G. Scott, *Gleanings*, etc., p. 231 ; for Eton and King's, see Willis and Clark ; for York, the *Fabric Rolls*.

[2] Viollet-le-Duc, *Dict. Arch.* iv, 263.

[3] *Ann. arch.*, iii, 237.

[4] See the article by Klotz in Didron, *Annales*, vol. v, p. 273.

for the strict and elaborate disciplinary regulations of the Florentine cloth-gilds.

An even deeper difference may be found in the mason's nomadic existence. A small proportion of these crafts-men would be permanently settled in large towns[1]; we find these, in German records of the fifteenth century, relegated to a separate category. For the vast majority were, in the nature of the case, wanderers from church to church, from castle to castle. Even in large English towns, stone houses were few and far between; we may probably say safely that 49 out of 50 were of wood, or even 99 out of 100. Therefore, whereas the saddlers' or tailors' gild had a local centre in each town, and could be organized on static principles, the only possible organization for the masons was provisional, elastic, and of far wider than merely local purport. It is signifi-cant that Parliament, attempting to fix flat maximum rates of wages, found its chief difficulty with the building trades. Wyclif, somewhere about 1380, is much concerned at the self-seeking which the gilds, he writes, encourage, and specially " men of subtle craft[s], as' freemasons and others," who " conspire together " to refuse statutory wages and to insist upon a rise.[2] In 1424, Henry VI approved a statute to the effect that " masons shall not confederate themselves in Chapiters and Assemblies," since as a result " the Statutes of Labourers be openly violated and broken " ; the holders of such chapters " shall be judged for Felons." No other gilds are thus dealt with; for there was no such necessity in their case. If the tailors had " confederated " to enforce higher wages than the Statutes of Labourers allowed, the local authorities could at once have clapped the offenders into prison and confiscated their gild funds. But the masons were here, there, and everywhere; and only

[1] Cf. Cunningham, pp. 3-4.
[2] *Select English Works.* Ed. T. Arnold, vol. iii, p. 332 ; I have printed this, and Henry VI's statute, at length in *Social Life in Britain*, pp. 490-491

in the largest towns, if at all, had they a gild-hall and seizable funds. So far they had a great advantage over other gild-folk; but, on the other hand, it was impossible for them to remain entirely invertebrate amid the general tendency of society to form into more and more elaborate associations. Already in 1424, therefore, they were holding central assemblies, or chapters, designed partly to protect, partly to control, the otherwise scattered groups or individuals, just as the modern Miners' Federation deals with its own members. It is significant that in Germany, which thenceforward becomes rich in masonic records, the first chapter for which we have documentary evidence is that of 1459, held at Regensburg, after preliminary meetings at Strassburg and at Speyer.[1] It was attended by nineteen masters and twenty-five journeymen, apparently the largest medieval numbers on record. Others were held alternately at Speyer and Strassburg in 1464, 1466, 1467, 1468, and 1471. The whole Empire was divided into four provinces, grouped round the lodges of Strassburg, Vienna, Berne and Cologne. The statutes of 1459 were confirmed in 1563 at a great Strassburg chapter, by seventy-two masters and thirty journeymen.[2] The word *chapter* in itself is significant, for it is a specifically monastic term; so, again, perhaps, is *parlierer*, the word used in German statutes for the lodge-master's deputy, the warden. It seems pretty certain that these fifteenth-century measures of central organization incorporated older and less formal traditions which dated from the days of masonic discipline within the abbey precincts. Each separate lodge may well have had, for many generations past, its own particular chapters. But it is difficult to escape from the conclusion that the General Chapter system was in fact an innovation. For instance, in 1356, two generations before we have record of any

---

[1] Klotz assumes chapters as early as the thirteenth century, but gives no proof; it is simply a guess. (*Ann. archéol.*, vol. v, p. 273.)
[2] Klotz, *l.c.*

General Chapter, the Mayor and Aldermen of London were obliged to legislate for the masons of that great city, " because that their trade has not been regulated in due manner, by the government of folks of their trade, in such form as other trades are " ; hence, a series of disputes which endangered the King's peace and the tranquillity of the city.[1] When, therefore, our two earliest ordinances of freemasonry, dating from the early fifteenth century, come to speak of the Chapter system, they claim a hoary antiquity for it.[2] According to one of them, the fourth chapter of Genesis shows masonry to have been the first art that was founded ; for Jubal, Lamech's son, invented masonry, and is called in the Bible *Pater habitancium in tentoriis atque pastorum.* " And he was Cain's master-mason, and governor of all his works when he made the city of Enoch, that was the first city that ever was made. . . . And this in part witnesseth [the] bible in the same X chapter [of Genesis], where he saith that Assur that was nigh kin to Nimrod [and] went out of the land of Senare and he builded the city Nineveh." Nimrod sent to Assur " XXXC of masons " and gave them a " charge " to govern themselves by ; this is the first masonic charge extant. " Abraham, as the chronicle saith, he was a wise man and a great clerk, and knew all the seven sciences and taught the Egyptians the science of geometry. And this worthy clerk, Euclid, was his clerk and learned of him." Many lords in Egypt had younger sons for whom they could not provide ; Euclid said " Will ye [that I] take your sons in governance, and I shall teach them such a science that they shall live thereby gentlemanly." They agreed . . . " And he taught to them the craft [of] masonry,

---

[1] H. T. Riley, *Memorials of London*, 1868. p. 280. But his *Right masons and setters* has been corrected by Mr. R. R. Sharpe to *mason layers and setters* (*Letter Book* 9, p. 51).

[2] *The History and Articles of Masonry*, printed in 1861, by Matthew Cooke, from the so-called Cooke-Baker MS. in the British Museum (MS. add. 23, 198). My summary starts from p. 23 of this edition.

and gave it the name of geometry." . . . "And he gave them a charge that they should call their each other fellow, and no otherwise, because that they were of one craft and of one gentle birth born, and lord's sons. And also that he that were most of cunning should be governor of the work and should be called master, and other charges more that are written in the book of charges." The Israelites learned masonry in Egypt and brought it with them to the Land of Behest. It is written in [1 Kings V] "that Solomon had iiii score thousand masons at his work. And the King's son, of Tyre, was his master-mason. And in other chronicles it is said, and in old books of masonry, that Solomon confirmed the charges that David his father had given to masons. And Solomon himself taught them their manners [with] but little difference from the manners that now be used." From India it spread to France "and other regions." Charles the second king of France [i.e. Charles Martel] "was a mason before that he was king" and loved them ever afterwards and ordained that they should have an assembly once a year. St. Adhabell [i.e. Amphibalus] came to England and converted St. Alban. St. Alban gave the first mason's charges in England. Athelstan's youngest son became a mason, learning "the practice of that science [in addition] to his speculative" and ordained their yearly meetings "as it is written and taught in the book of our charges." After this comes a great deal of repetition; the tale of Euclid is told again under form of Englet [*query*, Euglet ?]. Then we are told how Athelstan ordained "congregations" either yearly or triennially; and then follow the articles, one by one. Another manuscript of about the same time gives a very similar list of articles; but the variations are such as practically to disprove the claim of each MS. to represent an ancient and settled tradition.[1] This second

---

[1] J. O. Halliwell, *Early History of Freemasonry, &c.*, 2nd ed., 1844. A great deal of this early masonic poem is extracted in my *Social Life in Britain*, pp. 482 ff.

version is more moderate in its historical claims, tracing masonry no farther back than to the clerk Euclid in Egypt, except so far as Euclid had been anticipated, in a far less systematic way, by Nebuchadnezzar and his Tower of Babel, which was

> " So plainë work of lime and stone
> As any man should look upon;
> So long and broad it was begun,
> Seven mile the height shadowed the sun."

This author, again, claims Athelstan as founder of the craft in England; there can be little doubt that the suggestion came from the suggestion of *stane, stone,* in his name. For we see an analogous process in that earlier claim of descent from Charles Martel. The stone-axe, or stone-hammer, was almost as definite a badge of the mason as were the square and compasses; and nobody who has puzzled over medieval derivations will be surprised that the name of this distant king, already half-lost in the mists of legend, should have suggested a great patron to the fertile imagination of the later free-mason. For we can already trace this nearly two centuries earlier, at Paris, where Boileau's *Livre des Métiers* shows the masons claiming freedom from the burdensome duty of watch and ward at the walls and gates of the city. This freedom they shared with one or two other gilds, but the masons alone allege an historical reason for their pretension; they claim to inherit the privilege by direct gift from Charles Martel. We have here one of the commonest of medieval phenomena; an innovation claims for itself the sanction of immemorial practice; and this naturally happens most often in cases where the new idea seems to follow as a natural corollary from some actual fact of the past. For instance, those papalists who struggled to encroach upon imperial powers, or again the imperialists who would fain have encroached in the other direction, appealed alike to a real or imaginary antiquity. Rienzo, reaching forward to the future, easily persuaded himself and his friends that he was

K

simply reviving the past. Therefore these freemasons, who strove to bring the scattered traditions and practices of their craft into some sort of logical system, tried to consecrate their decrees with the imposing names of Tubal-Cain and Nebuchadnezzar and Charles Martel and Athelstan. The English traditions are bolder and more unhistorical than the French; for they go on to claim the direct patronage of royal sheriffs and great lords for their General Chapters. But these claims, however negligible as past history, are excellent evidence for the age in which they were forged. Athelstan, indeed, had nothing to do with the organization of the masons' gild; but these two writers of about 1420 were members of a group which was now struggling hard to create some such organization. Here, then, we are on real documentary ground at last, for England and for Germany. Here is a great gild, already grown to far wider dimensions than the ordinary craft gild, and conscious of its need not only for extension but also for intensive discipline. And the problem would be specially difficult, since the conditions would naturally, in this particular gild, create something more even than the common medieval gulf between strict theory and elastic practice. For the same causes which did so much to help the masons' gild to defy the Statutes of Labourers or public opinion, in defence of their own special interests, would also help the individual, or the small group, to go frequently on its own way with small regard for the rulings of the central authority; here, again, we have a close analogy in the present Miners' Federation. But it is important to study the ideal; even an unfulfilled ideal has, in the truest sense, a reality of its own. And this ideal was sufficiently realized in practice to differentiate medieval art very widely, in one most important respect, from that of to-day. That art, in its strong collectivism, contrasted sharply with modern individualism. The three greatest collectivist forces of the Middle Ages, under Church and State, were Monasticism, Knighthood,

and the Gild ; and even the laxest gild gave support to
the individual on the one hand, while it restricted him
on the other, to an extent which we may easily under-
estimate. It has been overlooked by writers on both
sides. When, for instance, we read that Gothic art
" was Christian in its impulse because it was freedom
itself . . . because it was bound by no hindering precedents,
but gave the fullest scope for personal expression . . .
no British monk or mason would for a moment consent
to be bound by any system or precedent he found hamper-
ing," then we are in the presence of an author who, however
valuable his practical work in modern architecture may
be, is writing here really at random, drawing unhesi-
tatingly upon his own imagination, and in complacent ignorance of real European facts.[1] There is a
very significant passage in the *De Altera Vita* of Luke,
Bishop of Tuy in Spain, written between 1260 and 1280,
when the artistic movement was still strong.[2] The
earliest Christian crucifixes had shown Christ clothed
and fastened to the cross by four nails, i.e. with feet
apart ; there is a famous crucifix of this kind at Romsey
Abbey. Gradually, sculptors found it more artistic,
and perhaps also more suitable for arousing devotion,
to drape the loins only, and to bring the feet together
with a single nail.[3] This movement was evidently new,
or comparatively new, in Spain at that time ; and Luke
writes with horror of the " heretics " who attempt to
shake the Orthodox Faith by " painting or carving ill-
shapen images of Saints ; in order that by gazing on
such images the devotion of simple Christian folk may
be turned to loathing. In derision and scorn of Christ's

[1] R. A. Cram, *The Gothic Quest*, New York, 1907, pp. 66, 72. See
farther in Appendix 8.

[2] This, and the passage from the Bishop of London's register, are
translated fully on pp. 473 ff of *Social Life in Britain*, with a phototype
from the Romsey crucifix. An illustrated article on this subject is in
Annales archéologiques, vol. iii, p. 357.

[3] The evolution is well described in Mâle I. pp. 84, 254-5.

Cross, they carve images of our Lord with one foot laid
over another, so that both are pierced by a single nail,
thus striving either to annul or to render doubtful men's
faith in the Holy Cross and the traditions of the sainted
Fathers, by superinducing these diversities or novelties."
In England, apparently, the evolution was later still.
The Bishop of London, in 1306, issued a solemn mandate
to the faithful of his diocese, "lest worse things befall."
One Tidemann, of Germany, had sold a crucifix to a
city rector for the enormous sum of £23 ; it must have
been a very elaborate work of art ; for at this time the
sum would have kept five yeomen with their families
for a year, and any freeholder possessing land to the
value of £20 per annum was bound by law to accept
knighthood or pay a fine. Worst of all, the people
appreciated this foreign crucifix; " the indiscreet populace flocked to it in crowds as to a true image of the cross."
Its eccentricity, unfortunately, is not very clearly specified ; it seems to have resided rather in the arms than
in the feet. But in some way the carving departed
seriously from orthodox tradition as delivered to the
bishop, and he feared lest "their souls should be imperilled." He emphasizes his own leniency to Tidemann,
who "claimeth to be an alien and a simple man, who
might probably and innocently have ignored the accustomed mysteries of the Crucifix and the image thereunto
attached." But Tidemann is to disgorge the money,
the rector must give up the crucifix (at present seques-
trated and safely imprisoned in a monastery) and then it
must be "borne forth from the monastery to some place
without our diocese, either at early dawn or late in the
evening, when it can be done most secretly and with
least scandal." In other words, the bishop deals with it
as the severest of his brethren dealt with the most incor-
rigible of their priests ; they banished them from their
own dioceses, and left the rest to Providence.

Moreover, equally invidious restrictions might be
imposed upon the artist, though in a different way,

by his own gild. There was no essential difference here between England and Germany, from which latter country we get a very significant episode.[1] The master-mason, Jodocus Tauchen, in 1456, was boycotted by his fellow-masons of Silesia because " they doubted whether he had properly satisfied all conditions according to the masons' customs, which were then kept more strictly than nowadays ; they doubted whether he had rightly learned his craft and had proved his capacity for the mastership by working his masterpiece publicly before the gild. Therefore they would allow none of the apprentices to work with Jodocus who had learned in their own lodges, nor would they receive any who had learned under Jodocus." Two years before, Jodocus had been chosen to carve the splendid ciborium which still exists on the church of St. Elizabeth at Breslau. Into this ciborium, notes Schultz, he introduced " new forms of ornaments, often ungraceful, which we must not lay to his charge as a very grievous crime, seeing that in those days every architect strove to invent novelties." This question of graceful or ungraceful ornament does not touch the present argu-ment ; certainly the ciborium as a whole is a fine piece of Gothic work ;

CIBORIUM OF THE ELIZABETHAN KIRCHE, BRESLAU, WITH JODOCUS TAUCHEN'S MARK.

and, if the facts were as these Silesian gild-masons con-tended, then Phidias himself would have been as vulnerable to their boycott as Jodocus was. The idea that a medieval artist had anything like modern freedom is a delusion difficult to account for. It is possible to argue that freedom is a bad thing in art and in religious belief ; but it is not permissible, in face of notorious facts, to assert that

[1] See the monograph by Alwin Schultz. *De Vita atque operibus M*[ri] *Jodoci Tauchen*, Breslau, 1864, pp. 3, 4, 10.

freedom existed in either field during the Middle Ages. If indeed all things are Christian in proportion to their freedom, then, in that respect, art conditions are more truly Christian to-day than they were during the thousand years before the Reformation.

The fullest and most interesting sets of pre-Reformation gild regulations are those of Regensburg in 1459 and of Torgau in 1462, printed by Janner on p. 251. They begin with solemn invocation of the Holy Trinity and the Virgin Mary, and the Four Crowned Martyrs—the *Quatuor Coronati*, masons who are said to have been martyred about A.D. 300 for refusing to carve pagan idols; the story may be found in *The Golden Legend* under November 8 (*Temple Classics*, Vol. VI, p. 139). Religious observances play as definite a part in these documents as in the similar and probably slightly earlier English statutes; we shall see the significance of this fact when we come to the later history of freemasonry. There are regular subscriptions for church services; each mason is to confess and communicate once a year, as had been commanded in the Lateran Council of 1215. At Strassburg, they must also attend the yearly service of the Quattuor Coronati. Again, they must obey the Church requirements of regular attendance at Mass on Sundays and greater feasts. The English statutes prescribe for Mass the simple and beautiful rhymed vernacular prayer which was often taught by priests to their parishioners—

> " Jesu, Lord, welcome thou be
> In form of bread, as I Thee see, etc."[1]

And the mason was taught, as the parish priest often taught his people, that the man who has heard Mass is safe for twenty-four hours from sudden death or loss of eyesight; a teaching against which the great Paris Chancellor, Jean Gerson, had vainly protested, pointing

[1] Halliwell, *l.c.*, *ad fin*; Myrc, *Instructions, etc.*, E.E.T.S., 1868, line 290.

out that common experience must frequently falsify it and bring discredit upon the Church. The English statutes add one promise which was homelier and far more secure from contrary evidence; the Archangel Gabriel measures and records every foot that the mason goes on his way to Mass. On the other hand, religion must not be made an excuse for idleness. There, as in all other gild or manorial records, we find occasional evidence that a large proportion of the red-letter festivals were not kept free from labour by workmen and employers, according to the strict prescriptions of the Church. " If a man makes holy days for himself during the week, instead of asking leave, these they count as unhallowed, and he shall not be paid."[1]

There is nothing here, except the special homage to the *Quattor Coronati*, which we might not expect to find in any medieval gild; nor is the apprenticeship system essentially different. The training lasts nominally seven years; sometimes no more than four or five, sometimes as many as twelve.[2]

At the end of this term, if he has given satisfaction, he becomes a " journeyman," i.e. a worker for day-wage, *journée*. Then he is in a position analogous to the Bachelor of Arts in the Middle Ages; for the Universities were gilds of teachers or students, following very nearly the lines of the other gilds. The B.A. had already a recognised, though only intermediate, status. In due time, if he could satisfy the masters of his competence, and pay the usual fees, he was admitted to their august

---

[1] Janner, pp. 125, 307 (1462). Compare this with the fact that, in the Eton Chapel accounts of 1442-3, the Freemasons are paid for the holydays on which they do not work, while the others are not. Fr. Denifle describes an account book of the painters' work at the papal palace of Avignon in 1346–7. Out of the 107 days covered by the account, 81 were work-days, and 26 Sundays and holy-days; of these, naturally, the Sundays must be either 15 or 16; this leaves 10 or 11 for the holydays; this would be nearly the normal proportion (ALKG., vol. iv, p. 606).

[2] Janner, p. 52; Gould, vol. i, pp. 145, 188.

confraternity. So also with the journeyman, with only one obvious difference and one less evident, though perhaps more important. The medieval journeyman was not, like the medieval bachelor, still a pupil. In discipline, it is true, he was still *in statu pupillari*; he worked, so to speak, under the overseer's rod. But in his craft he might be very far advanced, and separated from the mastership not by merit, but merely by jealous exclusiveness. For (and this is the second, though less often recognised point), we get increasing indications of a selfish and oligarchical spirit in the masons' gild, as in all the others. The masters formed a clique, with strong social and financial temptations to exclude younger men. Therefore they exacted heavier fees as time went on, and a more and more difficult " masterpiece," and sometimes (as in the Florentine wool-gild) insisted finally on the hereditary principle; no man could be a master who was not descended from masters. For this extreme exclusiveness in the masons' gild there is no evidence; yet, when it became common elsewhere, it would be natural enough for birth and family favouritism to play a considerable part here also: not, I think, to the extent of promoting really incapable men; certainly the statutes are careful to do what they can to secure the public against this. But, when the number of expectant journeymen was large (and for this we have evidence) it was natural that the master's son should have other advantages beyond which he would enjoy in the matter of the " masterpiece."

This " masterpiece " was to the journeyman what the public disputation in the schools was to the B.A. It comes first into prominence in 1514, in the Regensburg statutes; the requirements there are certainly very strict; and if (as it seems) the man was required not only to explain the making of a vaulted bay, a tower of certain specifications, etc. etc., but actually to have carried out such a work, then it must have been very difficult for him to reach the master's rank; many men who in them-

selves were sufficiently skilled must have found promotion
hopeless through sheer lack of opportunity.[1] In post-
Reformation France, the gilds gradually carried on
oligarchical selfishness to its farthest limits, as the following quotation from Gould will show.[2] None but a
master, it must be premised, might open a shop ; the
journeyman, as his name implies, was limited to the rôle
of employee.

" The achievement of the masterpiece was the
crowning point of the workman's career : and the
precautions to obviate fraud were very severe. The
nature of the test was decided by the authorities of
the craft, and sometimes the execution entailed months
of labour. The workman had to perform every operation under the immediate surveillance of the judges
in a locked chamber ; and no friends or acquaintances
were allowed to approach him lest they might assist
him with advice. If he failed to satisfy his superiors,
he was debarred from trying again for a certain period,
sometimes for ever ; and, until he had passed the
necessary examination, he could not exercise the
trade on his own account. Laudable in its inception
as this institution appears, it soon became the most
powerful buttress of the masters' monopoly. The
tests were so chosen as to entail an enormous expense,
although perhaps little skill, in their execution ; whilst
the workman was further hampered by the necessity
of paying high fees to the craft court, and providing
extravagant banquets for the masters of the trade. If
the poor journeyman was not ruined in his endeavour
to pass the ordeal ; if, in spite of all hindrances, he
rose to the position of master, the other masters had
at least the satisfaction of knowing that, in consequence
of the heavy strain on his resources, he must begin
business in a very small way indeed. The relations of

[1] Janner, p. 118.
[2] Vol. i, p. 189.

masters were exempt from these vexatious regulations. No apprenticeship, journey work, or masterpiece was required of them, and their fees were incomparably lighter. Louandre must be my sole authority for the almost incredible fact that masters have been known to procure the mastership for their sons at the age of four years! Apart from the fees payable to the guild, the judges, and the master or provost of the craft, whether elected by the craftsmen or appointed by the king, there were further sums due to the municipality. The greater portion of the revenues of certain towns arose from the fines inflicted on the trades. Nor was the unlucky candidate yet free to pursue his calling. In the feudal domains the lord of the manor stepped in and claimed *his fees*; in the royal domains the king received his share; and in some cases he was under an obligation to pay a certain yearly subsidy to his feudal lord. Under the feudal *régime* it was considered that the lord was the master of the crafts, and none had a right to exercise their calling except under his authority and during his pleasure. There were also some trades—Monteil says a great number—in which no journeyman could obtain the mastership, not even by marrying the daughter of a master; but in which the mastership was rigorously hereditary in the male line. The butchers of Paris were of this class."

Here we have the system pushed to its most vicious extreme, and in post-medieval times; yet in medieval Florence things were almost as bad. Modern scholars are inclined to attribute the constant and bitter class-warfare in that city, and in others of Northern Italy and Flanders, mainly to the exasperation of the multitude of journey-men oppressed by the small group of masters. When the former attempted to form a trade union of their own, this was strictly forbidden. In England, as we have seen, the Statutes of Labourers, emphasised by the Statute of Henry VI, practically forbade any effectual trade union of journeymen. In Germany, the masonic regulations of 1563, confirmed by His Imperial Roman Majesty Ferdinand I, for the whole Empire of Germany, makes the strike definitely illegal ; " *Item*, the journeymen shall never again make a union or combination to withdraw in a mass from any enterprise, and thus to hinder any building."[1] This is only an extension of the statute of 1459 : " *Item*, when a man capriciously takes his departure from the head lodge or from any other lodge, that same journeyman shall never ask for employment in that lodge for a year afterwards."[2] On the other hand, by the statutes of 1462, " any master may dismiss a journeyman from the building-work, so long as it be done decently [*gütlich*] and without wrath."[3] Also it must not be done except on a Saturday or a pay-day."[4] The journeyman, for his part, may take leave on any pay-day.[2]

The master was distinguished by his cap and gown ; here, again, Oxford and Cambridge have kept their medieval traditions. A modern M.A. might wear, without impossible singularity, the very gown and hood which we see on the tombstone of Hugues Libergier, who died in 1263. And, though the cap has passed through a strange series of metamorphoses between then and now, yet it still remains an essential part of the master's full-dress uniform.

The German statutes, beyond the religious conformity already emphasized, prescribe strict discipline.[5] The master-mason has under him a warden, *parlierer*, whose extra-artistic function is rather that of the sergeant-major. He and the master are responsible for settling all quarrels ; they exercise full judicial powers within the

---

[1] Janner, p. 288, art. 51.

[2] Ibid., p. 261 (art. 36).

[3] Ibid., p. 307.

[4] Ibid., 261 (1459).

[5] Well described by Janner, pp. 119–136. For the wardens of the Eton Chapel Lodge, see Willis and Clark, vol. i, p. 381.

HUGUES LIBERGIER, MASTER-MASON OF ST.-NICAISE AT REIMS.

lodge. The warden beats a board or rings a bell for the beginning and the close of work; he must come first and depart last of all. If a workman comes late, the warden puts a bad mark against him " on the under side of his stone." He must suffer no regular drinking (as apart from an occasional cup) until evensong. And he, like the workmen, is subject to a system of fines, which go partly to the master, partly to " the box." If he deliberately overlooks an offence on a journeyman's part, he is to pay double the journeyman's fine. He, like the journeyman (and presumably, *a fortiori*, the apprentice) must pay for anything he spoils.[1] For the formal drink-meetings, at which some of the most important business was transacted, correct table-manners are inculcated; button up your coat before you sit down; spill no more wine or beer than could be covered with the hand, and so on. The English rhymed statutes are even more explicit :

> " Goodë manners make a man . . .
> Look that thine handen be clean
> And that thy knife be sharp and keen . . .
> If thou sit by a worthier mon
> Than thyselven thou art one,
> Suffer him first to touch the meat . . .
> In chamber, among ladies bright,
> Hold thy tongue and spend thy sight."[2]

There is much idealism here; it is bound up with the supposition, certainly false, that " great lords " and sheriffs and mayors will come to the General Chapters, as well as " men of craft "; but we cannot afford to neglect the ideal of an institution, any more than its practice.

This brief account will serve for an introduction to

[1] We shall see in detail, later on, how strictly the employers enforced this law among the workmen at Eton Chapel.

[2] See Halliwell, pp. 38 ff. These rules bear a strong resemblance to other manuals of the time; see *The Babees Book*, E.E.T.S., p. 32, and *Social Life in Britain*, p. 90.

two real peculiarities of the masonic gilds ; peculiarities which probably developed in earlier times, but for which we get no documentary evidence until the Torgau articles of 1462. The first is, the notable development of the mark system. The other is the secret sign of recognition.

CHAPTER VIII

THE MASON'S MARK

MUCH has been done already to record the medieval masons' marks; but there is crying need for some scholar with sufficient leisure to assimilate these scattered records and work out a full synthesis. A good deal, however, is already certain or nearly certain. The large majority of those which we find are " banker-marks," that is, the mason's sign-manual which he set on his finished stone before it left the banker, or working-bench. And these signs-manual were partly a matter of choice, partly of compulsion. It was very natural that a man should like to mark his own work before finally parting with it; so far we must note a definite exception to the general rule of anonymity as stated in a preceding chapter. Many of the marks are capital letters, probably standing for the workman's Christian name[1]; and, even in the other cases, the man might well have as much affection for his own mark as Whistler had for his butterfly. Yet all the indications point to the probability that, originally, the mark system had not been invented by the workmen but imposed by their superiors, and that such compulsion remained an essential characteristic throughout our whole period, at least.[2]

The first marks we find are often very coarse and crude. The Norman pillars at Ely are covered with them.

[1] In Southern France, masons sometimes used their full name as a banker-mark.

[2] Cf. Gould, i, 149. All that I write here on the subject of banker-marks represents only an attempt to bring system into a hitherto unsystematic study. My observations rest often on necessarily brief inspection and hasty notes, sometimes even on memory. It is only on a mass of detailed observation that any certain theory can be founded.

Making all allowance for the ravages of time, and the far worse ravages of well-meaning " restorers " who have scraped the stones, we may see that these signatures were carelessly made; two or three are often found closely resembling each other, and we cannot be sure whether they were originally identical, or intentionally varied for different workmen who had chosen the same general type. Again, where two or more marks evidently come

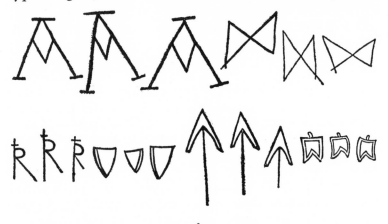

BANKER-MARKS FROM (1) ELY NAVE [ABOUT A.D. 1100], (2) ELY OCTAGON [ABOUT 1330], (3) GRANTCHESTER CHANCEL [ABOUT 1350] and (4) HARLTON [ABOUT 1450]. ALL ARE DRAWN TO SAME SCALE.

from the same man, they may differ a good deal in size and in general proportions. It is only in later work that we find the man's mark definitely standardized, each example answering much more closely to the other in size, in angle, and in depth of incision. This, together with the roughness of the axe-work and of the joints, agrees exactly with what we have other reasons to suspect, that these early Norman churches were built by hordes of half-skilled labourers, whom the clerk of the works and the master-mason had raked together as best they could;

so that their numbers, their clumsiness and their indiscipline called for constant and strict supervision. Each man was obliged to mark his stone when it was finished, and the taskmasters could thus verify the amount of his weekly work when pay-day came round. This theory, which from the first forces itself upon any observer of the facts, is rather strengthened than weakened, on reflection, by a phenomenon which becomes more and more evident in proportion as we look microscopically into those ancient walls. We find a large proportion of stones which

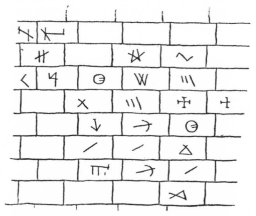

BANKER-MARKS IN GLOUCESTER TRIFORIUM.

are not, and never were, marked. This cannot be explained by supposing that banker-marks were sometimes made not on the face of the stone, but on the bed or the joint. An inspection of many hundreds of finished stones that lie about now among the ruins, and the agreement of other observers, will convince us that the rare marks found otherwise than on the surface are not banker-marks, but position-marks, to which we shall presently come.[1] And this is natural enough. The medieval

[1] A writer of real authority, Mr. John Hodges, speaks of banker-marks being placed on the bed of the stones; but he gives no evidence, and is apparently arguing simply from probabilities (*Hexham Abbey*, 1888, p. 32).

L

mason knew perfectly well that his surface, however carefully smoothed, was not destined for the public eye. In
medieval building accounts, when all the other charges
have been paid, we constantly find, *Item*, for so-and-so
many loads of lime. This was for lime-wash, with which
the walls were at once covered, to receive painting, in so
far as the funds might permit, later on. There is no
æsthetic reason, therefore, to account for an unmarked
stone. Yet many such there certainly are. In the
triforium at Gloucester, for instance, the surface is
extremely well preserved, and most of the marks rather
deeply cut; it is very difficult to believe that there ever
were marks, with a few trifling exceptions, where none
are to be seen to-day. And the ruined infirmary chapel
at Lewes Priory shows, or showed twenty years ago, still
more conclusive evidence. The floor had then been
recently excavated, laying bare the bottom courses of
masonry which had long been covered with earth. These
were in very perfect preservation, beautifully dressed
Caen stone with a surface like silk when the original thin
coat of limewash was peeled off. I stripped a few feet of
this with my own hands, and noted the marks carefully;
quite a large proportion of the stones bore no token
whatever. It seems impossible to doubt that there were,
from the very first, signed stones and unsigned.

And, on reflection, we may see that this fits in with the
rest. In any large establishment, the employés tend to
crystallize into two categories, a permanent staff and a
more or less casual section. We know this for a fact in
some medieval cases. Dr. Cunningham gives an admirable
example from a MS. register of Canterbury Cathedral
priory in the early fifteenth century. It contains a list
of regular servants of the monastery. " The heading
' Artifices ' includes workmen of different trades—carpenters, tylers, and masons, in numbers varying from five
to twelve. There are also a few carpenters who may be
regarded as the regular building staff of the monastery,
though some of them are specifically referred to as

retained for employment on the manors ; this establishment can be traced as existing without substantial change
from 1413 to 1448, though we do not get information
each separate year." Then came special building operations ; the first trace of them in the register is about
1428 : " We have a new heading, *Lathomi* [masons], and
find a staff of 20 stonecutters, 6 layers, 2 apprentices, and
4 labourers. These masons are described in 1429 as
Lathomi de la Loygge ; and we thus get a marked distinction between the ordinary staff, which is enumerated as
before, and the workmen who came and settled down for
a brief period and who formed a Lodge."[1] In many other
cases it is perfectly natural that some masons should have
been old and trusty enough to go on their own way even
while the majority needed to give strict vouchers for their
work. I suggested this once to an antiquary who is also
very familiar with publishers' work ; he replied that a
similar distinction existed in many large offices of to-day,
between men who can or cannot be trusted without
vouchers. And this theory is corroborated by the fact that
the best-cut stones are the least often signed. Even plain
capitals are seldom marked after the Norman period ; and
really artistic capitals, so far as my experience goes, never.[2]
Even good tabernacle-work is nearly always anonymous ;
the only exception I know is the Lady Chapel at
Gloucester, which was built so rapidly, and contains such
a mass of good stone-cutting, that many first-rate men
must have been engaged at the same time. Here, then,
we might expect to find even some first-rate men working
outside the permanent staff, and therefore needing to
prove from week to week that they were justifying their
engagement ; these would have to vouch their work, and

[1] P.3 ; Cf. Note 3, page 4.

[2] Mr. C. Symonds has drawn my attention to a remarkable exception ;
every capital in the east walk of the cloister at Lincoln bears the banker-
mark. ←⟨⟩— Here, as on the Peterborough keystone, the elaboration
of the mark suggests legitimate pride rather than compulsion. But, as
these all come in one walk only, they may be place-marks, as at Reims.

in fact we do find a few banker-marks here and there, on really elaborate stones. We know, from many entries in building accounts, that the best men were often paid not by the time but by the piece; this was called task-work; interesting instances will be found in Professor Lethaby's two books on Westminster Abbey.[1] Images, tabernacle-work, painted panels, etc., were constantly so paid; it was the most satisfactory arrangement to both parties, so long as both were honest; and a French episode of this kind seems very suggestive in the present context.[2] The chapter of Rouen had committed the making of their new choir-stalls to Philippe Viart, a master-carpenter with a great reputation. Philippe, of course, was responsible to the chapter alone; it was their business to keep him steadily to work. In 1466 they already found him too slow, and called in a master-joiner from Andely to report on Philippe's work. Next year, Sept. 3, he was called before the chapter and warned to go faster, or he would be dealt with by the civil magistrates—*auctoritate justiciæ secularis*. On Oct. 24 the chapter hastened the work by dismissing some of Viart's men, and giving the job to Rouen joiners, whom they now paid no longer by the day, like their pre-decessors, but by the piece. The only occupants of the lodge now are Viart with one assistant. On Nov. 24, Viart is seriously warned again; and next year (Jan. 19) the chapter finally expelled him, bag and baggage, wife

---

[1] Here, again, is an incident from Béthune in 1447, when the citizens built that town-hall of which we heard so much in the war. The mason engaged, Jehan Wiot, calculated the cost beforehand; the stonework would cost £693; the five corner-tabernacles would each need " four white stones, freestones from Lille," at £1 each; the masons' work would come to £17 per tabernacle (A. de la Fons), *Les artistes du Nord de la France* (Béthune, 1848, p. 81). At King's College, Cambridge, the statuary was actually estimated by measurement, at 5s. per foot (Willis and Clark, vol. i, p. 482). This was in or about 1515. See full text in chapter xi here below.

[2] See H. Langlois, *Les stalles de la cathédrale de Rouen* (Rouen, 1838), pp. 192 ff.

and children and all, from the lodge. At the same time, they demanded caution from him that he would not alienate his plans and drawings, on penalty of imprisonment and confiscation of his goods. Then they sent round one of their own workmen to recruit more joiners and hasten the work. He was absent 20 days, and was paid " for having visited Abbeville, Montreuil-sur-Mer, the Abbey of Fécamp, Hesdin, Brussels, Nivelles, Lille, Tournai, Arras, Amiens and other places." It may be noted here that such notices of recruitment of staff, or fetching of master-masons and master-carpenters from other places are very numerous (e.g. York Fabric Rolls, p. xix), and would suffice in themselves, apart from other evidence, to disprove the theory enunciated by Dr. Jessopp, and commonly repeated without caution to the present day, that nearly all the church-work in building and ornament was done by the village workman, or even by the youths and maidens of the place. Visitors to the famous rood-screen at Ranworth, for instance, are still told this.

This Rouen story, which might just as well have happened to a mason as to a carpenter, illustrates the theory sketched in the preceding pages ; and it throws light also upon two articles in the 1452 statutes, repeated almost word for word in 1563.[1] " All honest works and buildings which are carried on nowadays, and which stand in wage-work (to wit, Strassburg, Cologne and Vienna and Passau and other such-like work, and in the lodges thereunto appertaining) which by custom have hitherto been done and completed by wage-work—these same aforesaid buildings and works shall be continued in wage-work, and shall in no wise be turned into task-work, in order that the work be not interrupted by reason of the task-work, as far as may be " (art. 3). The fifth article is very similar, except for the final proviso that, if " the lords " (i.e the employers who order and pay for the building) insist upon the change " then [the master-

[1] Janner, pp. 252 (§§ 3, 5) and 273 ; Gould, i, 120.

mason] may do this according to the lord's desire, either in task-work or in wage-work"; if he makes the change without this excuse of following the employers' prescription, then the craft is to punish him. From this it seems to transpire plainly that the craft itself felt wage-work to be the more profitable system for the men, and resented the introduction of piece-work; the Rouen case shows clearly how the latter system could be used to put pressure upon men who were not working fast enough to suit the employers. For, while it is obvious how the piece-work system could be introduced in the case of carved capitals, a little reflection would seem to show that it could also be employed as a direct weapon against the ordinary hewers in the mass, though not directly against each individual, unless all the stones were standardized. The chapter of Cologne, for instance, could easily employ an expert to estimate how much each bay of plain wall-work ought to cost. We have many instances of such expert estimates in the Middle Ages. They could then say to the master-mason or the clerk of the works: " We will allow you so much, and no more, for such and such a measurement of plain wall; you will receive this sum for your hewers' wages; the longer they take about the job, the less will be their wages per diem." Under such pressure, the banker-mark system would enable the supervisor to reckon each man's rate of work, and to warn or dismiss the slower workman. Compare the corporation regulations imposed upon the London masons in 1356: " That the Master [masons] shall oversee that all those who work by the day shall take for their hire according as they are skilled, and may deserve for their work, and not outrageously."[1] Again, the English Masons' Charges of about 1480 insist more than once on this: the master is not to pay his underlings more than they really earn; (or, again, than they are worth to " the lord "—i.e. the

[1] Riley, p. 282. It must be remembered that this was eight years after the Black Death broke out; that the first Statute of Labourers, designed to keep down wages, dates from 1349 and the second from 1357.

employer). And § 8 runs : " That if it befal that any mason that be perfect and cunning come for to seek work, and find any unperfect and uncunning [mason] working [there], the master of the place shall receive the perfect and do away the unperfect, to the profit of his lord." [1]

The observation of ancient carpentry work seems to point in the same direction. Nobody seems to have found voucher-marks on the timbers of our old roofs, though position-marks are common enough, indicating how the beams are to be fitted together. A great beam could not be squared, and still less carved or moulded, in a day, or even a week. Therefore, even supposing that two or three men were not working simultaneously at the same timber, the master-carpenter had not the same easy method of calculation as the master-mason ; he could only check his men by comparing the state of the work at nightfall by what he remembered of it in the morning.

Finally, it seems a general rule that marks occur most frequently in the earliest and in the latest work, the two periods at which, from what we know in other ways, there would be most need of a business check upon the workmen. Mr. Hodges notes this fact, though he explains it differently.[2] The work of 1250–1350 is least marked, he says, because " a much finer surface was given to the masonry, and this led to the banker-marks being placed on the bed rather than on the exposed face of the stones." But for this assertion he gives no evidence ; and, in fact, the surface of the stones of the Lewes Infirmary chapel is far smoother than any that could be worked upon any but the most exceptional English stones ; yet they are frequently marked on the surface. Ely octagon, again, is covered with marks of more than average depth and size ; and, from what we know of the frequency of white-wash and paint, it seems rash to credit our ancestors with the modern feeling about smooth bare stonework. On the other hand, we have documentary evidence that the stone-

[1] Cooke-Baker, p. 118.
[2] *Hexham Abbey*, p. 32.

work of that octagon was begun and finished between 1322 and 1328; that is, a large number of masons must have worked there; and this would seem a far more natural explanation of the banker-marks.[1]

If this suggestion be true, and if we may expect to find most banker-marks where most masons were at work, or in circumstances in which some other cause called for strict business supervision—e.g. the contracts, fairly frequent in the fifteenth century, to finish the work within a given time—then we should expect more marks

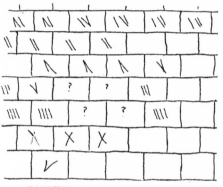

BANKER-MARKS AT DAMMARTIN.

in the earliest and in the latest period. Norman work was done largely, if not mostly, by hordes of comparatively unskilled labourers; many, perhaps, were serfs taken straight from the land.[2] In Perpendicular times, again, the contract system was growing up, and large numbers were often employed, with or without a definite time-limit. Here would come the call for as definite business organization as possible; the master-mason might well have to engage many men as yet unknown to him, and destined to drift out of knowledge again when the job was finished. Therefore, as the German statutes show us,

[1] For the rapidity with which some great works were carried out, see Lefèvre-Pontalis, p. 15, and especially Viollet-le-Duc, iv, 263.

[2] Even in transitional and early English work, the numbers engaged were often very large, as we see from the multiplicity of marks.

the system finally developed so far that each mason had his mark as a matter of course.

The banker-mark, therefore, was a business-voucher imposed upon the mason from above ; it was not, originally, " I will sign my stone," but " You must sign your stone." There are even indications which seem to point to something like military discipline ; the masons are distinguished by numerals, like soldiers in a file. This is very conspicuous in the ruins of Dammartin (Pas-de-Calais), and comes out fairly clearly from the chancel of the parish church at Calais. At Morat in Switzerland (anciently in Burgundy) the whole of the great tower of the walls on the land side is built of stones marked thus with the hewer's number. It seems evident, from these examples, that the later system under which the mason had his distinctive lifelong mark, like the knight's crest, was non-existent even in the later twelfth century, from which the Dammartin walls certainly date, and the Calais walls very likely, although the tracery is fifteenth century. But, however small may have been the mason's choice here at first, this still renders it perfectly natural that the man should, in process of time, accept his mark with more than mere acquiescence, and should become as proud of it as the soldier is of his uniform, which has its origin in similar requirements of discipline. Banker-marks become increasingly regular and artistic ; and, as we see with the master-mason of the keystone at Peterborough, or Jodocus Tauchen at Breslau, a man will sometimes display as an honour that which his remote predecessors had been obliged to accept as a token of obedience.[1] Therefore, the theory put forward in these pages cannot be pressed too strictly. It would mean, if it were taken as proved to the hilt, that the unmarked stones do, as a rule, come from the better workmen ; but we could not assert, inversely, that the better workmen never signed their stones, nor even that this anonymity

[1] For monograms and seals of master-masons see *Ann. archéologiques*, vol. v, p. 272, and viii, 147.

was the rule with them. We should be sure that they
need not; but this would not justify the inference that
they did not. When one man signed because he was
compelled, another might well do the same to mark his
great satisfaction with work that he was not ashamed of.
Certainly this is suggested by such a case as that of Great
Bardfield in Essex, where the remarkable stone rood-
screen and the nave pillars bear the same mark, constantly
repeated, though the whole may well have been done by
a single skilful mason.

In any case, these marks deserve far more scientific
attention than they have yet received as illustrations of
architectural history. If we had complete collections of
them in all the district archives, with equally exact records
of the tracery and the mouldings in each church of the
district, much could be done to trace the development of different schools, and perhaps even of
groups, or, still farther, of individual masons.
Great Bardfield is a case in point. We might
well doubt, on other grounds, whether the screen
and the piers are contemporary with each other,
but the banker-mark leaves no room for hesitation.

BANKER-
MARK AT
GREAT
BARDFIELD.

Still more interesting is a movement which can
be traced in the district of King's Lynn, and which
intensive study might possibly trace a great deal farther.
St. Nicholas at Lynn was begun and completed, as we
know from unimpeachable documentary evidence, between
the years 1399 and 1419. A few years after I had recorded
all the marks I could trace at that church, I happened to
revisit East Winch, five miles distant; and it soon occurred
to me that the piers and arches showed certain of the
Lynn characteristics. The next step was to search for
marks; and here there were two identical with those at
St. Nicholas.[1] A few years later, again, I visited Litcham

---

[1] Except that the St. Nicholas example is a little more elaborate. The
man may have made his mark more carelessly at St. Margaret's, at East
Winch, and at Walpole; or the less elaborate mark may be a younger
man's, imitated from an older colleague.

for the first time, some ten miles beyond East Winch.
There a striking feature of the Lynn window-tracery is
evidently repeated; the pillars, again, show certain
marked similarities; and there, again, is one of the

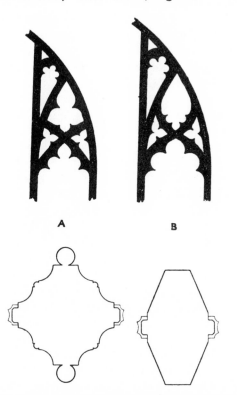

A   B

(A) THE AISLE WINDOWS OF ST. NICHOLAS AND LITCHAM, SHOWING A STRIKING
VARIATION FROM (B) THE USUAL WAY OF MANAGING THIS KIND OF TRACERY.
THE LEFT-HAND PILLAR-SECTION IS FROM LYNN, THE RIGHT FROM LITCHAM;
EACH HAS TWO SEMI-OCTAGONAL PILASTERS WITH CURIOUS CONCAVE MOULD-
INGS TO THEIR CAPITALS.

Lynn marks, and one of those which are to be found at
East Winch. Later research revealed similar migrations of
the St. Nicholas masons to other places in the district,
as the accompanying diagram will show. In Suffolk,
again, one and the same man worked at Cavendish and at

Long Melford, only a few miles apart. Here, then, is clear
light upon the persistence of style and the migrations of
the masons ; and, though a passing visitor can only find
this sort of evidence by great good luck, it can scarcely be
doubted that intensive study by local antiquarians would
yield far more fruitful results.

Nor is it only by marks that we can trace these migrations, if not of the actual artists, at least of their artistic
ideas. In the Lewes district of Sussex there is a group of
very remarkable capitals, dating from a little before or

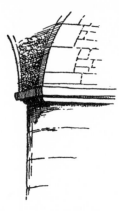

CAPITAL FROM PRITTLEWELL   CAPITAL FROM ST. ANNE'S, LEWES
        (ESSEX).   (SUSSEX).

after A.D. 1200 ;   they are to be found at St. Anne's,
Lewes, at another church in the Ouse Valley, and at Tels-
combe. A massive, almost squat circular pillar is surmounted by a square abacus ; and the transition from
round to square is managed by means of little carved
brackets at the four corners. This forms a remarkably
distinctive and successful design. At Prittlewell Priory, in
Essex, are round pillars of the same type, supporting a
square abacus. A cursory examination shows that, at each
corner, something has been cut away ; and it becomes
evident that here, also, the transition was originally
managed by four brackets, which had probably become

decayed, and which some churchwarden therefore removed altogether, leaving plain traces of mutilation. Now, Prittlewell Priory was a cell to Lewes, and the monks of Lewes had possessed Prittlewell church since Stephen's reign at least. These coincidences, therefore, can scarcely be accidental; and we may fairly take for granted that the Prittlewell capitals were wrought by the Lewes mason or by one of his companions. There is remarkable similarity, again, between the fragments of the great wheel window at St. Margaret's, Lynn, and the similar wheel windows on Peterborough west front. Here the connexion is not constitutional but merely local; all the good stone in Lynn and West Norfolk came at that time from Northamptonshire by the labyrinth of Fenland waterways. But it emphasizes the central fact, that the great school of medieval art was nearly always some great building.[1]

We may now come back to the personal side of the banker-mark; to its significance not for modern antiquarians but for the man himself who wrought the stones. The first definite and explicit evidence, apparently, comes from the Torgau statutes of 1462. The journeyman took his mark at a solemn admission-feast, partly at the master's cost and partly at his own. In the lodge, he was forbidden to engrave it on his work until the stone had been inspected and passed by the master or lodge-warden.[2] How necessary it was to check work in this way, we see from articles 51 and 61 of the same statutes. The warden himself, if he spoils a stone, must pay the cost of it to the lodge; again, if he passes as correct a badly-cut stone, he must pay 8d. and the defaulting workman 6d. In 1563, the statute runs: " No man shall change, of his

---

[1] Valuable information with regard to local schools may now be had from Mr. S. Gardner's *English Gothic Foliage Sculpture* (Camb. Univ. Press, 1927).

[2] Gould, vol. i, pp. 146–7; Janner, pp. 126, 299, 303, 306. For an instance of the way in which modern freemasons, like modern theologians, attempt to find symbolism in these natural proceedings, see Gould, i, 26.

own will and power, the banker-mark [*Ehrenzeichen*, lit.
" sign of honour "] which hath been conveyed and
granted to him by his gild ; but, if he purpose to change
it, let him do so with the favour, knowledge and consent
of the whole gild."

Before leaving this subject altogether, a word must be
said about position-marks, which have often been confused with banker-marks. The classical example here is
that of the west front of Reims Cathedral. At Notre-
Dame-de-Paris, a little earlier than this, some of the

POSITION-MARKS ON THE REIMS STATUES AND LINTELS.

elaborate statuary had been built into wrong places by
the setters, thus confusing the sequence of subjects which
had been thought out by the directing authorities and
worked out in the lodge. The Reims master-mason was
evidently determined to have no such confusion ; every
stone, therefore, was carefully marked. One symbol
denoted a particular side of a particular portal, another
denoted more exactly the place of the statue or statuette
within the lines of this general indication. For instance,
the general sign for the north side of the great central
portal is a crescent ; and, as there are five great statues

on each side, these are further marked with one straight line for the nearest to the door, two for the next, and so on. The plainest instance, conspicuous in any photograph, is St. Joseph, who comes fourth, and therefore bears a crescent with four lines. So, again, on the south side of the southern portal, where we have first Gabriel and the Virgin, then the Virgin with Elizabeth. The general sign for this side is a tau-cross (T), sometimes upright and sometimes reversed; masons often showed great indifference on that score. It can just be traced on

POSITION MARKS AT REIMS.

the Archangel Gabriel. The next figure is clearly marked with a ⊣II on a broad left-hand fold of the skirt. The third bears ⊣III a little below the right knee, the fourth has the T with four strokes a little above the right knee; and the angle-statue bears the same sign with five strokes in the lower folds of his mantle. The carved figures on the lintel have their own separate marks, first the generic T and then a little ring and cross, representing the consecrated Host, rising from one on the lowest stone to six on the highest. I record these, not only for their intrinsic interest, but because of their bearing upon an important artistic question. Efforts have been made to prove that the Salutation group was carved in the eighteenth century, on the strength of a date marked upon one of the figures in arabic numerals. But the place-marks show conclusively that this can only refer to some restoration, and not to the original figures; for no eighteenth century sculptor would have dreamed of marking his statues in this fashion in order that they might fit in with the mark-system of the confessedly thirteenth century figures on either side. Moreover, both

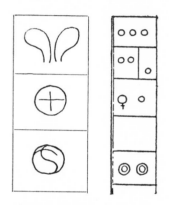

POSITION-MARKS AT WINCH-
COMBE.

statues are in the same piece with their brackets, which are of typical thirteenth century style. These two facts which I have not seen published elsewhere, and which can best be verified by climbing up to the level of the statues themselves, would seem to prove conclusively that the classical style of both statues is attributable, not to some later sculptor, but to a thirteenth century artist who had studied Greek statues in or from the Hippodrome of Constantinople; for another of these western figures, commonly called King Solomon, is obviously inspired by classical Greek art.[1] It can

[1] For this statue see ch. xx here below, page 417. M. Emile Mâle, in his brief contribution to this subject (*Revue Archéologique*, Jan. 1910, p. 142), has not noticed these proofs, which would seem more conclusive than the indirect arguments, however valuable, which he advances for the genuineness of the Visitation group. I pointed out the marks to the master-mason of the cathedral works in 1913; the fire of 1914 may have done much to efface them. But they can be traced, even by the naked eye, here and there on good photographs; e.g. in P. Vitry's great work on Reims Cathedral, tome i, pl. xiii, xvi, xxiv, lviii; also in the South Kensington Museum collection of photographs, *Sculpture, French*, xxv, c. 53, 554 (mark on Elizabeth's knee).

scarcely be a mere chance that the wonderful efflorescence of Gothic statuary with classically - modelled
draperies,as distinguished from such far more conventional
draperies as we see, for instance, on the west front of
Chartres, coincides with the generation which took Constantinople by storm and which carried off the bronze
horses which now adorn St. Mark's, at Venice.

Position-marks may also be traced in English buildings.
There is a very remarkable set at Winchcombe, cut on

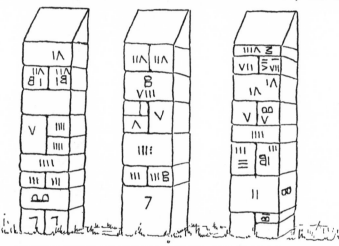

POSITION-MARKS ON THE BUTTRESSES, QUINCY-LE-VICOMTE.

the surface, as at Reims. They may occasionally be found
on quite simple work, as at the neighbouring villages of
Quincy-le-Vicomte and Bisernay in Burgundy, where the
little churches are of the same style and date, and were
therefore very likely built by the same group of workmen.
But position-marks were far more commonly placed on
the bed or the joint of the stone, and can therefore only be
studied in ruined buildings. A fan-tracery vault at Wells
Cathedral is now represented by a number of dislocated
stones preserved in one of the chapels ; each of these is
marked in Arabic numerals ; so also are some of the sculptures high up on the west front. At St. Mary Redcliffe,

M

Bristol, the restorers had the good sense to lay the discarded stones of window-tracery in the churchyard; each joint will be found marked with strange but strongly distinctive signs; this may be seen even through the railings, as we pass through to the south porch. At Fincham (Norfolk) the east window of a dismantled church lies in the present churchyard; it is fine flowing tracery of about 1350, and the joints are elaborately marked to secure correct fitting. Most interesting of all that I know in England are the carpenters' marks on the beams which form the framework of the New Inn at Gloucester, a building of the fifteenth century. The annexed diagram (in which the beams are shortened to bring all the joints into manageable space) shows clearly how the workmen provided against misfits during the erection.

POSITION-MARKS AT FINCHAM.

This chapter may fitly close with a brief sketch of the transition from medieval to modern freemasonry. It is well known that practically all the gilds were suppressed under Edward VI, on the pretext that their endowments were earmarked for superstitious purposes, except those of London, which were too formidable to touch. The masons escaped for similar reasons. They were here and there and everywhere, with ramifications and affiliations which may have been loose but were certainly very wide; they had no headquarters to be plundered and no concentrated main body to be crushed by a frontal attack; for long after the Reformation they led the same wandering life as before, coalescing and scattering and reforming again in kaleidoscopic groups, but with certain common traditions and practices which made them a real fellowship. The same qualities which made them objectionable to

Wycliffe and to Henry VI secured their survival through
that great religious and social revolution. When, therefore, in the late sixteenth and early seventeenth century,
there swelled up a wave of international sympathy among
scholars like Guillaume Postel and Grotius and other
cultivated people, then freemasonry became a natural
vehicle for the exchange of advanced political thought.
There was no government in Europe which would have
suffered the formation of a new international society;
but these humanitarian groups, otherwise unprotected

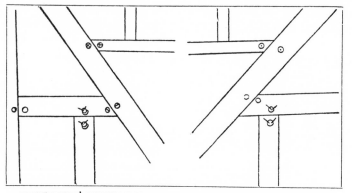

CARPENTERS' POSITION-MARKS AT THE NEW INN, GLOUCESTER.

and homeless, might imitate the hermit-crab and creep
into this pre-existing shell, admirably adapted to their
vague aspirations for brotherhood. " The admission of
love brothers, as honorary members of craft guilds, was
common enough; and this practice appears to have been
widely diffused both in England and Scotland at the
beginning of the seventeenth century. King James VI is
said to have been a mason in the lodge at Scone, John
Boswell of Auchinleck was present at a lodge in 1600,
and Elias Ashmole was admitted to a lodge at Warrington
in 1646. The building of St. Paul's after the fire gave a
fresh interest to the operations of builders, and Wren
was a member of the craft; but it was not till 1717 that

the institution of Grand Lodge took shape and that Freemasonry came to stand alone as a national institution, and to lose its close and direct connexion with operative masonry. The transition can be traced in connexion with the London Company of Masons, and even more distinctly at Dundee ; the old lodges of operative masons would be points at which the newly organized Free Masonry could readily obtain a footing. There seems to have been contact between the old organizations of craftsmen and the lodges of modern freemasons at Durham, Alnwick and Lincoln. Throughout the country generally, however, existing masonic lodges derive their status entirely from Grand Lodge, and have no links of connexion traceable with the bodies of operative masons who may have flourished in the same places in bygone times." [1]

---

[1] Cunningham, p. 10 ; a description all the more valuable since the author was himself a distinguished freemason.

CHAPTER IX

THE HAND-GRIP

IN the discussion of this subject, modern freemasons would seem to have an advantage, yet this is apparently counteracted by laws of secrecy, since Mr. Gould gives even less of definite evidence than Janner. But here and there we have direct documentary certainty, while in other directions we can rely with equal certainty upon attendant facts which seem to fit in exactly with the direct evidence.

Most masons, to begin with, led a nomadic life which contrasted with that of other artisans. In each case, on the completion of a building, the staff dispersed. Imaginative writers have pictured compact bands of masons, like the Free Companies of the Hundred Years' War, keeping together and passing on from church to church as those companies passed on from victory to victory. No evidence seems to have been offered for this; rather, all the evidence seems to be against it. In the vault of King's College Chapel, Cambridge, the banker-marks are indeed fairly uniform and continuous from beginning to end; but we know that the contract here was for three years, and the staff would naturally remain fairly stable. At other churches (e.g. Melrose and St. Nicholas, Lynn) the interest is, on the contrary, to see how men vanish and are replaced; again, the neighbouring churches testify to the dispersion of this large staff. Yet St. Nicholas certainly took less than eighteen years to build, and perhaps only ten or so, including the setting of the stones as well as the cutting. The mason, in this respect, was like the private tutor or governess of to-day; the very completion of his job meant a displacement and a fresh start from the beginning. A master-mason might take one or

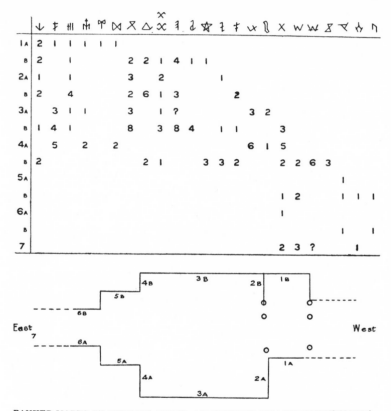

BANKER-MARKS AT MELROSE ABBEY, AS REVEALED BY A CURSORY EXAMINATION FROM THE GROUND, WITHOUT AID OF LADDERS.

The reader may trace, with the aid of the plan, how often each mark occurs on the lower part of each division of the building. The slant from left to right, which comes out from this tabulation, betrays the gradual falling-out of some masons and the arrival of others.

two of his most trusted associates on with him; but, from a work of any size, the majority would disperse.[1]

[1] This is treated more fully in Chapter X, where concrete instances may partly illustrate, partly modify, the generalizations attempted in this present chapter.

Here, then, was a problem far more pressing in masonry than in other crafts. The *Wanderjahre*, as the Germans call them, and the French *Compagnonnage du Tour de France*, which were only temporary and sporadic in other crafts, must have been general and chronic in the mason's.[1] He was out of his apprenticeship; was there work for him still in the same place? If not, he must go forth, and tramp on from village to village till he came upon masons at work. He probably possessed no tools; we find master-masons or carpenters leaving a few in their wills, but account-rolls seem to show that the lodge bought tools, and paid for their mending or sharpening (e.g. Dr. Stewart, *Ely Cathedral*, p. 94, and the under-smith already quoted at St. George's, Windsor, whose main duty was to keep all the tools in order). Moreover, the statutes themselves, as will be seen, definitely assume that the wander-fellow will have to borrow tools. How, then, was our wanderer to prove to the master-mason, when he found him at last, that he was a full-fledged competent workman, and not a mere half-trained tramp who would take a day's pay and spoil a piece of stone? There might be other ways, but for two we have a certain amount of documentary evidence; the pass-word and the sign. That evidence, it is true, is less early and less explicit than we might wish; yet it seems most probable that the conditions which we find in 1563 had developed far earlier, since they would follow logically from what we know to be the earlier conditions. Here, as on some other points, our only documents are German.

The young " fellow," *Geselle*, was advised at once to join the " brotherhood "; i.e. gild, or trade-union.[2] What happened if he refused to join we can only infer from the scattered indications of privileges granted to brethren, and (by implication) denied to outsiders. The 1462 statutes distinctly describe an initiation-ceremony, followed by a feast (§55) : " Every apprentice, when he

---

[1] See Appendix 9.
[2] Gould, i, 144 ff, esp. 146.

has served his time and is to be declared free, shall promise to the craft by his troth and honour, in lieu of oath, and on pain of losing the craft of a mason, that he will disclose or say to no man the greeting or the [handgrip] of a mason, except to one to whom he should rightly say it; and also, that he will put nothing thereof into writing."[1] The bracketed word represents the German *Schenck ;* and it seems a reasonable conjecture that this is used for *Handschenk,* a shake of the hand. The word may also mean *libation* (and drink certainly also formed part of the ceremony), but this sense would point to an even more crabbed and obscure syntax than that which we commonly find in these statutes.

For the greeting we have far fuller evidence, if Heldmann is to be trusted.[2] " If the wander-fellow seeks employment anywhere at a lodge, then he knocks thrice with his stick at the door, enters bareheaded, asks : ' Do masons work here ? ' and steps at once outside. As soon as he has gone out, all the masons who are at work put on their jackets, roll up their aprons, cover their heads with their hats and retreat to the room beside or over the lodge. Then one comes to the door, chisel in hand, and bids the wander-fellow welcome. The latter, as soon as he sees him, grasps his hand and whispers the following greeting in his ear :—

Stranger. God greet the honourable mason.

Mason. God thank the honourable mason.

Stranger. The honourable master [so and so] of [such and such a place], his warden, and the pious and honourable masons, send you hearty God-greetings to you and your honour.

Mason. Thanks to the honourable master [so and so], to his warden and to his pious and honourable masons ; and welcome in God's name, honourable mason.

When they have recognized each other as true masons by hand-grip, greeting and welcome, then the stranger is

---

[1] Janner, p. 289 ; Gould, i, 128, 146-7.
[2] Quoted in Janner, p. 140.

brought into the room of assembly, where the other brethren have meanwhile taken their places in order. . . . After the wander-fellow has performed his greeting, he says to the master: 'Honourable master! I beg thee heartily for God's sake to give me honourable employment.' If the master can give him work, he answers: 'With God's help, thou shalt have it;' otherwise he excuses himself by pleading impossibility." It is worth noting, here, that a consideration of the circumstances points to great probability of work for the wanderer. The very looseness of the organization worked in his favour at this moment, as it worked against him later on. In proportion as the lodge was easily disbanded when the work was done, it would be easy to take on another man while it was proceeding, especially if the master, as we know sometimes in the later Middle Ages, was bound by a time-contract. To pay five men for four months or four men for five months would cost just the same, while employer, and perhaps master, would benefit by recruiting.

Late as the above-cited evidence is, yet it receives remarkable confirmation from a medieval document which it is probable that Heldmann had never seen. David of Augsburg, a great Franciscan mission-preacher of the later thirteenth century, wrote a very interesting treatise against the Waldenses, who, from simple evangelical preachers of the Wesley-Whitfield type, had been driven into heresy and outlawry. David is distressed by their missionary activities, and especially by their systematic elusion of hierarchical vigilance, all the easier because the Waldenses were generally poor and obscure by birth. At the end of his treatise he has a little chapter: "How do Heretics recognize each other? Note, that it hath been told me by a certain priest who heard this in confession from a certain heretical woman, that, when heretics first meet each other, and know not each other, then they do and say as follows[1] :—

---

[1] This dialogue is given in French. The ordinary rule of secrecy in confession was naturally waived in the case of heretics.

A.　Take him by the ear.

B.　Welcome! will you speak, or shall I ?

A.　Speak; for it is my pleasure that you should speak.

B.　When we pray, we speak to God; when we meditate, God speaketh unto us.

A.　Now speak again, for this pleaseth me well.

B.　St. Paul saith, *Lie not.* St. James saith, *Swear not.* St. Peter saith, *Render not evil for evil, but rather contrariwise.*"

The collocation would seem equally significant, whether we suppose the wandering mason to have copied from the wandering heretic, or *vice versa*, or that similar circumstances have brought each to the same invention.

And this is to some extent corroborated by a document where we are on quite firm ground; the statutes of 1462.[1] Here we find a whole series of prescriptions :—

"[§ 105] And when a fellow travels, then when he comes to a new lodge shall he leave his master in friendship, and not in anger. [§ 106] And if a travelling fellow come before work is knocked off, he shall earn his day's wages. And every travelling fellow, when he has received the donation, shall go from one to the other and shall thank him therefor. [§ 107] And this is the greeting wherewith every fellow shall greet; when he first goeth into the lodge thus shall he say : ' God greet ye, God guide ye, God reward ye; ye honourable overmaster, warden and trusty fellows '; and the master or warden shall thank him, that he may know who is the superior in the lodge. Then shall the fellow address himself to the same, and say : ' The master ' (naming him) ' bids me greet you worthily ; ' and he shall go to the fellows from one to the other and greet each in a friendly manner, even as he greeted the superior. And then shall they all, master, and wardens, and fellows, pledge him as is the custom, and as is already written of the greeting and pledge ; but not to him whom they hold for no true

---

[1] Gould, i, 142 ; Janner, p. 309.

man, he shall be fined one pound of wax, xxiii. Kreuzer.
[§ 108] And every fellow when he returns thanks, if he
wish for employment, shall ask of the master, and the
master shall employ him till the next pay day, and deny
him not, that the fellow may earn his living ; and, should
the master have no more work than he can perform alone,
the master shall help him to find work. [§ 109] And every
travelling fellow shall ask first for a pick, thereafter for a
piece of stone and furthermore for tools, and that shall be
lent to him of goodwill. [§ 110] And every fellow shall
pray the other fellows, and they shall not turn a deaf ear ;
they shall all help ; ' Help me that God may help ye ' ;
and when they have helped him he shall doff his hat, and
shall say, ' God thank the master, and warden, and
worthy fellows.' "

Janner quotes a very interesting lodge-custom which
seems to be of considerable antiquity. When a mason
spoiled a stone, it was christened *Bernhardt*, " the spoiled
stone was carried on a bier to a place some distance from
the lodge, which was nicknamed *Charnel-house* ; all the
journeymen accompanied the corpse to its last rest.
Next after the bier, as chief mourner, went the author
of the crime ; and when he came back to the hut he was
subjected to a *Prutsch*.[1]   I believe that the Charnel-
house of the lodge at Regensburg has been recently
discovered, close by the so-called Eselsthurm [Ass-tower].
Pieces of finished stone were found among stone-cutters'
refuse, extending to a depth of some 12 feet below the
present surface ;   and the cathedral architect, Herr
Denziger, considers these to be ' evidently rejected

---

[1] A ceremony of a kind common in all medieval and some modern
universities. At that of Avignon, for instance, " the freshman . . . was
sentenced to receive a certain number of blows with a book or with a
frying-pan. On the highly philosophical principle that ' infinity may be
avoided,' it was, however, prescribed that each freshman should not
receive more than three blows from each of an unspecified number of
students ; but, if there were ' noble or honourable ladies ' present, the
Rector might, upon their intercession, reduce the punishment to one
from each operator."—Rashdall, *Univ. of Europe*, 1895, ii, 635.

masons' work.' "[1]   A similar case is quoted, if I am not mistaken, in *Annales archéologiques*, of carved work found buried just outside one of the doors of Notre-Dame-de-Paris.

A few other gild regulations call for notice here. Attempts were made to guard against temptations and abuses of different kinds.   Something like the modern contract system was already growing up ; it was perhaps thus that Chaucer's contemporary Henry de Yevele got some of his fortune, for by this system a man might well gain more by dealing in raw materials, and as an employer of other men's labour, than by his own purely artistic work.   He might even profit by sweated labour, employing an inordinate proportion of apprentices to the detriment of journeymen and employers.   It was to meet these dangers that the London Corporation legislated in 1356, and the German Chapter in 1459.[2]   The Londoners decreed : " No one shall take work in gross, if he be not of ability in a proper manner to complete such work ; and he who wishes to undertake such work in gross, shall come to the good man of whom he has taken such work to do and complete, and shall bring with him six or four ancient men of his trade, sworn thereunto, if they are prepared to testify unto the good man of whom he has taken such work to do, that he is skilful and of ability to perform such work, and that if he shall fail to complete such work in due manner, or not be of ability to do the same, they themselves, who so testify that he is skilful and of ability to finish the work, are bound to complete the same work well and properly at their own charges, in such manner as he undertook, in case the employer who owns the work shall have fully paid the workman."

The Germans prescribed (§§ 7, 8, 15) : " Those who have such work in hand may not undertake further than so far as concerns hewn stone work and that which pertaineth thereto, that is quarrying or hewing stone

---

[1] P. 134, quoting from *Verh. d. hist. Vereins d. Oberpfalz.* Bd. xxviii, s. 219.
[2] Riley, p. 281 ; Janner, p. 254.

lime or sand whether by task-work or by wage-work. But if the masons are needed to hew stone or to do mason's work whereunto they are able, a master may well set them to such work in order that the lords may suffer no delay in their work, and those who are thus set to work shall be unhindered by those ordinances if so be that they do it with good will. . . . *Item*, whatsoever master hath only one work or building in hand may have three apprentices . . . but if he have more buildings than one then he shall not have more than two apprentices on the aforesaid building, so that he cannot have more than five apprentices on all his buildings together."

These capitalistic tendencies come out clearly in such cases as that of Conrad Roritzer, in 1459.[1] He was head mason at the Cathedral of Regensburg, and received 64 Pfennige a week, all the year round ; his warden and his journeymen received 48 for the summer half and 30 for the winter. In addition to this, he had a quarterly allowance bringing his wages to more than 48 florins a year. At the same time he was controlling the building of St. Lorenz-Kirche at Nürnberg ; and, thirdly, he was paid extra for his sculpture, as piecework.[2] Thus, in that year, he carved " a great capital whereon the Mary stands," " a capital whereon St. Peter stands," " a capital next the tower, with a swine's head," seven other capitals, three saints' statues, and four hanging bosses ; for all this he received nearly 3 florins more. He seems, therefore, to have earned nearly three times as much as his workmen earned ; and, in all probability, if we could distinguish his work from theirs, we should say that this was well earned. But, none the less, it was an infraction of the earliest tradition that any mason should thus be allowed to multiply sources of pay, and to receive so much more than his fellows.

This piece of evidence (and more might be cited) goes some way to fill the gap which Mr. Kingsley Porter

[1] Janner, p. 173.
[2] So also Henri de Bruxelles and his partner at Troyes (Quicherat, ii, 209).

deplores. He quotes two very interesting texts for the evolution of the modern architect.[1] They are from sermons of the thirteenth and fourteenth centuries respectively. Nicholas de Biard, a famous Dominican preacher of about 1260, says, " Master-masons, with a rod and gloves in their hands, say to others ' cut it for me this way,' and labour not themselves, yet take higher pay ; that is what many modern prelates do." The other, from a MS. of the fourteenth century, is (as Mr. Porter points out) even more explicit : " Some work by word alone. Note how, in those great buildings, there is commonly one chief master who only commands by word of mouth, who seldom or never lays his hand to the job and yet takes higher pay than the rest. So there are many in the Church who have fat benefices, and God knoweth how much good they do ! They work in the Church with their tongue alone, saying, ' that is how you should do,' while they themselves do naught thereof." These quotations show plainly that in the later Middle Ages, and on great buildings, the chief master-mason's work was often noticeably differentiated from that of his subordinates[2] ; but the concrete case of Roritzer may make us hesitate to lay too much stress upon the preachers' epigrammatic way of stating the case. Roritzer may well have earned, now that he was at the top of the tree, comparative idleness for his hands, but comparative only. Even far on into the Renaissance, it would be difficult to find an architect who did not work at sculpture or painting also, to the very end of his life.

Another of the 1459 statutes (§ 6) is designed to secure artistic conservatism, or, it might be more correct to say,

[1] II. 189–191, where, however, *Berne* is a slip for *Biard*, *compass* for *gloves*, and *caementarium* for *caementariorum*, as may be seen by following his reference (*Romania*, vol. 18, 1889, p. 289).

[2] It is noticeable that Bishop Richard de Bury, towards the end of the fourth chapter of his *Philobiblon*, marks a distinct difference between those who are *architectonici in scientiis*, and the *subjecti mechanici*. This was about 1345. Note also the glory of the Master-Dyker at Ardres, in the story which I quote later, Chapter XVII.

artistic continuity. "*Item*, when a master, whosoever he be, who has such work and buildings in hand and in possession—when such a master shall decease, and another master shall come and find hewn stone-work there, whether such hewn stone-work be already laid or not, then shall the aforesaid master not remove such rightly-laid stone-work, nor cast aside the unlaid hewn stone-work on any account whatsoever, save it be with the counsel and know-ledge of other craftsmen ; in order that the lords and other honourable folk who cause such buildings to be made may not be put to unreasonable costs, and also that the master who hath died and left such work may not be put to shame. If, however, the lords [i.e. the em-ployers] are willing to let such work be removed, he may allow this so far as he sees no danger therein." This explains such well-known cases as the naves at West-minster and Beverley, where even the fifteenth-century masons have taken great pains to follow the thirteenth-century style, and the almost equally striking western bay of the nave at Eastbourne parish church.

The comparative rarity of such instances shows how much the recommendation was needed. The medieval mind, with its almost superstitious respect for antiquity in theory, had little self-control when the question of practice came in. We shall see this in a later chapter, when I have to deal with the wholesale vandalism of the Renaissance. That was one side of the vigorous vitality both of Gothic and of Renaissance art ; the weakest must go to the wall ; and, fashion being at least as potent then as it is now, the weakest generally meant the most ancient.

Another statute, and one for which we must give due credit to the fraternity, aimed at preventing unrestricted competition : it is put briefly in one of the English codes :—

> "There shall no master supplant another,
> But be together as sister and brother."[1]

Yet competition to a considerable extent was certainly permitted in practice, if not in theory. We have seen

[1] Cf. Cooke-Baker, the ninth of the articles between pp. 107 and 120.

how the English statutes of about 1480 actually lay it on the master's conscience, when a good workman comes fresh to the lodge, to turn off an inferior man in order to make room for the new-comer. It was common, again, for lay or ecclesiastical corporations which had great undertakings on hand to put the work up to open competition; Quicherat points out that this seems to have been the general practice as early as the fourteenth century, and quotes examples from the cathedrals of Paris and Troyes.[1] And elsewhere he quotes an instance of very definite and most successful " supplantation " of one master by another. The story is so instructive that it must be given at some length.[2] In 1381 the Chapter of Troyes Cathedral had money enough to erect a stone *jubé* (pulpitum, choir-screen). " Therefore Michelin and Jean Thierry made a plan which they presented to the canons in July 1382. This design, on parchment, seemed suitable; but, before accepting it, they wished to see it executed on a large scale. Therefore a flat surface was made between the vault and the roof of the cathedral; twenty cartloads of earth were hoisted up through the great tower and were beaten flat by a clay-worker who took six days to make the floor that was needed. The design was transferred to this surface; it succeeded completely, and the masters set to work."[3] A written contract was drawn up between them and the chapter, " and Jean Thierry with his companion worked at the job until October 27. Then came a revolution in the

[1] Vol. ii, p. 221.

[2] Ibid., p. 204.

[3] Quicherat seems to interpret this as a full-sized *elevation* of the Jubé, drawn upon the flat clay surface. But was it not a rough full-sized *model* ? For large drawings, we have evidence that the masons made a surface of Baltic boards, which would seem far cheaper and more effective than these twenty cartloads of earth. Brutails, p. 38, commenting on p. 260 of the second volume of Quicherat's Mélanges, discusses a passage in *Villard de Honnecourt* (pl. xxxviii) which seems to imply an earthen model of a moulded arch, though neither critic seems clearly to draw this conclusion.

ST. JOSEPH AT REIMS.

lodge. A stranger who had come to Troyes and who gave himself out for an abler workman than the rest, managed to gain the ear of the chapter. He offered a plan for a jubé which he vaunted as preferable to that which was being made. He appealed on his conscience to the canons, and from the canons to the public [who were contributing a great share of the cost], and at last he succeeded in getting the question referred to an assembly of citizens and workmen of Troyes, who awarded the prize to him. This successful artist was called Henri de Bruxelles. He came from Paris, and doubtless with a great reputation, since he was able to make conditions with the chapter and obtain all that he asked. A master-mason of his own choice was given to him for colleague, with a salary equal to his own and higher than that of his predecessors."

THE MASONS' LODGE AT CHARTRES.

We get a precious glimpse of the interior of the lodge from two panels of one of the thirteenth century windows at Chartres Cathedral. The tools, the molds, are practically those that were in use until our grandfathers' time, with the exception of the long crowbar-like chisel with which one mason is working at his statue. But the position of the statues themselves is, to the modern observer, remarkable. We should have expected the carver to set his figure upright before him ; yet he lays it flat upon the banker. Is there not here a very true and natural device ? The statue will, almost certainly, be set finally above the beholder's eye ; it may even be destined to stand a hundred feet or more above the pavement. Face to face with it, the carver cannot gauge this ; work-

N

ing at right angles to it, he can gauge it very accurately, by withdrawing now and then to the exact distance from which the statue will finally be seen. Even if it is to be set as high as the rows of Kings on the west front of Reims or Amiens or Notre-Dame, he needs only to lay his statue near the lodge door, and he can step backward until he sees it in its true perspective.

A further light on masons' methods is cast by the surviving drawings on parchment or paper, and the sketches on stone or plaster. The cathedral museums at Cologne and Strasbourg possess splendid examples of the former; and some from Italy have been published at different times in *Country Life*; and one or two by Didron in his *Annales archéologiques*, vol. v, pp. 87, 94. It is not generally realized, however, how many of the rough sketches have survived. Profiles of mouldings are scratched on the plaster of Raunds Church; when the chapel of St. John's College at Cambridge was pulled down, some tracery of about 1475 was found drawn on a smooth slab which is now in the Archæological Museum; others more elaborate, from roof-slabs of slate at Limoges, are figured by Didron. At Castleacre, the rigorous frosts of 1881 peeled a coating of plaster from one of the niches in the south transept, and revealed the original first coat, upon which,

MASON'S DESIGN ON A STONE FROM THE OLD CHAPEL OF ST. JOHN'S COLLEGE, CAMBRIDGE.

while it was yet wet, an elaborate decorated window had
been sketched, similar to or identical with the east
window at Watlington in the same county. A few years

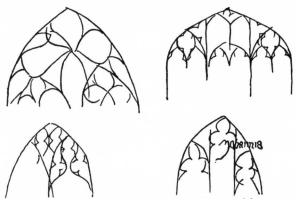

MASONS' SKETCHES FROM THE PILLARS AT (1) GAMLINGAY, (2) WHITTLESFORD,
(3) OFFLEY AND (4) BARRINGTON.

later other frosts destroyed this also; and in 1913 only a
few strokes were yet visible.[1] Spirited drawings of
figures are also sometimes to be found; the richest
fields for these, so far as I have been able to observe, are
the west front of St. Albans Cathedral, inside and outside, and the *pulpitum* at Sion in the Valais.

MASONS' SKETCHES FROM (1) THE SOUTH-WEST PORTAL OF ST. ALBANS AND
(2) THE CHAMBER WITH A FIREPLACE ON THE SOUTH SIDE OF LINCOLN MINSTER.

[1] See Appendix 10. I have dealt more fully with these and similar
graffiti in the twelfth of my *Medieval Studies*.

CHAPTER X

ETON AND KING'S COLLEGE

WE have here reached a point at which we may profitably study certain detailed evidence, mainly from the last four generations of the Middle Ages. This will be not so much a digression as a fresh view of artisan life from a different angle; and, at this stage of medieval art-history in England, the best that can be done is to present, from various viewpoints, as much as possible of the abundant documentary evidence; the reader may thus come to a better conception in his own mind than he would get even from the clearest-cut definitions of the author. For in this matter, as in many other departments of medieval life, we cannot make our verbal distinctions more exact than were the facts themselves. The same man will be called *mason, freemason, master mason*, just as at the University the same man might be called *master, doctor,* or *professor*. In this latter case, we know that there was originally no distinction, that only the latest generations of the Middle Ages began to differentiate the three titles, and that, even then, the differentiation was neither exact nor complete.[1] It is probable, therefore, that we shall never be able to define exactly the different masonic titles, and that they were seldom or never exactly differentiated in fact. But it is worth while putting the evidence together.

From very early times indeed we can trace class-

[1] Prof. Hamilton Thompson, under stress of necessary brevity, gives perhaps an impression of too definite differentiation in his valuable analysis, *Med. Build. Acc.*, pp. 15–18. The extracts given by Beissel (I., 182–3) show very clearly how often the terms varied.

distinctions in the mason's trade. The fact that those
" magistri Commacini " of the seventh century bore this
title of " master," solemnly rehearsed in the national
code of laws, points to one or more class of operatives
under them. Again, " in 1175, a contract was entered
into with one Raymundo, a Lambardo, for works done in
the cathedral of Urgel [in Spain]. He was to employ
four Lambardos, and, if necessary, *caementarii* or wallers."[1]
Here we have, clearly, the skilled Lombard masons contrasted with more ordinary workmen, whether we look
upon the *caementarii* as identical with, or separate from,
the wallers. As our study of this subject must here be
brief, it is best to begin with a series of notices from our
English Acts of Parliament and similar State documents
quoted in Gould (Chapter VII) and from the Eton and
King's College building accounts (Willis and Clark,
Vol. I, section vii, ch. v, ix, x). I give the evidence
chronologically.

In 1349 the masons all come under the general term
of *caementarii*. This, it may be observed, had been a
common name for them in much earlier times ; and in
1334 the architect of Salisbury spire is called, in a formal
document, indifferently *caementarius* and *lathomus*.

In 1350 the wages of " master freestone masons " are
fixed at 4*d*. a day, of other masons at 3*d*., and of their
servants at 1½d. The " servant " of this statute would be
analogous to (for instance) the modern plumber's " mate."[2]
This phrase *mestre mason de franche pere* is most significant for the probable origin of the term *freemason*.

In 1360 the " chief masters of masons " (*chiefs mestres
de maceons*) are to take 4*d*. a day ; others 2*d*. or 3*d*.
according to their worth.

In 1402 the masons are all comprised under the

---

[1] Gould, vol. ii, p. 316.

[2] I find this suggested analogy confirmed by a very valuable book
which has reached me only when this chapter is already in print (*Adderbury Rectoria*, by T. F. Hobson, F.S.A. (Oxfordshire Record Soc., 1926,
pp. 44 ff.). See farther in Appendix 11.

generic term of *cementers* in the Norman-French of the statute.

In 1425 all are comprised under the single term of *les masons*.

In 1441–2, the Eton building accounts show large numbers of freemasons employed upon the chapel, with accompanying rough-masons and hard-hewers. The accountant at first calls the freemasons simply "masons," and adds the full title only as time goes on. Six years later, an estimate for the same chapel work reckons the need of from forty to sixty freemasons, twelve to twenty-four "masons of Kent called hard-hewers," and twelve "layers," a term which explains itself. The freemasons, rough-masons, hard-hewers and carpenters were paid at the same rate of 6*d*. per day ; except that, whereas the freemasons were paid for the saints' days on which no work was done, the others were not.

In 1444 we have the first statutory occurrence of the name freemason—*frank mason*. Such freemasons, like master-carpenters, are to take 5*d*. a day, while the "rough-mason" and under-carpenter take only 4*d*.

In 1495 the statute is in English, and the word is *free-mason*. He and the rough-mason are now valued at the same wage, 6*d*. a day ; but, on the other hand, master-masons or master-carpenters who are also directing the work, and have not less than six men under them, may take 7*d*.

In 1508, at King's College Chapel, there were four "intaylers," or stone-carvers, and eighty-nine masons, all paid at a flat rate of 3*s*. 4*d*. a week, while carpenters had 6*d*. a day and labourers 4*d*. In the highest class of all were eight "setters" and three wardens at 3*s*. 8*d*. per week, and the master-mason at £13 6*s*. 8*d*. a year.

In 1513 the master-mason who contracted to finish King's College Chapel undertook to "keep continually sixty freemasons working upon the same works, as soon as it shall be possible for him to call them in," i.e. to recruit them either voluntarily or in virtue of the royal commission to impress men.

In 1515 the "freemasons, rough-masons and carpenters" of the City of London sent a petition to the King.

In 1548, for the first time in any statute, comes the threefold classification of freemasons, rough-masons, and hard hewers.

In Sir Thomas Elyot's Latin dictionary (1538) *caementarium* is translated "rough masons, which do make only walls."

In 1554–5 a Cambridge College "covenanted with Scott the rough-mason to make up the new wall and chimneys" (Willis and Clark, II, 470).

In 1564 an Act of Parliament, which repealed all previous enactments on the subject, dealt with apprenticeship to the various trades, specifying "carpenter, rough-mason, plasterer," etc., but strangely omitting freemason.

In Cooper's Latin dictionary (1578, founded on Elyot's) *caementarius* is translated "a dauber, a pargetter, a rough-mason," and *latomus* "a mason, one that cutteth or diggeth stones." Yet we have seen how, in 1334, these two words were treated as convertible terms; so also in the Ely Sacrist Rolls of about the same date.

In 1602 (to take one more quotation from the *Oxford English Dictionary*), at Burford, the "master freemason" and the "master rough-mason" who were engaged together on a job were paid 5*d*. each per diem.

The hard-hewers need not detain us long. In the Eton accounts they are evidently connected with the Kentish rag-stone, of which large quantities were used in the upper courses of the chapel.[1] Their job was rather that of the quarryman than of the skilled mason, and they probably worked with axes, not with chisels. A

---

[1] All farther references to Eton and King's College conditions may be verified from Willis and Clark, vol. i, pp. 380–425 and 470–97, with the illustrative documents in the Appendix.

stonemason of our generation has assured me that he has worked in the quarries under Edgehill with men who

HARD-HEWER AND FREEMASON AT KING'S COLLEGE CHAPEL.

could cut stone with an axe to as smooth a surface as others with their chisels; and certainly the axe was freely used quite late in the Middle Ages. The hard-hewer, then, dealt with stone in its most elementary forms; and it is probable that he was often regularly employed in preparing the work for his more skilled colleagues. The Eton accounts for 1450–1 show that, at the College quarry of Huddleston (Yorkshire), two classes were at work: "scapelers," who rough-dressed the stone, and "cimentarii." [1] The *Oxford English Dictionary* quotes from Palsgrave in 1530: "It is rough-hewn all ready; I will now fall a-carving of it"; and it is to this that Hamlet alludes: "There's a divinity that shapes our ends, rough-hew them how we will." Close observation indicates pretty plainly that the medieval sculptor, like his renaissance and modern brother, often got his

HARD-HEWER AND FREE-MASON AT BOURGES.

[1] Willis and Clark, i, 397; cf. ibid. 392, the accounts of 1445–6, when they bought 5,887 feet of stone called "ashlar rough-scapled" from the quarries. In the Oxfordshire quarry from which Adderbury Chancel was built, a good many of the masons were engaged for a while at scapeling (p. 43) and also at Bodmin (p. 12). At Adderbury one, at least, received a less wage for scapeling than when he was at work at the actual building; Mr. Hobson suggests that this was because the work was lighter; this, however, seems very improbable; the work would not be lighter, but rougher and less skilled.

work rough-hewn for him. One of the best examples is the portal of the north porch at Bourges Cathedral, where the stones are rough-hewn with the axe, and marked with ordinary banker-marks, all except one single edge which is worked with the chisel into masterly floral ornament.

The rough-mason, again, is fairly exactly described by Elyot ; and we have a still more detailed description of his job, at almost the same date, in the funeral accounts of the Earls of Rutland (*Journ. Brit. Archæol. Ass.*,

FREEMASON, LAYER, HARD-HEWER AND
LABOURER AT CHARTRES.

Ap., 1902, pp. 21 ff.). The first concerns a monument in Bottesford Church, " a beautiful alabaster tomb, with the recumbent effigies of Thomas, first Earl of Rutland, and his Countess, Eleanor. The Earl died September 20th 1543." The " alabaster-man " who made the two effigies was paid £20, according to contract. Then comes " paid to Lupton of Waltham, rough-mason, for four days' digging stone for the vault to be made with to bear the tomb . . . at 6*d.* the day . . . and to William West, labourer, for like days at 4*d.* the day." Next, " to John Lupton, rough-mason, for six days' work at the said tomb, the two walls and two arches to bear the tomb . . . 3*s.*" The " alabaster-worker " now gets £6 13*s.* 4*d.*

extra for farther work, and for setting his effigies upon the tomb.

In 1591, two Earls had one tomb between them. The carving was done by " Mr. Garret Johnson, tomb-maker " in London, who took £200 " for the making of two tombs and setting the same up at Bottesford " ; two other tombmakers, from Burton-on-Trent and Newark, were paid later for coming to advise " for the placing of the said tombs," 10s. and 4s. respectively. " Richard Brown, rough-mason, for taking down the chancel wall of both sides the chancel where the tombs be set up, and making up the same again, and for burning plaster and mending the chamber floor over the vestry, with other necessary works about the same tombs, for sixteen and a half days," receives 9d. a day ; the labourers who assist him get 4d. When Mr. Garret Johnson came down with his sons to supervise the job " whilst my Lord and my Lady stayed at Belvoir, they were given liberal allowance for their board and lodging and horse-food with the baker at Bottesford, " because he [Johnson] would not have them [his horses] at Belvoir, for fear of straying away and being ridden with some hunters." He was evidently, therefore, a man who could make his own terms.

This shows us pretty clearly the status of the rough-mason, when at last the word had crystallized into a fairly definite term. He may probably be identified, as a rule, with the " layers," or " setters," or " lathomi ponentes " of our accounts. He was the sedentary local artisan, the mason-of-all-work, the " general practitioner," in contradistinction to the freemason, who, like the modern Harley Street doctor, was usually concerned with more specialized and delicate work. We may trace this, again, in that statute of 1360 already cited, which enacts that the " chief masters " of masons (*maceons*) are to take 4d. a day ; " and the others 3d. or 2d., according as they be worth ; and that all alliances and covines of masons and carpenters, and congregations, chapters, ordinances and oaths betwixt them made, or to be made, shall be from henceforth void and wholly annulled; so that every mason and carpenter, of what condition that he be, shall be compelled by his master to whom he serveth to do every work that to him pertain[eth] to do, or of free stone, or of rough stone." Here, again, is another indication suggestive of the original derivation of *freemason* from *free stone*.

But Dr. Cunningham was very likely right in surmising that, however the term *free* might have grown up, it did gradually come to connote a certain constitutional privilege. We have an analogy here in other guilds; there, only those who were " free of the gild " enjoyed full privileges; all other folk were styled " foreign." The ordinary rough-mason, like the village carpenter and smith, was probably, as a rule, an ungilded man. He might be able to do ordinary stone-dressing and cutting as well as any other; but he lacked the free-mason's special artistic experience, and, again, he lacked the freemason's organization.

In the German freemasons' statutes we can see clearly that there was a class of masons who, having regular employment in large towns, were settled artisans and stood outside the general gild. Similarly, it is probable enough *a priori*, and the documentary evidence seems to prove it, that in England there was a whole class of masons in a small way who had enough simple work within their own district to keep them busy, and who, therefore, never went outside, except in exceptional circumstances. The Eton accounts, for instance, mention that four of the rough-masons were from Norwich: William and John Lynde, Thomas Rigware, and Thomas Sacrye. These were very likely pressed men. Another bears the name of a Norfolk village (Harpley). Such, then, would be the rough-masons. On the other hand, there were many others who migrated from one great building to another, and in that way found a sufficiency of work; these would, obviously, find it to their advantage to join the trade-union; and thus the class who originally

took their title as freestone-masons would now be able
to claim the freedom of the masons' gild; they would be
freemasons in a double sense.   And where, as at Eton,
as many hands as possible were needed for the work, there
the two classes would naturally work together.   For,
in such a building as that chapel, or in most of the colleges
at Oxford and Cambridge, there is little work that could
not have been done by the rough-mason.   The freemason
alone might be competent to design and to carve; but
the rough-mason could do all the rest, even including
the mouldings.   Moreover, vast quantities of these
mouldings at Eton, as we see from the accounts, were
imported ready-cut from the quarries.

With the very large number of workmen engaged at
both the royal chapels, a certain hierarchy was needed.
Henry VI prescribed this in his will; there was a Master
of the Works at £50 a year, and two Clerks of the Works
at £13 6s. 8d. each.   These were simply business men
and accountants.   Of actual artists or artisans (we have
seen how the two ideas were not yet separated) the Chief
Mason received £13 6s. 8d., the Chief Carpenter £10,
the Chief Smith £6 13s. 4d., and two Purveyors, to
provide men and materials, at £18 5s. 6d. for the two.
" Besides these [the master-mason, etc.], there were other
officers in each trade, called wardens (gardiani), whose
duty probably was to keep order among the men.   The
stone-cutters (lathami) or freemasons had a sub-warden,
as well as a warden; the carpenters and the plumbers a
warden only.   The warden of the freemasons, when the
works were in full operation, received £10 a year; the
others apparently were not paid more highly than the
rest of the men, but they were provided with livery once
a year.   In 1448 livery is charged not only for the officers
mentioned in the Will, but for the warden of the masons,
the warden of the carpenters, the lime-burner, the chief
labourer, and a journeyman smith (serviens faber).   The
clerk of the works, and the comptroller, were allowed
their food; but the workmen all paid for their own,

even the freemasons, who had a cook to themselves, paid for by the King." [1] And in the contract of 1512–13 for the completion of King's College Chapel, in which it was specified that sixty freemasons and many other workmen should be employed, one clause runs ; " And in case any mason or other laborer shalbe founde unprofytable or of ony suche ylle demeanour whereby the workes shuld be hyndred or the company mysordred not doyng their duties acordyngly as they ought to doo, then the seid Surveyour to indevour hymself to refourme them by such wayes as hath byn ther used before this tyme." [2]

We may now look more closely into these men's business ledgers, which have a good deal to tell us. Far more could doubtless be gleaned from the other surviving records of work at similar great buildings ; but an exhaustive survey of these might take a lifetime. I must confine myself here to the exceptionally interesting volume preserved in Eton College Library, and generously lent to the British Museum by the Provost and Fellows, in order that the wage-sheets might be tabulated by my former pupil, Mr. R. A. R. Hartridge.

Of the eighty-five freemasons employed during this year, from February 12, 1442, to February 11, 1443, only thirty were on the staff the whole year through. [3] Of the remaining fifty-five, some were engaged later ; e.g. Thomas East came in only for the last week of the year ; others quitted earlier, e.g. Thomas Jackson and John Bramhall worked only for the first fortnight. Of the forty-four who started on February 12, thirty-four are still working at Midsummer, and thirty, as we have seen, at the end of the year. These must have formed a good solid nucleus. They had seen others come and go during these twenty weeks ; Thomas Baset had

[1] Willis and Clark, vol. i, p. 381.
[2] Ibid., i, p. 610.
[3] I have not gone through these figures twice ; but I hope they will be always found correct within fairly narrow limits.

worked six weeks, only twice at full time, and disappeared ;
William Clarke had come twice and disappeared, to
reappear for a few fitful weeks later in the year. Many
of the still later recruits work steadily ; others pass rapidly
over our stage ; the twelve worst did only sixty-three
weeks between them, averaging scarcely more than five
each. Symkin Philpot works only two weeks, and one of
those half a day short ; Robert Gugman, after five weeks,
earned the note " deliuered ; he is not abull "—
cashiered ; he has earned a bad mark. John Reding,
docked of one and a half day's pay on November 18,
" for going without lycens," disappears after December 17.
He had been absent for eleven weeks during the year,
here and there, and at other times he had worked three
or four days short.

The rough-masons did far less work in the year. They
number, all counted, thirty-nine. For the first ten
weeks, none were engaged ; at last, on April 23, two
appear, and are joined by a third next week, by two more
the week after, and by one a fortnight later. Meanwhile
one has dropped off. Then begins the action of the
pressgang ; to these five, at a single stroke, were added
seven more next week, and six more in the next five weeks ;
we see very clearly how a haul of conscripted men had been
brought in. Meanwhile there was considerable leakage ;
Richard Bronge, after three weeks' work, was transferred to
the hard-hewer class, and the four Norwich men depart in
July with a unique testimonial : they receive 16½d. each
" in reward, at their going." Still, the numbers rise slowly
from eighteen on June 25 to twenty-seven (August 26
and next week). Then comes a drop to twenty-six,
and then, suddenly, to sixteen. They rise gradually
again to nineteen, (November 4), and then drop again
suddenly to nine ; from which they dwindle to two
(December 23). For three weeks, at Christmas, these
two are unemployed ; then they reappear for the last
three weeks of January, but drop out altogether in
February. The six shortest workers did together only

seventeen weeks, an average of less than three each.
Of the forty-one weeks accounted for, two men worked
thirty-five each, one thirty, and six others twenty or
more; the remaining thirty-two scarcely averaged ten
apiece. One, Pierce Halfyard, is four times described as
"brickman." Another, John Benham, comes on and is
tried for one week at the lower rate of 5d. a day; but
he then disappears.

The hard-hewers, again, rose by conscription at the
end of May from two to ten in a single week. They
reappear on the work even later than the rough-masons;
on May 21, two appeared, and eight more next week,
May 28, the same date on which the rough-masons had
suddenly been more than doubled. Five of these newcomers, after three weeks, absented themselves for six
weeks; after their return, the numbers crept up to
seventeen (October 17) and never again fell below ten.
They were unemployed during the Christmas fortnight;
and, of the eleven who were then on the staff, only four
did any work during the second week in January. With
each fresh descent in the scale of artisans, we find increased
difficulties of discipline. At the end of August, the
hard-hewers Richard Lilly and Richard Spenser are fined
" for ffyting," and Edmond Knight, in January, " for
keping of the hole owr'," of which we shall soon see the
full significance.

The last class which we need notice here are the
" laborers," who were doubtless employed in digging,
carrying loads, mixing mortar, etc. One, we are explicitly
told, was lading carts. Of these there were 175 during
the year; but their attendance was most irregular of
all; only three of all this crew worked regularly throughout the year. We start on February 12 with seven;
by June 25 the numbers have risen to twenty-eight; but
the high-water-mark is a little over forty, and we end the
year with only nineteen. The fines recorded are many
and significant. Seven are mulcted " for late cuming,"
or " for he com late," " for he com late divers tyme.'

The greatest difficulty was with the dinner hour, or rather the siesta which was a common medieval summer habit.[1] They evidently dined at twelve (or, possibly, half-past) and the first difficulty comes on May 21, when ten are fined " for keping of the hole owr'." This does not, I think, mean, (as others besides myself seem to have taken it to mean, reading it in Willis and Clark apart from the context) that the employers grudged the men a full hour for dinner. For the next entry of the kind (June 25) is more explicit, and throws a different light upon the quarrel. Robert Goodgrome is fined " for he wold keep his owris and not go to werke til the clocke smyte," and nineteen others at the same time are fined 2d. each because " they wolde not go to their' werke til ij of clocke, and al makith Goodgrome." Next week, three others are fined " for he was not at his werke at one of clocke." Evidently, therefore, the " whole hour " which the culprits took was the hour from one to two, and not the dinner-hour but supplementary. The fines seem to have been efficient ; for there is no farther entry of the kind.

We can trace the careers of this first batch, the rebels of May 21. Goodgrome, the leader, was one of the original seven with whom the wage-sheets begin. He did not put up a fight on July 2, but left the work altogether eleven weeks later. Ramsell, also, his partner in the first two rebellions, was quiet in July and left his job a week later than Goodgrome. Breserd, a rebel in May and June, was fined early in July " for shedding of lime "—he probably spilt a load—and disappeared a fortnight later. Bullok absented himself for three weeks after the May rebellion, then worked for three days, and then departed for ever. Knyth (Knight) rebelled again in June, was quiescent in July, and worked on

[1] Compare the Royal Statute of 1495: workmen are to have half an hour for breakfast, one and a half hours for dinner in the summer months (when a siesta was usual), and one hour in the other months ; for " none-meat " they were allowed half an hour. (Gould, vol. i, p.367.)

THE ANGEL CHOIR AT LINCOLN.

intermittently to the end of the year. Castell and Montford disappeared immediately after May 21. Clement rebelled again in June, but worked on nearly to the end of the year. Brynkeley, who had previously been fined for fighting, was fined on June 11 " for he com late divers tyme "; he disappeared, apparently, a few days before the July rebellion. Lente rebelled again in June, but not in July; after seven weeks' absence, he reappeared and was fined " for worstyld' [*wrestled*] and playde and ran a boute in werkyng tyme "; this punishment apparently sobered him, for he survived till November 19. A glance down the wage-sheet seems to show this week beginning May 21 as a critical time. Between April 30 and June 18, eighteen of the workmen then employed disappear either altogether or for a considerable number of weeks. There were forty-two at work on April 30, and only thirty-one a month later (May 28, the first revolt having occurred in the preceding week). On June 25, the week of the third revolt, there were twenty-five at work, of whom, as we have seen, Goodgrome and nineteen others were punished for taking the whole hour. Next week we have thirty-eight at work, but three are fined for taking the disputed hour. Next week again (July 9) there are only thirty-three, nine of whom disappear during the next fortnight. We cannot explain this by the hay-harvest, which was probably on when the numbers at Eton were high, and was well over at the time of this rapid leakage. See farther in Appendix 11.

Then, apparently, there was another great haul, probably of forced labour, to a considerable extent at least. In the next four weeks (July 23–August 13), twenty-eight fresh men come to the job, ten of them in a single week. Yet, of all these, fifteen disappear before the end of August, having only done twenty-six days of work between them, an average of less than two days each out of this whole month. Nor, here again, can we attribute this altogether to press of harvest work; for

o

of the rest, six stayed on till harvest must have been well over, drifting away at the end of September or in October.

This serious leakage naturally led to fresh efforts; and a great accession came in mid-August when, be it noted, harvest must almost certainly have been still going on. In the week ending August 20, there were only thirty-seven labourers; next week came thirteen fresh men, the record for any single week of the year; and, in the four weeks following, thirteen more. Yet these twenty-six new labourers brought only momentary relief. On September 17 there were indeed fifty labourers, but ten of these averaged only two days each during the week. On October 1, though five new men had been enlisted in the interval, the total had sunk to thirty-five; three weeks later they had risen again to thirty-nine; but only because eight more had been enlisted. On the last day of account, February 4, there were nineteen, of whom, as has already been said, only three had worked through the whole year. The batch of men enlisted between August 20 and September 17 show as unsatisfactory a record as the great haul of July 23–August 13. Twenty out of the twenty-six departed within a fortnight, and ten of these never completed even one full week's work.

It is impossible not to connect this with the fact that at Eton, as at King's, the men were partly enlisted through the press-gang. Of this we have definite evidence, more than once. As early as February 1441, when the building first began, the clerk of the works was commissioned to impress artisans of all classes that he needed. On June 8, the master-mason went on a journey of impressment; the struggles of the unwilling workmen and employers are related in Appendix 11. In October, a fresh commission of impressment was issued, with power to imprison the disobedient. Then again, on April 25, 1442, we find twenty shillings, a sum which would have paid a freemason's wages for forty weeks, given to Robert Westurley, " in Reward for purweing of Fremasons in diverse place of Engelond " for the Eton works.   This was probably money in advance for his expenses ; for we have documentary evidence of a haul at the end of May. Later, on June 16, 1444, the King " issued letters patent to the head mason of King's and the two clerks of the works, empowering them to commandeer, at market price, all the materials they might need ; and to conscript as many freemasons, rough-masons, carpenters, plumbers, tilers, smiths, daubers and all other artisans and workmen. . . . To arrest all these, and set them to work at our wages at our works ; and all whom ye may find contrary or rebellious in these afore-said matters, or in any of the same, to be committed to our prisons and confined therein until they find surety that they will serve in these our works aforesaid."[1]   This conscription system can be clearly traced in the wage-book.   I give details in Appendix 11, and may add two slight indications here.   Ralf Wolforth dis-appeared before July 30, and the clerk notes that he is paid nothing for his last day's work, " for he ran a waye."   Geoffrey Cawys, about July 4, is fined because " he wolde a ron a way " ; and in fact he disappears six weeks later.   The same may be implied by the term " delivered," which we have seen used for a mason's dismissal.   Others are fined " for playing," " for fieghtinge," " for telling of taylez," " for telling taille, and lettith of his felowes," " for he wille not do as he is bedyn," " for he wol not do nor labor buot as he list hymself."   Finally, there are punishments for careless damage ; " for breking of a bolle " [*bowl*], " for he lost a shovoll," " for breking of a shovoll," " for he brake a skepe " [*basket*].   For each of these last three offences, two persons were fined.   It is notable that

---

[1] Willis and Clark, vol. i, pp. 323, 384, 594. The term here used for head mason is *capitalis cementarius*, the others are called *lathami* and *cementarii*, which evidently refer to freemasons and rough-masons respec-tively, and exemplify once again how little precise definition can be found in these medieval terms.

these fines were most frequent in the earlier days of more stable work and less irregular attendance ; apparently the clerk of the works was obliged gradually to relax discipline as recruiting became more difficult.

The question of holidays has an interest of its own. The church holy-days were far more strictly kept at Eton Chapel than in any other case I have been able to note ; this is natural enough, considering that the work was being done for a royal saint. They amounted to forty during the whole year, including three days at Easter and six at Christmastide. One of these was the dedication day, June 4, still kept as a sacred day at Eton ; for this day all workmen received full wages. On all others the mass of the workmen lost their pay, the only exception being that of the freemasons, who were regularly paid 3s. a week, holiday or no holiday.[1] Thus a freemason might earn £7 16s. per annum, but a rough-mason could not earn more than £6 16s. 6d. At Easter-tide and Christmas there was naturally some irregularity of attendance beyond the statutory holidays. In the week before Christmas, the freemasons did 257 days' work ; in Christmas week, thirty-two ; in the week after, 125. Two more weeks had to elapse before normal regularity was restored among the men on the staff, and these were much reduced in number ; ten out of fifty-two make no farther appearance to the end of the book (February 4). The rough-masons show a still more irregular record ; eight were at work just before Christmas ; of these only two reappeared after the holidays, worked for three weeks, and then went off. The hard-hewers' and labourers' record resembles the freemasons' ; except that four of them did a little work even in the Christmas fortnight. Of those faithful three who alone remained all year on the staff out of the whole 175, two averaged four and a half days each in the

---

[1] Compare the Statute of 1402 : capenters, masons and tilers are forbidden to take wages by the week, or for the days or half-days on which they do no work. (Gould, i, 348.)

fortnight. Two others, comparatively recent recruits, averaged three and a half days each. The carpenters and sawyers took rather more holidays than the other workmen.

Let it be repeated that we have here a building work which is exceptional, though far from unprecedented. So far as the evidence goes, it seems clearly to contradict Thorold Rogers's assumption that the medieval artisan or labourer had constant and regular work. Moreover, as may be seen in Appendix 11, other account-rolls tell the same tale on this point. Instability of employment seems to come out clearly in all the records. By far the best generalization on these rolls, within reasonable compass, is Prof. Hamilton Thompson's *Medieval Building Accounts*, a Presidential address before the Somersetshire Archæological and Natural History Society in 1920. Next best, perhaps, is J. A. Brutail's *Deux chantiers bordelais* (in *Le Moyen Âge* for 1899–1901). Much may be learned also from Mr. Hobson's edition *Adderbury " Rectoria "* (Oxfordshire Record Society for 1926), and from Canon F. R. Chapman's privately-printed *Sacrist Rolls of Ely*. But the fullest collection of facts, and therefore the best foundation for exhaustive special study, is to be found in Beissel's book on Xanten, with which I deal also in my Appendix.[1]

---

[1] Just as I go to press, I learn from Mr. L. F. Salzman that he is at work upon an exhaustive study of building contracts and accounts, from MS. and printed sources, which will doubtless carry us a good deal farther.

CHAPTER XI

FROM PRENTICE TO MASTER

WE may now turn back again from these intimate details of two great building works to a more general survey of the subject.

We must avoid, to begin with, the idea that these men formed a definite type, apart from the society of their time. The general society of Chaucer's day had probably no better artistic taste than that of our own times. But two factors combined to narrow the gulf between the artist and his public. In the first place, the artist himself lived a more normal life than many of his modern descendants; and, secondly, the public were saved by the gild system from having any really bad art to choose from. If our ancestors had had the modern Hindoo's choice between old-method printed cottons with vegetable colours, and the newest Manchester stuff with crude aniline dyes, they might have chosen the new, as the Hindoo often does, not only as cheaper but also as more attractive. However, they had no such choice; the tree of the knowledge of good and evil in art had not yet been tasted. Cubism was not yet possible; but Turner's landscape was equally impossible.

The artist was a more normal man. He was exceptional only in so far as he came mainly from the poorer social strata; but so also did the lower clergy. The fifteenth century panegyrist might indeed boast that masonry took its beginning in the fact " that great lords had not so great possessions that they might not advance their free-begotten children, for they had so many; therefore they took counsel how they might their children advance, and ordain them honestly to live." [1] But this

[1] Cooke-Baker, p. 95.

did not pretend to be more recent than Euclid's day, far more remote than even the legendary Athelstan; and it would be difficult to name a single medieval artist, apart from a few churchmen, of whom we have any reason to suspect that his parentage was above the lower middle class, at the highest. Sometimes the craft ran in families; at different times in the late fourteenth and early fifteenth century, for instance, six of the family of Keldermans " drew the plans and worked at the building of a multitude of monuments in the Low Countries; churches, *beffrois*, castles, town-halls, and prisons." [1] At St.-Ouen-de-Rouen, again, we shall see a son succeed his father as master-mason, and Beissel gives reasons for believing that three generations in direct descent, with one collateral, worked in succession at Xanten (I, 104). At Ely, the monastery employed a family of hereditary goldsmiths for at least 200 years; the son of one of these becoming a monk, was finally raised to the see of Norwich in 1299. The master-goldsmith had a workshop in the Sacristy.[2] But, as a rule, their profession seems to have been determined rather by chance. The mason, with whom we are mainly concerned, might often come from the village, where some work was on hand, and where the master, needing another apprentice, took a boy from the plough-tail just as William Morris took errand-boys and made them into craftsmen. With Morris, this was due to the man's own driving-power; in the Middle Ages it was the gild system, which worked with the same rough accuracy of selection with which the public-school system worked fifty years ago. Many then drifted into schoolmasterships for want of anything better suited to their tastes and their possibilities; a certain number were found unsuited to the job and drifted out. Of the remainder, a few possessed enthusiasm and genius; many did honestly and well because they would

[1] L. de Burbure, *Notice sur les auteurs de l'ancien jubé de Bourbourg.* Lille, 1864.

[2] Chapman, *Sacrist Rolls*, vol. I, p. 151; a study of extraordinary interest.

have done honestly and well anywhere ; many, again, just passed muster. But the majority of masons came probably from the towns, where more work went on ; though not, in those days, so much more. Once out of his apprenticeship, the mason probably found the problem of employment far from negligible. In a few cases he might marry his master's daughter, ballad-fashion, and settle down early for life. But in most cases the building would be finished, and that job would be over, and now the quest for a new job must begin. This comes out very strongly from French and German records as well as from our own ; see Appendix 11.[1]

Most masons, therefore, except in a few good stone districts where work would be constant, must have been wandering men. When Prof. Hamilton Thompson stresses the lack of evidence for " bands of masons wandering about the country," he seems to refer only to the extreme theory that these bands were large and organized. There was frequent call upon the mason for some new adventure, where courage and energy would tell, but where blind fortune had her share also. Thousands succeeded ; but many, equally competent, must sometimes have drifted at the mercy of foul winds and currents and incalculable shoals. Perhaps in a few days, perhaps after many disappointments, our wanderer finds work again. It may be a small job in some village that will only last for a few months, or it may be at some greater edifice. When once he has come upon work that is in progress, he has good chance of employment ; for the

[1] Cf. *Cunningham*, p. 3 ; *Quicherat*, ii, 209 ; *Lefèvre-Pontalis*, p. 21 ; *York Fabric Rolls*, p. 200, with the statistics of the two royal chapels given in the preceding chapter ; it is worth while to compare others from more normal works. To judge by the figures which Heideloff gives from St. Stephen's Church at Vienna (p. 32) it would seem that, between 1404 and 1430, 74 masons were employed altogether, but their average tenure of office was less than four years each. The longest worked for twenty-four years ; the next two, for 17 and 14. At York Minster, 40 were employed in 1415, but only six in 1450. At Bodmin, in 1469–71, some were far more regularly employed than others.

master has very likely undertaken to finish within a given
time ; and, the more numerous his staff, the sooner he
can redeem his pledge. Just here and there the work is
big enough to last for generations ; the mason, therefore,
after full trial, may be put upon the permanent staff, and
even rise to the top. But, if we reckon the amount of
stone-building that went on, except at certain generations of intensest effort, as, for instance, the great
monastic and cathedral century from 1150 to 1250, and
if we follow this up with such documentary indications
as have survived, it would seem that the medieval mason
had little advantage over the agricultural labourer to
make up for his more unsettled life. In the later fifteenth
century, when wages were at their highest, the carpenter
gets nearly 6*d.* a day, the mason a little less, and the
labourer 4*d.*[1] In 1447–8, at King's College Chapel,
where the wages represent about the highest standard
of the day, seventy freemasons got 3*s.* a week each ;
twenty-four carpenters and carvers working on the stalls
3*s.* 4*d.* ; and forty labourers 2*s.*[2] About this time a
maidservant was paying 8*d.* a week for board and lodging at
Carrow Nunnery ; at Grace-Dieu Nunnery another paid
6*d.* a week ; at Swaffham Bulbeck the nuns charged 6*d.*
a week for boys' and girls' board ; two children, about a
generation later, paid 5*d.* a week. Between 1487 and 1532
we have boarding figures for carpenters and other workmen : these range from 10½*d.* to 11½*d.* a week. About
1480, a child is charged 10*d.* a week at Cornworthy
Nunnery ; a Winchester College boy's food and drink
are estimated at 8*d.* a week, and a fellow's at 1*s.* A
mason's food and drink are calculated at 1*d.* a day in
1444 and at 2*d.* in 1495, both by royal statute.[3] In the
early fifteenth century " the maintenance [of a labourer]
is valued at from 1¼*d.* to 2*d.* a day " ; at King's Hall,
Cambridge, from 1414 onwards, it is 8*d.*, 8½*d.*, 9*d.* and

[1] J. E. T. Rogers, *Six Cent. Work and Wages*, 1901, pp. 327–9.
[2] Willis and Clark, vol. i, p. 400.
[3] Gould, vol. ii, pp. 362, 367.

10*d.* a week, but the lowest figure predominates.[1] There
is room for a good deal of argument upon these data ;
some day, we may hope, much more evidence will be
collected and weighed ; but the figures do not seem to
leave much room for comfort if the mason had a wife and
(say) three surviving children. In a case of this kind, the
man himself was probably more fortunate than his family.

Nor must we imagine him to have had, in most cases,
much artistic inspiration. Take stock of any ordinary
medieval church, and you will see how little scope there
was for originality. Coton, by Cambridge, is quite
up to the average of a small village church, and perhaps
a little over. Here are four gargoyles on the tower ; in
these, no doubt, the carver had *carte blanche*. There are
four gable-crosses, on which again we will suppose him to
have had a free hand ; and, inside, a niche-bracket in
which an angel holds a coat of arms ; here, of course, the
subject was prescribed to him.[2] Beyond this, the ordinary
mason had no liberty at all ; in piers and capitals and
arches and window-tracery he had to follow the molds
drawn and cut for him by his master, almost as he would
have to follow them to-day. At a liberal computation of
all the working-hours spent upon the masonry of a
church, scarcely one-hundredth were spent upon work
where the mason had a free hand. On the Continent, and
in those parts of England where freestone is common, so
that the whole building is constructed of squared stone,
the disproportion would be found far greater. This is
specially noticeable in parts of Southern France and
Italy, where we might have expected the greatest artistic
efflorescence. Take, for instance, the little walled town

---

[1] J. E. T. Rogers, *Hist. Ag. and Prices*, vol. ii, pp. 497, 752 ; for the
other facts, see Dugdale-Caley, iv, 459 ; *Archæologia*, vol. xxv, p. 421 ;
Nichols, *Illust. of Manners, etc.*, 1797, pp. 80 ff. ; Leach and de Mont-
morency in *Journ. Ed.*, Oct. and Nov. 1910.

[2] Quicherat (ii, 1860) gives an instance from Rouen Cathedral in 1458,
where the head carver executed a stall after the model of which all the
rest were to be made. The Tower of Guilden Morden (Cambs.) is another
typical example, and gives much the same results as Coton.

of St.-Paul-du-Var, above Nice, which stands almost as
it stood in the Middle Ages, except for alterations which
a careful observer will detect at once.   There is more
dressed stone in it than there ever was in medieval Oxford
or Cambridge ; yet St. Mary's Church at Oxford contains more carved stone, and more elaborately carved,
than the whole of that Provençal town, or than the
cathedral city of Vence hard by.   Neither at Vence nor
at St.-Paul do the piers possess real capitals ; the windows
have not, nor ever had, any tracery.   Both buildings
show the master-mason's capacity as an engineer, and at
St.-Paul there is some real dignity of proportion ; but,
so far as the stone-cutting is concerned, there is scarcely
anything which could not have been done by one of the
rough-hewers of King's College Chapel.   If any reader
will try to take accurate stock of medieval mason work
as a whole, instead of choosing instinctively and unconsciously the most brilliant examples, he will probably be
startled to find how small a fraction was artistic except
in the sense in which we apply the word to an honest
deal table or chair.

All this, it is true, takes no account of the images
which were there before the Reformation.   The number
of such images may easily be exaggerated ; Bishop
Quivil's synodal injunctions in 1287 for Exeter diocese,
and the Totnes visitation of 1342, show how little was
required in Devonshire at that time, and how often even
that little was not forthcoming.[1]   Moreover, we have

[1] The only two legally required are one of the B.V.M. and one of the
patron saint of the church.   Two crosses are required, one portable and
one fixed, which would probably be a crucifix.   The deficiencies noted in
1342 are printed in *Eng. Hist. Rev.*, Jan. 1911, pp. 112 ff. ; a small selection
are translated in my *Five Centuries of Religion*, vol. ii, pp. 451 ff.   An
interesting sidelight on the patron saints comes from some French archi-
diaconal visitations in the diocese of Paris towards the end of the fifteenth
century.   " Whether through ignorance or through the secretary's negligence, the names of the parochial patron saints are too frequently changed
in the reports ; Gif, for instance, is successively attributed to St. Remi,
St. Maurice and even St. John ; the same phenomenon at Epinay-sur-
Orge and several others." (*Josas*, p. xxix).

evidence that a large proportion of these images, if not
the majority, were done in carvers' shops, and bought
and packed off in those days, just as in these of ours.
We have seen how Sacchetti shows us an artist who
had a whole cupboard full of life-sized crucifixes,
ready carved and painted for any customer who
might call. Prof. Lethaby suspects something of the
same in the famous church embroidery which has often
been ascribed to the nuns, as we have seen in Chapter IV.
Not only did the Eton Chapel authorities buy large
quantities of mouldings ready-cut from the quarries, but
we know that, long before, wrought marble was exported
in all directions from the Isle of Purbeck; and Devonshire churches are full of Dartmoor granite mouldings
wrought in the quarries on the moors. There were
busy factories of alabaster figures and tabernacles in
Derbyshire and Notts, driving a brisk export trade,
even beyond the sea.[1] The alabaster carvers at
Nottingham despatched in one consignment alone
no fewer than fifty-six heads of St. John the Baptist.
There were shops of " imagers " in London and
York. We have seen a Flemish artist carving statues
by contract; and at King's College, in 1515, it
was confidently calculated that statuary and tabernacle work could be got at five shillings per foot.[2]
The estimate runs : " Twoo Images of Kinges at the
west dorre in two tabernacles made for the same, Eyther
of viij foote high. Fowre at the south and north doorres
of the saide Churche, Eyther of vj foote high And xlviij
Images within the saide Churche. Every of them of three
foote high. Amounting in all to Clxxij foote. At the
fote, esteamed in workemanshipp which amounteth vnto
forty-five pounds. Xl ton of Yorkshire ston is estemed
to be sufficient for all the said Images. At vj Shillinges

---

[1] See Appendix 12, and especially Mr. A. Gardner's exhaustive article
in *The Archæological Journal*, vol. lxxx (1923).

[2] Willis and Clark, vol. i, p. 482.

viijd. the toon, thirteen pounds six shillings and eight-pence."[1] A great deal of such work could be rough-hewn to begin with by the carver's apprentices or journeymen; we need not wonder therefore that, just about this time, Thomas Drawswerd, the imager of York, rose to Sheriff, Lord Mayor, and Member of Parliament for the city. Another Lord Mayor of York, who died in 1508, was John Petty, the glazier. One item in his will is significant; he left to his brother Robert a good deal of glass, with " all my tools *and scrolls*."[2] It has often been noticed how medieval glass-painters used the same cartoon again and again, sometimes, in the same church, several times over for entirely different saints.

Traces of medieval shopwork may very frequently be found. At Chelsworth, in Suffolk, for instance, is a remarkably beautiful canopied tomb of the fourteenth century, which is put together with painful clumsiness. It was evidently carved by a first-rate artist, probably in London, packed and brought down in barrels (as we know in similar cases) and set up at Chelsworth by the local rough-mason and his men, who were incapable of puzzling out the right place for each stone. At Seaford the twelfth century capitals are in different pieces, evidently carved separately in the shop and put together without accurate fitting; Viollet le Duc gives a similar instance from St.-Denis. Still more startling is the Angel Choir of Lincoln, where some of the most beautiful sculpture in England suffers from the incapacity of the setters, who have fitted wrong wings to wrong bodies.[3]

---

[1] Willis and Clark, vol. i, p. 482.

[2] *Test. Eborac.*, vol. iv, 1868, p. 334.

[3] Compare the article on *The Luxor Shrines* in *The Times* for Jan. 15, 1924: " Each section bears on it in linear hieroglyphic characters clear indications of the position relative to the others in which it was to be erected, and it is assumed either that all the sections were originally

The so-called Galilee Porch at Lincoln would seem another instance in point ; the carving is beautiful in detail, but scarcely any two arches correspond to each other, and scarcely, it may be added, any two sides of the same arch. These, however, are probably not due to shopwork, but to the fact that one generation wrought the work in the Minster Lodge, and another less intelligent generation set it up.[1] Of definite shopwork, however, there is a clear example at Bristol Cathedral, from about 1330 or 1340. There, in the remarkable but uniform series of sepulchral niches, the artist has followed the fashion of his day in carving naturalistic foliage, hawthorn and maple and so on. But he has given to his hawthorn the characteristic winged seed of the maple, and, by a complementary error, mayblossom to his maple. It seems evident that he had worked from patterns which were stocked in the shop, and that he had mixed them up, being no direct observer of leaves and flowers. Moreover, this shopwork sometimes, at least, brought weariness to the workman. St. Antonino of Florence, a very keen observer of all classes of men in one of the busiest generations at that great city (he was Archbishop from 1448 to 1459), is explicit as to the temptations of the profession. " Illuminators of books, whether with

assembled outside the tomb, marked, and then taken to pieces for re-erection in the sepulchral chamber, or that they were so marked in the workshop according to the architect's design. While the carving and decorative work on the shrines are all carefully executed by skilful artists and craftsmen, those who actually put them in place would appear to have been somewhat negligent. In certain instances pieces are not in the position in which they were intended to be placed, and from the traces they bear it would follow that the workmen were either impatient or indifferent and did not trouble to correct their mistake when they found the pieces did not fit as they had been placed, but wrenched them into position. Whether the pieces were taken in their wrong order or the original fault lay with those who actually re-assembled them in the sepulchral chamber is immaterial. The fact remains that the whole shrine edifice is untrue."

[1] Professor Lethaby suggests that, as these angels are in Westminster style, they may have been brought from London.

the pen or with the brush, offend [against God] if they [labour] on holy days, or when they exact an excessive price, and especially when they temper their colours ill, by which reason they fade rapidly from the books, or when, for the sake of finishing quickly, they work carelessly." [1]

So far it is necessary to point out the limitations of the medieval artist ; and, while actually writing this page, I find support in the review of a book just published, the late Mr. J. D. Le Couteur's *English Medieval Painted Glass* : " Mr. Le Couteur shows that the medieval craftsman had little sentiment, but much willingness." (*Church Times*, December 10, 1926).

On the other hand, all this was instinct with the homely charm of a comparatively simple society ; it had " the breezy call of incense-breathing morn." An artist, even in the highest flights to which his profession then called him, could count upon wide public sympathy and appreciation, because he was expressing traditional and familiar ideas by methods which, in proportion as they departed from earlier conventions, drew nearer to easily-comprehensible realism. Giotto may have had carping critics among jealous fellow-craftsmen, or among church-men like that bishop of Tuy who, in his day, scented heresy in what is now the accepted form of crucifix. But, with the general public, he was sure of wide appre-ciation, since he painted what all men might understand. The most beautiful statues of saints realize ideals which were not entirely unfamiliar to any man who had any ideas at all. They were in the air, as motoring and aviation are in the air nowadays ; the very children were interested and sometimes imitative, as Giraldus Camb-rensis tells us of himself that, while his older brothers amused themselves with building castles and cities and palaces in the sand, he, " as a prelude to his later life, ever bent his whole mind to the building of churches

---

[1] *Summa,* pars. iii, tib. viii, c. 4, s. 11.

and monasteries in play."[1] It was what William Morris called it, a People's Art, appealing to all, with the strength and the limitations of that People's Religion to which all men must needs conform in those days, or suffer for rebellion. For that small minority of masons who were free to work out their own ideas, the Middle Ages were certainly a period of happy equilibrium.[2] Side by side with the men who carved the Annunciation groups at Reims or Chartres were others (or, possibly, the same men in other moods) who wrought grotesques which are difficult to publish in modern photography; portions of the Bayeux tapestry; the choir-screen brackets at Lynn; the prie-Dieu of Count Erhard of Württemberg, as elaborate as a bishop's throne, yet representing Noah's drunkenness with a realism as pitilessly complacent as that of the artist of St.-Savin.[3] We easily understand that often-quoted complaint of the monk Gautier de Coincy in the thirteenth century, that the clergy themselves are less interested in statues of Our Lady than in representations of Reynard the Fox.[4] So, for his part, the average artist would carve saints to order; but, where he was free, he often preferred to carve sinners.

The ordinary mason's satisfaction in his work was probably not far different from that of the modern mechanic. The one worked, as the other now works, at the sort of job which is most characteristic of his time, and which his time best understands; it is pleasant to row on a swinging forward tide. To say that the one was engaged, as the other is not, in furthering a professedly religious ideal, is to exaggerate in one very important

---

[1] For the whole passage, see my *Social Life in Britain*, p. 111. But castle-builders evidently far outnumbered church-builders; for Gerald's father " marvelled at this his custom," and took it as an omen of his future clerical career.

[2] To this Prof. Lethaby adds : " And the number larger in fellowship with them. In fact, it was a craftsman's age in the department of production."

[3] Didron. *Ann. arch.*, vol. ii, p. 169.

[4] Ibid., p. 269.

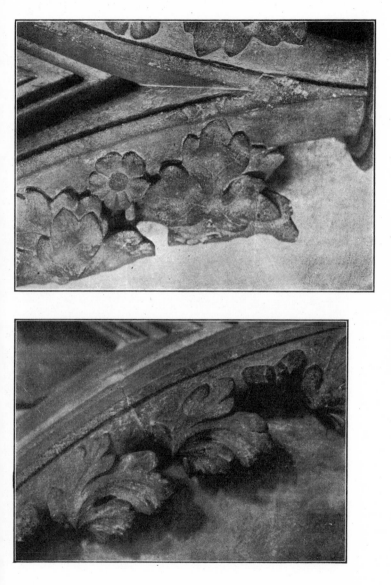

SHOPWORK AT BRISTOL CATHEDRAL.

208]

particular; there was a great deal of castle-work and city-work, as well as of church-work. And, even if we confine ourselves to the churches, we have no right to assume more religion in the man who cut and laid the stones than we assume of militarism in those who raised the towers and battlements. The king had to press men for his churches, as for his castles and his wars. To expound this fully would take us here too far afield; but I have given evidence elsewhere, and much more might be produced, to show that the masses under Catholicism were very like the masses under Protestantism, that the pre-reformation period can less strictly be called an Age of Faith than an Age of Acquiescence, and that the ordinary man's attitude to the priest might almost be summed up in the Northern Farmer's judgment on his own parson's sermons :—

"An' I niver knaw'd whot a meän'd, but I thowt a
    'ad summut to saäy,
An' I thowt a said whot a owt to' a said, an' I coom'd
    awaäy."

There was, indeed, something more than this; certain ceremonies which are now obsolete or obsolescent were more or less essential then. But ceremonies are not necessarily religion; and, apart from certain purely selfish thoughts about personal salvation or damnation, there is no serious reason for considering the medieval mason as more religious than the modern. His main advantage over the mason of to-day was that of rowing with the tide; an advantage enjoyed now by the mechanic.

But in acquiesence there is calm and content; and, apart from those who had more positive pride in helping to make God's house more beautiful than the castle, very many more would less consciously enjoy their connexion with the church. The walls at which they worked were intimately connected with the ceremonies which they took now as a matter of course, and to which on their

P

death-bed they would look more earnestly. A natural complement of sport on the village green and drink at the village alehouse was this of Mass at the church, and a grave, when the end should come, within its hallowed ground. But the inn and the game were uppermost in most men's minds.

The master-mason himself was not usually a man of inspiration. (See Appendix 13.) After all, honest routine carries the world very far, especially when it is the disciplined and purposeful routine of a vast collectivist force. Heroism is but a small part even of the soldier's job; Laurence Oates might have lived to eighty as an English gentleman, if that crisis had not come in which he showed himself a very gallant English gentleman. The ordinary master, then, would normally differ little from the foreman of to-day; only here and there might a splendid chance come to him; here and there, again, he might be in a manner transfigured by his intimate dependence upon some princely patron like Charles V of France, or some great and liberal churchman. The latter case was by far the commonest; at cathedrals and at great abbeys we sometimes find the master pensioned off, with no farther duties beyond advice and consultation, or with an easy job such as that of abbey porter.

Neither churchman alone, nor mason alone, could have done what churchman and mason did in harmonious partnership. The detailed descriptions which Henry VI left in his will, of Eton and King's College Chapels as he wished them to be built, give a fair idea of the interaction of employer's and workman's ideas.[1] It was not altogether unlike the partnership of married life; alternate inspiration and compromise. Each party knew what he himself wanted; and so much was common to both that the result was an harmonious whole. The ruins of a sanctuary like Castleacre in Norfolk, and the perfectly-preserved contemporary abbey-church of Lessay

[1] Willis and Clark, vol. i, pp. 366, 368.

in Normandy, tell the same tale, because neither was ever a house of the first magnitude. In buildings like these, we see how monk and mason must have inspired each other. Neither by himself would have created those solemn aisles, those masses of sculpture far more elaborate than the monk really needed for his religion, far vaster and costlier and more orderly than any artist or group of artists could have found money or leisure to achieve. No doubt there was some inevitable human friction. At one time the mason would say : " The governor wants *this !* " and, with a shrug of his shoulders, he would do the thing because " the governor " wanted it. Or, again, the monk would say : " I told the man to do *this* ; he persists in doing *that* ; well, well, we must bear with him !" Sometimes, no doubt, the churchman's suggestions were of real value to his workmen. But, in the large majority of cases, the employer then knew little more than he does nowadays ; he ordered and paid for a church of a certain size very much as he now orders a car according to certain specifications.

The fullest claim for the patron's control is perhaps that made by Mâle in his third volume (pp. 529 ff.). But the instances he there quotes, interesting as they are, seem scarcely sufficient on close analysis to bear all the weight of his argument. For example, even the pre-scription on which he seems to lay most stress was not really calculated to restrict an artist's liberty very far ; if a fifteenth century priest, ordering a picture, insists by formal contract that the Virgin's dress shall be " of white damask," must we not say that a modern lady might easily have been no less definite in commissioning a portrait by Millais, and can we really follow Mâle in his deduction that " the painter had nothing left to imagine " ? Even more interesting, perhaps, than any of the cases quoted by him is one which Paquot cites from the *Acta Sanctorum*, in the light it throws upon painter and patron. Poppi, in the hill-country of Central Italy, had its own local saint, San Torello, who died about 1282. The

story of his life and miracles, in its present form, probably
dates from about 1507, when his body was translated for
the second time ; but doubtless it records more ancient
traditions.[1]   The author records how " a certain Sienese,
the Lord Estagio by name, having fallen into disfavour
with his count, was banished to Poppi. There he noted the
miracles of San Torello, and commended himself to him
with the vow that, if he might come to peace with his
count, and dwell again in his own city, he would yearly
celebrate his feast and cause his image to be painted in his
own chamber. Not long after this vow his desire was fulfilled. So, having gained his pardon, he wished to fulfil his
vow, and summoned a painter, to whom he said : ' I will
that thou paint me a certain San Torello of Poppi ; by
whose favour I am come again into mine own country.'
Then said the painter : ' Hast thou his history in mind ? '
to whom the noble answered ' not very well.' ' Then
send for it,' said the painter, ' that I may learn the
fashion of his body and his raiment ; and then I will
paint him.' So this noble wrote a letter to send for the
saint's raiment and appearance. But, on the very night
before that day when the letter should have been sent,
Torello himself appeared in a vision to the painter ; and
in fashion as a Tertiary Friar.[2] That is to say, he was
clad in a tunic next his flesh, and over this a cloak ; his
head was covered with a cap [or hood] such as these
friars wear ; he was girt with a cord, and unshod, and he
seemed to bear a wolf in his arms. This, again, was the
fashion of his head : his hair neither curled nor lank, yet
white with age ; his brow broad and bald and smooth,
with few wrinkles ; his eyes of middle size, neither light
nor translucent, of a dark blue ; his nose neither too big
nor too small, but thinner towards the mouth ; his eye-
lashes with few and rare and short hairs ; his teeth white
and small and thick ; his ears little and thin, with few

[1] Molanus, p. 168 ; AA. SS. Boll. Mart., ii (1865), p. 498.

[2] *Fraterculi*. According to the Bollandists, he was not strictly a Tertiary,
but imitated their dress, as other solitaries often did.

A FRENCH WOOD-CARVER AT AMIENS.

convolutions; his chin small and curving towards the mouth, and very slightly dimpled at the tip. His skin and the hue of his face were between white and red; he was neither too fat nor too lean; his figure[1] was betwixt the fat and the lean, yet rather inclining to the latter; his shoulders broad; his body five feet long; his feet of a span-length; his gait moderate; his look neither very dark nor very placid; and as he stood he seemed quick and loveable, kindly and gracious. His hands were long, with slender fingers; his arms so long that when he stood erect and stretched them out he easily touched his knees with his hands. In this form, then, and in this fashion the friar appeared, turning to the painter and saying: ' My son, wouldst thou dare to paint a friar in this fashion, as thou seest me here ? ' The painter answered: ' Yea, my lord.' Then said the friar again: ' Paint in this fashion San Torello of Poppi; for I am formed and fashioned as he is.' Here he halted, and, having spoken, he vanished; so the painter, awaking from this vision, went forthwith to the Lord Estagio, and told him all that he had seen in his dream, and finished without pay the picture which he had promised."

It cannot be doubted that the business relations of patron and artist, in that simpler society, were more intimate than they are to-day. But we must face both sides of this old-world intimacy. Few of the modern writers who sentimentalize over the past could tolerate, for a few days even, the medieval lack of privacy. In the most luxurious palace of the Middle Ages there was perhaps less privacy than on a great Atlantic liner; in the numerous smaller crag-castles such as one sees on the Rhine or the Neckar, there can hardly have been more than on a modern tramp-steamer. The lord's family and the retainers lived more promiscuously, in many ways, than the upper-class artisan household of to-day. There, then, was the dark side; the brighter side comes out in the cheek-by-jowl familiarity which we get in Chaucer's

[1] The text has *loquela*, which makes no sense.

pilgrims. When class differences were so marked, and (it was generally admitted) so divinely appointed, then familiarity ran far less risk of breeding contempt. Therefore, when the business association between mason and employer was not merely transitory, it was probably, in most cases, very cordial and pleasant.[1] We may think of it in terms of the relation between a skipper of a century ago and the firm on whose business he sailed ; that relation comes out in the earlier chapters of *Monte Cristo*, and, better still, in Kielland's novel of *Skipper Worse*. Very similar, also, must have been the bond between the master-mason and his workmen ; they must have been very like an old-fashioned skipper and his crew, though with a good deal more of democratic licence. We may think of the masons bound together by their common interest in the work, no less lively than the sailors' common interest in their ship. We may even wonder whether they did not call the building *she*, living from hand to mouth in her service, often cursing her, yet with a general pride in her and a readiness even to suffer hardships and perils for her. One of the commonest types of miracle in medieval lives of the saints is that of the building accident which would have been fatal but for St. So-and-So's interposition.[2] Had they not also the seaman's alternate privations and carouses, sometimes tramping weary days or weeks or months for work, yet with a joy in their freedom, and a certain pride in it, and no little contempt for the settled artisan or country labourer, for the dog who bears the mark of the collar ? If, again, the artisan worked long enough at any church, he naturally became attached to it, and it to him. The *York Fabric Rolls* show us worn-out head-masons or

---

[1] Mr. Kingsley Porter (ii, 189) quotes an excellent example : " It is amusing to read in Gervase [of Canterbury] what infinite tact William of Sens was forced to employ to persuade the reluctant monks that it was necessary to destroy the charred fragments of the glorious choir of Conrad."

[2] Cf. Lefèvre-Pontalis, p. 9 ; Quicherat, ii, 178.

carpenters pensioned with a corrody or with a light job such as the porter's; here and there we get similar indications in monastic records. On the other hand, they show us the mason's solicitude to be buried in a church for which he has worked, and to which he is glad to leave a legacy. The fourth volume of *Testamenta Eboracensia* contains the will of John Petty, that artisan who had risen to capitalist rank and to the Lord Mayoralty of York. He is to be buried before the high altar of St. Michael le Belfry, under shadow of the Minster; and he hopes for all the soul-help the monks of Furness can give him: "To Furnes abbay xiijs iiijd., besechyng thame of clere absolucion, because I have wroght mych wark there." At Xanten, two successive master-masons in the first half of the fifteenth century left each about the amount of a year's pay to the fabric.[1] At Bordeaux, a master-carpenter of St.-Michel went on pilgrimages to Rome and Jerusalem, and left a sum equivalent to about £20 of present-day money to found a "year's mind" for his soul.[2] With these we may compare the celebrated mason's inscription on the west wall of the south transept at Melrose, close by his shield which he has carved over a door. The inscription runs, in modernized spelling:—

> John Morow sometime called was I
> And born in Paris certainly
> And had in keeping all mason-work
> Of Saint Andrew's the highë Kirk,
> Of Glasgow, Melrose and Paslay,   [Paisley
> Of Niddisdale and of Galway
> Pray to God and Mary baith   [both
>   And sweet St. John
> To keep this holy church from skaith.[3]

Several writers have noted what must probably strike all students of the original documents, that masons seem

[1] Beissel, i, 156.

[2] Brutails, p. 46.

[3] *Proc. Soc. Ant. of Scotland*, vol. ii, 1858, p. 166.

to have quarrelled rather oftener than most other artisans.[1]
It may have been that the mallet and the stone-axe were
specially tempting weapons ; there may also have been
stronger impulses of competition. The author of *Dives
and Pauper*, writing about A.D. 1400, notes this very
natural spirit in architecture as elsewhere. The section is
thus summarized in the table of contents : " Why it is

JOHN MORROW'S INSCRIPTION AT MELROSE.

to dread the solemn making of churches and good arraying
of them, and that fair service [that] is done in churches
of England is more of pomp and pride than to the worship
of God." And in his text (Com., i, c. 51, *ad fin.*), the
ecclesiastical teacher (*Pauper*) explains to the layman
whom he is instructing that all is well if this wealth of
building and ornament is done chiefly for devotion ; " but
I dread me that men do it more for pomp and pride of

[1] For instance, Lethaby, *Westminster I*, p. 184 ; Peckham, *Epp.*, R. S.,
vol. ii, p. 447 ; Peetz, p. 221. Compare Torrigiani's words : " Now
[Michael Angelo] Buonarroti had a habit of teasing all the rest of us who
were drawing [in the Church of the Carmine] ; and one day in particular
he was annoying me, and I was more vexed than usual ; so I stretched out
my hand and dealt him such a blow on the nose that I felt the bone and
the cartilage yield under my fist as if they had been made of crisp wafer.
And so he'll go with my mark upon him to his dying day." Benvenuto
Cellini, *Life*, bk. i, s. 13 ; tr. Macdonell, 1903, vol. i, p. 21.

this world, to have a name and worship thereby in the county, or for envy that one town hath against another, not for devotion but for the worship and the name that they see them have by array and ornaments in Holy Church, or else by sly covetise of men of Holy Church." *Dives* : " What fantasy hast thou that men do it not for devotion ? " *P.* : " For the people these days is full undevout to God and Holy Church, and they love but little men of Holy Church, and they be loth to come in Holy Church when they be bound to come thither [i.e. on Sundays and Feasts of Obligation] and full loth to hear God's service. Late they come, and full soon they go away. If they be there a little while, them thinketh full long. They have liever go to the tavern than Holy Church, liever to hear a song of Robin Hood or of some ribaldry than for to hear Mass or matins or any other God's service or any word of God. And, sith the people hath so little devotion to God and to Holy Church, I cannot see that they do such a cost in Holy Church for devotion nor for the love of God. For they despise God day and night with their evil and wicked living and their wicked thews [i.e. qualities]." After rebutting heretics who take occasion of this to carp at Churchmen as Judas carped at the waste of the ointment, *Pauper* adds : " Nevertheless, the waste cost of all these things, and other in Holy Church done for pride and vain glory, or of envy, one parish against another, or for covetise of the ministers in the Church, secular or religious, is greatly always to be reproved." This rivalry, natural enough in itself, is borne out by existing documents ; it is fairly common that the formal specification

JOHN MORROW'S SCUTCHEON.

for new work should run " like unto [some neighbouring parish]" with the addition, perhaps, of "or better, if may be." Henry VI's rivalry, when he built Eton and King's Colleges, with Wykeham's work at Winchester and other pre-existing buildings, may be found in Willis and Clark, vol. i, pp. 500, 596–7, 615. A Hull citizen's will of 1502–3 shows similar rivalry with King's Lynn. " I bequeath unto the said chapel [where I am buried] forty pounds in honour of the Sacrament, to make the ascent and descent at the high altar and the chapel roof at the elevation of God's Body and Blood, even as it is at the cathedral church of Lynn ; to wit, let an angel be let up and down until the end of singing, and the words *lead us not into temptation.*" [1]

Naturally also, in the realm of higher fancy, rival artists were as jealous in those days as in any other. Indeed, the jealousy may have been even greater then, in proportion as there was less room for the mere *poseur.* "Many a time have masters discussed," so Villard de Honnecourt tells us ; but those things discussed over the evening drink were questions rather of skill than of taste ; and, in the village inn of those days, if any man talked for mere effect, he was not likely to find the effect he sought. Again, that gild and apprenticeship system, which prevented any medieval artist from towering above the rest as Dante or even Chaucer tower among medieval poets, was still more unfavourable to the mere charlatan in art. The temptation in those days would rather be to boast one's own personal achievements ; the babbler of the medieval lodge would be of the Benvenuto Cellini rather than of the Huysmans type. The feelings which now find an outlet in talk might easily turn to tragedy

[1] *Testamenta Eboracensia*, Surtees Soc., vol. liii (1868), p. 209. Henry III issued a writ to Master John of St. Omer to cause a lectern to be made for the new Chapter-house at Westminster like the lectern in the Chapter-house at St. Albans, or more beautiful if it could be made (*Archæologia*, vol. lviii., p. 284). By *Cathedral*, the testator must mean one of the two great churches, probably St. Margaret's, but perhaps St. Nicholas.

among the artists of the Middle Ages. We have seen
how, when Dante wishes to illustrate the bitterness of
jealousy, he takes an example from the famous illuminator
Oderisi of Gubbio ; and the legend of the Prentice's
Pillar of Rosslyn has more than one medieval analogue.
At that famous castle chapel, so the story goes, the master
was determined to fashion one pillar which should outdo
even the lavish ornament of the rest. But for this he
needed further inspiration ; he must travel and note all
the best things that could be found elsewhere, just as
Villard noted on his drawing of the cathedral tower at
Laon, that it was the fairest he had seen in all his travels.
So the Rosslyn master-mason travelled as far as Rome,
and came home fully armed for the crowning work of
his life. But, during this long absence, his apprentice
had drawn inspiration from a nearer and deeper source.
He was in love, and for the girl's sake he imagined and
wrought a pillar so fantastically beautiful that the master,
on his return, saw himself hopelessly surpassed, and
brained the luckless youth with his hammer.[1] So runs the
legend ; and it has at least this basis of fact, that surviving
account-rolls show the master to have travelled in search
of models, after the common and natural practice,[2] and
on his return, to have drawn a large-scale design on
" Eastland boards," i.e. Baltic deals, upon which masons
frequently made their drawings or cut their molds.

Even this slight basis of ascertainable fact is lacking for
another famous legend of this kind, so famous that it has
even found a place in the Maurist Dom Pommeraye's
history of St.-Ouen-de-Rouen, and in Michelet's *Histoire
de France*. In a northern chapel of that great choir are
two fine sepulchral slabs comemorating three of the
St.-Ouen architects. The earlier bears a single figure,
marked by the style of its tabernacle-work as that of the
nameless master who designed and began the present
building. The other bears two figures, facing each other

[1] For another version see Appendix 14.
[2] Very interesting similar cases in Quicherat, ii, 177 and 210.

and standing upon lions, one of which seems to be showing his teeth at the other. These the popular imagination has interpreted after that fashion of its own which we shall see still more definitely illustrated in a succeeding chapter. These lions, said the good folk of Rouen to each other, are plainly symbolical; one is plainly enraged against the other; that is, one master was the other's mortal enemy. He holds in his hand the design of the more beautiful of the two great transept rose-windows, the southern. This, then, was the journeyman who wrought a fairer window than his master's; therefore the enraged master slew him; and there the masons with their lions face each other in grim defiance to all eternity. In this case, modern research has put us in possession of

THE TWO ARCHITECTS OF ST.-OUEN.

THE PRENTICE'S PILLAR AT ROSLYN.

the actual facts.[1] The left-hand figure is that of Alexandre
de Berneval, who died in 1440 ; so much is plainly recorded
in the inscription upon the slab itself.   It was Alexandre,
then, who built the southern transept.   But the right-
hand figure, as even the features on the tomb might
suggest, stands not for an older but for a younger man ;
and, in fact, we know now that Colin de Berneval succeeded to the mastership on his father Alexandre's death,
and built the northern transept.   Round his figure on
the great slab there is no inscription, and the reason is
simple enough : Colin's piety prepared this memorial for
himself and his father ; Colin chiselled the old man's
epitaph, but no son succeeded to chisel Colin's, and no
friendly hand troubled itself to add this natural finishing
touch to the memorial.   At Coton, in Cambridgeshire,
a half-finished tombstone has been built into the chancel
wall and may well have a similar history ; it is possible
that some mason prepared it for himself, but was cut
short by death, and found no friendly successor.

   These legends of Rosslyn and St.-Ouen, apocryphal as
the latter certainly is, and as the former may well be, do
at least testify to tragic artistic rivalries in the past.   For
the social historian the tale that is merely *ben trovato*
may have quite as much significance, and sometimes even
more, than if it were demonstrably true to actual fact.
We have in these two legends a commentary upon the
sententious pronouncement of the Bolognese professor,
Benvenuto da Imola, that " the love of glory doth so
indifferently fasten upon all men, that even petty artisans
[*parvi artifices*] are anxious to earn it."[2]

---

[1] Quicherat, ii, 216 ff.

[2] *Comentum,* vol. iii, p. 309 ; the whole passage in *Social Britain,* p. 469.

CHAPTER XII

WANDER-YEARS

THERE are many districts of England and of Northern France in which, when once we have familiarized ourselves with the churches, we can come very close indeed to the medieval artist. The interested observer can thus, through the land and folk of to-day, make friends with the land and folk of a distant past, and live among the ghosts that haunt the mouldering stones. Let me take, for instance, north-west Norfolk, the corner from which I can best write from memory. Here we have traces of more than one artist in the strictest sense ; a few examples will suffice, out of many. The great wheel-window of St. Margaret's at Lynn was splendid both in design and in execution ; at Middleton is a fine string-course of foliage all round the chancel ; in the little church of Pentney are two dripstone-heads of remarkable dignity and beauty even through partial defacement, and an east window which, except in size, is worthy of a cathedral. All these are of the thirteenth century ; in the next, we find the choir-stalls of St. Margaret's and the great Flemish brasses ; singularly beautiful fragments of a screen at Southacre ; the whole church of Snettisham, from Galilee-porch to spire ; and the window-tracery at Old Walsingham and at Beeston-by-Litcham, which we may sit and watch in the sunlight and reflect what the artist's just pride must have been when he first saw his own work perfect and new and white, imprinted from his brain upon the stone as a seal impresses itself upon the wax. In the fifteenth century we get far less real beauty of detail. The great west window of St. Nicholas at Lynn may well have made its author proud, and the vaulting of the porch; but the corbel-figures, though interesting and good for their time, are far inferior to the smaller and less elaborate heads at Pentney. It is rather in their size and symmetry that these latter churches impress us; the carving had often become sadly mechanical, but the proportions of a great church like Swaffham, or the far smaller East Winch, are very finely conceived. These date from about the time when, to judge from the written documents, there was a serious attempt to organize freemasonry throughout England. So far as time-indications go, the Cooke-Baker MS. might have been written by the actual master-mason of St. Nicholas at Lynn.

This church exemplifies the dictum that there is no school of architecture like a great building.[1] We know its dates very nearly; it was not begun before 1399 at earliest, and it was finished at latest in 1419. Apart from the large number of unsigned stones, eleven masons have left numerous banker-marks on pillar and arch and window. Of these, six went on to work at other churches in the district; we may trace not only their marks but, in some cases, similarities of style. How they drifted from one work to the other we shall never know exactly, yet we can trace them as through a glass, darkly. Tantalizing as the actual documents often are; painfully as they often leave us at the point where we are most curious to learn, yet there was enough common atmosphere to justify a great deal of cross-inference; and, with much probability, we may eke out what we know for certain of England by what we know for certain of Germany or France. Thanks to Blomefield and other antiquaries, we know a good deal of the history of this particular district; and, having so often amused myself with dreaming of a mason walking beside me on those roads, or showing me his own work in those churches, I venture in this chapter to think these

[1] For transference of artistic ideas as a by-product of business relations between Oxford and Gloucester, see Prof. Willis in *The Gentleman's Magazine*, 1860 (July–Dec.), p. 272.

things aloud. It is all make-believe; yet I think there will be nothing of importance in this story for which vouchers could not be given, in the sense that it, or something like it, did really happen.[1]

By the autumn of 1417 the masons had finished at St. Nicholas, and the carpenters were finishing the roof and the glaziers were beginning at the windows. There was a tradition among their employers answering to the country labourer's Harvest Home when a great job was finished, the men were often given drink to make merry, with a sheep or a pig if there were many of them. So these Lynn masons roasted their pig in the lodge, and helped it out with cakes and ale. Some slept next morning till noonday; none was inclined to start that day for his new work. But the different parties spoke with each other, and ordered everything for the morrow. Then, at daybreak on that September morning, they heard Morrow-Mass at the altar of the great church which they themselves had reared from the ground; and after Mass they took the chaplain's special blessing, and lingered a moment to look round for the last time. The first to break silence now was Roger Piggott, by nature the most taciturn of all, who, with his wife and his slip of a girl, had been among the latest comers to the lodge, and who, in general, opened his mouth scarce a dozen times a day. He had been singling out his own mark here and there on the arches; and now he said in a hoarse whisper, almost to himself: " Aye, they will mount up at the Day of Doom ! " " Mount up whither, man ? " " Mount up to my reckoning, William Hindley. There's nothing heavier than stones in a common way; and I guess there must be some twenty or thirty hundred-weight of mine here in this church, all cut as honestly as a man can cut them. So the blessed St. Nicholas will see to it that every stone goes into my scale at Doomsday; and the Devil may pull as hard as he will at the other, yet I trust that mine shall weigh him down." So he passed

[1] Se Appendix 14.

his hand lovingly over the nearest pillar; and all men streamed out silently, marvelling that Roger could talk like a clerk when it came to saying farewell to his own work. Then they went out into the glimmering sunshine, and crossed the great market place, and down the narrow lane past St. George's Gild-hall to the ferry; for they wished to see the last of Geoffrey Billing, freest man of hand and of speech in the whole lodge, who was bound for Walpole with his wife and children, and with John Franklin and Thomas Goddard for his work-fellows. The crabbed uncouth old ferryman took them with few words into his ancient boat, for all the world like Charon

KING'S LYNN FROM THE RIVER, ST. MARGARET'S CHURCH IN CENTRE, ST. NICHOLAS ON LEFT.

in the Æneid or in the Inferno. First he made them pay their fare, and looked well to the coins; for he had no special regard for mason-folk in general, and somewhat less than ordinary respect for Franklin and Goddard, who drank often at the Ferry Boat Inn and were quarrelsome in their cups. Then he put off from the slimy shore, right into the swinging tide, with a few swift silent eddies to break the oily surface, and mists curling up from the water, so that the boat and the boatful were almost hidden before they reached the other shore, from whence Margaret Billing's cry of farewell sounded eerie and despairing over that dim distance. And indeed she was in no merry mood; for now this Franklin and this Goddard would be brought far closer to her husband in

Q

the smaller Lodge of Walpole. But that must be; that was in the way of business; so the wayfarers landed at West Lynn, and followed the old Roman bank, clear

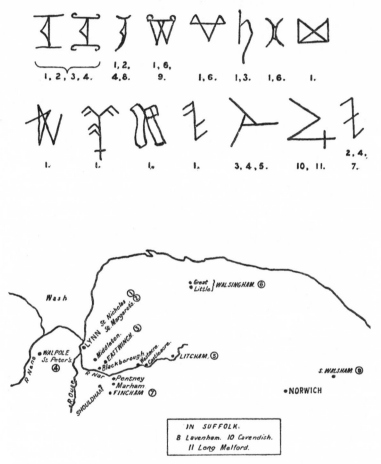

WANDERING MASONS IN NORFOLK.

above the marshes, with a whole day's journey to Walpole before them.

The rest turned back over the market-place, down Jews' Lane and along by the precinct-wall of the Austin

Friars, and so to the East Gate, where they divided again. Hindley was bound for Litcham; while Roger Piggott and Walter Foster and Sandro of Genoa had heard of work at Walsingham. So these four, with a hearty farewell to Hugh Rose, took the causeway to Gaywood, and thence past the Bishop's Palace, and over the sandy heath of Leziate, to their rough night-quarters at Gayton. Here the host gave them plenty of straw in a stable-corner, with cold bacon and ale; and next day also the whole party rested at Gayton for Alison Piggott's sake, who went heavily because she was great with child.

On the third day, William Hindley went on to Litcham; and there we may leave him for a while. As a man who had done good work for Lynn, he was now set over the half-dozen masons and wallers and labourers recruited from the Litcham neighbourhood; and there he followed old John Ford, the master-mason of St. Nicholas, in his trick of the St. Andrew's Cross in the window-tracery, and in the main section of the pillars, and the engrailed abacus to the pilasters. So much, then, for Hindley at Litcham.

But the others (except Walter Foster, who pressed on now to the end of his journey) got no farther than the five miles across Massingham Heath; for Alison soon wearied again, and Sandro would not leave Roger. For when Sandro's father, the drunken shipman from Genoa, had brought him here to Lynn and had perished soon afterwards in a tavern brawl, then it was Roger who took charge of the fourteen-year-old boy and persuaded John Ford to take him on as apprentice; for the lad was as quick and imitative as a monkey, and looked like a monkey with his black eyes under shaggy black hair, and could be as mischievous as any ape. With all that, he had thoughts which flashed out at times and surprised these Englishmen; and it was he, almost before he had learned to handle a chisel for himself, who put into John Ford's head the main motive of that great west window, with a hovering as of angels' wings and a great cross in the centre that rose quite naturally from the steps that were needed to

give room for the great west door. This the boy had set
out one night on the tavern table, dipping his forefinger
in his beer ; and Ford generously acknowledged his debt
with praise and with money. But at other moments
Sandro tried old John's patience sorely ; and then Roger
had always stood by him, sheltering him like a father even
though he cuffed him like a father, and doing his best to
keep the boy from his inherited vice of drink ; so that
these two loved each other like Jack Sprat and his wife.
All men might have seen that, even as they went across
Massingham Heath. There was Roger, with his long face
and long nose and long beard and long body, set upon
one of the shortest pair of legs that ever carried mortal
man, stepping forth firmly and steadily with Alison on
his arm, while Sandro went before and behind and around,
and would have helped Alison also if she could have
borne with his uneven steps. But his laughter and his
talk constantly weaned her from darker thoughts ; and
at Massingham the three found straw again, and good
bread and cheese, and sound ale. And, what Alison cared
for even more than meat and drink, here they found
a good friar in the inn, a limitour from the Franciscans
of Walsingham, who was come to preach for to-morrow's
Mass at Massingham ; for this was the eve of the Nativity
of the Blessed Virgin, and all folk knew that the Blessed
Virgin was more truly present at Walsingham than in any
other place, and that the long trail of starlight which
some men call the Milky Way is indeed the Walsingham
Way, divinely ordained as a guide for pilgrims to her
shrine. This truth Brother Laurence did not fail to
impress upon his hearers next day, on that September 8,
1417 ; and then, after Mass, Alison besought him to
hear her in confession. For she had worse fears now
than ever before, and she knew that the friar had more
powers of absolution than the parish priest. Of all the
eight children with whom she had travailed, only one
was now alive, the little girl whom she had left at Lynn
as sewing-maid to the Black Ox by St. Margaret's Church ;

and now she herself was aged before her time with hard work; and her pains might well be worse than ever before, and less hope than ever for this ninth child's life, and less reason to hope. So she made her full confession, and was shriven, and went home to the inn to face the morrow in greater calm of spirit. And there at the inn was Brother Laurence again; and, for his sake, the host made them all welcome, and gave Sandro more ale than was good for that Italian head, and stood at his door to watch the little company move slowly northward across the common. As they went, Brother Laurence spoke words of comfort to Alison for her seven lost children, all duly baptized and taken in the age of innocence to Heaven, where they waited to greet their mother after her weary pilgrimage on earth. And, finding how sorely she feared for herself, and how she envied the good fortune of Margaret Billing at Walpole, (for at Walpole St. Godric of Finchale was born, and St. Godric's girdle was sovereign for women in peril of childbirth), then the good friar told her how God's providence was everywhere greater than St. Godric; and he went on to cheer her in Scripture words that seemed suited to her state. For he cited from Isaiah those words which speak of God's care for all men, and of pardon earned by patient suffering: "Comfort ye, comfort ye my people, saith your God; speak ye comfortably to Jerusalem, and cry unto her that her warfare is accomplished, that her iniquity is pardoned, for she hath received of the Lord's hand double for all her sins. . . . He shall feed his flock like a shepherd; he shall gather the lambs with his arm, and carry them in his bosom, and shall gently lead those that are with young." So with this they came to the farther edge of the common, and Alison sat down on a bank by the wayside, for, though the words had put fresh heart into her, her strength was not equal to her spirit. She besought him to say that last sentence over again; but at that moment there appeared, just over the little rise to their left, coming from Little Massingham and making northward like themselves, a peasant with an unladen ass. The men hailed him, and he bent round to wait for them, for he was a Walsingham man well known to Brother Laurence. Sandro, who by this time was mellow and pious with ale, swore that here was the finger of God; and, as the peasant and the ass and the poor woman led the way slowly forward, then the artist

ON MASSINGHAM HEATH.

in him awoke also, and he dreamed of a flight into Egypt that he would carve some day, when he should become master-mason in his turn. Meanwhile, he went forward, singing all that he could remember (and more too, for he had a lively imagination) of the ballad of Walsingham:

> " Unto the town of Walsingham
> The way is hard for to be gone
> And very crooked are those paths
> For you to find out all alone."

And he bawled so lustily and so long that, long before they were come to Rudham, his throat was very dry again ; and at Rudham, too, there was good ale ; for the traffic was brisk everywhere along this Pilgrims' Way. It was a merrily pious and almost unctuous Sandro that went into this Rudham inn ; and the rest of the company had reached Tatterset before he caught them up, merry still, but with a wild and boisterous flux of speech ; for he was now at his usual middle stage of liquor ; a few cups more, and he would presently be quarrelsome-drunk. They heard him chant as he came up, from a poem which was new in those days, and which all the company had often heard in scraps from minstrels at the ale :—

> " Heremites on an heap, With hookëd stavës
> Wenten to Walsingham, And their wenches after,
> Great lubbers and long, That loth were to work. . . .
> I found there friars Of all the four Orders,
> Preaching the people For profit of the belly,
> And glosing the gospel As them good likëd,
> For coveteise of copës Construed it as they would.
> Many of these master friars May clothen them at liking
> For their money and merchandize Marchen together."

" Peace, man ! " said the friar. " Half an hour agone thou thyself wast glosing of God's providence."

" Providence ! nay, wise men know better. Who is the best-deserving creature in this company ? is it not this poor woman, who can scarce stay herself on the beast's back until the journey's end ? And who next, but her good man, who can do naught to mend all this and must needs trudge on as dumb as an ox ? Yet there in the inn at Rudham I found the lord's bailiff, who had just taken a dead man's best beast for an heriot, and this fellow was merry in his cups, ailing naught and caring naught " :—

> " The most part of this people That passeth on this earth,
> Have they worship in this world, They willen no better ;
> Of other heaven than here Hold they no tale."

" Peace, fellow," repeated the friar angrily, " thou

annoyest this poor woman for whom thou professest pity.
Take heed to that which the Wise Man saith : ' As he
that taketh away a garment in cold weather, and as
vinegar upon nitre, so is he that singeth songs to a heavy
heart.' " But the untimely jester was not to be silenced,
"Aye, Brother Laurence ; the devil can cite Scripture to
his purposes, and the friar, the friar—

> ' Alas,' quoth he, ' I am in the well ! '
> ' No matter,' quoth she, ' if thou wert in hell. . . .'
> The friar he went all along the street,
> And shaking his lugs like a well-washen sheep. . . . "

"Thou knowest that ballad of *The Friar and the
Well* ? " Here Roger took two steps forward, and caught
Sandro by the arm. The younger man kept his look of
defiance for a moment ; but he saw something in Piggott's
eye which spoke even more plainly than Brother Laurence ;
and, shaking himself free, he fell to the rear and shuffled
on in sulky silence.

In silence the rest now trudged on before him ; and,
soon after sunset they were at Walsingham, where
Brother Laurence found them food and lodging. Here,
therefore, Alison found some measure of rest, while the
men took to their work, and presently the brand-new
parish church began to rise in place of that little Norman
building, patched up in all sorts of later styles, which
the prosperous folk of New Walsingham had grown
ashamed of for its smallness and its gloom, so that they
were willing to spend freely now upon a greater sanctuary
built in the latest style. But poor Alison's forebodings
came true in the end, and the new-born babe was buried
at the mother's breast ; and some folk said that it was
a happy release for both. So Roger became a more
silent man than ever, and presently he lost even his
friend Sandro ; for men missed the Italian from the
lodge for ten whole days on end, and some said he was
drinking in one of the villages round, and others said that
he was praying ; and presently Brother Laurence came in
with the tidings that they had taken him into the friary

as a novice. Here was a nine days' wonder! some crossed themselves, and others jested; but Roger turned without a word to his stone again, and smote on in settled gloom; his mallet clicked like a mill-wheel, but he was very desolate at heart.

And then the nine days' wonder grew old; and the next news was that Sandro had gone out again, casting his frock to the nettles. In his later life, when he went about as a Lollard, and before he was converted again to an equal extreme of orthodoxy, this Walsingham incident was one of his sorest points; we have it in his own words, in the poem that he wrote against his old masters :—

> " Off I cast my friar's clothing
>   And wightly went my gate.
> Other leave me took I none,
>   From them when I went,
> But took them to the devil each one,
>   The prior and his convent.
> Out of the Order though I be gone,
> Apostata ne am I none,
> Of twelve months me wanted one,
>   And odd days nine or ten.
> Away to wend I made me bound,
> Ere time come of professioun;
> I went my way throughout the town
>   In sight of many men."

And so far he was right; as a novice, he had taken no vows; apostate he was not; yet all orderly folk looked askance at a man who, having once put his hand to the plough, had looked back. And so also, among others, did Roger Piggott; who, a few days later, knocked at the Walsingham friary and besought admission as a novice, to redeem his friend's vow. Then, though the friars refused him at first (for he would never have made a priest and a limitour) yet he was so humbly insistent, and so anxious to do any menial work in the convent, and so determined to offer himself otherwise as a lay-brother to the canons of the great Austin Priory, that the Franciscans took him at last, and never found cause to repent.

So Roger wrought no more stones for New Walsingham church.

Meanwhile, Sandro drifted off towards Norwich, where, as he heard, great things would soon be doing. Halfway, at Bawdeswell, he found a great barn a-building, and offered himself for the rough work in carpentry, being jack of all trades and master of none. The carpenter was a slender choleric man, true son to his father Oswald the reeve, who by this time had feathered his own nest in a small way, and sat all day long in his chimney-corner, talking of old-world chaffer and old-world quarrels with the miller. He harped always on the perversity of the modern world, and on those fair spring days of forty years agone, when he had ridden on his pilgrimage to the holy blissful martyr at Canterbury, by the side of a king's squire named Geoffrey Chaucer, who had many cousins at Lynn and elsewhere in those parts of Norfolk and Suffolk ; and, since the old man had the brown jug always beside his chair, Sandro came and listened nightly to his stories for a few weeks. But at last, by mishap, he broke an axe-haft at his work; and (for he had overdrawn two weeks' pay, and no fine was to be got from him), his choleric master laid wait for him next morning on the Norwich road, to take the runaway and put him in the stocks. Therefore Sandro rose a little before dawn, and went not eastward to Norwich but westward to Litcham, where he found William Hindley and got a few more days' work, though indeed the lodge was full already. William was a man of business, somewhat hard and unimaginative ; else (said Sandro openly to his fellows), the man would never have copied the tricks of St. Nicholas so slavishly, but would rather have struck out something new for himself. So Sandro knew himself for a stranger and a sojourner on sufferance at Litcham ; and, hearing news of fresh wars in France, and of masons pressed to go overseas for the Regent Bedford, he took the road to Lynn and the ship to France, with half-a-dozen Bohemians like himself, and one sober married man, caught on the road and taken from his wife and family, who was justly aghast to find himself in such company. Once in France, Sandro did as more than one mason did before and after him, quitting the mallet and chisel for the longbow, and shooting Frenchmen by rule instead of rabbits and fat swans against the law. So he fought under Suffolk on the heath of La Brécinière, where he was beaten and ran away, to fight again at Cravant, where, of our Scottish enemies alone, 1,200 were left on the field, and it was a glorious victory; but Sandro came back to Lynn with a broken head, less master of himself than ever. He heard that Hugh Rose was still working at East Winch, and Hugh had always been as friendly to him as the Good Apprentice can well be to the Idle Apprentice; so to Winch Sandro went, and worked for a whole fortnight without overstepping the bounds of mellowness in liquor; for he knew that Hugh was a frequent water-drinker and somewhat more precise in this matter than most mason-folk. But, on the fifteenth day, Sandro spent twelve long hours on end at the Green Dragon, from dawn to dark; and on the sixteenth morning he was taking a hair of the dog that bit him, when in strode Hugh, and took him by the arm without further ceremony, and brought him to his work. There he stood, looking at his banker like a naughty unwashed child, and saying that, if only the good God would let him be drunken for two days out of three, and if Hugh Rose would give him good stone to fashion freely out of his own head, then he would show these tailed English folk how the carvers wrought in Italy. But the rest only heaved their shoulders and laughed; so Sandro took up his tools with a curse, and, for the next hour, sent the chips flying faster than any two of the rest; after which he went out for five minutes, and came back wiping his mouth, and overflowing again with marvellous tales of war and adventure. Thus then it went on, with alternate April showers and sunshine in the Lodge, for the next few months, until Hugh Rose's death. But here we must go back, and see a little more of Hugh's own life, and how he had come to East Winch in 1417 and how he worked there now.

On that September morning on which he parted from his last four companions, and must now go forth alone, he had looked wistfully after them for a few minutes, and then turned to seek his own new work. Keeping inside the town walls for half a mile, he then turned out through Gannock Gate, and so along the causeway that ran through the marshy Chase to Hardwick and Middleton. There he left Lord Scales's castle on the left hand, and Blackborough nunnery on the right, and came to the edge of the gentle hill that looks down upon East Winch, and sat down for a while by the roadside to brood at ease over the prospect that lay spread before him. For, in such level country as this of West Norfolk, a very small eminence gives a wide perspective; and many thoughts come crowding in upon the lonely wayfarer who has cause and leisure for meditation. Sir John Howard of East Winch had resolved to build a new church, worthy of the growing honours of his family, which had begun nearly a century and a half earlier with his great-great-grandfather, the good Judge Sir William, and were destined in the near future to grow far greater by for-tunate marriages, until at last these Howards should become Dukes of Norfolk. One day, therefore, when Sir John had come into Lynn, where his ancestor had first come to honour and where the family had frequent business, he had bidden John Ford to his lodging at the Golden Lion, and had asked him to name some trusty mason for his purpose. So Ford had brought Hugh Rose with him; and it was agreed that Hugh should come to East Winch as soon as St. Nicholas was finished, and should there recruit an apprentice and three journeymen to work under him, and should rebuild the church from ground-stone to ridge-tile. All this was in Hugh's mind, as he sat now and looked down upon his future work. His eye swept the whole horizon from north to south;

band after band of woodland and stubble and fallow, stubble and fallow and wood, deepening afar into transparent grey, and then swelling gently up again, on the blue horizon, into the wooded ridge that looked down, within a radius of ten miles, upon nine abbeys and priories besides those of Lynn; Flitcham and Wendling, Castleacre and Westacre, Pentney and Marham, Shouldham and Wormegay and Blackborough. And here, in the very midst of that large and liberal landscape, the little church of East Winch was set as an eyetrap, with the line of road leading inevitably down to it, and a momentary glint of sunlight upon tower and village, and, behind, the clouds and their wandering shadows. In space, that little white building filled only the tiniest part of the picture; yet the whole landscape seemed to exist only for its sake. Therefore to Hugh, who had the quiet meditative eye of a shepherd, and who saw things more in their breadth than in detail, this scene at this moment seemed prophetic of all his future work. He thought of old John Ford's words, so often repeated to him or to others in the lodge: " Make it worthy, young man "—worthy, as Chaucer uses the word for the quiet dignity of his knight, and yet a more homely word than ours, as all life was more homely then than now—" Make it worthy, though the thing in itself were no more than a pig-sty." And that is why, to this very day, Hugh Rose's church stands there in quiet dignity, looking down from its bank to the high-road, and looking up to the road from Lynn. It is of no great size; for this is a small village, and Sir John was a man of no unusual substance for a country knight; yet in its height of arch and clerestory, and in the proportions of chancel and nave and aisles and tower, there is a suggestion of something more than a mere village church; striking, yet unboastful, thoroughly honest both in detail and in mass, making the most of every foot of stone and every penny of money that was put into it. All this, as men may see it realized now, was already in Hugh's mind when he rose from the turf by the roadside and went down to the Green Dragon at East Winch. Five years he worked at the church, he and his journeymen; and in his first year he married the reeve's daughter; and at the end of the fifth, when carpenters and tilers were already busy with the roof, he was taken with a mortal fever. For, as we have seen

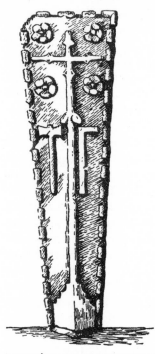

MASON'S TOMB AT EAST WINCH.

already, he was a frequent water-drinker, and that was a perilous diet in those days; else men would not have distinguished certain of their fellows with the name of Drink-water or Boileau or Bevilacqua, and such surnames would have been commoner than they are. The rector honoured Hugh with sepulture in his own church, and Sandro, who truly missed him as much as any man, often talked in his cups of the tomb that he would carve for him, if only Sir John or some Lynn merchant would trust him with the stone; the figure of a true master-mason, gowned and capped, with angels bending over his head on either side; such a tomb, in short, as Italian marblers would make, and such as no man had seen in England. But, in the end, it was Geoffrey Billing who came over from Walpole to take Hugh's place; for in this year 1423 the masons and carpenters had nearly finished at Walpole, and the glaziers would soon be at work, and Geoffrey was glad enough to leave a lodge where things went mainly after the fashion of John Franklin and Thomas Goddard. There he undertook the tomb himself; and each of the journeymen at East

Winch paid a penny a week for the next half-year, and the Warden of the Trinity Gild at Lynn sold at a low price (for he had known Hugh and loved him) one of those foreign tombstones in which the Gild always dealt, and Geoffrey, as a labour of love, wrought it himself, not after any Italian dream, but in good straightforward English fashion, with a cross and four roses and the mason's hammer and square, and battlements all round the edge to recall the Heavenly Jerusalem; and there it is to the present day.

William Hindley trudged the highway less, and prospered more in the world, than all the rest. He finished Litcham in uninspired but blameless fashion, so much to the satisfaction of all folk that news came of him to Norwich, where there was no lack of building work on hand. Here, he settled for a while, and, being a personable man, and having saved while most of his fellows spent, he married a not unprosperous mercer's daughter and thus gained burgher's right in one of the busiest towns of all England. And when Sir Thomas Erpingham, Shakespeare's White-headed Knight of Agincourt, resolved to build a great new gateway that should add honour to the Cathedral Close, and three master-masons of Norwich made drawings for the new work, then William was inspired to imitate, after such fashion as was here possible, the great central arch of the west front at Peterborough, and thus to outdo in size and height that old St. Ethelbert's gate which he could not rival in detail. So this was the drawing which pleased Sir Thomas and the lord prior; and thenceforward William was a made man; and in process of time his fame reached the canons of York, who wanted a new master to build their choir; and men may still read the record of how they fetched him over to their work: " By way of reward to William Hindley, by grace of the Dean and Chapter, in subsidy and recompense for his outlays, both in the matter of conveying his wife and children and goods from the city of Norwich to York, and also in defence of

ERPINGHAM GATE, NORWICH.

the suit which has been prosecuted against him in London, maliciously and without just cause, by his adversaries, the sum of one hundred shillings." [1]

---

[1] *York Fabric Rolls*, Surtees Soc., p. 80. The editor speculates : "Could he have thrown up a situation contrary to agreement, or was he in debt ? "

R

CHAPTER XIII

SYMBOLISM

WE have seen how M. Émile Mâle emphasizes the power of tradition, and the comparative infrequency of innovation, in medieval art. Both this general tradition and these occasional innovations have often been attributed to the direct action of the Church. There is a special tendency to over-emphasize the force of medieval symbolism; Ruskin certainly exaggerated here, taking a few remarkable buildings for his text and knowing little of the exact documentary history of the Middle Ages; and Ruskin's imitators have stumbled into still wilder fancies. Even Émile Mâle seems to exaggerate also; every student of this subject must acknowledge a heavy debt to him, yet there are implications in his valuable volumes which are scarcely reconcilable with the full documentary evidence. Here and there we do find evidence for an ecclesiastic giving fairly minute directions to the artist. Mâle makes full use of Abbot Suger's extraordinarily valuable account of his own prescriptions to the workmen at St.-Denis. This, no doubt, is in the main accurate; but it has been pointed out by careful students that the abbot seems, naturally enough, to magnify his own office here, and to minimize the factor of artistic, quite apart from ecclesiastical, tradition. Again, Jocelin of Brakelond tells us how Abbot Samson of St. Edmundsbury did this; and Gregory of Tours gives us the case of Namatia.[1] This lady's husband, who was bishop of le Puy, died in 423; and the widow built the basilica of St. Stephen there. " She was wont to hold a book on her knees, reading therefrom tales of the

[1] P.L., vol. lxxi, col. 215.

deeds of the men of old, and pointing out to the painters
what they should show forth on the walls." But, when
we come to the great centuries of Gothic art, it would be
almost as difficult to find a parallel for this lady's artistic
activities as for her marital experiences. In the vast
majority of cases the ecclesiastical patron seems simply
to have prescribed the subject in general, just as a sports-
man of to-day will ask a painter to supply him with a
horse-race, a fox-hunt, or a flight of wild-fowl. The
artist then worked this subject out in accordance with
tradition or with his own fancy. Henry VI.'s specifications for his two royal chapels accord pretty exactly with
this supposition. Yet the hierarchy, if they had thought
it worth while, could easily have gone much farther than
this, and could have drawn up one or more manuals for
the direction of artists. Mâle suspects the existence of
such books, but he gives no evidence; and it is scarcely
credible that, if any serious effort had been made, no
trace of it should be left. For the direction of parish
clergy in preaching and catechetical instruction, as we
know, a large number of manuals were composed, some
of them by diocesan synods or provincial councils;
and when Jean Gerson, in the early fifteenth century,
pleaded emphatically for the better instruction of parish
priests, he suggested that some still more authoritative
manual should be drawn up to supersede this hetero-
geneous multitude. In the Eastern Church there was
indeed an art-manual which enjoyed something of the
authority of these ordinary preachers' manuals; a book of
about 1180, surviving only in a later réchauffé discovered
by Didron in a convent at Mount Athos, and accessible
now in print.[1] Yet this book itself never had any formal
authority; and painters took the liberty of adding to
it, generation by generation. In the West there was not

[1] Dionysius, Ἑρμηνεία τῶν Ζωγραφῶν, 2nd ed., by A. Constan-
tinides. Athens, 1885. I am now informed by Prof. E. H. Minns that
the book is far more recent than Didron thought, and there is little in it
which can be directly traced back to the Middle Ages.

even this rudimentary centralization of artistic tradition ; and it seems fairly evident that some of the things which seem most striking in their uniformity—the schematic presentation of the Seven Liberal Arts, and so on—are mainly confined to great monasteries and cathedrals, finding no echo in the ordinary churches.[1]

Far more potent, doubtless, was the more indirect ecclesiastical influence ; artists caught hints from priests just as the Pre-Raphaelites did from Malory and from Tennyson ; and, in the later generations, there was very intimate action and interaction between the spectacular side of the miracle play and the didactic side of church art. The oft-quoted sentence, " The Church was the Poor Man's Bible," admittedly contains a very great deal of truth ; the problem at the present stage is to fix as nearly as possible the limits of that truth.

Here, as so often elsewhere, the falsehood of to-day has grown quite naturally from the distortion of what was yesterday's epigrammatic catchword. When young Goethe was a student at Strassburg, he discovered the beauty and significance of the Minster there ; and from Goethe, through Scott, came one strong factor in the English Romantic Revival. Victor Hugo, again, owed much to Goethe ; and *Notre Dame de Paris* emphasized and stereotyped what the great German had only sketched. There, for instance, we read in the second chapter of the fifth book : " From the beginning of the world, down to the end of the fifteenth century, architecture is the great book of the human race. . . . It fixed, under an eternal, visible, palpable form, all the floating symbolism [of the past]. . . . Thus, during the first six thousand years of the world's history, from the most immemorial pagoda of Hindostan down to the cathedral of Cologne, architecture is the great written document of mankind."

A great stone thus cast into world-literature is naturally followed by ripples which widen in proportion as they subside and travel farther from the original word of

[1] Schlosser, *Beiträge*, pp. 147 ff.

THE WEST WINDOW OF ST. NICHOLAS AT LYNN.

genius that started them. The modern form of Victor Hugo's thought, naturally magnified by ecclesiastical bias, may be not unfairly reproduced here in quotation from a recent newspaper report. The reporter is giving the impression left on his mind by a lecture delivered to a meeting of Anglican churchmen at the Church House, organized by the *Catholic Literature Association*, (*Church Times*, May 13, 1921). The speaker was a prominent University teacher ; and, though the report may be far from verbally faithful, yet it shows how his words were understood by the representative of a very ably-conducted paper ; and, thence, the instruction which that paper communicated, on a subject of primary importance in religious and artistic history, to several thousand educated readers who are mainly dependent upon periodical literature of this kind.

The report runs : " Fr—— followed, with a delightful and extremely informative speech. Going back some six or seven hundred years ago, ' long before the troubled seas of the Reformation,' he pointed out how the Middle Ages had always been taught by one thing, art. The nature of God, the doctrines of religion, the virtues of saints were all taught by art, in pictures, statues and windows, so that it had been very justly said that in the Middle Ages the cathedral was the Bible of the Poor. It was the thing that everyone saw, which in every detail taught the Catholic Faith. Sometimes the individual parts seemed a strange jumble, but they all gave exactly the same teaching and the same message, and though it was art, it was also science. It was never left to individual fancy ; it was a very strictly ordered science, a science of symbols ; for everyone looked at everything that he saw with his outward eyes as having a deep spiritual meaning, so that everyone in those days was a natural sacramentalist. And that symbolism the Church did not allow to run riot, but restrained it by very strict rules, and the artist did better work because he was disciplined ; while the people, both simple and educated, learned, loved and prayed." This is rather an extreme case, yet not unfair to choose ; for something very like it may be read in most modern books or magazine articles dealing with the subject. Nor is it confined to ecclesiastics ; imaginative masons, at the other end of the scale, have supposed all the grotesques in medieval art to be anti-clerical satires. These exaggerations spring from the fact of which Julius v. Schlosser complained, that medieval art has too often been treated either by art-lovers who had not read the documents, or by documentary scholars who had no feeling for art. The latter, naturally enough, get little popularity ; it is the former who pass on to journalists these distorted echoes from great imaginative writers of the past. It needs some historical reading and reflection to realize that not one poor Englishman in a score had ever set eyes upon a cathedral in the Middle Ages, and that there was far less unity of faith then than is commonly represented. But the briefest reflection ought to have warned this lecturer that he must not claim " the nature of God " as a thing adequately set forth in medieval art, wherein the Almighty is represented, perhaps more frequently than not, as an old man crowned with a triple tiara such as the popes wear.

But there is one book written by a real scholar and needing more serious treatment, since it has perhaps done more than any other to foster exaggerations on this subject ; this is Didron's *Christian Iconography*. Didron was one of the leaders of the Gothic revival in France ; his *Annales archéologiques* rendered priceless services in their day, and he had a wide knowledge not only of the churches themselves but of many medieval documents. Yet, as an enthusiastic churchman, he was tempted everywhere to exaggerate the rôle of his Church ; and sometimes, as may be traced by anyone who will carefully sift his arguments and follow up his references, he did this in the very face of contradictory evidence from the actual records to which he was appealing. For instance, he writes (p. 6 of Vol. I in the English translation): " A sculptured arch in the porch of a church, or an historical glass painting in the nave, presented the ignorant with a lesson, the believer with a sermon which reached the heart through the eyes instead of entering at the ears. The impression, besides, was infinitely deeper; for it is acknowledged that a picture sways the soul far more powerfully than any discourse or description in words." He then quotes from Venantius Fortunatus: " ' If any should inquire why, contrary to common usage, I have given personal representations of holy people in this sacred dwelling, I answer: ' Among the crowds attracted hither by the fame of St. Felix, there are peasants recently converted, who cannot read, and who, before embracing the faith of Christ, had long been the slaves of profane usages, and had obeyed their senses as gods. They arrive here from afar, and from all parts of the country. Glowing with faith, they despise the chilling frosts; they pass the entire night in joyous watchings; they drive away slumber by gaiety, and darkness by torches. But they mingle festivities with their prayers, and, after singing hymns to God, abandon themselves to good cheer; they joyously stain with odoriferous wine the tombs of the saints. They sing in the midst of their cups, and, by their drunken lips, the demon insults St. Felix. I have, therefore, thought it expedient to enliven with paintings the entire habitation of the Holy Saint. Images thus traced and coloured will perhaps inspire those rude minds with astonishment. Inscriptions are placed above the pictures, in order that the letter may explain what the hand has depicted. While showing them to each other, and reading thus by turns these pictured objects, they do not think of eating till later than before—their eyes aid them to endure fasting. . . . A great part of the time being spent in looking at their pictures, they drink much less, for there remain only a few short minutes for their repast.' "

Note here how little the actual text bears out Didron's

main contentions. In the first place, the pictures are
evidently spoken of only as a *pis aller*. And, secondly,
there is no hint here that the pictures were supposed to
be more impressive than more explicit teaching by word
of mouth or by books. On the contrary, it is implicitly
confessed that they actually need the written word to
help them out : " the letter " has to " explain what the
hand has depicted." And such was the common practice
all through the Middle Ages, down to the artists whose
lives Vasari wrote, and of whom he often records how
they put long explanatory legends to their pictures.[1]
Moreover, this was not only implicitly confessed in the
Middle Ages, it was also explicitly asserted. Rabanus
Maurus, Archbishop of Mainz (d. 856), one of the greatest
of medieval theologians, is most unfavourable to painting
as a means of edification in comparison with the written
word. " For," he says, " writing is of more profit than
the vain pictured form, and it brings more ornament to
the mind than the feigned painting of colours, which
show not rightly the figures of things. . . . This [writing]
serves our ears, our eyes, our gaze ; that [pictorial art]
offers only a little solace to the eyes. . . . This latter,
when new, is pleasant to the sight, but burdensome
when it is old ; it will soon fail, and it is no faithful
guardian of truth. Consider who were the inventors and
followers of these things. . . . The Egyptians were the
first to paint light and shade ; but it was the Lord who
graved letters on the rock." [2] Again, St. Bernardino of
Siena is quite explicit here. Speaking of his *I.H.S.*
monograms, which he used as a stimulus to devotion, he
says that they may serve as a continual reminder to us,
" like the pictures which recall to you the Blessed Virgin
or other saints, which pictures are made only in memory
of the said saints. Note, therefore, that there are four
kinds of letters, each better than the other. The first

---

[1] Cf. also Schlosser, *Beiträge* (*Sitzungsb.*, vol. cxxiii, 1891), pp. 15 ff, and
Libri Carolini in Migne P.L., vol. xcviii, pp. iii, 23.
[2] P.L., vol. cxii, col. 1608.

kind are gross letters for rude folk, as for example pictures; the next, for men of middle sort, are middle
letters, as, for example, written letters; and these are
better than the first. The third are vocal letters, found
for those men who desire actively to busy themselves for
charity's sake, pleading and discoursing, in order that
they may be learned and may teach others; and these
excel the two first. Fourthly and lastly come the mental
letters, ordained by God for those who desire to per-
severe always in contemplation; and this is more perfect
than the others and exceeds them all." [1] Sensible folk in
the Middle Ages were a great deal less medieval than
some of their more enthusiastic modern champions. It
is not only paradoxical, but anachronistic, to suppose that
pictorial art was ever more valuable for religious teaching
than the written or spoken word. Orthodox Catholics
can be found who feel equally strongly in our own day.
" Could the people really understand [this multitude of
subjects] since even educated people of to-day need
scholars to explain them ? " [2] But modern sentimentalism
often chooses, for its vain regrets, just the very things
from which the best men of the past were struggling hard to free themselves. That ignorance of letters,
which is sometimes treated now as a virtue in religion,
was in its own time commonly and rightly regarded as a
defect. Nor is this false perspective confined to history;
a *Spectator* correspondent quoted, some five-and-twenty
years ago, the comment of a lady friend whose cook had
cheated her : " I *did* think the woman was honest, for
she could not even read ! "

---

[1] *Opp.*, ed. de la Haye, 1745, vol. i, p. 282. (*Fer. II post dom. vi quad.
serm.* 40). Again, when he complains that " innumerable [religious]
errors are multiplied among the people," he does not trace this to lack of
pictures in the churches, but to lack of preaching from the pulpit ; a
population which hears no preaching (he insists) grows up " incomparably " more irreligious than a population which has no Mass. (*Serm. X.
in Domin. Prima in Quadrag.*)

[2] J. Buteux, in a paper read before the Soc. d'Émulation d'Abbeillev
(*Mém. S. d'E. d'A.*, 1852, p. 714).

We cannot do justice to medieval symbolism unless we realize how truly it was born of the popular mind. To say (with the writer first quoted) that the different parts all gave exactly the same teaching, and that it was never left to individual fancy but was a very strictly ordered science, is almost the direct opposite of the truth. It would be truer, on the contrary, to say that it was born in the popular mind, born of childlike impulses, and treated like a child's toy, to be played with and distorted and broken and finally forgotten; and then, perhaps, picked up again, and again broken and distorted and forgotten.[1] To put it thus is to exaggerate in the contrary direction, but only by omitting, and not by mis-stating, facts. There was indeed an effort, in certain quarters, to create a science of symbolism in the Middle Ages. But those who attempted this worked, like the scholastic philosophers, on a basis which they had inherited by no choice of their own; a basis built up, in great part, from popular fancies which had gradually crystallized into tradition, and must thenceforward be accepted even by serious thinkers, under pain of condemnation for suspicious free-thought. The symbolist period in medieval writings coincides very closely with the beginnings of the scholastic period. But, whereas the paramount importance of its special subject-matter kept scholasticism alive, after a fashion at least, to the very end of the Middle Ages and beyond, yet the difficulties of making symbolism into a science were perhaps equally great, and the subject itself had obviously far less importance. Aquinas accepted the popular eschatology, and wove it into his philosophical system with marvellous labour and skill. An equally great mind might, by the devotion of a life-time, have welded popular ideas of artistic symbolism into an equally harmonious and durable whole;

---

[1] This transpires, though only indirectly, from such a monograph as Canon J. Fossey's *L'art religieux dans les diocèses de Rouen et d'Évreux*. We there see how often popular taste was a more potent factor than ecclesiastical direction; cf. pp. 97, 99, 104, 106, 121.

but the game was evidently not worth the candle. There never existed, therefore, a complete and authoritative system of symbolism in medieval art. Some of the most important points were left to individual choice, others were interpreted differently by different writers, or by the same writer. Émile Mâle's valuable volumes show how much was systematized ; yet it is equally important, at the present time, to show how much was left unsystematized, and how little of the system (so far as that word can be strictly used) was imposed by the hierarchy from above. The most distinguished of all symbolist writers was only a bishop ; he wrote only in his private capacity ; he quotes no papal or conciliar confirmation of his symbolic interpretations ; he sometimes suggests alternative, and even contradictory, interpretations of the same thing.

Julius v. Schlosser, in his *Beiträge zur Kunstgeschichte u.s.w.*, traces admirably the earlier indications of symbolism. These point strongly to the popular imagination as chief formative factor ; it was not so much that things were fashioned after symbolic rules, as that rules were invented to account for the fashion in which the things themselves had grown. Most men, in the early days of Christianity, sought for " types," strove to explain the visible by reference to the invisible ; and, when nearly all men lean one way, the result will roughly reflect the crowd-mind. The Middle Ages found something supernatural in the remains of antique art ; hence those legends of Virgil the Magician, frequently connected with some striking edifice or statue. There was something devilish in those ancient figures, with their resemblance to life, and their mysterious posture or expression of face. And, as men sought for hidden meanings here, they sought no less busily in the sphere of orthodox religion. We miss the whole spirit of the Middle Ages unless we bear constantly in mind that the pagan gods were as truly existent as the Trinity or the Virgin Mary. In goodness, of course, the differences

were immeasurable ; but in existence there was no
practical difference ; as truly as Christ was God, so
truly were Jupiter or Mahomet or Thor existent devils.
Therefore men strove equally hard, and perhaps even
earlier, to find a hidden meaning in Christian as in pagan
art. As early as the fourth century a church resting on
twelve pillars is treated as symbolic of the twelve apostles.
Later, when St. Michael's chapel at Fulda rested on
eight pillars, these were intrepreted as the eight beati-
tudes. Abbot Angilbert is often quoted for the symbolism of the Abbey of St.-Riquier, which he describes
as built on a triangular plan, in honour of the Trinity.[1]
But Schnaase shows, from Mabillon's engraving of this
abbey taken from an old MS., " that symbolism had little
influence even here ; or at most a very subordinate
influence." The three churches are not contemporaneous,
or part of any single plan ; and the shape of the monastery
can be called triangular only in a very loose sense : strictly
speaking, it does not form a triangle at all, but an irregular trapezoid quadrangle ; and the drawing shows
that what prevented it from becoming a more regular
quadrangle was a stream which interfered with the plan.
" It was probably, therefore, an afterthought of the
pious abbot to bring in this allusion to the Trinity."[2]
    In all this, therefore, there was nothing official ; it
was simply the working of the popular mind, or of popular
instincts at the back of more cultivated minds. Men
found in these chance coincidences, exact or loose, the
same sort of mystic truth which they found in the freaks
of nature. The Dominican Johann Nider tells us how,
at the Council of Bâle, a certain distinguished Spanish
ecclesiastic said to him : " I have heard, on good authority, from merchants who have dealt among the Saracens
in the kingdom of Granada, that they have seen there a
fruit-tree whose fruit, however it be cut, is always distinguished by the clear appearance of an image of the

[1] E.g. Didron, vol. i, p. 62 ; vol. ii, p. 32.
[2] Vol. ii, i, p. 295.

THE DOOM AT AUTUN.

crucifix on the cut surface."[1] The story occurs also in one of the thirteenth century friars, who tells us he had seen the fruit himself in the Far East ; I think it is in Odoric of Pordenone. Here we have, in all probability, the banana, of which each section can easily be made by imagination into an image of a crucifix.

A similar childlike faith in chance analogies inspires a twelfth-century book on symbolism, quoted by Schnaase from an unprinted MS. at Düsseldorf (Vol. II, part i, 1850, p. 291). The church walls (says this writer) signify the people ; they are four in number, to show that people flock hither from all four points of the compass. To the west they meet in the corner-stones, as Jews and Christians meet in belief in the Gospel ; eastwards the walls form a semi-circle to show the oneness of the Church. The stones are foursquare, to denote the four virtues (Wisdom, Power, Temperance and Justice). The cement is Charity ; when they are once fixed in their place there is no more sound of axe or hammer ; this betokens that the times of persecution for the Church are over. The windows are square at the bottom, in token of the four cardinal virtues, and round at the top, that they may serve God in perfection ; the glass is brittle, in memory of the brittleness of human prosperity. It is obvious how much this depends not merely upon fancy, but also upon chance conditions. If all this had been a matter of disciplined science, if " the Church had restrained it by very strict rules," how could the round apse and the round arch ever have gone out of fashion ? This mystical oneness of the Church and this religious perfection of the windows were mainly destroyed—were being destroyed, perhaps, at the moment when this pious man was writing—by the Cistercians, that religious Order which perhaps, of all others, was in closest touch with the papacy and in highest favour with the hierarchy. Almost without exception Cistercian churches have a square east end ; and they were among the first to adopt

---

[1] *Formicarius*, Douai, 1602, p. 292.

the pointed arch. One fact, however, this Düsseldorf manuscript may go some way to explain. It has often been noted that, while the pointed arch won its way through its obvious structural advantages, yet the merely ornamental arches, such as window-tops and blind arcades, often remained round for some time after. This has generally been explained by conservatism and by æsthetic preference ; but symbolism also may possibly have had something to do with it. Yet this symbolism was itself an afterthought. Schnaase, two generations ago, pointed out how Durandus's symbolism rests on the Romanesque style, and how it entirely ignores the pointed arch, which had been in use for more than a century, and was by far the most noteworthy feature of the buildings which Durandus saw rising around him.[1] Again, contemporary with the Düsseldorf author was John Beleth, Master of the Schools at Notre Dame de Paris. His *Explicatio Divinorum Officiorum* is mainly concerned with liturgical symbolism, but deals occasionally in the other matters. He, again, shows us how little we must look for strict scientific accuracy ; he tells us in his second chapter that " it is absolutely necessary for the Church to be turned towards the East " ; yet he admits that " some will and do this matter otherwise," as indeed we know from many surviving examples.

This brings us to the classical work on symbolism, Durandus's *Rationale Divinorum Officiorum.* Guillaume Durand was bishop of Mende in Southern France ; he died in 1296, and was thus contemporary with St. Thomas Aquinas and St. Bonaventura. Though he was a bishop, he wrote here only as a private person ; he wished to expound the inner meaning of Church rites and buildings and ornaments as methodically as those saintly scholastics were expounding their heritage of religious dogma. But he was a man of intellectual distinction ; and therefore it is particularly significant to note his omissions and his uncertainties. Much of what he tells us is as obviously

[1] *Gesch. d. bild. Künste,* vol. ii, pt. 1, 1850, p. 297.

invented as the Düsseldorf MS. The four walls here signify not the multitude of people, but the four cardinal virtues. On the other hand, the bell-rope, we are informed, betokens humility, because it hangs downwards ! (Lib. I, c. 1, § 17 ; c. 4, § 8.) Here, again, is his treatment of the ostrich's egg. (Lib. I, c. iii., § 42.) These eggs had been frequent ornaments in Mohammedan mosques ; crusaders brought them home ; and by this time they were sometimes hung in Christian churches. For their presence there Durand first finds the same reason which we ourselves should find ; the eggs were a great curiosity, and he thinks it natural to hang them in the sanctuary " in order that people may thus be brought to church and be the more impressed." But this is not enough ; and " some allege " the following reason. The ostrich is a bird which forgets her own eggs in the sand ; but at length she is reminded of their existence by the sight of a certain star ; whereupon she returns to them and cherishes them by the glance of her eye. In like manner the sinner is allowed by God to lie wallowing in his sins ; but, if he come back to his Maker, then he is cherished by the regard of the Divine Face, even as Luke says that, after the great denial, the Lord looked upon Peter. This is only a specially marked instance of the spirit which pervades the whole book. As Didron says : " Durandus always loves to find an exaggerated symbolical meaning, even at the expense of reason " (I, 273 n.). Pecham, the contemporary Archbishop of Canterbury, finds an explanation equally symbolical but more natural : " Ostrich eggs are hung up in churches and placed before the eyes of prelates for this reason, to warn them against imitating ostriches in their carelessness for their young " (Job xxxix.).[1]

Yet Durandus is our least unsystematic authority. John Beleth, perhaps his nearest rival, is uncertain even as to an important detail of the General Resurrection. Of all the medieval artistic themes, next to the Crucifixion

[1] *Epp.*, R.S., vol. iii, p. 88.

or the Virgin and Child, perhaps the commonest is the
Last Judgment. But here the artist must ask, on the
very threshold: In what form will mankind then rise
from the dead, clothed or naked? Beleth cannot tell
us; nor was there ever, I believe, any pretence of an
authoritative decision. Beleth writes: " Men are
accustomed to ask on this point, whether folk will be
naked or clothed after the Day of Doom. It would
seem that they will be clothed, since angels are always
wont to appear in clothes. . . . On the other hand, it
would seem that they will be naked, for the reason that
we shall be in the same shape as Adam was before his
sin, and even in fairer shape. But let us not presume to
decide anything, whether of the clothing or of its quality,
except this one thing, that there will be neither deformity
nor infirmity."[1] Yet, only one generation earlier than
this, the question had been confidently answered, quite
differently, by the so-called Honorius of Autun. In
his dialogue called *Elucidarium*,[2] the Disciple asks: " Tell
me, what sort of bodies shall the saints have? . . .
will they be clothed, or naked? " To which the Master
answers: " They shall be naked; yet shall they shine
with all comeliness. . . . The salvation of the blessed,
and their gladness, shall be their vesture; for the Lord
shall endue their bodies with the vesture of salvation,
and their souls with the garment of gladness. And, even
as there are here [on earth] divers kinds of flowers, white
in the lilies and red in the roses, so we believe that there
will be divers graces of colours in the bodies of the
blessed, so that martyrs will be of one colour and virgins

[1] *Explicatio*, chap. 159. So also the author of a theological dictionary
of about 1300 (Brit. Mus., MS. Reg. VI, E.6, fol. 58). He discusses this
question, and decides doubtfully in favour of nakedness.

[2] A MS. of the *Elucidarium* describes the author as *Scholasticus* of Autun
Cathedral. But the attribution of the *Elucidarium* has been called in
question; and Wattenbach, followed by other scholars, refer the author
to Augsburg, which would be equally reconcilable with the surname
Augustodunensis. Dr. R. L. Poole is inclined to accept this latter attribution.

THE ANNUNCIATION AT REIMS.

of another; and these shall be counted to them as
garments."[1]   This is the more interesting, since Honorius
wrote about 1130, and the new cathedral at Autun was
dedicated in 1132; and there, on the great west portal,
is one of the earliest surviving Dooms.   If medieval
sculpture was so definitely dictated by Church authority
as we are often told, then it would be strange to find the
theologian and the artist at variance on so important a
point; remarkable, even if the one were writing in
Southern Germany and the other working in Central
France, and still stranger if the theologian was really none
other than the local *scholasticus*, the master of the
cathedral theological school.   For, in fact, all the
blessed are clothed at Autun; it is only the damned
who are cast down to hell in their naked deformity.
Mâle, therefore, conveys only a half-truth when he
writes: " Medieval art did not love the nude, and
was glad to avoid it; but on this point it was
necessary to follow the teaching of the Church."[2]   For
there was no definite Church teaching here; therefore
individual artists and individual patrons took their own
way.   Even as they rose from their graves, the dead
were sometimes clothed, as at Notre-Dame-de-Paris.[3]
A Doom of about 1170, on the northern portal of Bâle
Cathedral, gives an intermediate rendering of great
interest; the last trumpet has found men naked (as all
medieval folk slept naked almost always in bed), but they
are hastily clothing themselves.[4]   Before God's throne,
although the artist often marks the contrast, as here at
Autun, between the blessed in their clothes and the

---

[1] Migne, P. L., vol. clxxii, col. 1170. Mâle, by a slip, refers to chap. x;
it is, in fact, chap. xv of the third book.

[2] Mâle, ii, p. 474.

[3] Ibid., p. 482.

[4] Here, again, there was no certain tradition. Honorius tells us that
the trumpet shall sound at midnight and at Eastertide, as an exact parallel
to Christ's resurrection; Vincent of Beauvais tells us that we must interpret the term *midnight* only mystically; and Honorius himself writes
inconsistently on the subject.

S

naked reprobates, yet sometimes the damned also appear
in their garments : thus it is in the windows of Bourges,
and in Herrad's *Hortus Deliciarum*.[1] In this latter case,
the artist conceives a unique scene ; in order to render
the resurrection perfect he shows the wild beasts and
birds and fishes giving up the limbs that they have
devoured. Unique, that is, at least in the sense that

DRESSING FOR JUDGMENT, FROM THE CATHEDRAL OF BÂLE.

few or no parallels can be found in surviving Western
art ; yet it lends itself to obvious artistic effect, and the
sculptor or painter might have found emphatic justification in theological literature.[2] Honorius and Vincent
expatiate on this subject with equal emphasis. The
former writes :

[1] Martin and Cahier, p. iii, facing plate 171 ; Herrad, plate lxviii, for
which see the next scene also.

[2] Dr. M. R. James informs me that this *motif* is of Eastern origin, and
is borrowed ultimately from the apocryphal *Apocalypse of Peter*. He
adds that the *Hortus Deliciarum*, from which my instance is taken, was
largely copied from Byzantine MSS.

D.—" Sometimes a wolf devoureth a man, and the man's flesh is converted into wolf-flesh; then a bear devoureth the wolf, and a lion the bear; how shall the man arise from these?

M.—That which was man's flesh shall rise again; that which was of beasts, shall remain. For He, who was able to create all things from nothing, knoweth well to separate these things. Whether therefore men be eaten limb by limb through beasts or fishes or fowls, all shall be so formed again at the resurrection that not a hair of their head shall perish.

THE BEASTS GIVE UP THEIR DEAD.

D.—But if all their hairs, and their nails that have been clipped, return to their place, will not the men be deformed?

M.—We must not understand that they will be restored to their former place; but, even as a potter may break a fresh-thrown vessel and make the same clay into another, not caring what was handle at first, and what was bottom, so doth God form, from the self-same matter [as before], another body far unlike to this present body, since all deformity and infirmity have given place to full integrity and comeliness." [1] Vincent writes: [2] " And in [the Resurrection] each shall arise in that form wherein

[1] *Elucid* III, 11; P.L., vol. clxxii, col. 1164.
[2] *Spec. Hist.*, bk. XXXI, c. 113 (ed. Douai, p. 1326).

he had originally his proper being. Therefore the rib taken from Adam shall arise not in Adam, but in Eve; seeing that, when woman had been created, man was more perfect than before with regard to the conservation of the species. But, seeing that the human body is most perfect in comparison with all inferior bodies, therefore the flesh of oxen, eaten by man and changed into his flesh, shall arise in the latter; yet not in its first form (even as the clay will not, from which Adam was moulded), but under the form of human flesh. . . . Nor need those parts which have fallen from the body return to the same parts wherein they were at first, but, even as a statue, when it is recast, may have matter of the former nose in its foot and of the former foot in its nose." Such, then, were the opportunities neglected by the sculptors of all the great cathedral Dooms; and, on the other hand, they took liberties which neither Honorius nor Vincent would have allowed. For there are scenes among the damned (e.g. on the portal of the north transept at Reims), of which we must say, either that the carver took his own way without the least regard for his ecclesiastical patrons, or that the cathedral dignitaries were not always fit persons to direct religious representations.

If there was any one subject upon which a hierarchy, definitely established from the earliest times, could have indoctrinated the artists with a definite tradition upon a point of capital importance, that was the representation of the Founder of Christianity. Yet, if the so-called Abgarus portrait be genuine, it must be confessed that thousands of sculptors and painters were permitted to ignore it. Moreover, there is no certain tradition even as to the fundamental question: Was the Saviour's face beautiful, according to human standards, or are we to take literally the words of Isaiah, " There was no sightliness, that we should be desirous of Him " ? On this question there has been " a regrettable controversy among the most distinguished persons in the Church." Some argue that the acknowledged ugliness of earlier

Byzantine types was due to the explicit teaching of Doctors of the Church, and especially of monks; others, that it sprang from mere artistic decadence and clumsiness. Again, some paintings and sculptures represent Christ as bearded, others as beardless.[1]

Nor was the symbolism more authoritative, or much more certain, even in those later generations in which the interaction of plastic art and theatrical art tended to stereotype a series of religious tableaux. Two books stand out here far above the rest ; the *Biblia Pauperum* and the *Speculum Humanæ Salvationis*—Bible of the Poor and Mirror of Human Salvation. Manuscripts of both are extremely numerous. The former dates from the end of the thirteenth century at latest, and was printed as early as 1460. The latter can be dated exactly, it was composed in 1324. The books themselves, and the influence exercised upon them and upon the Miracle Play by the *Hundred Meditations* on the Life of Christ,[2] are admirably described by Mâle. Both books deal with Gospel history in a series of types and antitypes ; yet, even at this date, and with these increasing opportunities of standardization, there is still much laxity of private choice. For instance, when we come to the Annunciation, the *Biblia Pauperum* parallels this scene with two others, Eve and Gideon. The *Speculum*, on the other hand, gives three: Gideon, the Burning Bush, and Rebecca meeting Eliezer. Again, for the Harrowing of Hell the *Biblia Pauperum* compares this scene with Goliath and David ; in the windows of King's College Chapel at Cambridge the type is Israel going forth from Egypt.

But perhaps the iconography of the Virgin Mary shows the strongest proof that these things were far less imposed from above than allowed to grow up from

---

[1] *Bulletin de la Soc. des ant. de Picardie*, 1846, pp. 320 ff.: discussion of a paper communicated by Abbé Bourgeois. The question is treated casually also in *Mém. Soc. d'Émulation d'Abbeville*, 1852, p. 760.

[2] A book often ascribed to St. Bonaventura, but really composed by another Franciscan, his disciple, Joannes de Caulibus.

below, and to struggle with each other until one survived
and set thenceforward an almost exclusive standard.
Even in the Annunciation scene we find wide differences.
At Bâle, possibly even as late as A.D. 1200, the conception
is charming, but primitive and almost childish. But the
groups of Reims and Chartres are thoroughly representative of Durandus's age, when we might look upon the

convention as fully de-
veloped and fixed for all
time. They are of wonder-
ful grace and simplicity;
two tall figures side by
side ; the angel holding a
flower, perhaps a lily but
perhaps of no botanical
character ; a flower from
Paradise. As early as about
1250, at least, the lily
sometimes comes in be-
tween the two figures;
and this seems to be
intended in the Annun-

THE ANNUNCIATION, FROM THE
CATHEDRAL OF BÂLE.

ciation on the great candelabrum given by Barbarossa to
Aachen in about 1165.[1] But in the best age the figures
themselves tell their own tale ; and to the Reims group in
especial, we may exactly apply Dante's description of the
same scene as plastically represented in his *Purgatorio* :—

> Giurato si saria ch' ei dicesse : *Ave* . . .
> Ed avea in atto impressa esta favella,
> *Ecce ancilla Dei*, propriamente,
> Come figura in cera si suggella.[2]

Later, however, the scene changes, and, as many
artists or mystics might judge, not for the better. The
angel loses much of his earlier dignity, and becomes a

[1] Schnaase, vol. iii, p. 792.

[2] *Purg.* x, 40. One would have sworn that he was saying Hail ! and in
her attitude were imprinted these words, *Behold the handmaid of the Lord*,
as exactly as a figure is imprinted with a seal on wax.

transfigured page-boy, bringing a lily; the Virgin herself kneels at a *prie-Dieu*, reading her psalter; and a pot
of lilies stands between. However we ourselves may
decide as between Fra Angelico's Annunciation and that
of Reims, there can be no question that they represent
different artistic traditions. And this was instinctively
recognized by the multitude, who in this case, as in that
of the changed fashion of crucifix, invented a miraculous
story to account for it. Myrc, the canon of Lilleshall,
whose writings throw such valuable light upon the
religion of the man in the street during Chaucer's lifetime, addresses his hearers as follows: " Thus, good men,
you have now heard of this annunciation. Then be there
some that ask why there standeth a wine-pot and a lily
between our Lady and Gabriel at her salutation. Thus
was the reason; for our Lady at her salutation conceived
by sight. And that was the first miracle that was wrought
in proving of Christ's faith. And fell thus that a Christian
man and a Jew sat together talking of the coming of our
Lady. And there, as they were, a wine-pot stood between
them. Then said the Christian man to the Jew: ' We
believe right as the stalk of the lily groweth, and con-
ceiveth colour of green, and after bringeth forth a white
flower without craft of man or any impairing of the
stalk; right so our Lady conceived of the Holy Ghost,
and afterwards brought forth her son without stain of
her body, that is the flower and chief fruit of all women.'
Then said the Jew: ' When I see a lily spring out of this
pot, I will believe, and not otherwise.' Then anon
therewith a lily sprang out of the pot, the fairest that
ever was seen. And when the Jew saw that, anon he fell
down on knees and said: ' Lady, now I believe that
thou conceivedest of the Holy Ghost, Jesu Christ, God,
Son of Heaven, and thou a clean maiden before and
after.' And so he went and was christened, and was a
holy man afterwards. For this reason, the pot and the
lily are set between our Lady and Gabriel."[1]

[1] E.E.T.S., 1905, p. 108.

Equally fluid, for an even longer time, perhaps, was the tradition of the Virgin's colours. Until about A.D. 1300, it is actually the exception for her to appear in a blue cloak, or with any conspicuous blue in her garments. By 1400, it has become still more exceptional to find her without that blue mantle : indeed, the ordinary untechnical visitors to continental picture-galleries have a comfortable feeling that they do know one thing for certain : Mary can always be recognised by her azure cloak. Yet, if they study the older stained glass with any care, they will find that green, red and golden yellow are by far the Virgin's favourite colours.[1] For this there was a very natural reason : the Queen of Heaven must be royally arrayed ; red and green, side by side with gold, were the two most aristocratic colours for dress in the Middle Ages ; ecclesiastical disciplinarians, for instance, while very closely prescribing the shape and fashion of clerical costume, gave very wide latitude as to hue ; the only colours definitely forbidden were green and red. The artist, therefore, naturally clad his Queen of Heaven in crimson and green and gold ; yet, in so doing, he exemplified the weakness of ecclesiastical symbolism. Honorius of Autun, indeed, would wholly or partially excuse him ; for Honorius describes how, when the youthful Mary lived in the Temple at Jerusalem with other consecrated maidens of her age, and whenever they were set to work, it was always the crimson or the gold embroidery that fell to Mary's lot, and therefore the others called her Queen.[2] Yet later medieval moralists were never weary of rebuking the ordinary girls' love of finery by reminding them that the Blessed Virgin had

[1] See Appendix 16. At Chartres, though " la Belle Verrière " shows the B.V.M. in a splendid blue mantle, this is exceptional. I can here speak not only from personal observation but with the concurrence of the custodian who knows every corner of the cathedral. The four remaining paintings in St. Albans Cathedral, of the Virgin beside the Cross, are excellently reproduced in colour in *Archæologia*, vol. lviii (1902), pl. 18. Not one of the four is in blue.

[2] *Spec. Eccl. De Nat. S. Mariae*, P.L., vol. clxxii, col. 1000.

been noted for the plainness of her dress, and Pelbart, the great Franciscan Mary-encomiast at the end of the Middle Ages, quotes Albert the Great and Epiphanius and St. German to this same effect. She did not indeed go about in sackcloth, not being an ecclesiastical penitent ; yet " her garments were not very precious or coloured or notable. . . . She always wore a shift and tunic, and over this a religious cloak of self-colour, such as religious women were wont to wear in those days."[1] It would be difficult, I think, to find one among the thousand representations which conforms to this description of a cloak self-coloured with the tunic of natural grey. Cloak and tunic are generally in studied contrast with each other, even after the convention of the blue cloak has come in.[2]

And although, when once that revolutionary change began, it was almost everywhere victorious within a generation or two, yet we may find striking exceptions even in those later times. These may be studied in London, at the National Gallery. No. 20 (Early Westphalian, fifteenth century) shows only a scrap of blue under-robe beneath an ample cloak of brown velvet. In No. 1331 she wears a heavy mantle of bright brocade without a hint of blue ; this is by the Sienese Bernardino Fungar, about 1500. Moreover, there was no authoritative ruling even as to the colour of her hair. It is almost always portrayed as golden ; yet Pelbart tells us that it was " dark," and " temperately tending to black."[3]

Lastly, even after some generations of standardization, the conventional colours for Christ's dress were not thoroughly fixed. The rule had gradually been formed in the Passion Play that Christ in His human life should

[1] *Pomerium Sermonum de B. Virgine*, bk. VII, pt. ii, art. 3, c. 7 (ed. Hagenau, 1515, f. 80 a.). Cf. Molanus, p. 164, where the original quotations show that " self-colour " means undyed wool, the grey now called " natural."

[2] Moreover, this is so not only with the representations of Mary after the Assumption, glorified in heaven, but just as often during her days of suffering on earth, and even at the foot of the Cross.

[3] See *Five Centuries of Religion*, vol. i, p. 160.

be in dull purple or purple-brown; the risen and
glorified Christ in the crimson of victory. In King's
College Chapel this comes out with special clearness; even after the Resurrection, in the garden scene
with Mary Magdalene and at the supper of Emmaus,
Christ is clad again in the humble colour of humanity,
because His divinity was then unrecognized. Here is
a clear and comprehensible distinction; yet, so little
was the matter definitely regulated, that we find
constant variations of
importance. Even at
King's College Chapel,
in the Ascension scene,
when the triumphal
crimson seems clearly
called for, we find purple;
and in other churches the
whole colour-convention
seems to be ignored, as
in Ste.-Madeleine-de-
Troyes, where the win-
dows are of the fifteenth
century.[1]

ALEXANDER'S CELESTIAL JOURNEY.

The symbolism which
dilettante imagination
loves to find in the minor
decorations of medieval
churches is repudiated by the best authors of all parties.
The animals, the flowers, the grotesques were almost
universally inspired by purely artistic considerations,
or at most by familiar tales such as Reynard the
Fox, or the Arthurian legends, or well-known fabliaux.
Monsieur Mâle, as an orthodox Catholic, and Prof.
Hirn, as a detached observer, would equally repudiate
the contention that "the grotesque and even the
obscene carvings will be found to have been designed
for a specific purpose . . . the coarse element was

[1] See Appendix 17.

designed to produce a purely moral impression."[1]   Still
less support, if possible, could be found for the theory
propounded in certain masonic writings, that the
grotesques form a systematic body of satire directed
by the medieval freemasons against the clergy.[2]

There is a whole window at Chartres dedicated to the
legends of Charlemagne and Roland ; in many great
churches, again, (e.g. Bâle, Freiburg, St. Mark's at Venice)
we have the legend of Alexander's sky-ride with the help
of his two gryphons.[3]   The great king hit upon the ingenious device of harnessing those monsters to a chariot
in which he had placed two lofty spears, baited at their
points with tempting flesh.   The gryphons, in their
perpetual struggles to reach the bait, flew higher and
higher ; and Alexander was thus enabled to survey all
the kingdoms of the world.   Sculptured examples range
from the crude portal of Remagen on the Rhine to
beautiful and delicate misericords in the Minsters of Wells,
Beverley, Chester, Lincoln, Gloucester and Cartmel.

---

[1] S. Heath, *The Romance of Symbolism*, 1909, p. 212. The book is
scientifically worthless, but fairly typical of the irresponsible writing
which often passes current on this subject.

[2] Reflexions which may serve to moderate the exaggerations of modern
symbolists will be found in the following pages by real scholars : Schnaase,
Gesch. d. bild. Künste, vol. ii, pt. i, 1850, pp. 290, 367, 369 ; vol. iv, 376 ;
Y. Hirn, *The Sacred Shrine*, pp. 80 ff. ; J. v. Schlosser, *Beiträge*, pp. 115–
16 ; Mâle ii, 73–5, 82, 363, 391 ; Ch. Cahier, *Nouveaux mélanges*, vol. i,
1874, p. 117. De Gourmont allows himself here and there some very
entertaining exposures of the symbolistic theories which Huysmans has
swallowed uncritically from other authors (pp. 150–2, 159 ff.).

[3] For an excellent study of this story in art, see Prof. R. S. Loomis in
The Burlington Magazine, April and May, 1918. He has collected more
than twenty examples, apart from illuminations in MSS.

CHAPTER XIV

THE PEOPLE'S MIND

WE see, then, how narrow are the limits within which, with any truth, we can call medieval symbolism a Science. Yet it remains true that a certain number of churchmen, at different times and places, tried to erect it into a science; some, like Durandus, by writing for the public, and others, like Abbot Samson, by prescribing to their own workmen. All this, and the elaborate doctrinal schemes followed in certain great buildings, are excellently set forth in M. Mâle's two volumes, and they are well deserving of study. But, here again, it is necessary to go one step farther, and to inquire how far the ordinary worshipper understood what may have been in the designer's mind.

It would seem impossible to doubt that the splendid statuary of a cathedral like Chartres impressed contemporaries far more than it impresses the average beholder of to-day. The workmanship itself must have created something of the same effect which the heathen statues had upon the people of Rome or Naples—awe and reverence. Much of their symbolism, again, was most simple and evident; St. Laurence with his gridiron, St. Sebastian with his arrows, other martyrs bearing the sword. But what did people in general make of those numerous and elaborate reliefs (for instance) on which Ruskin comments so minutely in his *Bible of Amiens* ? Here, as in the last chapter, it will be well to start with a statement of the fashionable modern theory as conceived by an able and orthodox author. The professor of medieval philosophy at Louvain, Maurice de Wulf, deals with this subject in his lectures delivered at Princeton

University, *Philosophy and Civilization in the Middle Ages*. He writes (p. 150): "The *Rationale Divinorum Officiorum* of William [Durand], Bishop of Mende, shows in detail how the cathedrals are at once marvels of art and symbols of prayer. The Church of Amiens, which was the most perfect of the great French monuments, is a striking demonstration of the æsthetic resources of the original scheme. That of Chartres no less brilliantly

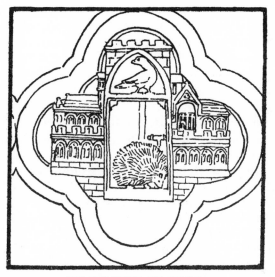

THE HEDGEHOG OF AMIENS.

exhibits its iconographic resources. Each stone had its language. Covered with sculpture, it presents a complete religious programme. It is for the people the great book of sacred history, the catechism in images." Let us test this by a concrete example from the cathedral which is here instanced as most perfect, that of Amiens.

These beautiful quatrefoils, which others besides Ruskin have taken as the high-water mark of medieval symbolism, contain a whole series of references to the twelve prophets. The illustration for Zephaniah is taken, as modern students have shown, from Chapter II, verse 14, which runs thus in the Roman Catholic [Douay] version : " The Lord will make the beautiful city a wilderness . . . and the bittern and the urchin shall lodge in the threshold thereof." *Urchin* is used here, of course, in its primitive sense of *hedgehog* ; the Revised Version has " the pelican and the porcupine." Therefore the artist has shown us a building, with two birds and a hedgehog.

But though, indeed, the best men of the Middle Ages knew their Bible very well, yet we have overwhelming evidence not only for popular ignorance, outside the most elementary sayings or events, but also for the Bible-ignorance even of the ordinary clergy. When we ask ourselves, therefore, what this medallion would convey to all but a very small minority of beholders, we must conclude that, if they puzzled themselves about it at all, they would be likely to interpret it by their notions of animal symbolism. But animal symbolism, much as it interested our forefathers, was far from being orderly and scientific ; if it had been, it would probably have interested them less. The most elaborate treatise on the symbolism of Bible animals is that of Petrus Berchorius, prior of St.-Éloi at Paris, who died in 1362. It will be instructive, therefore, to see what he has to tell us on this subject ; we shall find here, as we find in Durandus, the sum-total of much venerable tradition, augmented from the author's own reading or fancy, and cast into methodical didactic form.[1] Certainly Berchorius gives us plenty of moralizations on this subject. " The urchin or hedgehog is a little beast that . . . is clothed (as Aristotle saith) with prickles in place of hair . . . for all the nutriment of his body goeth to make prickles. Such, my dear brethren, are rich and worldly folk, who have a little body (that is, little grace and virtue) . . . but are thick-set all round with thorns, that is, with riches, that are prickly and disquieting to the mind and heart." And then, again, " Isidore telleth us that the hedgehog

[1] *Opera*, ed. 1730, vol. ii, p. 371.

climbeth trees or vines, casteth down the fruit or the grapes, and then rolleth in them as they lie on the ground ; thus, when he is stuck all over with fruit, he goeth home to nourish his young therewith. Therefore he is a type of evil men who hold high office in the Church ; for such men climb into high offices as into trees, and thus get and collect and accumulate fruit (that is, worldly wealth), not attending to the profit of the people subjected to them, but only to their own gain . . . for in these days such men enrich their relations from the

qe eſt le ḣerecum

THE GUILE OF THE HEDGEHOG.

patrimony of Christ crucified. . . . Alas ! how many hedgehogs of this kind we have in the Church ! '' And so on for a whole folio column. But then, suddenly, the wind changes, and we find that the hedgehog is the type no longer of a bad man, but of the perfect Christian. For this beast, according to some medieval naturalists, has five different stomachs, arranged one after the other for different stages of digestion. Therefore, in this, he resembles the righteous man, who has five different processes of meditating upon God's word ; which five processes Berchorius thereupon proceeds to explain in detail. Again, by rolling himself into an impenetrable ball against dogs and other foes, the hedgehog presents a type of the truly religious and contemplative life, self-sufficient and securely guarded from temptation or distraction. Moreover, Aristotle, in the sixth chapter òf the ninth book of his *Historia Animalium*, tells us of a man at Byzantium whose tame hedgehog foretold the weather by running in or out of his cave. So " all hedge-hogs—that is, all good men—have a presentiment and prevision of impending evil weather [in religion] . . . that is, of the pains of hell." And, even as this aforesaid Byzantine set himself up for a weather-prophet on the strength of his hedgehog's infallible instinct, so there are many folk in this world who exploit what they have learnt from others as though it were their own native wisdom. Thus Berchorius has a text for every argument; all is extremely persuasive and extremely edifying; but it leaves us still doubtful whether the hedgehog symbolizes a child of God or a limb of the devil. What, then, could the ordinary worshipper at Amiens make of these beasts which might be painted in black or in white according to individual fancy? For this is no isolated instance; it could be paralleled from more than one of those famous medallions, and from dozens of places elsewhere. Mâle says no more than the truth: " There were multitudes of variations [in animal symbolism]. I know several fourteenth century books in which animals are taken as typical of vices; there are no two which agree exactly " (ii, 357). He rejects no less emphatically the attempts to read symbolism into floral ornaments and grotesques.[1] Giraldus Cambrensis, writing about A.D. 1200, tells us that he himself invented the symbolism in his *Topographia Hibernica* out of his own head, and that the Archbishop of Canterbury commended him for it.[2]

The want of system in symbolical moralization, and the indifference of the medieval mind to consistency or even ordinary probability in this field, may easily be tested by reference to one very common book, and

[1] Ibid., pp. 73, 82.
[2] *Opp.*, R.S., vol. iii, p. 334.   Cf. Schlosser, *Beiträge*, p. 169.

TOOTHACHE AT WELLS AND AT LINCOLN.

another fairly accessible. The *Gesta Romanorum* was perhaps the most popular of all collections of anecdotes designed to help the clergy in their sermons and their religious teaching. It dates from the thirteenth century, and one of the earliest versions of the book has been translated by Swan and printed in Bohn's series. Tale 121 is a famous medieval story, alluded to in *The Owl and the Nightingale*, of a jealous old knight who, having killed a nightingale because it pleased his wife with its song, gave her in scorn the bird's heart to eat. This knight, the moralizer assures us, is a type of Christ ! No. 140, again, is a tale very discreditable to the Emperor Heraclius : yet " the Emperor is God." After Tale 171, again we are told : " My beloved, the Emperor is God "; yet, this time there is actually no emperor in the story ! Again, the Early English Text Society has published two fifteenth century translations of the same tales, with somewhat different moralizations, yet not less repugnant to common sense. The tenth story in the collection, for instance, is that of an emperor who made a tyrannous law " that each man should hold, upon pain of death, the day of his birth as an holy day." With the aid of Virgil and his magic arts, this emperor discovered that a certain smith regularly broke the law. Upon which the moralist assures us that the Emperor stands for " our Lord Jesu Christ, the which hath ordained for law that each man should keep the Sabbath day.[1] Virgil . . . is the Holy Ghost, which setteth up a preacher to show virtues and vices, not sparing no more the rich than the poor. But nowadays, if the preacher saith sooth, or telleth who breaketh the commandment or the will of Christ, forsooth he shall be threatened of the enemies of Christ, i.e. evil men, which neither loveth God neither their neighbour. . . . In time before, [men] were devout, blessed and meek ; and now they have no devotion, and be cruel

---

[1] I have pointed out elsewhere that the puritanical idea of Sunday as equivalent with the Jewish Sabbath has its roots in the Middle Ages. (*Medieval Village*, pp. 255, 272, and App. 34).

T

and wicked and have no soul; and therefore he that will
say sooth now, may be silent, and have a broken head."
All these reflections are ordinary medieval common-
places; but there is only the faintest excuse for them in
the actual stories. In the face of facts like these, can we
believe that the Amiens hedgehog, any more than the
majority of symbolical representations on that magnificent façade, conveyed any religious or moral teaching
of primary importance to the multitude in general?
The whole pile would, of course, impress them with
solemn admiration; the array of statues and bas-reliefs
might well attune their thoughts to devotion, as music
does, or as the statues of gods and demi-gods had raised
men's thoughts in Greece and Rome; but, of the religion
of the Lord's Prayer or of the Parables, there is far less
even at Amiens (let alone, in a village church) than could
be conveyed in a few simple discourses from the pulpit.

It is sometimes pleaded that such an application of
common-sense tests is anachronistic; that medieval
folk themselves had never any difficulties here, and that
the fault lies really in modern critics, purblind with
book-reading and ignorant of the true mind of the past.
But, on the contrary, the ignorance and the anachronism
lie in this apologetic plea; a large proportion of medieval
clergy were often in serious difficulties with the symbolism of the Church. One of the most valuable of the
books written for the instruction of parish priests is the
Festial of John Myrc, a contemporary of Chaucer. On
p. 261 of the E.E.T.S. edition, Myrc (whose book is
written as a guide to his fellow-priests) warns against the
popular errors bred by even the most familiar of symbolical representations. "Then, for [*i.e.* because] these
four evangelists be likened to four divers beasts, and be
so painted in four parties of Christ [*i.e.* at the four angles
of a square in which Christ occupies the centre]; that
is, for Mark a lion, for Matthew a man, for Luke a calf,
and for John an eagle, therefore many lewd [*i.e.* unlearned]
men and women ween that they were such beasts, and

not men. But they that so understand, they shall know [that] they be so likened to these beasts, for Christ's doings in the Gospel that they wrote was like to these beasts' kind "—that is, Matthew emphasizes Christ's human nature, Luke His sacrifice, as the Jews slew calves under their law; Mark, His resurrection (and we all know that a lion's cubs are born dead, and are roused to life by their father's roaring); John, the ineffable mysteries upon which, like the sun, only an eagle can gaze undazzled. Myrc himself seems not to realize that this symbolism comes originally from Ezekiel. And, in another passage (p. 124), he warns his fellow-priests against common folk who sometimes ask them awkward questions. "For it is oft seen that lewd men, the which be of many words and proud in their wit, will ask priests divers questions of things that touchen to service of Holy Church, and especially of this [Easter] time; and, gladly [they ask] such priests as cannot make a suitable answer, so for to put them to shame. Wherefore I have titled [i.e. set down] here divers points which that been needful to each priest to know; so he that will look and hold it in his heart, he may make an answer, so that he shall do himself worship, and other [folk] profit." And, apart from this plain confession, we have other explicit evidence for popular and priestly ignorance. It is not only that we find how a master-glazier himself, after describing many saints or subjects in the windows for which he is charging, specifies in one case simply a window of two lights, "wherein is one great prophet."[1] The pseudo-Chaucerian tale of Beryn is as valuable for certain sides of social history as Chaucer himself; it shows us the pilgrims reaching Canterbury at last. But in the cathedral, instead of interesting themselves in the images of saints or prophets or kings, they are described as going about and "goggling with their heads" at the blazoned windows, in which they try to recognize familiar coats

[1] A. de la Fons, *Les Artistes du nord de la France*, p. 53; the date is 1425.

of arms. Here was what they could understand; these coats would be known to them, among other ways, through inn signs; for it is probable that many of these— the Red Lion, Blue Boar, Black Bull, and so on—were originally the arms of knights or squires who were lords of the town or village, or who commonly put up at the hostelry and hung their shields outside. The Swiss reformer Zwingli, as we shall see later on, deprecated the destruction of glass, on the ground that people did not

THE THREE KINGS, AT MILAN.

worship the saints in the windows, as they did those carved in niches or painted on walls.

Again, Chaucer's contemporary, the friar who wrote *Dives and Pauper*, tells us that " it is a common saw " that a bishop's mitre has always two lappets hanging down, to " betoken that this land [of England] hath been twice renegade and perverted: that is false; for sith this land took first the faith the people was never renegade " (Precept viii). But the author himself goes on to assert that the double

AN ARCHBISHOP, TWO EMPERORS, AND A KING.

horn of the mitre betokens the bishop's knowledge of both Testaments, the Old and the New. Yet nothing is more certain (for it is familiar to antiquarians of all religious schools) than that none of the clergy, originally, wore any headdress whatever in church; that the mitre came in only about A.D. 1000 at earliest; and that it was then a round cap without horns. But, gradually, it evolved a depression in the middle, like the modern "Trilby" hat; and, finally, it took the horned shape familiar to our two symbolists. Myrc, again, warns his hearers in his *Festial* against a common delusion as to the three Magi. The midmost of these was commonly represented turning his head backward as he rode. Says Myrc: "Ignorant men have an opinion that he had slain a man, wherefore he turned backward; but God forbid that this opinion were true!" At Emneth, in Norfolk, where there is a flat tomb carved with a long cross elaborately floriated at the top, something after the fashion of a wheel with spokes, the common folk attributed it to a legendary local hero, Hickafrick or Hickathrift. This man, in defence against the petty tyrant of his fields, had taken his own waggon-pole for spear and the wheel for a shield, and had thus driven off the lord and his minions. It was the tomb that suggested the story, just as the cross-legged monuments, a type conceived from purely artistic motives, have been interpreted as symbolical of crusaders. Very similar is the story of numerous votive offerings still to be seen in the Church of Sant' Agostino alla Zecca, at Naples. There, the popular imagination has been struck by a remarkable life-sized figure, extraordinarily realistic, representing a saint (I think, St. Agatha) pierced to the heart by a long dagger thrust in at the collar-bone. This statue has interpreted itself, in the people's mind, as the patron saint of the dagger-thrust; for there are still more stabbing-cases in Naples than in any other European city of equal population. Therefore men who had a vendetta on hand have vowed their weapon as an offering to the saint ; so that we see, hanging beside the altar, a large number of triumphant stiletti. The many unoccupied nails intermingled with these trophies tell a still more dismal story. At different times men have borrowed these votive daggers from the shrine, as lucky weapons, more likely than any other to do the deed. In many cases the borrowed stiletto has had no luck ; the borrower himself has fallen ; his vow has never been

VOTIVE STILETTI.

performed, and there stands the empty nail in testimony of at least two fatal frays.

Very similar, in all probability, is the explanation of the celebrated " Toothache Capital " at Wells Cathedral. Hard by this carving lies Bishop Bytton, who died in 1274, in the odour of sanctity, and whose tomb was specially frequented by sufferers from toothache. The guide-books, even the most authoritative, labour to explain how a tomb which could not have been placed there much before 1300 should have dictated the sym-

bolism of a capital which, to all appearance, dates from
the same time as its neighbours; that is, a century
before Bytton's death. The central tower, they point
out, fell down; we may therefore presume that it
crushed some of the capitals, and that this one (with
two other grotesques showing teeth) was carved after
Bytton's death, in obvious allusion to the good bishop's
dental miracles. This would bring the making of these
capitals into the episcopate of Burnell; and that would
explain why, side by side with the toothache head, is a
figure extracting a thorn—or let us call it a *bur*—from its
foot.[1]

But the carving of
this capital is so char-
acteristic of an earlier
date, and resembles its
fellows so closely in
style, as to render this
theory improbable from
the very beginning.
Even in the rare cases
(as in the naves of
Westminster Abbey and
Beverley Minster) where
the later artists have
taken great pains to

TOOTHACHE AT OVER (CAMBS).

imitate the older work, no trained architectural eye could
possibly mistake one for the other; neither the craftsmen
nor their patrons had any idea of exact imitation in the
modern sense; their instincts were not antiquarian but
creative. On the other hand, a quite contrary explanation
of the capital would be in full accordance with medieval
facts. This toothache-caricature is, in fact, a common
medieval motive; it occurs, for instance, in a cloister-boss
at Lincoln Minster, and as a gargoyle at Over (Cambs)
among other similar grotesques, for none of which we
can offer any probable symbolic explanation. Moreover,

[1] E.g. Dr. Dearmer's *Wells Cathedral*, 1898, p. 92; cf. 89, 125.

at Grandson in Switzerland (anciently in Burgundy) there is a still closer analogy. The capitals in that remarkable church are of very nearly the Wells date, perhaps fifty years earlier, and proportionately ruder. Here, on the south-western respond, is a series of five grotesques all connected with medicine. The left-hand figure is in an attitude difficult to describe here, but unmistakable to all who are familiar with medieval medical methods.

TOOTHACHE AT GRANDSON.

The next is solemnly feeling his pulse; the third and fourth represent respectively the thorn and the toothache, just as at Wells; the fifth is unfortunately obscured by the organ-gallery; its mouth is wide open, and it is very likely showing its tongue to the doctor. We have here, therefore, a series of grotesques based upon common daily scenes, analogous not only to the two Wells subjects under discussion, but also to the equally famous subjects from that same cathedral, of the cobbler at his work, and of the fruit-stealers and their fate. Moreover, the general analogy is equally close;

at Grandson, as at Wells, there are one or two Biblical or definitely religious subjects among a large majority of capitals representing either plain foliage or evident grotesques.

With this clue, let us reconsider the relation between Bishop Bytton and the toothache grotesques. One of the most conspicuous of these is within easy sight of the bishop's tomb. It is likely enough that we have cause and effect here; but in which direction did the current run? We may avoid all artistic improbability by supposing that here, as at Naples, it was the pre-existent carving which suggested miraculous influence to a miracle-hungry people. The bishop, so holy in his life that men naturally prayed to him in death, appears as the patron of toothache, just as the Naples saint with a dagger at her heart appears as the patroness of the dagger-thrust. Even if we neglected the evidence of style, it would be more in consonance with medieval mentality that the impressive carving should suggest the miracle, than that the miracle should suggest a carving which fits in so well with all the other Wells grotesques.[1] So it was also, by confession of orthodox modern symbolists, with the legend of St.-Denis and other saints having walked some distance after decapitation, bearing their heads in their hands. First came the symbolist, who represented decapitated martyrs as holding their own heads; then " that popular error throve whereby they were fancied to have taken up their several heads after death, and carried the same to the place where their remains were worshipped." [2] P. Saintyves reckons that there were about eighty saints reputed to have carried their own heads.[3]

These may be illustrated by a still stranger incident. St. Nicholas, Bishop of Myra, became in the later Middle

[1] Schlosser (*Beiträge*, p. 7) gives a similar case from Greek antiquity.

[2] Cf. *Five Centuries of Religion*, vol. i, pp. 49 ff. The words are those of the Jesuit Father Henschen in the later eighteenth century.

[3] *Les Saints Successeurs des Dieux*, Paris, 1907, ch. ii.

Ages the patron saint of children, especially schoolboys. Yet what specially distinguished him in life was the multitude of pagans whom he baptized in Asia Minor.

THE MURDEROUS HOST.

Therefore he was commonly represented beside a baptismal font, in which stood three naked pagans. It was a common rule of medieval symbolism (as it had been of Greek and Roman symbolism before it) to represent the saint, or the hero of any event, as larger in stature than the other actors in the scene. Therefore, as time went on, these three pagans were mistaken for three boys; the round barrel-like font became a pickling-tub; and the legend was invented that St. Nicholas, putting up at an inn, found there a cannibalistic hostess. The host, under persuasion of this woman, had killed three children and pickled them ; St. Nicholas was divinely warned of the event ; and, instead of eating them, he restored them to life.[1]   The story appears early, in a sermon attributed

[1] A. Maury in *Revue archéologique*, 1847, p. 615. Père Cahier refers the legend also to a misunderstood symbolism, tracing it to a story of three officers whom St. Nicholas miraculously freed from prison. (*Vitraux de Bourges*, pp. 257 ff.) Mâle agrees with Cahier (ii, 367–8, 420–1). Canon Corblet traces the legend also to misunderstood symbolism ; Abbé Laroche, who criticizes this view, gives no serious reasons for his objections (*Rev. de l'art chrétien*, 1891, p. 105).   There is a representation of this scene, almost obliterated, on the south wall of Honington Church (Suffolk).

to St. Bonaventura.[1] It became very popular not only in
the Middle Ages but far beyond ; it figures as the characteristic Nicholas-miracle at the foot of the statue erected

A MIRACLE OF ST. NICHOLAS.

at Auxerre in 1774 by the Confrèrie de St.-Nicolas on the
house by the river-side.

Even more remarkable is another episode in the iconography of St. Nicholas, whom this pseudo-Bonaventura

[1] See Appendix 19.

celebrates as " distinguished among the saints of his own day by most noteworthy and stupendous miracles." [1] The Golden Legend tells us how, " the first day that he was washen and bathed, he addressed him right up in the basin ; and he would not take the breast nor the pap but once on the Wednesday and once on the Friday ; and in his young age he eschewed the plays and japes of other young children." Another version was that, when the saint was baptized, he stood upright in prayer to receive

ST. NICHOLAS, FROM A BOOK OF HOURS.

the chrism upon his forehead.[2] This story is admirably illustrated in the beautiful triptych by Gerard David which was shown in the recent Exhibition of Flemish Art at the Royal Academy in London, and which, by the liberality of the owner, I am permitted to reproduce here. But, at a very early date, this representation was misinterpreted by the popular imagination. The trouvère Robert Wace, who wrote a metrical Life of St. Nicholas not later than A.D. 1155, tells the story in great detail. St. Nicholas,

[1] An excellent little monograph is that of A. Marguillier, *St.-Nicolas*, in the series of " L'Art et les Saints," published by Laurens of Paris. It contains more than thirty illustrations, from a tenth century painting to nineteenth century chap-books. Much light is thrown upon the introduction of Nicholas-worship into the West in the eleventh century by Prof. G. R. Coffman, *A New Theory concerning the Origin of the Miracle Play* (Menasha, W.S., 1914). There is also a study of the legend, with illustrations from St.-Étienne-de-Beauvais, in the 1854 volume of *Mémoires de la soc. académique de l'Oise*.

[2] Marguillier, p. 12.

TWO MIRACLES OF ST. NICHOLAS.

though an unknown stranger, was by divine inspiration suddenly elected by the people of Myra as their bishop; and nobody was more excited by this miracle than his hostess.

" The hostess of the house where he had lodged and slept that night, hearing that he was ordained and set in the bishop's see, for the joy that she felt at this news left her child in the bath; for that evening she had made a fire and the child was in an earthen vessel. For in those days men made vessels of that sort, *pan* was the name. So was this mother confused, and so beside herself with joy, that she left her child on the fire. The fire burned, the water waxed hot, and then it began to boil, to wallop and to roar; and the child within the pan, whose body was tender and new, sat within this boiling water and played with the bubbles at its will; never in this boiling water did it feel the smallest hurt.

THE CHILD IN THE BATH, FROM A BRASS AT LÜBECK.

When the Mass [of Nicholas's consecration] was over, then the mother bethought herself that she had left her child in the bath upon the burning fire. Then she went running homewards and crying upon her child by name. When she had come within her house, as a woman distraught, she found the child in all health, safe and sound within the boiling pan. Then she took her child and brought it before the whole people and told them the miracle that had befallen her. The people held

this for a great marvel; much did St. Nicholas wax
forthwith in great renown throughout that country.
Painful would it be for me to recount, and painful for
you to hear, the great miracles and kindnesses which he
did to many Christian folk." [1] It is remarkable that
Wace's version of the story is a century older than the
Golden Legend, and, again, that, two centuries and more

THE CHILD IN THE BATH, FROM AUXERRE CATHEDRAL.

before David, about the middle of the thirteenth century, it was represented in the windows of Auxerre Cathedral, and again on one of the great episcopal tombs at
Lübeck. In the Auxerre picture, lest there should be any
doubt in the beholder's mind, one devil is seen stirring
the fire, while another is busy with the bellows. Yet,
though that is the order in which the two versions of
this episode have come down to us both in writing and

[1] R. Wace, *St. Nicolas*, ed. N. Delius, Bonn, 1850, p. 6.

in picture, it can scarcely be doubted that here, as elsewhere, popular imagination rather exaggerated the
legend than toned it down, and that the baptism
developed into the caldron-bath, not the caldron-bath
into the baptism.[1]

Strangest of all, perhaps, is the story of St. Wilgeforte,
which I have told more fully elsewhere.[2] The most

TWO NICHOLAS-MIRACLES.

ancient crucifixes, as we have seen, commonly represented
Christ as clothed in a long Byzantine robe, and with
flowing hair.[3] When, in the Middle Ages proper, the
present type grew up and carried all before it, then in a
few generations the surviving examples of the older type
lent themselves to misinterpretation. There are historical indications which suggest that the new legend

[1] The caldron-bath is also figured on the Nicholas-reredos in Bayeux
Cathedral. For another favourite Nicholas-legend, developed in great
detail in the stained glass of Auxerre Cathedral, see Appendix 19.

[2] *Five Centuries of Religion*, vol. i, p. 546.

[3] For the scandal caused in sixth century France by a half-unclothed
crucifix, see Schlosser's quotation from Gregory of Tours (*Beiträge*,
p. 9).

grew up through a misunderstanding of the most famous, perhaps, among these archaic crucifixes, the *Volto Santo* of Lucca.[1] This image, reproduced in medieval embroidery upon a chasuble now preserved at Stonyhurst, was described in 1888, before it had been identified by an experienced antiquary, as " a singular female saint with a beard, and hanging upon a cross fully clothed."

ST. WILGEFORTE.

This is exactly how it struck some fertile imagination of the Middle Ages, at a date when the four-nail clothed crucifix was well out of fashion. The figure being thus mistaken for a woman, a popular legend was invented to account for it. She was daughter to a King of Portugal ; she prayed God to preserve her from marriage by disfiguring her ; He gave her a beard, the princely suitor thenceforth disdained her, and her angry father crucified her. She was soon worshipped all through Europe as Santa Liberata, Sanct Oncommer, Sainte Wilgeforte, Maid Uncumber; and we know from Sir Thomas More that, before her statue in St. Paul's Cathedral, the *femme incomprise* would offer oats to obtain deliverance from her husband (*Eng. Works*, 1557, p. 194). The story of this popular misconception is told at some length by the Jesuit fathers in the Bollandist *Acta Sanctorum*, under the date of July 5. St. Wilgeforte is still worshipped in the little church just outside the Abbey of St.-Wandrille in Normandy ; there you may see before her statue offerings no longer of oats but of wheaten bread ; and her votaries come no longer for deliverance from husbands,

[1] This is traced by the Bollandist Fathers in A.A.S.S., Jnl. v, 50 (ed. 1868).

but for dyspepsia or for difficulties in earning their daily bread.

And, as ancient artistic traditions were thus misunderstood and distorted, so also were ancient ceremonies. The Pope, on certain occasions, keeps up the original tradition of the Lord's Supper, and communicates with his face to the people. The Middle Ages, which had gradually changed this primitive Eucharist into the Mass, wherein the priest turns away from the people to face an altar, evolved their own interpretation of a phenomenon so strange and disconcerting as this ancient tradition had already become. Giraldus Cambrensis, a man distinguished not only for his birth and learning but also for his ecclesiastical dignity, tells us that the custom was introduced to obviate such abuses as took place under Pope Sylvester II. That Pontiff was conspicuous in his own day for learning ; moreover, he had studied in Spain, and the Spanish schools, with their proximity to Mohammedan culture, were always ill-famed for the Black Arts. Sylvester, therefore, earned the reputation of a sorcerer ; and Giraldus tells us that he was accustomed to slip the consecrated wafer, at Communion, into a little bag that hung at his neck, in order to utilize it in these nefarious practices. Therefore the rule was introduced that the Pope should face the people, who can thus assure themselves that he actually puts the host into his mouth and swallows it. It is generally admitted now that the fable of Pope Joan originated in a similar miscomprehension of ancient symbolic ceremonies.

Finally, the saints themselves, and some of the greatest, have had their phases and even their eclipses in the popular mind. This is admirably brought out by Dr. A. van Gennep in the *Revue d'histoire franciscaine*, vol. iv, 1927, pp. 113 ff. Certain saints, in Savoy, " have not been suppressed in the strict sense of the word, but replaced, often through similarity of names. The fact is specially remarkable in the case of St. Francis of Sales, who, in popular devotion, has replaced St. Francis of

U

Assisi." "He has driven him out of his oldest and most venerable sanctuary in Savoy, at Chambéry"; after the fifteen years' break at the Revolution, the people had forgotten the original dedication of the cathedral, and there were no protests when, at its re-dedication, St. Francis of Sales was imposed as the patron saint. "St. Clara is nowhere invoked in Savoy nowadays; but St. Clair, who cures sore eyes, is still prayed to in old sanctuaries." There has been similar confusion between St. Antony the Hermit, and St. Antony of Padua (pp. 118, 140–1, 144–5). Such confusions would have been altogether impossible if symbolism had had a firm hold on the popular imagination; St. Antony the hermit with a pig at his side could never have been confused with his Paduan namesake holding the Child-Jesus in his arms.

Medieval symbolism, therefore, was less the child of science than of ignorance; it was born and bred less in reflection than in imaginative impulse. No doubt some of the above-quoted instances may be said to illustrate legend rather than symbolism; but the two shade off imperceptibly into each other; both are born of the same spirit. Symbolism did indeed work under a certain sense of ecclesiastical discipline; but the creative energy was far stronger than the controlling forces; and here, even more than in the field of theological dogma, the learned classes were forced to accept what tradition had handed down to them, and to weld it as best they could into a philosophical system. Nor, in facing this fact, are we belittling medieval art in any way; rather the contrary. That was what William Morris called it, a People's Art; and the very considerable leaven of symbolism which worked in it was largely a people's symbolism. Indeed, it sometimes shocked the best and most learned men. Wyclif was not more disgusted by the ordinary pictorial representations of the Trinity, with their gross anthropomorphism, than (as we shall see) post-Reformation Popes were; and Gerson, the blameless Chancellor of Paris University in the early fifteenth century, publicly expressed his indignation at the so-called *Ventre Notre-Dame*.[1] In a Christmas-Day sermon, Gerson said to his congregation : " We ought to avoid with great care the false painting of any story in Holy Scripture, in so far as it can be well done. This I say partly by reason of an image which is in the Carmelite [friars' church at Paris] and other like places ; images [of the Blessed Virgin] which show in her womb a Trinity, as though the whole Trinity had taken man's flesh within the Virgin Mary. And, more marvellous still, there is a hell painted therein ; and I cannot see wherefore men do such work ; for, in my judgment, there is neither beauty nor devotion in such paintings ; and this must be a cause of error, and of indignation or indevotion." The editor of Etienne Boileau quotes this as one example of the exuberance of popular imagination : " The eccentricities of taste had revelled in giving all sorts of forms [to images] ; there were moving statues, ' with wagging eyebrows and eyes ' ; there were statues that opened ; '*item*, the *Ventre de Notre Dame*, opening, wherein is the Trinity ; and the said work of art has St. Peter and St. Paul at its two flanks.' " (Inventory of Charles V [of France, 1337–80]).[2]

Moreover, this childlike activity of imagination was matched with a childlike forgetfulness.[3] Not only were these new fancies built on the ruins of past and forgotten facts, but the whole system fell gradually into oblivion. In the seventeenth and eighteenth centuries, until the Romantic Revival, there survived scarcely a glimmer of these ancient orthodoxies, even among the orthodox, except in the commonest and simplest matters. The

[1] Quoted by A. N. Didron (*Christian Iconography*, vol. ii, p. 60), who points out that this fashion of representing the Incarnation was in fact heretical, and that a similar heresy, in a less startling form, was implied in the symbolism of many chasubles worn in his own day (1843).

[2] E. Boileau, *Métiers de Paris*, 1879, p. 43, n. 2.

[3] Quicherat shows how inattentive even the medieval clergy might be, for generation after generation, to the most conspicuous inscriptions in their own churches (ii, 179).

learned Didron has to correct the far more learned Montfaucon, one of the greatest of all ecclesiastical antiquaries. At Chartres, the cathedral where, above all others, we might expect the true traditions to have been kept alive among an unbroken succession of canons and dignitaries, a great deal is still in doubt; Mâle, who is probably the best living authority, disagrees with Bulteau, of the last generation, who made the cathedral his lifelong study. At Reims, nobody can put a certain name to the most remarkable of all the male figures, which is even more reminiscent of Greek statuary than the Annunciation group; it is commonly called Solomon by modern antiquaries, but this seems to rest upon uncertain conjecture and analogy. The kings and queens which decorate some of the greatest of French churches are, at bottom, as uncertain in their nomenclature as the similar series at Wells. Santa Zita of Lucca became naturalized in England as St. Sithe; and, in despite of her emblem which might have kept him straight, the learned Roman Catholic symbolist, Fr. Husenbeth, mistook her for St. Osyth.[1] If these things had really been recognized as integral parts of a great religious science; if the Church had truly felt them to constitute one of the most important factors in her teaching, is it possible that nine-tenths of this symbolism should have become a mere playground for the modern antiquary? It is with these very important reservations, therefore, that we must accept modern statements as to the universality and paramount religious importance of medieval symbolism.

---

[1] See *Notes and Queries*, series xii, vol. xii, pp. 107, 180, 216, and *The Times* correspondence columns for May 31 and June 9, 1927, with earlier and later letters.

CHAPTER XV

THE POOR MAN'S BIBLE

LET us apply this same test of recorded fact to the proverbial saying, "The Church was the Bible of the Poor." No doubt, in most cases, the church wall was indeed the only Bible that the poor man had; but how far did art, whether pictorial or plastic or scenic, really represent the complete and unadulterated Bible?

We have already seen the stress which theologians, when they were writing most seriously, laid upon the details of the Bible text. It will be still more evident to anyone who reads the originals with their context, that those speculations of Honorius and Vincent are dictated by the necessity of conforming their conceptions of the Resurrection to such stories as that of Eve and Adam's rib, and to such details as those

EVE AND THE SERPENT, FROM SANT'
AMBROGIO AT MILAN.

of 1 Cor. xv, taken in their most literal sense. It is true the Middle Ages were less in love with the literal sense than the modern world is, whether Catholic or non-Catholic. Mâle writes very truly: "Since the Council of Trent the Church has left the method of symbolism in the shade, and has clung by preference to the literal sense of the Old Testament; so that the exegesis founded on symbolism, which the Fathers of the Church use constantly and almost exclusively, is generally ignored nowadays."[1] Still, though the Middle Ages laid most stress upon what they defined as the allegorical, moral or anagogical truths of the Bible, yet even the literal sense was to them absolute and authoritative. The mood which modern folk call *bibliolatry* is as prominent in the scholastic philosophers as in the Anglican divines of the seventeenth century; perhaps even more prominent, except in so far as private judgment was then forbidden, and the interpretation even of the literal sense was reserved for the Church. Aquinas, for instance, teaches that the author of Holy Writ is God, in whose power it is to signify His meaning, not by words only (as man also can do) but also by things themselves. It follows, as the first consequence of this authorship, that the Holy Scriptures can never contain an untruth in their literal sense; rather, we must believe all that stands in the Bible as God's Word. For not only all that relates to matters of faith and morals, but its historical contents also are truths for which God stands sponsor. Therefore, if (for instance) anyone said that Samuel was not the son of Elkanah, it would follow that the Divine Scriptures would be false, which would be to contradict the Faith, however indirectly. Even the Council of Trent, in its fourth session, characterized the Old and New Testament as " dictated either orally by Christ, or by the Holy Ghost."

Everything written in the Bible, therefore, must in its literal meaning be literally true; but a great many of the most important Biblical texts are not capable of representation in plastic art; therefore the painter or sculptor, like the theologian, found a far more congenial field in allegory. Even in the greatest cathedrals there was no serious attempt, and there scarcely could have been, to bring the Bible before Christian folk with anything approaching the completeness with which Catholic or non-Catholic can now study the volume at the cost of

---

[1] II, 179. The whole of this section explains very clearly the genesis of medieval allegorization.

a few pence. The common medieval word for this book was *Bibliotheca*, " the library " ; for such, indeed, it is. How much of this could, at the very best, have been taught by painting and sculpture ? Many of the finest psalms are quite incapable of full pictorial representation ; a very inconsiderable proportion of the most magnificent chapters in the prophets could be thus conveyed ; it would be impossible to paint or carve anything which should express St. Paul's triumphant ending to the eighth chapter of Romans, or the splendid rhetoric of the Epistle to the Hebrews. Nobody ever attempted this, and for the best of reasons. Nor did the artists or their patrons grapple with more than a small fraction of the history and romance which might have been expressed. Is there any evidence that the tragedy of Jephthah and his daughter was ever represented ? or the idyll of Ruth and Boaz ? apart, of course, from a single little statue in a Jesse-tree, which might serve as a theme for some preacher who should tell the people the whole story. Yet we have evidence that, even to the ordinary clergy, the idyll of Ruth was a sealed book. The Knight of La Tour Landry wrote a manual for his daughters' education with the help, he tells us, of two priests and two other clerics. He undertakes to tell the story of Ruth, but from pure imagination ; beyond the name of the heroine and the simple fact of her widowhood, there is no single point of contact with the actual Bible story.[1] Nor did the clergy ever prompt a full artistic rendering of many among the finest scenes even in Judges and Samuel and Kings and Chronicles. As to the Gospels, many incidents in the life of Christ are among the most frequent themes ; yet His blessing of the little children is seldom or never portrayed, and there is scarcely any attempt to give a full representation of the parables. The good Samaritan is, indeed, sometimes represented in great churches as a type of Christ Himself ; but far less often than stories of the saints. As to the Sower, the

[1] See the E.E.T.S. edition, p. 119.

Vineyards, the Talents, and others which would have lent themselves as easily to pictorial representation, these have left little or no trace upon our churches. Mâle points out how, while the painters' handbook current in the Greek Church deals with forty parables, the Western Church portrayed four only in the thirteenth century—the Good Samaritan, the Wise and Foolish Virgins, the Prodigal Son and Dives and Lazarus (II, 287).

Apart from great cathedrals like Amiens and Reims, which have been untouched by the Reformation, enough remains in almost every part of Europe to give us an idea of the state of our churches in the past. Most of the paintings have been destroyed, and a large proportion of the carvings; but there is no reason to suppose that Bible themes have thus perished in greater proportion than others. On the contrary, since a good deal of the destruction has been prompted by a party zeal which magnified the Bible and despised the saints, it is reasonable to suppose that, if there is any disproportion among the survivals, this is in favour of Biblical pictures. Yet how few these are, as compared with their rivals in popular and ecclesiastical favour! Indeed, a moment's reflection will show us how few, at the very best, art could have reproduced of those things which fascinated the English people when the full Bible was at last opened to them. Then, men hung on the lips even of lay readers in the churches, a new world of history and drama, of lyric and elegiac poetry and of rhetoric, was revealed to the weaver and to the peasant. Thus we suddenly inherited a mass of literature which far outweighed the whole body of vernacular prose and poetry that England had produced during those thousand years of the Middle Ages, and which made it possible for the next generation to produce Spenser and Marlowe and Shakespeare and Hooker and Bacon.[1]

Learned men, indeed, studied and commented every verse of the Bible in the Middle Ages; but, in default

[1] See especially R. G. Moulton, *The Literary Study of the Bible*.

LEVIATHAN CAUGHT.

of a healthy general public opinion, they constantly wasted themselves in fanciful trivialities. The famous *Hortus Deliciarum* reproduces, pictorially, an idea founded on Job xi, 20, 21, of which Martin and Cahier trace the germ as far back as St. Jerome in the fifth century, and thence down through St. Gregory the Great and St. Odo of Cluny to the Abbess Herrad v. Landsberg; and Mâle has added two other names to this honourable list.[1] The former authors thus describe the picture: " God the Father has thrown the line, with the hook of the Cross, into the depths haunted by Leviathan. The line is Christ's genealogy: His descent from Adam is indicated by a series of medallions enclosing the busts of the patriarchs; the bait is none other than the mortal flesh of the Divine Redeemer. The monster has snapped at the visible body; but he has been caught by the hook, in virtue of the invisible divinity of Christ, placed out of his reach." It is, in fact, one of the medieval methods of explaining the Atonement to the popular mind; it ranks side by side with that other simile, immortalized by the great schoolman Peter Lombard, that God made a mouse-trap for the Devil and baited it with Christ's human flesh.[2] It was in these materialistic and unspiritual forms that a great deal of religious teaching was naturally conveyed to multitudes who neither possessed the Bible itself, nor could have read it if they had possessed it.

And this medieval Bible of the Poor differed widely from the real Bible not only in its omissions but in its additions. The apocryphal gospels, books which no scholar would venture to defend in modern times, ranked then in art side by side with Matthew and Mark, Luke and John. Especially popular was the legend of Joachim and Anne and the birth of the Virgin Mary. " This story," writes Mâle, " apocryphal as it was, had not been rejected by the Medieval Church. On the Feast of the

---

[1] Martin and Cahier, *Vitraux de Bourges*, p. 19; Mâle II 480, who instead of *patriarchs*, would interpret, *Kings of Judah.*

[2] *Sent,* bk. III, dist. xix.a.

THE KISS AT THE GOLDEN GATE.

Nativity of the Blessed Virgin it was customarily read to the faithful. From time to time a bishop might evince certain scruples : ' I would read you this book to-day,' said Fulbert of Chartres [about A.D. 1020], ' if it had not been condemned by the Fathers ' [1] ; yet this did not prevent him from telling the whole story of Anne and Joachim in another sermon for the Feast of the Nativity. Certain churches were so indulgent to the legend that they introduced it into their lectionaries [e.g. at Coutances and at Caen]. . . . The meeting [of Joachim and Anne] at the Golden Gate is the most frequent of all these subjects. The artists at the end of the Middle Ages clung to it with marked predilection ; it was, in

(a)   (b)

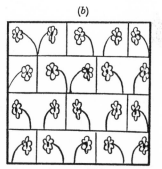

WALL PATTERNS FROM (a) RINGMORE (DEVON) AND (b) HAREFIELD (MIDDLESEX).

fact, the only way that had yet been imagined of representing the Immaculate Conception. Men repeated, although doctors [like St. Bernard] had condemned the error, that Mary had been conceived at the moment when Anne kissed Joachim. Therefore a fourteenth century Italian artist, in an exquisite picture, shows us an angel bringing the heads of husband and wife together for this holy kiss." [2]

[1] It was condemned even by two popes, Innocent I and Gelasius ; cf. Appendix 21.

[2] II, 314–16. In the Bâle painting here reproduced, the angel's scroll is inscribed *Mariam paries almam*—"Thou shalt give birth to the gentle Mary."

Moreover, the majority of medieval paintings were not even thus remotely connected with the Scriptures; they were not even from the apocryphal legends. To begin with, a large proportion of the walls was often covered with some geometrical pattern, such as imitation stonework with leaves or flowers in the corners, or a simple imitation of brocade. Then, among actual figures, by far the largest number represent no scene, but just a single saint, bearing his or her traditional emblem. Only a minority of English churches (except those of unusual size and importance), can have had so complete a series of pictures as Bede describes in the church which Benedict Biscop built.[1] "Fifthly, he [Benedict Biscop] brought with him pictures of sacred representations, to adorn the Church of St. Peter which he had built, namely a likeness of the Virgin Mary and of the twelve Apostles, with which he intended to adorn the central nave on boarding placed from one wall to the other; also some figures from ecclesiastical history for the south wall, and others from the Revelation of St. John for the north wall; so that everyone who entered the church, even if they could not read, wherever they turned their eyes, might have before them the amiable countenance of Christ and His saints, though it were but in a picture, and with watchful minds might revolve on the benefit of our Lord's incarnation, and having before their eyes the perils of the last judgment, might examine their hearts the more strictly on that account."

Any traveller in France may verify for himself how small a proportion of the representations are directly Biblical, especially if we except the single figures of prophets or apostles with their emblems, figures which would need much verbal explanation to give them anything beyond a superficial religious message. Moreover there was much carelessness in the use of scriptural subjects. A great deal was borrowed from the apocryphal gospels; at Amiens, for instance, the scene of Christ's

[1] Ed. Giles, vol. iv, pp. 368–9.

birth is not more conspicuous than the fabulous scene succeeding it, where, at the moment when Mary and

THE IDOLS OF EGYPT.

MOSES BREAKING THE TABLES.

Joseph and the babe enter upon the land of Egypt, every idol in that country falls in a moment from its pedestal. Moreover, of actual Biblical events, some of the best-

known are inexcusably distorted. The famous inlaid
pavement at St. Remi-de-Reims represents Moses breaking the Tables of the Law not against a calf, but against
a human-shaped idol. An English fifteenth century
window represents the combat of David and Goliath;
the former, in direct contradiction to the Bible text, is
fighting in plate-armour (*Ass. Arch. Soc. Reports*, 1925,
plates). The Twenty-four Elders of the Apocalypse are
not usually, perhaps never, represented according to the
Bible text, clad all in white robes, though certainly this
might have lent itself in capable hands to striking artistic
effect. In the southern rose-window of Chartres, and in
the Lady Chapel at Wells, the artist has arrayed them in
such colours as pleased his own fancy. A similar carelessness may be noted in the beautiful and perfect series
of windows which fill the choir of Conches, in Normandy.
Each of these lofty lights contains three scenes, one above
the other, as follows :—

1	2	3	4	5	6	7
B.V.M., Magdalene and John	Agony in Garden	Jesus mocked (palm)	Crucifixion	Rising from tomb	Appearance to B.V.M.	Pentecost
Entry to Jerusalem	Judas-kiss	Crowning with thorns	Jesus bears Cross	Harrowing of Hell	To Magdalene in Garden	Ascension
Last Supper	Jesus before Caiaphas	Scourging	Pilate washes hands	Descent from Cross	Peter leaps into sea	Thomas doubting

It is plain that several of these scenes are misplaced.
It is just possible that this has been done by the
clergy at some " restoration " ; but, when the windows
are studied on the spot, it is difficult to avoid the con-

clusion that the artist himself was responsible, and that he mixed up his cartoons.

This carelessness is quite in keeping with the frequent subordination of Bible to saint-worship. Here, as fairly typical of an important church, we may take that of St. Loup, the west front of which is described in the *Bibliothèque de l'école des chartes* (vol. ii, 1840–41, p. 255) : " Such are the admirably-preserved sculptures of the portal at St. Loup. We have recognised very few which recall the Gospels, the Apocalypse, the Bible or the general traditions of Christianity. Most seem to us to represent the deeds of St. Loup ; those which we have not been able to explain by well-known legends are probably intended to represent less important events which were still living in men's memory when the church was built." No doubt, within the church, there was a good deal of painting also ; but the most conspicuous portion for the general public was utilized for these scenes in the life of the local saint.

Mr. Kendon has carefully analized the data collected from Mr. Keyser's indispensable list of the paintings which remain in all our English churches. He writes (p. 10)[1] : " It is true enough that the medieval artist seems to miss innumerable opportunities, the rich mines of story in the Old Testament are almost untouched ; for though many representations of Old Testament scenes appear, these are generally if not always subsidiary, to be understood rather as examples, symbols, foreshadowings of New Testament events, than as containing any intrinsic interest or instruction. The gospel narrative too is only thinly drawn upon, and always in those parts where the two doctrines of the Virgin Birth and the Atonement may be illustrated. . . . The Nativity,

---

[1] *Mural Paintings in English Churches during the Middle Ages.* (John Lane, 1923.) This book, in spite of certain technical inaccuracies, is the best known to me, among those easily accessible to English readers, dealing with this part of the subject ; it has an admirable reproduction in colours of the Chichester painting.

then, and the Passion, Crucifix and Resurrection constitute the best examples of narrative art, and close to these, with perhaps less still of dogma, and more of human

ST. CHRISTOPHER.

" On whatsoever day thou hast seen Christopher's face, on that day, to be sure, thou shalt not die an evil death."

interest, come the histories of the saints, and, in especial, those of the martyrs. . . . The point which it is important to emphasize is that, out of the vast fields of legend and history from which they might have selected, the artists were strangely limited in their choice, especially in the matter of Scriptural histories."

There were three subjects which were normally found in every church, though visitation records show us that some of them were sometimes lacking or in bad repair. These were the Crucifix, the Mary and Child, and the Patron Saint of the church. Two others are extremely common, and probably existed originally in the large majority of churches; St. Christopher and the Doom. St. Christopher was generally on the north wall, exactly opposite the south door, which was the usual entrance.[1] There is the best of reasons for his popularity and his position; the sight of him was talismanic. As Molanus writes (III xxvii, p. 317) : " Men are wont to paint him in halls and in churches where he can easily be seen. Nay, I hear that in many places of Germany he is painted outside the church, about the entrance or on the outer wall. In some places the cause of this is indicated by verses under the picture, as, for instance :—

> Christophori sancti speciem quicunque tuetur
> Ista nempe die non morte mala morietur.[2]

But, as we have elsewhere spoken of this as vain, it would seem a better deed to put his image in some other decent place, in order that no occasion may be found for this vain error from his position." Elsewhere (II, xxxv, p. 100) Molanus has told us how the synod of Cambrai, in 1565, " stigmatized as abominable the vanity and superstition of those folk who promise for certain that men shall not quit this life without penitence and sacraments who have worshipped this or that saint ; so also we must blame as a most vain superstition whatsoever of the kind is found written beneath holy images. Let us

---

[1] At Amiens Cathedral, he is carved in gigantic proportions outside the south-west door.

[2] ' Whosoever seeth the representation of St. Christopher, on that day surely he shall not die an evil death.'

x

therefore say farewell to those verses concerning Christopher [above quoted], or

> Christophore sancte, virtutes sunt tibi tantae,
> Qui te mane vident, nocturno tempore rident,

or

> Christophorum videas ; postea tutus eas."[1]

Still more frequent, and beyond comparison more impressive, was the Doom. This, like many of the other subjects, had travelled far since the earlier Christian centuries.[2] The mosaic in SS. Cosma e Damiano at Rome is as impressive artistically as it is morally instructive. Christ stands there against a splendid sunrise sky ; blue and amber and crimson. On either side are His sheep ; not sheep and goats, but sheep on either side. This simple and consoling conception, however, did not endure. When the Church had to preach to more barbarous nations, she adopted grosser methods. She preached most emphatically, both in word and in pictures, the paramount importance of hourly reflection on hellfire.[3] There is no modern religious denomination, not

[1] " St. Christopher, so great are thy virtues, that they who see you in the morning laugh at night-time " ; " Look at Christopher, and afterwards go safe on your way." This was a far more serious consideration then than even in our own day. For sudden death meant death without the last absolving rites of the Church ; and theologians seriously discussed whether the man who died thus had a right of burial in holy ground, though they always, I believe, concluded finally on the merciful side. Sudden death in a tournament, however, deprived him of all Church offices. This legend that the sight of the saint's image preserved from sudden death is probably of fairly late origin ; St. Christopher was not otherwise conspicuous ; only seven or eight churches were dedicated to him in the whole of England (F. Arnold-Forster, Studies in Ch. Ded., vol. iii, pp. 5, 348).

[2] Readers may follow this up in a very interesting article recently published by Mr. Theodore Spencer, on Chaucer's Hell, a Study in Medieval Convention (Speculum, April, 1927, p. 177).

[3] Mr. Kendon writes very truly that the Advent Sunday sermon in Myrc's Festial is a sort of spoken Doom : " Above him shall be Christ his doomsman, so wroth, that no tongue can tell," etc.

THE LADDER OF SALVATION AT CHALDON (SURREY).

even the Salvation Army, which emphasizes this subject
so frequently and so pitilessly as medieval orthodoxy.[1]
Kind-hearted men made it their duty to describe these
horrors from the pulpit.   The Franciscan Berthold of
Regensburg, whom Roger Bacon singles out as the greatest
preacher of the thirteenth century, asks his hearers to
imagine themselves kindled to white-heat in a white-hot

FROM WORCESTER CATHEDRAL.

universe, until the Day of Judgment ; thenceforward to
live on, under far worse tortures, for as many years as
there have grown hairs on all the beasts bred in this
world since the days of Adam ; and even then to bear in
mind that all this would be but the beginning of their
everlasting torments.   St. Francis himself had appealed
as plainly to hell-fire as General Booth.   And this is a
subject which might truly justify Didron's contention
that the picture taught our forefathers more than the

[1] See *Five Centuries of Religion*, vol. i, pp. 441 ff, and the sixteenth of
my *Medieval Studies*, " Infant Perdition in the Middle Ages."

written or spoken word ; for a village painter could depict
devils more horrible than even Berthold's eloquence
could describe. No antiquarian can fail to have remarked,
what Mr. Kendon notes in his book on English wall-
paintings, that these primitive artists are far more successful in representing the damned than the blessed.
He notes also the great frequency of such representations ;
109 survive in English churches alone ; the subject is
even commoner than the Crucifixion ; moreover, it is
worked out with far more elaboration of detail, and at
proportionately greater cost. We have explicit testimony,
also, to its doctrinal efficacy. In the life of St. Methodius
we read how this effected the conversion of King Bogoris
of Bulgaria, and, indirectly, the accession of that country
not to the Roman Church, but to that of St. Methodius
the Greek. For the saint was something of an artist ;
and he reinforced his word by painting such lurid pictures
on the walls of the royal palace that the King gave way.
Even our John Lackland, we know on good authority,
was impressed for a moment by the Doom in Lincoln
Cathedral, though he had refused to take the Holy
Communion at his own coronation-mass, and was reported
never to have communicated since he reached the age of
discretion.[1] Similar evidence comes from the touching
prayer which François Villon composed for his old
mother. For certainly these are the most vivid of all
medieval picture-lessons, and often the most artistic
also. Below, the dead rise from their tombs in ecstasy
or doubt or despair ; above, sits the stern Christ of
Judgment, with Mary pleading on the right hand and
St. John on the left. In the midst is Michael weighing
the souls in his balance, a motive borrowed from Greek
pagan art, where we see Hermes (for instance) weighing
Achilles and Hector in his balance before their final
combat. In the Christian version, a fiend clings to the
evil side of the balance hoping to drag it down.
Thence the two streams of souls part to right and

[1] *Magna Vita S. Hugonis*, R.S., pp. 290 ff.

to left, on one side to Abraham's Bosom and to the Heavenly Jerusalem, on the other to the Jaws of Hell, amid a terrible medley of caldrons and furnaces and devils with pitchforks or red-hot pincers. In the most elaborate Dooms both sides are often clad, to show by their insignia that the Judge is no accepter of persons; evil Emperors, Kings, Popes, Bishops, Priests

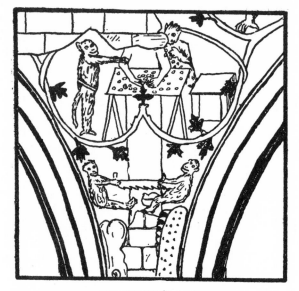

THE USURER'S FATE.

and Monks lead the crowd down to hell, even as virtuous dignitaries lead the procession to heaven. In the later Middle Ages this Doom was generally painted over the chancel-arch; and often, as in the now destroyed paintings at Felsted (Essex) the seven Deadly Sins were represented between the nave arches on either side. Of those sculptured Dooms that remain in great cathedrals, perhaps the finest is at Bourges. One of the most elaborate, and the most lurid, since it has lately been repainted in its original flaming colours, is at Berne. A very early series, extraordinarily lifelike and impressive in spite of its anatomical incorrectness, is at Worcester Cathedral.

These representations must be borne in mind as a pendant to those glorious porticoes and façades which treat happier subjects with still higher art. That symbolic blazoning shows at its best on some of the French west fronts. There we see one very real side of medieval faith; saints and prophets in solemn majesty at the doors, tier after tier with innumerable angels in the deep arches above them; then, higher still, kings of heroic proportions looking down upon the city; above that, perhaps, Christ crowning the Queen of Heaven. But very real also is this other motive of the Doom; and it may even be said that, of the two, this is the more characteristically medieval. At Wells there are no tortures; but this is very exceptional. For certainly it was an integral part of their faith; and, while we cannot understand medieval religion without bearing in constant remembrance the pious man's upward thoughts to Christ and His saints and heaven, so the picture must be incomplete unless we realize also that he was haunted by fears which scarcely exist for this present generation, in any form which our ancestors would have recognized as truly representing their own. St. Bernardino of Siena was not only one of the greatest mission-preachers of the Middle Ages; he was also a learned scholastic and a great restorer of the original Rule of his master, St. Francis. His nature was friendly and exceptionally sympathetic; but in more than one sermon he assures us that the blessed shall rejoice in the torments of the damned. Here, for instance, are his words in a lententide sermon: [1] " Fourthly, the damned ought to be tortured for ever by reason of pleasure [*jucunditatis*]. . . . Now, in the damnation of the reprobate, God's glory is all the greater in proportion to their multitude and greatness. Similarly all the greater is the beauty of His justice in proportion

[1] Serm iii, post 1, Dom. Quad. (Opp., Venice, 1745, p. 77).

as their vices and sins are more evident ; and, added to those sins, the most obdurate contumacy which nothing can soften. Nor would God's praise and glory, which is nothing else than His lofty and clear and widespread fame, be complete, if He had not perpetual praise and glory for His justice, even as for His goodness and mercy. Therefore at last the works of His glory will be fulfilled, even as those of His mercy also ; therefore His praise and glory whereof we have spoken shall be fulfilled in both [blessed and damned]. And, even as continual praise of thanksgiving shall everlastingly resound His

mercy in those that are saved, even so shall wailing and lamentation, sighs and bellowings and cries resound His justice in the damned ; therefore, to the ears of the blessed, Hell shall sing to Paradise with ineffable sweetness. Nor would there be in that place a pleasant and completely perfect sweetness of musical song, if

THE CALDRON OF PURGATORY.

this infernal discant from God's justice were lacking to the chant of His mercy : as it is written in Psalm [101] : ' I will sing of mercy and judgment.' Nor is any solemnity altogether complete which hath chant alone, without organ or discant. Therefore, together with the saints of the realms above, ' let us sing unto the Lord in glory, for He hath cast the horse and his rider ' to wit, the wicked and the devils, ' into the sea ' of the torments of hell : [1] that is, the wicked and the devils, for that reason that the Lord is just in all His ways and holy in all His works ; for He is three in one, just and loving and great and glorious, and to be blessed in all His works and to be praised to all eternity."

[1] Exod. xv, 1, 21 ; modified by St. Bernardino to suit his purpose.

In this, St. Bernardino is thoroughly orthodox ; he expresses the mind of the scholastic philosophers in general, and the ordinary teaching from the pulpit ; and we cannot understand the medieval representations of the Last Judgment without mental reference to this among other things. Even so great a thinker as St. Thomas Aquinas, who is remarkable for nothing more than for his sanity and balance, accepts it as the people accept it. He knows for certain that more folk will be damned than saved ; he knows that the flames of hell are not only moral but material actual fire ;[1] he knows that the blessed will look down from heaven and see the accursed writhing in hell beneath them, and that this proof of God's justice will add to their bliss : " The righteous shall rejoice when he seeth the vengeance " (Ps. lvii, 10).[2] Moreover, it is upon this that he bases his theory of heresy. If indeed hell be such as this ; if such be the omnipresent peril of hell ; if salvation from this unspeakable eternity depends upon the last moment of life, and upon a man's faith at that particular moment— and in all those matters Aquinas had no real choice ; they had been settled by tradition, and he must needs base his philosophy upon them—then his plea for the constant vigilance and action of the Inquisition is irrefragable. The nonconformist may at any moment pervert a conformist and send him to hell. As Berthold of Regensburg puts it : If I had a sister in a country wherein was only one single heretic, yet I should be afraid for her soul on that one heretic's account. Though many modern writers repudiate this medieval teaching, yet there is not one orthodox Catholic, I believe, who would dare to contradict St. Thomas's premises, or who

[1] From his commentary on Peter Lombard's *Sentences*, bk. IV, dist. 50, quaest. ii, art. 4, printed as Supplement to *Sum. Theol.*, pars iii, quaest. lxxi, art. I.

[2] Ibid., quaest. xcv, art. ii, iii. So also Vincent of Beauvais, *Spec. Hist.*, bk. 131, ch. 129 : " Although to the righteous their own joys suffice, yet for greater glory they behold the pains of the wicked which by [God's grace they themselves have escaped."

can undertake to break a single link of the chain which leads inexorably from those premises to that terrible conclusion. On the contrary, divinity professors at Rome, with express papal approval, have reminded their hearers even in this twentieth century that the principles remain untouched, though in practice it may be impossible or unwise to enforce them; and that those modern apologists who now minimize the Catholic Church's right to inflict bodily punishment, for religious nonconformity, upon all baptized persons of whatever religious denomination, are flying in the face of all orthodox tradition.[1] But these apologetic efforts have one very real significance; they show how anxious are even the most orthodox Roman Catholics to break here with their past; and the hell-fire booklets of Father Furniss, which were scattered abroad by tens of thousands within our own recollection, are now almost unprocurable even in the second-hand bookshops of their native Ireland; they have been quietly suppressed within the last twenty years or so. The Doom, then, may be called typically medieval; it has seldom been painted since the Reformation even in Roman Catholic parish churches, though it is fairly frequent in wayside shrines [2]; and, among all the most civilized peoples of to-day, the representation is tolerated only as a relic of the past. The portals of Reims and Amiens, on the other hand, appeal to educated modern Protestants and Agnostics more than they did to the less thoughtful of the population in their own Middle Ages.[3] But we

[1] See the eighteenth of my *Medieval Studies*. No writer, so far as I know, has ventured to challenge the accuracy of the statements in that monograph, except upon one doubtful point which is irrelevant to the present purpose.

[2] There is, however, one remarkable exception in the south transept of St. Remi-de-Troyes. Here is a large painted window of about 1850, almost ultra-medieval in the crude realism of its torments, signed by the artist: " Ch. Champigneulle, 40 Rue Denfer Rochereau, Paris."

[3] See Salimbene's casual notice of vandalism, which I quote later, in ch. xxii. It must be noted that I am here comparing *educated* modern amateurs with *the less thoughtful* of the Middle Ages. If we were to compare the whole modern with the whole medieval population, we should have to remember that, in Prof. Lethaby's words, " Those that could do could see."

must remember that, for one great building which impressed by this exalted imagery, there were literally hundreds of parish churches not only painted crudely with the Doom, but which presented the saints themselves in a fashion scarcely more refined. It was far easier for the ordinary craftsman to portray horror than beauty, where

HOLY AND UNHOLY IN POPULAR ART.

he had to steer between the Scylla of insipidity and the Charybdis of sensuous realism. The great mission-preacher Geiler complained, in about 1500 : " Nowadays, there is not an altar but a harlot stands thereon. When the painters paint a St. Barbara or St. Catharine, they paint her like a harlot. . . . What sort of piety does this breed in a young cleric when he prays his *confiteor*, and sees these pretty statues in front of him ? "[1]   Fr.

[1] Quoted by Kawerau, *Murner*, p. 76, where Murner is quoted as saying the same for himself, a generation later than Geiler.

Jarrett (p. 265) quotes a similar complaint from Savo-narola : " These young men go about saying of this woman or that, there is a Magdalen, there the Virgin, there a St. John ; and then you paint their faces in your churches, which is a great profanation of divine things. You painters do very ill. Did you know, as I know, the scandal you cause, you would certainly act very differently ; you fill the churches with vain things. Think you the

THE MARRIAGE FEAST AT CANA, FROM THE CHOIR
STALLS OF MONTRÉAL.

Virgin should be painted as you paint her ? I tell you she went clothed as a beggar, she went in rags."

Thus the large majority of church representations were neither Biblical nor even narrative in any way, except so far as the saint might speak through the emblem that he bore. Mr. Kendon points out that saint-image pictures are far more frequent than saint-narrative pictures ; and also, a significant fact, that, out of the 139 saints of which representations still remain in English churches, only 69 are persons of sufficient importance to find a place in the *Golden Legend* of Jacobus de Voragine.

Most of the points which I have emphasized in this chapter can be verified by any reader who has moderate facilities for travel, and who takes the trouble to analyse for himself the witness of cathedrals or parish churches. The importance of medieval imagery has been, and still is, very seriously distorted by modern antiquarian or religious zeal. The whole of Fr. Jarrett's chapter on Art is written in a key of exaggeration which, though natural enough, takes us very far from the medieval facts.[1] The pictures needed much help from the spoken word ; but preaching and catechetical teaching were more rare, even in the later Middle Ages, than in any modern church. An eloquent preacher might, no doubt, make a very striking point by appealing to the witness of the walls at his side.[2] But, after reading a great many medieval sermons, I can testify that such appeals are rarely recorded. In all Myrc's *Festial*, as Mr. Kendon notes, there is only one direct reference, and one indirect. St. Bernardino of Siena is a very valuable witness here ; for we have three volumes of his vernacular sermons taken down in shorthand as he spoke them. I do not remember any reference to pictorial symbolism in them ;[3] and, if this be so, it is significant ; for, although those sermons were delivered in the public square, it is unlikely that there was no imagery in view. It is true, the word-pictures of poets are in close harmony with the art of their day ; we see this very clearly, for instance, in Dante's *Purgatorio*. We cannot doubt, therefore, that the poor, in proportion to their intelligence, were deeply coloured in their thoughts by such carvings and paintings

---

[1] *Social Theories of the Middle Ages*, 1926, pp. 236 ff. The author generously acknowledges his debt to Jacques Maritain, for whom see Appendix 22.

[2] I mean, by appealing to them as driving home some religious truth, and not merely, for example, when Bromyard refers to the " fair paintings and images," in the east window. See Appendix 23.

[3] Except, of course, the monogram I H S, which St. Bernardino himself did so much to popularize.

as they might see every week or even every day. But these influences were far from being purely religious; and the things that they loved most were often either mainly or altogether spurious, or at least mixed with much alloy. One of the most touching pictures in Dante is that of the half-civilized peasant who has come to Rome to adore the Vernicle (*Parad.* xxxi 93) :—

> " Like a wight,
> Who haply from Croatia wends to see
> Our Veronica, and the while 'tis shown,
> Hangs over it with never sated gaze,
> And, all that he hath heard revolving, saith
> Unto himself in thought : ' And didst thou look
> E'en thus, O Jesus, my true Lord and God ?
> And was this semblance thine ? ' "

Yet, among that man's modern co-religionists, the majority of educated persons would decline to pin their faith either upon the authenticity of this portrait, or on the truth of the legend that it was miraculously imprinted on the napkin with which St. Veronica wiped the sweat from Christ's brow on the way to Calvary.

It falsifies our perspective altogether, therefore, if we concentrate on the cathedrals and forget the parish churches, which served for a far larger body of worshippers than did the cathedrals, and which, in their totality, perhaps cost more in money and in labour. Even if we granted, in over-generous concession, that the thousand statues or painted figures of Reims formed a full body of religious doctrine, the question of the villager would still remain ; and the villagers formed the overwhelming majority of medieval souls. We ourselves, contemplating the cathedrals, do truly feel ourselves compassed with a great cloud of heavenly witnesses. Let us not presume to minimize these artistic glories and their enduring effect on generation after generation of mankind ; but, on the other hand, let us avoid exaggeration.

Do even the most magnificent cathedral façades to the average beholder, or even to any but an exceptional beholder, bring home the reality and sanctity of religion more truly than, for instance, John Bunyan's *Pilgrim's Progress* ? And would it be less false to history if we formed all our conceptions of the teaching given to seventeenth century Protestant villagers upon the *Pilgrim's Progress*, than it is to judge of those villagers who formed 90 per cent. of the medieval population by the spiritual advantages that may be enjoyed in contemplation of the Cathedral of Chartres ?

To sum up, then, we have the strongest evidence that medieval art was, from the point of view of religious teaching, an imperfect substitute for the spoken or written word. From the very first, common sense might suggest its comparative inferiority, and abundant documents show that common sense is right. The equivocal nature of symbolic teaching is proverbial; one of the best and most natural of ancient stories is that of James VI and the Professor of Signs.[1] A large part of medieval symbolism was at no time generally understood, and was rapidly forgotten even by the clergy; that religious and educational revival which we call the Counter-Reformation had no use for it. In its nobler and more permanent constituents, it adds a glory to the highest Gothic art, and often a simple grace to the work of those every-day craftsmen, who, after all, wrought by far the greater number of medieval buildings, and are too often forgotten in comparison with the cathedral masons. It is essential that we should subject mere irresponsible talk to the criterion of plain fact. For, in the long run, this is not only a practical necessity, but even the most edifying course to the best minds of all parties. Cardinal Newman's apology may serve for all of us : " Nor is this the sole consideration, on which an author may be justified in the use of frankness after the manner of Scripture in speaking of the saints; for their lingering imperfections surely

[1] See Appendix 24.

make us love them more, without leading us to reverence them less, and act as a relief to the discouragement and despondency which may come over those who, in the midst of much error and sin, are striving to imitate them ; according to the saying of St. Gregory on a graver occasion, ' Plus nobis Thomae infidelitas ad fidem, ·quam fides credentium discipulorum profuit.' "[1]

---

[1] " Thomas's unbelief, even more than the faith of the believing disciples, has helped us to faith." (*Hist. Sketches*, vol. iii, 1873, *advt.* p. xii.)

CHAPTER XVI

ART AND RELIGION

THE thirteenth century achieved an equilibrium of art and religion which, though neither so complete nor so stable as it is often represented, was yet very real. Through the Dark Ages, art had been preserved mainly in the cloister, by monastic money and even sometimes by monastic hands. In many cases, also, it had been penetrated by a genuine and deep devotional spirit. Though Tuotilo of St. Gall is acknowledged now to be partly legendary—for our records date from a century later than his actual day, and Ekkehard, who describes him at length, is unquestionably so inaccurate as to confuse between different generations at that monastery— yet at least his story is in all respects *ben trovato*, and an unregenerate modern historian of art might echo those contemporary words : " Curses on the man who made so fine a fellow as this into a monk ! " The legend of his work at Metz rests also upon real facts ; monks did indeed, here and there, wander forth from their abbeys to work for churches outside. Some, again, like that Roger of Helmershausen, who called himself Theophilus, collected small groups of pupils, and jotted down practical notes for their use. But a careful analysis of the facts indicates that all this tradition was monastic mainly in the sense that it was sheltered within the monastic precincts. Nearly all these practical recipes of the Middle Ages can be traced back to Greek or Egyptian paganism. The two arts which monks themselves seem most to have practised are metal-work and illumination. Neither of these is distinctly Christian in its origin or in its general character ; they are Christianized, if at all, only by the addition of certain details which are in no way essential to the general artistic effect.[1] We may see this in the Gloucester candlestick at the Victoria and Albert Museum ; or, still better, in the thirteenth century huge bronze candelabrum of Milan Cathedral. The central boss, occupying perhaps one-fiftieth of the whole mass, contains four groups from the Adoration of the Magi ; but most of the rest is undenominational ; with very little change of detail, and none of general effect, the candelabrum might light a temple of Buddha or of Vishnu. Moreover, even the details in our churches were not always distinctively Christian. We have seen how ostrich-eggs were borrowed from mosques ; and the *baldacchino* of Roman churches was originally, as its name tells us, simply a hanging of those brocades for which Baldak, or Bagdad, has always been famous. It is probable that the great statue of Peter in his own church at Rome, whose toes have been kissed away by generations of worshippers, was originally a Jupiter.

For early Christianity had been strongly puritan in the matter of art ; and, when at last it adopted painting and sculpture, it accepted pre-existing pagan traditions for its basis. Remi de Gourmont, though he hated and despised Protestantism, was driven to energetic protest against the sentimental figments of Huysmans on the subject of medieval art. " The worship of saints and of sanctified deities," he writes, " begat churches. The Catholic churches, like the temples of ancient Egypt, are tombs ; they were not built in honour of God alone ; their pretext was almost always to shelter the corpse of a saint or a miracle-worker, the

[1] The pre-Christian tribes of Europe had excelled in elaborate metal-work ; and their laws show clearly how great a value was attached to metal-workers in comparison with other craftsmen. In almost every code a higher fine must be paid in redemption for killing a goldsmith than for any other. " The goldsmith has almost everywhere the highest ' weregeld.' From the 30 to 50 *solidi* [gold pieces] which are prescribed by the Salic and Alamannic Laws, it rises among the Burgundians to 100, or even 150." (J. v. Schlosser, *Beiträge*, p. 175.)

simulacrum of some traditional deity scarcely even re-baptized by an innocent piety. . . . [Huysmans] tries to prove that there is, or rather that there has been, a Catholic, symbolic and mystic art, far above profane art, especially in expression. . . . There is a Catholic art ; there is no such thing as Christian art. Evangelical Christianity is essentially opposed to all representations of sensible beauty, whether imitated from the human body or from the rest of nature. . . . Whenever Christianity, through its monks or its revolutionaries, has tried to force itself to closer conformity with apostolic teaching, it was compelled to reject all that there was in the Roman religion of paganism in beauty, and consequently of sensualism. There is no Christian art ; it is a contradiction in terms. . . . The pagan origin of the symbolism of the catacombs is certain ; it was mythology which supplied the decorative elements to the tombs of the first martyrs. . . . The martyrs who refused incense to idols would have been very surprised if they had been told that the censer would become a pious article of furniture."[1] The best churchmen of the Middle Ages, as we shall see, made no attempt to confuse art with religion.

Yet in practice the two were inextricably intermingled, when once the Church had committed herself to the Græco-Roman rather than the Jewish attitude towards art. " Catholic art . . . is the natural and logical sequence of pagan art."[2] It refused that complete breach with the past which the earlier Fathers had aimed at, and which others again attempted at the Reformation. The Church needed churches, and for them she needed artists ; thenceforward there was continual interaction. The ubiquitous character of the medieval Church can scarcely be exaggerated. In England, which represents about the average, there was more than one parish church to every hundred families, without counting chapels or wayside shrines. The proportion was even

[1] *La Culture des Idées,* ed. du *Mercure de France,* 1916, pp. 139–155.
[2] Ibid., p. 140.

greater in the towns than in the villages. Norwich had about 50 churches when its total population was more probably 8,000 than 12,000 souls, Lincoln had 49, York 41.[1] And these buildings entered not merely into religious life but into men's daily affairs. As the priest claimed authority over all baptized folk from the cradle to the grave and in almost every act of their lives, so the consecrated building was more their home than it is nowadays, even in modern Roman Catholic countries. A modern French church is sometimes placarded with notices asking the worshippers, among other things, not to bring packages into the sacred building ; but in Italy the peasant woman still brings in her market-basket, and sets it down under the pulpit if she stops to listen to a sermon. Lawsuits and university disputations and degree-ceremonies were regularly carried on in medieval churches. This had its irreverent side ; litigation and theatrical performances were often forbidden, though not with complete success. At Strassburg, one of the Burgomaster's most regular places and times for business was his pew in the cathedral during Mass. Saintliest ecclesiastics did not shrink from doing business during the sacred office ; St. Hugh of Lincoln, in the chapel of Château-Gaillard, held an animated dispute with Richard I, before he passed on to the altar and " attended to naught else but the divine service."[2] Of Henry II, who was quite an average God-fearing man as medieval kings went, Giraldus tells us that " either forgetting his own sacramental unction as king, or putting it out of his mind, he would scarce lend to God's worship just the time of consecration in the Mass ; and even during that time (perchance by reason of his royal cares and the heavy business of the State), he was more busy with his councillors, and with talk, than with devotion to the sacrament."[3] " When he went intoh is chapel,"

[1] Baldwin Brown, p. 119.
[2] Magna Vita S. Hugonis, R.S., p. 251.
[3] Giraldus Cambrensis, *De Instructione Principum*, 1846, p. 72.

says another contemporary, " he would spend the time
in whispering and scribbling pictures."[1] The chronicler
of Battle Abbey tells us how the Abbot of Westminster,
a few days after Henry II's coronation, was so anxious
to get confirmation of a charter of privileges for his
abbey, that he came to the king during Mass and got the
king to read and approve it ; the king then sent for the
chancellor and got it sealed ; then came up the Bishop
of Chichester and protested against the charter. All
this certainly took place during Mass, and apparently
almost at the foot of the altar.[2]

But there was a better side to all this, and we must
beware of judging it from a narrowly modern point of
view ; it was partly childish, but it was also in great
part childlike. The people felt that this was their own
building, their one natural meeting-place outside the
family fireside. We must not think of it as a place of
complete equality ; the squire had a right of sitting
apart in the chancel with the clergy, and Chaucer, among
others, shows us how neighbours struggled for precedence
in accordance with their competing social claims.[3] Yet
the Church had kept a good deal of ancient Christian
democratic tradition ; and, among the large majority
who acquiesced more or less completely in her authority,
the sacred building was a real home ; so that they nestled
within its walls with some true portion of that spirit of
adoption whereby we cry *Abba, Father,* the Spirit itself
bearing witness with our spirit that we are the children
of God. It was bound up with a spirit of local patriotism,
narrow but intense ; the inhabitant even of the next
village or town is spoken of in market-regulations as a
" foreigner " ; when different villages repair on solemn
festivals to the nearest cathedral, each with the banner
of its own local saint, there are fierce struggles for precedence, often ending in bloodshed and sometimes in

[1] Radulphus Niger (ed. Anstruther), p. 169.
[2] *Chron. de Bello,* 1846, p. 72.
[3] *Cant. Tales,* B, 3091 ; cf. *The Medieval Village,* pp. 283 ff.

death.''[1] On the other hand, within the parish there was a strong sense of social solidarity. The mere sight of men's faces and sound of voices in peaceful surroundings, and in homage to a single ideal, however vaguely understood, exercises a progressive humanizing influence. However the hierarchy was feudalized, there was at bottom the theory of the equality of all souls ; and this was realized to some extent in the community of worship and of the Sacraments. There is equal religious and artistic significance in that story, dear to Burne-Jones and his friends, of the Merciful Knight who spared his enemy and for whom, next time he knelt before the crucifix, the Christ-figure bent down from that cross to embrace him. Provided that men thought at all (a proviso as necessary for the estimate of medieval as of modern society) there was the daily thought of Christ suffering and redeeming, and, still more, of the Virgin Mary as mediator, side by side with the strict Judge who sits aloft over the chancel arch, and shows five bleeding wounds that cry for vengeance like Abel's. The parish church, then, was where faces and voices met ; a sort of spiritual (and sometimes, even material) market-place. Under stress of great sorrow, it was still more ; refreshing, uplifting, and affording the one hope there was for the dead.

In many ways, therefore, churchman and artist were natural allies, and art was kept in natural touch both with the religious idealist up above and with popular ideas down below. Probably the craftsman's personal preference would generally have been for a completer independence ; but the Church paid him and the Church did much to

---

[1] E.g. Grosseteste, *Epistolæ*, R.S., p. 75. The author of an admirable recent study of a single Burgundian village writes : " Formerly, inter-parochial hatred was general ; villages hated and insulted each other ; on the feast of the patron saint something was lacking to the full festival if there was no fight among the young folk. . . . When, about 1840, the first Arbigny girl married an Uchizy man, there was a sort of riot in the parish on the wedding-day. (Ch. Dard, *Uchizy en Mâconnais*, Mâcon, 1926. p. 144.)

call the tune, if not directly, at least indirectly, in the sense that the building must be constructed to serve ecclesiastical purposes and traditions, even when the funds were raised by mere layfolk. Therefore, although it is likely that the hierarchy did little more to shape art directly than to shape vernacular literature—and in that field its influence can be calculated with some approach to exactitude—yet the indirect influence of the Church was immense. The thesis of the communal origin of the ballad is often defended on the ground that the requirements of ballad poetry were practically dictated by communal conditions ; [1] and in that same sense we may emphasize the ecclesiastical character of medieval art.

To claim more for it than this would seem inconsistent with historical facts. The theory of a direct connexion between art and religion is paradoxical, to say the least, in the face of what we know about society in the thirteenth century, or, again, in the age of Pericles. The generations which produced our greatest cathedrals were those in which we can trace a strong spirit of doubt, both philosophic and popular. University scholars were then condemned for formulating difficulties strikingly similar to the difficulties felt by the majority of thinking people in this twentieth century ; and it would be absurd to suppose, even if we had not explicit evidence to the contrary, that the teachers who were bold enough to provoke these censures were the only men who thought thus in their hearts ; or, again, that this ecclesiastical condemnation did in fact reverse the current of their thoughts. Moreover, there is evidence for widespread popular unbelief also, in cruder forms.[2] So again with the age of Pericles, as no less an authority than Jebb has pointed out.[3] This was the age of perfect Greek art, and also of

[1] E.g. G. L. Kittredge, on pp. 20 ff. of *English and Scottish Popular Ballads*, ed. Sargent and Kittredge, (Houghton, Mifflin & Co., 1904.)

[2] Cf. *From St. Francis to Dante*, Chapter XXIV.

[3] *Has Art thriven best in an Age of Faith ?* This rare pamphlet, embodying a lecture given at Glasgow in 1889, seems never to have been reprinted. I summarize it in Appendix 25.

widespread scientific scepticism. Ruskin generalizes from these facts : " The religious passion is nearly always vividest when the art is weakest ; and the technical skill reaches its deliberate splendour only when the ecstasy which gave it birth has passed away for ever." [1] And at another time, in *The Stones of Venice* : " The more I have examined this subject, the more dangerous I have found it to dogmatize respecting the character of the art which is likely, at a given period, to be most useful to the cause of religion. One great fact first meets me. I cannot answer for the experience of others, but I never yet met with a Christian whose heart was thoroughly set upon the world to come, and, so far as human judgment could pronounce, perfect and right before God, who cared about art at all. . . . I have never known a man who seemed altogether right and calm in faith, who seriously cared about art." [2]

It is true that certain forms of religion appeal specially to the artistic temperament ; but so also do certain forms of irreligion. Of Perugino, whose actual pictures would never have suggested this, Vasari tells us that he could never get any notion of God into that hard head of his. [3] Of all present races, it is probable that the most artistic are the Chinese, among whom the educated classes are said to be conspicuous for their lack of religious enthusiasm.

The Middle Ages provide no true exception to this general law in social history. Not only was the medieval Church never mistress of man's artistic emotions, but she never claimed to be, except so far as she asserted a right of censorship over all men's actions, in the interest of her dogmatic traditions. Bishop Baldock of London might, for his own diocese, forbid an artistic crucifix as

---

[1] *The Queen of the Air*, library edition, vol. xix, p. 384.

[2] IV. *St. Mark's*, § 58, ed. vol. x, p. 125.

[3] It is interesting to connect this with what Sacchetti tells us of superstition in Perugia, and the connexion between superstition and infidelity. See Chapter XIV above.

heretical; but I believe that no pre-Renaissance popes ever attempted to regulate art in general, any more than they attempted to revise the notoriously corrupt text of the Vulgate Bible. Charlemagne, it is true, attempted both. His Bible-revision, with the similar work of Roger Bacon and his school, marked the only great forward steps in that field during the last nine centuries of the Middle Ages; next in importance came the work of another Englishman, Stephen Harding. And in art, as we have seen, Charlemagne intervened also, with sound sense though not with enduring success. There were other individuals, as we shall see, who strongly objected to grotesques and obscenities, especially in churches. An inconvenient reformer like Savonarola might persuade people for a moment to make bonfires of lascivious pictures and expensive artistic superfluities; but Savonarola himself became food for the faggot, chiefly because of his determined opposition to the reigning clerical tendencies of his time. When at last popes became seriously interested in art, they were far from sharing Savonarola's attitude towards morals, or Charlemagne's towards image-worship.

The puritanism of great medieval religious reformers is very notable. The remarkable reform of Cluny is often quoted in the contrary direction, but by an anachronism. It is true, Cluny had probably a very large part in that movement which produced Glaber's often-cited " white robe of churches " in the first half of the eleventh century. But the reform itself had begun a century before this; and we need evidence for any real revival of art under Cluniac influence during the first and purest generations. Moreover, the churches of which Glaber speaks were probably what we should consider extremely plain; it is only in the century after his death, roughly from 1070 to 1170, that we have evidence for Cluniac workshops and a whole school of remarkable sculpture and metal work. But by that time there was a good deal of worldliness in the congregation; the Cluniacs as a whole did not even declare definitely for Gregory VII in his quarrel with Henry IV ; and the Abbot of Cluny kept friendly relations with the emperor. Therefore it is obviously impossible to argue from what we know of A.D. 1100, when the Cluniacs were among the wealthiest bodies in the Western world, back to 910, when they had started on a career of evangelical poverty. It follows that, pending the production of entirely new evidence, Cluny cannot be quoted as exemplifying an alliance of pure art with pure religion.

For the next great reformers, the Cistercians, we have abundant evidence of puritanism ; indeed, among the modern orthodox there are not a few who accuse them here of straitlaced Phariseeism. They were anxious above all " to follow, naked, the naked Christ : " from this followed logically their determination " that nothing savouring of pride or superfluity should be left in God's house." [1] The Cistercians, writes Abbé Vacandard, " vowed to remove from their lowly chapels everything which might flatter curious eyes and charm weak souls. They banished painting and carving, as vain things that were good for worldly folk. The same prohibition extended to fine tissues and precious metals ; the very crosses might not be plated with silver or copper, they were to be of wood." [2] This dates from their very beginning ; it is expressed in St. Stephen Harding's " Charter of Charity," which is the constitutional foundation-stone of the Order.

And these Cistercians, zealous for reform, did not hesitate to plead openly and definitely here against the Cluniacs, whom they rightly recognized as representatives, in that day, less of Benedictine strictness than of monastic relaxation. St.-Bernard, in his letter to Guillaume de St.-Thierry, wrote with a satirical emphasis which would not have been fully endorsed by cultured

---

[1] Migne, P.L., vol. 185, col. 1011 ; cf. *Five Cent. of Religion*, vol. i, p. 278.

[2] *Vie de St.-Bernard*, 2nd ed., vol. i, p. 101.

Anglican puritans like Milton and Selden; and yet St.
Bernard, like those men, had been brought up in the
literary tradition of the Roman classics, as they were
taught in his own day.[1] The size and elaborate ornamentation of the Cluniac churches, says the saint, seem
distinctive less of Christian worship than of Jewish rites.
All this gilding and these sensuous attractions, are they
meant to secure " the admiration of fools, or the offerings
of simple folk ? " " To speak plainly, doth the root of
this lie in covetousness, which is idolatry ? and do we
seek not [spiritual] profit, but a gift " ? according to the
worldly law which often renders ostentation a successful
bait for further endowments. " Men's eyes are feasted
with relics cased in gold, and their purse-strings are
loosed." The net result is, that " the Church is resplendent in her walls, beggarly in her poor ; she clothes her
stones in gold and leaves her sons naked ; the rich man's
eye is fed at the expense of the indigent." He is specially
severe upon the magnificent hanging chandelier of bronze
which was one of the greatest ornaments of Cluny. The
very floors, again, are pictured, so that men spit in the
face of an angel. For simple and uneducated folk, St.
Bernard does permit some of these attractions ; they
may need artificial stimulus ; but for his fellow-religious
he is inexorable. The grotesques which adorn the Cluniac
cloisters do but distract the truly pious mind ; " we are
tempted to spend the whole day in wondering at these
things, rather than in meditating on the law of God."
It will be noted that Bernard, like Charlemagne, emphasizes
not any hidden meaning supposed to underlie these
grotesques, but their want of meaning. Schnaase writes
very truly : " We possess a series of passages, from the
twelfth century to the fifteenth, in which ecclesiastical
writers mention animal representations, sometimes with
sharp blame, as contrary to the dignity of a sanctuary,
and sometimes with praise for their vivid execution, but
never with the slightest reference to their symbolical

[1] See Appendix 26 for fuller text of this and similar utterances.

character, though this could not have passed unnoticed if symbolism had been usual here. Therefore these fully-instructed men either did not assume any such meaning, or held it to be so little disseminated as to require no refutation." [1] I have already noted how St. Bernard, speaking bitterly of the wastefulness of such objects, gives no hint of monks' time or energies squandered on these artistic treasures, but of money wasted which might have gone to feed and clothe the destitute. Moreover, this spirit of St. Stephen Harding and St. Bernard lived on among many Cistercians of the next generation. It comes out very strongly in the *Dialogue between a Cluniac and a Cistercian*, of about 1180. There, the Cluniac is shocked at St. Bernard's satire: " I have read it, and marvelled how he could so reprove those insignia of our religious devotion (whereby we honour God), as to hold us up to scorn." To which the Cistercian answers: " Did those unknown authors of your Order imagine

FROM FUNERAL BRASS OF ABBOT DELAMERE AT ST. ALBANS (HERTS).

that, at the Last Day, Christ would thus say (among other things) to the Elect: ' *Come, ye blessed of My Father* [2] *for ye have made a golden chalice in My honour, and a chasuble with golden fringes* ; ' and that He would make some contrary speech to the damned ? "

Petrus Cantor, the famous precentor of Notre-Dame-

[1] Vol. ii, pt. 1, p. 376 ; see the whole discussion from p. 369 onwards.

[2] Martène, Thes., vol. v, col. 1585. On the verge of the Reformation, Abbot Tritheim repeated what others had said before him, that magnificent monastic buildings were only too often concomitants of spiritual decay (*Opp. Pia*, p. 884). For further evidence see *Five Cent. of Religion*, vol. i. For a very interesting further example of Cistercian puritanism, about 1230, see Renan and Leclerc, vol. i, p. 71.

de-Paris, wrote at the time when this *Dialogue* was being composed. He also takes the puritan standpoint ; these great monastic buildings are often raised from the proceeds of usury or " the deceitful lies of hireling preachers," and " men sin even in building churches," for these preach rather pride than Christian humility.[1] So thought St. Francis also, insisting that the poverty of the brethren's churches would preach better than words. Thomas of

FROM FUNERAL BRASS OF BISHOPS BURCHARD
AND JOHN AT LÜBECK.

Eccleston tells us how loyal the English friars of the first generation had been to that ideal.[2] "At Shrewsbury Brother William, the minister, being zealous for poverty, ordered the stone walls in the dormitory to be removed and mud walls put in their stead, which was done by the brethren with admirable meekness and at great cost." And again, " Under Brother Agnellus the brethren had so strict a conscience regarding the building of houses and the possession of pictures that the visitor acted with great severity because of the windows in the chapel at Gloucester ; moreover, he deprived a brother of his hood

[1] *Verb. Abbrev.*, chap. lxxxvi.
[2] *Monumenta Franciscana*, R.S., pp. 18, 29.

because he had decorated a pulpit with pictures, and he inflicted the same penance upon the Guardian of the place because he had permitted the pictures to be painted."

Humbert de Romans (about 1270), criticized severely the architectural indulgences to which by this time even the Cistercians had become accustomed : " There are some, among whom there is such excess in buildings, either in number or in cost or in elaboration of ornament [*curiositatem*], that they surpass even worldly folk." He is indignant also " that there is an excessive costliness in books, and especially in the books of Religious, who ought specially to profess poverty. St. Jerome would have us care not so much for beautiful texts, as for texts carefully corrected." [1] He writes as General of the Dominicans, who had begun in the same spirit of puritanism with the Franciscans, though perhaps with rather less militant directness. [2] And in the fifteenth century, when all Orders of Friars sadly needed recall to their first simplicity, grave warnings were uttered by another Dominican, St. Antonino, Archbishop of Florence. [3] He was a great canon lawyer and a confessor of vast experience ; his knowledge of mankind and his common sense enabled him to get near as any other man to that reconciliation of usury and religion which had been begun by earlier thinkers, and especially by St. Thomas Aquinas. But, in the matter of art, he agreed with St. Bernard and St. Francis. Taking his text from Gratian, the first book of the *Corpus Juris Canonici*, he wrote : " Note that St. Ambrose saith [Gratian, pars. i., dist. 86, c. 18], ' It is specially proper for the priest to adorn God's temple with suitable honour, in order that God's hall may shine with such ornaments also.' Yet he saith not that we should

---

[1] De la Bigne, *Bib. Max. Patrum*, vol. xxv, pp. 465, 633. It will be noted here again that his objection to these illuminated volumes is not waste of monks' labour, but waste of money : by this time, even the illuminations were mainly done by paid workmen.

[2] E.g. the statutes of 1228, printed by Ehrle and Denifle (*Archiv.*, vol. i, p. 225).

[3] *Summa Major*, pars. iii, tit xii, cap. x, § 2.

make superfluities, pomps, and many vanities of coats of
arms, of paintings, of golden vessels and so forth. . . .
St. Jerome [*ibid.*, pars. ii, causa xii, c. 71] in his epistle
to Nepotianus, saith : ' Many folk build walls, and rear
columns for the church ; we see gleaming marbles, and
the roofs are bright with gold ; the altar is adorned with
gems ; yet no care is taken to choose the ministers of
Christ.   Let no man here plead against me that the
temple of the Jews was rich ; that it had a golden table,
golden lamps, dishes and cups and covers of beaten gold.
Such things were then approved by God, while the priests
slaughtered beasts for sacrifice—that is, while the people
were as yet carnal, and God's worship was sought in
outward and sensible things ' ; but then Jerome con-
tinueth [1] : ' Yet all these things were preparatory and
figurative, and were written for our correction, upon
whom the ends of the world are come [1 Cor. x. 11].
Now, however, when our Lord, as a poor man, has consecrated the poverty of His own house, let us bear His
cross and look upon delights [2] as dirt.'   St. Bernard also
reprehendeth the vain and monstrous pictures of churches,
and the filth and carelessness of sacred things, as of altar-
cloths and so forth."   And elsewhere, speaking of architecture and art in general, he writes : [3] " The reprobate
Cain is the first of whom we read that he built a city, and
therefore houses. . . . After the deluge, the tyrant
Nimrod was the first who led others to build the tower
of Babel. . . . Spacious palaces and excessive buildings,
beyond what is convenient, are not pleasing to God ; the
Patriarchs lived in tents." . . . St. Antonino then speaks
of *latomi* and *caementarii*, and continues : " Stone-cutters
are joined with these, whereof some hew stones and bring
them to a rough shape, whence others complete divers
finished works, others carve statues and figures, as marblers
also ; and these cannot make many frauds in their works,

[1] I.e. this parenthesis is Antonino's gloss upon Jerome.
[2] Gratian has *divitias*, not *delicias*.
[3] Ibid., pars. iii, tit. viii, cap. iv, § 8.

for such works are manifest to all men ; yet they can demand an excessive price for their labour ; nevertheless, if experts in art esteem the work at such a price, we must believe them."[1] We have seen how the author of *Dives and Pauper*, himself in all probability a friar, is emphatic as to the non-religious character of a great deal of church-building. St. Bernardino of Siena counts it a sin in artisans to make superfluous and sumptuous curtains, shirts in which the embroidery is worth ten times the material, costly caps or garlands for ladies, or playing-cards.[2] Dean Colet, in his famous Convocation sermon of 1511, complained that the goods of the Church were too often spent on sumptuous edifices.[3]

These quotations may suffice out of a far larger number which might be produced. Art devotees in the Middle Ages were of almost all sorts, but they were seldom or never canonized saints. St.-Eloi, who is frequently quoted, is no real example here ; there is, I believe, no evidence for his having practised art-work from the moment of his conversion onwards. Fra Angelico would be a nearer instance, if we are to choose the best case we can produce from about a thousand years of history. The heroes of the most romantic episodes in medieval art history are not the hierarchy but the lay public. They are not saints, but the better sort of ordinary people ; this will come out more clearly in my next chapter.

But let me here repeat that it is no part of my thesis to deny the intimate connexion between the art of any age and the religion of that age. Many indications of this connexion will be obvious to everybody ; and, quite recently, Emile Mâle and other authors have shown that the pilgrimage-routes did as much as the trade-routes

---

[1] " The parishioners of Totnes in 1488 appointed a committee of ' supervisors ' to visit all the bell-towers for miles around, and afterwards built one at Totnes ' according to the best model'."—*Hist. MSS. Comm.* III, 235–346.

[2] *Opera*, ed. de la Haye, vol. i, p. 161 ; cf. iii, 160 (elaborate music offensive to God's ears).

[3] Knight's *Life of Colet.*, 1823, p. 247.

for the spread of new ideas in art, or perhaps even more.[1] It is my aim only to clear this question and to guard against exaggerations. However real and potent and ennobling may be the religious emotion inspired in us by art, or the religious emotions which inspired certain artists in their own day, let us not forget that this does not appeal equally to all men ; and, again, that there are other high religious appeals quite independent of art. We shall best learn, and best enjoy, by taking each on its own merits. And, when either theologian or artist is tempted to complain that something in the atmosphere of his own day frustrates his efforts, will he not then, in proportion as he has the real root of the matter in his soul, hear a voice descending from that which he is aspiring to reach : " What is that to thee ?   Follow thou Me."

Yet there was, at certain times and places, what may be called a real Religion of Art. Vasari has told the story of Cimabue and the Borgo Allegri, the Suburb of the Joyful, in words which modern historians dare not endorse as accurate, but which are not beyond the bounds of probability ; the anecdote may be accepted as *ben trovato* so long as we refrain from undue emphasis.[2]   " He afterwards painted the Picture of the Virgin, for the Church of Santa Maria Novella. This picture is of larger size than any figure that had been painted down to that time ; and the angels surrounding it made it evident that, although Cimabue still retained the Greek manner, he was nevertheless gradually approaching the mode of outline and general method of modern times. Thus it happened that this work was an object of so much admiration to the people of that day—they having then never seen anything better—that it was carried in solemn procession, with the sound of trumpets and other festal

---

[1] E.g. *Revue de Paris*, Oct. 15, 1919. " L'Art du Moyen âge et les pèlerinages."

[2] *Lives of the Painters*, ed. Bohn, vol. i, p. 41. As the editor points out, the suburb almost certainly drew its name from the Allegri family.

demonstrations, from the house of Cimabue to the church ; he himself being highly rewarded and honoured for it. It is further reported, and may be read in certain records of old painters, that, whilst Cimabue was painting this picture, in a garden near the Church of San Pietro, King Charles the Elder, of Anjou, passed through Florence, and the authorities of the city, among other marks of respect, conducted him to see the picture of Cimabue. When this work was thus shown to the King, it had not before been seen by any one ; wherefore all the men and women of Florence hastened in great crowds to admire it, making all possible demonstrations of delight. The inhabitants of the neighbourhood, rejoicing in this occurrence, ever afterwards called that place Borgo Allegri ; and this name it has ever since retained, although in process of time it became enclosed within the walls of the city."

But we have a far more remarkable story, upon far better evidence, from about the year 1155. It is told at length by Henry Adams in *Mont St.-Michel and Chartres*. But Adams was a superficial student, and the whole book, in spite of the author's real ability and the interest of his subject, is full of false impressions. Under a style which implies a vast reserve of learning from which the writer is drawing almost at random, he conceals a frequent ignorance of the most important documents ; and, in this particular case, writing apparently at second-hand, he mistakenly applies to Chartres a description which does, indeed, cast a very valuable sidelight on that cathedral, but which in the original source, points in direct and full detail only one corner of Normandy.

For Chartres, we have a brief but valuable record in a single sentence from the pen of a contemporary archbishop of Rouen. In a letter to the Bishop of Amiens, he says : " At Chartres, men began in their humility to drag carts and waggons for the building of the cathedral ; and their humility was even illuminated by miracles."[1]

---

[1] Mabillon, *An. Bened.*, vol. vi, p. 392.

Next comes a little treatise, written shortly after this, by Haymo, Abbot of St.-Pierre-sur-Dives, in Normandy. He tells us that the movement began at Chartres, but dismisses this in as few words as the archbishop. Then, turning to what he can speak of in his own district, as an eye-witness, he tells a story of extraordinary interest.

From Chartres, he says, this wave of enthusiasm spread over most of the Île-de-France and Normandy, " and many other places." It was part of a sudden religious revival.[1] He begins by describing the religious decay of his own generation—a generation which " had almost forgotten God." " If it had not been for this revival," he says, " Christ would have found no faith and no faithful people left on earth. . . . All had wandered away from God : all had become abominable in their iniquities." But then came this new awakening : " God called men while they were still in their worst sins, and offered them new and hitherto unheard of methods of returning to Himself. New and unheard of, I say ; for who ever saw, who ever heard, in all the generations past, that kings, princes, mighty men of this world, puffed up with honours and riches, men and women of noble birth, should bind bridles upon their proud [and swollen] necks and submit them to waggons which, after the fashion of brute beasts, they dragged with their loads of wine, corn, oil, lime, stones, beams, and other things necessary to sustain life or to build churches, up even unto Christ's abode ? Moreover, while they draw the waggons, we may see this miracle that, although sometimes a thousand men and women, or even more, are bound in the traces (so vast indeed is the mass, so great is the engine, and so heavy the load laid upon it), yet they go forward in such silence that no voice, no murmur, is heard ; and, unless we saw it with our eyes, no man would dream that so great a multitude is there. When, again, they pause

[1] Compare Salimbene's description of " The Great Alleluia " in Northern Italy (A.D. 1233). This and similar revivals are described in chapter III of *From St. Francis to Dante*.

on the way, then no other voice is heard than confession
of guilt, with supplications and pure prayers to God
that He may vouchsafe pardon for their sins ; and, while
the priests there preach peace, hatred is soothed, discord
is driven away, debts are forgiven, and unity is restored
betwixt man and man." . . . . As for the children,
" you might see them, with their own little kings and
leaders, bound to their laden waggons, and not dragging
with bowed backs like their elders, but walking erect as
though they bore no burden, and (more wonderful still)
surpassing them in nimbleness and speed. Thus went
they in a fashion far more glorious, holy, and religious,
than any words of ours could express.

" When they were come to the church, then the
waggons were arrayed around it like a spiritual camp ;
and, all that night following, this army of the Lord kept
watch with psalms and hymns. Then waxen tapers and
lights were kindled in each waggon ; then the sick and
infirm were set apart ; then the relics of the saints were
brought to their relief ; then mystical processions were
made by priests and clergy, and followed with all devotion by the people, who earnestly implored the Lord's
mercy and that of His Blessed Mother, for their restoration to health. If, however, the healing were but a little
delayed, nor followed forthwith after their vows, then all
might have been seen putting off their clothes—men and
women alike, naked from the loins upward, casting away
all bashfulness and lying upon the earth. Moreover,
their example was followed even more devoutly by the
children and infants who, grovelling on the ground, not
so much crept from the church porch upon their hands
and knees, but rather dragged themselves flat upon their
bodies, first to the high altar and then to all the others,
calling upon the Mother of Mercy in the new fashion of
prayer, and there extorting from her surely and forthwith the pious desires of their petitions. . . . Who
indeed would not be moved, nay rather, whose stony
heart would not be softened as he watched that pious

humility of the innocent children dragging their naked ribs along the bare ground ? Who would not be pricked to tears by those lamentable voices crying aloud to Heaven ? Who, I ask, would not be bent by those tender hands and arms stretched out to be beaten with rods ? For it did not suffice them (though that surely were admirable at so tender an age !) to cry so long with the voice of weeping ; it did not suffice that so many tears should be shed ; but, of their own accord, they must needs add bodily pain also, to obtain the healing of these sick folk. The priests stood over them, shedding tears while they beat with their scourges upon the tender limbs thus exposed, while the children besought them not to spare their strokes, nor withhold their hand in too great mercy. All voices echoed the same cry, ' Smite, scourge, lash, and spare not.' . . . After each miracle a solemn procession is held to the high altar ; the bells are rung ; praise and thanks are rendered to the Mother of Mercy. This is the manner of their vigils ; these are their divine night-watches ; such is the order of the Lord's camp ; these are the forms of new religion ; these are the rites, the heaven-taught rites, in their secret watches. For here nothing carnal is seen ; nothing earthly of any kind ; all is divine, all is done as in Heaven ; heavenly altogether are such vigils, wherein nothing is heard but hymns, and lauds, and thanks."

It is a remarkable story ; and, in spite of the author's rhetorical style, we need not discount it more than we ordinarily discount the heightened colours of a tract written for edification. But we must look closely into Haymo's actual words, and pay special attention to certain points neglected by every author I have seen who refers to this treatise. In the first place, all this was part of a general and sudden religious revival in those particular districts—a spasmodic revival, suddenly waking people from their religious indifference. Secondly, Haymo knows no past precedent for this religious fervour in connexion with architecture. And, thirdly, in a later part of his letter, he plainly implies that it was as sudden in its passing-away as in its rise. He says in so many words, concerning the dragging of chariots to the Cathedral of Chartres : " He who hath not seen these things will never see their like again." Yet in 1145 we are only at the beginning of the great era of cathedral-building ; this same popular effort which Haymo describes at Chartres would have been welcome all through France, not only during all Haymo's lifetime but far beyond. We have, therefore, his explicit authority for treating as exceptional and isolated phenomena the few scattered notices which can be adduced from other sources as even roughly parallel to this incident of 1145.

Here and there, as we have already seen in dealing with Montalembert's evidence, a monk or a group of monks are commended for their special enthusiasm in actually helping the builders with their own hands. The author of the metrical Life of St. Hugh of Lincoln tells us how, in about 1190, " with wondrous art he built the fabric of the cathedral, whereunto he supplied not only his own wealth and the labours of his servants, but even the sweat of his own brow ; for he oftentimes bore the hod-load of hewn stone or of binding lime." Earlier than this, in 969, the monastic chronicler of Ramsey lauds the enthusiasm even of the hirelings : " These workmen continued their labours as much from fervour of devotion as from love of gain ; some bore stones, others made mortar, and others again hoisted both on high by means of a mechanical wheel, so that, the Lord giving increase, the walls rose from day to day."[1] Again, not infrequently the monks or canons contributed of their own money to the building. At the Cathedral of Autun, in 1294, the chapter taxed itself at 160 livres for the year ; and 93 livres of this were actually paid ; then again at 43 livres, apparently all paid up ; the total receipts from all sources amounted to 400 livres. At Troyes Cathedral, in 1380, the only contribution of the kind was an entrance-fee

[1] *Hist. Rames.*, R.S., 1866, p. 41.

for each newly-elected canon of 13 livres odd.[1] At St. Albans, under Abbot John I (1195–1214), the monks gave up their wine for fifteen years in order to further the building of a new refectory and dormitory.[2] But the emphasis laid on instances of this kind is, to some real extent, a testimonial to their rarity. At Westminster, in about 1452, the new Abbot Millyng's " enthusiasm for the building was, as might be expected, reflected in sacrifices made by the monks themselves. They agreed each to contribute one mark a year towards the work, and to forgo entirely their annual visit to Battersea, for which the sum set aside was five pounds." This was for the building of the nave, to which Archbishop Langham, a former abbot, had contributed very liberally, and which was liberally helped also by Millyng's next successor but one, who from his own personal income, gave more than the equivalent of £6,000 modern.[3] " There are few things in the whole history of the monastery," writes Canon Westlake, "which make more pleasant reading" But when we remember that the abbot had a baronial income and lived in baronial state, and that the monks, vowed by their rule to poverty, were exceptionally well fed and clothed, and enjoyed their own private incomes, in defiance both of the Rule and of papal statutes, then the sacrifice is reduced to more ordinary proportions. Though these monks ceased, for some years, to indulge in a joy-ride and feast which cost the abbey about £2 per person in modern values, yet the Westminster customal, with numerous other documentary indications, show that their standard of comfort, even after this sacrifice and their money-contribution, would still remain that of a well-to-do merchant. Moreover, all that abbots and ex-abbots and monastery together contributed to this building, as a whole, was small indeed compared with the offerings of the royal family. Not long before this

[1] J. Quicherat, *Mélanges*, vol. ii, pp. 185 ff, 194 ff.

[2] *Gest. Abb.*, R.S., vol. i, p. 220.

[3] H. F. Westlake, *Westminster Abbey*, 1923, p. 192.

self-denial on the monks' part, Richard II had settled upon the fabric fund the whole revenues of one confiscated alien priory (Folkestone) and great part of another (Clare).[1] The Westminster walls were thus raised by money originally given by far-distant benefactors for widely different objects. And, though other sacrifices of this Westminster kind have sometimes been quoted, yet, when all are collected, they seldom or never give evidence for anything even remotely approaching the enthusiasm described by Haymo.

---

[1] Westlake, *l.c.*, p. 187.

CHAPTER XVII

ARCHITECTURAL FINANCE

LET us begin here with a perfectly typical instance for which a mass of detailed evidence survives, the great collegiate church of St. Victor at Xanten, on the Lower Rhine. At this city St. Victor was said to have been martyred in 286, with other comrades of the Theban Legion who refused to burn incense to the imperial gods; and, according to a legend which meets us first in 1224, the church dedicated to him was founded by the Empress Helena. In Germanic legend the town is even more famous: " There grew up in the Netherlands a noble King's son, his father's name was Siegmund and his mother Siegelind, in a wealthy city, far and wide renowned, there on the Lower Rhine. Xanten was its name; Siegfried was the name of that doughty warrior."[1] In the later Middle Ages it was one of the most prosperous towns on that great highway of commerce. The Provost of the Victorkirche was one of the outstanding ecclesiastical dignitaries of the province; and the great church itself still survives as a monument of art. What is more important for our purpose, its records are extraordinarily abundant for the last four centuries of our period, and they have been worked through with exceptional diligence by Father S. Beissel, S.J. I cannot do better, therefore, than summarize here the sixty pages

[1] *Nibelungenlied*, Ab. II.

in which he deals with the finance of the fabric fund.[1]

How, he asks, did the Provost and Chapter raise that sum (equivalent to 3 million marks in the year 1889, or £150,000 sterling) which they spent on their great church between 1175 and 1560 ? And he enumerates the following sources.

(1) One of the prebends, on the foundation, had been assigned to the master-mason ; he received a canon's pay.[2] In 1374, the Chapter changed this ; the prebend was assigned to the building fund, and a separate agreement for wages was to be made whenever a master-mason was hired. This prebend defrayed about a quarter of the yearly expenses.

(2) The fabric fund had possessions of its own, from different benefactors ; in 1509 it possessed twenty-two houses, mostly in Xanten, and twenty-seven in 1547.

(3) If vicars or altar-priests chose to be non-resident, the Chapter applied to the fabric fund such sums as were offered at the absentee's altar. But there is no evidence that it took any of his regular income ; and Beissel notes that even the rule of partial confiscation seems to have fallen into abeyance.

(4) Fees for burial within the church ; or for ringing the great bell in honour of a funeral.

(5) The offerings at certain alms-boxes within the church.

(6) Frequent gifts from the Duke or Duchess of Cleves, when they came to Xanten.

(7) Contributions from the so-called Skittle-Gild (*Kegelgilt*), a social-religious brotherhood of extraordinary interest, though a full description here would take us too

---

[1] *Die Bauführung des Mittelalters*, Freiburg i/B., 1889. For this valuable book see farther in Appendix 11. The present subject fills pp. 9–70 of part ii.

[2] And also, argues Beissel, a canon's full constitutional privileges ; but this seems very improbable, if only because the cup-bearer had also a full prebend, and the three cooks shared two between them, and the three bell-ringers shared another (I., 97).

far from our subject. Its activities ranged from policing the town (in virtue of a legendary grant from Constantine and his Empress Helena) to skittle-play and periodical feasts. "The canons took part in this game, to which they were very partial. The old Chapter statutes had indeed prescribed 'No member of the Chapter shall haunt taverns or play at dice or skittles'; but on the margin of this manuscript a fifteenth-century hand has written: 'That was no wise man who inserted this sentence against skittles; for this is a decent bodily exercise, and one which holy and pious men use for their recreation.'" The entrance-fees for this gild went to the fabric.

(9) It became customary, at last, for all well-to-do folk to leave something to the fund at their death. Men often left their armour; this was hung for view in the choir until a purchaser turned up, and a man was occasionally paid for scouring it from rust.

(10) It was common for sick folk to vow, for their recovery, their own weight in wheat to the fabric. The Duchess of Cleve, on one occasion, had herself weighed by the side of the common sufferers.

(11) Fines from evil-doers; especially the frequent statutory fines imposed upon the clergy on duty when they came late for the services.

(12) "Conscience money," which is best described in Beissel's own words. "Archbishop Wilhelm v. Gennep [of Cologne] had indeed prescribed, in his diocesan statutes of 1354 and 1356, that all unjustly-gained possessions which were not to be restored to their rightful owners should be applied to no other purpose than the fabric-fund of Cologne Cathedral. But these prescriptions do not seem to have been legally binding in Xanten. For, on the one hand, the Chapter statutes commanded the master of the building-fund frequently to remind curates and chaplains who heard confessions in the church that they must warn all penitents to apply such [ill-gotten] goods and their alms to the fabric of Xanten.

And, on the other, the accounts contain many items which show that these prescriptions were not without effect."[1]

(13) When there was a special call, the richer citizens met it promptly : e.g. in the crisis of 1463 we find " a considerable list of richer folk who gave from 7½d. to 15s. The town clerk is set down for 4s. 6d. . . . A poor woman gave him 13d., that the widow's mite might be represented also." But, in face of the fact that, in 1473, the best masons below the master received 3s. 9d. a day for their summer-wage, Beissel would seem a little over-enthusiastic over these gifts of 15s. from the richer folk.[2]

(14) For special emergencies, a general collection throughout the city. For instance, " In 1439, when one of the new bells cracked, the clerk of the works, Johann v. Goch, had it taken down and laid in the church. Then he ordered the carpenter to make a great chest by the *pulpitum* ; and, when it was finished, he called upon everybody to fill it with kettles and pans that might be used for casting the bell again."

[1] Compare the following anecdote from Cæsarius of Heisterbach, who wrote about 1230 (*Dial. Mirac.*, dist. ii, c. 33). " There was at Paris a certain most wealthy usurer, Theobald by name. This man, having very many possessions and infinite moneys collected from usury, was smitten with godly compunction and came to ask counsel of Master Maurice [de Sully], bishop of that city [from 1160 to 1196]. He, being most fervent for the building of the Church of the Mother of God [i.e. Notre-Dame as we see it now], advised him to give his money to the fabric of that work. The usurer, having some suspicion of such counsel, went to Master Petrus Cantor [Precentor of Notre-Dame], and told him of the bishop's words. Petrus answered, ' This time he hath not given thee good counsel ; but go and let a crier call throughout the city that thou art ready to make restitution to all men from whom thou hast taken anything beyond thy bare capital.' He did thus ; and then returned to the Master saying : ' My conscience is witness that I have made all restitution to all who came unto me ; and I have yet many goods left.' Then said Petrus : ' Now thou canst give alms with a good conscience.' "

[2] It must be borne in mind that the different moneys in use at Xanten were far inferior in value to the English sterling coinage of the time, in spite of the similarity of names. So also with the contemporary French coinage.

(15) When these more ordinary sources were insufficient, they sold works of art from their treasury to be melted down. Thus, in 1422, they got leave from the Archbishop to sell in favour of the fabric fund " a little chest which is unnecessary for divine service, and which is only an ornament to our church. It is covered outside with gold and chased [or *embossed*], and some jewels are set therein." And they wrote to their agent in Cologne : " It is necessary to get this done quickly, before anyone else make any complaint, and thus (which God forbid !) may perhaps set a hindrance and a bar to our permission, as indeed is to be feared." It was broken up and partly sold in fragments to different goldsmiths, partly given in payment to separate creditors.

(16) They invested gifts and legacies in " rents " ; in other words, invested the money at interest, by a process which had been forbidden as usurious by earlier Church Law, but for which the more reasonable commercial ethics of St. Thomas Aquinas and his successors had by this time procured official allowance.

(17) They sometimes sent their officials to beg through the city, or even abroad as far as into Friesland.

(18) In their utmost extremity the Chapter intervened with its own possessions or income. In 1398 it gave 375 Mk. to the fabric fund ; and it often gave over to the clerk of the works a greater or less portion of the dues which it could claim from its serfs or subjects.

(*a*) Thus, the fund sometimes benefited by the bargains by which the Chapter sold to their serfs not indeed complete freedom, which was rare on the part of ecclesiastical landlords, but freedom from some of the most galling servile disabilities.

(*b*) This, however, still left the peasant subject to the " heriot," by which, when a man or woman died, the best beast, or other best possession, was taken as a fine by the landlord before he admitted the next heir to the holding. This, one of the most invidious of all feudal dues, brought in to the Xanten Chapter, in the single year 1468, 1,082½ *solidi*, equivalent to the average yearly earnings of four masons. Among the items thus taken from the peasants were gowns, beds, cows and horses ; and we find only one excused altogether " because he was poor," while from two others, because they were poor, the Chapter took only 7½ and 9 *solidi* respectively, i.e. the price of a gown. A horse " of little value " was priced as low as 12, but they averaged about 50 and even ran up to 72. Cows averaged about 25 or 30. Of these takings the Chapter at first gave a certain proportion to the fabric-fund, but in 1485 and 1486 the whole.

(19) Letters of indulgence. " We find in the archives of Xanten a whole series of bulls of indulgence, wherein the pope and the bishops, in virtue of their plenary spiritual powers, promised and guaranteed the remission of all penalties for sin to those who helped the building of the Victorkirche with money or labour " (p. 27). The average income from this source in the early sixteenth century was nearly 100 Mk., or three times the yearly income of a master-mason.

(20) But, at frequent intervals, a special celebration was held, provoking special indulgences and contributions. This was called the *Victortracht* ; relics were carried round, special services and solemn processions were held, the Duke and his family were invited, famous preachers were invited and entertained, and " two preacher-friars of Kalkar, Johann v. Bentheim and his companion, undertook to make the indulgences known in Holland and Friesland, for which the Chapter granted them 20 Mk. for their travelling expenses " (p. 69). This was a profitable outlay ; they brought back 382 Mk. to the fabric. This was in 1487, the most elaborate Victortracht of all. The whole expenses this year amounted to 404 Mk., much of which went in wine to great folk and their servants ; receipts came to 1,855 Mk., leaving a clear gain of 1,451 Mk.

In 1514 another offertory box was set up in the

Victorkirche, for those who wished to earn indulgences by contributing to the building of St. Peter's at Rome. Here, as Beissel points out, is a painful reminder of the great religious revolution ; three years later, the enormous extension of these indulgences provoked Luther's open resistance.

Brutails, again, has admirably analysed the finance of the fabric fund at St.-Michel-de-Bordeaux.[1] The town council voted a little money ; there was a Lententide sermon in aid of the work; there were certain collectors

VOTIVE PILLAR-BASE AT BABRAHAM (CAMBS).

authorized to beg. The canons also distributed earthen-ware money-boxes which shopkeepers kept on their counters, from 15 to 20 dozen per annum. Here also, indulgences played a great part. At the cathedral, " the archbishops contributed to the repairs. The word ' liberalities ' has been wrongly applied here ; the fact is that this generosity was forced upon them by judges' authority ; the Chapter prosecuted them several times " (p. 24). One of the most abundant sources was that of testamentary legacies. A certain amount of work was given gratuitously by artisans. " Finally, there were the voluntary subscriptions of the parishioners. Some clubbed

[1] *Op. Cit.*, pp. 20 ff.

together to pay part of a workman's wages, just as nowadays, when a well-known church is being built, the faithful will offer a pillar, a stone, or so on.[1] Huguet Bauducheau, who has given his name to a street in Bordeaux, and several of his fellows received only part of their wages from the fabric-fund ; the rest was paid by subscribers. One of these having ceased to pay his subscription, Bauducheau threatened to leave; the fabric-fund took over the subscriber's engagement in order to retain him " (p. 25).

Similar, though less detailed, is the evidence we get from three monographs published, in a limited edition, upon the fabric-accounts of the cathedral and the churches of St.-Jean and Ste.-Madeleine at Troyes.[2] They show much the same kind of voluntary subscriptions, in number and in relative value, as were raised for the different war-memorials in England in 1919. Legacies, of course, were more frequent ; again, we get such an item as " a mantle of silk, brought by Sir Jehan Pougeoise [priest], who had received it in confession to be employed

---

[1] There is an inscription of about 1450 rudely scratched on the base of a pillar at Babraham (Cambs.) " Beverach and Kateryn Sant offyrit [offered] this gobyite," i.e. this goblet, or block of stone. The name Beverach occurs thrice in Bishop Brantyngham's issue-roll of 1370 (ed. Devon, 1835, pp. 28, 42, 311) ; this man was apparently a royal clerk. The heart seems to indicate that Beverach and Katherine were affianced or married. Compare the story in Cæsarius of Heisterbach (about 1230 ; dist. viii, c. 63). " There was a citizen of Cologne, rich and powerful, named Karl, father to the Lord Karl who was formerly Abbot of Villers. He, having heard that the Apostles would judge the world, said within himself : ' Sin is a heavy thing, and anchor-stones [probably the great basalt blocks which are quarried on the Rhine] are of great weight Therefore I will buy stones of that sort for the proposed building of the Apostelnkirche [at Cologne] ; in order that, at the Day of Doom, when my good and my evil deeds are placed in the balance, these judges, the Apostles, may cast the stones into my scale that holds the good works, and they will forthwith weigh it down.' So he bought a shipload of stones, and had them carted and laid hard by the Apostelnkirche."

[2] (a) *Comptes de l'œuvre de l'Église de Troyes* ; (b) *C. de la fabrique de l'ég. St.-J.* ; (c) *C. de la fabrique de l'ég. Ste.-M.* ; all published at Troyes by Bouquot in 1854 and 1855. The editor was Alex. Assier.

for the fabric-fund," which was sold at £2 10*s*. (*a*, p. 23). Indulgences, again, were a principal source; Assier enumerates six bulls or episcopal letters to this purpose between 1415 and 1462, i.e. the period with which he is concerned for the cathedral. He writes (*a*, 57) : " The general ' pardons ' brought in to the Chapter considerable sums, which the managers style ' recepte extraordinaire.' That of 1452 produced more than £1,000 [i.e. something like £6,000 in purchasing power at the present day]. Copies [of the bull] in Latin and in French were carried into the provinces; friars preached in Lorraine, in Picardy, in the dioceses of Nevers and Reims and Soissons, and in Burgundy; thousands of pilgrims visited the Cathedral of Troyes. Jean Belin, *miraclier*, furnished great *miracles à mirouer* [i.e. holy medals with a mirror], which were sent to pious subscribers. Day and night, confessors and preachers plied their holy office, the *miracliers* sold *miracles*, great and small, and gilded *enseignes* of St. Peter [to whom the cathedral was dedicated]. The preachers received gifts of Beaune wine; the guardians and *miracliers* were fed with bread, wine and flesh at the expense of the fabric." At St.-Jean the church kept " fair garments of black damask and other stuff " which it hired out for funerals or weddings : " *Item*, received from Perrecin, that he might have the fair garments for the day of his wedding, 10 sols " (*b*, 22). And, contrary to the tradition among modern antiquaries that pew-rents date from the Reformation, these formed one of the most profitable sources at St.-Jean in 1508 (*ibid.*, 21).[1] So at St. Lawrence, Reading, " Seat rents appear to have been a source of church revenue from very early times. Anno 1441–2. ' Et de iiijd. de dono uxoris Johannis Tanner ptoj setell.' [' *Item*, of 4*d*. given by John Tanner's wife for a settle.'] A similar sum was paid by the wives of Robert Hover, John Strode, and Thomas Benham,

---

[1] For the antiquity of the pew-system, which in Italy dates at least from the twelfth century, see *Medieval Village*, pp. 252 ff.

but 6*d*. was given by the wife of Nicholas Carter—for a *front* sitting no doubt. The seat rents in 1498 amounted to 6*s*. 6*d*. The women only would appear to have been accommodated. The seatholders at this time were the wives of Thomas Smyth, . . . Hudson, ' bocher,' John Carpynter, the mother of Agnes Quedamton, the wife of Will. Hasylwood, John Ffauxbye, Will. Watts, Will. Jonson, Bartylmew Capper, Robard Dyer, John Darling, Will. Doyntre, baker, Mathew and Nicholas Goldsmyth.

1515–5. ' Also hit is aggreyd that all women that shall take any seate in the seid church to pay for the same seate vj except in the mydle range and the north range be neth the font the which shall pay but iiij and that every woman to take her place every day as they cumyth to church excepte such as have ben mayors wyfes.'

1520–1. ' Setis. *Item* of my lord (the abbot) for his moder sete iiijd.'

A touching entry. Hugh Farringdon, in his promotion to the abbacy, though a man of humble extraction, did not overlook, or forget to provide for, the comfort of his poor aged mother."[1]

We have seen how great a part was played by hired preachers and by licensed collectors who carried the church's wonder-working relics far afield. Two concrete instances will throw light on this system, which many good churchfolk reprobated as perilous and unedifying. The learned and pious Guibert, Abbot of Nogent in the early twelfth century, tells us of a fact within his own experience. The " most famous church " of which he here speaks is doubtless the Cathedral of Laon, close by his abbey, which was burned down in 1112 and sent round its shrine for help. We have a contemporary book of miracles performed by the shrine on this tour ; and it is noteworthy that the large majority of these belong to the three classes of miracle which Guibert exposes as most unsafe to trust in. He is himself writing an elaborate treatise *On the Relics of Saints*, and exposing the abuses

[1] C. Kerry, *Hist. of St. Lawrence, Reading*, 1883, p. 77.

which often crept in.[1] He proceeds: "But why do I accuse the multitude, without citing specific examples to rebuke this error? A most famous church sent its servants thus wandering abroad [with its shrine], and engaged a preacher to seek alms for repairing its loss. This man, after a long and exaggerated discourse on his relics, brought forth a little reliquary and said, in my presence, ' Know ye that there is within this little vessel some of that very bread which our Lord pressed with His own teeth; and, if ye believe not, here is this great man '—this he said of me—' here is this great man to whose renown in learning ye may bear witness, and who will rise from his place, if need be, to corroborate my words.' I confess that I blushed for shame to hear this; and, but for my reverence of those persons who seemed to be his patrons, which compelled me to act after thei wishes rather than his, I should have discovered the forger. What shall I say? Not even monks (not to speak of the secular clergy) refrain from such filthy gains, but they preach doctrines of heresy in matters of our faith, even in mine own hearing. For, as Boethius says, I should be rightly condemned as a madman if I should dispute with madmen."

In this light we may read that vivid picture from Matthew Paris of the building at St. Albans under one of its greatest abbots—John de Cella (1195–1214).[2] He employed a too-ambitious master-mason, who tempted him into great schemes, and " added carvings that were impertinent, trifling, and costly beyond measure." The work stuck half-way; winter frosts came on and split the unprotected stones; the building began to crumble away, " so that the ruins of the images and flowers moved beholders to laughter and scorn. So the artists [*artifices*] departed in despair, nor were they paid their wages for

---

[1] Migne, P.L., vol. clvi. col. 621: Herman's *Treatise on the Miracles* is *ibid.*, col. 963.

[2] *Gest. Abb.*, R.S., vol. i., p. 219. We must allow a little for Matthew Paris's rhetorical style.

their work." The abbot appointed another mason, and assigned certain revenues to the fabric; "yet that unlucky work never grew visibly . . . whereat he grieved inconsolably. Therefore he added many gifts of gold and silver, if perchance he might give increase to the work; and he sent preachers throughout all the domains of St. Alban, and through many other dioceses, sending relics with them, and a certain clerk named Amphibalus, whom God, through the merits of St. Alban and St. Amphibalus, had raised from the grave after he had been four days dead, in order that he might supply ocular evidence for faith in the miracles of those saints; by this means he heaped up no small sum of money. Yet that ill-fated work sucked up all this as the sea sucks up the rivers; nor did the fabric yet grow happily." Even when the master-mason changed again, the church grew scarce two feet in height during thirty years. These relic-tours, therefore, were strongly deprecated by some of the more earnest church folk; we have seen in Chapter XVI how Petrus Cantor complained that the great monastic buildings were frequently raised from the proceeds of usury or " the deceiful lies of hireling preachers."

This was a natural effect of medieval relic-worship. We may feel that Achille Luchaire, great scholar as he was, exaggerated in his dictum that " the real religion of the Middle Ages was relic-worship." Yet there can be no doubt that the cult of relics, in those days, played a far greater part than even in the least educated districts of Roman Catholic countries of to-day. We have already seen how that exceptionally popular relic, the corpse of Edward II, paid for all the new work at Gloucester and created a new style in architecture. Similar instances may be found down to the very end of our period. Two entries in Landucci's diary may here be placed side by side :—

" 12th June [1482]. At this time there was much talk of the worship of an image of Our Lady at Bibbona, or rather in a tabernacle about a bowshot from Bibbona. It is, namely, a Virgin seated and holding the dead Christ in her arms, after He has been taken down from the Cross; which is called by some a Pietà. This worship began on April 5, when it was transfigured: that is, it changed from blue to red, and from red to black and divers colours. And this is said to have happened many times between then and now, and a number of sick persons have been cured, and a number of miracles been performed and quarrels reconciled; so that all the world is running there. Nothing else is talked of at this moment; I have spoken to many who tell me that they themselves have seen it transfigured, so that one must perforce believe it." The result was, that a church was built at Bibbona in honour of this image.

Then Landucci notes on June 19, 1484: "In this July a worship of the Virgin Mary at Prato began; people rushing there from all the country round. It worked miracles like that of Bibbona, so that building was done and great expense incurred." The further story of this building may be read in the editor's note.

Still more significant are the records of the indulgence-system. This is always in the foreground, even when we are dealing with cathedral cities of the first rank, populous and wealthy and marching in the forefront of the civilization of their age. The system had grown gradually; but it had received a sudden and enormous impulse from the Crusades; before the middle of the thirteenth century its obvious financial advantages had enabled it to strike root deeply and widely in every department of Church life. The greatest preacher of that century, Berthold of Regensburg, might complain publicly that thousands went to hell in the belief that they had bought remission of their sins "for a penny or a halfpenny"[1]; but such objections had no appreciable effect; rather the increase went on at an accelerated

[1] *Predigten,* ed. Pfeiffer, vol. i., p. 394; cf. 543 and *passim;* or my *Medieval Studies,* 2nd ed., 1915, p. 24.

pace. At Sens, in 1295–6, the indulgences brought in more than one-third of the total receipts to the cathedral fabric fund.[1] At Evreux, they had begun at least as early as 1203, though in a rudimentary form. Innocent III, writing on behalf of the cathedral building fund " to all faithful Christians to whom these letters may come," continues : " We beseech you all, we warn and exhort you in the Lord, and enjoin upon you for the remission of your sins, to grant your alms, from such goods as God hath given you, for this rebuilding, in order that thereby, and by your other good deeds, ye may be able to attain to everlasting bliss." [2] At St. Albans, about 1400, a monk drew up a list of indulgences obtainable at a single altar of the abbey church. He is apparently limiting himself to those granted in his own lifetime, yet these amount to nine.[3] And he complacently describes a similar source of income, those " letters of fraternity " which Langland couples in his poem with papal indulgences.[4] " Moreover, all benefactors who, from the goods God hath given them, pay anything for themselves or for those who are dear to them, living or dead, to the fabric of our Church, or of any of the abbey buildings or for the sustenance of the monks . . . become participants with us in the Masses which are daily celebrated by a hundred monks or more,[5] in their night-services and fasts and alms-giving and vigils, processions, scourgings, prayers both public and private, and all other [spiritual] benefits earned in this abbey or in the cells thereunto apper-taining." This system, reposing upon much the same

[1] M. Quantin, *Mémoires lus à la Sorbonne* (1868), pp. 209, 222.

[2] Abbé F. Blanquart, *Documents et bulles d'indulgences*, etc., Rouen, 1893.

[3] *Gesta Abbatum*, R.S., vol. iii, p. 544.

[4] See Chaucer, *Summoner's Tale*, and *Piers Plowman*, B. III, 47 ff.

[5] This number is greatly exaggerated for this date. King Offa, it is true, was said to have founded the abbey for 100 monks. In about 1200 the *Gesta Abbatum* leave us to infer that, counting the dependent cells, there were about 100 in all. But in 1380 we have the exact number, 56 (Dugdale-Caley, vol. ii, p. 209) ; and at the Dissolution there seem to have been only 39.

theological presuppositions as that of indulgences, contributed powerfully to the commercialization of church-
building. It is not only that a Lollard like the author of
Piers Plowman's Creed draws some of his arguments from
the magnificence of the church and domestic buildings
of a Dominican friary, nominally vowed to poverty.
The very different author of *Piers Plowman's Vision*
confesses himself a grateful and obedient nurseling of
Holy Church. He had, again, a keen sense of beauty ;
some of his word-pictures are among the best that have
come down to us from the Middle Ages. Yet he is as
scornful as any Lollard in face of the false spiritual pre-
tences by which much of the money was raised for
building and adorning the churches which were being built
or rebuilt so busily in that age. His Lady Meed—the per-
sonification of ill-gotten gain, the Almighty Dollar of the
Middle Ages—makes neither profession of serious religion
nor promise of amendment, yet she has no difficulty in
making her peace with those who boldly claim to speak for
the Church.[1] She has only to confess herself to a friar and
give him a noble, or, in modern terms, a ten-pound note :—
" Then he absolved her soon ; and presently he said,
' We have a window a-working, will sitten us full high   [cost.
Wouldest thou glaze that gable, and grave therein thy name,
Secure should thy soul be heaven to have.'
' Wist I that,' quoth that woman, ' I would not spare
For to be your friend, friar, and fail you never . . . .
And I shall cover your kirk, your cloister do maken   [cause to be made
Walls do whiten, and windows glazen,
Do paint and portray, and pay for the making,
That every segge shall sayen I am sister of your house.'   [person.
But God to all good folk such graving defendeth,   [forbids
To writen in windows of their well-deeds,
Lest pride be painted there, and pomp of the world ;
For Christ knoweth thy conscience, and thy kind will   [natural
And thy cost and thy coveteise, and who the chattels owed.
Therefore I learn you, lords, leave now such works,
To writen in windows of your well-deeds,
Or to cry after God's men when ye deal doles,
Lest ye have your hire here, and your heaven also."

[1] B. III, 47.

Later, again, Langland returns to this subject, and shows us very clearly how thoughtful and earnest men regaided it in Chaucer's day. He obediently accepts the current theory of indulgences, little as he can reconcile it with other religious principles ; but he is still more definitely convinced of an immutable moral law in the background (B. VII, 173).

" Now hath the pope power, pardon to grant the people,
Withouten any penance to pass into heaven ;
That is our belief, as lettered men us teachen
    Quodcwmque ligaveris super terram,
    erit ligatum et in celis, etc.[1]
And so I believe loyally (Lord forbid it else !)
That pardon and penance and prayers do save
Souls that have sinned seven sithes deadly.   [times
But to trust to these triennials, truly me thinketh, [three-year Masses
Is not so secure for the soul, certes, as is Do-Well.
Therefore I rede you, renkes, that rich be on this earth [counsel, fellows.
Upon trust of your treasure triennials to have
Be ye never the bolder to break the ten hests ;   [commandments
And namely ye masters, mayors and judges   [specially
That have the wealth of this world, and for wise men be holden,
To purchase you pardon and the pope's bulls.
At the dreadful Doom, when dead shall arise,
And come all before Christ, accounts to yield,
How thou leddest thy life here, and His laws keptest,
And how thou diddest day by day the doom will rehearse ;
A pocketful of pardon there, nor Provincials' letters,
Though ye be found in the fraternity of all the four Orders [of friars],
And have indulgences double-fold, but if Do-Well you help,
I set your patents and your pardons at one pie's heel ! "

Concerning which, scholars debate whether it is the last stale remnant of a pie-crust, or the heel of a magpie.

This brings us back to the indulgence-system proper. The matter can be studied most easily, for the later Middle Ages, in the Papal Registers. The British Government is gradually publishing a Calendar of these docu-

---

[1] Matt. xvi. 19. " Whatsoever thou shalt bind upon earth, it shall be bound also in heaven."

ments, whether Letters or Petitions, concerned with this country. From about 1300, when the entries begin to be fairly full, down to 1464, the date at present reached by the *Calendar of Papal Letters*, we may trace a steady increase in these indulgences for building. Let us take the last monastic and the last secular case recorded, both from 1462 (vol. xi, pp. 618, 636). On behalf of the monks of Christchurch in Hampshire Pius II grants an indulgence, "a relaxation in perpetuity of seven years and seven quarantines of enjoined penance," to all who, on certain two feast-days of the year visit the church and give alms for its repair. A like indulgence is given on behalf of the gild which has lately been founded in the parish church of Baldock for the maintenance of the fabric. Account-rolls sometimes tell us how much these papal grants cost; the canons of Troyes, in 1382, paid 6 livres (about £25 in modern money) for one from Clement VII. The *York Fabric Rolls* give a whole collection of indulgences for the Minster fabric (pp. 158, 235 ff.); so do the muniments of every cathedral wherever they have survived. By the middle of the fifteenth century the system had reached vast proportions. Henry VI, in 1441, obtained the most generous indulgences for building his new collegiate church of Eton. A plenary indulgence, i.e. as much as could be obtained in past centuries by a crusade in Palestine, was now offered to all who, during the King's lifetime, should worship at Eton on the feast of the Assumption and contribute to the fabric. " Archbishop Chicheley wrote to the Bishop of Exeter ordering him to publish them in his diocese, and describing them as more ample than any hitherto issued by any pope. . . . It would appear that the payment made to the Roman Court ' for one Indulgence ' amounted to more than £158."[1] This kind of thing began to scandalize thoughtful churchmen still more. The greatest of Oxford Chancellors about this time was

[1] Issue Roll, Easter, 20th Hen. VI, quoted by H. Maxwell-Lyte, *Hist. of Eton Coll.*, 1911, p. 11. See Appendix 28.

Thomas Gascoigne, who wrote his *Liber Veritatum* about 1450. Here, he speaks very plainly about indulgences.[1] " I know that the officials of one cathedral church [viz., York], enjoin and command all parish priests in their province to bid their penitents, in Lententide, pay somewhat of their goods to the cathedral church; and the priest enjoins for a penance upon a poor man who has not fourpence, to pay forty pence to the Minster; and another priest has taken his own church and parish on farm from the Minster officials. I know one who pays five shillings a year to the Minster for his parish; and this very parish priest straitly enjoined upon every man in his parish that he should pay a certain sum that year to the cathedral church; so that certain poor folk paid to this priest forty pence [each] for the fabric, yet he who laid the injunction upon them had the parish to farm for five shillings." This, he tells us on another page, happened in about 1440; and he adds: " A doctor at the Council of Bâle wrote there a long discourse on papal indulgences, wherein he saith that he hath found no indulgences granted and sealed, after the fashion current in these days of ours, within the first thousand years of the Christian era; and that no saint ever expressed them in the form which is used nowadays. . . . Sinners nowadays [*moderni peccatores*] say ' I care not what and how many sins I commit before God's face; for I can get at once, with the greatest ease, plenary remission of any guilt and penalty by means of an absolution and indulgence granted to me by the pope, whose written grant I have bought for fourpence or sixpence or won as a stake at tennis.' For these indulgence-mongers scour the country, giving a letter [of pardon] sometimes for twopence, sometimes for a good draught of wine or beer, sometimes as a stake at tennis, sometimes for hire of a prostitute, sometimes for carnal love." Less than two generations after these words were written, the still busier trade in pardons for the fabric

[1] Ed. J. E. T. Rogers, pp. 1, 121, 151.

THE BUTTER TOWER AT ROUEN.

of St. Peter's at Rome created the crisis which brought Luther forward.

Very similar was the system of selling relaxations of Lententide fast. At Mâcon, in Burgundy, in 1518, " the bishop granted permission to eat meat on Monday and Tuesday after *Dimanche Gras*, and milk and butter during Lent, to all who should contribute to the repair of the bridge. The same permission, again, was required by the inhabitants, on the same conditions, in 1547, 1548, 1549 and 1550. This shows that, even as late as this, the custom of abstaining from dairy-food during Lent, and from meat on Quinquagesima Monday and Tuesday, had not yet died out in the diocese of Mâcon." [1] A more striking example is the Tour de Beurre at Rouen, built between 1485 and 1597 from similar contributions. Ruskin, who was familiar with the tower and its story from his boyhood, wrote in later life : " It is ridiculous to attribute any great refinement of religious feeling, or height of religious aspiration, to those who furnished the funds for the erection of the loveliest tower in North France, by paying for permission to eat butter in Lent." [2]

Another source of income not infrequent, yet still stranger to modern ideas, was the system of fining unchaste clerics for the benefit of the fabric. I give many references on this subject in the notes to the last chapter of *From St. Francis to Dante* ; another may be added here by way of illustration, from p. 314 of the calendar of the register of Bishop Stafford at Exeter (ed. Hingeston-Randolph, 1886). The bishop, visiting St. German's Priory in 1400, " found that John Pengelly, Nicholas Julyan, John Brystowe, and Bernard Page (*alias* Skelly), canons, had been guilty of scandalous and immoral conduct. He commanded each of them to be put to open penance. Pengelly was to sit on the floor in the middle of the Refectory, at meal time, and have nothing

---

[1] *Nouvelle Hist. de l'Abbaye de Tournus,* par un chanoine de la même Abbaye, Dijon, 1733, p. 246.

[2] *Works,* library ed., vol. xii, 1904, p. 45 note.

but bread and water, once in the day every Friday for seven weeks; for a whole year he was to confine himself strictly to the choir and cloister, and not to walk about the road and speak to any women (whether of doubtful character or not), unless he had a trustworthy brother in his company; he was not to undertake any manner of office within the said priory throughout the year; and he was to forfeit out of his allowance for clothing one noble, to be expended on the fabrick of the Church: should he rebel, the Prior was to shut him up *in ergastulo ipsius Prioratus* ['in the prison of the said Priory'] for eight days, and allow him no flesh meat. Julyan was also condemned to sit on the floor of the Refectory 'duabus sextis feriis, inchoando die Veneris proximo post festam Sancti Michaelis Archangeli' ['for two Fridays, beginning from the Friday next after Michaelmas'] and to have only bread and water once in the day: for a quarter of a year 'a festo Sancti Fidis' ['from St. Faith's Day,' Oct. 6] he was to be confined to the cloister and choir; and to forfeit 40*d*. out of his allowance for clothing, to be applied to the fabrick of the Church; moreover, he was to sleep in the common dormitory. The same penance was assigned to Brystowe; and Page was to abstain from fish and wine for two successive Fridays, and contribute 40*d*. to the fabrick fund. The Bishop wrote to the Prior (from Launceston Priory) September 18, requiring him to see to the execution of the sentence in each case, 'in virtute obediencie nobis prestite' ['in virtue of the obedience rendered unto us']."

We must therefore distinguish clearly, though not, of course, absolutely, between the short period or periods of enthusiasm and the long years of reaction or weariness. The records seem to show conclusively that such remarkable self-sacrifices as have been quoted on the part of monastic or cathedral chapters were, naturally enough, short-lived. Apart from these most remarkable buildings of all, which in France were mostly begun and

ended within the single reign of Philip Augustus—apart,
that is, from an architectural period which has no rival
between the great Cluny revival and the still more epoch-
making Renaissance—great medieval buildings often
grew by fits and starts. Quicherat notes this at Troyes,
and adds truly that we have here no isolated phenomenon.
The step between Autun in 1294, when every canon was
to pay something like 10 livres, and Troyes in 1380,
when they simply imposed an entrance-fee on newcomers,
is most significant.

Let us not fall, however, from the exaggerations of
encomiasts into an equal exaggeration of unsympathetic
criticism. The general medieval interest in building was,
as I have noted already, quite as strong as the modern
interest in machinery. Men's motives were mixed as
they are now and always have been ; but the fact remains
that the building or rebuilding of a church was generally,
and perhaps always, a matter of strong local interest.
We have an excellent example of this in the story of
Bodmin. In vol. vii of the *Camden Miscellany* (1875)
there is a most instructive account-book of the rebuilding
of this parish church in 1469–71. " The whole sum
expended," says the editor, " was £268 17s. 9½d. ; in
addition to which, windows, trees and other materials,
and labour were contributed." This cash, by itself,
would be equivalent to about £5,000 at the present day.
" Everyone seems to have given according to his means,
and up to his means. Many who gave money gave labour
also, many who could not give money laboured as best
they might, and others gave what they could. We have
gifts of lambs, of a cow, and of a goose ; and one woman
in addition to her subscription sold her crokke [brass
cauldron] for 20d. ; and all found its way into the common
treasury. No age or sex seems to have kept aloof. We
find a ' hold woman ' contributing 3s. 2½d. ; while the
maidens in Fore Street and Bore Street gave subscriptions, in addition to the sums received from the Gilds
of Virgins in the same streets. The Vicar gave his year's

salary, and the 'parish pepell' who lived in the town contributed 19*s*. Much of the zeal shown may, we think, be attributed to the influence exercised by the Gilds." Of these religious gilds there were more than forty in all. The accounts end up with a list of individual contributors, 460 in all, which must have been nearly all the adults in the little town, or perhaps quite all, since it is evident that a quasi-compulsory collection was voted ; a certain number are listed as defaulters (pp. 39–41), and some are even distrained ; Joachym Hoper is dead, and nothing can now be got out of him ; but from John Harry, who owes two shillings, " a pot has been taken, which is now with the mayor," and so on. We must remember also that by this time a good many church contributions, at first voluntary and individual, had by long continuance become compulsory and universal ; this was one of the main complaints among layfolk in the early sixteenth century. We must remember also that there was probably papal indulgence for all contributing to this work—the Calendars of Papal Letters unfortunately stop for the moment a few years short of 1469—and, certainly, all pious folk believed that the contribution would mitigate their pains in purgatory. But, after all legitimate discount, we have still a very pleasant picture of a small community working together at a common religious cause.

There is a pleasant sidelight, also, in the Xanten accounts. We have seen how there was a chest into which folk cast their old brass and pewter for the recasting of the bell ; and the actual operation called forth a similar effort. It was difficult to bring the furnace to the heat necessary for so great a mass ; fresh bellows and fresh smiths were hired from the neighbour city of Wesel, and, in order to keep the blast constant for so many hours, the local grammar-school boys were enlisted. " They were paid in beer and·cakes, while the ordinary workfolk received bread and meat, or fish on fast-days."[1]

[1] Beissel, pt. i, p. 116.

But Beissel explodes the legend that the very asses contributed their labour to these holy causes, toiling up
with their loads from stage to stage of the scaffolding.
Jakob, the master-mason, did indeed raise all his heavy
stones with the help of an *asinus*, but this was a sort of
crane, named after the beast as the other is named after
the bird ; it was probably what we see sometimes in old
illuminations, a sort of gallows with horizontal beam and
two wheels, not unlike the original velocipedes. In any
case, its mechanical nature is proved by the fact that the
clerk of the work accounts in 1356 " for the great pin for
the wheel in the ass, 12*d.* ; item, for smaller nails for the
ass, 14*d.*"[1]

It must be remembered, however, that religion was not
the only force which kept men together. Patriotism, like
religion, was in those days intenser in proportion as it
was narrower. No unbaptized person, with infinitesimal
exceptions which were practically neglected, could come
to heaven ; all were enemies of Christ ; this gave a sort
of artificial coherence to Christendom, though, even so,
strict measures had to be taken against merchants and
others who were ready, for the sake of gain, to supply
the enemy even with materials of war. In the same
way these smaller political units of the Middle Ages, in
spite of their continual intestine quarrels, gained often a
certain hysterical cohesion from their hatred and fear of
the enemy outside. It is sometimes asserted that
" nationalism " is a post-Reformation phenomenon ; it
is not probable that any thoughtful person will believe
this after reading Luca Landucci's diary, lately translated
into English. This shows war as a chronic phenomenon in
fifteenth century Italy, just as it had been for centuries
before ; moreover, the loss of life and the bestialities
were all the worse because it was not the larger area, " my
country, right or wrong," but the smaller, " my province,
right or wrong," and because a man could scarcely travel
fifty miles from his own capital without coming upon

[1] Ibid., p. 102.

hostile soil. This it is which lends point to the words
with which Lambert of Ardres (about A.D. 1200) describes
the fortification of his native town in the Pas de Calais :
" The Count shut it in, and surrounded it himself with
a most mighty moat after the fashion of the moat at
St.-Omer, such as no hand had conceived hitherto in the
land of Guisnes, nor no eye had seen. Wherefore no
small multitude of workmen came together to make and
dig this moat aforesaid ; who, howsoever vexed by the
hardships of the season and pinched by the great famine
and afflicted by the labour and heat of the day, yet
chattered together and lightened their labour oftentimes with merry words whereby their hunger was
appeased. Moreover, many oftentimes came together to
see these great Earthworks ; for such poor folk as were
not hired labourers forgot their penury in the joy of
beholding this work ; while the rich, both knights and
burgesses and oftentimes priests or monks, came not
daily only, but again and again to refresh their bodies
and see so marvellous a sight. For who but a man
stupefied and deadened by age or cares, could have failed
to rejoice in the sight of that Master Simon the Dyker,
so learned in geometrical work, pacing with rod in hand,
and with all a master's dignity, and setting out hither
and thither, not so much with that actual rod as with
the spiritual rod of his mind, the work which in imagination he had already conceived ?—tearing down houses
and granges, hewing to the ground orchards and trees
covered with flowers and fruit, seeing to it with the utmost
zeal and care that the streets should be cleared, on work-
days even more than on holidays, for all convenience of
traffic, digging up kitchen gardens with their store of
potherbs or of flax, treading down and destroying the
crops to make straight the ways, even though some
groaned in the indignation of their hearts, and cursed
him under their breath ? There the peasant folk with
their mud-waggons and dung-carts, dragging loads of
pebbles to be laid upon the road, cheered each other to

the work with strokes and hearty blows on the shoulders. There, again, laboured the ditchers with their shovels, the hoe-men with their hoes, the pickers with their pick-axes, the beaters with their wooden mallets, the shavers with their shaving irons, and the stone-layers and wallers and rammers and paviours with their proper and necessary gear and tools, the load-men and hod-men with their hods, and the turfers with their oblong sheets of turf, cut and torn at the master's bidding from all the meadows around ; the catchpolls too, with their rods and knotted clubs, rousing the labourers and busily urging them to their work ; and ever in the forefront the masters of the work, weighing all that was done in the scales of their geometrical plan ; moreover, all these labourers were driven and constrained to this work through a continual time of travail and grief, of fear and pain." Writers have generally confined their attention too much to the great churches, and forgotten the villages and castles. Of all the writers on medieval art whom I happen to have read, Prof. Baldwin Brown is the only one who gives full value to the military side ; as indeed he is the writer who has gone most carefully to actual medieval sources, and taken most pains to verify his references.[1]

Finally, we must note that there is no evidence for the same healthy influence of public artistic opinion in the Middle Ages as in the Periclean Age. Not that there was no real influence, but the public was, so far as we can judge, far less sure of its own judgment and far less able to enforce this, than at the best periods of Greek art. *The Times Literary Supplement* for May 14, 1925 makes a significant comment on the attitude of Robert de Clari, one of the French barons who took and sacked Constantinople in 1204. " Characteristically, he is ignorant of the meaning and value of the classic art still preserved in the town, and is only interested in works of a supposedly miraculous nature. Santa Sophia, the chapel of the Emperors, the church of the Apostles, chiefly struck

[1] *Arts in Early England,* vol. i, p. 7.

BB

his imagination ; but he describes in his naïve way many other things, including the equestrian statue of Heraclius, and the Hippodrome with its wealth of statues, which (Clari assures us) ' of old moved by magic, but nowadays never work.' To think of the last noble relics of classic Greek sculpture treated as examples of black magic and melted down to make bronze coins for these Frankish barbarians ! " In the matter of art, we cannot put the medieval knight or rich citizen side by side with the magistracy and aristocracy of Athens. Nor can we infer the same eager and critical attitude on the part of all the workmen themselves. Villard de Honnecourt shows us how masons discussed problems with each other ; but the gild system, while it kept the work up to a certain level, tended to discourage the highest originality. Apart from such limitations as we have seen Bishop Baldock imposing upon Tidemann of Germany, there is much significance in the German masonic statute of 1459, repeated later : " The mason shall in no wise blame his master's work, neither openly nor in secret—unless indeed the master work contrary to the ordinances of the Masons' Gild ; then may any mason speak against him."

CHAPTER XVIII

THE PURITAN REVOLT

I AM using the word *puritan* here in its purest and least invidious sense ; the sense in which it is applicable equally to St. Bernard and to Milton. I mean, the spirit which refuses to divorce art from morals ; which protests against being compelled to choose between the two ; and which, if so compelled, would attach even greater importance to morality than to art. This has been already anticipated to some extent in Chapter XVI ; in this present chapter, I shall deal more especially with the attitude of orthodox puritans towards Church images.

The equilibrium of thirteenth century civilization is often greatly exaggerated in our times ; especially the static and monumental character of the Church. That appearance of completeness and finality which Aquinas gave to Christian philosophy did not impose upon his contemporary Roger Bacon, who criticized the saint's work in very much the same terms in which Huxley might have criticized it. We have seen how doctors were burned or forced to recant at thirteenth century universities for saying very much the same things as pass from mouth to mouth in the sceptical circles of to-day. The fact that such recorded cases amount, perhaps, to less than a hundred at different times and places, is no proof that there were not far larger numbers who never fell into the hands of the authorities, or whose condemnation-records have not come down to us. Moreover, a still more significant fact, we have evidence for popular nonconformity growing *pari passu* with popular education. Expanding trade, wider experience of the world in general, swept away the narrower tutelage of the earlier Middle Ages. The original prohibition of usury broke down altogether; entirely new definitions had to be framed in order to legitimize even ecclesiastical revenues; a pope's definition conflicted with a saint's; and, as trade and commerce still went on expanding, even the pope's and the saint's definition were commonly neglected. New growth was bursting old bonds everywhere; many medieval ideals (as Bishop Lightfoot once put it) had already outgrown their strength before the thirteenth century was over. Art among others, and especially the imager's art, with accompanying image-worship, outgrew its strength.

The evidence I have already had occasion to quote may prepare the reader to learn, without surprise, that a good many of the best churchmen felt more and more serious misgivings in face of the popular imagery of their day. Things had been different in the past. Origen, the greatest of all the early apologists, had not only admitted the heathen accusation that Christians neither worshipped nor possessed images; he actually gloried in the fact. Christians, he says, repudiate images for religious reasons: it was one of the Jews' great contributions to world-religion that they expelled from their state " all painters and makers of images . . . an art which attracts the attention of foolish men, and which drags down the eyes of the soul from God to earth." And, again, what reasonable man can refrain from smiling at these heathens, many of them even educated men, who " imagine that by gazing upon these material things they can ascend from the visible symbol to that which is spiritual and immaterial." [1] But this was about A.D. 240; and, some five centuries later, Pope Gregory II (or the official of

[1] *Contra Celsum*, Bk. IV, c. 31; vi. 14; vii. 44, 62-7; viii. 17-19. I deal with the matter more fully on p. 429 of *Five Centuries of Religion*, vol. ii.

the Roman Court who wrote in his name) argued complacently upon the assumption that the Apostles themselves had worshipped images.[1] For, by this time, the historical facts were completely obscured by the current practice ; nobody now cared for that ancient puritan tradition, in a Church which welcomed imagery more and more warmly in proportion as she found herself confronted with the problem of converting, without alienating, vast multitudes of heathens. Charles the Great did indeed attempt to regulate this matter, just as he strove to secure a pure text of the Vulgate Bible ; nothing testifies better to this emperor's greatness than his care for details both in Church and in State. " In the image-quarrel, he took sides not indeed for the worship of images, but for their retention [in the church]. ' Let us not adore them,' he says expressly, ' but let us not destroy them.' He even recommends their multiplication, not only to adorn the churches but also to commemorate great patriotic events. Yet he blames certain iconographic eccentricities. Why should we represent the earth and the moon in human form, or fashion doubleheaded monsters, or fabulous creatures half-man, halfbeast ? ' That which is contrary to Scripture,' he writes in a striking sentence, ' is contrary to nature.' Yet these censures missed their mark, and the traditions against which they were aimed persisted still for a long time in iconography." [2] They persisted, as we shall see, until the Reformation and the Counter-Reformation of Trent agreed in condemning them.

The great medieval schoolmen were obliged to accept past tradition as the basis of their philosophy ; not necessarily the earliest Christian traditions, but such as passed current in their own day because they came down

[1] The puritanism of primitive Christianity is brought out very strongly by Remy de Gourmont, writing from a very different standpoint. He claims it as one great asset of Roman Catholicism that it is " le christianisme paganisé " (La culture des idées, pp. 136, 149).

[2] André Michel, Histoire de l'art, tom. I, pt. ii, p. 939.

from their father's and their grandfather's day. Therefore the typical belief of the Middle Ages proper, even among the most learned churchmen, is that which we find in the *Summa Theologica* of St. Thomas Aquinas. He decides that " the same reverence should be paid to the image of Christ, as to Christ Himself. Since therefore Christ ought to be worshipped with the adoration of *latria* [i.e. the adoration paid to God] it follows that His image should be worshipped with the adoration of *latria*." [1] And he backs this up with an historical assertion : " The Apostles, by the personal inspiration of the Holy Ghost, handed down for the observance of the Church certain things which they did not leave in writing . . . and, among these traditions, is the adoration of Christ's images. Wherefore St. Luke is said to have painted the image of Christ which is kept in Rome." St. Antonino, of Florence, in that *Summa Major* which was possibly even more read than St. Thomas in the later Middle Ages, repeats the same (pars. 3, tit. xii, cap. ix, § 1).

Yet, in face of what actually went on, misgivings sometimes crept in. William of Auvergne, one of the greatest medieval bishops of Paris, writing about 1230, complains not only of the pagan idols still cherished by old women in his day, but also that, just as the ancient Greeks and Romans often thought their idols were gods, so " perchance there are many simple folk also in our day who make no distinction in their prayers between the images of saints and the saints themselves ; nay, those prayers which they should make to the saints, they make to the images themselves." [2] " There is another pagan superstition," he continues, " the relics whereof subsist still among many old women even in Christendom. For they say that all images acquire a certain virtue in the sixtieth

[1] *Sum. Theol.*, pt. iii q., xxvi, art. 3. This orthodox philosophy rendered it difficult for later authors to explain why a piece of dead wood or stone must be worshipped with higher worship than the living Virgin Mary (Pelbart, *Pomerium*, lib. xii, pt. i, art. 1).

[2] This, as the author of *Dives and Pauper* points out (Com. I, c. 4), is sheer idolatry, whether it be done in ignorance or not. See Appendix 29.

year from their [first] making, and keep it thenceforward for so long as they endure ; to these images, therefore, they have directed their censings and fumigations and words and incantations as though these were true gods, gods made with men's hands."[1]

Complaints increase as time goes on. Chaucer's friend, Eustache Deschamps, wrote a balade on the theme " that no graven images should be set in our churches, save only the Crucifix and the Virgin, for fear of idolatry."[2] In it he writes : " For the work [of imagery] is a pleasing shape ; the painting thereof, whence I complain, and the beauty of the shining gold, make many inconstant folk to believe that these are gods for certain ; and, in their foolish thoughts, they serve these images which stand around in the churches, wherein we place too many of them. This is very ill done ; in brief words, we should not have such images."

His contemporary, the friar who wrote *Dives and Pauper*, blames the equivocal attitude of the official Church towards the Cross, and says : " This blindeth much people in their redynge [i.e. *interpretation*]. For they meane [i.e. *think*] that all the prayers that Holy Church maketh to the Cross, that she maketh them to the tree that Christ died on, or else to the cross in the church, as in that anthem, *O crux splendidior*. And so for lewdness [i.e. *ignorance*] they be deceived, and worship creatures as God Himself."[3] Sacchetti, about the same

---

[1] *De Legibus* (*Opera*, ed. Regnault, Paris, 1516, vol. i, fol. 33, col. 3).

[2] *Œuvres* (Soc. d'anciens textes français), vol. viii, p. 201.

[3] Com. I, c. 4 (ed. Berthelet, 1534, f. 15.v°). Cardinal Gasquet, on p. 75 of his *Monastic Life in the Middle Ages*, quotes this author as *disproving* the Protestant delusion that, " by allowing this customary reverence [to the Cross], the Church had given occasion for the growth of serious superstition among the common people, amounting in reality to practical idolatry." In order to make out his case, he quotes the words of *Dives and Pauper* which precede and succeed this frank admission on the author's part, but *suppresses the whole of the passage which I here quote in the text*, and gives no reference which would enable the reader to check an omission which he marks by only three dots. See Appendix 29.

time, was preaching against similar abuses. The Holy Crucifix of Lucca, though its hoary antiquity gave it surpassing virtue in the minds of such old women as William of Auvergne rebuked, and such semi-pagans as our William Rufus, and such sinners as Dante satirizes in the twenty-first canto of his *Inferno*, was estimated at its true value by this intelligent and plain-spoken Florentine novelist, Sacchetti. This fashion in images, he writes, this attribution of more virtue to one than to another, is sheer idolatry ; so far is it from edifying, that it makes reasonable men doubt of the faith ; the Perugians believe more in their Sant' Ercolano than they do in Christ ; the vicious system is encouraged by priests and monks to bring grist to their own mill.[1] This last accusation is borne out by Church councils of about the same time.

Roughly contemporary with Sacchetti, again, was the Bohemian Mathias von Janow, often called Mathias Parisiensis, because he had been professor of divinity at that university. To him (about 1370), the question of church images is already among the most serious. He writes :

"Alas ! nowadays certain associations [*collegia*], and the multitude of those who call themselves masters of the Church and wise men, have decreed in God's name in the Church [*decreta Dei in ecclesia posuerunt*] to the effect that images of wood or stone or silver or such like should be adored and worshipped by Christians, though Holy Scripture saith openly and expressly, ' Thou shalt not adore nor worship them ' ! a thing which can by no means be held or defended from the assertion of Thomas Aquinas or from other doctors ; *and Holy Church, although she has admitted images and statues to be honoured and reverenced, yet she has never taught or decreed that they should be adored or worshipped,* as may be seen in the Corpus [of Canon Law], in the Faculty of Law. . . .

---

[1] *Sermoni*, Florence, 1857, pp. 214 ff. ; Novella, 157 *ad fin* ; Novella, 169. I give this evidence and that of the Councils more fully in *From St. Francis to Dante*, 2nd ed., pp. 309 ff. and notes.

They have decreed also, and have commanded in their synods that men should preach to the people, *that folk may piously believe God's virtue, and the virtue of the saints, to reside in painted images of stone or wood,* and therefore that the miracles which are seen or reported to be wrought by them are wrought by God through and on account of these images ; and therefore whosoever believes this, or puts faith in such an image and takes refuge in it doeth no wrong ; nay, they say it is impossible that he should do wrong, nor are simple folk to be corrected and rebuked for fleeing to images in times of their need, or to relics of the saints or other such dead things that have neither merit nor virtue. Moreover, they have decreed that we should not preach against such abuse of statues or relics ; for they say that Christian folk do not err in such matters. Yet who doth not understand how pernicious these things are to rude and carnal Christian folk, if only he reflect how the common folk of to-day, not having the spirit of the Lord Jesus, can by no means be raised in mind to spiritual things, but, impelled only and chiefly by carnal judgment and fancies, they prize only bodily things, and marvel and fear in the presence of such things, pouring out their whole soul to these things."[1] In another place he points out how, in comparison with famous statues like the Holy Rood of Lucca, " men pay slight attention, or none, to the Body of Christ, present in the same place. The reason whereof is that the unlearned people, following their senses only, are strongly moved by such images and by their splendid and artificial appearance ; and that all such folk are prone to idolatry, seeing that they circumscribe their concepts or their imagination more easily, and limit it more gladly, in the creature than in the Deity, since the creature is nearer to their natural faculties. . . . Yet by this I intend not to deny that images may reasonably be made and

[1] F. Palacky, *Die Vorläufer des Husitenthums in Böhmen*, Prag, 1869, pp. 78–80. The sentences I have here italicized have been marked by Lord Acton in his copy.

placed in the church, since all Holy Church holdeth thus, and men commonly say that such images are the lay folk's Bible. Let the Church, therefore, be adorned with statues ; I oppose not this, nor gainsay in any wise, provided that we be on our guard against the devil's wiles here as in other things." And elsewhere the author speaks even more plainly for his orthodox intention : " I submit these words, all and several, and myself also, to the Holy Catholic Church, my most sweet mother, and bride of Jesus Christ."

St. Bernardino of Siena (d. 1444) was distressed by remnants of pagan superstitions among the worshippers at St. Peter's in Rome, and indignant that such open sinners as usurers should treat the images as other folk did and do still, " defiling the saints painted on the walls by touching their countenances with shameless hands and then rubbing over their own faces."[1] His older contemporary, Cardinal Pierre d'Ailly, one of the greatest figures at the Council of Constance, propounded to that Council, among other necessary articles of reform, " that so great a variety of images and pictures should not be multiplied in the churches."[2] A few years later, the still more distinguished Cardinal Nicolas of Cusa, as bishop of

THE TRINITY AND THE FOUR
EVANGELISTS
(FROM A BOOK OF HOURS).

[1] *Opera*, ed. de la Haye, vol. ii, pp. 53, 256.
[2] V. d. Hardt, *Mag. Œcum. Const. Concilium*, vol. i, p. 423.

Brixen, complained that the Tyrolese, his flock, " generally " worshipped the saints only for selfish and material
reasons, " for the prosperity of their crops and their
herds," and therefore witchcraft was particularly abundant
in those mountain districts.[1] As Papal Legate in Holland,
he publicly proclaimed that " to call upon this or that
saint for this or that thing, is a relic of paganism." [2]

The idea that the average church building of A.D. 1500
was filled with imagery presenting an harmonious body of
teaching, is quite anachronistic.[3] We have abundant
indications, slight enough individually yet convincing in
their totality, that, where there was not great neglect,
there was often great confusion. Very significant is a
Lincolnshire document of about 1480 printed by Trice
Martin in *Archæologia* (vol. lx, p. 366). It is a petition
to Chancery ; i.e. a protest against the strict law and an
attempt to secure the King's protection in the name of
equity. The first half runs : " All the parishioners of
Grayingham, near Kirton in Lindsey, who are tenants of
our Lord the King, beseech that, as a dispute has arisen
between Robert Conyng, parson of one half of the church
of the said town of Grayingham, and the said parishioners,
touching an image which the said Robert has had set in a
place within their said Church to the great nuisance of
the said parishioners, so that they cannot well see the

[1] Van Steenberghe, *Nicolas de Cues*, p. 160.
[2] F. A. Scharpff, *Nicolaus v. Cusa*, Mainz, 1843, p. 181. On this point
the reader may find a mass of interesting details in Dr. van Gennep's
Essai sue le culte populaire des saints franciscains en Savoie (*Rev. d'hist.
franciscaine*, Avril–Juin, 1927, pp. 113 ff.). He shows that in this
district, which he knows intimately, the cult of saints is prevalently utilitarian ; those survive who have the reputation of curing some constant
and frequent trouble among the country folk. Thus " St. Antony of
Padua has succeeded in keeping his place, because he was the first inter-
cessor who specialized in the recovery of lost articles. And, since mis-
laying is a durable and widespread defect, therefore St. Anthony of Padua
retains really popular worship in parts of Savoy, whereas St. Francis of
Assisi and St. Clare have fallen into oblivion, except, perhaps, among
the educated middle-class and the lower local nobility."
[3] Unless, of course, it had been newly built or restored.

elevation [of the Host] nor divine service performed in the said Church. And because they would complain of it, he has caused to be denounced as excommunicated all the said parishioners who would gainsay him or hinder him in his will in this behalf. And because they have obtained an inhibition of the said denunciation from their Archdeacon, the said Robert has summoned the said parishioners to be before the Bishop of Lincoln within a short time to come, to bring them into court and vex them as much as he can of his malice."

We need not wonder that, while high ecclesiastics murmured their misgivings, common folk were saying the same things more and more insistently and with less and less ecclesiastical caution; and here was one of the currents which led to the religious revolution of the sixteenth century. Then it was that the miracle-play and the image went through the furnace of affliction. In 1565, St. Charles Borromeo forbade the Passion Play altogether, and all other theatrical representations on Church Holy-days, throughout his province of Milan.[1] Pope Urban VIII, in 1628, forbade at last such representations of the Trinity as had scandalized Wyclif two hundred and fifty years earlier; he prescribed, under penalty of anathema, that all figures should be burnt which portrayed the Three Persons " in the shape of a man with three mouths, three noses, and four eyes." Benedict XIV, in 1745, recalled and confirmed this condemnation.[2]

What, then, had caused this change in the orthodox attitude towards medieval symbolic art? The story is admirably told by Mâle in his concluding chapter (vol. iii, pp. 525 ff.); yet we may be permitted to add a little to what he says, and to suggest certain points of view which he scarcely treats with full justice.[3]

---

[1] Dejob, p. 212.

[2] Didron, *Christ. Icon.*, vol. ii, p. 61.

[3] Very useful also is a much smaller volume by Dr. Charles Dejob. *De l'influence du Concile de Trente sur la litt. et les beaux-arts chez les peuples catholiques*, 1884.

Nearly all the heretics (he points out), like nearly all the orthodox reformers, had taken a puritan view of art. But the heretics had, of course, gone farther, and repudiated the whole system of ecclesiastical imagery. Thus the leaders of the Counter-Reformation, the fathers of the Council of Trent, had to deal with the acknowledged abuses of images, while they insisted on their use. In their twenty-fifth and last session, after formally anathematizing all who denied purgatory, they cursed with equal solemnity all opponents of images. After this the decree proceeds : " Yet, if any abuses have crept into these holy and salutary observances, this Holy Synod is vehemently desirous of abolishing such altogether, so that no images of false dogma may be set up, giving occasion of perilous error to simple folk. And if ever it chance that stories and narrations of Holy Scripture are sometimes expressed and figured, as this is expedient for the unlearned multitude, let the people be taught that the Deity is not figured on this account, as though It could be seen with the bodily eyes, or expressed in colours or shapes. . . . Moreover, let all wantonness be avoided, so that images be not painted or adorned with provocative beauty." This was in November 1563 ; and in 1570 appeared the book of Molanus, " *Concerning Pictures and Sacred Images*, treating of the Avoidance of Abuses with Regard to them, and of their Signification." A posthumous edition, with fresh matter, in 1593, was entitled " *Of the History of Holy Images*, for their true Use against Abuses, in four Books." The author, whose native name was Ver Meulen, was professor at Louvain, and of a learning which impressed the learned Baronius. Writing in the face of heretics, he is concerned to emphasize those apologetic words of the Council " if any," " if ever," and to insist that the worst abuses of which he speaks are rare (p. 228). Again, after describing several types of picture, he is careful to add his opinion that, though reprehensible, they are not actually such as to " give occasion of perilous error to simple folk " (75). Later on, it is true, he is less definitely on the defensive, and reminds his readers how the St. Christopher guarantee had lately been condemned at a provincial Council as " an abominable vanity and superstition " ; but we shall understand his attitude best if we look first at these earlier instances which he does indeed blame, but refuses to bring under the anathema of the Council, and denies to the parish priest the right of making any change except by authority of his bishop. And, farther to understand this question, we must bear in mind that Molanus was evidently not an artistic nature, and that he deals with the subject from the point of view of the ordinary theological professor of the Counter-Reformation.

" I think " (he writes, p. 70) " that there is not even one [image which gives occasion of error to simple folk] in our Churches, although they seem, or at least might seem, such. For in certain places, in the story of the Annunciation and the Lord's Incarnation, there is painted a little human body, among rays diffused by the Holy Ghost, descending to the most blessed Virgin's womb ; which picture might seem to offer an occasion not only of perilous but even of heretical error. For Valentinus has long been held a heretic by the Church, for teaching that Christ brought His body from heaven, and passed through Mary only as through a pipe ; wherefore St. Antonino [1] doth sharply reprove this picture, saying ' reprehensible, also, are painters who paint things contrary to the Faith ; when they represent the Trinity as one person with three heads, which is a monster in nature ; or, at the Annunciation, a little fully-formed child, Jesus to wit, sent into the Virgin's womb, as though His body were not taken from the substance of the Virgin ; or the child Jesus with a hornbook, whereas he learned not

---

[1] The great Dominican teacher, Archbishop of Florence, 1448–59, whose authority on moral questions was perhaps even more studied, in the later Middle Ages, than that of Aquinas. The quotation is from his *Summa*, pars. iii, tit. viii, c. 4, § 11.

from man.'[1] Again, at the Last Judgment, some portray the Blessed Virgin and the Baptist in prayer, a representation which would seem to savour of what St. Augustine hath condemned, to wit the dogma of the salvation of the damned through prayers and intercession of the saints, and to be in direct contradiction to Gratian [cause xiii, q. 2][2]. . . . Again, some portray the Archangel Michael with scales, weighing the soul in one and its virtues in another. They represent the Devil standing at the soul's scale and striving to press it down in so far as he can ; while, on the other side, Michael with his sign of the Cross hinders the Devil's attempt, and seems to add something more to that scale from the merits of Christ's passion and cross. But from such a representation some would easily infer that those attain to eternal life whose good works outweigh the bad, while those in whom the bad outweigh the good are left to the Devil.[3] . . . Moreover, some

[1] To this St. Antonino himself adds : " Nor are they praiseworthy when they paint apocryphal things, as the midwives at the Virgin Birth, or the Virgin Mary at her Assumption leaving her girdle to the Apostle Thomas by reason of his doubting, and things of that sort. Also when in the stories of saints or in churches they paint curiosities which avail not to excite devotion, but laughter and vanity, as apes, and dogs chasing hares, and so forth, or vain ornaments of apparel, this seemeth superfluous and vain."

[2] Molanus seems here to have lost hold of medieval symbolism ; for the praying St. John is generally the Evangelist and not the Baptist, though by no means always, especially in Germany and the Netherlands. Mâle, who notes Reims as an exception in France, holds that the German examples teach another story ; not intercession but : " Here is He whom I foretold." Yet on the main point he agrees with Molanus (II, 472). " The theologians had affirmed that, at the Last Day, no prayer could move the Judge ; but the humble crowd of the faithful did not believe this. They continued to hope that, at that day, the Virgin and St. John would still be powerful intercessors, and would save more than one soul by their prayers."

[3] The annotator quotes here an example of such interpretation, from a medieval Dominican legend. A usurer, in a vision, saw his soul thus weighed by Michael ; the vices were " infinitely heavier " than the virtues ; only he had been accustomed to say the rosary of the Virgin Mary every day. Therefore she now intervened, cast a rosary into the lighter scale, and the heavier at once kicked the beam. The usurer was converted by this vision to amendment of life.

represent St. John the Evangelist as the spouse at the marriage-feast of Cana. Yet, as Catharinus saith, we must by no means believe that he was the spouse at that wedding whereunto Jesus was called ; for in that case our Lord would have dissolved the marriage ; yet He came, as holy expositors rightly teach us, to honour and approve it. If, on the other hand, He had dissolved it, He would rather have supplied the heretics with an argument for disapproval of marriage. To this we may add that Salome, mother to the sons of Zebedee, coming to Christ with her sons the Apostles James and John, is [sometimes] portrayed bringing her sons like little children to Christ. For from this picture it would seem that a man might well argue : 'Lo ! Christ chose children for Apostles, for these were the two against whom the ten were angry : wherefore then should it not be lawful to give Church benefices to children ? ' And, lastly, that Charles Martel, that great Duke of Brabant who was grandfather to the Emperor Charles the Great, is painted as receiving imposition of hands or absolution from St. Giles ; or, as another representation hath it, an angel announceth to Charles the remission of his sin, with a verse added :

Aegidii merito, Caroli peccata remitto,[1]

which seems to answer to that story of St. Giles wherein it is written that, at the revelation of an angel, and at the prayers of St. Giles, this King of France . . . was forgiven a great crime, which he had not dared to confess to any man, on condition that he should desist therefrom for the future. And that this was added at the end : Whosoever should call upon St. Giles, for whatever sin, if he ceased from the practice thereof, then he might believe without doubt that God had forgiven it him. But, seeing that this story is partly in contradiction with Holy Scripture and Church tradition, which demand sacramental absolution, it would seem also that the image which expresseth

---

[1] " By the merit of Giles, I remit Charles's sin."

this story should be relegated among those which give occasion of error to simple folk."

The extreme caution of the conclusions here drawn by Molanus (he will not say that these things *do* fall under the Council's anathemana, but they *seem* to fall) and the care with which he proclaims the subordination of his own judgments to those of popes or bishops, whenever popes or bishops might see fit to pronounce themselves, lend all the more significance to these examples which he quotes. Moreover, the reader will see that, in two at least of these cases, what he reprehends is not rare, as in his apologetic mood he had pleaded, but normal and almost universal. Mary and John praying at the Doom, with Michael weighing the souls, are among the most unchanging features of medieval symbolism. Yet all these he would willingly sweep away.

He refuses to go so far as Erasmus in reproof; yet he realizes how many artistic conventions repose on popular imagination (90). And on one point he agrees with Erasmus, in his *Institution of Christian Matrimony*, though he knows that the book has been condemned by the Council of Trent. He entirely disapproves of unnecessary nudities, e.g. David and Bathsheba, or Salome dancing alluring dances before Herod. He transcribes Erasmus's blame of the farcical element introduced by artists; " as, for instance, when they portray Mary and Martha receiving our Lord to a feast, the Lord speaking with Mary, and John as a youth talking secretly in a corner with Martha, while Peter drains a tankard. Or again, at the feast, Martha standing behind by John, with one arm over his shoulders, while with the other hand she seems to mock at Christ, unaware of all this. Or again, Peter already rubicund with wine, yet holding the goblet to his lips." These were probably the extravagances of Flemish painters.

More serious are his criticisms of the scenes from Christ's, or Mary's, life. He realizes that the former sometimes come from the apocryphal *Book of Christ's*

cc

Infancy (83). He reprobates the figment, based upon this same book, that Mary was conceived by the kiss of Joachim and Anne at the Golden Gate (393). He approves of the attempts to follow definite and ancient tradition of portraiture, especially in these holiest pictures of all; but here he has to wrestle with the discordance of early written authorities (164). Epiphanius had described Mary as " of a colour that recalled wheat, with yellow hair and keen eyes, of a yellowish hue and as it were oil-coloured in the pupils." A Greek of the eleventh century described her as " somewhat dark [*subfusca*], with tawny hair and tawny eyes "; yet Pelbart, in the fifteenth, is certain that she was dark-haired.

It would be too long a task to follow Molanus farther through his iconographical difficulties; but here again we must note how careful he is to give no handle to iconoclasm (84). " It seemeth to me (yet I subject mine opinion to the correction of others), that it is not expedient to remove or change pictures of this sort, if some folk's weakness would be troubled thereby, so long as no provincial synod decrees otherwise in that particular case. Let us tolerate and permit some things for the sake of the weak, even as our Mother Church tolerates and permits certain things. How many opinions does she tolerate in published books ? She tolerates *Vitaspatum*,[1] though Pope Gelasius and his council once reprobated the book.[2] She tolerates Jacobus de Voragine's *Golden Legend*, which some men call *The Leaden Legend*; for, as Melchior Cano saith, ' This book was written by a

---

[1] A collection of stories of the early Fathers of the Desert, varying much in date and in authority, which the Middle Ages regarded as the foundation of monastic history. An English version of a Syriac redaction of this collection has been published by E. A. Wallis Budge, 1907.

[2] The reference here given is to the first volume of the *Corpus of Canon Law*, Gratian [pars. i], dist. xv. But I can there find no mention of this book in the long list of volumes reprobated; on the contrary, the list of books recommended contains certain lives extracted from the kernel of this book. The other list, however, contains the name of Cassian, and Molanus may be thinking of this.

man of iron mouth and leaden heart, and certainly of small gravity or prudence in mind ' ; words which he hath borrowed from Ludovicus Vives. She tolerates much which hath been already published in divers histories, things uncertain, fabulous, apocryphal and lacking all verisimilitude, only taking care that they be not read in Church. . . . Therefore, that which the Church tolerates in books, let us also, with her, tolerate in pictures, which the Fathers have justly named the Scriptures of the Simple. Meanwhile let the simple be taught what they ought to learn, what not to learn, from images of this sort. Let painters and sculptors be taught to avoid at least the more notable and important errors in that which they set up. This, after all, is easy, since the more notable errors scarcely exist except in images which, when all things are considered, are rare."

CHAPTER XIX

REFORMATION OR RENAISSANCE ?

MUCH of the evidence given in Chapter XVIII is rehearsed more briefly in Mâle's concluding chapter, entitled : " How did Medieval Art End ? " Since my own answer to that question differs on some important points from his, it is the more necessary to present his point of view fairly.

" It seems," he writes, " that the rich iconography [of the Middle Ages] had never been more living and fertile than at the beginning of the sixteenth century. How is it then that, a few years later, it dissolved and soon disappeared without leaving any traces behind ? The first idea which occurs to us is, that the medieval tradition in France was killed by the art of the Italian Renaissance." At first sight, we say that the mark of medieval art was humility ; as for that of the Renaissance, " its hidden principle is pride ; henceforth man is self-sufficient and aspires to be a god." This art did indeed come into France with Francis I, and conquered rapidly : " but this new conception of art did nothing to modify the old iconographic dispositions." Mâle gives examples of a Nativity and an Assumption, and concludes : " Thus Italian Renaissance art, penetrating into France, did nothing to destroy the old French iconography ; it conformed itself thereunto. . . . If the tradition of the Middle Ages is dead, the slayer is not the Renaissance, but the Reformation. It is the Reformation which, by compelling the Catholic Church to watch every aspect of her own thought and to concentrate herself violently, put an end to that long tradition of legends and poetry and dreams."

How is this ?   " One of the first consequences of the Reformation was to render Catholics suspicious of their old religious drama.   They perceived for the first time that the authors of the miracle-plays had mingled the Gospel text with a thousand fables, a thousand platitudes, and a thousand coarsenesses.   They had to admit that the Protestants were not altogether wrong in saying that these detestable poets ' changed the holy words of the Bible into a mere farce.'   The happy age of innocence, in which everything is graceful, was now past and gone."   The municipality of Amiens raised difficulties in 1541 ; the Parlement of Paris, in 1548, expressly forbade the gilds to represent " the mystery of the Passion of our Saviour, or other sacred mysteries."   The miracle-play lingered on here and there, but the edict of 1548 had given it its death-blow.   And " its disappearance had serious consequences for Christian art.   We have shown how the mystery-plays had in a great measure created the iconography of the later Middle Ages. . . . When they disappeared, no traditions remained but those which lingered still for a while in the workshops. . . . Thus, by the end of the sixteenth century, our artists suddenly found themselves facing the subjects of Christian art without traditions [to guide them].   Their pride was doubtless flattered by this ; for Italy had taught them that a great artist owes no debt but to himself ; yet Christian art did not gain by this.   In that dying tradition there was more poetry and tenderness and pain than any man, even a genius, could put into his work.   That is how the Reformation, by killing the medieval theatre, struck an indirect blow at iconography."   And, at this very moment, in 1563, came that decree of the Council of Trent which regulated Church images.   " There was a fresh consequence of the Reformation.   The Protestants had declared war against images, and they must not be permitted to have legitimate motives for mocking the

credulity of the Catholics or their want of moral deli-
cacy." The clergy were still the guides of the artists;
" but one thing is evident, that this clergy felt none of
the scruples which the Reformation awoke in men's
minds." Canons and bishops saw no reason why pagan
legends, even Mars and Venus or Bacchus and Ceres,
should not figure in churches. Again, " nothing testifies
more clearly to their tolerance than those [carved] stalls
of the fifteenth and sixteenth centuries. There is no
room in them for things of heaven; they represent daily
life "—the water-carrier, the tallow-chandler, etc.; or
again, fairy-tales or satirical fabliaux. It is a mistake to
suppose that these things were done behind the backs of
the clergy; in 1458, for instance, the canons of Rouen
were shown by Viart, in his workshop, specimens of the
little grotesques with which he adorned the still-existing
stalls of the cathedral, " and they went away thoroughly
satisfied."

Such was still the orthodox mind about 1530. " Everything beautiful deserves to be gratefully received. Beauty
is heaven-sent; every fair work, be it pagan or Christian,
is a message from God. Had not the Pope opened his
Vatican to all the marvels of ancient art ? " But at last,
" at the Council of Trent, the Church examined herself.
She asked herself whether she had always done her duty
conscientiously; and she promised herself to be more
strict with herself in future. Iconoclastic Protestantism
had condemned art; the Church saved it; but she
wished it to ·be without reproach " (534). With this
idea, men like Cardinal Paleotti came forward. They
fought the Protestants, but were compelled to fight them
on the ground not of imagination, but of reason and
common-sense. Molanus tries to explain how the
Christopher and Nicholas and George legends could have
grown up. " Thus, poesy recoils before good sense.
Unluckily, pure reason has never inspired artists; and
henceforth there was no hope that the story of St. George
would ever give birth to a masterpiece. It is not only

the old popular Christianity of the Middle Ages which
is condemned by the new spirit ; [Molanus condemns]
also that pathetic Christianity which we may call Franciscan Christianity." And " this appeal to austerity was
only too well heard. Strange to say, on this point the
Renaissance conspired with the Church." For Molanus
and his friends hated nudities, and the Renaissance had
a taste for ample and elaborate drapery.

" Thus an age of decency and reason announced itself.
After 1560, everything conspired to kill medieval art.
With the miracle-plays, the iconographic traditions of
the past began to disappear ; at the same moment the
Church reviewed those traditions, discovered that most
of them were stamped with the excessive credulity of
past ages, and asked the artists to abandon them. Medieval
art must needs succumb. Its charm was that it had kept
the candour of childhood. This art resembled the medieval
Church itself ; it resembled faith which does not discuss,
but sings. Such an art could not even be touched with
doubt. . . . The art of the Middle Ages, which was
nothing but simple faith and spontaneity, could not
survive that spirit of examination which owes its outburst to the Reformation. Henceforward there can be
only one resource for the Christian artist ; to stand face
to face with the Gospel and interpret it as he feels it.
Thus will Rembrandt do, and thus will Poussin ; for,
henceforward, Catholics will be no more supported by
tradition than the Protestants themselves in this new age
which begins at the Council of Trent ; the artist will now
owe nothing to anyone but himself. So, from time to
time, we shall have a few men in Europe capable of inter-
preting the Gospel in accordance with their temperament or their genius ; but there will be no longer, as in
the Middle Ages, a collection of traditions respected
everywhere and capable of raising the most moderate
artist above himself. We shall still have Christian artists ;
we shall no longer have a Christian art."

With these melancholy words Mâle closes his valuable book ; but let us look more closely into the facts and the inferences.

First, the iconography of the greatest age of Gothic art had owed comparatively little to the miracle-play. The main creators here, apart from the artists themselves, had been learned ecclesiastics here and there, such as Abbot Suger at St.-Denis, or Abbot Samson at St. Edmundsbury, or the authors of a good many surviving sets of verses which were composed as explicatory legends to be painted under some great series of pictures.[1] The influence of the miracle-play, so admirably traced by Mâle in that third volume, is, as he points out in its place, mainly late ; it belongs to an age when Gothic art was already running fast to seed ; it coincides, for instance, with the shopwork of the English alabaster factories. What effect need the disappearance of the miracle-play have had (to choose among the best-known and most obvious examples) upon the portals of Chartres, the serious quatrefoils on the west front of Amiens, or the sportive panels on the *portail des libraires* at Rouen ?

Secondly, it is historically incorrect to date this dissatisfaction with the medieval sacred drama from the Reformation. Here, as in so many other fields, the Reformers did no more than insist loudly, and often brutally, on things which pious and orthodox folk had murmured more discreetly for some time past, and in which satirists had long found theme for mockery. Chaucer shows no respect either for the tragedy or for the comedy of the religious drama ; either for Herod strutting on high or for the farce of Noah bringing his wife to ship. A contemporary of his, who may or may not have been a Lollard, but who certainly bases all his criticisms on religious and moral assumptions which most modern Christians would admit, is far more outspokenly critical of that drama. It had been invented (men had

[1] E.g. those published by Dr. M. R. James in Camb. Antiq. Soc., 8vo Series No. XXVIII, pp. 156 ff., and XXXVIII, pp. 13 ff.

pleaded in earlier days), to strengthen the faith of the multitude ; yet to this author it is mainly objectionable because the mixture of truth and fable, of edification and folly, has resulted in a weakening of faith.[1] An extraordinarily interesting light comes to us from the York records.[2] In 1425 a Franciscan friar, William of Melton, " Doctor of Divinity, and most famous preacher of the Word of God, came to this city and in his various sermons commended to the people the aforesaid play [i.e. the elaborate series of Bible-plays which were performed from dawn to dark, each scene by a trade-gild or a group of gilds, on Corpus Christi Day]. He affirmed that the play, in itself, was good and most laudable. Yet he said that the citizens of the said city, and other foreigners who flowed in upon that holy-day, busy themselves greatly not only with the said holy-day pageant but also in gluttony and drunkenness, shoutings and songs and other insolences, paying no attention whatever [*minime attendentes*] to the Church service appointed for that day. And, sad to say, they thus lose the indulgences granted in that matter by Urban the Fourth of blessed memory [a long list of indulgences for attendance in church on Corpus Christi and following days]. And therefore it seemed salutary to this friar William, and he would fain bring the people of the city thereunto, that the play should take place on one day and the Corpus Christi procession on the next, so that folk might flock to church on that holy-day and attend divine service for the obtaining of these indulgences." It was enacted, therefore, that the pageants should thenceforward be played on the eve of the feast. But, as the editor tells us, " the influence of Willelmus soon passed ; the people

---

[1] Compare the extracts from Robert Mannyng of Brunne, printed on p. 402 of *Social Life in Britain*, and from a preacher of about 1400 in *Medieval Garner*, p. 570, and in *Life in Medieval Europe*, p. 191.

[2] *York Memorandum Book*, vol. ii, Surtees Soc., 1914, pp. 124, 156–8 ; cf. introd., pp. 46 ff. The version of Friar Melton's action given in *The Cambridge Hist. of Eng. Lit.* is strangely distorted.

obtained two holidays, but continued to perform their plays on Corpus Christi day and relegated the religious procession to the following day."

The second York incident was in 1431. The goldsmiths complained of the insupportable burden of having to produce two scenes of the play. " On the other hand, since the stonemasons of this city murmured among themselves concerning the pageant assigned to them in the Corpus Christi play, wherein Fergus was scourged, seeing that the matter of that pageant is not contained in Holy Scripture, and that it caused rather laughter and shouting than devotion, and sometimes quarrels and contentions and fights arose therefrom among the people, and that they could seldom or never perform and play that pageant by clear daylight, as the earlier pageants do, therefore the said masons desired greatly to be relieved of this their pageant, and to be assigned to some other which is in accordance with Holy Scripture, and which they can perform and play by daylight." [1]

The City Council sympathized with both the petitioning gilds, and transferred to the masons the pageant of Herod, which hitherto had been one of the two assigned to the goldsmiths.

Very nearly at this same time, St. Antonino was writing at Florence. He was not only a scholar and archbishop but also a man of remarkable practical insight and knowledge of the world. We find him complaining that, in general, " the [theatrical] representations of spiritual things which are made nowadays are mixed with

---

[1] The episode of Fergus (otherwise called Belzeray), resting upon the same sort of apocryphal foundation as that of Joachim and Anne, deals with a Jew who laid hands on the Virgin's bier, and whose hands clave to it by miracle. It is one of the scenes carved on the north side of Notre-Dame (figured in *Medieval Garner*, p. 701). The story is given fully in the *Golden Legend* (Assumption of B.V.M.), and it was one of those painted on the walls of Eton College Chapel for the instruction of those royal scholars. Since it dealt with the last scene of all, the Assumption, it was natural that dusk should come on before the masons were called upon for their performance.

many jests and buffooneries and masquerades."[1] And, a generation later, in 1469, we get a most significant glimpse of this theatre in an ordinary French village. The Archdeacon of Josas, in the Diocese of Paris, reported on his visit to St.-Vrain (Seine-et-Oise): "Note, that the rural dean gave leave for playing the play of St. Sebastian on Our Lady's Day in September, and on the Sunday following. The players were Michel Datilli, Geoffroy Levain, Jean Bérault, Roger Cordier, and Pierre Jeudi, with Guillot Bardon, who dwelleth at Lèdeville, and Antoine Simonnet of Marolles. They rehearsed their play in the Chapel of St.-Vrain, denying God and fighting with each other."[2] A Hungarian friend tells me of a common proverb in that country, answering to the English slang: "A went for B bald-headed"; it runs: "A went for B as Christ went for the shoemaker." This records a similar occasion, on which one performer taunted the other for his trade, and all dramatic proprieties were suddenly swept away by professional rivalry. It was quite natural, therefore, for any reforming saint to discourage the miracle-play; and here St. Charles Borromeo, however he might shock the multitude, was creating no real religious breach but rather drawing an inevitable inference from saints of the past. In 1565 he, like the Parlement of Paris, prohibited the Passion Play: moreover, he forbade all theatrical representations on the Church holy-days.[3] Reformation and Counter-Reformation did indeed sweep much away; but to describe the age which there ended as "the happy age of innocence" seems almost as bold as it would be to apply that same regretful phrase to French society

---

[1] *Summa Major*, pars. iii, tit. viii, c. 4, § 12.

[2] *Visites archidiaconales de Josas*, ed. Alliot, 1902, p. 336.

[3] Dejob, pp. 212–14. His severity against actors in general was such that the municipality of Milan protested formally to the Pope; they complained that this puritanism "scandalized and shocked the innocent, and left the guilty no alternative but hypocrisy or despair." Yet in this St. Charles was following medieval Canon Law, and the sentiments of great medieval ecclesiastics.

before 1789. The world of 1500 had outgrown things that were often far from innocent, and no longer even happy. The reluctance of the York masons cannot have been an isolated incident.

So, again, with a great deal of the carved or painted things with which the mystery-play was bound up. When Mâle writes (p. 536) " a good half of the masterpieces which we admire in our churches were inspired by fables," we recognize this as true of later medieval art, and probably even of the thirteenth century. But can we recognize the same indisputable truth in the words with which he continues ?—" These legends had been more fruitful and beneficent than any history whatsoever, in the days when they were taken as authentic ; but those days were past." Is not this modern antiquary out of harmony, on that point, with all the best Christian thought ? Great fathers like Origen had not known these legends ; even St. Gregory the Great, in the Dark Ages, had despised and ignored the fable of Constantine's leprosy ; Monsignor L. Duchesne pointed this out in his edition of the *Liber Pontificalis.* If, in the thirteenth century, Catholics believed implicitly in things which Gregory the Great had despised, and which no educated Catholic defends nowadays, this was not because the inventions were more fruitful and beneficent than the truth, but because men lacked certain methods of approach to truth which have been constructed by the labour and ingenuity and sincerity of twenty succeeding generations of mankind. It can scarcely be doubted that St. Bernard or Roger Bacon would have repudiated any sentimental hankering after what they had once recognized as fables, as vehemently as Luther or Calvin did. Their last word would not have been a regretful " but those days are past ! " but rather an energetic " let them pass, and God will give us better days in their stead ! " " Instead of thy fathers thou shalt have children, whom thou mayest make princes in all the earth."

And such was the attitude of really great churchmen,

when once the Renaissance had begun to open men's minds to historical truth. Ludovicus Vives, the great Spanish humanist and educational reformer of the first half of the sixteenth century, had no hesitation in calling upon all straightforward minds to winnow boldly the chaff from the wheat. He wrote : " With what serious patience did the ancient Greeks and Romans seek the truth, and what pains they took to set it clearly forth ! " But the men who have come after them have almost entirely lost that factor of [accurate] memory and that of prudence. . . . Even in the books which are supposed to be Latin, such as the *De Vitis Philosophorum*, or the moralized *Gesta Romanorum*, what need was there of so great falsehoods ? Why could they not find the moral teaching which they sought in the real deeds of the Romans ? But let us suppose these things, grave as they are, to be within the bounds of toleration. What is it when this same licence of lying has crept into holy things, or rather has been openly borne into them ? For example, the traditional teaching concerning Constantine's leprosy and his bath in children's blood ; of the leprosy of Vespasian, of Gamaliel, of Berenice, the Acts of Christ and of the Blessed Virgin ? [1] We cry and bark at lesser things than this, and at these falsehoods we connive ; yet, if these come into the hands of impious folk, they turn our holiest and most earnest piety into a mockery fit to be hissed from the stage. Nor are we more religious in our traditions of things that stand nearer to us. [Each nation has its own false patriotic histories.] Nor do we keep truth more exactly when we write the lives of the saints ; though here all should have been exact and precise ; each has written their deeds according to his own affection for the man, so that the story is dictated

[1] These last two will be recognized as the already-mentioned apocryphal legends of Joachim and Anne and the Childhood of the Lord. The Leprosy of Constantine, a legend despised by St. Gregory, became in due time the foundation of Constantine's fictitious Donation to the Roman See, which was implicitly believed for nearly 700 years and upon which the medieval papal claims were to a great extent founded.

not by truth but by the writer's mood. How unworthy of saints and Christian men is that history of the saints which men call *Golden Legend* ? I know not wherefore it should be called golden, seeing that it is written by a man of iron mouth and leaden heart. What can we name that is baser than this book ? Oh, how shameful it is to us Christians that the most excellent deeds of our saints have not been handed down more truly and exactly, whether for the knowledge or for the imitation of their great virtue, seeing that the Greek and Roman authors took such care in writing of their own warriors and philosophers and sages ! " [1]

Again, Melchior Cano was one of the greatest among the bishops who sat on the Council of Trent.[2] In his *De Locis Theologicis*, written about 1550, when we come to the eleventh book, we find him insisting upon the impossibility of separating theology from history, and the consequent necessity of treating ecclesiastical traditions critically, though not, of course, with hypercriticism. The current story of Trajan freed from hell by the prayers of Pope Gregory, accepted implicitly by Dante and in another sense by the author of Piers Plowman, he rejects as a mere fable, and regrets that it had been believed " not by the multitude only, but even by St. Thomas [Aquinas] in his youth." Although, from Cyprian onwards, many Fathers have described the three Magi as kings, and this is therefore the reigning opinion, "yet this common tradition in the Church affords absolutely no proof [of its truth]." Again, though antiquity has consistently handed down the tradition that the Miracle of Cana took place on the anniversary of the Epiphany, yet " we can take no certain proof from the public commemoration of seasons." He knows that many cherished traditions are false ; that the legend of the

---

[1] *De Causis Corrupt. Artium*, lib. ii *ad fin* ; *Opera*, Bâle, 1555, p. 371.

[2] Modern orthodox authorities like *The Catholic Encyclopædia* and the Freiburg *Kirchenlexikon* speak of his " imperishable name," " worthy of a place next St. Thomas Aquinas," " epoch-making work," etc., etc.

Eleven Thousand Virgins is absurd ; that " certainly
the story of St. Thomas the Apostle is an apocryphal
fiction, since not only has [Pope] Gelasius said this [in a
passage embodied in Canon Law] but Augustine also
[in more than one passage]." [1]   He is well aware of the
weakness even of the early Church historians—Philo,
Sozomenus, Eusebius—" among ecclesiastics, there is not
one who can be taken as a thoroughly trustworthy
[probabilis] historian."   Is there nothing trustworthy,
then, in past records ?   Yes ; but only if we make proper
distinctions ; some are far more trustworthy than others ;
but in the least trustworthy class stand " edifying "
writers.   Among the pagan Greeks and Romans, on the
other hand, " some, impelled either by love of truth or
by the shamefastness of native modesty, have so abhorred
lying that we ought perhaps to blush to find that certain
Gentile historians have been more veracious than our
own.   I say it rather with grief than in contumely, that
[Diogenes] Laertius wrote the Lives of the Philosophers
far more strictly than Christians have written the Lives
of the Saints ; and that Suetonius has rehearsed the
affairs of the emperors with far more impartiality and
integrity than Catholics have rehearsed, I do not say the
story of the emperors, but [even] of martyrs, virgins and
confessors.   For those ancient authors, when dealing with
good emperors or philosophers, do not suppress either
their faults or the suspicion of fault ; again, with the
wicked, they show even such colour of virtue as these had.
But very many of ours [nostri plerique] are either slaves
to partiality, or even deliberately invent so much that I
am not only ashamed but disgusted at them."   Vives,
he continues, has very justly pilloried these men " who,
in the place of piety, have thought good to invent lies
for religion's sake " ;   the net result is that even truths
are rendered dubious.   " Such men sometimes paint us
the saints such as the saints themselves, though they

---

[1] This story of St. Thomas is among those which Mâle enumerates as
specially dear to medieval artists.

could have been, would have refused to be. For who
can believe that St. Francis, when the lice had been shaken
off, was wont to put them again upon himself " ; or,
again, an equally absurd story about St. Dominic ?
The book *Vitaspatrum*, commonly ascribed to St. Jerome,
has very little in it that Jerome actually wrote. " Of the
same sort also is that foolish and barbarous book of the
Nativity of St..Mary " [i.e. of Joachim and Anne] " and
many other things which Erasmus has most diligently
and justly refuted. . . . Therefore the Church of Christ
is sadly incommoded by these men who think they cannot
excellently set forth the noble deeds of the saints unless
they trick them out with fictitious revelations and
miracles.   Wherein human impudence hath spared
neither the holy Virgin nor Christ our Lord, but men
have done with their histories as with other saints,
allowing their frivolous human fancies to mingle therein
with many vain and ridiculous details.   In former years,
when I was at the Council of Trent, I heard from some
that this evil was remedied by Aloysio Lippomano,
Bishop of Verona, who had published a History of the
Lives of the Saints after a uniform and serious method.
But I have not yet been able to see this, nor has any
other come into my hands which, to me at least, would
seem trustworthy.   It will be a hard and burdensome task,
yet most profitable to all Christian folk, that someone
should now supply a work worthy of the Saints, of the
Church, and of Christ."   Meanwhile, however, the
printing-press and the censorship are often responsible
for the popularity of gross errors.   Cano knows of a
priest who " is fully convinced that there is no falsehood
whatsoever in anything that has once been printed," for
how can he believe that the authorities would not only
permit lies to be printed, but actually fortify them with
the privilege of exclusive copyright ?   " The multitude
reads those books all the more incautiously, because it
sees them approved not only by the civil magistrates, but
even by those who are definitely appointed as censors of

THE COBBLER ON THE CANON'S STALL.

doctrine in Christ's Church." The common herd demands religious fiction, and supply follows the demand. Moreover, these manufacturers of falsehood "imagine that they have the more liberty in this matter, since they see most famous authors taking it as a true rule of history to write those things which are vulgarly counted as true. Nor do I here excuse the author of the book called *Speculum Exemplorum*,[1] nor even of the history entitled *Golden Legend*. For in that book you will more often read monstrosities of miracles than real miracles; for it was written by a man of iron mouth and leaden heart, and certainly of small gravity or prudence in mind." Even Vincent of Beauvais and St Antonino of Florence, in their laborious compilations, "have taken less trouble to relate true things and certainties, than to rake together every detail that they could find written in any booklet [*schedulis*] whatsoever."

Here, then, are facts which we have to consider side by side with what Mâle gives us. He quotes to us frankly and fully from Molanus; but he seems not to suspect how much support Molanus could have claimed from like-minded predecessors in the Middle Ages, and from contemporaries in the Counter-Reformation. He writes sadly: "This cold-blooded little chapter of Molanus marks clearly the end of a chapter in human history." True; but even in the history of art we must sometimes look coldly at the facts; nor do all our natural regrets for a vanished world excuse us from a careful and two-sided analysis of the causes. That early Protestantism was often hasty and bungling is admitted nowadays by all reasonable and well-informed writers; it is as much of a truism as the complementary fact that very serious corruptions sheltered under the wing of the

---

[1] Possibly the *Speculum Morale*, compiled as a complementary volume to the great encyclopædia of Vincent of Beauvais by an anonymous sub-contemporary; or perhaps Herolt's *Promptuarium Exemplorum*, of which a translation by Mr. C. C. S. Bland will shortly be published by Routledge and Co.

Catholic Church. All men are now agreed that some change was then needed ; again, all are agreed that the surgery was often clumsy and ill-informed, and that, here and there, the changes created worse difficulties than they were designed to overcome. But, when we have said this, have we in fact said more than truth must allege against all surgeries, literal or metaphorical, in the light of four centuries of later experience ? Ambroise Paré was one of the great surgeons of all time, and he was roughly contemporary with Molanus and Cranmer. Would Paré have dealt with a case of appendicitis any more successfully than Cranmer dealt with the reform of the Liturgy ? Was any worse injustice done at the Reformation than by the orthodox emperors of early Christianity, who forcibly suppressed the schools of Athens, who made it penal for any man thenceforward to worship as the whole Empire had worshipped for centuries past, and who robbed the temples of a booty far exceeding all the spoils gathered by Henry VIII and the Protestant princes of Germany ? Let us ask ourselves therefore, as coolly as Molanus might ask himself in the light of modern knowledge, what was the alternative which would have saved medieval art ? Suppose that no Lollard or Lutheran or Calvinist had ever existed ; suppose that the sores of the Church had been left entirely in the hands of practitioners like the Fathers of the Council of Trent ; suppose these to have been unsoured and unjostled, doing their tranquil and reflective best without any heretics to shake their nerves ; what then would have happened to the painter and the sculptor ?

What was to be done with that " good half " of subjects which had inspired the best of Gothic art, and which were in fact fabulous ? Long before Luther, the Renaissance had begun to open men's eyes here. That fable of Constantine's leprosy, for instance, was exploded almost simultaneously by the humanist Lorenzo Valla in Italy and by Cardinal Nicholas of Cues in Germany. How was the new light to be concealed from the ordinary

educated man, from the merchant, for instance, like
Ralph Hythlodaye, whom More takes for the narrator
of his Utopia ?   How could it be permanently concealed
from these men that the whole story of Joachim and
the Nativity of the Virgin Mary was fabulous, and that,
as Cano saw, there was no real certitude in the fact that
events of this kind had been attached by immemorial
tradition to certain days of the year ?   And, if the merchant might learn the truth, why not the artisan and
even the peasant ?   Would our imaginary perfect reformers
have condescended to that policy of the modern *Action
Française* ?   Would they have held that the uneducated
must be encouraged to accept dogmas which his educated
director believes to be false ?   Will the historian of four
centuries hence be more impressed by the Reformers who
cut out certain acknowledged fables, or by the Anglican
bishops who have retained St. Anne (with added emphasis)
and St. Catharine of Alexandria in their Revised Liturgy,
though there are at least two ecclesiastical historians on
the bench ?   Mâle does not suggest that the *Golden Legend*
could possibly have maintained its sway throughout this
new age of enlightenment ; except, of course, in the
sense in which Cinderella and Balder, Atalanta and
Theseus will always live on.   It must go, then, but how
must it go ?   All the medieval heresies, or nearly all, had
demanded sharp surgery here.   Lollards had died for
their belief, shared by orthodox pietists like the author
of *Dives and Pauper*, that these unrealities led men into
actual idolatry.   The best of them were guided by moral
principles which were latent in the highest art of the
thirteenth century itself.   They did not stand alone in
the conviction that, for religion's sake, art must now be
brought back more closely to truth and to everyday
morality ; these heretics differed from the most earnest
men among the orthodox mainly in their resolve to
grapple themselves with a problem from which the
authorities persistently shrank.   Was it the fault of those
who tried to moralize religious art, if that art had drifted

so far from morality that the operation must prove fatal ? When a surgeon, removing the morbid tissue, finds that he has extinguished all that was left of life, do we fairly describe him as the slayer of his patient ? We cannot justly judge the Reformers without bearing constantly in mind that the Tridentine Fathers practically admitted the necessity of much of this surgery ; " the Church reviewed those traditions, discovered that most of them were stamped with the excessive credulity of past ages, and asked the artists to abandon them." We need not enter here again into the question of image-worship in general ; we are dealing with the image simply in so far as it is bound up with medieval artistic traditions ; and, on this point, we find that Trent agrees in the main with Protestantism. How, then, can it be seriously contended that it was Protestantism which killed medieval symbolic art ? The Renaissance, more than a century before Luther, had begun to show that a good half of this art reposed upon legends which would not bear examination. The Council of Trent, after Luther, recognised this fact, and practically proscribed a great deal of medieval iconography. The average Catholic dignitary of the seventeenth century had less sympathy with Gothic statuary than high Anglicans like Andrewes and Cosin and Laud.

The Renaissance had been steadily putting these legends, one by one, into a prison in which they must needs die of cold and starvation. Popes and cardinals, in later days, confessed that these legends deserved to die. In the meanwhile, a revolutionary mob (to picture Protestantism at its worst) had burst into the prison and cut the prisoners' throats. Therefore, even if we confine ourselves, as hitherto, to the purely theological side of the question, must we not decide that the slayers were more truly those who made it impossible for the legends to live, and whose descendants approved of the death, than those who hastened this end by rough methods which the others would have repudiated ?

Even if we were dealing with Protestant countries only, justice would compel us to take these things into account. But we are concerned also with that half of Europe which remained Catholic, and which has generally been more active in the pursuit of art than any Protestant land. How could the Reformation have killed Gothic art in France and Italy and Spain, if it had really been vigorous in those lands? The religious revolution has done practically nothing to affect image-worship in those countries, because image-worship corresponds to a deep and imperious instinct in a multitude of hearts. If the medieval symbolism, and all those other characteristics which distinguish Gothic from Classical or Renaissance, had been half so deeply rooted, how could that art, almost within a single generation, have withered more hopelessly in France and Spain and Italy than in England? Does not the root of all misconception in this matter lie here, that modern critics often imagine a closer nexus between special forms of art and special religious denominations than has ever existed in fact? I deliberately choose here the word *denomination* rather than *faith*, because I have given evidence elsewhere for the conviction that the fundamental faith or unfaith of the medieval multitude differed far less from that of the modern multitude than is commonly supposed, and that an intensive study of medieval life, by students of all schools, will make this increasingly evident.

CHAPTER XX

PROTESTANTISM AND ART

I MUST use the term Protestantism, in this chapter, in its most ordinary sense, as applying to all the churches which, in the sixteenth century, cast off the Roman obedience. This definition is in accord not only with the sense in which many generations have been accustomed to understand the word, but also with its obvious etymology. All Anglo-Catholics, for instance, are in a position of protest against certain essential Roman Catholic claims ; in some cases, it is perhaps that protest alone which distinguishes them from Roman Catholics. Medieval art, on the other hand, was unquestionably produced by people who accepted those claims in a sense in which even the extremest Anglo-Catholic does not ; and if it be true, as Mâle argues and as many believe, that medieval art was the exact expression of medieval religion, then Mâle is plainly right in dividing as he does, between Protestant and Roman Catholic ; and those who, like myself, are inclined seriously to question his conclusion, are yet bound to follow in the line of his arguments. But we must bear in mind what he seems sometimes to forget, that this division, like all other things in this actual world, is less absolute in fact than in logic, and especially that, in England, the Elizabethan settlement was designedly vague enough to leave room for a very great deal of what is now called Anglo-Catholicism inside the prevailing Protestantism. The most extreme of Anglican Protestants is accustomed, in the Creed, to assert his belief in the Catholic Church. Protestantism, therefore, covers a number of religious bodies, in many cases widely divergent, of which the

Anglican Church is on the whole the most conservative. And we may ask : " Is there anything in the general theory of Protestantism, reasonably interpreted, that is necessarily fatal to medieval art as a whole, apart, that is, from such details as have been condemned or discouraged by enlightened Roman Catholics themselves ? Or, if not in theory, has Protestantism in practice been such that medieval art could not live with it ?

The subject has already been discussed more than once at some length. Readers who are especially interested in it should refer to the debate between Messrs. Eugène Müntz and N. Weiss in the *Revue des Revues* for March 1 and July 15, 1900, and in the *Bulletin de la Société du protestantisme français* for October 15, 1900 ; also to Mr. Joseph Crouch's *Puritanism and Art*.[1] The French articles, as the less accessible, ought to occupy us most here. Weiss being a Protestant pastor, and Müntz an art-historian apparently holding liberal Catholic views, they naturally differed on a good many points. Müntz was evidently less familiar with his patristic authorities and his Church history than with art matters proper ; Weiss, again, is principally concerned to defend his own co-religionists, and does so with some heat ; but I will attempt to put down nothing here which is not either agreed between the two disputants, or vouched with good evidence by one or other of them.

As there are many forms of Protestantism, so there have been many degrees of friendliness or enmity to art. Calvin, on the whole, was the least friendly in theory, and his followers have been the most inartistic in practice. Yet even Calvin was far less definitely inimical to art than is generally imagined. Like Luther, he recognized it as one of God's gifts. In his *Institution*, which sums up his whole doctrine, he writes : " Yet am I not so scrupulous as to judge that no images should be endured or suffered ; but, seeing that the art of painting and carving images cometh from God, I require that the

[1] Cassell and Co., 1910. See Appendix 30.

practice of art should be kept pure and lawful. . . . Therefore men should not paint nor carve any thing but such as can be seen with the eye ; so that God's Majesty, which is too exalted for human sight, may not be corrupted by fantasies which have no true agreement therewith."[1]

Luther went a great deal farther. " I do not hold that the Gospel should destroy all the arts, as certain superstitious folk believe. On the contrary, I would fain see all arts, and especially that of music, serving Him who hath created them and given them unto us. . . . The Law of Moses forbade only the image of God ; the crucifix is not forbidden." He would have church walls painted with the Creation, Noah building his ark, etc. ; he thought all lords ought to paint the walls of their mansions with Bible scenes.

In practice, again, Luther corresponded with Dürer and was a warm friend and patron to Lucas Cranach. " One of the first specimens of Lutheran art was the reredos at Montbéliard, executed by Hans Leonhard Schaufelein and the ' Master of Messkirch,' which is now at the Museum of Vienna. This picture contains no less than 157 subjects, borrowed with one or two exceptions from the Gospels, and accompanied by long legends in German. Many parables will be noticed in it, a field rarely exploited by Catholic art. It was painted after 1526. . . . It was only at a later date that the principality became iconoclastic, under the influence of the reformers from French Switzerland." Again, " Long after Cranach's death, Lutheran churches continued to receive paintings."[2] They were mostly second-rate ; but they showed that Protestantism as such had no theory of destruction for religious art. Nor were they always second-rate ; among early Protestants we may name some really great artists ; Holbein, Dürer, Jean Goujon, and Bernard Palissy, who worked indiscrimi-

[1] *Instit.*, bk. i, c. xi, § 12.
[2] Müntz, pp. 490, 491.

nately for Protestant and Catholic patrons.[1] True, these men had mostly learned their art in Catholic surroundings ; yet their very existence may keep us from drawing too hard a line of division between the two creeds. Müntz, who rehearses these and others, adds, " Such names authorize us to assert that the Reformation, as formulated by Luther, was by no means exclusive of art." We must not, however, attempt to dispute the general fact, that Protestantism was less favourable to art in churches than was the Catholicism of that time, and of a thousand preceding years. But, at its strictest, it was less unfavourable than the earliest Christian orthodoxy had often been ; and we must remember, again, that even Lutheranism and Calvinism combined did not control a full half of Europe. There was nothing, therefore, to hinder a strong Catholic reaction ; if thirteenth century art had really been a vital and growing thing in 1500, there was nothing in the mere existence of Protestantism to prevent the orthodox half of Europe from continuing, or if possible improving upon, the medieval traditions. What really rendered this impossible was partly the fact that the movement had run its natural course, and partly that great and pious Roman theologians often condemned, or at least discouraged, many of the things to which Protestantism was inimical, and that the general public also looked upon the old traditions as somewhat outworn. The orthodox masons of York come as really into this problem as the unorthodox iconoclasts.

But it remains for us to look more closely into Protestant practice during the first century of the Reformation. Here, again, the harm wrought by revolutionaries is sufficiently notorious, and it is a fact which must be taken full account of at every point. Although, as we have

---

[1] Dürer never officially broke with Catholicism, but his letters and diaries contain, as Müntz says, " regular professions of Lutheran faith." Holbein was perhaps rather a sceptic than an acknowledged Protestant ; but certainly he was not orthodox.

seen, much that was then destroyed was also condemned or discouraged by the Council of Trent, yet undoubtedly there was a great deal of vandalism among objects that were dogmatically innocuous, or that had lost much of their dogmatic significance with the progress of time. Here again, however, it is necessary to guard against the exaggeration of ignorance and cheap rhetoric. When we read that, " through the destruction of the monasteries by Henry's cut-throats . . . most of the very noblest examples of Gothic in England have utterly perished from the earth,"[1] it is as well to turn from this to the able and zealous Catholic Montalembert, who knew England very well, and who noted regretfully that " if we wish to form an idea of the majestic grandeur of monastic buildings, we must visit England. The work of devastation has been less complete and irreparable there than elsewhere."[2]   On this point of Protestant vandalism, Weiss has no difficulty in convicting even Müntz of unjustifiable exaggeration. Both authors agree in emphasizing Zwingli's attitude in Switzerland.[3] Radical as this reformer was in many of his ideas, he was far from a complete iconoclast. He had great admiration for ancient art : " I yield to no man in admiration for pictures and statues," so long as they were not worshipped. Therefore he expressly protected the stained glass, since it led to no risk of idolatry.[4]   With regard to the rest, he wrote a diatribe against images, and at his instigation the Zürich magistrates proclaimed that, in each parish where the majority should so decide, all images that were an object of worship should be removed and destroyed. The result was a very considerable destruction. Calvin, on the other hand, protested more generally

[1] R. A. Cram, *The Gothic Quest*, p. 125.

[2] *Moines d'Occident*, l. xviii, ch. v (ed. 1882, vol. vi, p. 247).

[3] Pp. 484, 511 respectively.

[4] In incidental agreement with the author of *The Tale of Beryn*, who, as I have pointed out in an earlier chapter, represents his fifteenth century pilgrims as indifferent to the religious meaning of the windows.

against images : " I know the common proverb, that images are the books of unlettered folk, and that St. Gregory hath thus spoken : but the Spirit of God hath judged otherwise ; " i.e. Jeremiah x. 3, and Habakkuk ii. 18. He was persuaded that, under the Reformation, all folk would learn to read ; and in any case " all that men learn of God through images is frivolous and even abusive."[1] Later, in the same book, however, he writes less strongly, in the passage I have already quoted earlier in this chapter. This was in 1535 ; in 1562 civil wars in France led to a great deal of image-breaking, and Calvin pronounced definitely against this. God, he wrote, has not commanded us to destroy idols except in our own houses ; and he condemned the Protestant image-breakers of Lyons. Nor, even among the rank and file of the Huguenots, was iconoclasm ever " the rule," as Müntz asserts. Weiss shows that it was mainly confined to one brief period, in the fury of civil war (1562) ; and in the later phases of the struggle, destruction was mainly military, and was not confined to one side only ; at Dijon and Chartres, for instance, the Catholic leaders melted down Church plate and ornaments as Charles I did the plate of the Oxford colleges. And he quotes an orthodox writer of the time who confesses how, at Orléans, " the [Huguenot] lords and ministers took a good attitude, and showed that they approved not such abominations. . . . Proclamation was made to do no damage to the churches, nor to scratch a single image."[2]

Still less can we speak of systematic destruction in Germany as a whole. When Luther's former ally Carlstadt broke images and glass at Wittenberg (1521), Luther came out from his hiding-place at the Wartburg

[1] *Instit.*, bk. i, ch. xi, § 5.

[2] Weiss, p. 516, cf. p. 514 *note*, where he points out that, of all the 500 and more condemnations pronounced against Huguenots by the Parlement of Paris between 1547 and 1550, one only is against an act of iconoclasm.

to protest. Next year he preached openly against Carlstadt : we are free to possess images or not ; only, for fear of abuse, it is better to have none.

Let us therefore avoid as much as possible this emphasis upon differences which, after all, are sometimes artificial. As Catholicism and Protestantism profess alike to have one and the same ultimate aim, so in fact, when we take each at its best, the fundamental common factors far outweigh the divergent details. It may often be necessary to give these details far more than their face value ; so long as one side or the other insists upon them as principles, they must be treated as principles in general discussion. St. Paul was seldom more in earnest, or more persistent, than when he discussed circumcision with St. Peter. But, while details thus force their importance inexorably upon us, we must never so treat them as to lose sight of deeper principles. We must discuss side-issues so as to show their relative unimportance, not so as to give them an artificial value.

A great deal of what is commonly written about medieval architecture seems thus to put the cart before the horse. It seems to rest upon two vicious assumptions, one demonstrably false and the other unprovable, if not improbable.

First, that our Gothic cathedrals are the natural and inevitable expression, in stone, of the Christian faith, and of one special form of that faith, the Roman Catholic. *A priori*, this theory is not without a certain specious verisimilitude. If we chose to argue merely from our own emotions in face of the statued porches or the solemn altar-services, then those who regard these things as the inevitable expression of the highest Christianity would have as much right to their conviction as (for instance) Renan had for the opposite feeling, that the Parthenon was a more elevating work of art than Amiens. But we have not here a question of feeling and taste alone ; it is even more directly a question of history and experience. If Amiens Cathedral were indeed the Roman Catholic

faith crystallized into stone, then the popes would have
been the first to foster Gothic art, and the last to let it
go ; indeed, why should they, under any conditions,
ever abandon that expression, any more than other
natural expressions, of the Catholic faith ? Yet, as a
matter of history, we may say with literal truth : The
nearer to Rome, the farther from Gothic ![1] Even if it
be an exaggeration to assert, with at least one responsible
writer, that only one Gothic church was built in Rome ;
yet it is unquestionable that no medieval city of comparable size and importance showed anything approaching the same indifference to, or even dislike for, Gothic.
Roughly speaking, the nearest examples here are the
cities nearest to Rome, which lay most definitely under
the papal eye, if not directly under papal government,
during the whole Gothic period. Venice had much Gothic
of an Arab cast ; and Venice was one of the least papal of
cities in Italy ; later, under Fra Paolo, she came near to
asserting actual independence. The builder of the great
Gothic basilica at Assisi, Frate Elia, did in his later years
actually repudiate papal authority and join the Emperor
Frederick II. Florence has a good deal of semi-Gothic
work, and Florence in the fourteenth century was in rebellion against the popes, who not only excommunicated her
but adjudged her citizens to slavery. In France and in
Germany, again, the least Gothic districts are those
nearest to the Italian frontier, or to the great trade-
routes from Italy. Moreover, from the first moment
of the great papal revival onwards, when the popes rose
victorious from their struggle against the constitu-
tionalists at Constance and Bâle, they set their faces

[1] Lord Braye, in his recent reminiscences, praises his beloved Catholic
college of Prior Park for its " eighteenth century plan of magnificent
rectitude in design," in which he finds a congruity with the genius both
of the Latin liturgy and of the imperial Roman Church, and which he
contrasts most favourably with " the Pugin-Ruskin school " (*Times Lit.
Sup.*, July 28, 1927, p. 515). Many will agree with him even as a matter
of taste ; but in the present connexion the one thing that matters is the
historical fact.

more definitely against Gothic architecture than the
English Protestants. If, as might well happen, some pope
were elected in our own day who was entirely ignorant
of Gothic art, and if he were suddenly kindled to enthusiasm by such volumes as those of Émile Mâle, he would
have to end his days in ignorance of all that could not
be picked up from books and photographs ; his knowledge
of this particular subject would necessarily be the second-
hand knowledge of (for instance) an American too busy or
too poor to travel in Europe. Indeed, the American
might well have an advantage here ; for it is possible
that some American town no larger than Rome may
possess a really good piece of modern Gothic ; Boston,
for instance, is building or has built a small memorial
church which shows an understanding of the Gothic
forms which could hardly be found in Rome. Not only
geographically, but aesthetically, the splendid English
minsters of the Middle Ages are farther from Rome
than Rome is from Constantinople. Again, not only
does a detached modern critic like Remi de Gourmont expose the impossibility of those theories which
may be said to culminate in Huysmans, but some
thoroughly orthodox art-lovers have at all times raised
their voices against it. At Abbeville, at Amiens, scholars
might be found repudiating it two generations ago,
when it was in the bloom of early youth.[1] " We must
drop the term *Christian Art*, and recognize that Gothic
speaks no more to the soul than other styles, unless it be
to the souls of Catholics who insist on finding symbolism
where none exists and nobody has ever thought of putting
it. . . . We might say of the medieval architects, as of
the ancient authors, that, if they came back to life, they
would often be greatly astonished at the ideas which we
attribute to them." The first of these sentences is significant even in its exaggeration ; the second is not even
exaggerated.

[1] *Mém. Soc. d'Émulation d'Abbeville*, 1852, pp. 747 ff., 761–2 ; *Bull.
Soc. Ant. de Picardie*, 1846, pp. 324 ff.

There is far more historic, as well as æsthetic, probability in deriving Gothic art from the traditions of the
half-nomad northerners who hunted, and reared cattle,
and tilled scanty patches of corn amid primeval forests
where the pines and beeches run up to eighty feet before
they throw out their first branches. Prof. Lethaby
quotes many such suggestions on pp. 87–90 of *The Legacy
of the Middle Ages* (Oxford, 1926) ; and he himself sums
up : " Our last sight of Gothic before it disappeared is
a fringe of much crocketed pinnacles like pine-trees
ranged along a peaked horizon. The northern forests
had nurtured a people who could do no other than
build according to their ideals ; not knowing but only
doing. As the Greek expressed lucidity and serenity,
so northern art had the mystery of the great forests
behind it."

Moreover, it is significant that the apostles of that
other theory—Huysmans and his followers—have been
men whose general outlook on life would have appealed
far less to any of the great saints or philosophers or
moralists of the Middle Ages, than to the average Thor-
worshipper of the German forests, or to the freethinker
of Renaissance Rome. Is it indeed worth while to make
a single proselyte at the cost of such theories as these ?
Is it not far more honourable to human nature, and at
the same time far more consonant with obvious facts,
to conclude that the purely religious element in Gothic
is that which appeals not only to all religious minds, of
whatever creed, but also to every truly religious chord
in what may be, predominantly, an irreligious mind ?
I do not say, of course, that the appeal is equal in every
case ; but only that the differences are dependent far
more on artistic than on religious temperament. Among
Romans or Southern Italians, only a minority truly
appreciate the greatest French Gothic. On the other
hand, we may well doubt whether Huysmans ever felt
it in every fibre of his being, or drank it in with such
physical enjoyment, as the Protestant Ruskin who ended

in something like Agnosticism, and William Morris who had no use whatever for organized religion.

The second assumption is complementary to the first. Not only (we are told) did Roman Catholicism in fact create Gothic art, but no other spirit could by any possibility have created it. Here, of course, we have a theory immune against all attack from the ground of plain historical fact; speculations as to what might have happened are as secure from absolute disproof as they are wanting in conclusive proof. But we have a right to judge them by this principle of medieval philosophy: *Quod gratis asseritur, gratis negatur*; if a man brings no sufficient reasons for his assertions, neither do I need formal reasons for my disbelief. Let us suppose for a moment that, instead of Christianity conquering the polytheism of the barbarian invaders, the religious victory had gone the other way. With the help of pagan classical literature and art and institutions (of which we may reasonably suppose these polytheists to make use, and perhaps even as freely as the Catholic Church did) they would gradually have settled down from the turmoil of the Dark Ages into long medieval centuries, during which commerce and culture would rapidly develop; and, until commerce had reached its full modern development in the banking system, the most obvious form of investment would have been in building. So far the hypothesis would seem entirely reasonable; it is very much the story of Arabic culture. These men would have built more and more ambitiously; why not, then, as high as a Gothic cathedral? Italian churches never ran so high in the Middle Ages, nor did those of Southern France; it was not religion that created this aspiring height; it was something in the northern mind and in northern experience. Is it a mere chance that those forests of pillars, branching into vault-ribs high overhead, were characteristic of populations familiar with taller and thicker forests than the south ever produced in those centuries? It is at least far more probable that the

THE CENTRAL GABLE AT WELLS.

contrast between Amiens and San Francesco at Assisi
(which might easily be greatly increased by choosing two
other examples) is due rather to such considerable differences of social or business outlook and environment
as we know to have existed between north and south,
than to the almost negligible
religious differences between the
mind of a Picard and an Umbrian
in the thirteenth century. Is not
the romance element in Gothic even
greater than the Christian ?

In detail of ornament, there is
no reason why this architecture of
the supposed northern polytheists
should have differed much from
the Gothic that we know. They,
also, would have copied the Saracen
and Persian brocades that they
bought, and Byzantine imagery and
scroll-work, and those intricate patterns that the Celts loved, but had
not invented, and the ruder patterns
on the Viking ships. They too
would have taken Constantinople by
storm, and carried back with them
not only classical Greek statues but,
more valuable still, Greek ideas in
art. There would seem no reason
why their temples should not have
been as full of gods and demi-gods
and heroes as Chartres is of saints.

SOLOMON AT REIMS.

Charles the Great, whose ideas here
as elsewhere ran before his time, counselled the representation of heroes as well as of saints. If our
hypothetical artists had filled the windows with warriors,
why should those figures have been less artistically
effective than the famous De Montfort medallion at
Chartres, or those De Clares in the choir windows of

EE

Tewkesbury ? Their funeral effigies might have been
practically identical with many of the best that we have
in Europe ; and the statues of kings or queens or heroes
round their portals might, in many cases, have been
indistinguishable from those of Chartres. Or take, again,
that figure from Reims of which Viollet-le-Duc kept a
cast in his studio, and enjoyed the questions of his classical
friends : " What is this Greek statue that I have never
seen before ? " It is commonly called Solomon ; but
by general confession there is no certainty in the attribution ; who would dare to say that it has anything so
distinctly Christian in figure or in face that it could not
have been fashioned to represent Ulysses himself, or that
Viking Ulysses who first discovered America ? The main
principles of Gothic art are to be found rather in construction than in detail.[1] Those piles of wall and buttress
and tower, massed in alternate light and shade, sometimes
frowning but mainly content to impose by their majesty
of height and skyline, might as fitly commemorate some
line of earthly kings, flanked by their warriors and
ministers, as Christ with His royal ancestors and His
saints. In one sense, the two motives may be a whole
horizon apart ; they may be as different as sunset is from
sunrise. But that is not to the present point ; in a
Claude or a Turner, who will undertake to tell us with
certainty whether the sun is rising or setting ? Would
two intelligent visitors from Mars, standing far enough
from the façade of Wells to grasp the whole general
effect, necessarily agree with each other as to the heavenly
or the earthly character of figures and canopies which
both would admire as artistically effective ? Therefore,
if polytheism had won that victory which I have taken
the liberty of suggesting, would not the zealous poly-
theist of to-day, the Huysmans with his disciples, be

---

[1] For Ruskin's estimate of the value of mass and projection, and of
those effects which are more likely to be suggested by natural scenery
than by dogmatic religion, see the extract from *Seven Lamps of Architecture* (ch. iii, § 23–4) which I give in Appendix 31.

insisting to us that here is the one supreme inimitable art, built upon the glorious creed of Thor and Odin, and crowned with an æsthetic success to which no other creed could conceivably have attained ?

True, all this refers only to the general constructive and decorative principles of Gothic, and takes no account of the spiritual expression in such a group, for instance, as the Annunciation at Reims. There indeed, and in the Beau Dieu d'Amiens, and in a thousand Mary and Child groups, we have something as distinctive of Christianity, and sometimes of Catholic Christianity alone, as the great Buddha statues are of Buddhism, borrowed though they originally were from Greek models. But, among all these, it is only the Mary and Child that we may think of as normal in the ordinary village church; and villagers formed in those days the overwhelming majority of the population. No doubt there is often considerable grace of line even in the most rapid village daub; but this

LE BEAU DIEU D'AMIENS.

did not appeal to the worshipper as it appeals to the modern artist. Otherwise we cannot account for the fact, acknowledged by so earnest a modern Catholic as Maurice de Wulf, that Catholics as well as Protestants came to despise Gothic art.[1] Ruskin scarcely exaggerated when he wrote : " Observe, the change of which I speak has nothing whatever to do with the Reformation, or with any of its effects. It is a far broader thing than the Reformation. It is a change which has taken place not only in reformed England and reformed Scotland, but

[1] *Philos. and Civil. in the Middle Ages*, 1922, p. 8.

in unreformed France, in unreformed Italy, in unreformed Austria."[1] Dejob, again, emphasizes very truly the remarkable neglect of the finest medieval art by these orthodox art-writers of the Counter-Reformation. " Ver Meulen, though he knows the works of the old masters, does not seem touched by the faith which breathes from most of them. As to [Cardinal] Paleotti and the other Italian theorists, they scarcely make passing mention of the primitives. . . . Shortly afterwards, these precursors, in whose name men have attacked Raphael in our own day, fell into an oblivion comparable to that into which our medieval literature fell about the same time ; but a much more surprising oblivion, since men had only to open their eyes to see the works of the ancient masters, whereas our *Chansons de Geste* had, so to speak, disappeared."[2]

But, while expressing my belief that a great deal of the most popular writing on this subject has not only ignored historical facts but has shown a want of serious thought, let me not seem to exaggerate in the other direction. A religious creed, and the buildings and ornaments wrought by the men of that creed, may be as closely related as soul and body ; I would not quarrel with the metaphor, though it seems to me to partake of exaggeration. Yet it is very hazardous to insist too much on the relation even of soul and body. The story of Socrates and the professional physiognomist is proverbial ; if, again, we possessed no signed bust of any Roman emperor, and had to identify the faces from what we know of their histories, what disputes would there not be among learned and unlearned ! and how few would be found to have named even the twelve Cæsars aright ! In the light of such considerations, let us beware of too hasty identifications between art and religious dogma. What differentiates Lincoln Cathedral, in its present Protestant hands, from Amiens is indeed mainly peculiar

[1] *Lect. Arch. and Painting*, IV, § 115 (Library ed., vol. xii, p. 139).
[2] P. 251.

to the Roman Catholic faith ; yet the far greater artistic differences between Amiens and St. Peter's at Rome are not denominational.

This does not mean that there were not many artists who felt religious inspiration while they worked, or that there are not far more worshippers now who from those works derive religious inspiration. It leaves us free to love Gothic art, to worship Gothic art if we will, but not to worship it in the name of one creed and to the exclusion of all others. Here, as everywhere else, those feel truest and deepest who do not entirely ignore that other men's deepest feelings may also be true.

CHAPTER XXI

THE ROOTS OF THE RENAISSANCE

HERE, then, we must again make an effort to clear our minds, and not to assume a closer connexion between the art and the religion of any period than the facts will warrant. That connexion was exceptionally close in the early thirteenth century; yet, even for that period, it is generally exaggerated. Here, for instance, let us turn again to a modern writer who is eminently suitable to illustrate my point. Why, asks Mr. Cram, has America lost the artistic spirit? And he continues : " Were the answer to this sought seriously . . . we should find that all the Christian art that exists, whether it be architecture, sculpture, painting, music, craftsmanship, owes its life and its glory to one power, the Catholic Church, and we should find also that, although Protestantism has held dominion in Germany, England, Scandinavia, and the United States for several hundred years, it has produced no vital art of any kind ; such sporadic instances as have occurred possessing no connexion whatever with the dominant form of theology. We should also find that the decadence of art has been almost unbroken since the period called the Reformation. I argue nothing from these facts, I wish only to call attention to them."[1] These words are no unfair sample of the sort of writing which, because it flatters strong sectarian prejudices, is sure of success within a fairly wide circle, and, through its boldness of assertion, even outside the fold. This confident appeal to history is backed up neither here nor elsewhere by any shred of tangible historical evidence ; the facts from which Mr. Cram will

[1] *The Gothic Quest*, p. 85.

not argue, but upon which he will composedly take his stand and lift up his voice to command our attention, are simply exploded fictions.   The whole passage is thoroughly typical of a whole school which descends ultimately from Ruskin, but which, substituting rhetoric for thought at every fresh step, and having by this time become separated from its living source by two or three generations of commonplace writers, lives now upon Ruskin's exaggerations and has forgotten that great man's qualifications.   Here, for instance, is what Ruskin himself wrote (*Stones of Venice*, iv, § 53) : " There being no beauty in our recent architecture, and much in the remains of the past, and these remains being almost exclusively ecclesiastical, the High Church and Romanist parties have not been slow in availing themselves of the natural instincts which were deprived of all food except from this source ; and have willingly promulgated the theory, that because all the good architecture that is now left is expressive of High Church or Romanist doctrines, all good architecture ever has been and must be so—a piece of absurdity from which, though here and there a country clergyman may innocently believe it, I hope the common sense of the nation will soon manfully quit itself.   It needs but little inquiry into the spirit of the past, to ascertain what, once for all, I would desire here clearly and forcibly to assert, that wherever Christian Church architecture has been good and lovely, it has been merely the perfect development of the common dwelling-house architecture of the period ; that, when the pointed arch was used in the street, it was used in the Church." And, elsewhere, Ruskin points out the notorious fact that Gothic art was even more despised in Roman Catholic countries, from the sixteenth century to almost the present day, than in Protestant countries.   Nowhere are the churches more inartistic to-day than in Tyrol, which has been untouched by the Reformation.

Therefore, in correction of modern pleas which, on the face of them, seem grossly exaggerated, and which certainly have as yet made no pretence of adequate documentary vouchers, let us here follow very briefly the course of the Renaissance, and mark its actual effects upon art. For much of this present chapter which is not merely common knowledge, I have given documentary evidence elsewhere ; the rest will be supplied here.

The movement which we call Renaissance can be traced back very far indeed. In one very real sense, it began at least as early as the Norman Conquest of England; at that period came a great revival of art and letters, and therefore of thought, both orthodox and unorthodox. Side by side with Lanfranc and Anselm were Berengar of Tours, who anticipated some of Luther's work, and many little-known thinkers who harked back to those ancient Gnostics, the rationalizers of early religion.[1] A century later, there came in simultaneously the complete Aristotle, upon which Aquinas and the other schoolmen based so much of Christian philosophy, and the Arab Averroes with a philosophy that was fundamentally and irreconcilably anti-Christian. The number of condemnations which have survived, from Paris and elsewhere, suffice to prove that there was, under the surface, a strong current of University thought no more friendly to orthodox Catholicism than the average University thought of to-day. Petrarch complained that, in Venice, orthodox Christian philosophy was laughed at as a " back number " ; Padua was a hotbed of Averroism ; and Marsilius of Padua, with the Englishman Ockham, worked out theories of Church and State which practically reduced the Pope himself to a mere figure-head. Petrarch, with his pupil Boccaccio, began to revive the serious study of classical antiquity ; Rienzo based his revolution in Rome upon ancient pagan precedent. Therefore this classical revival, even if we date it only from Petrarch, is a whole generation older than Lollardy,

[1] This was admirably brought out in a paper read by Prof. Alphandéry before the recent *Congrès d'Histoire du Christianisme* at Paris, which will be printed in the official report of that Congress.

just as Valla and Cusanus began systematically to destroy medieval legend by the solvent of historical research nearly a century before Luther's revolt.   Vives and Melchior Cano derive from Valla and Cusanus; therefore, even though no heretic had ever existed, orthodoxy must have discovered, sooner or later, that there was one only too real sense in which the Golden Legend must be called the Legend of Lead.

Moreover, popes themselves at last began to lead the way in this direction.   When, with the final failure of the Council of Bâle (1443) the papacy emerged more despotic than before, then (as Creighton points out) it became a definite papal policy to side-track this pressure for ecclesiastical reform into the direction of culture; popes staved off the Reformation by supporting the Renaissance.   Men might be as pagan as they chose, so long as they made no claim to be Bible-Christians, or radical reformers in morals, or rivals to the temporal sovereignty of the popes.   For that temporal sovereignty was now a more practical reality than it had ever been before; now, at last, the popes were real and firmly-seated princes of the City of Rome; and they set themselves deliberately to dazzle their subjects, far and near, by the most princely displays of earthly splendour. Their palaces, and the new church of St. Peter's which was now to replace the ancient building, ranked among the marvels of the world.   To raise funds for St. Peter's, indulgences were multiplied tenfold, though so devoted a papalist as the Oxford Chancellor Gascoigne had already complained of the system as intolerable.   It was these Petrine indulgences, as everybody knows, which first brought Luther forward.   The policy of side-tracking had failed; there were now two breaches in the ecclesiastical dyke, Reformation and Renaissance; for indeed that encouragement of culture soon proved, from the narrowly ecclesiastical point of view, a short-sighted policy.   Modern Catholic historians on the Continent, who are generally far better-read and abler in every way than their English brethren, recognize clearly that the worst enemy of orthodoxy has been not the Reformation but the Renaissance. It is not Protestantism which has gradually converted France into a country more anticlerical than Great Britain, or which has prompted (if we are to believe the Catholic newspapers) far worse cruelties in modern Mexico than in Tudor England.

The more we insist upon the connexion of medieval art and religion, the more we must recognize how fatal this long sapping movement must have proved to Gothic art. That connexion, even when all exaggerations have been stripped away, was admittedly very strong. If it weakened visibly from the mid-thirteenth century onward, this was partly because rationalistic opposition to the Church was rapidly increasing at that same time. In any case, therefore, the Renaissance was likely to undermine Gothic art in something like the proportion in which it undermined orthodoxy; but, as the movement gained momentum, and especially when popes and princes gave it their whole-hearted support on the artistic side, then social and economic forces came into play also; and from thenceforward its victory was assured and irresistible.

Having thus noted the indirect action upon art through religion, let us go back to trace the more direct effects of this movement.

Here, again, the earlier manifestations are too often ignored. Father Cahier finds traces of Renaissance debasement in the France of the later fourteenth century.[1] He writes: " The confident expansion of this new art [more realistic than that of the thirteenth century] had its dangerous rock, as all human things have. By carrying men out of themselves, it tempted them to find pleasure in outward show rather than in inward principle. This inconvenience could only have been avoided if faith had kept her full sovereignty, or even increased it, in order to hallow these [purely] human

[1] *Nouveaux Mélanges*, 1877, pp. 187 ff.

accessories. That, unfortunately, was not the case. The
outer world, at this time, grew abruptly and suddenly in
action and in influence, while there were neglected, but
powerful causes which sapped men's hearts and minds. . . .
The desertion of several Christian populations was being
prepared by turbulence and immorality ; and, when art
was in full flower, towards the end of the fifteenth century, its sap was already running dry."

What is here said of France might be said more emphatically of Italy. Perrens brings out clearly the first
stages of Renaissance art in Florence.[1]   After instancing
Giotto and his disciples, and quoting examples from 1360
to 1374, he continues : " If the nude was ill seen under
ample draperies, the magnificence of the costumes, and
the glorious feasts of a city where everyone lived in the
open air, in the sun, under a blue sky, were food for art.
And the nude was not quite absent, as may be thought.
In Rome, and probably elsewhere, there were races of
naked men as in the old games of Greece, and obscene
processions as in the circuses of the Roman Empire, while
the loose morals of the artists hardly induce a belief that
they lacked occasions to study the nude. A change
was promised not so much in art as in the condition
of the artists. In old Florence an architect, a sculptor,
or a painter was a tradesman like any other, and not
distinguished from a mechanic ; for example, a varnisher
was classed with a painter. . . . Under the oligarchy,
in the relative calm that came with oppression, a
taste for art as well as for letters began to develop in
Florence as elsewhere." The study of the antique
flourished ; and " by it Christian art was relegated to a
second place. Building was continued, and churches
were decorated, and it is a mistake to imagine that the
Medici wanted to turn their compatriots from a religion
that teaches submission to the great ; but there were
churches everywhere ; what was wanted were palaces,

---

[1] *Hist. of Florence, from the Domination of the Medici*, tr. Lynch, 1892,
vol. i, pp. 200 ff.

and in palaces pious pictures being out of place, hunting-scenes, tournaments, amorous and mythological adventures, served to recall ancient art, now so long forgotten as to appear quite fresh. . . . That Brunelleschi had lost what a few may call the sentiment of religion, which is only the tradition of the hieratic art of ancient times, we need not doubt. He built churches and palaces upon the same antique models. . . . But, like Giotto, he had the taste for natural forms. . . . He advanced art in the direction of truth and reality, and, in building temples for churches, incurred, like many others, the reproach of being a pagan. Not an unjustifiable reproach, certainly, but those who flung it at the fifteenth century ought to have included the fourteenth also. Piety and chastity were then not more frequent ; and, if the sentiment of religion was less rare, religion itself was wanting in purity. The Scaligeri of Verona, the Estes of Ferrara, the Della Polentas of Ravenna, the Malatestas of Rimini, the Visconti of Milan, Castruccio, Robert of Naples, and also [Pope] Clement V in his *lupanar* at Avignon, equalled the Medici in their appreciation of the famous mythological nudities which are said to have ruined Christian art. The only difference was that in the fourteenth century commissions for this sort of work were few, as it was not yet the fashion. If Giotto, of joyous and pagan temperament, only painted sacred and serious subjects, it was because he did not solely paint for pleasure, but also for bread. The strong impulsion of the Renaissance was necessary to force artists to free themselves from the prevailing taste by disinterested study, and little by little to transform it." Benozzo Gozzoli was a sceptic, ready to work either in the religious or the profane style ; Perugino's religious scepticism was notorious and impenitent. Lippo Lippi was the most profligate of all in his private life, but " his subjects were always religious . . . because his cloistered life procured him countless commissions . . . a proof that the paganism of the Renaissance did not exclude a taste for religious pictures."

Savonarola succeeded momentarily in stemming the more open paganisms and obscenities, and in converting a few painters, " but faith did not bring them back to the Christian traditions of art " ; " no sign of Christian faith is to be seen in the remarkable works of Simone del Pollaiuolo (1457–1508)." It was still fashionable to pay for sacred subjects, and profitable to paint them, but the great thirteenth-century tradition of art was already dead. New social ideas, and new economic forces, were sweeping it away.

New social ideas ; for the Middle Ages had their own natural thirst for novelty and change. I cannot help believing that the generality of men were no more artistic then than they are now ;[1] and that, if they did not show the frequent modern preference for thoroughly bad art, it was because there was no thoroughly bad art for them to choose. The apprenticeship and gild system, which hindered the highest flights of all, rendered impossible the vilest lapses ; those baser things against which Morris fought were never to be bought in the medieval market. But, if they had been, many men would have preferred them, just as thousands of purchasers in India prefer crude Manchester stuff to their own traditional native prints, not only because it is cheaper, but also because it is newer and more glaring.[1] So, in the Middle Ages, novelty attracted more than abstract beauty. Men tired of the noble architecture of the thirteenth century, and invented what we call the Decorated style ; they tired of that spiritual grace which is the main claim of Gothic statuary in comparison with that of antiquity ; they went on therefore, stage by stage, to complete realism. Then, again, the newer Perpendicular style (or, in France, the Flamboyant) gained a victory rather of fashion than of excellence ; and finally the Classical styles, new again after a sleep of a thousand years, began

---

[1] I must warn the reader that Professor Lethaby is unable to accept the opinions hazarded in these two sentences; but they express my belief, and therefore I leave them for what they are worth.

to drive out all the rest. Eugène Müntz counts it as a
very remarkable testimony to the originality and pene-
tration of the future Pope Pius II that, in spite of his
contempt for " the pictures of 200 years ago," he has
real admiration for Giotto as the harbinger of a new
school which " has now reached the summit of art," in
other words, of the Renaissance school.¹ About this same
time, " under Nicholas V [1447–55], glass-painting gave a
last flicker before its systematic exclusion from Italian
churches; or, at least, before it ceased as an independent
art, and became the handmaid of painting proper, and was
reduced to the meanest of rôles, that of mere copyist."²

Thus, in the story of the Renaissance, we find the
plainest corrective to all exaggerated identifications of
Gothic art with any religious denomination, to the
exclusion of others. Such exaggerations break down at
once when we note how differently dogma and art reacted
to this new current which attained its full strength in
the early sixteenth century. Theologically, the Renaissance was a solvent of Roman Catholic tradition; but,
artistically, it was welcomed as the logical consequence
of that tradition. The fact that medieval Church ceremonies were borrowed from pagan Rome is (argues de
Gourmont), " the best proof of the antiquity and also of
the excellence of Catholicism. . . . The most ancient
religions are the best; it is a great absurdity to try
reducing children's games to reason; it is great madness
to attempt the purification of religions." And again :
" A young Catholic poet has called the Blessed Virgin
' cette belle nymphe ' ; there is the true tradition of
popular Catholicism " : " Leo X and Julius II could
truly boast the name of *Pontifex Maximus* ; they were
truly successors not only to St. Peter but also to the
High Priest of Jupiter Capitolinus."³ Therefore, under

¹ *Les arts à la cour des Papes*, 1878, p. 222. The whole passage is most
significant for the Renaissance estimate of medieval letters and art.
² Ibid., p. 76.
³ *La Culture des Idées*, pp. 137, 138, 174.

these Renaissance popes, it is natural to find pagan art gaining ground in the churches of Italy. Rimini is here a classical example ; again, " at a time when Bembo, a pope's secretary and a future cardinal, spoke of ' the hero Jesus Christ ' and ' the virgin goddess,' we need not be surprised that Philaretus sculptured the loves of Jupiter and Leda upon the very gates of the Vatican.[1] But we may find the same movement even north of the Alps. This is brought out by Didron in two essays of his *Annales archéologiques*. In the first (xii, 300) he discourses on " paganism in Christian art " ; in the second (xiii, 242) he describes and figures a painting of the Virgin Mary as Venus. It is an Assumption in a triptych of perhaps shortly before or after 1500, which he ascribes to a pupil of the Van Eycks or of Memling, and even guesses at the possibility of ascription to one of those masters himself. The engraving fully bears out his description : " The Mother of God is painted standing, absolutely naked, her dishevelled hair falling round her with the intention of supplying a garment which they certainly do not supply." And he adds in a footnote : " This Venus-Virgin was originally even less veiled than she is at present."

[1] Perrens, *l.c.*, p. 465.

CHAPTER XXII

RENAISSANCE AND DESTRUCTION

THE foregoing chapter has shown how naturally the revived pagan art began to supplant that of the Middle Ages ; let us turn now to the subject of deliberate destruction. The demolition of ancient work had been common enough in the Middle Ages ; but now at last, for the pleasure of popes and princes, it became chronic and systematic.

That famous White Robe of Churches, that sudden rush of new buildings, which marked the Cluniac revival, had involved considerable destruction of older edifices. In the words of the Cluniac Ralph Glaber, who is our authority for the whole episode, " the fabrics of churches were rebuilt, though many of these were still seemly and needed no such care ; but every nation in Christendom rivalled with the other, as to which should worship in the seemliest buildings." So again with the great outburst of architecture about A.D. 1200 ; so, again, when the Perpendicular style invaded England. The Totnes visitation of 1342 not infrequently insists that a church should be rebuilt because it is " small and dark " ; in other words, Norman or simple Early English. This was one side of the vigorous vitality of medieval art ; the weakest must go to the wall, and that weakest was nearly always the most ancient. In English churches, especially of the Perpendicular period, we commonly find fragments of Norman doorways or arcades built in with the ordinary rubble. A large number of early tombstones have been thus utilized for the walls of Bracebridge Church, near Lincoln, and of Little Shelford in Cambridgeshire. One fine medieval tombstone is

built into the tower staircase of Castleacre in Norfolk;
another, at Little Malvern, has been built into the
roof of an opening at the east end, where it can only
be detected by a person adventurous enough to clamber
into this niche. We have more records of vandalism
in tombs, perhaps, than in any other feature; in this
matter, we cannot distinguish between one medieval
century and another. At Troyes Cathedral, in 1385,
a new choir-screen was built and the old (which
to us would probably have seemed the nobler) was pulled
down. " The work employed fifteen men per diem. In
this clearing process they met with six tombs, four of
them to known persons, but they were unable to identify
two of the skeletons, though certain indications showed
that one was a bishop and the other a monk. The chapter,
without troubling farther about these illustrious dead,
caused them to be buried in plain coffins at threepence
apiece," the masons receiving fivepence a day.[1] When
Queen Philippa was buried in Westminster Abbey,
wrought iron rails were employed from the tomb of Bishop
Braybroke in St. Paul's Cathedral, to grace the queen's
sepulchre. Part of Philippa's own tomb, not long after,
was disfigured by building that of Henry V up against it.[2]
Henry V's queen, Katharine, had her own tomb cast
out from the Lady Chapel in 1502 : " Her coffin was to
lie unburied for more than two centuries and a half." [3]
A whole batch of seven early thirteenth century tombs
at Wells, and another batch of ten Perpendicular tombs
at Hereford, commemorate earlier bishops some of whom
perhaps never had monuments, but others had probably
been destroyed. The famous Johann Busch tells us
himself of what he did at Sulte, near Hildesheim. " Bishop
Brunyng, of Hildesheim, founded [the Abbey Church of
Sulte] . . . and lieth buried there by the choir door, in
a raised tomb which beareth the image of a bishop with

---

[1] Quicherat, *Mélanges*, vol. ii, p. 211.
[2] Lethaby, *Westminster I*, p. 251.
[3] Westlake, *Last Days*, p. 101.

mitre and crozier. When we reformed the monastery, we took that image away and put it in front of the principal altar . . . calling it that of St. Godhard [who had first founded the Church of Sulte before the monastery was founded], because my Lord Brunyng, though he had been a holy man, was not canonized. And we levelled Bishop Brunyng's tomb with the ground." This was about 1420.[1] The monk Odo of St. Maur, writing in 1058, describes the beauty of Count Burchard's tomb, erected in the abbey church some forty years before. It bore, he says, " on his breast a gilded cross with the letters *alpha* and *omega* ; I also, in my boyhood, saw this with mine own eyes ; but all this has been utterly destroyed since, as we may see to-day." [2] Richard of Barking, abbot of Westminster, was buried in the Lady Chapel " beneath a tomb of marble, which was destroyed in the time of Abbot Colchester." [3] William of Malmesbury tells us that the tomb of the famous Joannes Scotus Eriugena had been destroyed before the date at which he was writing : this was done by Abbot Warin (1070–1081), who at the same time cast out the tombs of St. Maidulf and other great abbots of the past.[4] Abbot Curteys of St. Edmundsbury, between 1436 and 1441, was compelled to fulminate against " the improper removals of sepulchral monuments from the cemetery of the [abbey] church." [5] Some of the latest medieval work at Melrose Abbey destroyed, wholly or in part, large numbers of ancient tombs ; the walls " appear to have been founded on, or at least partially to cover, the tombstones of a previous generation. . . . Under it [the east wall] we find numbers of sepulchral stones showing black-letter inscriptions, and portions of incised figures, apparently crosses, etc., peeping out

[1] *Lib. Ref.*, bk. i, c. vi, p. 409.
[2] Migne, P. L., vol. clxiii, col. 860.
[3] Dugdale-Caley, vol. i, p. 271.
[4] R. L. Poole, *Ill. Hist. Med. Thought*, 2nd ed., 1920, p. 282.
[5] Dugdale-Caley, vol. iii, p. 114.

below the base of the wall."[1] But perhaps the worst record comes from St. Albans, where there were two wholesale raids. Paul, the first Norman abbot (1077–93), did " what can in no way be excused ; he destroyed the tombs of his venerable predecessors the noble abbots, whom he was wont to call rude and unlearned, either despising them as English, or in envy, since almost all had been born of royal stock, or the noble blood of great lords." [2] Abbot Robert, again (1151–66), " in the first construction of the chapter-house which he was about to build, caused the bodies of the old abbots to be buried too meanly [*abjecte*] and without counsel of discreet men, at the counsel of his mason ; wherefore, when the mason was cut off by apoplexy, the memory of the place was lost." [3]

What was done with tombs was done in every other quarter. St. Albans had a remarkable school of painters in the early thirteenth century ; the remaining fragments are now guarded with pious care, and inspire critics to almost lyrical rhapsodies : " I can scarcely conceive of anything finer than this series of paintings as viewed from the west end of the church." Yet " those paintings were probably all whitewashed over at the end of the fourteenth or early in the fifteenth century, as it may be noticed that a fifteenth century bracket, which we know held the figure of St. Richard in 1428, has been inserted into the middle of the lower picture of the first painting." [4] For neither the ecclesiastical guardian of a church, nor the artist who worked upon it, felt anything like the modern conservatism. The saintly and learned Odo Rigaldi, Archbishop of Rouen from 1248 to 1267, more than once entered in his register a command that church windows, not yet glazed, should be walled up for convenience of the worshippers. Artists, again, were

[1] *Proc. Soc. Ant. Scotland,* vol. ii, 1858, p. 174.
[2] *Gest. Abb. S. Albani,* R.S., vol. i, p. 62.
[3] Ibid., p. 183.
[4] *Archæologia,* vol. lviii, pp. 281–2.

naturally far more concerned to show their own powers
and to go their own way than simply to patch up their
predecessor's work, or to continue it with the fidelity
of a pupil carrying out a master's designs. The magnificent thirteenth-century wheel window at Lynn, resembling but surpassing those in the west front of Peterborough Cathedral, had apparently become ruinous by
about 1450. Instead of renewing it, the mason inserted a
Perpendicular design more curious than beautiful, and
used the old work to mend the roof of a turret staircase,
where it was only discovered at the restoration of
1870. Very few people, in 1450, would have admitted
Ruskin's Lamp of Memory : " Let us think, as we lay
stone on stone, that a time will come when those stones
will be held sacred because our hands have touched
them. . . . The greatest glory of a building is not in
its stones, nor in its gold. Its glory is in its age. . . . I
think that a building cannot be considered as in its prime
until four or five centuries have passed over it, and that
the entire choice and arrangement of its details should
have reference to their appearance after that period." [1]
The medieval view was far more childlike than this.
Those who looked forward at all were convinced that
the world had not many years more to last ; few medieval
expressions are more constant and uniform than this,
that the world was at its last stage, deserving dissolution
and destined soon to be dissolved. Men's childlike
exuberance of invention was matched by childlike impatience and love of novelty : " There is more respect
and consideration shown at the present moment to our
cathedrals than was ever paid them in the Middle Ages." [2]

Our modern churchwardens have had their reasons for
loving whitewash, but their forefathers had reason also.
Constantly, in building accounts, we find a final entry :
" *item*, for so many loads of lime," to wash the building
over. It was not only that limewash is one of the most

[1] *Seven Lamps*, VI, x (p. 339 of the pocket authorized edition).
[2] *York Fabric Rolls*, p. 68, note.

PERPENDICULAR SUBSTITUTE FOR THE
LYNN WHEEL-WINDOW.

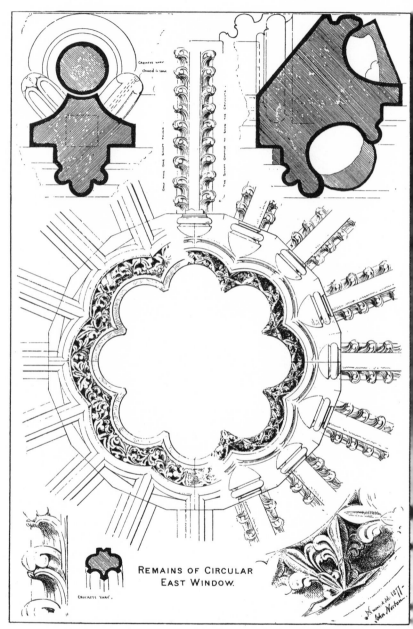

REMAINS OF CIRCULAR
EAST WINDOW.

THIRTEENTH-CENTURY WINDOW FROM ST. MARGARET'S, LYNN.

valuable preservatives of stonework, but men loved it
for itself ; it made their work look fresh and new.   The
White Tower, one of the glories of London, was thus
distinguished and kept in constant brilliancy by royal
command.   The *Liberate Rolls* of 25 Hen. III contain
a prescription to the Keeper of the Tower " to cause
all the leaden gutters of the great towers through which
rain water should fall from the summit of the same tower,
to be carried to the ground ; so that the walls of the
said tower, which has been newly whitewashed, may in
no wise be injured by the dropping of rain water, nor be
easily weakened."   And in 1380, at Troyes, where the
north transept, though only sixty years old, was already
tarnished by weather, the cathedral chapter caused the
whole gable and the rose window, with other portions,
to be whitewashed.[1]

Moreover, it must be recognized that the childish
love of destruction for destruction's sake was present
also in the Middle Ages.   Not only were many churches
destroyed then, as now, for military reasons in war-
time ; the thing was often done also, for military
reasons or otherwise, in times of peace.   The Emperor
Charles V, champion of orthodoxy, ready to burn an
unlimited number of heretics, deliberately swept away
the church and nearly all the other buildings of one of
the most beautiful abbeys in Europe, St. Bavon-de-Gand,
in order to build a fortress which should overawe the too
democratic citizens of Ghent.[2]   Rufus's wholesale destruction of churches for the sake of his own hunting in the
New Forest may be ascribed partly to the irreligion of a
monarch who, though he feared the Holy Face of Lucca,
had little respect for any other religious idea, even as
religious ideas were commonly conceived in his own
time.   But the Cistercian monks destroyed many churches

[1] Quicherat, *Mélanges, II*, 203.

[2] The whole story in V. Fris, *Hist. de Gand*, Brussels, 1913, pp. 192–3.
I give a bird's-eye view of the abbey, taken just before its destruction,
in the 2nd volume of *Five Centuries of Religion*.

in the thirteenth century, and so did sheep-farming abbots in the early sixteenth.[1]   Then, in war-time (which, after all, was almost chronic in some of what are now among the most prosperous districts in Europe), very much was destroyed out of pure wantonness, as by Cromwell's troopers in later days. Father Denifle's two bulky volumes, *La désolation des Églises*, etc., give abundant evidence of this for the single country of France after the Hundred Years' War ; more harm was often done by the French royal troops, the francs-archers, to their own churches, than by the English invaders. More than one collection of miracles, again, testifies to the wanton vandalism of soldiers or desperate gamblers, and records the vengeance taken by saints whose images had been outraged.   The chronicler Bourdigné, for instance, writing in 1521, tells us how " in the village called St.-Côme-de-Ver, in the said country of Maine, as the francs-archers aforesaid had (according to their wont) done several insolences and derisions against the holy relics in that church, and against the sacraments and ceremonies of the Church, finally one of them came behind the said church of St.-Côme, hard by the [great] glass window which giveth it light, where the said franc-archer found an apple-tree laden with fruit, which apples he plucked one by one, and threw them for his pleasure against the painted window of the church. And, having thrown several without being able to strike or break the glass, then it befel that, cursing and blaspheming, he cast one wherewith he smote the crown on a pictured St. Cosmas that was in the window ; which apple stuck there amidst the glass for a whole year's space, in the sight of all people, without decay or corruption ; yet on the other hand all the other apples that hung on the tree fell to the ground from that day forward, and rotted in the twinkling of an eye, as though poisoned and infected by the touch of that wretch who had laid hands on the tree ; who nevertheless escaped

---

[1] Documentary evidence for this may be found in my *Medieval Village.*

not our Lord's judgment and vengeance. For, in that night following, the arm wherewith he had cast the said apples was stricken with palsy."[1] And, finally, there was the vandalism of the general public. The friar Salimbene of Parma tells us of an old noble whom he had known in his boyhood, somewhere about A.D. 1230. " He came and dwelt hard by the Cathedral Church, which is dedicated to the glorious Virgin, wherein he daily heard Mass and all the daily and nightly offices of the Church, each at the fit season ; and, whensoever he was not busied with the offices of the Church, he would sit with his neighbours under the public portico by the Bishop's palace, and speak of God, or listen gladly to any who spoke of Him. Nor would he ever suffer children to cast stones against the Baptistery or the Cathedral to destroy the carvings or paintings ; for when he saw any such he waxed wroth and ran swiftly against them and beat them with a leather thong as though he had been specially deputed to this office ; yet he did it for pure godly zeal and divine love, as though he said in the Prophet's words ' The zeal of thine house, hath eaten me up.' " Again, the diary of the Florentine apothecary Landucci gives us, no less casually, just the same sort of evidence. When Michael Angelo had completed his colossal statue of David, and it was being slowly moved from his studio to its place in the public square, precautions were taken against the vandalism of the Florentine populace : " During the night, stones were thrown at the giant to injure it ; therefore it was necessary to keep watch over it." [2]

All this destruction was now immensely hastened by that economic development which was one important factor in both Renaissance and Reformation. Bishop

[1] *Chroniques*, vol. ii, p. 329, translated in *Medieval Garner*, 1st ed., p. 721.

[2] Landucci, p. 214 (May 14, 1504).

Creighton put it with his usual epigrammatic clearness :
" [In the fifteenth century] it was not because there
was a multitude of eager and able architects that churches
were built ; but because a number of wealthy wool
merchants wished to commemorate their munificence,
and had no better way of doing it than in pulling down
the old parish church and building another. We see
what the fifteenth century built, not what it destroyed.
Yet we admire as rare gems the fine Norman, Early
English, and Decorated churches, on a smaller scale,
which still remain in the lucky villages which did not
produce a wealthy man, who ground down the people
during his life and then built a new church to serve as
a chantry to himself." [1]   In short, the wool-merchant was
now doing on a smaller scale what popes and princes
were doing in papal and princely proportions. Nowhere,
perhaps, in any civilized community, has there been such
wholesale and persistent vandalism as in the City of
Rome. Here, if anywhere, the modern artist may
moralize sadly on that which man hath made of man.
The story is told briefly by the Jesuit professor Grisar
in his *History of Rome and the Popes in the Middle Ages*,
and by the still more learned Lanciani in his *Destruction
of Ancient Rome* (Macmillans, 1899). And it is so vital
to the whole thesis of this present book, that I give it
as far as possible in Lanciani's own words.

From the moment when this city began to revive from
the torpor of the Dark Ages, and the times of worst
ignorance and immorality among the popes, it began also
systematically to pursue the revival of its own art through
the destruction of Græco-Roman work. Rome became
famous for delicate work in the purest white marble,
inlaid with mosaics of the most costly materials ; and it
was one of these Roman workmen, Peter, whom Henry III
employed for the magnificent shrine which he erected
in honour of Edward the Confessor in Westminster
Abbey. This work, exported thus to far-off England (or,

[1] *Life and Letters*, ed. Louise Creighton, vol. i, p. 413.

to give another instance, to Aachen), has generally been called *Cosmati*, after the most famous family which earned a living by it. But in fact it demanded the energies of several families, which seem to have formed a sort of close corporation. We find the " filii Pauli " in about 1150, the " filii Cosmati " about 1180, " Vassalecti " from 1153 to 1275, and a fourth branch from 1143 to 1209 : " For three centuries this guild lived and prospered and accomplished its work at the expense of the ruins of ancient Rome."[1] For the bulk of this work, the pure white foundation was obtained by cutting up Greek statues of Parian marble; and the other precious materials were broken from porphyry columns, ancient mosaics, and every place where rare Eastern stones could be found. The first influential voice heard in remonstrance against these practices of the marble-cutters, and the utter abandonment of the Roman monuments, is that of Petrarch. But the great poet pleaded in vain ; for the destruction did not decrease in the Middle Ages and it waxed even greater in the Renaissance. Chrysoloras, the master of Poggio Bracciolini, says, referring to marbles taken from this source : " The statues lie broken in fragments, ready for the lime-kiln, or are made use of as building material. I have seen many used as mounting steps, or as curbstones, or as mangers in stables." In 1426, the papal authorities gave a company of lime-burners leave to destroy the Basilica Julia, claiming half the produce of the kilns ; a host of other monuments were thus destroyed. " ' In the early years of Paul III ' (1534–1550), says De Marchi, ' many torsoes and statues discovered in digging cellars, in planting gardens and vineyards, and in opening new streets, used to be thrown into the kilns, especially those sculptured in Greek marble, on account of the wonderful lime which they produced. Paul III issued most cruel regulations to the effect that no one should dare thus to destroy ancient statuary

---

[1] Lanciani, p. 181 ; my other quotations come from succeeding pages of the same book.

under penalty of death.' As a matter of fact, however, these ' most cruel regulations ' of Paul III did not produce a lasting effect. We may suppose that the destruction of the masterpieces of Græco-Roman art may have diminished for the time being, but it was by no means suppressed. The spoliation of marble and stone edifices went on with increasing activity to the end of the sixteenth century. We must not forget that another edict of the same pope, dated July 22, 1540, put at the mercy of the ' deputies ' of the Fabbrica di S. Pietro [i.e. St. Peter's Church at Rome] all the monuments of the Forum and of the Sacra Via ; and they did not hesitate to profit by the pontifical grant to the fullest possible extent. Pirro Ligorio, the architect, discussing the best way of obtaining a particularly fine plaster, suggests the use of powdered Parian marble, ' obtained from the statues which are constantly destroyed.' . . . Fra Giocondo da Verona, adducing testimony from his own experience, says that some Roman citizens boasted of having had the foundations of their houses and palaces constructed with ancient statues. . . . So important was the exercise of this industry of lime-burning at the Circus Flaminius that the whole district received the name of Lime-pit (calcarario, calcararia). . . . In fact, none of the important excavations with which I have been connected, either in Rome or on neighbouring sites, has failed to bring to light remains of one or more lime-kilns. I mention two examples as specially worthy of note. A lime-kiln was found in the palace of Tiberius on the Palatine hill by Rosa, in 1869. It was filled to the brim with fine works of art, some calcined, some intact. Among the latter were the veiled bust of Claudius, now in the Museo delle Terme ; a head of Nero ; three caryatides, in nero antico ; the exquisite little statuette of an ephebus in black basalt, published by Hauser in the *Mittheilungen* for 1895, pp. 97–119, pl. 1 ; a head of Harpocrates, and other minor fragments. In February 1883, in the excavations on the south side of the Atrium of Vesta, a pile of marble was found about 14 feet long, 9 feet wide and 7 feet high. It was wholly made up of statues of the *Vestales maximæ*, some unbroken, others in fragments. The statues and fragments had been carefully packed together, leaving as few interstices as possible between them, and the spaces formed by the curves of the bodies were filled in with chips. . . . These beautiful statues had been piled into a regular oblong, like a cord of wood, by some diggers of marble, who had carefully filled the spaces between the statues as they lay side by side, in order that no empty spaces might be left. By what fortunate accident these sculptures were preserved it is difficult to guess ; but one thing at least is certain—a great quantity of other marbles belonging to the House of the Vestals must have perished by fire. Two kilns and two deposits of lime and of charcoal were found in the course of the same excavations." Lanciani gives a list of specially papal demolitions (p. 201). " Alexander VI destroyed also a Forum, a temple, and part of the Baths of Diocletian. His successor, Julius II " (1503-1513), had too many wars in hand to afford much time or money for destroying ancient monuments ; but he laid the foundations of the present St. Peter's, and destroyed the old church.[1] " The loss occasioned to art, history, and Christian antiquities by the destruction of the venerable basilica is simply incalculable. The west half of the greatest temple of Christendom was levelled to the ground with all its precious decorations in mosaic, fresco, sculpture, in marble and in wood, with its historical inscriptions and its pontifical tombs, among which were those of Celestine IV († 1243), Gregory IX († 1241), Boniface IX († 1404), Innocent VII († 1406), Eugene IV († 1447) and Nicholas V (†1455). Three other churches also disappeared in the pontificate of Julius II. . . . No great losses are recorded under the rule of Leo X. . . . The only act of vandalism which can be brought home to him is the destruction of a certain part of the Via

[1] The destruction had been begun by Nicholas V (Müntz, 1878, p. 105).

Tiburtina, called La Quadrata, the embankment of which was supported by great walls of travertine. The stones were removed to St. Peter's." After which he sums up (p. 202) : "All sense of the beautiful, all appreciation of art, seems to have been lost for a time among the Romans. While other cities in Italy were raising churches, town-halls, exchanges, fountains, palaces, and splendid private houses which command admiration at the present day on account of the graceful simplicity of their proportions and the finish of their work, the builders at Rome did little more than pile up and jumble together fragments of older structures without regard to form or fitness. Tivoli, Viterbo, and even Corneto, were in this period far superior to Rome in their public and domestic architecture. They can point to splendid examples of the skill and taste of their master masons of the fourteenth century, while we Romans have absolutely nothing to show that is comparable."[1]

In another volume, Lanciani emphasizes the full responsibility of the Renaissance for vandalism.

" In the long and sad history of the destruction of ancient Rome, the Middle Ages are perhaps the least guilty—less guilty, at any rate, than the period of the Renaissance which followed. In spite of their enthusiastic love for ancient art and classic civilization, the great masters of the Renaissance treated our monuments and ruins with incredible contempt and brutality. The original cause of this state of things must be found, strange to say, in the increasing civilization of the age, in the softening and refining of former habits, in the development of public and private wealth, which was pushing popes, cardinals, patricians, bankers, and rich merchants to raise everywhere magnificent palaces and villas, churches and monasteries, aqueducts and fountains, harbours and bridges, castles and towers. All these constructions of the golden age, which justly form the pride

[1] *Ancient Rome*, Macmillans, 1888. My quotations come from the preface, xvi ff.

of my city, and make it unique and enviable by the whole world, were built, stone by stone, with materials stolen from ancient ruins. . . . The cinquecento excavations did more harm to the monuments of imperial, republican, and kingly Rome than the ten centuries of preceding barbarism. . . . The next period, which runs from the middle of the seventeenth century to the end of the eighteenth, ranks also among the saddest in our history, because it marks the almost complete destruction of medieval buildings. Under the pretence of restorations and embellishments, the authorities laid their hands upon the most noted and the most venerable churches of the city, which had until then preserved their beautiful basilical type in all its simplicity, purity and majesty."

He goes on to enumerate, from 1665 onwards, thirteen great churches thus spoiled ; and he adds : " The system followed in restoring these churches was everywhere uniform. The columns of the nave were walled up, and concealed in thick pilasters of whitewashed masonry ; the inscribed or sculptured marble slabs and the mosaic pavements were taken up and replaced by brick floors ; the windows were enlarged out of all proportion, and assumed a rectangular form, so that floods of light might enter and illuminate every remote, peaceful recess of the sacred place. For the beautiful roofs made of cedar wood, vaults or *lacunaria* were substituted. The number of entrance-doors was trebled ; the simple but precious frescoes of the fourteenth century were whitewashed, and the fresh surface was covered with the insignificant productions of Francesco Cozza, Gerolamo Troppa, Giacinto Brandi, Michelangelo Cerruti, Pasquale Marini, Biagio Puccini, and other painters equally obscure. All these profanations could be accomplished, not only without opposition, but amid general applause, because such was the spirit of the age." It needed a special art-lover like Vasari to raise any protest against the demolition of medieval work. He laments the destruction of a very valuable fresco by Pietro Cavallini in San Marco at Florence, which, with many other similar works of art, was whitewashed over, " with little feeling or consideration," by the Dominicans, the brethren of Fra Angelico. In 1560, at S. Spirito in Florence, the monks destroyed a priceless fresco by Simone Memmi.[1] In fact, though there was perhaps more religious painting done now than ever before, and though purely pagan subjects were still only a minority, yet the prevailing taste was strongly anti-medieval.

Again, there is perhaps no matter for which iconoclasts have earned bitterer curses than for their destruction of stained glass, one of the most precious heritages of medieval art. Much of this, of course, was done deliberately for religious reasons ; but surely, if any excuse can be admitted for this destruction, that is the best that could be pleaded. When popes themselves decreed the destruction of certain representations, without for one moment taking their artistic merits into consideration, must not the average thinking man of to-day recognize some palliation for a similar destruction of imagery which proclaimed doctrines inextricably intermingled, *at that time*, with superstitions and cruelties which no man dares to defend at the present day. The worship of the Virgin Mary, the doctrine of Transubstantiation, were things for which hundreds had suffered the cruellest of deaths, and for which other thousands or even millions were still liable, under Roman Catholic law, to be burned at any time. This system was deliberately described, by incomparably the greatest Roman Catholic historian who ever wrote in the English language, in terms which will be questioned by few scholars who have actually studied the Inquisition records, and searched their own hearts unsparingly as to the real meaning of those documents.

[1] *Lives of the Painters*, Bohn, vol. i, pp. 179, 184. Yet Cavallini had enjoyed such a reputation for personal piety in his own day that, as Vasari says, it is no wonder a crucifix made by him actually spoke to St. Bridget, and that a Virgin of his " should have performed, and still be performing, an infinite number of miracles." For farther instances of vandalism see Schlosser, *Beiträge*, pp. 93, 123, 143.

" The principle of the Inquisition," wrote Acton, " is murderous " ; and, again : " The murder of a heretic was not only permitted but rewarded . . . it was a virtuous deed to slaughter Protestant men and women, until they were all exterminated."[1] In the face of a system which can be thus described by a man of ency-clopædic learning and supremely conscious of the his-torian's responsibilities, which of us will refuse some measure of sympathy, at least, to men who believed that the highest of all arts is the conduct of life ; and that, if even the most marvellous picture is murderous of soul and body, then the world will gain by its disappearance ? This, after all, is what inspired Savonarola, though of course his definition of soul-murder would have differed widely in many ways from that of the Reformers. A century earlier, the same religious zeal in face of the relics of an earlier worship had inspired Urban V, one of the three best popes of the fourteenth century. " On the throne of St. Peter, he lived as a monk faithful to the smallest details of his Rule " ; he always confessed before saying his Mass ; " the impulse which he gave to art was no less strong than that which he gave to letters and to science " ; and he had the courage to bring the papal court from Avignon back to Rome, if only for a few months. But he fought hard against what he con-sidered immodesty in the fashionable dress of his day ; and, under the foundations of the vast palace which he was building, he deliberately buried a statue of Hercules and other objects of pagan art " in order to abolish the memory of idolatry."[2] St.-Francois de Sales, again, de-stroyed many medieval statues in his diocese as unedify-ing.[3] Would there not have been equal moral justification for any Protestant ruler who, if he had had the power, might have destroyed artistic representations which

---

[1] *Letters to Mary Gladstone*, 1904, pp. 141, 185.

[2] G. Mollat, *Papes d'Avignon*, 1st ed., pp. 105, 109 ; J. B. Joudou, *Hist. de la ville d'Avignon*, 1853, p. 393.

[3] *Rev. hist. franciscaine*, vol. iv, 1927, p. 207.

tended to assert the world-authority of the Pope ; that is, of another ruler who claimed over all baptized persons the power of life and death for differences of belief, and who frequently put that claim into practice ? Christ of the Bible, when Peter rushed into the crowd and cut off the ear of Malchus, reproved that action in words of unmistakable rebuke : " All that take the sword shall perish with the sword." Yet the Bible of the Poor, at Reims, tells us a very different story. The incident there is portrayed not according to the Gospels, but after the mystic gloss which represents it as an exercise of legitimate judicial authority ; not a disorderly affray, but as a solemn and deliberate execution. A passage wrongly attributed to St. Gregory the Great, but really from St. Ambrose, is incorporated in Gratian's *Decretum*, the first book of that *Corpus Juris Canonici* by which the Church, and to a great extent the State also, was regulated almost entirely for the last three and a half centuries of the Middle Ages. It is from a commentary upon Luke xxii, 50 and John xviii, 10, with which we must compare Matt. xxvi. 51, and it is headed : *The Roman Church, by her Profession of Faith, hath cut off the ear of Error.* In the text we find : " Peter, therefore, cutteth off the ear. But why Peter ? Because it is he who hath received the keys of the Kingdom of Heaven. For he doth condemn who doth also absolve, since he hath received the power both of binding and of loosing. So he smiteth off the ear of him who listeneth ill ; he smiteth off with the spiritual sword the inward ear of him who understandeth wrongly." And the commentary upon this runs : " Peter, at our Lord's passion, cut off the ear of Malchus, and the Lord restored it again ; note thereby that it is Peter's duty to cut off spiritually the ear of him who understandeth wrongly, for he hath the power of binding and loosing. Note also that, if such men be converted, God will restore their hearing."[1]
This, then, is the doctrine which the Reims sculptor has

[1] Pars. ii, caus. xxiv, q.1, cap. 17.

PETER AND MALCHUS AT REIMS.

represented in preference to the Bible story. Instead of
the generous ill-regulated impulse of the disciple, plung-
ing hastily into the crowd with a blow which was mis-
directed even more from the spiritual than from the
military point of view, here we have a judge quietly and
deliberately executing justice upon an offender paralysed
by his sense of guilt. Malchus clings to the operating
Peter with the same passive resignation with which, in
our childhood, we clung to the dentist's chair. This
distortion of Bible facts, however, was perfectly natural
in the circumstances. By the time this group was carved,
in the middle or the latter half of the thirteenth century,
popes were asserting the right of wielding not only the
spiritual but also the earthly sword, even against emperors
and princes. Not only did they claim to make and
unmake kings, and to transfer whole populations from
one ruler to another, but they had more than once set
armies in motion to enforce that claim. It is more than
probable, therefore, that this was in the mind of the
man who conceived the Reims group ; and it is practically certain that the sculpture would convey that impression to those who took the Reims portals for their Bible.
Therefore, as we can say of the Doom, that it was not
only a work of art but even more definitely a sermon,
so these two Reims figures must be considered in that
double aspect ; and any inartistic person who might care
for nothing but the moral lesson would be more truly in
the mind of the Church than a beholder of the most
sensitive artistic fibre who remained indifferent to that
lesson. But the moral in this case is, at bottom, political ;
the group, in its inner meaning, begs a party-question
no less important than that question of the flag which
stands so definitely in the front rank, at the present
moment, in South Africa and in Germany. If this
relation of Peter to Malchus, of the Church to the State,
could have been expounded to one of the earlier Christian
emperors, or even to Charles the Great, it would have
seemed as revolutionary to him as the Declaration of

GG

Independence. Any earthly ruler, therefore, who might have demanded the defacement of that Reims group would simply have been paying the Church the compliment of taking her to mean what she said. " If, indeed, it stands there mainly to teach a lesson, then I cannot tolerate a lesson which seems to me so false." If that lesson had been expounded to the Huguenot-hating Louis XIV, these statues would probably have run more risk of destruction from him than even from Henry IV in his Huguenot days. And in that case would not the dispassionate outsider have judged that, in this lamentable affair, the original fault lay with those who had mixed up good art with bad or questionable politics ? Consequently, regrettable as most of the sixteenth-century vandalism was, yet a great deal of it could at least plead such religious reasons as appeal perhaps to the majority of Christians to-day, and moral reasons which appeal to all men who refuse to admit heresy-hunting as an integral part of the Christian's duty to God.

If, therefore, as lovers of art, we feel bound to curse any of our predecessors, let us reserve our heartiest maledictions for those who, having no objection to the doctrines—being, indeed, professionally bound to burn such fellow-Christians as might publicly object to these doctrines—yet destroyed acres (it might almost be said) of priceless glass, through pure artistic indifference or actual dislike of those most characteristic medieval glories. Here again, instead of making my own summary from the sight of existing French cathedrals and the study of the pertinent monographs, let me translate from Olivier Merson, who gives the whole story briefly in his monograph on stained glass.[1]

" Now, if so many monuments of our national art have been destroyed, we must not seek the causes of this merely

---

[1] *Les Vitraux*, Quantin, 1895, p. 100. Our English churches, in spite of all ravages, contain probably twice as much medieval stained glass as there is in all the churches of Italy ; and I am told that Spain is not much better in that respect.

in the savagery of the religious wars or in the effervescence
of revolutionary rage, nor again in the folly of the ' black
bands ' or in human negligence. The very men who
ought to have been interested in preserving the glass have
often decided, nay, even commanded, its destruction.
At Notre-Dame-de-Paris, the chapter replaced all the
windows of the twelfth, thirteenth, and fourteenth
century with white glass. The canons of Reims, between
1739 and 1768, wrought this same act of vandalism in
the lower windows of their cathedral. Similar work was
done by the monks of St.-Remi-de-Reims ; and a worthy
Benedictine (Dom Chastellain, in order that his name
be not ignored), a learned man, we may suppose, wrote
with ineffable serenity on this matter : ' In order to give
this great basilica an air of majesty and magnificence
which it hitherto lacked, the monks, not content with
having put nearly all the windows into white glass a few
years earlier, undertook now to whitewash the church
again from top to bottom, which lasted from October
1755 to October 1757, and made it look quite new.'
Similarly at Chartres, in 1757, the canons took it into
their heads to replace the borders of twelve clerestory
windows in the choir with white glass ; and later (in 1773
and 1788) they ordered the total demolition of six of
these windows in order to throw a better light upon a
marble group by the [contemporary] sculptor Bridan,
representing the Assumption. In 1786, when Bridan
was finishing his work on the spot, the chapter had already
destroyed a great window of stained glass above the
temporary choir installed in the nave, near the south
transept. How many misdeeds were committed by
ordinary parish priests, when their hierarchical superiors,
and the best educated among the clergy, showed such a
burning love for white glass and whitewash ! Yet, in
spite of all, many thirteenth century windows have
managed to escape from untoward circumstances."

Here, again, is Canon J. Fossey's account of the carved
reredoses, in wood or stone, over a considerable portion

of Normandy.[1] He can enumerate sixteen survivors; but he adds: "How many charming compositions of this kind were destroyed by the bad taste of the seventeenth and eighteenth centuries! Scarcely any one of these is in its original place. They have been banished either to the nave-walls, or even into the sacristies."

The men who did all this were untouched by the Reformation; but the Renaissance had cleft an impassable chasm between them and medieval art. Modern French Gothic, both in building and in furniture, is definitely inferior to English of the same date; and perhaps nowhere is this so marked as in glass, which the monk Theophilus specified as the unique glory of France.[2]

---

[1] *L'art religieux dans les diocèses de Rouen et d'Évreux* (Évreux, 1920, p. 94).

[2] Here, again, I must insert a protest from Professor Lethaby: "No, superior, in not being so *sham.*" Yet I cannot help thinking that, from this point of view also, the comparison holds good; the church of Bonsecours above Rouen, and the west front of St.-Ouen, seem as reprehensible shams as equivalent buildings of the same date on our side.

CHAPTER XXIII

RENAISSANCE AND CONSTRUCTION.—(1)

LET us now turn from the negative to the positive aspect of the Renaissance. This chapter will be found to owe a heavy debt to a stimulating modern writer on economics, Werner Sombart. The main theory of his two monographs on *War and Capitalism*, *Luxury and Capitalism*, and of his greater *Modern Capitalism* seems as sound as it is striking ; and here and there it is possible to reinforce his argument by earlier instances than he has adduced.[1]

The thesis of the two books may be put into a single sentence ; modern capitalism was not produced so much by any popular demand or popular effort, as by the pressure of war and luxury ; it has been rather imposed from above than grown up from below. Modern industry on a large scale (*Gross-Industrie*) is differentiated from earlier and simpler society, among other factors, by two of supreme importance : the Contract System and Standardization. Both of those factors are due mainly to war and to luxury.

In one sense, the monks are the parents of modern Gross-Industrie. It was they who continued, or revived, that wholesale exploitation of the land which great Roman capitalists had practised in their *latifundia*. It was they alone who had capital enough to build on a scale rivalling or surpassing kings and princes. This capital, for many generations, they used more wisely

---

[1] *Krieg und Kapitalismus*, Leipzig, 1913 ; *Luxus und Kapitalismus*, Leipzig, 1913 ; *Der Moderne Kapitalismus*, vol. ii, pt. ii (Munich and Leipzig, 1919). I shall refer to these as K.K. and L.K. and M.K. respectively.

than other folk. What the serf would never have done for himself, he did under compulsion for himself and for the monk his master. The peasant was too content with mere animal nourishment for himself and his family, and too much hampered by narrowness of outlook and petty jealousies, to have brought things forward at anything like the rate which they actually took. The real capitalists, until the rise of a powerful merchant class, were the Benedictines and other almost equally wealthy Religious.[1] Petrus Cantor of Notre-Dame-de-Paris, one of the most pious and learned of the later twelfth century theologians, emphasizes this strongly. The luxury of contemporary building seems to him positively unchristian. Great folk everywhere are raising palaces as proud as the Tower of Babel ; monks castellate their dwellings, in order to obtain farther security for their great wealth. If Peter had been told that this movement which he describes, after growing steadily for three centuries more, would suddenly bring men farther in a couple of generations than in the whole of those three hundred years, then he would probably have looked upon the world as past redemption.

Yet this is what history shows us. The prince or great baron or monk of the thirteenth century was a strong man armed ; but the last generations of the Middle Ages produced a stronger than he had been. We have already seen how, two centuries after Peter, the author of *Dives and Pauper* finds more worldliness than religion in the great buildings of his own day.[2] The kitchen of the great cathedral monastery at Durham, which is still standing as a remarkable architectural monument, cost a sum equivalent to something like £15,000 in modern purchasing power. That of Canterbury Cathedral cost about the same ; and, though a good deal of the food cooked in both found its way, sooner or later, to the

[1] Fuller evidence in the opening chapters of *Five Centuries of Religion*, vol. ii.
[2] Com. I, chap. li.

poor, yet this was far less than is commonly represented, and great abbeys often sold, instead of giving away, their offal and even the bones from the kitchen. One of the mainsprings of the Franciscan movement was a revolt against Benedictine capitalism ; yet one of the most imposing buildings in Italy was built over St. Francis's bones within a few years of his death ; and, when the author of *Piers Plowman's Creed* wishes to draw a satirical contrast between ideal and practice, he chooses the magnificent edifices of the professionally-mendicant Dominicans.

The Monastic Orders, then, did much to hasten the growth of wholesale production on a great scale ; and war provided an even greater stimulus. I know no author who has brought out the influence of warfare upon art so well as Prof. Baldwin Brown ; it cannot be expressed better than he has expressed it in a single page : " Nor was war less prolific [than religion] in commissions to the artist. Imperiously practical, as it has just been called, war demanded of all its impedimenta active service and not show, but the conditions that made the medieval an artistic epoch so wrought here, that display became one of the most effective agents for the work in hand. It was not for mere show, but for added efficiency in the camp and in the mêlée, that the sun was made to glint on the warrior's surcoat of crimson silk and gold, on the ridge and hollow of the fluted mail, on the embossed leather and the Damascene filigree in the iron of the horse trappings. The helm which kept safe his head within its walls of steel marked at the same time with crest and plume his progress through the ranks, while the sword with which he hewed his way had won by service its right to the gold and gems and costly fancies of the craftsmen lavished on its hilt. A whole minute and sumptuous art, that of heraldry, was brought into being to exalt his personal distinction and pride of race, and he confronted the foe with the insignia of his person and line emblazoned on his shield ; all the arts of the time vied with each other to give to his tomb a glory that should be record and praise in one."[1]

But we are dealing here with a special stimulus, the stimulus to Gross-Industrie. We have already seen, in Chapter XVII, how the citizens of Ardres were conscripted wholesale to fortify that town ; and there are many similar medieval records on a smaller scale. It may be safely asserted, I think, that in every city the compulsory levy for raising or repairing walls, whether in labour or in money, preceded by many generations, or even by many centuries, such a contribution as the paving-rate or any similar modern levy. Aigues-Mortes was evidently built by concentrating labour on a very great scale ; so was a princely castle like the now-vanished Coucy ; so, as we know from documentary evidence, was Windsor Castle. Most significant is a note quoted from the Close Rolls of 28 Henry III by Prof. Lethaby : " In 1244 the king ordered the same keepers to see that the Knight's Chamber in the Palace of Westminster should be finished before Easter, even if they had to employ a thousand men. This employment of a thousand men is a characteristic exaggeration in the king's speech, of which there are many examples. The Sheriff of Kent in 1244–5 was instructed to prevent stone being taken to London except for the works of Westminster. London was to suffer a great deal on account of these same works!"[2] Of special interest, again, is the passage in Lydgate's *Troy Book* in which he describes Priam's royal haste to build that city ; a passage which enlarges upon the scene in far fuller detail than the original from which Lydgate borrows :

> " And all about the countries environ
> He madë seek in every region
> For suchë workmen as were curious,
> Of wit inventive, of casting marvellous,

[1] *Arts in Early England*, vol. i, p. 7.

[2] Lethaby I, p. 150.

Or such as couldë craft of ge[o]metry
Or werë subtle in their fantasy ;
And for every that was good deviser,
Mason, hewer or crafty quarrier,
For every wright and passing carpenter
That may be found, either far or near ;
For such as couldë gravë, grope[1] or carve,
Or such as weren able for to serve
With lime or stonë, for to raise a wall
With batailling and crestës martial,
Or such as haddë cunning in their head,
Alabaster, either white or red
Or marble gray for to polish it plain,
To make it smooth of veinës and of grain.
He sent also for every imager
Both in entaille,[2] and every portrayer
That couldë drawe, or with colour paint
With hewës freshë, that the work not faint ;
And such as could with countenances glad
Make an imagë that will never fade,
To counterfeit in metal, tree or stone
The subtle workë of Pigmaleoun,
Or of Appollo,[3] the which as bookës tell
In imagery all other did excel,
For by his crafty working curious
The tomb he made of King Darius."[4]

These words describe, with no more than natural poetic licence, what we have seen Lydgate's patron Henry VI doing, a generation after the lines were written, at Eton and King's College. Moreover, bishops and city councils must have done much the same, according to their powers, when those vast cathedrals were built which surpassed even the great monastic churches in magnificence and in haste of execution. Monk, citizen and prince are all combining to fan the flame of Gross-Industrie in the building art.

For work on this scale, both in size and in haste,

[1] Carve deep and hollow, as the French use the word *fouiller*.
[2] Sculpture.
[3] Apelles ; cf. Chaucer, *Wife of Bath's Prologue*.
[4] *Troy Book*, E.G.T.S., extra series, 1906, vol. i, p. 138 (probably written somewhere about 1410).

necessarily created the contract system. St. Antonino of Florence, writing about 1420, speaks of it as a growing practice ; [1] but it was the princes of Italy, and especially the popes, who made it quite normal a generation later.

Traces, of course, may be found much earlier. Quicherat has published the analysis of a document of 1261 which shows distinct traces of modernity. The abbot of St.-Gilles in Languedoc, backed up by the *operarius*—i.e. the monk who supervises this part of the abbey business and revenues—makes a contract with Martin, a master-mason of Vauvert. Master Martin undertakes to order, devise, and direct the building work, to decide what must be bought, and to keep watch over the supplies. For his trouble, he takes 100 *sols tournois* [equivalent to £1 5*s*. sterling of then English money] at Pentecost, as the equivalent of a suit of clothes. In addition, he gets a wage of two sols for every work-day on which he commences before midday. He can claim, any day of the year, food for himself and his horse. If he chooses to eat outside, he takes the ration of two monks in bread and wine.[2] If he prefers to eat in the abbey, he will sit at the abbot's table, or in his absence, at that of the prior or of the judge, but only on non-fast days ; and then his portion shall be that of a monk, valued at three deniers.[3] On fast days, he will fetch from the kitchen " a monk's *generale* and pittance," a phrase which Quicherat glosses, on what seem far-fetched and doubtful grounds, as " half as much again as a monk's fast-diet." This master-mason evidently intended to live only the summer months at St.-Gilles ; for the agreement binds him, for the period between Martinmas and Whitsuntide,

---

[1] *Summa Major*, pars. iii, tit. viii, cap. 4, § 8.

[2] Doubled, as we shall presently see, to make up for his missing all victuals except bread and wine.

[3] Twelve *deniers* went to the *sol* ; this, therefore, would be ¾*d*. of contemporary English money. But this valuation apparently comprised only the two dishes ; the bread and wine, accounted for elsewhere, being here omitted.

" to come with all speed whensoever anything unexpected occurs in the course of the works, if he is sent for by the abbot or the *operarius*."

Much nearer to the modern contract is the indenture for the construction of Fotheringhay Church, made in 1434–5, between the representatives of the Duke of York and William Horwood, freemason, of Fotheringhay. This indenture system had already become common in war. Our armies were regularly thus organized in the Hundred Years' War, after the earlier tentative stages. A certain great captain would bind himself by indenture to supply the king with so many men, at so much per man and per day, according to a regular tariff.[1] This captain would then often indent with minor captains, each of whom undertook to bring a certain quota at a certain price ; and these, again, might raise their quotas by indenting with smaller men. The Italians, the great business men of that day, were doing the same. Long ago, in the crusade of 1204, the Venetians had entered into a regular business contract with the Crusaders. In 1337, again, Ayton Doria of Genoa contracted in regular form with the King of France. He was to supply twenty war-galleys, fully equipped and manned, at the rate of 900 gold florins per month and per ship. The king accepted forty galleys at that rate, and used them for four months ; this bargain cost him 144,000 florins, a sum equivalent to the whole budget of one of the great medieval Hanse cities.[2] Sombart's comment upon this and similar incidents runs : " It was war which created the Stock Exchange."

But a princely baron like the Duke of York very naturally carried his military experience into his business at home. He indented to raise a church as he might have indented to raise a division for Agincourt, in which battle he lost his life. We must not exaggerate the

---

[1] For example, the indenture of the Earl of Kent with Edward III in 1360 (Rymer, *Foedera*, vol. iii, 1825, p. 510).

[2] Sombart, K.K., pp. 33, 51, 65.

connexion of ideas ; it may well be that building contracts in similar form were drawn up long before this
surviving contract for Fotheringhay. We must not
exaggerate, but neither must we ignore the fact that the
same movement may be traced in both fields, and that
it would be natural for each to influence the other.
After giving, in great detail, the size and description of
the new nave and tower required, even down to such
small items as the mouldings, the contract proceeds :
" And of all the work that in this same indenture is
devised and rehearsed [i.e. nave and tower], my said Lord
of York shall find the carriage and stuff ; that is to say,
lime, stone, sand, ropes, bolts, ladders, timber, scaffolds,
gynnes [*machinery*], and all manner of stuff that be-
longeth to the said work ; for which work, well, truly
and duly to be made and finished in wise as it is before
devised and declared, the said William Horwood shall
have of my said Lord £300 sterling ; of the which sum
he shall be paid in wise as it shall be declared hereafter.
That is to say, when he hath taken his ground [*laid the
foundation*] of the said kirk, aisles, buttresses, porch and
steeple, hewn and set his ground-table-stones, and his
ligements [i.e. string-courses] and the wall thereunto
within and without, as it ought to be well and duly made,
then he shall have £6 13s. 4d. And when the said William
Horwood hath set one foot above the ground-table-
stone, as well throughout the outer side as the inner side
of the said work, then shall he have payment of £100
sterling.[1] And so for every foot of the said work, after
that it be fully wrought and set, as it ought to be, and as
it is afore devised, till it come to the full height of the
highest of the finials and battlement of the said body,
hewing, setting and raising . . . [*sic*] of the steeple, after
it be passed the highest of the embattlement of the said
body, he shall have but xxxs sterlings till it be fully ended
and performed, in wise as it is before devised." Here,
then, all is calculated on a general scale ; five pounds for

[1] The copyist seems to have mistaken C^ii for C^s.

every foot in height up to the battlements, and thenceforward, nothing being left to raise but the tower, only thirty shillings a foot.[1] The contract was stringent in other directions also. " During all the said work the said Will. Horwood shall neither set more nor fewer freemasons, rough-setters nor layers thereupon, but such as shall be ordained to have the governance and oversight of the said work under my Lord of York will ordain him and assign him to have. And if so be that the said Will. Horwood make not full payment of all or any of his workmen, then the clerk of the work shall pay him in his presence, and stop as mickle in the said Will. Horwood's hand, as the payment that shall be due unto the workmen cometh to. And during all the said work the setters shall be chosen and taken by such as have the governance and oversight of the said work by my said Lord ; they to be paid by the hand of Will. Horwood . . . . And if so be that the said Will. Horwood will complain and say at any time that the two said setters, or any of them, be not profitable nor sufficient workmen for my Lord's avail, then by oversight of master-masons of the country they shall be deemed ; and if they be found faulty or unable, then they shall be changed, and others taken and chosen in. . . . And if it so be that the said Will. Horwood make not full end of the said work within term reasonable [which shall be specified beforehand] then he shall yield his body to prison at my Lord's will, and all his movable goods and heritages at my said Lord's disposition and ordinance." [2]

It will be noted that we have in this indenture another definitely modern feature ; a specified penalty for breach

---

[1] Compare this with Dunmow Priory, where in 1533 the monks paid a mason for $9\frac{1}{2}$ feet of steeple which he had built for them; the price was £11 0s. 7d. (*V. C. H. Essex*, vol. ii, p. 153).

[2] Dugdale-Caley, vol. vi, pp. 1414 ff. For other contracts, besides those noted in Prof. A. Hamilton Thompson's *Med. Build. Docts.*, p. 19, see Brutails, pp. 26-7, 54, 74 ; *Kirby Muxloe* (bricks laid at 1s. 6d. per thousand). Portions of Westminster Abbey were done by " task-work " from 1253 onwards.

of contract. This occurs much earlier, in a document which I have printed elsewhere.[1] Among the muniments of the Cistercian abbey of Dunes, in Flanders, is a contract of about A.D. 1200 with a hired scribe. He is to finish a book in as good letters as the specimen which he had begun ; he undertakes to do no other work till this is finished ; if he breaks this promise, he shall be " kept in prison and in iron bonds . . . never to go forth until the said work shall have been altogether completed. . . . And, for the keeping of the aforesaid articles, the said [scribe] hath pledged [to his employer], by his faith, his own person and heirs, and all his goods, whether movable or immovable, present or future, without right of appeal to any tribunal outside the bishop's court." And, naturally, this fixing of a definite sanction for the contract became more and more general, though, equally naturally, the crude resource of imprisonment was replaced by a money-penalty, as society became more civilized. This comes out clearly in the arrangements of Henry VII's executors for the completion of King's College Chapel. Here, though the contracts are not yet in quite the stringent modern form, yet they mark a definite stage between ordinary medieval small-business and the capitalistic Gross-Industrie of to-day. The master-masons engage to finish the work at the rate of £100 per bay ; on the other hand, one " binds himself, his heirs and executors, in £300 of good and lawful money of England," for the due performance of his part. The four master-glaziers who first contracted for the windows were to receive 16d. per foot, and bound themselves in 500 marks for performance of the job. The two to whom this contract was transferred accepted it under bond of £200. It is evident that all these artists were also capitalistic contractors.[2]

But let us go back to illustrate Fotheringhay, perhaps

---

[1] *Social Life in Britain*, p. 102.

[2] Willis and Clark, vol. i, pp. 610, 616, 618. For another contract see *Gould*, vol. i, p. 304.

the most interesting of all our contracts, from the generalizations of St. Antonino, who at that same moment was working and writing in Florence. There, capitalism and the Gross-Industrie were more advanced than in England, and there is a very modern ring in the Saint's advice to confessors for dealing with the men of business whose souls they were directing. He is treating now of " architects or builders "—*de architectis seu aedificatoribus.* After the uncomplimentary passage which I have quoted earlier, tracing back this art to Cain and Nimrod, two of the least respectable among all Old Testament figures in medieval tradition, he notes that the holy patriarchs were content to live in tents, " knowing that they had here no continuing city, but expecting a house not made with hands, a most spacious house in heaven." He then goes on to specify the ordinary artisan's temptations to idleness or dishonest work, and finally deals with what we may call the contractor. " If men are paid by the yard for the building they do, the employer supplying them with all the materials, then they commit fraud if, for the sake of doing more work and earning more, they work not properly but carelessly, whereby the building is rendered feeble and unprofitable. Thirdly, when they undertake to construct a building at their own expense, supplying all the materials for a certain price specified between builder and employer, then they sometimes cheat by not putting lime enough, or not supplying other things in their right place, in order that they may spend less of the stuff which it is their part to supply, whereby the building is rendered insufficient. Nor could they be excused on the plea that, if they chose to supply what is agreed upon, and to labour diligently, then they would earn very little, so small is the sum that they receive ; for it is their duty to take heed hereunto at the outset ; but they do this in order that they may get the job rather than other men."[1]

This brings us to the most important stage of the

[1] *Summa Major*, pars. iii, tit. viii, c. 4, § 8.

evolution which we are tracing. Two generations before these princely executors put the Cambridge work into the hands of capitalists, the same stage had been reached in Italy, and especially at Rome. The old medieval system no longer sufficed for this rush of enormous and costly buildings ; the patriarchal and personal methods of earlier centuries must now give way to something like the methods of the modern joint-stock company. In the Middle Ages, the master of the works had hired workmen for the job ; had bought the materials (it was a step forward when, as at St.-Gilles, not he but the contracting master-mason was responsible for those materials) ; had put all these ingredients, so to speak, to simmer together ; and from this caldron the complete building had finally emerged. Even at King's College, where the executors were dealing with masons and glaziers who possessed considerable capital, and who could contract to turn the building out at so much per bay, so much per turret, so much per pinnacle, these capitalist head-workmen did not supply the materials. It was left to the great princes of the Continent to arrive at this final stage of commercialization. The earlier part of this story is brought out by Müntz,[1] and the later by Sombart.[2] The movement had begun in the earlier fifteenth century ;[3] but quite definite is the contract between Paul II and Bernardo di Lorenzo for building the palace and church of San Marco at Rome, a contract repeated almost verbally from a previous agreement of Pius II with Bernardo's predecessors. And now, writes Müntz, " an attentive study of the contract . . . which we have had copied from the secret archives of the Vatican, permits us to go still farther and to assert that Bernardo [and his three partners] participated in the building of the Palace of San Marco not as architects but as plain contractors. In fact, they pledge themselves,

---

[1] *Les arts à la cour des Popes*, II (1879), pp. 20, 25, 52, 55, 290.
[2] *M.K.*, pp. 773 ff.
[3] Müntz, I (1878), 46 ff., 104 ff., 157 ff., 164, 169.

ST. JOHN'S COLLEGE LIBRARY.

for a flat rate of 19 *grossi* for each yard of masonry, to dig the foundations, raise the walls, and so on. The notary, at every point, takes care to mark that these works are to be done in conformity with measures given to the contractors. Does not this seem to prove that the plans were drawn by others ? Nothing is more frequent, in the fifteenth century, than this sort of agreement. Thus, in the reign of Nicholas V, Beltramo di Martino, of Varese, had undertaken to rebuild the gallery of St. Peter's, under penalty for failure. Under Paul II, similar contracts are equally abundant. At San Marco itself we see two artists, far more celebrated than the preceding, helping as plain contractors ; these are Giuliano da San Gallo, and Theo del Caprino. Giuliano (or, as our documents call him, Julianus son of Francis of Florence), seems to have been specially charged with the masonry. Theo, on the contrary, with a large number of other ' stone-cutters,' was busy with cutting the blocks of travertine needed for the building. He received nineteen [soldi] of Bologna per ell. Sometimes, however, we find him doing more interesting work; window-frames, marble fire-places, and so on. But (it will be said), if such eminent artists consented to work like plain artisans, sometimes at task-work and sometimes at day-work, then they must have had, above them, some very eminent chief ; a master of imposing genius ; how, then, can this master's name have remained unknown ? That name is no longer a secret for my readers. I have shown that, in March 1466, Giacomo da Pietra-Santa figured among the witnesses of the contract signed with Bernardo di Lorenzo. . . . Shall we be accused of rashness if we identify him with, we need not say the architect, but one of the architects of San Marco ? "

On a previous page, Müntz writes : " The number of supervisors of the works at San Marco (*superstites, præsidentes*) seems at the first glance so considerable that we can scarcely understand how all this multiplicity failed to hinder the regularity of the pope's enterprises.

But, if we note the pecuniary situation of the different employés, and not merely their title, we soon find that there was very great inequality between them. Those who received ten florins a month were evidently above those who took only two. The former were real head-architects; the others were simple overseers, foremen, or accountants." He proceeds to show that nearly all the artists recorded in the account-rolls are North Italians, or even Germans; scarcely any were Romans, or from Roman territory in the wider sense. He then continues : "At San Marco, and probably also at the Vatican and at St. Peter's, the following system was employed. The work in gross was undertaken under a separate agreement with a company of contractors and architects; the secondary work was done sometimes by the task, sometimes by the day [the wages ranged from 18 *Bolognesi* for the best master-masons, to 4 for the lowest labourers]. The orders for payment are generally collective; but it does not seem that the workmen were divided into squads, as Filareto supposed. In fact, the number comprised in the same order varies almost with every payment. Take, for instance, the payments made to the German master Giovanni di Pietro; once, beyond his own wages, he draws those of four labourers; another time, the wages of eleven ' fellow-wallers and stone-cutters,' and of twenty-two labourers. This last mention shows that the masons were not even always separated from the stone-cutters."[1]

Worldly princes followed this same course, in proportion as their revenues and their circumstances permitted; the Field of the Cloth of Gold was a natural sequel to this Renaissance display in Rome and under the richer

[1] Something like this seems to emerge from the Bodmin accounts; at least two different " fellowships " are mentioned, but their membership seems to vary. (See Appendix 11.) It looks as though the smaller men worked, on a precarious tenure, under the others; and it may go some way to support my explanation of unsigned stones (chap. viii). For farther notice of the advance of these popes towards modern Gross-Industrie, see Müntz, 1878, pp. 84, n. 3 and 104.

despots of Italy. At the moment when Paul II was building his magnificent palaces, in 1468, Charles the Bold celebrated his wedding at Bruges. One hundred and thirty-seven painters and carvers were employed . . . "They were called in from Tournai, Brussels, and Antwerp, from Hainault, from Cambrai and Arras, Valenciennes and Douai, Louvain and Ypres. As Hugo van der Goes was of the number, mingled among the rest without distinction, we cannot believe that they were mere daubers."[1] Their work for this one festivity totalled at least 983 days. Jacques Daret, "maistre peintre," received 24 *sols* a day ; the lowest pay was 5½ and the average was 12 *sols*, 1½ *deniers*. Special account is taken of the expenses of an artist who spent six days going and coming and "riding round to Ghent and Audenarde and other good towns, to fetch in all the best workmen of the country, both painters and others."[2] All this was only the logical consequence of the pressgang exercised by medieval princes here and there from early times ; but the fact that Gross-Industrie was now growing so much more frequent implied a real social change. And, as Sombart notices, it began first with the popes, masters of vast wealth from the taxation of Christendom, and with the despotic princes of Italy and Flanders, who again had specially rich sources of taxation. Thence it spread to France and Spain ; only later did it reach England.[3] Moreover, it was very naturally associated with the recrudescence of slavery in the later Middle Ages. In Italy, that system had never died out altogether ; it revived very much with the growth of commerce and luxury ; there were slaves at Rome, real slaves in the Carolina plantation sense, until almost modern times. In 1310, a systematic raid is

[1] A. Michiels, *Hist. de la peinture flamande et hollandaise*, vol. ii, p. 260. A very interesting account of Prof. Cartellieri's fuller and more recent studies on this subject in *The Times Lit. Sup.*, February 1, 1923, p. 69.

[2] Ibid., 417.

[3] *L.K.*, pp. 78–91.

recorded to have brought 12,000 slaves into the Italian market ; in 1355, another raid brought 7,000. However we may discount medieval figures, this is quite characteristic of that commercialization of society which was one factor in the Renaissance. Sombart specifies the slave-traders in chronological order ; the commerce began first with Jews, then the Venetians took it up, then the Genoese, then the Portuguese ; last came the French and the English.[1] In most European countries, the ancient Roman slave had gradually become a medieval serf, and the serf was becoming a free man ; the Italian Renaissance harked back here, as elsewhere, to the traditions of Pagan Rome.[2]

---

[1] *L.K.*, p. 148.

[2] See an article on this subject in *The Review of the Churches* for July 1927, and de Gourmont, *l.c.*, p. 147 : " The Roman popes made Rome into the twin capital of Christendom and of Paganism."

CHAPTER XXIV

RENAISSANCE AND CONSTRUCTION.—(2)

SO much for the extent to which the Renaissance brought us on to Gross-Industrie through the contract system. But, as Sombart points out, this is not all; it brought us onward also to modern methods of standardization. The movement in this direction was inevitable; architecture and its ancillary arts could not become a Gross-Industrie without some considerable advance in the standardization of materials.

Some things, of course, were standardized in very early times. Here, again, war provided a stimulus. A "sheaf" of arrows seems to have meant something definite from the first time we find the word mentioned; and Sombart traces military standardization down to its final perfection under Louis XIV. In the building arts, nails were very early standardized, to some extent at least. The still surviving phrase "tenpenny nail" marks a time when nails of the largest size ran at tenpence per hundred. Into the art (we may call it) of writing, the Universities introduced definite standardization; a *pecia* contained 16 columns, each consisting of 62 lines, with 32 letters to the line.[1] Two *peciae* made a *quaternio*, from which we get *quire*, the French *cahier*, and the well-known poem of "The King's Quair." This standardization may be traced in a rudimentary form from about 1300; in the fifteenth century it was so definite that it was incorporated in the University

---

[1] Wattenbach, *Schriftwesen im M.A.*, Leipzig, 1896, p. 185; cf. H. Rashdall. *Univs. of Europe*, I, 191 ff., 415 ff.

statues of Bologna and Padua.[1] This, of course, must not be taken too literally in practice; here as with all medieval statutes and medieval measures, we must allow for considerable variations; yet the standardization was so much of a reality that Savigny is able to quote a MS. of the late thirteenth or early fourteenth century in which the whole book is transformed—it may be said also, deformed—by the scribe's exact reckoning of his *peciae*. "Each part consists of 24 *peciae*, so that the whole runs to 48; and in fact this is noted at the beginning and end: 'here begins' (or 'ends') 'the 1st *pecia* of the 1st part,' and so on. For most of these *peciae* he does in fact take half a *quaternus*, or four pages; but, since the *pecia* mostly comes to an end before these four pages are filled, he leaves the rest blank; indeed, more than once he leaves a whole blank leaf, which is then cut away." The universities did much also to standardize book prices, both new and second-hand.

But it was a combination of military requirements and of luxury that produced one of the earliest instances of standardization in architecture, and probably the most striking instance until we come to these popes of the full Renaissance.

Sombart is probably right in picking out Avignon as the first " modern " princely court, the definite predecessor of the Milanese court, or of Fontainebleau under Francis I.[2] If the visitor will take a tape-measure with him to that enormous fortress-palace of Avignon, built almost entirely within about twenty-two years (1336–1358), he will find that every stone within his reach, on the wall-surface, is of exactly the same thickness. The official curator of the building has assured me that this

---

[1] F. C. v. Savigny, *Gesch. d. röm. Rechts im M.A.*, 2nd ed., vol. iii, pp. 580 ff. In Peterhouse Library, several fifteenth century MSS. have the scribal prices noted at the end; calculation shows that there was a recognized rate of so much per word or per letter.

[2] Compare the details given by G. Mollat, *Les Papes d'Avignon*, 1st ed., p. 348.

rule has scarcely any exception throughout that mountain of masonry. Many hundreds of workmen, therefore, were employed during these twenty-two years in cutting these innumerable stones to one exact standard; only thus could the layers have laid at double rate, and the popes have satisfied their feverish haste to finish the building. It must have been almost as great an innovation, in its way, as when Louis XIV set his army of builders to work on day and night shifts, so that there was no moment of repose, at his palace of Versailles.[1] Later in the same century, we get similar evidence, though naturally on a smaller scale, from Troyes Cathedral. The masons were ordered to supply fifty stones of three feet in length, a hundred of two-and-a-half, and fifty of two feet; the whole two hundred to have a uniform height and breadth of one foot.[2] A century later, there was evidently still more standardization at Bordeaux. There were ordinarily three classes of stones: (1) *queyrons*, *doublerons* or *demi-pierres*, measuring $1 \times 1 \times 1$ foot; (2) *pierres*, 2 feet by 1 foot, and (3) *grandes-pierres* of irregular dimensions.[3] The first two classes were bought at a recognized market price per hundred or per thousand.

And, earlier than this, we find even sculpture being sold by the foot. In 1447, the Hotel de Ville of Béthune was burned down, and the municipality set themselves to replace it by a structure worthy of their civic prosperity. They commissioned a painter to make " two portraitures or devices " of the building, and paid him £5 for " the labour and subtilty therein expended." They chose the design which seemed most suitable; and then, " shortly afterwards, the mason-work of the building was adjudged to Jehan Wiot, mason and carver

---

[1] *L.K.*, p. 115.

[2] Quicherat, II, 198.

[3] Brutails, p. 72; cf. 59, 69–71, 88 ff. Nails were still more definitely standardized; ibid., p. 91. The Xanten, Eton, Bodmin and Adderbury accounts seem to imply something like the same standardization in the fifteenth century.

in hard sandstone, for the sum of £693, while Amand
Millon demanded £198 for the carpentry-work. Wiot,
under cross-examination by the master of the works [i.e.
the business representative of the municipality, like the
operarius of St.-Gilles], declared that, apart from ordinary
wall-stones, he would need for the lower courses xx feet
of soeulles, listeaux, planques and steps for winding
stairs, at 18*d*. the foot.[1] For the encaulements, he said,
xxiii white stones will be needed, parpains of 2½ feet and
3 feet, from the Bouvignies quarry, at 2*s*. 6*d*. ; while the
xiii white stones, also called parpains, which have been
furnished by Jehan Pinchon, master-mason to my lord
Duke of Burgundy at his castle of Hesdin, will serve for
the borderings of white stone, for the pavillons and for
the boss-work. The five tabernacles at the angles, with
mouldings or leaf-work, whereon the arms of several
lords will be carved, and the pinnacles surmounting their
canopies will need white stone, freestone of Lille [*franques
pierres de Lille*] ; four, at £4, will suffice for one tabernacle. Note also that each tabernacle, canopy included,
will cost £18."

It was natural that this standardization of art should
begin in this most highly-commercialized corner of
Europe, where literature also was organized into a trade
as it was organized nowhere else. But, a few generations
later, we find even England estimating her statuary by
the foot-rule. Here is an extract from the estimate of
about 1515 for King's College Chapel :

" Two images of kings at the west door in two tabernacles made for the same, either of 8 feet high. Four at
the south and north doors of the said church, either of
6 foot high ; and 48 Images within the said church,
every of them of three foot high. Amounting in all to
172 foot, at 5*s*. the foot, esteemed in workmanship,

---

[1] There must be an error here ; probably the MS. has XXc—i.e. 2,000,
which at 18*d*. the foot would cost £150. So also with the XXIII and
XIII directly after. I am obliged to leave several words untranslated ;
but this does not affect the document as an illustration of method.

which amounteth unto £43. Forty ton of Yorkshire
stone is esteemed to be sufficient for all the said Images.
At 6 shillings 8d. the ton, £13 6s. 8d." [1]
About the same time, we find a farther standardization
of materials. Glass was imported in standard quantities
from Normandy and Rhineland; it was reckoned, as
arrows were, by the sheaf.[2] And artist glaziers undertook, not only at King's but elsewhere, to produce
painted windows at so much per foot. In 1477–8, tiles
were standardized in England by Act of Parliament;
there are exact specifications for all sorts of tiles, with
heavy fines for contravention.[3]

With this same movement, came a similar growth of
taste for symmetry, in contrast with the irregularities
which delight our modern eyes so much in medieval
work. Not but that the Middle Ages themselves had
sought symmetry, and had often been driven by mere
necessity to the inequalities that we love in them. The
great trade-halls of Bruges and Ypres were already far
on the way to modern standardization. Again, French
antiquaries have long emphasized the remarkable growth
of new towns in the south and the centre, especially
during the thirteenth century; towns which may very
commonly be distinguished by their very names, as
Villeneuve, Villefranche, La Bastide.[4] These were often
built upon a plan almost as regular as a Roman camp or
a new American town, and for much the same business

---

[1] Willis and Clark, vol. i, p. 482.

[2] E.g. *Test. Eborac*, vol. iv, Surtees Soc., 1868, p. 334 (1508 A.D.); the
York Fabric Rolls supply similar evidence. The movement may be
traced in every industry; at York, in 1420, the price for chipping bows
was 1s. 4d. per 100; for boring horns, 1s. 3d. per 1,000 (*York Memo.
Book*, Surtees Soc., 1912, vol. i, p. 48).

[3] Statute of 17 Ed. IV, chap. iv. See Appendix 32.

[4] A very interesting summary of these researches, with added matter,
has been printed by Prof. T. F. Tout (*Medieval Town Planning*, Manchester Univ. Press, 1s. 6d.). The French articles may be found in
Annales archéologiques, vol. vi, pp. 71 ff. and 302 ff.; xi, 335 ff.; xii,
24 ff.; xiv, 361 ff.

reasons. The business then was military; here, again, it was war that stimulated men to something more elaborately mechanical, and therefore more standardized, than the village or the town had ever become so long as it had been left to automatic development. And here, again, luxury worked strongly for the same subordination of individual choice to a regularized collective plan. The utility of fortification and the architectural taste of the princely patron pointed in one and the same direction; both required greater and more uniform masses of masonry. Before Charles V had swept away the thousand pleasing irregularities of what may be called a great abbey-village at Ghent, in favour of half a dozen uniform smooth bastions, popes had begun to do much the same for their own city. " Early in the fifteenth century the modern spirit, so methodical in all things and so fond of straight lines, began to manifest itself in the cutting of spacious streets through the ruins and rambling habitations of the city. By a bull dated March 30, 1425, Martin V re-established the office of the commissioners of streets (magistri viarum). [Eugenius IV, Nicholas V, Paul II, Sixtus IV, and Alexander VI followed the same policy.] It cannot be denied that these improvements in the material aspect and welfare of the city involved great losses on the archæological and historical side. . . . Follow Poggio Braccolini in his ride through the city in 1447, the year of the election of Nicholas V. Beginning with the Capitol, Poggio describes the southern platform of the hill, where the Caffarelli palace now stands, as covered with the colossal remains of the temple of Jupiter; but a few decades later columns, capitals, and frieze had disappeared so completely that archæologists since then have found serious difficulty in determining which of the two summits of the hill was occupied by the Capitolium and which by the Citadel."[1]

Finally, even ordinary noblemen, when they were rich or extravagant enough, followed the example of their

[1] Lanciani, *l.c.*, p. 204.

betters. A wave of semi-modern standardization swept over the French castles; where the baron could not afford to pull down and rebuild altogether, he did his

THE CASTLE OF BURY (LOIR-ET-CHER)

best to reduce it to the same sort of regularity which it pleased the popes to impose upon the Roman streets. Viollet-le-Duc, in one of his inimitable illustrative sketches, has shown how this process was applied to the château of Bury. The great towers were gutted from top to bottom, and then fitted with a uniform set of windows for domestic convenience. True, these are far more beautiful than the modern sash window usually is ; but the slippery slope is evident ; and we may see how far the material requirements of the Renaissance, the demands of fortification or of growing comfort or of wider industry and commerce and culture, impelled men to constructions which threw into the shade, even when they did not directly involve the destruction of, much that our present generation would most have prized in the art of earlier centuries.

This, and a good deal more if this be not enough, may be urged in answer to Mâle's plea that Protestantism, not Renaissance, killed Gothic art. For the Renaissance was an earlier, a deeper and a wider movement than Protestantism ; in one not unreal sense, it was the mother of Protestantism. It was a complex current fed by many side-streams that tended all in the same direction ; indeed, a current so strong that it swept nearly all the minor currents of its time into that direction. Everything, in the sixteenth century, thus conspired to one general end, the making of a new world. And, of this general revolution, English Protestantism was in many ways among the most conservative currents. Elizabethan and Jacobean domestic architecture remained still Gothic in its general principles. Scarcely any new churches were built, indeed, because the old had long been there, and were still preserved at least as carefully as in any other land, more carefully than in most. Yet, even so, a certain amount of new work was built in the true Gothic spirit. The construction of Bath Abbey Church was continued after the medieval design all through Elizabeth's reign ; and the whole was consecrated under James I. John Williams, Bishop of Lincoln, built a real Gothic library at St. John's College, Cambridge, in 1624;

and the great entrance-hall of Christ Church, Oxford, was even later. Yet all this time, and through succeeding generations, Continental orthodox authorities were destroying Gothic work at a rate which was scarcely limited except by the limits of their purse. The Abbey of Cîteaux, mother of the whole Cistercian Order, would have been entirely rebuilt in the style in which one great existing wing was built, if only the Revolution had not come and put an end to farther vandalism. To realize the devastation wrought thus in the French monasteries, we must look through the splendid collection of bird's-eye views of all the abbeys of the congregation of St.-Maur, made about 1690 and published in 1871 by M. Peigné-Delacourt under the title of *Monasticon Gallicanum*. The churches, it is true, had in most cases been spared ; but, of the rest of the abbey buildings, more than half had been rebuilt in some more modern barrack-style. In South Germany and Austria, even more destruction had been wrought. At the same moment at which the Bishop of Lincoln was building St. John's College library, the monks of the great abbey of Admont rebuilt their whole monastery with the exception of the precinct wall, which, as an outlying feature devoted to mere utility, was suffered to partly retain its ancient medieval character. The contemporary engraving of this building, and of the tomb of the saintly founder, substituted at the same time for the old Gothic tomb, are, after all, entirely in keeping with other examples more easily accessible and far too numerous for rehearsal here. I need only instance the whole of the great abbey buildings at St. Gallen, or the orthodox ornamentation applied to the choir arches at Chartres Cathedral and at St.-Maclou-de-Rouen. And this same contrast may be traced down to the present day.[1] Modern French Gothic churches are, almost without exception, inferior to those built at the same date in England.

[1] This is clearly brought out in Montalembert's monograph on " Vandalism and Catholicism in Art " (*Œuvres*, vol. vi, 1861). See Appendix 33.

Their stained glass is scarcely ever tolerable, and generally of a vileness beyond all description. Their furniture, and especially the machine-made imagery turned out from the shops round St.-Sulpice at Paris, has become a byword even among the orthodox. One architect of real talent, a man far beyond his time, Pugin, was mainly converted to Roman Catholicism by his dislike of the current Protestant architecture of the early nineteenth century; but, once within the fold, he was accustomed to confess bitter disappointment.[1] The new Cathedral at Westminster, with all its striking qualities, does not pretend to be Gothic; indeed, the absence of any such pretence is among its most striking qualities. It is difficult to understand how anyone familiar with both English and Continental buildings can, after carefully weighing all the evidence, seriously contend that Protestantism was the true destroyer of Gothic art.

[1] See Appendix 34.

CHAPTER XXV

CONCLUSION

IT seems impossible, in face of the facts, to believe in a past age in which a large body of men worked as religious artists (in the full modern sense of both terms, *art* and *religion*) upon a series of monuments which succeeding ages have been able only to destroy or to caricature. The vast majority of masons either did not possess, or had no opportunity of developing, more artistic sense than that of the modern skilled mechanic. A small minority were not only stone-dressers but also stone-carvers ; yet these were probably no more numerous, in proportion to population, than the exhibitors at our art galleries of to-day. Moreover, even of this minority only a small fraction showed real originality. " The artists of the fifteenth century imitated with almost the same docility as those of the twelfth. Imitation is still the great law of [medieval] art. . . . There were a few artists, at the end of the fourteenth century and during the fifteenth, who were able to invent. . . . But the illumination of service-books was as much an industry as an art. The head of the workshop alone was a real artist ; he alone took the liberty of making discreet innovations."[1] Those words might as truly have been written about stone-carving as about illumination. Again, the extent to which glass-painters copied each other and repeated themselves has long been recognized. " Moreover, it is a popular fallacy that the medieval glass-painter was a sentimentalist, a man of high ideals, who worked chiefly for the love of God's Church and its adornment, and to that end was content to labour

[1] Mâle, II, 71 ; cf. Cennini, introd., pp. 16, 18.

479

for very small wages. In reality this was far from being the case."[1]

We are apt to forget sometimes that the great period of Gothic art in England, from the Conquest to the Reformation, covers four centuries and a half, or a considerably longer period than that which divides the Reformation from the present day. We are surveying, therefore, the aggregate results of fifteen generations of medieval work; or rather, we survey what time has spared from those four hundred and fifty years. In England, where so many monasteries lived on as cathedrals, and the parish churches have been comparatively respected, we have still perhaps a quarter of what was standing in 1530, especially if we count the fragments; for instance, a single bay of a cloister often enables us to judge of the rest. In France and in Italy, a larger proportion of medieval work has perished, and more, perhaps, by rebuilding than by revolution. If so much has survived anywhere, this is due mainly to a peculiar product of modern civilization, the antiquarian sense. It would scarcely be an exaggeration to say that the Gothic work of the thirteenth century has seldom found such a terrible enemy as it had in the Gothic builders of the later Middle Ages. Medieval art, like the French Revolution, " devoured its own children."

Let us, therefore, temper our regrets, though regrets there must always be. Something has certainly been lost, partly or wholly, of those factors which made for the greatness of medieval painting and sculpture. There was in those days a sense of unity in purpose, and a patriarchal simplicity of intercourse between man and man, which we must do what we can to recapture. But those who feel this most strongly seem least able to tell us how it is to be achieved. Much of what charms us in the past is due to the simplicity of comparative inexperience, the naturally childlike mind. But it would

---

[1] J. D. le Couteur, *English Medieval Painted Glass*, S.P.C.K., 1926, p. 18, cf. L. F. Salzman, *Med. Eng. Industries*, Oxford, 1923, p. 309.

seem almost a contradiction in terms to aim consciously at simple inexperience; and, in fact, those who lash their flanks to be childlike are too often merely childish. Nor does the gild system seem a real remedy, unless we are content to take it with all its apparently inseparable limitations. A socialist society could doubtless suppress all really bad art but only at the expense of a great deal that is best. There are certain sides of the art of a man like Jean-François Millet which a medieval carver would never have been fully free to develop except in caricature.

Therefore, while repudiating pusillanimous content with things as they are, and while refusing to believe that whatever exists is therefore right, must we not yet accept a great deal of what we deplore, for the present at least, as an almost inevitable consequence of changes which we cannot reverse? Changes, moreover, which, after weighing both sides carefully, we would no more wish to reverse than we wish to go back to the nursery? One mere schoolboy experience struck to me a clear note of warning which constantly sounds again amid speculations in social history. Our village furniture-dealer in Essex, after selling a fine rapier with bullion-gold tassels to an older schoolfellow, and precious fragments of fifteenth-century glass to me from the Bishop of London's palace at Much Hadham, pressed upon us a pair of leather breeches, the last that had ever been seen in the village; a garment which, to his certain knowledge, had been worn for forty consecutive years by a labourer not very long deceased. The leather was almost as stiff as tin; it might have lasted several lives longer, as it had doubtless lasted several before; but it was a more curious thing to have seen and handled, and to ponder upon at a distance, than to possess. There were volumes of patriarchal poetry in that relic; but who would go back into it? Who can seriously weigh the beautiful thatched cottage, when, as so often, it is insanitary and indecent within, against even the most hideous of those

I I

buildings which are helping the modern labourer to live under less degrading conditions ?

For the conditions are less degrading on the whole, even in the towns. Durkheim's *Division du travail social* makes short work of a great deal of nonsense about the noble savage, as compared with his modern descendant. Much as we still need to improve conditions of labour, we must not attempt to go back to the pre-machinery days when every man made for himself whatever he himself wanted. The savage, if he needs a boat, must make it for himself ; if he needs a pair of boots, he must make them. This results not in individual originality, but in its opposite. Take a hundred savages at random ; their separate likes and dislikes resemble each other far more nearly than those of a hundred cotton-operatives, even of those whose daily work is most mechanical. For, during those labour-hours themselves, the modern workman has some time for reflection ; and, when his work is over, he steps out into a world whose variety and whose stimulus differentiates it by a whole horizon from the world of the savage. One will play football, others watch the game, others go to the tavern, or to the public library for a glance at the newspapers ; the hundred Lancashire operatives would show differences of taste quite unknown to the simple savages. Those who complain of modern life as monotonous, and of modern men as lacking in individuality, are superficial observers who mistake one part for the whole. True, we do want to get at the ideal of More's Utopia ; six hours of compulsory breadwork for every man or woman, and not more than six hours for any ; that, if it could be fully carried out, would be enough to get all the world's work done, and would give all men " time to stand and stare." But, while we keep this in view, we must not allow any natural impatience to make us unjust towards certain real lines of past progress, or to stampede us into specious side-avenues which history shows to be blind alleys.

So long as we believe man to be in any sense master

of his destiny, one man's cry of despair is for the rest a call to action. "From that time forward," writes Mâle concerning the early sixteenth century, "the Christian artist had but one resource left : to stand face to face with the Gospel narrative, and to interpret it as he feels it." But where is the harm in this ? Have we not here a change of world-view which, rightly taken, might be fruitful of still higher art ? May we not answer Mâle from Goethe's *Faust* ? "If you don't feel it, with all the pains in the world, you won't get hold of it." Rembrandt thus stood face to face with the Gospel narrative ; he felt it in many cases more vividly than any medieval artist ; and his "Raising of Lazarus," apart from its purely technical excellences, has all the life and the religious feeling of the very best thirteenth century work. For it was one of the few great deficiencies in that art that it neglected not only most of the parables but some of the most striking Gospel scenes, such as : "Suffer ye the little children to come unto me." If true religion inevitably expresses itself in true art ; if that is indeed a universal law which (as we are told) kept Europe straight for a thousand years ; if from a people's churches, with their ornaments, the philosophic observer can with certainty infer that people's faith, why then has there not grown up a whole school of art capable of impressing these medievally-neglected things upon the least educated of our populations ? Is there no need nowadays for a Bible of the Poor ? Why are the churches filled, so far as modern art is concerned, with those Stations of the Cross, and those sickly saint-statues from Paris, which are a laughing-stock to all art-lovers even among the orthodox ? There must come a change of heart somewhere ; but where is it to come from ?

It is constantly said that this must come from the artisan ; we must make a more human being of him, and then we shall have better art.

By all means ; and, if I thought this present volume might give legitimate excuse for those who deny or ignore our duty of doing all we can for the artisan, then it should never have been printed. But is not the problem here very much like the problem of War and Peace ? Much can indeed be done by wise measures of detail, but these will be abortive in the long run unless they contribute to a corresponding change of heart.

Let us not forget the fine achievements of the present day at Buckfast Abbey, where the monks have nearly completed a task rare even in the Middle Ages, of building their own church. They have laboured unremittingly for twenty years, never more than six monks, and for most of the time five only ; and now the work is almost done. Similar work, I am told, is being done at one spot in America, without denominational religious inspiration, and without encouragement from those who talk loudest about bringing the world back to medieval art ; work similar, that is, in organization, though there the workmen are co-operative wage-earners. Such instances must, in the nature of the case, be exceptional; yet they may help us much in the way of example. But how are we to bring back the days in which all workmen worked truly, and had joy in their work, or, at least, had content ?

First of all, I should say, by recognizing actual facts. There never was such an age ; it is a great exaggeration to imagine it, and those who seek it in the past are wasting precious time and energy. We cannot say they are doing nothing ; those also did something who sought the philosopher's stone ; but their discoveries would have been far more fruitful if they had built upon a firmer basis of ascertained fact. Nobody would be more astonished and amused than our ancestors of seven centuries ago if they could listen to those who often speak now in their name. From at least the middle of the thirteenth century, when the great Franciscan Berthold of Regensburg was telling his contemporaries from the pulpit what he thought of them, one great theme has been the guile of artisans ; their idleness and their shoddy work, except under the strictest supervision. Indeed, from an earlier date than this. Honorius, so-called of Autun, wrote about 1130: succeeding moralists, such as John Gower and St. Antonino of Florence, repeat the same complaints with wearisome emphasis. We must discount what they tell us, but only as we discount the pessimist of our own day.

That, then, seems the first condition; that we should worship the past only where it truly deserves our worship, and that we should blame the present only in so far as it truly falls short of that past. Therefore let us turn away from the journalists who bawl in our ears that this world is a mere Bedlam of feverish competition and dissatisfaction and unrest. Some of us have lived longer than they, and have seen quite as many varieties of human nature, at home and abroad; yet, the older we grow, the more we become aware of, and the deeper respect we feel for, one great class whom these philippics almost ignore; the multitude of good quiet folk who are neither feverish nor over-competitive. Those revivalist preachers are themselves their own fever and pain. Richly paid, they are struggling for more; popular already, they thirst hydroptically for real fame; and their own disquiet gives them this illusion of world-unrest. Meanwhile, millions live on tranquilly in the conviction that man is as much master of his fate as he ever has been; and those millions are the modern analogue of the medieval artisan whom we wish to multiply. They are to be found in all trades and all professions; sometimes they are even masters of some big business. In so far as the medieval artisan was really content with his work and his wage, these men are his true descendants. There is as much honesty and disinterested work now as in the thirteenth century; and, in so far as it can be truly said that the output per man is smaller now, this is mainly due to modern liberty, and to the hesitations which accompany every change, however good in itself. The workman is under far less strict compulsion now, and has far more competing interests. Yet we would not willingly curtail either his liberty or his interests ; let him be free to choose ; let him have the greatest possible variety of choice, even at the risk of his choosing ill. There are very many, unfortunately, who feel their breadwork as drudgery ; and this we must do our best to mend. But these men have nearly always far shorter work-hours than their forefathers ; and, assuming sense and self-control in the man, who shall say that this alternation of drudgery and leisure does not give as fine opportunities, both for self-culture and for public work, as were ever enjoyed by the medieval artisan ? It is lamentable that there should also be so many whose life is drudgery without leisure ; but of this also there was far more in the Middle Ages than we are commonly told. If we can ever arrive at anything near the Utopian proportion of work-hours to leisure, then the problem will probably solve itself *ambulando*, and human nature will find its own balance between work and play. But neither machinery nor the present social structure is a necessary obstacle to this Utopian solution. The problem, it must be repeated, resembles the problem of War and Peace. A world which really desires peace can get it ; a society which really desires six hours of work for all, and no more for any, could arrange that also without abolition of private property and without reducing us all to a general dead level of life.

We possess already, and let us never for a moment forget it, a mass of honest and disinterested work under the most various forms. It is not always organized and gilded ; let us by all means do whatever seems possible to organize it and to give external encouragement. To some extent it is already a conscious and coherent force in our Garden Cities. Plain living and hard thinking are the foundation of success here ; and, if the modern artist is restless, this is often because he is fighting all the while for a far higher wage and wider reputation than that of the medieval artisan. In those days, he was restricted by circumstances; in the greater freedom of modern society, he has "chances in life" which his predecessor had not; and he gambles on those chances. Yet, again be it said, there are millions who do not thus bow the knee to Baal, and who are none the less helping us forward because they are so inconspicuous among us, and because they accept this world as neither too good nor too bad for human nature's daily food. They work and rest, feed and sleep in reasonable content; they meet other men's eyes frankly and reach out loyally for other hands, trusting in their fellows and trusting in the dear old brown earth; and it is these men's seed that shall inherit the earth. In so far as the medieval craftsman was what William Morris loved to dream of, it is in such men as this that he survives, and will survive for ever and ever, through every change of outward form and every shifting circumstance. The man who knows what he can do, and is honestly doing it, lives on *sub specie aeternitatis.*

In painting alone, how many heroes of this kind there have been in modern times! The old English watercolour school, and men like Jean-François Millet, have lived the artist life in a sense of which any age might be proud. Of J. S. Cotman and David Cox and W. L. Leitch, to name three almost at random, we have records worthy of a biographer like Izaak Walton. But, however many such there may have been or may still be, there are not yet enough; and the equilibrium of the modern world is still in one way inferior to that of the thirteenth century, even when all exaggerations have been cleared away. Then, a man worked longer hours but could often take greater pleasure in the work itself; now, the average artisan has less direct pleasure in his work, and looks more to relaxation or books outside that work. Even here the difference is, I believe, far less than is commonly assumed; the masons and carvers with whom I talked as a boy and whom I question again nowadays, are not discontented with their job, nor do they describe their fellows as discontented. But unquestionably, in the past, there were more masters in a small way; and I must here quote the warning of a wise friend : " It was workman's art, and not sham artists' ' designs ' ' worked out ' by practically slave labour. . . . Then, there was some all-pervading folk-spirit, vitality, story, *a flow of force.* . . . My one little point of anxiety is lest arguers should seize on your facts and say : ' There was no more story, folk-spirit, craft in the Middle Ages than now ; it was always like *this* ; sham Gothic is the same as real Gothic, and Liverpool Cathedral is of the same kind as Lincoln Cathedral. Work was always as hateful as it has now been made with efficiency-movements and stop-watches.' "

I would here venture to amend only two phrases, in the first and in the last sentence. I do not think the words " slave labour " do truly describe the difference between even the commonest modern mason and the men who did the ordinary walling of a medieval church, let alone those who had to standardize the stones for that Avignon palace. And, with regard to modern work, I do think there is another way, a way not merely flattering but essentially true, of looking at the problem.

The nearest modern approach to the folk-spirit of medieval architecture would seem to be in a good many laboratories and machine-shops ; and I believe the analogy to be far closer in this than is generally assumed. I do not speak here only of the great masters of creative work ; men like Pasteur, pursuing his own branch of research " moved, like the even motion of a wheel, by the love that moves the sun and the other stars."[1] and bending daily before the altar in homage to the faith of his birth ; or, on the other hand, Alfred Loisy resolutely facing all the spectres of the past, unmoved by excommunication, intent only upon finding and communicating what he felt to be the truth. Far below these great figures, all through the laboratories and workshops, there are not only thousands who enjoy their

[1] Dante, *Paradiso,* xxxiii, 144.

work, but a select few who take it religiously. They have
the folk-spirit to help them, in this age in which the
very children understand vaguely, and have the keenest
interest in, the working of motor-car and wireless and
aeroplane. Nor are they supported only by this crowd-
interest, as universal as that which existed formerly in
the building arts ; there is also much the same belief,
even to exaggeration, in the value of their industry.
We have nowadays, also, something like the same array
of workers, from the prince or the parson who have
turned aside from their life-job to join the army of inventors, down to Stephenson the peasant and the errand-
boy Edison. There is also much of the same self-sacrifice,
from the heroism of a few who would rather starve than
cease to learn, down to the many who will give up an
extra hour or two for the sake of finishing the job in a
better way ; a sacrifice that is not felt, since in fruitful
labour there is something like the absorbing excitement
of the chase. And, among many who neither consciously
formulate it in their own minds, nor have tongue to talk
of it to others, there is the same uplifting conviction
that this is, in some real sense, a great and sacred work ;
that, since each fresh step reveals so much, and has such
power to rivet the attention, therefore the way itself
must be divine ; that here is one of the many fruitful
paths in this labyrinthine world ; one of those roads
which, however they may twist and turn, lead surely
upwards to the City of God. That feeling is present
even in those who would express it in very different
words ; and a melancholy Jaques among the medieval
masons might well have fathered Mr. Bertrand Russell's
words concerning Pure Mathematics. " Remote from
human passions, remote even from the pitiful facts of
nature, the generations have gradually created an ordered
cosmos, where pure thought can dwell as in its natural
home, and where one, at least, of our nobler impulses
can escape from the dreary exile of the actual world."
At bottom, this is curiously like the answer of St. Catharine

of Siena to those who wondered how she could keep her perpetual serenity amid the drudgery of uncongenial household duties : " I make a little corner of my heart in which I can live with Christ."

Very similar is the artist's problem ; he cannot banish machinery ; he must strive to rise superior to it ; so to use it as not abusing it. There is hope for this and future generations in Mr. Kipling's Scottish engineer.[1]

" That minds me of our Viscount loon—Sir Kenneth's kin—the chap
Wi' Russia leather tennis-shoon an' spar-decked yachtin' cap.
I showed him round last week, o'er all—and at the last says he :
' Mister M'Andrews, don't you think steam spoils romance at sea ? '
Damned ijjit ! I'd been doon that morn to see what ailed The Throws,
Manholin', on my back—The cranks three inches off my nose.
Romance ! Those first-class passengers they like it very well,
Printed an' bound in little books ; but why don't poets tell ?
I'm sick of all their quirks an' turns—the loves an' doves they dream.
Lord, send a man like Robbie Burns to sing the Song o' Steam ! . . .
Uplift am I ? When first in store the new-made beasties stood,
Were Ye cast down that breathed the Word declarin' all things good ?
Not so ! O' that world-liftin' joy no after-fall could vex,
Ye've left a glimmer still to cheer the Man—the Arrtifex !
That holds, in spite o' knock and scale, o' friction, waste an' slip,
An' by that light—now, mark my word—we'll build the Perfect Ship.
I'll never last to judge her lines or take her curve—not I.
But I ha' lived an' I ha' worked. ' Be thanks to Thee, Most High ! ' "

This, then, is what we find in the modern world, and must take account of. We cannot keep machinery out, even if we would ; is it not our real task to humanize it ? An acute German observer thinks that in Britain we do not go the right way to work here : " we choose to ignore production by machinery ; we deny the possibility of any considerable artistic worth to anything not done by hand ; we refuse division of labour."[2] Is it not possible that these problems may finally be worked out better in America than with us ? Will not a new art grow there from a frankly practical stem ? For us, much

[1] *Seven Seas*, p. 43, " McAndrews's Hymn."
[2] *The Athenæum*, September 21, 1912, p. 317.

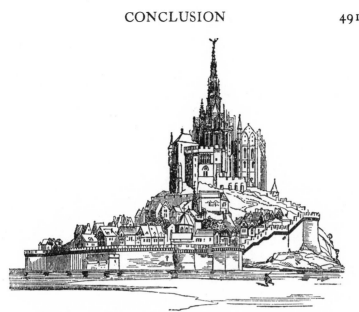

MONT ST.-MICHEL.

of the charm of the Gothic building lies in its natural and obvious adaptation to the practical requirements of its day. The typical picturesque in architecture is a crag-castle, or the crown of towers round a walled city ; the supreme example that comes first into our mind is the abbey-fortress of Mont St.-Michel, but the towers of Rothenburg on the Tauber are almost equally remarkable. Yet in all these cases it is the fact which shapes the art, not the art which controls the facts ; it is by taking full practical advantage of every ledge and every bit of cliff or slope that the masons have reared those walls and towers over which we linger with unfailing delight. So also, in our own day, if we are to make things as we want them to be, we must begin by taking things as they are.

It is necessary that a large number of modern buildings should be on an enormous scale. Quite apart from megalomania, which enters into this problem as into

ROTHENBURG (BAVARIA).

others, there is an undeniable need of vast structures. Therefore a new architecture of steel and concrete has grown up ; and some men are growing up to the new conceptions implied by this enormous revolution. The late Sir Thomas Jackson, one of those who combined real scholarship with fine artistic taste and wide experience, wrote quite truly : " It is from the demands of utility that the best suggestions for advance in architecture have come in the past, and to them we must look in the future."[1]   Here is robust sense and lofty optimism, in contrast to the reactionary writers whose theories amount in plain language to this, that we must substitute hand-work for machinery, and steadily keep the common people to one particular form of religion, in order that connoisseurs may enjoy the art which, under such hothouse treatment, the multitude will secrete for us. Thoughtful artists value such ideas at their true worth ; and it would be difficult to express their feeling better than it has been recently expressed by one of them, in protest against the

[1] *Times Lit. Sup.*, November 22, 1923, p. 777.

exaggerations of a modern prophet. " Your criticism of modern industrial theory," he writes, " has been magnificent. It has never failed to be destructive. You have destroyed the gods which many a striving craftsman was tempted to worship. Surely that is sufficient for one man to accomplish. The creative ideas must come from the craftsmen themselves. If, fearless, they will go on producing the best they know, they will soon make a new economic system. And perhaps then they will enjoy your appreciation of their beautiful economy. But no craftsman cares a rap when you tell him that he ought not to work in the place he has selected as being the best suited for his work, or that people ought to buy ugly things merely because they are made in their own village. Show the craftsman that he is not as free as he thinks he is, and you will earn his eternal gratitude."

Let us apply this to America and the sky-scrapers and the necessary development of modern architecture. The craftsman here will not be free ; but free he never really was, at any time of really living and great art. The mass of craftsmen will be doing monotonous work, yet not necessary servile, any more than that of the medieval quarryman or the hard-hewer. A minority will be using their brains a good deal, in the adjustment of girders and the laying of concrete. A much smaller minority, again, will be doing higher supervision ; and one or two, at the top, will be real creators, real locomotives dragging the whole huge train along. What is there to be afraid of here, and why should not America succeed ?

The present volume has grown out of a course of American lectures, and is necessarily coloured by an experience, however brief and partial, of that country. It is strictly relevant, therefore, that I should repeat here, in this connexion, something of what was said there in a smaller company before whom even a semi-formal speech easily degenerated into a frank confession of the feelings of the moment, feelings called forth by that very visit and those experiences.

Men had told me that I should find the country and the people widely different from my own. I was struck, on the contrary, with the essential similarity of both, at least as far west as Ohio, and as far south as Baltimore, though this, of course, is not very far. And, everywhere, I was haunted by those lines of George Herbert :—

> Religion stands on tip-toe in our land,
> Ready to pass to the American strand.

Here is a land that was colonized from ours at the very time when Protestantism had justest causes of protest ; a land where the basis of law is still English common-law ; and in which, as in our own country, freedom has broadened down from precedent to precedent in spite of lapses and infidelities. Here are vast tracts, and a teeming population, in which experiments once tried in Europe can be tried again on a greater scale, and of which we may also say in art what Samuel Daniel, three centuries ago, said concerning the almost Roman universality which this new continent might give to the English tongue :—

> " And who, in time, knows whither we may vent
>   The treasure of our tongue ?   To what strange shores
> This gain of our best glory shall be sent
>   To enrich unknowing nations with our stores ?
> What worlds in th' yet unformed Occident
>   May come refin'd with the accents that are ours ?
>
> Or who can tell for what great work in hand
>   The greatness of our style is now ordained ?
> What powers it shall bring in, what spirits command ?
>   What thoughts let out, what humours keep restrained ?
> What mischief it may powerfully withstand ?
>   And what fair ends may thereby be attained ? "

The fact that there is much materialism in a country does not debar it from final excellence in art or in literature. I have already expressed my conviction that the art of arts is the conduct of life ; of our own lives first, and then of the lives which depend in any way upon us ;

and here, in spite of all that can be said on the other side, my belief is that America, as a whole, will stand comparison with any existing society, and must be ranked higher than some of the vaunted societies of the past. It is easy to exaggerate the moral and artistic disadvantages of money-getting. There is profound truth in Dr. Johnson's remark that a man is seldom more innocently employed than when he is making money, so long as we import no prejudices of our own into Johnson's plain words, but take them in their literal sense, and analyse straightforwardly the lesson they convey. In the light of sober experience, we have reason to distrust the persons or the peoples which boast that they are not money-getters. They are generally of that sort which makes a merit of carelessness and lack of foresight, and which tries to console itself for failure by despising the grapes that hang out of reach. Let a man first prove that he can make money, and then show his superiority to the mere money-getter by superior employment of that wealth and of his time. Some at least of the most artistic populations in history, for example, the Athenians and the Florentines, began as money-getters. On the other hand, medieval Rome was dead to healthy commerce and handiwork; it contained one of the most thriftless hand-to-mouth populations in Europe, and it produced practically no art beyond that of the few mosaic-workers who preyed on the great works of their ancestors. The popes had to import their artists from money-making districts. Britain, the nation of shopkeepers, has produced perhaps the finest body of poetry in the world. Art and literature, therefore, have nothing to fear in the long run from steel and steam and electricity; at the worst, we have only to wait till these things have found their equilibrium, as the Middle Ages had to ripen into that equilibrium of the thirteenth century.

But, however these things may be, one thing seems more and more certain; in our struggle for a better world, we cannot afford to neglect any good, whether in past history or in present society. And here there is no reason why the Protestant, in the truest and broadest sense of that word, should not join hands with Catholicity in its truest and broadest sense. Indeed, if we avoid artificial limitations of what ought to be sufficiently plain words, and artificial party exclusiveness, there is no real opposition between the two terms or the two ideas. *Protestant Catholic* is no more of a contradiction in terms than *Roman Catholic*, that time-honoured medieval phrase which is somewhat out of favour with the modern Roman Church. In proportion as a man clings to what seems Catholic (that is, universal) truth, he is bound to repudiate all that seems inconsistent with, or contradictory of, such universal truth. St. Paul and St. Peter were Protestants against idolatry ; St. Paul was a Protestant against the exclusive sectarian view of circumcision ; in far more recent times, some of the greatest of all Roman Catholics have protested most emphatically against religious abuses which were also among those most stoutly repudiated by our Reformers. And the one hope for the unity of Christendom—we may go farther, and say, for the harmony of all honest minds—lies in the acceptance of the widest field that is common to the largest number of thinking people. Indeed, I have recently heard something very like this, in public, from the lips of a prominent and earnest Roman Catholic ; corporate union seemed to him, at least for the present, outside of practical politics.

In all this discussion, we are in danger of losing sight of Walter Savage Landor's true order of things : " Nature I loved, and, next to nature, art." Or, as it has been put less formally in our own day : " Verses are made by fools like me, but only God can make a tree." The art of arts, let it be said again, is the art of life ; the accumulation and the harmony of all impressions and all human activities. In the Middle Ages, the men who corresponded to our present academics and critics, the people who wrote in Latin, were convinced, almost to a man, of the

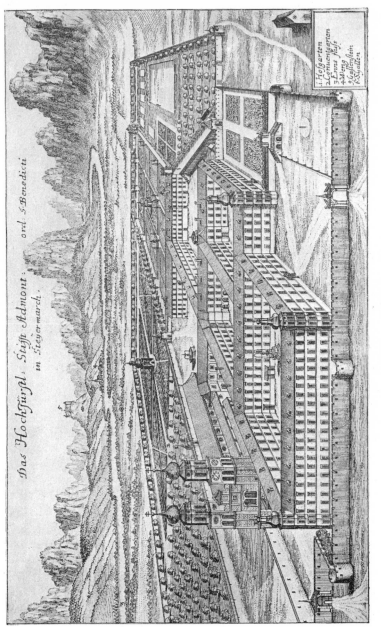

Das Hochfürstl. Stift Admont, ord. S. Benedicti in Steyermarck.

1. Hofgarten
2. Convent garten
3. Enns Fluß
4. Werg
5. Gallenstein
6. Scholen

THE ABBEY OF ADMONT, STYRIA.

497]

hopeless and debasing inferiority of their own age to classical antiquity. They repeated this with an iteration that is wearisome to the modern reader. Meanwhile the medieval artisan, doing his own work as best he could, labouring in rivalry with his brethren, but also in harmony with them, and, as time went on and the work became greater and more complicated, labouring by the hundred in obedience to one single master—the artisan, I say, silently achieved what the scholastic philosopher knew to be impossible, and evolved something far greater, in its own way, than Greece or Rome had ever known. That was, in the main, the achievement of the common man, with whom it had been a toss-up whether he ploughed the land and made your bread, or stitched the leather and made your shoes, or made you these cathedrals. It was a product not of any part of the age alone, but of the whole age, of all humanity at that time ; it reflects the general tone of society. We see it even in the difference between the English and the French village churches. Here at home we have our elms, our meadow sloping down to the quiet brook, and the church most natural to those surroundings. There, in France, we have the sunburnt coteaux ; much of the field-work is in the more delicate task of vine-dressers, working among the fragile clear-cut tendrils and leaves, as distinguished from the simplicity or the old-world monotony of the plough and the cornfield.[1] Most French churches, therefore, ran higher

---

[1] Brutails notes how, at Bordeaux, when an artisan was settled enough to possess a house, there was generally a garden and a little bit of vineyard also (p. 44). Let us compare this with the fact that French flamboyant, even in its latest stages, never descended to the shallow platitudes of leaf-ornament which are too common in our Perpendicular. Even as far north as Amiens, "the culture of the vine and the vintage busied as many hands as the harvest" (A. de Calonne, in *Mém. Soc. Ant. Picardie.* 1880, p. 456). There may be some exaggeration here; the facts quoted, though strong, are not conclusive; also, there were far more vines in medieval England than now; *e.g.*, the manor of Trumpington had a vineyard. But, on the whole, the contrast was very great then, as now.

KK

than ours ; they were more costly, and the French sense of sculpture is more delicate. But, whether here or there, as we move among these buildings, we are the dreamers, they the dream. Something as far-off and as tranquil as sunset divides their world from that which we move in ; their dusty work-day has worn onward into evening and faded into afterglow ; the trees stand in arabesques against the sky ; they have " a darkness that we feel is green " ; it is a time of twilight and of dews. All that was once fully-modelled is now cut out and stencilled in flat filigree ; the tree is as beautiful as ever, yet with a very different beauty. In a sense it is conventional and imperfect now ; since we see it in only two dimensions ; and our actual eyes will never grasp its full modelling, for we are travellers passing on before to-morrow. Thus, in the long-drawn vista of the centuries, we see medieval life and art through a glass, darkly ; we may not see it face to face, but it has none the less a reality of its own, and, to many minds, a beauty beyond that of full sunlight ; moreover, highest of all, a mystical beauty. These common sights are capable of evoking the same emotions as the porches of Chartres in the sunlight under a June sky, or its aisles in the twilight, when the jewelled windows stand out as the only realities in all that solemn gloom.

In every religion there are things deeper even than the sacraments ; and those deeper things are common to all true faith. This is not to say that all creeds are the same, but that some essential elements, at least, are common to all. In every country and every age, mystics have arrived at remarkably similar results ; and if either art or nature stirs us to certain thoughts, it is commonly because these existed already in germ, and because the eye, in this case, brings that same stimulus which Sir Thomas Browne ascribes in his own case to music. Side by side with hours in English or Continental churches, I cherish unforgettable memories of open-air Catholic litanies, and open-air Revivalist hymns. Once on the

Upper Rhine, between Rheinfelden and Bâle, and once
on its middle course, near the castle of Altenahr in the
Ahrthal, and again in the Black Forest, I have had the
same experience. A delicious deep summer twilight after
a splendid day; a wayside shrine; and a group of workfolk, dark against the fading sky, led by one voice more
earnest than the rest, almost painful in its tense devotion,
chanting, alternately with the crowd, versicle and response
of a vernacular litany. Again, earlier still, in the
summer evenings of adolescence, driving to Westacre
Church, under the shadow of the priory ruins. The
road turns suddenly down to the ford under a
little steepish slope of hill, waste and barren at the
top, the neglected remnant of a common. There,
up against the sky, in the slanting sunlight, was
always a group of worshippers to whom the church
seemed too narrow; we heard them singing "Hold the
Fort!" or "We shall meet on that beautiful shore."
Here in Norfolk, as there in Rhineland, was an unmistakable reality of tone; rough or metallic voices which
broke the cloying melody of those popular tunes; all the
softening and harmonizing effect of distance. Here, as
there, the voices rose and fell upon the breeze and died
away into the distance; the hour and the open air and
the woodland scenery purged them of all commonplace
everyday associations; they went up like incense; and
when, an hour later, we ourselves were singing our last
hymn in Westacre Church, and the sun had stolen through
the northern windows, to fall upon the white angel-tomb
in the chancel, then in our hearts we all bore that other
open-air music also. For nobody has the monopoly
either of religion or of religious art; nor need we to fear
that either the one or the other is dead. We may get
now, as men got in the past, as much of either as we are
willing to pay the just price for; Baron von Hügel, we
are told, always insisted on that word *cost* in religion. In
the material sense, we may get religion on Isaiah's terms,
without money and without price; but, in the spiritual

sense, every man in every age must work out his own salvation.

And that is why I am steeled against the attempt to put a sectarian ring-fence round Gothic art, with a sectarian turnstile for admittance. The attempt is as absurd in practice as it is in history; for nature laughs at these artificial obstacles. For one man who persuades himself that, because he loves Chartres, therefore he must accept the theological formulæ of the men who built it, there will always be many others who love its self, and perhaps love it more deeply, without the need of such illusion. It is the case of Lovelace's " I could not love thee, dear, so much, loved I not honour more "; it is the case of William Morris, of whom it might be said as truly as of Matthew Arnold that " he was never a Romantic in the bad sense of the word— namely, an artist who will submit to the lie of the soul for the purposes of his art." And it is the same, in different degrees, with thousands more who reverence these buildings, who reverence their builders and all truth in the religion with which these men are connected, yet who thank God daily that they were born in an age in which men are free to be Protestants, or Catholics, or both, or neither. Among those thousands I have the right to count myself. It was Gothic art, sixty years ago, that first kindled in me the love of the Middle Ages. Afternoon service at St. Margaret's, Lynn, where even children might sit in the choir-stalls, and we walked to our places (*horresco referens!*) over two of the most beautiful monumental brasses in the world, and sat there under some of the fairest thirteenth century stonework and fourteenth century wood-carving in England, is an unforgettable recollection. In Westminster Abbey or one of our cathedrals, or sometimes at Mass in France, there is a glow of feeling and a rush of thoughts which warms and illuminates like sunshine. We are wrong if we do not welcome these things; but we are wrong also if we identify them too closely with the Christian religion.

ST. MARGARET'S CHANCEL, LYNN.

They may help us to worship God in spirit and in truth ; but, on the other hand, they may stand between us and God. They were not there in the earliest days ; the best of the primitive Christians did without them.[1] If we care deeply for these things which St. Bernard and St. Francis neglected, it may possibly be because we have higher artistic sensibilities than they, but it certainly is not because we are more religious. The indiscriminate identification of art and a particular religion is no real compliment to either.

And, in one very real sense, it would seem positively unchristian ; it would seem to shut us off from Christian hope. For, if we take even the most eloquent of these lamentations over the past, they do but recall the dignified melancholy of Lucretius—*mortalem vitam mors immortalis ademit*—our mortal art has been swallowed up in immortal death. But this, put into Bible words, is tantamount to a proclamation that the gates of hell have prevailed against medieval art ; and to this the Bible-Christian will answer with St. Paul : " God forbid. . . . Death is swallowed up in victory ! " After Attila's pillage, St. Jerome cried in despair, " When Rome falls, what is left standing ? " But it was then that St. Augustine sat down to write his *City of God*. That brave and inspiring book has two abiding lessons for all time. First, that we have no need to regret the passing of a former civilization, so long as we ourselves have faith and courage enough to save what treasure there is to be saved from among the ruins.

[1] This remains true, even if we take the Catacomb pictures of Rome at the earliest date assigned to them. In perhaps the majority of cases, these are simply pagan motives adopted by the Christians ; again, they do not represent the official teaching of the Church at that time. It is incredible that all the early apologists should have spoken of image-worship as non-existent among Christians, if this repudiation had not been true in fact. For, it must be remembered, they had every temptation to exaggerate in the other direction ; the pagan accusations of atheism could have been refuted in a single sentence if they had been able to say " we do in fact secretly paint Christ and the Virgin Mary and the saints, and say our prayers before them."

And, secondly, that this change should bring us not despair but hope ; the things which have perished beyond recall are those which were doomed to perish ; true, the New Jerusalem must be built with the sword in one hand and the trowel in the other ; yet for those who build in the spirit, and on a spiritual foundation, there can be no final failure. In the material sense, Rome is fallen ; ancient Rome is indeed fallen ; but " there remaineth a Sabbath-rest for the people of God." [1]

[1] Augustine, *De Civ. Dei,* bk. xxii, c. 30.

APPENDIX I.—(Chap. I, p. 16)

ART AND THE BLACK DEATH

THERE are several historic cases—e.g. Siena cathedral and St. Nicholas, Great Yarmouth—where we know for certain that important work was begun, was interrupted by the Black Death, and still survives in its embryonic state. But, apart from these, it is possible that a careful search might reveal others where, from internal evidence alone, we may surmise something similar. There is some-thing very puzzling, for instance, about the church of Evington, just outside Leicester. Two of the windows of the south aisle show a strange mixture of earlier mouldings and details with later tracery-design; here is a figure of the eastern one, from R. and J. A. Buckler's *Analysis of Gothic Architecture*, Vol. I, 1849, p. 25. It seems possible that the

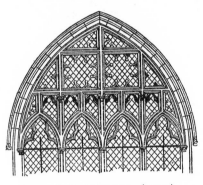

WINDOW AT EVINGTON, (LEICS).

lower half, up to the four main arches, was done at some time between 1290 and 1320, and lay in the mason's lodge awaiting completion whenever the funds should permit, as we know to have been constantly the case. When the building was resumed after the Black Death (and there is much in the church pointing to such a later date), then some comparatively unskilful mason may well have continued the job; he would be almost obliged, of course, to follow the original mouldings; he would very naturally imitate such original details as the open soffit-cusp; but he was quite unequal to designing a system of tracery worthy of those beginnings ; the head of the window is almost ludicrous in its clumsy incoherence and stiffness. The western window shows a similar, though less obvious, contrast between the lower and the upper parts, the detail and the main tracery. Thus the immediate and temporary shock which the Black Death gave to masonry, as to everything else, may well have helped the progress of that easier and cheaper style which had already been invented at Gloucester or in London, or had emerged in a more general way from the drift and nature of things in the early fourteenth century. I cling personally to the theory of origin set forth in my text, in reliance upon the documentary evidence from Gloucester, and the inferential evidence from Bristol. All that we know at present seems reconcilable with the supposition that (1) the style *originated* in the exigencies of the Gloucester work and the natural application of Bristol methods to those exigencies ; and that (2) it was rapidly *assimilated* by other clever masons, and by Yevele in particular. The Bristol eccentricities, which cannot be altogether separated from the peculiar east window of the Lady Chapel and the equally peculiar tomb-recesses in the Berkeley Chapel, might lead naturally to some such work as that of Gloucester. This Bristol work may be studied in the excellent little twopenny volume in *Notes on the Cathedrals* series (Swan, Sonnenschien and Co.), and Yevele's achievements in Lethaby, *Westminster I*, p. 220, and *Westminster II*, pp. 140-2.

APPENDIX 2.—(Chap. II, p. 29)

MONTALEMBERT AND OTHERS

(A) Montalembert's References

Les Moines d'Occident, Bk. XVIII, ch. 5. (Ed. 1882, Vol. VI, pp. 239 ff.)

L ET us take his assertions one by one, and test them by the actual documents.

(1) (p. 241) St. Benedict (writes M.) provided for artists, upon whom he "imposed only one condition, humility." No medieval commentator has yet been alleged who understood St. Benedict's *artifices,* except in the sense of *artisan,* not excluding the ' fine arts," but, as always in the Middle Ages, laying as much stress on ploughman and shoemaker as on painter and sculptor ; or, rather, laying more stress on these plainer *artifices* in proportion as they were more numerous and indispensable. See Dom Martène's *Commentary on the Rule,* s.v. *artes* in Chapter LXVI, and Turrecremata's commentary, which stresses not ornament but utility.

(2) (242) "The teaching of these various arts [architecture, painting, etc.] even formed an essential part of monastic education." The footnote refers us (without page or chapter) to a previous assertion about "the monasteries of Hildesheim." When we have run this down (p. 176) we find it refers to two bishops, St. Bernward, who in his youth learned "versification, logic, painting and carving" at the monastery of Hildesheim, and his successor, St. Godehard, who formed a group of young students very profitable to his diocese for their services "in reading, writing, and painting." The emphasis in both cases is on the unusual energy of these saintly bishops ; and we know from many other sources that at this time (993–1038) Hildesheim was one of the most conspicuous art-centres in Western Europe. It is no detraction from the merit of these two saints to point

out that we have here not the normal monastic education, but a very exceptional episode.

(3) Then follows a list of great abbeys renowned for the arts. Nine are specified; for only five are medieval references given, and in only one of those does the evidence speak of work done by the monks themselves (Hirschau, for which see my discussion of the evidence in Chapter II).

(4) Hence, Montalembert proceeds to quote individual instances of monastic artists, in order to prove that " the majority of monks who were celebrated for their virtues, their learning or their devotion to the liberty of the Church, were equally distinguished by their zeal for art, and often also for their personal talent in carving, painting or architecture. The Rule was broken to permit, or even to command, artist-monks, when their conduct was exemplary, to leave their cloister and travel for the improvement of their talent or the development of their studies." One single example is quoted out of all the five centuries with which Montalembert deals, that of the semilegendary Tuotilo (for whom see above, Chapter IV).

(5) Abbot Ceolfrid of Wearmouth (about A.D. 690) sent " architectos " at the request of the King of the Picts. But Bede, who tells us this, gives no hint that these workmen were monastic.

(6) " Church architecture has everywhere owed its most remarkable advances to monks." This is a rash generalization even for the years before 1150; and no serious writer would maintain it nowadays for the period 1150–1550. Montalembert cites the Cistercians for his thesis, without thinking of their reprobation of all but the most necessary ornaments. The Cistercian puritanism did compel the artist to pay more attention to structure than to ornament; but this effect was accidental; they furthered art in the same sense in which we say that Attila, by making it difficult for energetic and self-respecting folk to live on the mainland, founded the great city of Venice. He cites the Cluniacs, ignoring the fact that early Cistercians condemned Cluniac magnificence of building and furniture as a hindrance, rather than a help, to religion. Finally, he names twenty-one great abbeys from different parts of Europe, without one word of proof that a single stone was laid or carved there by a monk.

(7) England is the country where, at the present day, we can most clearly see how magnificent the medieval monastic buildings were. This, of course, is perfectly true; the Reformation

destroyed less here than was destroyed abroad by rebuildings in the classical taste and by the Revolution.

(8) "When we say that the innumerable monastic churches scattered over the whole face of Europe were built by the monks, this assertion must be taken in its literal sense. They were, in fact, not only the architects but also the masons of their buildings " (etc., etc., as quoted already in Chapter II). For this, the following evidence is given.

(*a*) *Architects.* "We will quote only one example out of a thousand " : Ansteus, Abbot of Metz at the end of the ninth century, is recorded to have possessed " no ignoble skill in architecture." The fact is, that it would not be easy to quote twenty clear instances of monastic architects—perhaps not ten, out of the whole of Europe during the ten centuries of medieval monasticism. Moreover, the context of this Ansteus case seems to imply clearly that his workmen were outsiders.

(*b*) *Without outside help*, as a general rule. Only one instance is given : " This is expressly stated in the life of St. Ethelwold, monk and bishop of Winchester, AA, SS, O.S.B. saec. v. p. 618." M. can scarcely have looked at this passage himself, for it tells how St. E. " *commanded* his brethren frequently to labour *together with the artisans and workmen* "—i.e. the masons or carpenters and the unskilled labourers. Thus, even this " frequent " and partial help of monks themselves appears distinctly as an exception ; if it had been the regular practice, why should St. E. need to command it, and his biographer record it as a noteworthy factor in his government of this monastery ?

(*c*) *Chanting psalms.* A single case again, from Ramsey, where the actual document seems rather to contradict than to support M.'s assertion ; it distinctly relates how, in this rebuilding of the abbey church, " workmen were hired." We have seen (Chapter III) what to think of the injunction of psalm-singing for monastic labour.

(*d*) *Interrupting their work only to go to choir.* Again one single individual is quoted ; a contemporary tells this as an instance of his singular zeal.

(*e*) *They undertook dangerous work.* A single case again, in which it is not distinctly asserted that it was the brethren who did the dangerous work, though they certainly were working on the building at the time.

(*f*) *Ordinary monks were sometimes architects in chief.* A single obscure instance, in which the original Latin does not, in fact, clearly support this assertion.

(*g*) *Abbot Ratger of St. Gall* worked in the quarry at the great columns. This citation is correct.

(*h*) *An abbot himself* escorted certain columns of porphyry from Italy to Belgium. True again.

(*i*) *Herluin, first Abbot of Bec*, worked like a simple labourer. But the chronicler distinctly quotes this as an example of his special humility, and, so far as he helps us either way, implies that Herluin's fellow-workers were not monks. Lanfranc, Herluin's successor, only laid a foundation-stone, and the chronicler there speaks of buildings wrought, not " by the hands," but " at the expense of the poor [cloisterers]."

(*j*) *Abbot Hugh of Selby* did the same as Herluin. Montalembert has misunderstood this ; Hugh helped not to build but to clear the foundations, and was so humble that he grappled with accumulated filth from drains which ordinary workmen would not touch.

(*k*) *Hézelon of Cluny* was called " the mason " from his occupation. I cannot find that the reference to Mabillon supports this ; and I suspect that here, again, we have a second-hand reference or a note misunderstood. Hézelon is reported to " have done more for the construction of the new church than any other man except the Kings of Spain and England " ; but this implies financial, not artistic activity.

(*l*) *Frederick, a monk of noble birth*, shamed a fellow-monk who refused to carry a hod of mortar, by shouldering it himself. Here Montalembert misquotes ; his document does not tell us that the culprit, or the other workmen, were *monks* ; as for Frederick, his act is quoted here again as an instance of humility so striking as to deserve immortality.

(*m*) *When the lay-brother system grew up*, the choir-monks still worked with the lay-brethren. He quotes the Tritheim-Hirschau case as " furnishing the most positive proof in this matter." Tritheim says nothing of the kind ; the reader has seen his actual words in Chapter II, and it is strange that Montalembert could so have misinterpreted them.

(*n*) " *Vast workshops* had been organized [within the monasteries], in which all the other arts were practised." No reference is given. See Chapter III for the very narrow limits within which these words are at all true.

(*o*) *Extraordinary versatility* of these artists. So it was with all medieval artists; they were far more jack-of-all-trades than those of to-day.

(*p*) *St.-Eloi* is instanced, but he was a goldsmith *before* he became monk; and all records, I believe, are silent as to his doing art-work *after* his conversion.

(*q*) *Mannius, Abbot of Evesham.* Here M. is correct.

(*r*) *Foulques, precentor of St.-Hubert.* So also here; but this is the *only* artist whom the chronicler mentions, among a list of monks of that day, whose eminence he records for posterity.

(*s*) *Hermannus Contractus* was skilled in clockwork. Correct.

(*t*) *Abbot Thiemo* was " *architect*, goldsmith, and painter." The word italicized is not in the record, but is supplied by M.'s imagination.

(*u*) (p. 256) *Miniature* is dwelt upon, with a constant assumption that all works found in monastic libraries were written and painted by monks; whereas it is admitted now, practically on all hands, that nearly all miniature-painting in the later Middle Ages was due to hired professionals, even when they lived in the abbey precincts. Montalembert gives a few individual instances, mainly borrowed from the laborious researches of Père Cahier, but not always correctly. He specially brings Cluny forward; yet it is for Cluny that Cahier confesses himself least able to specify individual monastic artists, in spite of the general implication, for what it is worth, in the *Cistercian-Cluniac Dialogue* (see Chapter III).

(*v*) *And wall-painting.* Here M. specifies *St. Gall ;* but without proof that a good deal of the work was not done by hirelings; *Reichenau,* without proof that any of it was done by actual monks; *Wearmouth,* where Bede, though cited in favour of this theory, implies the contrary. *Fontenelle* and *Luxeuil :* here we have correct cases of individual monks painting the walls. Then *St.-Savin,* whose " beautiful frescoes still excite the admiration of artists." For this we are referred to Mérimée's magnificent monograph, but without page-reference; it is only after we have laboured through fifty-six pages that we find Mérimée flatly contradicting Montalembert, and attributing the paintings to artists imported from Greece. M. then cites the *Cluniac Churches ;* these, it is true, were generally painted, but M. gives no evidence that the monks did the work. *Methodius,* an Eastern monk, is known to have painted; here the citation is correct; but Methodius comes outside M.'s subject, " The Monks of the West."

This is the result of a close analysis of the first twenty-one pages. The rest is of the same sort. Here and there we get an indubitable monastic artist; elsewhere M. claims credit for the monks where he can prove no more than that the work was done in or for the monastery (e.g. Benedict Biscop and St. Philibert, p. 260), or even where his documents clearly imply hired workmen (Tegernsee, p. 261). Then, summing up, he appeals to the enormous number of medieval art-works which have survived even the Reformation and the Revolution, as proof positive of "the elegance and perfection to which *the monks* had succeeded in bringing their work" (italics mine). The remaining ten pages of this chapter refer to the monks' contributions to music, and are probably far more correct.

It is not creditable to medieval scholarship that writing of this kind should have passed for two generations as authoritative, and that a book should still be quoted as classical in which the author constantly begs the most important questions, and sometimes slips even into categorically false assertions upon essential points. For I have had occasion to point out equally frequent and serious inaccuracies in equally important chapters of social history, to which Montalembert has given wide currency (*Monastic Schools in the Middle Ages*, pp. 9, 29, and *The Medieval Village*, Appendix 4e). It is a testimonial to the generosity of modern scholars, but far from flattering to their acumen and industry, that this imposing array of inconclusive or inaccurate footnotes should have held their ground for nearly eighty years.

(B) Lefèvre-Pontalis

This author again, though far more scientific than Montalembert, assumes a great deal beyond what his actual documents show. I will take all his cases in order (pp. 28 ff.).

(1) *Adam.* The reference is to a book not in the Cambridge University Library; but if, as the brief notice says, the man was *maître de l'œuvre*, then he was far more probably a mere business director than an architect in the artistic sense.

(2) *Albaldus.* The context implies here that this monk was a supervisor rather than an architect.

(3) *Alquerus.* The context weighs only slightly in the direction of actual artistic work; it is quite possible that the passage speaks of Alquerus as building this monastery only in the sense in which Alan of Walsingham built the Ely octagon.

(4) *Deusdet* does seem really to have been an architect, in the sense of skilled artistic director.

(5) *Gallebertus*, as the text clearly shows, was neither artist nor architect, but business supervisor of the workmen, and collector of funds for the building.

(6) *Geraldus de Latofavo* " built the church" ; but (as Lefèvre-Pontalis himself warns us on p. 5) we can never, in default of farther evidence, take such an expression more literally than in the sentence " Louis XIV built the Palace of Versailles."

(7) *Gerardus*, Abbot of St.-Jouin.   This book again is not in our library ; but the words *diriger la construction* do not carry us farther than supervisory work.

(8) *Giraudus* of St.-Benoît.   Not in library ; here, again, he is only called *maître de l'œuvre*.

(9) *Gislebertus* of St.-Ouen.   So far is Ordericus Vitalis, who is our witness here (Bk. VIII, c. 24, P.L., vol. 188, col. 635), from implying that this monk was an architect, that he lays all his stress upon the money which the man contributed from a fund at his disposal, and other moneys which were raised for the building fund.

(10) *Guinamandus*, a monk, did certainly " carve with wondrous art " the tomb of St.-Front at Périgueux.

(11) *Guirannus* was *operarius* at St.-Victor de Marseille ; but, as Mortet points out (p. 189), this word means not handiworker, but business director.

(12) *Hebertus* " built " certain things, but there is no proof that this is used in any but the broadest sense.

(13) *Hezelo* also " built " a great deal at Cluny, but the context clearly forbids the stricter interpretation here ; he " built more than any mortal man except the Kings of Spain and of England."

(14) *Humbertus* " built " a priory ; but there is no farther implication.

(15) *Hunaldus*, it is clearly implied by the text, was not a handiworker but an overseer.

(16) *Joannes*, a canon, " had built [a church] from the very foundations," but there is no architectural implication in the text.

(17) *Joannes* of Vendôme was certainly an artist, though not a model monk ; see my text in Chapter IV.

(18) *Joannes Bénézet* " built " the famous bridge of Avignon ; but we are not told in what sense, and the reference is to a MS. at Avignon.

(19) *Martinus* seems really to have been the sculptor of a tomb.

(20) *Odolricus* of Tours evidently was a painter-monk.

(21) *Odolricus* of Conques seems really to have been an architect.

(22) *Omblardus* was a painter-monk.

(23) *Paganus* " built a fishpond," by damming up one end of a marsh ; but there is no farther implication.

(24) *Petrus* of Conques seems to have had architectural skill, like Odolricus.

(25) *Petrus* of Redon is called " the mason." (Text not in University Library.)

(26) *Petrus* is summarized by Lefèvre-Pontalis as " architect " of a church ; text not in University Library.

(27) *Poncius* was the " builder " of a monastery, and the Duke of Aquitaine " ordered the building " ; but the text is by no means conclusive as to Poncius's architectural functions.

(28) *Poncius Rebolli*, a canon, was *operarius*, a word which we know to mean ordinarily " supervisor."

(29) *Radulphus*. I am again unable to verify.

(30) *Raymundus*, a canon, was " supervisor," *operarius*, of certain buildings.

(31) *Savari*. I cannot verify.

(32) *Selva* " built " a church, at the command of the local prince.

(33) *Theodardus* " built " a small priory. He was a monk, and is also called *magister*, a word which Lefèvre-Pontalis seems to misinterpret altogether, taking it in the sense of " architect." The text runs, " dominus Theodardus, qui fuit præceptor et magister," and seems clearly to imply that he was a schoolmaster.

(34) *Thetbaudus* was merely a supervisor, and colleague of Albaldus (No. 2).

(35) *Valerius* was really a monk-glazier and painter.

(36) *Walterus*. I cannot verify.

(C) THE EARLIER APOLOGISTS

We may take as typical the learned Belgian Benedictine Haeften, whose work still ranks as a monastic classic, yet who shows incidentally how little documentary evidence there is for any regular practice of what we now call *art*. (*Monasticarum Disquisitionum Libri XII*. Antwerp, 1644, lib. IX, tract. ii, disq. 2, pp. 546 ff.) He adopts, to begin with, the ancient vague definition of *artes* (p. 183, col. 2) ; yet the Benedictine *artes* are

BODMIN CHURCH.

kitchen and cellar-work, baking, gardening, etc.; compare the definition of *art*, which he borrows from St. Thomas Aquinas, on p. 560. With regard to any kind of manual dexterity, he fetches his evidence mainly from the earliest fathers of the Egyptian deserts, and from occasional instances in the Dark Ages. He does indeed take one instance from the end of the thirteenth century: " St. Peter Celestine " (i.e. the Pope of the *Gran Rifiuto*) " was wont to bind books, or to sew his own garments or those of his brethren, in order that the Devil, that Evil Tempter, might always find him busy with labour." But thence Haeften strays into post-reformation times, and quotes a Cistercian of that date who asserts (apparently out of his own head) that the early Cistercians practised painting! Yet it is on the authority of books of this kind that the legend has grown up. The authors were often diligent and accurate scholars, but hypnotized by very natural prepossessions in favour of their own Order. They seldom indulged in anything like the exaggerations dear to apologists in modern times; they stood too near to the actual facts. They lived in countries where the monastic tradition had never been broken; they knew how little art-work their own fellow-monks were doing; and they did not venture to guess that their medieval ancestors had lived so very differently. Still, they naturally caught at all such brilliant exceptions as they could find; and, preoccupied with these, they took no notice of the mass of negative evidence.

No Order did more for art than the Cluniacs; it was their influence which was largely responsible for that " white robe of churches " which the West put on soon after A.D. 1000; they had very great influence over French and Spanish and West German architecture; the wealth of ornament in their churches and church furniture attracted severe criticism from St. Bernard and his Cistercians. Yet it is remarkable how the Cluniac customals, and those of the monasteries which submitted to their influence, not only fail to support the legend of regular monastic handiwork, but sometimes imply the contrary; see Marrier, *Bibliotheca Cluniacensis*, col. 659.a; 670.d; 1365.d.

Compare also the data in the *Consuetudines Monasticæ*, edited by Dom Bruno Albers. Vol. I, pp. 144–5, we find *opus manuum*, but with no hint of " art," in the sense of carving or painting or metal-work. So again in Vol. III, pp. 42, 91, 101, 109, 119; these last two places rather imply the contrary, as does also p. 83. In Vol. IV, pp. 80, 125, 146, 227, there is no hint of

" art " ; while pp. 137, 146, 168, 228, imply that there was no custom of " artistic " work. For instance, there is provision for sharpening the knives of the scribes, but not for the tools of carvers. In Vol. V, pp. 55, 99, 150, give no indication, while p. 108 has again an unfavourable implication.

Even Prof. Baldwin Brown, whose command of the documents is usually exact and critical, seems not to realize the force of the negative evidence, and to generalize incautiously from a few known cases (Vol. I, pp. 236, 240).

Finally, there is a passage in *Theophilus* which seems to have escaped notice in this connexion. He describes the ideal workshop to be built ; a long hall in three separate closed compartments ; one greater room for the baser metals, and two smaller for the silversmiths and goldsmiths respectively. All the windows are to be three feet high, two feet broad, pierced at intervals of five feet and raised only one foot from the ground, in order to give the most convenient light to the workmen ; for the same reason, the main axis of the building must run east and west (lib. III, c. 1). Here we have a very definite type of building, similar in many respects to the lay-brethren's hall at Fountains and other Cistercian houses. If such buildings had been regular and customary, even at great monasteries only, no doubt we could not expect them to be so clearly identified as the refectory and dormitory, but at least they ought to be as easily recognizable as are the calefactorium, library, prison, etc. Yet, among all the minute researches which have done so much honour to our architects and antiquaries, has any led to the identification of any such building ? Let me repeat here, again, that I throw no doubt upon the exceptional existence of monastic workshops ; indeed, we know of a workshop at Ely for the [lay] goldsmith ; I only hold that the silence or negative implications of customals and other intimate records, taken with the absence of any such customary building among monastic ruins, weighs very heavily against the theory that the average monk, at ordinary times and places, was in any sense a regular practician in any sort of artistic handicraft. Indeed, it is difficult to reconcile the actual evidence even with the theory of an organized art school for lay workmen, maintained and patronized by the monks within their own precincts, except when some considerable building work was on hand. At such times there would, of course, be a mason's lodge, carpenter's shop, smithy, etc. ; but these would probably be temporary wooden buildings.

(D)

W. PAGE. *The St. Albans School of Painting.* (*Archæologia*, Vol. LVIII, 1902, pp. 275 ff.)

This is a far more scientific study; but we must remember that the author is concerned only with a single great monastery. From about 1200 to about 1250 there are seven monastic artists traceable at St. Albans, among nearly a hundred monks with perhaps a dozen lay-brethren.[1] Six of these artists are choir-monks,[2] with one lay-brother, of whom we know only that he is called Alan Painter in the obituary, and died in 1245. Of these six, it is fairly evident that three had gained their artistic rank before they ever took the vows. Mr. Page twice alludes to this as a probability in footnotes; but I think it might be put a good deal more strongly. They are called *Magister*; whereas the monk's proper title was *Dominus*, or *Frater*; and thus in fact Anketil and Richard are called. It would be difficult, I think, to find an instance of a monk called *Magister* who had not earned that title *outside* the monastery; i.e. as master in the schools or in the workshop; or, later on, as having earned a University degree. The evidence, therefore, points to the probability that these men took the vows only late in life; and, when Mr. Page writes that Walter of Colchester, the "incomparable painter," "must have *become a monk at* St. Albans about the year 1200 or a little later," it would seem far safer to substitute *migrated to* for the words I have here italicized. Again, the reader would not gather definitely that the goldsmith Solomon of Ely is known to have been a layman; his biography may be found in Chapman's *Ely Sacrist Rolls* (I, 152). Farther, it is important to note that the obituary printed in Matthew Paris, *Chron. Major*, R.S., Vol. VI, pp. 269 ff. specifies only that one painter, Alan.

[1] In 1200, the abbot decreed that the number of monks should not exceed 100, unless the newcomer were of special dignity or learning, or patronized by "some powerful man whom we could not gainsay without perilous offence." *Gest. Abb.*, vol. i, p. 234.

[2] Supposing, that is, that we may identify Baldwin the saint with Baldwin the artist. But the name is not sufficiently rare to make this certain; and, of our only two texts, one speaks of *Master* Baldwin *the goldsmith* (without *Sacrist*) and the other, *Sacrist* Baldwin (without the title of *master* or *goldsmith*). *Gest. Abb.*, vol. i, pp. 190–1205. Still, as two of the other artists became sacrists, this adds to the probability in Baldwin's case.

Still, there was certainly at St. Albans a flourishing art school for those two generations, and certainly the directors and the best artists were monks, by final if not by original vocation. But that monastic school did not outlast the century: " With the close of the thirteenth century the monks at St. Albans appear to have ceased to work themselves at mural painting, sculpture, or the kindred arts, or to have designed or superintended the buildings of the monastery " (p. 285).[1] Moreover, no serious attempt has been made, I believe, to prove that there was any other such monastic school of painting and sculpture as this St. Albans school of 1200–1250, even at the greatest English monasteries during those crowning generations of monasticism. For writing and illumination the evidence is far stronger, though here also the lay artist has got the upper hand by the end of the thirteenth century. One proof of the exceptional character of St. Albans may be found in this, that the great cathedral monastery of Canterbury, when it made the celebrated shrine of St. Thomas à Becket about 1220, committed the design of the work to Walter the monk of St. Albans, and its execution to Walter in association with Elias de Derham, canon of Salisbury (p. 279). But Mr. Page's study certainly deserves the close attention of all who are specially interested in this subject.

---

[1] Moreover, garrulous as the later chroniclers of St. Albans often are as to the brethren's achievements, there is scarcely any mention of art.

APPENDIX 3.—(Chap. II, p. 31)

HECKINGTON CHURCH

THIS extraordinarily beautiful parish church, between Boston and Sleaford, has been claimed as the work of the monks of Bardney, to whom the revenues of the parish were appropriated. But Prof. Hamilton Thompson has recently shown that the church was almost certainly built before the appropriation took place, and that we owe it to a rich and generous rector. The Heckington authorities, to their credit be it recorded, have accepted the correction ; a large stained-glass window had already been designed for the south transept, in which there was a cartoon of monk-masons labouring at the fabric ; this cartoon will not now appear. In the earlier times, when monasteries were often great schools of building, the fabric of their appropriated churches naturally profited by this ; the little church of Pentney in Norfolk, for instance, has a small late thirteenth century east window of perfect design, and two splendidly-modelled heads supporting the dripstone of the priest's door ; it is difficult not to connect this with the fact (which we know from existing stones taken from the ruins) that active building was going on about that same date at the priory. But, in the later Middle Ages, this appropriation system led rather to the neglect of our parish churches ; I have given full evidence for this in *The English Historical Review* for January 1911, and in *The History Teachers' Miscellany*, December 1925 to July 1926. Adderbury seems to have been a brilliant exception ; and this was appropriated to New College, not to a monastery.

APPENDIX 4.—(Chap. V, p. 78)

ARTISTS' PRICES

THE details for parish churches may be found in a visitation which I printed in *The English Historical Review* for January 1911. New chancels are estimated at prices varying from £10 to £17 ; but no doubt there would be in each case a considerable amount of material from the old building which could be utilized in the new. A new vicarage costs £13 6s. 8d. ; a vicarage-hall alone, from £4 to £5 ; a tithe-barn £12 ; on the other hand a rectory *plus* churchyard and wall is twice reckoned at £40. The chancel windows might be glazed for £3 6s. 8d. See No. 3, Manaton ; 22, Diptford ; 42, 43, Ermington ; 45, Walkhampton ; 56, Lifton or Dunkerton ; 57 (ditto) ; 58 ; 65 ; 72 ; 75 ; 79; 87, in which last, by subtracting the price of a new *legenda* [£3 6s. 8d.] we may infer that the glazing of the chancel was roughly estimated at £3 6s. 8d. also. Similar quotations of price may be found in the Visitations printed with Stapeldon's Register (ed. Hingeston-Randolph, pp. 155, 185, 195, 198, 345-7, 397, 409). Our visitors value the books also : e.g. a fresh set of *libri matutinales* is estimated at £4 ; it is rare to find such trustworthy evidence as to the cost price of medieval books under normal conditions.

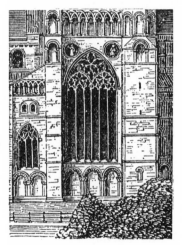

TRANSEPT WINDOW AT DURHAM.

In these cases, however, the visitor is evidently estimating only for the most summary and necessary work. When it was done with much elaboration the cost might be much higher. The rebuilding of Bodmin Church in 1469, with granite pillars and window-tracery and a new roof and glass windows, cost more than £270, though the tower was left alone. Adderbury chancel, rebuilt after 1408 with real elaboration of detail, cost about £400. (See Appendix 11.)

For the bishop's throne at Exeter, see P. Freeman, *Arch. Hist. of E. Cathl.*, new ed., 1888, p. 51. Other valuable indications of price are scattered about the notes to this volume : e.g. the thirty-eight small Purbeck marble shafts cost 5s. 6d. each in 1316–7 (p. 126). Compare this with Westminster Abbey, where the great marble piers of the nave (1387–1403) cost £40 each, and those supporting the central tower £60 and £80 (Rackham in *Trans. Brit. Acad.*, 1909, p. 42). At Ely, about 1340, the three bays east of the octagon cost £760 each (*Anglia Sacra*, Vol. I, p. 647). At Durham, about 1350, the great six-light window in the north transept cost £100 to cut and set up, and £52 to glaze (*Hist. Dunelm. Script. Tres.*, p. 131). A very interesting specification of a chancel in 1264, with total price (£13 6s. 8d. plus the stone of the demolished building) may be found in the Hist. MSS. Commission's ninth report, p. 39b. For total costs at Westminster Abbey under Henry III, see Lethaby, *Westminster I*, p. 173 ; for the nave, Rackham *l.c.*, p. 89 (he calculates total nave at £21,000) ; for Exeter Cathedral, Freeman, pp. 82, 132. These may suffice for the present purpose, out of the mass of surviving evidence.

APPENDIX 5.—(CHAP. V, p. 82)

Sacchetti, Nov. 191.

"THIS man (Bonamico) was in his youth the pupil of a painter named Tafo, and he lived in the same house with him ; and at night he slept in a room which was next to his master's, and only divided from it by a thin brick wall. It was the custom of the master painters to call up their apprentices very early in the morning to begin their painting, especially during the winter time when the nights were long ; and Tafo having followed this custom for half a winter, awaking Bonamico very early, the matter began to displease Bonamico, for he was a man who preferred to sleep rather than to paint." The rest of the tale describes the trick by which Bonamico got his morning sleep, in Tafo's despite.

APPENDIX 6.—(Chap. V, p. 83)

SCRIBAL LAMENTATIONS

WATTENBACH, *Schriftwesen im Mittelalter*, 1896, pp. 498 ff. The metre, and sometimes even the grammar, cast an unfavourable light on the average scribe's Latin scholarship.

Qui librum scripsit, multum sudavit et alsit :
Propitietur ei deus et pia virgo Maria.

He who wrote the book, sweated sore and froze : may God and the gracious Virgin Mary have mercy on him.

Daz ist awss, gib mir trincken !
That is done ; give me a drink !

Finito libro pinguis detur auca magistro.
Now that the book is finished, let the master [scribe] have a fat goose.

Libro completo saltat scriptor pede leto.
The book is done, and the writer dances with gladsome foot.

Detur pro penna scriptori pulchra puella.
Let a pretty girl be given to the scribe in reward for his penwork.

Qui me scribebat multum potare solebat.
He who wrote me was wont to drink deep.

O penna cessa, quoniam manus est michi fessa.
Cease, O pen, for my hand is weary.

Pro tali precio nunquam plus scribere volo.
For such a price as this I will never write again.

Scriptor opus sciste (i.e. siste), tenuit labot iste nimis te.
Writer, cease work ; this labour hath held thee too long.

Hoc opus exegi, pennas sepissime fregi.
I have finished this job ; very often have I broken my pens.

Pennula scriptoris requiescat plena laboris.
Let the writer's pen, so full of labour, now find rest.

Explicit hic totum
Infunde, da mihi potum !
Et si melius scripsissem
Nomen meum [non]¹ apposuissem
Et sic est finis per totum
Deo gracias !

This is all done ; pour out, and give me a drink ! And if I had written better I would [not] have put my name. And so here is the end altogether, God be thanked !

Ich habe dyss büchelyn geschribin
Das lon ist zu dem byer blebin.

I have written this book ; the money remains in the beer [-house].

Ach ! Ach ! ich was fro, do ich schreip finito libro.

Ah, ah ! I was glad when I wrote *Here endeth the book*.

Ach got wie fro ich was, do dis buches ein ende was.

Ah God, how glad was I when this book came to an end !

O Maria wol fro ich was, da ich schraib deo gratias.

O Mary ! glad indeed was I when I wrote *God be thanked*.

Dis het ein end, Des frowt sich hercz und hend.

Here is the end, heart and hand rejoice thereat.

Datum in domo, ubi nulla copia, sed summa inopia.

Written in mine own house, where there is no plenty, but utter want.

Finis letificat, incepcio sepe molestat.

The end rejoices us ; the beginning is often irksome.

Congratulor incausto quod ulterius scribere nolo.

I congratulate the ink, for I will write no farther.

Explicit hoc totum, pro Christo da mihi potum.

Here is the very end ; for Christ's sake give me a drink !

Compare E. Müntz, *L'Art à la cour des papes :*

" L'invention de l'imprimerie fit juger bien lourd le travail de la transcription par ceux qui continuaient à l'exercer encore. On peut voir les doléances répétées de Satriano à Sixte IV auquel il énumère les cahiers qu'il lui a fallu remplir ; aussi se promet-il de la libéralité du pape, qu'on ne lui laissera point terminer ses jours dans une si pénible tâche que celle de copier des livres. La calligraphie et l'enluminure avaient passé à l'état d'industrie qui faisait vivre bien des familles ; et l'on voit ces professions classées parmi les *métiers* de plusieurs villes, comme à Venise, à Bruges et à Gand, sans parler de Paris et de Bologne."

¹ I have bracketed this word, which seems to spoil both metre and sense.

APPENDIX 7.—(CHAP. V, p. 83)

THE ARTIST'S STATUS

RENAN writes : " The fourteenth century had not reached [the stage at which ancient Greece and Rome and the Renaissance stood]. All that century through, the artist is still a mere artisan, the architect is a master-mason, and the musician is a minstrel ; there is no distinction between the painter or sculptor and the decorative painter. From the time of King John [d. 1364] and especially of [his son] Charles V, a considerable change does indeed begin, which was destined to be continued at the Court of Burgundy. The artist becomes the favourite, the guest, and often the secret agent and confidant of the princes ; the architect has the title of sergeant-at-arms ; the painter is a valet-de-chambre. They enter royal households side by side with the lower attendants—spicers, tailors, etc. ; and these offices were not empty titles. . . . Jan van Eyck was sent on several missions by the Duke of Burgundy. . . . Unfortunately the courts were not then centres of sufficient refinement to serve as schools of taste. The artists whom these sovereign favours left untouched struggled painfully along amid the vulgarities of bourgeois life. With the exception of the *jongleurs* they formed no gild ; the painters were a branch of the saddlers, and the gild regulations imposed upon them were such precautions as one takes to avoid the frauds of lower artisans."[1] And, as he points out elsewhere, the higher social status of the artist coincides with the decline of the art ; " he is no longer the manly and intelligent artisan of the twelfth and thirteenth centuries ; he is a skilful valet, fit for all kinds of services, adding saddlery to his painting, and secret commissions to works of real art ; a man who ranks in the prince's household with the fool,

[1] V. le Clerc et E. Renan, *Discours*, etc. (reprinted from the *Hist. Litt. de la France*), 2nd ed., vol. ii, 1865, p. 208. But Renan seems here to forget that the masons certainly had their gild at Paris as early as 1260.

the minstrel and the tailor " (*Rev. d. d. Mondes*, Vol. XL, July 1862, p. 222).

Under Pius II, the first pope who represents every side of the Renaissance, Paolo Romano " was admitted to the great dining-hall, while Master Giovanni [who bore the title of ' Sculptor of the Apostolic Palace '] was relegated to the second hall, with the tailors, cooks, porters, couriers, grooms, sweepers, muleteers, water-carriers and so forth. Let us add, however, that three copyists (*scriptores*) and two architects (*Marianus magister lignorum* and *Magister Albertus murator*) lived also in this unaristocratic society " (Müntz, 1878, p. 259).

In Britain the fullest artists' inscriptions seem to come rather from the north. At Bridekirk in Northumberland we have, on an early font :

> He was Richard who me wrought,
> And me to grace with joy he brought.[1]

There is a similar testimonial by the mason to himself in the precincts of Aberdeen Cathedral. For John Morrow at Melrose see my text and illustration in Chapter XI. At Cottan, near Bayeux, the central boss of the choir vault bears seven reptiles joined in one single head with the inscription *MCCCXLVIII fist maistre Helie le Lou clore ceste voute* : " In 1348, Master Elias Wolf put the keystone to this vault."[2]

---

[1] M. H. Bulley, *Ancient and Medieval Art*, 1914, p. 310.

[2] *Annuaire des 5 dépts. de la Normandie*, vol. xxxv., 1869, p. 536.

APPENDIX 8.—(Chap. VII, p. 131)

"THE GOTHIC QUEST"

IT is necessary to say a few words about this book, which was treated seriously by the late Dr. F. J. N. Figgis, and which, by inspiring a good deal of modern journalism, is partly responsible for some very regrettable exaggerations. Men are naturally disposed to listen to what a successful architect has to say about architecture; and in these cases, when the author writes not only confidently but with something more than the ordinary emphasis of conviction, most readers take it for granted that he has at his back an array of actually observed or acknowledged facts. In this case, however, it is plain that he has not only neglected to study the ordinary original records of the Middle Ages, but has even failed to note a great deal of the architectural evidence from surviving buildings on this side of the Atlantic. He shows complete ignorance of the survival of Gothic in England after the Reformation, and of its almost total extinction in the unreformed countries; yet these facts are obvious even to the most superficial student of architecture at Oxford and Cambridge, or in most districts of the Continent.

He imagines the Middle Ages to have been free from the struggle for "useless wealth" (p. 24). Yet, in fact, medieval contemporaries complain, as strongly as modern writers, that their whole world is subservient to the Almighty Dollar; *pecuniæ obediunt omnia* is one of the commonest of quotations; a great part of the celebrated poem of *Piers Plowman* is a sermon on this text.

He writes airily about the Monastic Orders (pp. 68, 123, 124, 125), but in painful ignorance of their actual history; and here, as usual, his own mistakes form the foundation of his argumentative superstructure. On p. 57, again, he imagines St. Thomas Aquinas to have invented a generalization, which in fact is quoted textually from St. Paul's speech (Acts xiv. 17). His quotations from French and German are mis-spelt in a fashion which betrays elementary ignorance of the languages (pp. 20, 36). And, seeing that the whole argument of the book is designed to prove the complete dependence of medieval art upon medieval theology, it is worth while to deal more fully with two of Mr. Cram's theological points.

On p. 43, the Inquisition is reckoned among " the manifestations of the Pagan Renaissance " as distinguished from " the mighty glories of Church and State in the thirteenth century." The Inquisition was created, of course, in the early thirteenth century, when medieval civilization is generally reckoned to have been at its highest point. In the Renaissance period it was practically dead everywhere but in Spain and in Italy, the two countries which were least touched by Protestantism and which therefore, according to Mr. Cram's general thesis, ought to have shown the highest examples of religion, morality, and art. He calls on the world, on this same page, to repent and to " base our forms [of art] on those developed by Christianity to express Christianity "—i.e. on the Gothic " style." This protest should be addressed in the first place to Italy and to Spain. On p. 46, once again, the Inquisition is reckoned as a Renaissance product ; and Mr. Cram opposes it as a representative of Paganism to St. Thomas Aquinas and St. Louis, the representatives of Christianity. Yet it was St. Thomas who laid the philosophical basis for the Inquisition, and whose iron chain of logic, starting from orthodox premises and ending with the Christian duty of manslaughter for religious differences, is so embarrassing to apologists of to-day, who can neither dispute his assumptions nor break any link of his logic. St. Louis was not only a patron of the Inquisition, but he told his intimates that the knight's duty, if he heard antichristian talk from a Jew, was to thrust his sword into the unbeliever's belly as far as it would go.

On p. 97, again, Mr. Cram depreciates the spiritual value of sermons in comparison with " a noble and imposing service, complete in its reverent and solemn ritual " (p. 97). Yet this would be contradicted by some of the best churchmen of the Middle Ages. The author of *Dives and Pauper* (who was Chaucer's contemporary) writes " it is more profitable to hear God's Word in preaching, than to hear any Mass." Much the same had already been said by one of the greatest of all the Dominican Ministers General, Humbert de Romans, under whose ministry St. Thomas Aquinas wrote ; and this was repeated by St. Bernardino of Siena. In fact, it was based upon an ancient patristic

text enshrined in Canon Law—Gratian's *Decretum*, pt. ii, c. 1,
q. 1, §94. I have devoted a couple of pages to these authorities
in *Five Centuries of Religion*, Vol. I, pp. 124 ff. It is probable
that St. Bernard or St. Francis or St. Thomas Aquinas, if they
had met with Mr. Cram's plea, would have rejected it as emphatically as St. Bernardino did.

I have treated the book seriously only because it has sometimes been so treated by others. The loose reasoning and the
recklessness as to facts call for serious criticism, since one of
the main difficulties of modern medieval studies is created by
the welcome which attends random writing of this kind, so long
as it ministers to the prejudices of one or other religious sect.

APPENDIX 9.—(Chap. IX, p. 167)

THE WANDERING WORKMAN

GOULD (Vol. I, p. 149) has an interesting description of the *Wanderjahre* and the *Compagnonnage* as they appear in the light of post-Reformation documents. We must remember, in reading this, that we are dealing not only with a later date than that with which I am concerned in my text, but also that Gould is composing a composite picture from a good many different crafts ; but, with this caution, the story throws a good deal of light upon our subject.

"As regards the mark, although we have no evidence that this custom was a general one, and indeed in many trades its observance would have been well-nigh impossible, yet in a few the members were required to choose a mark, and place it on all their work ; for instance, the cutlers of Nuremberg and the joiners. He might have added the cutlers of York. We thus find the mark appearing in shops where the number of workmen employed was considerable, and where it might become necessary to distinguish one man's work from another's ; and we can easily understand that with the ordinary tradesman, such as the baker, butcher, shoemaker, it was not necessary, and therefore not in use. Yet at Amiens, to guard against fraud, the bakers were obliged to mark their bread, each with a distinctive sign of his own. The mason's mark thus loses [in Germany] much of the recondite symbolism which enthusiastic writers have attributed to it, and becomes reduced to a mere trade regulation arising out of the exigencies of the handicraft. Whether or not it afterwards received any mystic interpretation need not now be discussed, as it is fully treated of elsewhere. Our young journeyman is now ready to commence his travels, which, in different trades, extended over a longer or shorter space as the case might be. The *rationale* of this pilgrimage is readily explained. It kept down the number of masters by prolonging the novitiate, it served to bring all the different and independent guilds of a trade into a close harmony of usage, and it helped to propagate the improvements, which, in any particular locality had been engrafted on the specialities of a handicraft. This, in an age of slow locomotion and gradual dispersion of news, was highly beneficial; but, above all, it served to widen each craftsman's ideas and judgment, to complete his trade education, and to rub off any local prejudices. But, in order that a journeyman might be able to travel, special institutions were necessary. In the earliest times, the craftsman, on entering a new town, applied at the first shop of his trade that he came to, for work for eight or fourteen days, and if the master was able to employ him he did so, if not he recommended him to another master. Failing to find work in any shop, the craftsman received a night's lodging, supper and breakfast, in the house of the master whose turn it was to receive, and at his departure next morning a small sum of money sufficient to carry him to the next town. Later on, the masters arranged with some tavern-keeper to afford the necessary board at their expense. This tavern was then the house of call of a particular trade, where the journeyman could at once obtain information if work were procurable, and where the masters could leave notice if they required any extra assistance. The landlord and his wife were styled father and mother, their children and domestics, male and female, brothers and sisters. Later on still, when the journeymen established their own fraternities, these houses became their places of meeting, and some one, either a journeyman or a master, was deputed to call there every day at noon in order to welcome, and provide work for, new arrivals, or if such was not possible, to attend to their bodily comforts by partaking *with* them of a stoup of liquor. The supper and bed were furnished at the expense of the fraternity, to whose treasury, however, the masters also contributed. The newcomer, unless work were found for him, usually received a small sum of money to carry him forward. This was called the *Geschenk*—the donation or present. We thus see that a journeyman could travel from one end of Germany to the other, without exercising forethought as to his expenses, and yet without feeling that he was in any way subsisting on charity."

MM

APPENDIX 10.—(CHAP. IX, p. 179)

MEDIEVAL WALL-SCRATCHES

THE fullest attempt to collect these, yet a very rudimentary
attempt, is perhaps in the twelfth of my own *Medieval Studies,*
entitled " Medieval Graffiti." These are, as a rule, unquestionably
far superior to those of later date which may be found by their
side in much larger numbers. A good many of them are mere
names, as nowadays ; but some of these may be later than
1530, and therefore not legitimately within our scope. Others,
however, are definitely the work of a parish priest or clerk in
his idle moments, since the title is added to the name. The
most interesting are rhymed saws in Latin or English, notes by
the workmen concerning their work, dates of completion, or
sketches from animal or plant life. The writing nearly always
betrays an educated hand, and a number of the sketches are
evidently by real artists. Others, again, are very evidently
by amateurs ; yet these also, as Professor Lethaby has pointed
out, follow the usual medieval artistic traditions. The most
interesting that I know of this class are on the thirteenth-century
jubé (pulpitum) of the upper cathedral at Sion in the Valais ;
here some knight or squire, apparently of about 1300, has drawn
mounted knights in armour and battle-scenes.

But all or nearly all (to come back to our starting-point) are
greatly superior to the usual mean scrawls of to-day. Perhaps
the real difference here is in the *personnel ;* in rendering the art
of writing almost universal, we have necessarily vulgarized it
also in a certain sense ; and the man who scratches a picture
now is not an artist or a knight, but the vulgarest among our
tourists. In other words, only educated people did the medieval
scratches which may be found here and there in our churches ;
while those who scratch or use their pencils nowadays are only
the uneducated.

APPENDIX 11.—(CHAP. X, p. 181)

THE WITNESS OF THE BUILDING ACCOUNTS

(A) ETON CHAPEL

LET us first note the records of impressment, as given by Maxwell-Lyte, *History of Eton College*, 1911, pp. 11–13.

"In February, 1441, William Lynde was appointed clerk of the works for life, and invested with very considerable powers by virtue of the royal prerogative. The letters patent issued in his favour authorized him to impress as many stone-hewers, carpenters, masons, plumbers, tilers, plasterers and other artificers as he might require, and to imprison all such as should refuse to work for the King at reasonable wages. He was also empowered to procure stone, timber, iron, lead, glass, tiles and other materials, and carriage for the same by land or by water, at the King's expense. Somewhat similar directions were at the same time given to a certain Thomas Wight. A little later, the right to take workmen and carriage in the King's name was conferred upon the master-mason, the warden of the carpenters, and the warden of the masons, each of the principal crafts having a separate chief, who bore the title of warden. . . .

. . . Various difficulties had to be encountered. On June 8, Robert Westerley, the King's chief mason, was empowered by letters patent to impress men for the works at Eton, and he was instructed by the Earl of Suffolk to secure at least fifty of the best stone-hewers in England. He accordingly went to Burford and to Oxford, and selected twenty-four men suitable for the purpose. Inasmuch, however, as his proceedings threatened to interfere with the erection of All Souls' College, Archbishop Chicheley obtained from the King an order exempting his workmen from arrest, provided that the best twelve of them should be transferred to Eton. Lynde in his turn complained that the Archbishop kept the picked men and sent him only 'the refuse of theym alle,' deserters and the like. Eventually, on October 3, John Wynwyk, the new warden of the masons at Eton, procured a commission to take as many stone-hewers and masons as might be necessary, even in the fee of the church, with power to imprison the disobedient. This commission was renewed six months later. At the end of May, John Hampton and William Lynde were authorized to take artificers of all kinds and to commit those who would not work to prison in Windsor Castle. The number of men actually employed seems to have varied considerably in different weeks, the average being about sixty-nine between July 1441 and February 1442, and about 116 during the following twelvemonth." The exact average for this following twelvemonth is, I think it will be found, 122.28. This is the twelvemonth covered by the annexed table of attendances.

The special commission for impressment was issued this year " at the end of May." Specially high and low figures are here marked by differences of type, until Christmas week, when attendances naturally become abnormal.

This list shows clearly the effect of the fresh commission for impressment issued " at the end of May." Either these letters were dated somewhere about May 20, or Westerley acted about that time in certain reliance upon immediate letters of authority ; the attendances, which had gradually dwindled to 89, suddenly go up to 123, and thence in almost unbroken increase to 192. Equally significant is the tale of the labourers' numbers during the hay-harvest and the corn-harvest, in so far as we can assume these to have taken place that year at average dates. It may be that the rise of ten on June 2 was due to the close of the hay-harvest ; yet the numbers through the harvest itself had been ten more than the average of the whole year. During the barley-harvest they are still higher, though here, again, a leap of eighteen may mark the close of that period. During the wheat-harvest the numbers are nearly half as high again as the average ; here, for the third time, we get a further leap just about when we should expect the harvest to close ; but, during the next five weeks when field-work must have been at its lowest ebb, the numbers are so far from rising that they diminish by more than 30 per cent. ; and thence they dwindle still, almost without exception, until the natural slump at Christmas. Evidently, therefore, these numbers of labourers at Eton were not mainly, perhaps not at all, dictated by agricultural conditions. The main factor was the pressgang, which had far more effect than the close of harvest can have had. Indeed, the harvest probably facilitated impressment : the officers need only go into the field to make an abundant haul.

ETON CHAPEL WAGE-LIST FOR THE TWELVEMONTH, 1442-3.

	February			March				April				
	12	19	26	5	12	19	26	2	9	16	23	30
Freemasons ..	41	41	46	46	47	49	49	41	48	48	47	47
Rowmasons ..	—	—	—	—	—	—	—	—	—	—	2	3
Carpenters	3	3	3	3	3	3	3	3	10	9	9	10
Sawyers	2	2	2	2	2	2	1	2	2	4	4	4
Smiths												
Daubers	—	—	—	—	—	—	—	—	—	1	1	1
Jackers	—	—	—	—	—	—	—	—	1	1	1	1
Tilers	—	—	—	—	—	—	—	—	—	1	—	—
Hard Hewers ..												
Labourers	7	4	4	4	4	3	7	19	24	26	25	27
Total workmen engaged	53	50	55	55	56	57	60	65	85	90	89	93

	May				June				July				
	7	14	21	28	4	11	18	25	2	9	16	23	30
Freemasons ..	50	48	41	49	50	55	52	44	48	46	53	53	49
Rowmasons ..	5	4	5	14	15	15	17	18	20	16	19	19	23
Carpenters ..	11	10	4	16	16	18	18	19	20	24	29	34	50
Sawyers ..	2	2	2	2	2	2	2	2	2	2	4	6	8
Smiths ..	—	—	—	—	1	1	1	1	1	1	1	1	1
Daubers ..	2	2	2	2	2	1	1	1	1	1	1	1	3
Jackers ..	1	2	1	1	1	1	—	—	—	—	—	3	3
Tilers ..	—	—	1	1	—	—	1	1	—	—	—	1	—
Hard Hewers ..	—	—	2	10	10	10	5	4	4	4	5	9	13
Labourers ..	23	26	23	28	33	26	34	38	42	33	34	40	35
							Hay harvest				Barley harvest		
Total workmen engaged ..	94	94	81	123	130	129	131	128	138	127	146	167	185

	August				September				October				
	6	13	20	27	3	10	17	24	1	8	15	22	29
Freemasons ..	55	55	49	53	56	54	55	54	54	48	55	56	55
Rowmasons ..	21	22	27	27	26	17	15	15	18	20	20	19	19
Carpenters ..	41	48	48	37	32	26	15	10	13	11	9	9	11
Sawyers ..	8	8	4	4	4	4	2	—	2	2	2	2	2
Smiths ..	1	1	1	1	1	—	1	1	1	1	1	1	1
Daubers ..	2	1	1	1	1	—	—	—	—	—	—	—	—
Jackers ..	—	—	—	—	—	—	—	1	1	—	—	—	1
Tilers ..	—	—	—	—	—	—	—	1	—	—	—	—	—
Hard Hewers ..	10	12	13	14	14	15	14	13	13	15	15	17	16
Labourers ..	32	37	49	40	47	42	43	37	35	38	38	40	34
	Wheat harvest												
Total workmen engaged ..	170	184	192	177	181	158	145	132	137	135	140	144	139

	November				December					January				Feb 4
	5	12	19	26	3	10	17	24	31	7	14	21	28	
Freemasons ..	53	54	53	55	55	53	52	32	35	38	43	47	47	49
Rowmasons ..	8	8	8	8	8	2	2	—	—	—	2	2	2	—
Carpenters ..	20	10	11	11	12	12	12	1	—	7	9	8	10	12
Sawyers ..	2	4	4	4	4	4	4	—		4	4	4	4	4
Smiths ..	1	1	1	1	1	1	1	—	1	1	1	1	1	1
Daubers ..	1	1	1	1	1	1	1	—		1	1	1	1	1
Jackers ..	1	—	—	—	—	—	1	1	1	2	2	2	—	—
Tilers ..	1	1	—	—	—	—	—			1	1	1	1	1
Hard Hewers ..	14	13	16	16	14	13	11	—	—	4	8	9	9	10
Labourers ..	29	25	21	23	23	25	20	4	4	6	6	8	21	17
Total workmen engaged ..	130	117	115	117	118	111	104	38	41	64	77	83	96	95

But a study of the individual absentees seems to suggest occasional runaways back into the harvest field. Taking those who drop out and reappear after a considerable interval, we find *Salmon* absent from May to the end of October ; *Taillour*, from May to the end of June, then again from mid-September to the end of October ; *Longe* drops the last three weeks of June ; *Adam*, all April and May. *Lente* is absent for half July and all August ; *Benet, Goodbyn, Meret* and *Towe*, disappearing almost simultaneously early in July, reappear on September 17 and October 15 respectively. *Crese's* absence coincides very nearly with theirs. All these five look as if they had gone off for harvest ; on the other hand, of ten men recruited on July 23, whereas four did not work out a whole week, the other six worked all through until September 10 or beyond ; so did two of the five recruited on August 13.

(B) ADDERBURY (Oxon), 1408–1418. (Oxfordshire Record Society, Vol. VIII, 1926, ed. T. F. Hobson, F.S.A.)

At Adderbury, the whole was directed by a freemason named Richard Winchcombe, whose career Mr. Howard traces in a very interesting study (pp. 34 ff.). He probably served his apprenticeship in the Gloucester lodge ; Mr. Howard shows good evidence for tracing his hand at four other churches in the district ; and we know from documentary evidence that he was supervisor of the work at Oxford Divinity School from 1430 to 1440. He seems to have come only intermittently during the first four years ; his manual work was that of cutting the great east window. An apprentice worked with him, and Winchcombe received pay for this double work at five different rates, varying from 4s. 10d. to 6s. 1d. per week. The editor confesses himself unable to suggest reasons for these variations ; is it not probable that they represent the different proportions of master's and apprentice's contributions to the work, since Winchcombe himself was evidently irregular in his attendance ? Other masons are paid 3s. a week (cut down to 2s. 6d. during the three months of shortest daylight) or 2s. 6d. (cut down to 1s. 8d. for those three months). This, as the editor points out, is in close accord with the practice at York Minster Lodge about 1350. Part of the work is done by contract. Winchcombe cuts 338 feet of stone for the parapet, weathering-ledge, and copings at 2½d., 1d., and

6*d*. respectively per foot; the glazing and the carpentry of the roof are done entirely by contract.

The editor does not deal directly with the question of regular or casual employment; but a good deal can be worked out from the accounts. Besides Winchcombe and his apprentice, fifteen masons at least were on the job during these eight years. If the "Thomas Mason" of the record is a different man from "Thomas Clerk," and if "the apprentice's father," who is more than once mentioned, is different from all whose names are recorded, then we have seventeen in all. In the seven years during which actual mason-work was done, there is no year in which more than nine were employed, and this total was reached only in 1414 and 1415. Nor were these all at work for the whole year; in 1414 five of the nine worked only thirty-five weeks each, and another only three; next year, the lowest six averaged only twenty-five weeks. In earlier and later years, the unemployment was still greater. Only two, Reed and Saltcombe, are regular workers through the seven years; Rudyfer and Cropredy worked each for a little over three, and Clerk for about two and a half. Three, at least, put in only ninety-five weeks between them in the whole time; possibly two others put in even less. It may be that these men who appear for so short a time at Adderbury had regular work elsewhere, and lost no more time by the change than it would take them to tramp from one place to another. But it would seem improbable that things fitted in so exactly for them; and the wage-list, as it stands, lends no support to Thorold Rogers's theory that employment was not only well paid at this time, but constant also.

Very interesting is the question of the "plumber's mate," which the editor discusses on pp. 44 ff., developing, with far fuller evidence and a surer touch, the idea to which I had come independently from the Eton and Bodmin accounts. I cannot do better than transcribe Mr. Hobson's summary, which is backed up by a conclusive series of concrete instances from the different rolls[1] (p. 44).

"Generally it appears that the skilled worker, as distinct from the unskilled labourer, is employed in company with an underling or assistant. The descriptive name used for such an assistant in these rolls is 'servitor,' 'serviens,' 'deserviens' or

[1] To these might be added *Finchale Priory* (Surtees Soc.), pp. lxvi, cccxciv; *Durham Acct. Rolls* (Surtees Soc.), pp. 406, 586, 610, and the Bodmin evidence which I give later on.

'famulus.' In other records, e.g. the Ely Rolls, the name 'garcio' or, more rarely, 'pagius' is used. The skilled crafts-man of those days was, it seems, accustomed to have the help of an inferior worker, who prepared his materials, handed him his tools, and generally played the part of the modern 'mate.' Sometimes the day wage for the two together is stated, often it is shown that the assistant receives a lower rate of pay. Much modern criticism has been directed against the institution which our comic papers call 'The Plumber's Mate,' the plumber as special instance taking the blame, if blame there be, which might be cast upon the shoulders of all skilled workmen. It is suggested that the custom or institution, or whatever it may be called, is not after all completely modern and that the four-teenth and fifteenth century worker, where trained skill was in question, was usually employed in company with a 'mate.' The instances which occur, in the Rolls here printed or in earlier or later Adderbury Rolls or in other records, such as the Ely, York and Durham Rolls, may be classed under three headings :

(1) A class of labourers, 'laborarii' or 'laboratores,' is men-tioned as assisting and working for or waiting upon the skilled men.

(2) A skilled man is hired and an assistant is also hired to work under or with him or for him.

(3) A skilled man is hired and it is specially recorded that his ' serviens ' or ' famulus ' is also hired to work with him."

(C) BODMIN CHURCH, 1469–1472. (*Camden Miscellany*, Vol. VII. *ad fin.*)

At Bodmin, as at Adderbury, not only did the wages vary from man to man, but the same man's wages varied from work to work. Normally, seven of them received 6*d.* a day each. Another gets 9*d.* with " his man " ; and by comparison we may see that he got 5*d.*, the " man " 4*d.* John and Thomas Hancock, for pillars and windows and arch, get 6*d.* ; for gutter-stones and verges they get 5*d.* Skilled masons when they are doing quarry-work get 6*d.*, exactly as when they are at the church (p. 16). One other, however, gets only 3*d.* a day at the quarry (*ibid*). A good deal was done by task-work (13, 24, 28). The William Mason of p. 38 and William Freemason of p. 49 are apparently the same. There were apparently nineteen masons in all during the three years that the work lasted; but these did not all work simultaneously, nor regularly. By the end of 1470 (p. 25) the work had evidently been going on for considerably more than a year, perhaps for two whole years. The time-sheet of the nineteen masons can be worked out correctly within a few days, since, even where the accountant has not reckoned these himself, the payments show how long the men had worked. We shall find that the nineteen masons had, in this time, worked not more than 3,609 days altogether, probably a few less. This comes to an average of almost exactly 190 each; that is to not very much more than half the working year. We cannot work out any man's separate contribution, because they are so often lumped together; e.g. p. 13. "*Item*, delivered to Richard Richowe and his fellows for the task-work of the said walls of the south side, and on the north side, £12." It is evident that this represents somewhere about 550 days, since the better masons drew 6*d*., and nearly all the others 5*d*.; but we have no means of discovering how long Richowe worked, as apart from his "fellowship," nor, again, how many of the nineteen masons were in that fellowship.

But it points to a system which is of extreme interest, and for which other accounts may perhaps yield even more definite evidence. If it were always Richowe and his fellows, as it often is, we should conclude that he, as master-mason, ruled the whole lodge as a matter of course. Certainly he seems to be the head man, and contracts to supply labour to the large price of £22 in all, or at least 11,000 days' work; no other mason's contract, I think, is made until quite the end, when John Hancock undertakes to do certain pillar-work for £2 (p. 26). But it is disconcerting to find that, whereas Robert Wetter and Petrok Gwelys are definitely counted as Richowe's fellows (p. 14), the very next entry runs: "*Item*, to Petrok Gwelys and his fellowship for drawing and scapeling stones at Pentewyn." Next page, after "Richowe and his fellows," we have Wetter and Gwelys "and the fellowship." Next page, again, "*Item* to Robert Wetter, William Hayn, and Witford at quarry, fifty-two days: *item*, to same fellowship, Robert and his fellows, at [the] church." On p. 20, "To Robert Wetter and his fellowship at [the] moor . . . fifty jornays [i.e. days] . . . *item* to Hayn, mason, twenty-five jornays; *item* to Whitford forty-two days for the same work." And finally (27) while the task-work for the pillars, porch and south wall is paid to Richowe and Wetter in common, there is

another item " to masons at the moor in Lent," which runs,
" Ric. Richowe twenty-one days ; *item*, Rob. Wettor twenty-
seven jornays ; *item*, Ric. Witforth twenty-six days ; item, Will.
Hayn twenty-six days." From this it would seem to emerge
that Wetter, Hayn, Whitford (and, for a while, Gwelys) formed
a stable nucleus of masons, while the others came and went ;
that this band was under command of Richowe, who is certainly
the most prominent man in these accounts ; and that Wetter
was next in command. If English freemasonry was as definitely
developed and organized as it is sometimes contended, this was
certainly a *lodge*, with its *master* and its *warden*. But it is quite
possible that the men themselves would not have used those
technical words, and that the organization was looser than (for
instance) at Eton.

Another point which emerges clearly is what all must have
suspected who have looked with any attention into Cornish and
South Devon churches, that the granite pillars and window-
tracery, so frequent there, was done upon the moors and brought
down. References to this come on pp. 13, 16, 20, 27 ; and it
is quite possible that Richowe and his fellowship were normally
working at the moor, where they had a sort of permanent workshop, and that they were brought down to Bodmin or other
churches as occasion served.[1] Again, we find Wetter, Hayn and
Whitford working at the quarry also (16), thus illustrating that
statute of 1360 which prescribed that the mason, when required
by his employers, should " do every work that to him pertaineth
to do, or of free-stone or of rough stone." Indeed, we find
Gille and Hancock making " pinnes " by the thousand ; i.e.
wooden pegs for the roof-slates (24). And, to conclude this
brief study, we find on pp. 14, 15 that the men did a certain
amount by candle-light in winter, though the gild statutes
expressly forbid this except for mere practice-work.[2] The
timber-work of the roof here, as at Adderbury, was done by

[1] The present Vicar, Mr. Leonard Browne, has kindly supplied me
with photographs and descriptions which show the pillars and the
tracery to be of the type common at this time in Devon and Corn-
wall granite ; the pillars plainly clustered and the capitals adorned
all round with a simple flattish four-leaved flower. The moor
comes close down to Bodmin ; but the nearest place where there is
plenty of granite would be from eight to ten miles distant, towards
Brown Willy and Rough Tor. The quarry, at Pentewan, is some
thirteen miles distant.

[2] See *Social Life in Britain*, p. 484, art. 10.

contract (24). The "plumber's mate" ("his man," "his servant," etc.) may be found on pp. 12, 16, 23, etc. And we have a valuable indication of time; it seems pretty clear that the whole porch took sixty-five days to build, and that five masons were engaged upon it, on and off (p. 30).

(D) XANTEN, on the Lower Rhine.

S. Beissel, S.J., *Die Baufuhrung d. Mittelalters, Studie uber die Kirche des hl, Victor zu Xanten.* 2te Auflage, Freiburg i/B. 1889. (3 parts, separately paged.)

This is, so far as I know, the fullest and most thorough analysis of a large series of building accounts that has ever been published. It runs to 600 octavo pages, and deals with a series of accounts which is almost unbroken from 1356 until far beyond the Reformation. This collegiate church of St. Victor was among the richest in one of the most prosperous districts of Europe; five times the head of the Chapter (Provost) was raised to the cardinalate; and two of these became popes. Beissel's monograph is worthy of the subject; it contains whole pages giving the yearly variations in workmen's wages, in the price of corn and other necessities, and in the even more varying values of the many different kinds of coin current in the district during those centuries. It would form an indispensable foundation for any exhaustive study of medieval building methods.

(1) It corroborates very strongly the evidence of other records as to the casual employment of ordinary workmen; and even, sometimes, of master-masons.

Xanten had one peculiarity until 1374; the master-mason was a member of the Chapter, with a canon's pay. I have already expressed my doubts whether he had, as Beissel assumes, the full constitutional rights of a canon; if only because two other canonries were shared between the three cooks, and one other between the three bell-ringers. But at least it meant that he was well paid and had a secure position. It possibly meant, also, that the job went rather by favour than by capacity, as was too often the case with all Chapter prebends in those days, so that the *Magister Lapicida* was too little of a working mason and too much of a figure-head.

Certainly the system does not seem to have been working well when our accounts begin (Part I, p. 106). In 1358 a new chapter-house was begun, and the mason-prebendary, Master Jakob, engaged another master-mason from Douai to work with him. " But Master John of Douai did not stay long in Xanten; he moved on. His place was taken by Master Riquinus; but he also stayed only three weeks. . . . So far as we can gather from the accounts, these masters got no higher pay than Master Jakob's other workmen. When Master Riquinus went off suddenly, the Clerk of the Works, Heinrich v. Tyzel, was in great straits; for it seems that he got on ill with his workmen and that the frequent changes were laid at his door. So he sent a hasty messenger to Rheinberg, to fetch Jakob the mason. Jakob came indeed, but he also soon went off. The only one who stuck to his work was Master Jakob's second workman, Hannekins or Little Harry. Next year, Master Jakob cut molds for his assistants from boards, and from these they worked at the tracery of the new windows. But at the beginning of winter he had only one assistant (*socius lapicida*) and, when necessary, two labourers. About twelfth-night came a new journeyman from Cleves, and soon afterwards a third. But soon the whole lodge was broken up. At the beginning of Lententide, 1360, Master Jakob gave notice to the clerk of the works that he would seek his fortune elsewhere. Two of his journeymen followed him; the third stayed four days longer, and then departed also. The clerk had to buy from Master Jakob's wife the necessary tools for continuing the job, and a number of stones that belonged to her husband. Then he besought Master Heinrich v. Mainz, Master Jakob's brother, to undertake the continuation of the work. He consented, and began on April 4 with one journey-man, Tilkin. On Sunday after the Assumption [August 15] he began building the vault. When it was finished, the clerk of the works gave him 3 mark [the equivalent of seventy-two days' pay for a mason] [' for a gown and a courtesy '], that is, a reward for his trouble, with which he might buy a new gown. He took them and went; for the chapter-house was finished."

In 1374 Master Jakob died; the Chapter threw the income of the prebend into the fabric-fund, and engaged each later master by a separate contract. Master Conrad of Cleves was appointed; he was building at the same time upon the collegiate church at Cleves; he and his journeymen went backwards and forwards from one to the other (I, p. 118). Only two were working regu-larly at Xanten. In 1396 the work was under two masters from

Cologne, one engaged definitely for four years, and the other working under him (p. 125). The journeymen were often changing (p. 126). Again, in the period 1421–3, " four to eight journeymen worked under Master Gisbert, often changing " (p. 137; fourteen mentioned by name, of whom two were masters). In about 1472 some sort of local school seems to have grown up, and the changes are apparently fewer (p. 168). Yet between 1493 and 1518 the local men, though they formed a steady kernel, are in a minority, and Beissel notes how many came from more distant parts (pp. 193–4).

Against the foregoing evidence, we must put the fact that the small permanent or quasi-permanent staff worked regularly. This is brought out by the following table (Part II, p. 157) of the days' work actually done by the master and his men during a period of two and a half years. The master, he notes, was probably a good deal absent on other business, and Hermann went often to fetch consignments of stones. This latter reason seems scarcely to hold; in that case, the payments for his travel-days would be traceable in the accounts, and could be added to the rest.

Days worked by	1435		1436		1437
	Summer	Winter	Summer	Winter	Summer
Master Gisbert	118	67½	157	70	77
Johann Bertkens	113	72½	181	72	89½
Hermann v. Wintern ..	113	72½	138½	74½	73
Theodorich Moer	112½	73	168½	74	85
Hermann v. Offenburgh ..	—	—	35½	—	89
Tilmann v. Köln	—	—	24½	—	89

(2) At Xanten, as usually elsewhere, the masons were paid less for a winter than for a summer day. Beissel has worked out very carefully the average of cessation for holy-days in the years 1358 and 1495. In each case, the men had almost exactly five working-days per week. Thus, he concludes, " The workmen of ancient days had less work, yet more pay," than in 1889.

(3) Very interesting details are given, though late in date, for the house-rent of master and journeymen. In 1529, the rent of the master's house was 4½ mark, or about one-seventh of his yearly pay (II, pp. 148, 160). In 1539, the journeyman mason's

house-rent was counted at 7½*d*. a week, his daily pay being 19*d*. ;
in 1543 the ratio was 9*d*. a week and 30*d*. a day (pp. 148, 164).

The most important Xanten evidence on other points is
emphasized in my text.

(E) BORDEAUX

J. A. Brutails, *Deux chantiers bordelais* (1486–1521), reprinted
from *Le Moyen Age*, 1899–1901.

This is almost as instructive as Beissel's book, though far
briefer and dealing with far scantier documents ; it is an admirable work of scholarship.

The wandering and casual side of artisan life comes out on
pp. 30, 43–4, 51–2, 56–7. True, " a certain number of the workmen had evidently a settled residence at Bordeaux : Botarel
[the master-mason], who preceded the [two] Lebas, was bound
to employ by preference the masons of the parish " of St. Michel.
" A number of artisans at Bordeaux possessed a house, with a
garden and a little vineyard." But these were the exceptions,
" a priori, it is not very probable [in the ordinary mason's case,]
given the nomadic habits of the journeyman of the past, who
travelled from one fabric to another. Huguet Banducheau and
Yvonet Alain were faithful to the lodge [Huguet worked at least
from before September 1485 to June 16, 1497]. But many workfolk only just appear in the registers ; they were taken on, and
worked a few days or months, and then went on their way. I
have already pointed out that the workmen's names show an
origin foreign to our provinces."

On p. 62, Brutails gives full details for one of the two regular
men, Yvonnet Alain, during nearly two years. The number of
calendar days was 612 ; counting one Sunday and one holy-day
per week (as at Xanten and Eton Chapel), we get a residuum of
437 real working days. Of these he did 406. And on p. 60 Brutails
notes that when masons were engaged by the month or the year,
these steady wages were far lower than the day-wages. Upon
this he comments : " The large number of holy-days celebrated
by our forefathers has often been remarked ; even if we confine
ourselves to the material side, like certain economists who
reckon human beings by the kilogram, when the workman finds
healthy distraction outside his work, it is good for him to take
frequent rest. Perhaps France would not have been capable of the
gigantic effort which she made at the end of the eighteenth and

the beginning of the nineteenth century, if the preceding generations had been overtasked, like a great part of our present population, by unremitting labour." This comment is valuable, but it rests to some extent upon unsupported assumptions. We have strong evidence for a great deal of overwork in the Middle Ages, especially among the peasants, who formed the enormous majority of the population. And, again, contemporaries assure us that these overworked men did not always spend the holy-days in " healthy distractions," but too often fell by reaction into license and intemperance. For this evidence I may be permitted to refer to Chapters XVIII–XXV of my *Medieval Village.*

(F) Kirby Muxloe

The Building Accounts of Kirby Muxloe Castle (1480–1484), by A. Hamilton Thompson. (Leicestershire Archæol. Soc. *Transactions,* Vol. XI, 1920, pp. 193 ff.)

The editor has dealt so fully with these in his introduction that a brief notice may suffice here. The documents seem to give the same testimony as other similar records to the differences between winter and summer pay, the casual employment of some of the workmen, the " plumber's mate " ; the " warden " working under the master mason ; the equality of payment between freemason and rough-mason ; the intermittent attendance of the master-mason, who had evidently other jobs to superintend ; and the deliberate imitation of other work in the neighbourhood. Professor Thompson has, however, brought out certain peculiarities. At this Leicestershire castle, " for the most part the labourers seem to have been Welshmen, who were probably hired at Powell's recommendation [Powell was head of the labourers and received 4*d.* a day as winter-wage in comparison with their 3*d.*] Local men were hired occasionally " (p. 194). Again, there was a great deal of brickwork here, and nearly all the men engaged on this work seem to have been of Flemish origin, though one had also lived in Norfolk (p. 205). These foreigners were specially engaged upon the *pictura muri*—i.e. variegating the brickwork in patterns of different colours, as may still be seen in buildings like St. John's College, Cambridge. For a short time, six of the bricklayers worked as rough-masons (p. 206). A good deal of bricklaying was done by task-work, at 1*s.* 6*d.* per thousand (p. 210).

(G) Modern Sicily

A friend has pointed out a passage in which Professor A. Marshall saw, through modern conditions, a clear picture of what was probably normal in the Middle Ages. (*Principles of Economics,* 5th Ed., 1907, p. 687).

"Inconstancy of employment is a great evil, and rightly attracts public attention. But several causes combine to make it appear to be greater than it really is. When a large factory goes on half-time, rumour bruits the news over the whole neighbourhood, and perhaps the newspapers spread it all over the country. But few people know when an independent workman, or even a small employer, gets only a few days' work in a month ; and in consequence, whatever suspensions of industry there are in modern times, are apt to seem more important than they are relatively to those of earlier times. In earlier times some labourers were hired by the year : but they were not free, and were kept to their work by personal chastisement. There is no good cause for thinking that the medieval artisan had constant employment. And the most persistently inconstant employment now to be found in Europe is in those non-agricultural industries of the West which are most nearly medieval in their methods, and in those industries of Eastern and Southern Europe in which medieval traditions are strongest. . . . One instance, which has come under the present writer's observation, may be mentioned here. In Palermo there is a semi-feudal connexion between the artists and their patrons. Each carpenter or tailor has one or more large houses to which he looks for employment : and so long as he behaves himself fairly well, he is practically secure from competition. There are no great waves of depression of trade ; the newspapers are never filled with accounts of the sufferings of those out of work, because their condition changes very little from time to time. But a larger percentage of artisans are out of employment at the best of times in Palermo, than in England in the centre of the worst depression of recent years."

APPENDIX 12.—(CHAP. XI, p. 204)

SHOP-WORK

(*a*) Sir W. St. John Hope, as reported in *The Architect* for August 12, 1892, p. 74, speaking of alabaster works : " It would be, as Mr. Hope remarked, very interesting if anyone could find evidence as to the precise locality of the workshop from which they all came. The procedure of purchase must have been very similar to that in a monumental mason's shop or yard at the present day. The customer selected his kind of monument out of those in stock, and gave instructions as to the armorial bearings to be added, and perhaps as to the effigy. This extremely prosaic method of business was prevalent in the thirteenth as well as in the sixteenth century."

(*b*) From an able review of F. H. Crossley's *English Church Monuments*, in *The Church Times* for May 12, 1922.

" Some of the freestone effigies illustrated in this book were obviously the work of local carvers with rudimentary skill, and such examples might be multiplied from country districts throughout England. But the Purbeck marble effigies of the thirteenth century came from well-known centres of the trade ; and, later on, the alabaster workers of Nottingham and the neighbouring towns developed an industry which found its way far and wide. As a result of this centralization of manufacture there was no effort, except perhaps in rare cases, at portraiture. Mr. Crossley has done well to give an abbreviated version of four contracts for tombs, two of which relate to monuments of alabaster. The Chellaston carvers who contracted in 1419 for the tomb of Ralph Greene and his wife at Lowick, in Northamptonshire, were to furnish ' a counterfeit of an esquire armed at all points,' and ' a counterfeit of a lady lying in her open surcoat.' More than a century and a half later two Burton tomb-makers covenanted to make ' a very faire decent and well-proportioned picture of a gentleman with furniture and ornamentes in armour ' for a

NN

tomb at Somerton in Oxfordshire, while the representations of his son and daughters on the side were to be 'usual pictures.' In fact, a customer got for his money the conventional figures which the craftsman wrought from stock patterns. It was, nevertheless, the case that the craftsman worked with rare inspiration. If some alabaster effigies, like those of the Duchess of Suffolk at Ewelme and Chichele at Canterbury, are probably portraits, it is equally certain that the majority are not; but there are few in which the maker has not achieved a singular effect of nobility and calm. Realism was a comparatively late growth in the art."

APPENDIX 13.—(Chap. XI, p. 207)

THE MASTER'S METHODS

(*a*) Report of a lecture on the methods of construction at Gloucester Cathedral, by Professor R. Willis (*Gentleman's Magazine*, September 1860, p. 274).

"THE whole building, indeed, is full of peculiar and ingenious fancies. What is more peculiar than the slender arch below the great arch of the tower looking like a piece of carpentry done in stone, and apparently holding up the vault ? . . . All this appears to be characteristic of a school of masons who were extremely skilful, and glad of an opportunity of showing their skill, as a modern engineer likes to carry his railway through a chain of mountains when he has a plain valley before him, merely to show his skill. . . ." Professor Willis concluded by saying that " he admired the ingenuity of the Middle Ages, but whatever may be said of their science as shown in their masonry he believed they had none. They were perfectly practical and ingenious men ; they worked experimentally ; if their buildings were strong enough there they stood ; if they were too strong, they also stood ; but if they were too weak they gave way, and they put props and built the next stronger. That was their science, and very good practical science it was, but in many cases they imperilled their work and gave trouble to future restorers."

(*b*) Compare what Quicherat says of the methods by which Villard undertakes to teach figure-drawing (II., 282).

" Doubtless these principles were very loosely applied. . . . They aimed at reducing different attitudes to simple lines or geometrical figures, after an approximative fashion. They helped the memory to certain conventional attitudes ; the artist's eye and hand thus learned certain tricks which (as Villard claims) ' made his work easy,' because they saved him the trouble of any closer study of nature. His ' art of portraiture,' therefore, is simply a routine, just as his illustrative drawings are only patterns for certain selected subjects. Anybody may see this who is familiar with thirteenth century art ; these poses which Villard represents are just those which were most popular with the sculptors and illuminators of that time."

APPENDIX 14.—(CHAP. XI, p. 219)

THE PRENTICE'S PILLAR

A slightly different version is given by A. Kerr in *Proc. Soc. Art. Scotland*, Vol. XII, 1877, p. 232.

" AT the west end, about half way up the wall, are three heads. One in the south-west corner is that of a man with a cut above the left eye, described as the head of the apprentice who finished the Apprentice Pillar ; in a line with it, over the second pillar of the south side, is the head of a woman weeping, popularly designated that of the mother of the apprentice ; and in the north-west corner is the head of an old man frowning, representing the master mason, all of which refer to the tradition connected with the ' Apprentice Pillar.' The model of this pillar was taken from an original in Rome. On its arrival in this country, the master mason distrusted his ability to finish it without seeing the original, and therefore went to Rome to examine it. In his absence one of his apprentices dreamt that he had finished the pillar, and undertook the task, which he finished with the most complete success. On his return the master mason's envy was so inflamed that he seized a mallet and killed him by a blow upon the head. An almost similar tradition is preserved at Melrose, in connexion with the building of the east window of the abbey church."

APPENDIX 15.—(Chap. XII, p. 224)

VOUCHERS FOR CHAPTER XII

A TALE in Cæsarius of Heisterbach (Dist. viii, cap 63) suggested Roger's trust in the weight of his stones for the Day of Doom. The story of the building of St. Nicholas may be found in E. M. Beloe's *Our Churches*, or in H. J. Hillen's *History of Lynn*. For the Howards of East Winch, see *The House of Howard*, by G. Brenan and E. P. Statham, Vol. I, pp. 11 ff. For the scraps of poetry, *Piers Plowman* and Wright's *Political Songs* in the Rolls series. For St. Godric, his Life in the Surtees Society series; for Chaucer's connexion with Norfolk, the numerous and valuable publications of Mr. Walter Rye. For the mason and his dead friend's tomb, Beissel, p. 157 (1438).

For the rest, see F. Blomefield's *Hist. of Norfolk*, under the different parishes mentioned. I have permitted myself one change of dates, in antedating William Hindley's call to York; but the thing itself might just as well have happened in the first half of the fifteenth century as in the second.

APPENDIX 16.—(CHAP. XIII, p. 264)

THE VIRGIN'S ROBES

TO the evidence given in the text, let me add notes taken during my last two or three visits to France. In all cases not otherwise specified, the glass is anterior to 1300.

Troyes, (*a*) *Cathl.,* North-east Chapel. B.V.M. four times in green and red, once in green and purple. Lady Chapel, four representations, only one in blue. Choir clerestory, north-east window, many scenes, not once in blue, though once the child in her lap wears blue. In another window, crowned in heaven, she is conspicuous in blue. (*b*) *St.-Urbain.* Apsidal chapels, both north and south, are full of scenes in life of B.V.M. ; never in blue ; oftenest in green, then crimson, then dull purple.

Coutances, Cathl., central window of apse. Crucifixion, green and brown, with Christ-child white (or very pale green (?)) and brown. In other apse windows, three times in bright green and golden yellow ; once green and brown ; once green and crimson. West window, centre of circle, purple and green.

Séez, Cathl., east window of Lady Chapel (perhaps early fourteenth century), green, crimson and white. Central top window of chevet, brilliant yellow cloak and white veil, more conspicuous than blue robe showing underneath.

Lisieux, Cathl. Even the modern imitations of thirteenth century windows, being by people who knew something of archaeology, choose what colours they like for B.V.M.

Conches. Though these fine windows are late fifteenth century, yet the tradition of the blue mantle is by no means uniform.

Évreux, Cathl. South side of chevet, one crimson and gold, one white and gold, one golden robe with blue mantle. North side, heliotrope mantle with tiny traces of blue robe showing beneath. Another (early fourteenth century), pink robe and gold mantle. In the side chapels of the chevet (windows of early fourteenth century), we find plum-coloured cloak, with blue robe scarcely glimpsed beneath ; again, gold and white ;

gold and crimson; gold and pink (two cases); one case with blue mantle over gold robe. In the nave (early fourteenth century again), three times with blue mantle; otherwise brown and gold, plum-colour and green. Nave clerestory, twice in pure white from head to foot, though the glass cannot be much earlier than 1400.

Rouen, Cathl. North aisle of choir (1320 ?), brown robe, green cloak, white veil.

St.-Ouen. Chevet of Lady Chapel (1300 ?), green and crimson. Central window of choir clerestory, green robe, old gold mantle and inconspicuous blue scarf. In the other choir windows (1320 ?), thrice with blue mantle, once in green and crimson.

Bourges, Cathl. Choir clerestory, Mary in plum-colour, green and white, Child in blue. Yet Stephen and Peter, in adjacent windows, show each a mass of blue mantle. Choir triforium, Mary in crimson and green, Child in blue. Christ, next to this, is all draped in blue and gold.

Beauvais, Cathl. North-west chapel of chevet; crucifixion, green and white; coronation, all white (1320 ?). Central chapel, three times in green and yellow, four times in green and pink. In the top medallion of the left-hand window, a pink robe with greenish blue mantle. South ambulatory, second chapel from east, top medallion, green and yellow. Clerestory of apse, crucifixion, green robe and light blue mantle.

St.-Germer, Lady Chapel. Green and plum-colour; green and crimson; green alone; yellow and crimson; red robe, blue mantle; yellow mantle with just visible bit of blue robe.

Sens, Cathl. Apse, green and mauve; green and crimson.

Auxerre, Cathl. Lady Chapel, middle window, crimson and orange; white, orange and blue; green and purple; green robe, blue mantle. North-west window, green and crimson. East window (Jesse Tree), green and purple. Apse (great crucifixion), green and purple.

Amiens, Cathl. North transept, right-hand lancet, two nativities; in one Mary has a blue mantle, in the other plum robe and green mantle. Christ crowning the Virgin; she wears mauve and gold.

APPENDIX 17.—(CHAP. XIII, p. 266)

COLOURS OF CHRIST'S DRESS

THE instances here quoted are all, where not otherwise stated, from the late fifteenth or early sixteenth century, when the miracle-play conventions had had more than a century to influence pictorial art.

Rouen, Cathl. Apse. In the southernmost of the two at the end of the south aisle (thirteenth century) are several scenes of the Passion, in which there is evidently no idea of a definite scheme of colour for Christ's robes.

Rouen, St.-Godard. Easternmost window of north aisle. Heliotrope before Resurrection, crimson afterwards, including the Magdalene scene in the garden (*noli me tangere*), where Christ has no spade, but a cross and banner.

Rouen, St.-Patrice. Chevet. Same scheme as at St. Godard, except that in the Magdalene scene there is a spade instead of the cross and banner.

Rouen, St.-Vincent. (*a*) Life of St. Peter in north aisle. Here the convention is complete ; the risen Christ is in crimson, while in earlier scenes He is in dark heliotrope. (*b*) Chapels in the chevet, Passion and Resurrection. Here again the pre-Resurrection convention is complete. In the garden scene He wears a crimson robe thrown open to disclose the wounded side, just as in the scene with St. Thomas. Also, instead of the usual spade, He carries a cross.

Conches. (*a*) Upper windows of choir. Dark heliotrope in all scenes before the Resurrection, crimson afterwards in all cases, even with the Magdalene and St. Thomas. With the Magdalene He carries a spade. (*b*) Last window but one in choir. A greenish grey garment before, except that the mocking scene has a white garment, in deference to the Bible story. (*c*) Last window. The risen Christ is everywhere in a sort of reddish purple, quite different from the pure crimson which appears in many other parts of the window. In *noli me tangere*, still the same robe and the same triumphant cross as in the Harrowing of Hell. (*d*) North aisle. Last Supper. Crimson robe with purple cloak just showing on left shoulder.

Évreux, Cathl. (*a*) Lady Chapel. A large number of pre-Resurrection scenes. Here the colour ranges from a reddish purple to a tawny brown, almost Franciscan in some cases, while in others it inclines to claret. The one exception is the Transfiguration ; here again the garment is pure white, as in the Bible narrative. (*b*) In another window (about 1420) crimson never appears at all ; purple-brown robes for the Resurrection, Harrowing of Hell, Ascension, etc. (*c*) North aisle of nave (thirteenth century). In Raising of Lazarus, white robe with green mantle ; Last Supper, green robe and blue mantle ; Garden scene, white robe and spade.

Great Malvern. Choir windows. In the mockery scene, purple-brown. Entry to Jerusalem and Deposition from Cross, frankly crimson. Last Supper, crimson, rather dark, but apparently not intentionally darkened.

Pont de l'Arche. North aisle. Nearly always dark heliotrope ; but in the miracle of the loaves and fishes a crimson over-mantle is more conspicuous than the heliotrope robe.

English Alabasters in Rouen Museum. No. 71, Harrowing of Hell ; no red robe, only a loin-cloth. Again, in the Judas-kiss scene, the robe has no trace of purple-brown, only of gilding. No. 70, Judas-kiss ; white robe lined with dark blue or purple. Entombment, white lined with dark green. Rising from Tomb, white lined with dark grey or green.

Troyes, St.-Urbain. Choir chevet (thirteenth or early four-teenth century). Christ rises from tomb not in crimson, but in dull purple. *Ste.-Madeleine.* Fifteenth century windows ; no trace of the convention of purple for the Christ on earth and crimson for Christ triumphant.

Rouen, St.-Ouen. North ambulatory, early fourteenth century ; Christ on Palm Sunday in pale lilac robe with bright green mantle.

APPENDIX 18.—(CHAP. XIV, p. 272)

ANIMAL SYMBOLISM

THE peacock and pea-hen, in Berchorius, show, if possible, more plainly than the hedge-hog how fluctuating and arbitrary were the preachers' methods of exposition, even in the late fourteenth century. (*Reductorium Morale* lib. VII c. 62 (pp. 212 ff).) According to this learned monk, the peacock typifies (1) The avaricious man (flesh hard to cook, slow to decay). (2) The devil (serpentine neck and head, fiendish voice). (3) The envious man (he envies pea-hen's eggs and breaks them). (4) The envious and secretive preacher, who does not publish his sermons. (5) Devil again. (6) Pea-hen is emblem of Religion (with her 12 eggs). Peacock stands for the persecuting worldlings. (7) The proud man. (8) The perfect Religious. (9) The vain man. For the peacock's cries in the night come from wounded vanity; he wakes up in the darkness, believes that he has lost his beauty, and makes night hideous with his complaints. (10) The just man (whose voice terrifies devils, just as peacock's voice terrifies serpents). (11) Pride (for he climbs tree; this predicts rain, which symbolises ill-fortune). (12) Lust, since the usual proportion is that of one cock to five hens; on the other hand, the preacher may interpret this as charity. (13) The good prelate (protects his hens from the fox). (14) The worldling (who recognises his own and loves his own). (15) Transitory beauty, with attendant sin and shame. (16) Good men; for we know from Augustine that the peacock's flesh never putrefies, however long it be kept; thus he symbolises the incorruptibility of real goodness. Yet, in spite of all these sixteen elaborate moralizations, we know as a matter of fact that the peacock came into Christian art through pagan artistic tradition, in which it symbolized immortality, either because of its periodical renewal of its splendid feathers or because of that belief, shared by St. Augustine, in the incorruptibility of its flesh.

APPENDIX 19.—(CHAP. XIV, pp. 283, 287)

ST. NICHOLAS

THE pickling-tub is one of the most frequent of this saint's miracles in art. The stalls at Fribourg, in the great church dedicated to St. Nicholas, contain only two scenes from his life ; the murder of the children and his raising them from the dead. The Auxerre shrine of the eighteenth century has only two scenes again, the children in their tub and one of his sea-miracles.

The earliest literary account of this incident, in the pseudo-Bonaventure sermon, runs as follows (*Opera*, Mainz, vol. III, 1609, p. 220a) :—

"Fourthly, St. Nicholas followed Christ to some extent with regard to the tokens of his power in miracle-working, for he was distinguished by most noteworthy and stupendous miracles among the saints of his own day, even as Holy Church saith of him in her prayer : 'God, who hast adorned St. Nicholas with innumerable miracles'; some of which are in his legend and others I have told above. For I will quote one [here] ; and it is written elsewhere than in the Legend itself. For two scholars, noble and rich, carrying much gold with them, being on their way to learn

ST. NICHOLAS AT HONINGTON (SUFFOLK), FROM A ROUGH SKETCH.

philosophy at Athens, desired first to see St. Nicholas, that they might commend themselves to his prayers ; and they came to the city where the Bishop dwelt. Their host, seeing how rich they were, was driven by the devil to slay them and cut them piece-meal like swine and salt their flesh in a barrel. St. Nicholas, having learned this through an angel, came forthwith to the host's dwelling and pointed out what he had done ; he rebuked him sternly, and by his prayers he brought the boys back to life. Since therefore he imitated Christ in miracle-working, therefore we may apply to him that which is said of Christ : ' The children of them that afflict thee shall come bowing down to thee, and all that slandered thee shall worship the steps of thy feet ' (Is. 60. 14)."

Another most characteristic miracle is told by the Augustinian canon Myrc, for the instruction of parish priests and their flocks (*Festial*, E.E.T.S., 1905, p. 14, spelling, and a few obsolete words, modernized) :—

" Then after, for great miracles that were wrought here, it fell that a Jew let make an image of Saint Nicholas, and set it in his shop among his goods, and bade him keep well his goods while he was from home, or else he should dearly abide it ; and so went his way. So, when he was gone, thieves came and stole his goods, and bore them away. So when this Jew had come home and found his goods stolen, he was mad wroth with St. Nicholas, as it had been St. Nicholas himself, and thus spake to him : ' I took thee my goods to keep, Nicholas, for great trust I had in thee ; and now thou hast thus foully served me. Thou shalt abide it each day, till I have my goods again.' Then, as these thieves were busied in sharing these stolen goods, St. Nicholas came to them and said : ' How you have made me beaten for these goods ! ' and showed them his sides all bloody. ' Go,' said he, ' and bear his goods again, or else vengeance shall fall upon you, and you shall be hanged each one.' Then said they to him : ' Who art thou that pratest this to us ? ' Then said he : ' I am Nicholas, God's servant, that the Jew betook his goods to keep.' Then were they sore afeard, that anon, that same night, they bore again all his goods. Then, on the morrow, when the Jew saw his goods brought wholly again, anon he took baptism, and was afterwards a true Christian man, and had the blessing of Heaven."

APPENDIX 20.—(CHAP. XIV, p. 289)

CHOICE OF PATRON SAINTS

Facsimile of a paragraph in *The Universe* of June 17, 1927 :—

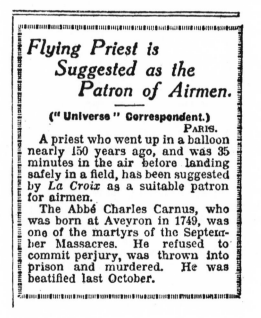

Flying Priest is
Suggested as the
Patron of Airmen.

(" Universe " Correspondent.)
PARIS.

A priest who went up in a balloon nearly 150 years ago, and was 35 minutes in the air before landing safely in a field, has been suggested by *La Croix* as a suitable patron for airmen.

The Abbé Charles Carnus, who was born at Aveyron in 1749, was one of the martyrs of the September Massacres. He refused to commit perjury, was thrown into prison and murdered. He was beatified last October.

APPENDIX 21.—(CHAP. XV, p. 299)

THE LEGEND OF ST. ANNE

THE foundation of this in the *Protevangelium Jacobi* (" Fore-gospel of St. James "), which in its earliest form may go back as far as A.D. 150. From this comes all the medieval legend of Anne and Joachim. St. Augustine and St. Jerome repudiated this kind of apocryphal literature ; Innocent I solemnly condemned it. St. Bernard, in the famous *Letter to the Canons of Lyons* (Ep. 174), in which he condemns the new-fangled Feast of the Immaculate Conception of the B.V.M., reprobates the legend ; the only support he knows is a story of a vision which he repudiates as apocryphal, and which is now universally abandoned (see, e.g., E. Vacandard, *Vie de St.-B.*, 1897, vol. II, p. 85). So, though the Joachim legend flourished in the Eastern Church, it had no real success in the West until about 1280, when Jacobus de Voragine incorporated it in his *Golden Legend.* This made the fortune of the story : St. Anne now became one of the most popular saints in the Roman Church. In 1378 the papacy formally authorized her worship, by a decree addressed to the Church in England. The cult grew to such an extent that in the eighteenth century it was necessary for Benedict XIV to condemn the teaching that Mary, like Christ, was conceived and born of a virgin.

APPENDIX 22.—(CHAP. XV, p. 317)

SCHOLASTICISM AND ART

(a) The most recent and accessible English writing on this subject is in Fr. Bede Jarrett's *Social Theories of the Middle Ages*, 1926, pp. 236 ff. The author acknowledges his debt to Jacques Maritain, for whom see section B. of this Appendix; and it seems evident that his reliance upon this author, and even sometimes his reliance upon the far more learned and accurate Émile Mâle, betrays him into reading a good many modern imaginations into the medieval moralists. It is remarkable, to begin with, how few lines even he and Maritain, though both are special students of scholastic philosophy, can find in all those scores of volumes concerning art, even though art, in those days, was held to include the ploughman and the shoemaker quite as definitely as the painter and the sculptor. What little they find, they seem to expound rather after the methods of medieval or seventeenth century exegesis than by those of modern history; a couple of words in the original give them an excuse for explanations which, I cannot help thinking, would have seemed strange to the original writer. In this way even Fr. Jarrett, who is more moderate, and who confesses that he has ventured to disagree sometimes with Maritain, produces a picture of the Middle Ages which seems strangely discordant from what we know otherwise about those times. " Medieval man was by nature a philosopher . . . by education a scientist," is a statement which, I cannot help thinking, will convey to the ordinary modern reader an impression diametrically opposed to the truth. Again, " In the eleventh and twelfth centuries, which were the real formative ages of mediaevalism, *writings and criticisms on art abound.*" The words I have italicised convey a statement of great importance, for which, so far as I can see, Fr. Jarrett supplies no real vouchers, nor any other author whom I have met with. " Everywhere was to be found symbolism of a most elaborate kind," conveys an exaggeration as great as the assertion that the medieval artist, having learned " the precise meaning of nature " from " Fra Tomaso Aquino," had thenceforward a sacramental view of nature and taught it sacramentally to the beholders ; that in short, " he was most concerned to prevent anyone supposing that a tree was only a tree." And we have the more right to be sceptical on such points when we note a good many slips. For instance, he bases an argument on the alleged " fact " that " the carica- tures begin in the fifteenth century and are never malicious," which, of course, is far from the truth. Nor, again, was Libergier the builder of the Cathedral of Reims, as the words plainly imply on p. 266. Again, Fr. Jarrett gives only inconclusive words from a modern writer in support of his assertion that " the artist, whether architect or sculptor or worker, was duly honoured at his trade " (p. 267). This, in the sense in which the whole context implies and in which the public are accustomed to hear it sometimes proclaimed, is an assertion which has never yet been supported by solid evidence. But this, after all, is only one of many chapters in Fr. Jarrett's book ; and Maritain's monograph challenges closer attention.

(b) *Art et scholastique*, par Jacques Maritain, Nouvelle éd. (Rouart, 1927).

The first thing which will probably strike any attentive and unprejudiced reader is the extraordinarily small number of really pertinent quotations from the scholastics. To begin with, the pseudo-Dionysius is frequently quoted ; yet he was no scholastic philosopher, though scholastic philosophers imagined him to have been St. Paul's disciple and constantly appealed to his authority. Again, neither he nor the scholastics proper devote themselves to the consideration of " fine art " in the more specialized sense, though they occasionally drop an *obiter dictum*, or borrow a passing illustration from it.[1] To them, all " mechanical arts " are in the same category ; the ploughman is an artist in the same sense as the sculptor or the painter. This is perfectly natural ;

[1] I use " fine art " as a convenient term, but hope that readers will not take it as begging any vital question. It may well be pleaded that a good ploughman is as real an artist as Titian ; yet, even so, we can scarcely avoid distinguishing sometimes between " fine arts " and " mechanical arts," if only to express special refinement of subject or of treatment. We may say one man has fine hair, another coarse, even when we think both equally beautiful, or that the coarse is more beautiful than the fine. There is a very real sense in which all good work is " art " ; yet this is not the usual connotation of the word, and, though an artist may gain by refusing to recognize certain distinctions, I feel that a philosopher ought to note them.

at the time when Aquinas was writing in Paris, the painters were
enrolled in the saddlers' gild, for the reason that saddles were
commonly painted. It may be pleaded, again, that to draw no
distinction between " fine art " and handicraft is a healthier state
of mind than to be hypnotized by the modern tendency to divorce
the two; but is it not a philosopher's duty to notice these
differences, even though they be only differences of degree ? And
why choose, as matter for a volume of 350 pages, a subject concerning which there is so little to be legitimately said ? This deficiency
is fairly obvious in Fr. Jarrett's chapter, where the greater part
is filled with things that are in the author's mind and that he
reads backwards into the minds of these philosophers. But in
Maritain it is far more conspicuous ; for here, after all, is not
merely a chapter but a whole volume. Therefore, if so little that
is directly to the purpose can be found in this volume, then
probably the plain man's first suspicion will not be far wrong,
and we shall conclude that philosophers who did not distinguish
between a painter and a saddler, writing for a public to whom
this distinction was equally irrelevant, were philosophers who had
not devoted much thought to theories of " fine art " in the more
specialized sense. And this impression is rather strengthened
by the pains which Maritain takes to squeeze from his scholastics
something which may seem in some way consonant with modern
thought. This comes out in his difference of opinion with Père
de Munnynck on the Idea of the Beautiful in scholastic philosophy
(p. 265) ; a difference which would scarcely have been possible
if St. Thomas and his successors had made up their own minds
more definitely, and recorded their conclusions more clearly.
But it comes out far more strongly on pp. 122, 323, where
Maritain boldly substitutes his own contradictory ideas for the
words of St. Thomas, on the plea that, if St. Thomas had devoted
more direct thought to the matter, and written more explicitly,
this is what he would have said. The saint here agrees with
Aristotle, that it is the business of the state authorities to control
the artist, by compulsion if necessary, in the exercise of his
art. In order to escape from a conclusion so inacceptable to
modern readers, Maritain pleads that St. Thomas, here, would
doubtless allow to the " fine arts " that indulgence and
freedom which he and Aristotle explicitly allow to the
speculative sciences. But is not this plea a plain example of
what Bossuet stigmatized as " the worst of intellectual vices,
the belief that things are so because we should like them to

oo

be so ? " When St. Thomas, in enumerating the mechanical arts, so carefully includes " fine art " and distinguishes all alike from the speculative sciences, do we not pay him a very poor compliment by supposing that he would have meant just the opposite if he had possessed M. Maritain's modern advantages and M. Maritain's clearness of thought ? The whole passage shows how the author, while persuading himself that he follows St. Thomas, is really voicing the catchwords of a modern clique. The Scholastics, all through this book, are scarcely more than a convenient excuse for temperamental divagations.

What, then, is M. Maritain's temperament ? He is as pessimistic as Roger Bacon was in the thirteenth century. He is convinced— or rather, like Bacon, in his imperfect acquaintance with social history he takes it for granted—that " the world from which the saints of old fled into the desert was no worse than ours is " (179). He imagines, in still more glaring contradiction with the documentary evidence, a " Middle Age that was tumultuous and passionate, but heroically Christian, making an imprint upon our civilization which four centuries of modern culture have been powerless to efface " (318). This was " an incomparable age, in which an ingenious people was fashioned in beauty without even perceiving it, as the perfection of religion is to pray without being conscious that we pray " (34). With this imaginary age he contrasts a Reformation and a modern world which are almost equally indebted to his own fancy. Though his special study claims to be in scientific theology, he imagines Luther to have hated art (209, 329), and, stranger still, claims to be contradicting the " Lutheran " doctrine when he explains to his readers that, in spite of original sin, our fallen nature " may be cured by Grace " (314). As for the modern world, it is " the corpse of the Christian world ; and its miserable state makes us yearn with special intensity for the reinvention of a true civilization " (168). It " impresses upon human activity an actually inhuman fashion, and an actually diabolic direction, since the final end of all this delirium is to prevent man from remembering God . . . Consequently it is bound, in logic, to treat as useless, and therefore as reprobate, everything which, in any way whatsoever, bears the mark of the Spirit " (60). " What makes the condition of modern art so tragic is, that it must be converted before it can find God again " (183).

Compared with all this emphatic pessimism, the suggested remedies are feeble indeed. He confesses that the clock cannot be put back, and the Middle Ages will never return (166). Protestants, of course, "are doing nothing," for Christian art (310). But, unfortunately, even in France, "Christ's spouse, our Mother Holy Church, is decked out with horrors. She, who is so fair within, is so hideous in all that shows her forth outwardly; all men's efforts tend to make her grotesque. In the first days, her body was given naked to the beasts. Then artists devoted their souls to her adornment; then vanity has come in, and at last shop-work; and, when they have thus tricked her out, they make a laughing-stock of her. They are beasts of another kind, less noble and more wicked than lions " (309). The heresies of Jansenism and Quietism, and the fresh direction given to art by the Council of Trent, have all had their share in this sad result (311); " the great churches of Lourdes are more tragic, to any reflective eye, than the ruins of Reims Cathedral " (313). So true is this that Léon Bloy, a modern Catholic, who has " an incalculable historical importance from this point of view " [i.e. of the anguish felt by enthusiastic souls], was driven to write, " We may meet with unlucky and exceptional folk who are both artists and Christians; but we cannot have a Christian art " (170, 314). For the Faithful themselves do not present a favourable soil. "Mysticism is the fashion, but asceticism is not so fashionable. It is a terrible mistake to believe that we can separate the former from the latter, and from its most certain laws." What, then, is to be done with such a society as this, a society which can indeed be stirred to sentiment, but not to self-denial and self-control? Here, apparently, Maritain himself has nothing but vague sentimentality to offer us. Two, at least, of his proposed remedies are painfully reminiscent of the *maître de danse* in the *Bourgeois Gentilhomme*, who argues that, since all the evils in the world come from want of harmony and measure, and since dancing teaches harmony and measure, therefore it is the one mistress-art of all. All true art (argues Maritain) depends upon Contemplation; but " Adam sinned because he failed in Contemplation; and from that time forward there have been divisions among mankind " (141). Again the artist fails if he lacks Prudence; but " the upshot is that, generally speaking, Catholicism alone is able to reconcile Prudence and Art, by reason of the universality, by reason of the very *Catholicity*, of Her wisdom " (328). St. Thomas Aquinas is solemnly quoted to us, in Latin, to prove that " concupiscence has no limits " (130); but from this truism we

gather no tangible results. When our author seems on the point
of giving us a definite lead, he evaporates into vague generalities.
" Christian art is defined by the subject with which it deals and
the spirit by which it works ; we say ' Christian art,' or ' a
Christian's art,' as we say ' a bee's art ' or ' a man's art.' It
is implanted in the Christian soul, by the brink of the living
waters, under the sky of the theological virtues, among the
breezes of the seven gifts of the Holy Ghost. It is natural that
it should bear Christian fruit " (111). And again : " To speak
quite definitely, faith and piety in the artist are not sufficient
for his work to produce a Christian emotion, since such an effect
always depends upon some contemplative element . . . and
Contemplation itself, according to theologians, demands not
only the virtue of Faith, but also the influence of the Gifts of
the Holy Ghost " (317). And, once launched upon this slope of
sentimentality, Maritain comes to the conclusion upon which
French authors so often converge, starting from the most varied
premises : " It would seem that, in modern times, the French
genius has a mission analogous [to that of Athens in antiquity],
but a mission which lays upon her the task of serving a loftier
universality than that of pure reason ; namely, the full
Catholicity of natural and supernatural truth " (325).

Meanwhile, there stares us in the face the painful fact that in
France, as elsewhere, dogmatic faith is on the decline ; Maritain
does not, I think, allude directly to this, but naturally it colours
his thoughts and damps his hopes. " Will this new epoch [in art]
never live except in our yearnings ? The elders have done their
work and are doing it ; everything now depends on a few young
men of twenty—and also, alas, upon the general conditions of
human life ; for every artistic epoch is a function of civilization
as a whole. The one thing certain is, that an art subject to the
law of Grace is something so difficult, and demands such rare
balances, that man is incapable of it by himself, even though
he be a Christian, and as poetic as you will. God's spirit is
needed " (175). " When we consider its human conditions,
and the present state of men's hearts, the success of that renewal
for which we hope seems strangely problematic. A rose cannot
blossom upon a dead branch, let alone upon a heap of sawdust.
I do not for a moment profess to say what will be. I do not
seek to know what poets and novelists will be doing to-morrow. I
am only trying to point out how certain deep-rooted desires in the
art of our time are stretching out in the direction of a Christian

Renaissance ; I am looking forwards to a possible future ; to what might be, and ought to be if man did not always betray those deposits which are entrusted to him. It seems to me then, that modern poetry, at least wherever it has not chosen despair instead, is aiming in art at that of which the Virgin is the perfect examplar to all time in the domain of holiness ; namely, to do common things in a divine way."

Therefore, the book as a whole seems singularly ineffective. We really learn very little about the scholastics, for the simple reason that they had so little to say about " fine art " in the modern sense, and apparently heeded it so little. They may have known, but they did not care ; M. Maritain professes to care a great deal, but he does not know. Yet this is a problem for which knowledge and patience are as necessary as desire.

APPENDIX 23.—(CHAP. XV, p. 317)

ART IN THE SERMONS

DR. G. R. OWST informs me that direct references of this
kind are, so far as his wide experience goes, infrequent and
rather commonplace. He sends a rough list, which may be of use
to anyone who wishes to pursue this subject further. (a) Bromyard,
Summa Predicantium s.v. *mundus* (wheel of fortune), *compassio*
(grinning corbel), *conversatio* ("fair paintings"), *luxuria* and
munditia (marble and painted stone tombs of the rich; cf.
Myrc's *Festial*, p. 85). (b) *Jacob's Well* (E.E.T.S., pt. i), p. 203
(robbing the poor to build churches; cf. Bromyard s.v.
bona fama). (c) Myrc's *Festial*, pp. 171 (roods and images),
187 (Peter and Paul), 108 (Annunciation), 261 (evangelists as
four beasts). Also the following descriptions seem influenced by
typical paintings: pp. 155 (hell-mouth), 238 (devil described),
268 (heavenly hierarchy).

APPENDIX 24.—(CHAP. XV, p. 319)

THE PROFESSOR OF SIGNS

From *Deliciae Literariae*, by Joseph Robertson, 1840, p. 205.

"KING JAMES VI, on removing to London, was waited upon by the Spanish Ambassador, a man of erudition, but who had a *crotchet* in his head that every country should have a Professor of Signs, to teach him and the like of him to understand one another. The ambassador was lamenting one day, before the King, this great desideratum throughout all Europe, when the King, who was a *queerish* sort of man, says to him, ' Why, I have a professor of signs in the northernmost college in my dominions, viz., at Aberdeen ; but it is a great way off, perhaps 600 miles.' ' Were it 10,000 leagues off I shall see him,' says the ambassador, ' and am determined to set out in two or three days.' The King saw he had committed himself, and writes, or causes to be written, to the University of Aberdeen, stating the case, and desiring the professors to put him off some way, or make the best of him. The ambassador arrives, is received with great solemnity ; but soon began to inquire which of them had the honour to be professor of signs, and, being told that the professor was absent in the Highlands, and would return nobody could say when, says the ambassador, ' I will wait his return, though it were twelve months.' Seeing that this would not do, and that they had to entertain him at great expense all the while, they contrived a stratagem. There was one, Geordy, a butcher, blind of an eye, a droll fellow, with much wit and roguery about him. He is got, told the story, and instructed to be a professor of signs, but not to speak on pain of death. Geordy undertakes it. The ambassador is now told that the professor of signs would be at home next day, at which he rejoiced greatly. Geordy is *gowned*, *wigged*, and placed in a chair of state in a room of the college, all the professors and the ambassador being in an adjoining room. The ambassador is now shown into Geordy's room, and left to converse with him as well as he could, the whole professors waiting the issue with fear and trembling. The ambassador holds up one of his fingers to Geordy; Geordy holds up two of his. The ambassador holds up three; Geordy clenches his fist and looks stern. The ambassador then takes an orange from his pocket, and holds it up; Geordy takes a piece of barley-cake from his pocket and holds that up. After which the ambassador bows to him, and retires to the other professors, who anxiously inquired his opinion of their brother. '*He is a perfect miracle*,' says the ambassador, 'I would not give him for the wealth of the Indies!' 'Well,' say the professors, 'to descend to particulars.' 'Why,' said the ambassador, 'I first held up one finger, denoting that there is one God; he held up two, signifying that there are the Father and Son; I held up three, meaning the Father, Son and Holy Ghost; he clenched his fist, to say that these three are one. I then took out an orange, signifying the goodness of God, who gives his creatures not only the necessaries, but the luxuries of life; upon which the wonderful man presented a piece of bread, showing that it was the staff of life, and preferable to every luxury.' The professors were glad that everything had turned out so well; so, having got quit of the ambassador, they next got Geordy to hear his version of the signs. 'Well, Geordy, how have you come on, and what do you think of yon man?' 'The rascal!' says Geordy, 'what did he do first, think ye? He held up one finger, as much as to say you have only one eye! Then I held up two, meaning that my one eye was perhaps as good as both his. Then the fellow held up three of his fingers, to say that there were but three eyes between us; and then I was so mad at the scoundrel that I *stecked my neive*, and was to come a whack on the side of his head, and would ha'e done it too, but for your sakes. Then the rascal did not stop with his provocation here; but, forsooth, takes out an orange, as much as to say, your poor beggarly cold country cannot produce that! I showed him a whang of a bear [i.e. *barley*] bannock, meaning that I did not care a farthing for him, nor his trash neither, as long's I hae this! But, by a' that's guid,' concluded Geordy, 'I'm angry yet that I didna thrash the hide o' the scoundrel!'"

APPENDIX 25.—(CHAP. XVI. p. 327)

SIR RICHARD JEBB'S PAMPHLET

HAS ART THRIVEN BEST IN AN AGE OF FAITH ? A paper read before members of the Glasgow Art Club, March 25, 1889. (Glasgow, Veir and Richardson, 1889.)

SIR RICHARD begins with a clear definition : " I am using the phrase, ' an Age of Faith,' in the special sense in which it has sometimes been employed—viz., to denote an age in which the artist, and those for whose delight he works, are alike possessed by an untroubled faith in some form of religious doctrine ; and when the artist, in treating of religious themes, is at once expressing and satisfying a religious enthusiasm." He first considers the subject generally, and confesses that, at first sight, history might seem to answer *Yes* (p. 6). " The development of Greek sculpture and of Italian painting lends some apparent force to the contention that Art has never been so excellent as when it has been inspired by religion ; it was the glow of a devout faith that lifted the imagination of Greek sculptor and Italian painter into a region of beauty higher than they could have reached by any weaker aid." But he concludes that this answer, however plausible at first sight, is not in accordance with the real facts. First, he takes the case of Greece (p. 9) : " The period during which Pheidias flourished was from 450 to 432 B.C. At that time the popular religion was still, indeed, in full external vigour ; there was no decadence in the ritual of the temples, the sacrifices, and the festivals. But, by the side of the popular religion, there was also an esoteric religion, that of men who could no longer believe in the Homeric gods or the temple myths, but who cherished a more simple faith in a divine government of the world. And there were also some who had cut adrift from all religious belief. Pheidias was the friend of Pericles ; the society in which he lived was doubtless that of the keenest intellects of his day. Glorious as were the forms which he gave to the popular gods, it is most improbable that the spirit in which he worked was that of one who regarded them with the devout faith of the simpler folk ; rather, it must have been purely the spirit of the artist and the poet—in imaginative sympathy with a popular belief which was not his own." And again (p. 11) : the artistic productions of earlier ages in Greece are rude and marked by a rigid adherence to traditional types. " They belonged to an age of simple dogmatic faith. In the age of Pheidias there were many men who, like the Ionian Herodotus or the Athenian Nicias, stood firmly on the ancient ways ; there was also a believing multitude ; but it was not, in respect to most of the finer minds, an age of faith." So, again, with Italy in the fifteenth century : " The influence of the Renaissance had, as a matter of fact, been to weaken the hold of doctrinal Catholicism on the cultivated classes. But this did not directly affect Art. The point which I desire to mark is this : that the period at which Italian painting was best was not that at which the hold of religious faith on artists was strongest ; and that the heightened excellence of Art was due to a cause wholly independent of religion, just as little was the decadence of Italian painting towards the end of the sixteenth century connected in any way with a decline of religious faith " (p. 15). " If, then, we ask what is the teaching of history on this point, the answer must be as follows : Religion has indeed supplied Art with its loftiest.themes, and has received in tribute some of Art's greatest achievements ; but the artistical result has owed its excellence to an artistic, and not to a religious motive. When Raphael painted a Madonna, the very nature of the subject constrained him to present human beauty in the highest and purest form that he could conceive. But, as an artist, he would do this equally, whether he was or was not in mental accord with the doctrinal teaching of his church. If to any this seem a truism, I would only venture to observe that it has not always, and to all men, seemed a truism. We have sometimes heard language held by critics of repute which implied that for us, in this age and in this country, the supreme inspiration of Art had for ever passed away, along with that attitude towards Catholicism which prevailed in medieval Europe." And, finally, on the wider question of art's relation to morality and religion, he concludes (p. 21) : " Art, whether consciously or unconsciously, must always be producing some moral effect on those who view its works. And Art is doing moral good in the way proper to it as Art, when, whatever its form or subject, it brings the beholder's mind into a genuine relation with natural beauty—in other words, whenever it enables the beholder to see the beauty of the created universe, animate or inanimate, with a new vividness of perception. And to do that is to serve Religion in the largest and truest sense of the word, in a sense which would have been acknowledged equally by John Knox and by St. Francis; for, when Art is most herself, then it is that she gives visible form to the precept of that sublime hymn—that utterance in which the Catholic Church of medieval Christendom is so wholly at one with our own age, in every Christian communion—

'O all ye works of the Lord, bless ye the Lord; praise Him and magnify Him for ever.' "

APPENDIX 26.—(Chap. XVI, p. 331)

ST. BERNARD AND PETER THE PRECENTOR

(*a*) St. Bernard. *Letter to Abbot William of St.-Thierry.*

" I SAY naught of the vast height of your [Cluniac] churches, their immoderate length, their superfluous breadth, the costly polishings, the curious carvings and paintings which attract the worshipper's gaze and hinder his attention, and seem to me in some sort a revival of the Ancient Jewish rites. Let this pass, however : say that this is done for God's honour. But I, as a monk, ask of my brother monks . . . ' tell me, ye poor (if, indeed, ye be poor), what doeth this gold in your sanctuary ? ' And indeed the bishops have an excuse which monks have not ; for we know that they, being debtors both to the wise and the unwise, and unable to excite the devotion of carnal folk by spiritual things, do so by bodily adornments. But we [monks] who have now come forth from the people ; we who have left all the precious and beautiful things of the world for Christ's sake ; who have counted but dung, that we may win Christ, all things fair to see or soothing to hear, sweet to smell, delightful to taste, or pleasant to touch—in a word, all bodily delights— whose devotion, pray, do we monks intend to excite by these things ? What profit, I say, do we expect therefrom ? The admiration of fools, or the oblations of the simple ? Or, since we are scattered among the nations, have we perchance learnt their works and do we yet serve their graven images ? To speak plainly, doth the root of all this lie in covetousness, which is idolatry ; and do we seek not [spiritual] profit, but a gift ? If thou askest : ' How ? ' I answer, ' In a strange fashion.' For money is thus artfully scattered in order that it may multiply ; it is expended that it may give increase, and prodigality giveth birth to plenty ; for at the very sight of these costly yet marvellous vanities men are more kindled to offer gifts than to pray. Thus wealth is drawn up by ropes of wealth, thus money bringeth money ; for I know not how it is that, wheresoever more abundant wealth is seen, there do men offer more freely. Their eyes are feasted with relics cased in gold, and their purse-strings are loosed. They are shown a most comely image of some saint, whom they think all the more saintly that he is the more gaudily painted. Men run to kiss him, and are invited to give ; there is more admiration for his comeliness than veneration for his sanctity. . . . The church is resplendent in her walls, beggarly in her poor ; she clothes her stones in gold, and leaves her sons naked ; the rich man's eye is fed at the expense of the indigent. The curious find their delight here, yet the needy find no relief. Do we not revere at least the images of the Saints, which swarm even in the inlaid pavement whereon we tread ? Men spit oftentimes in an Angel's face; [this is so shocking to the latest orthodox biographer of the Saint, that he takes the liberty of omitting it (*Life of St. Bernard*, by A. J. Luddy, *O. Cist*, p. 109). Otherwise, however, Fr. Luddy makes no attempt to minimize the bearing and the effect of this letter.] Often, again, the countenance of some Saint is ground under the heel of a passer-by. And if he spare not these sacred images, why not even the fair colours ? Why dost thou make that so fair which will soon be made so foul ? Why lavish bright hues upon that which must needs be trodden under foot ? What avail these comely forms in places where they are defiled with customary dust ? And, lastly, what are such things as these to you poor men, you monks, you spiritual folk ? Unless perchance here also ye may answer the poet's question in the words of the Psalmist : ' Lord, I have loved the habitation of Thy house, and the place where Thine honour dwelleth.' I grant it, then, let us suffer even this to be done in the church ; for, though it be harmful to vain and covetous folk, yet not so to the simple and devout. But in the cloister, under the eyes of the Brethren who read there, what profit is there in those ridiculous monsters, in that marvellous and deformed comeliness, that comely deformity ? To what purpose are those unclean apes, those fierce lions, those monstrous centaurs, those half-men, those striped tigers, those fighting knights, those hunters winding their horns ? Many bodies are there seen under one head, or again, many heads to a single body. Here is a four-footed beast with a serpent's tail ; there, a fish with a beast's head. Here again, the forepart of a horse trails half a goat behind it, or a horned beast bears the hind quarters of a horse. In short, so many and so marvellous are the varieties of divers shapes on every hand, that we are more tempted to read in the marble than in our books, and to spend the whole day in wondering at these things rather than in meditating the law of God. For God's sake, if men are not ashamed of these follies, why at least do they not shrink from the expense ? "

(*b*) Petrus Cantor. (*Verbum Abbreviatum*, c. 86.) Nearly two generations later than St. Bernard.

" Christians ought rather to exhort each other, saying : ' We have not here a lasting city, but we seek one that is to come . . . ' As one prelate said to another, ' What meaneth this loftiness of your buildings ? Wherefore have ye towers and bulwarks withal ? Thou shalt not thereby be better defended against the Devil, but all the nearer to him.' Moreover, this lust of building is testified by the palaces of princes, reared from the tears and the money wrung from the poor. But monastic or ecclesiastical edifices are raised from the usury and breed of barren metal among covetous men, from the lying deceits and deceitful lies of hireling preachers ; and whatsoever is built from ill-gotten gains is in much peril of ruin ; for, as Ovid saith, ' A sordid prey hath no good issue.' For example, St. Bernard wept to see the shepherds' huts thatched with straw, like unto the first huts of the Cistercians, who were then beginning to live in palaces of stone, set with all the stars of heaven. But oftentimes to the Religious themselves, as to other men, their own offence becomes an instrument to punish them for this disease of building ; for the construction of comely and ample houses is an invitation to proud guests. Even the granges of the monks are oftentimes castellated in self-defence."

APPENDIX 27.—(Chap. XVII, p. 346)

ARCHITECTURAL FINANCE

(*a*) It is instructive to summarize the different sources of revenue for the fabric fund at Autun Cathedral in 1294, as analysed by Quicherat (*Mélanges*, vol. II, pp. 185 ff).

These are (1) Tax on the Chapter. Receipts £160 5*s.*; arrears £68 17*s.* (2) From vacant benefices in diocese, which Pope allows to be taxed, £12 10*s.* (3) Indulgences, £24 18*s.* 4*d.* (4) Subscriptions (from clergy ?) at Pentecostal synod, £12 11*s.* 7*d.* (5) Casual receipts, including several legacies, all from peasants except one *magister*, a clerk, £34 19*s.* 5*d.* (Includes also almsboxes in different churches.) (6) Alms-boxes in other churches, regularly kept for this work; also. shares of indulgences, £10 17*s.* 2*d.* (7) Additional Chapter tax, £42 13*s.* 3*d.*

Among the expenses is an item of £1 10*s.* for the scribes copying the letters of indulgence.

(*b*) Again, Quicherat analyses the Troyes Cathedral fabric fund receipts from 1373 to 1380 (ibid., p. 194). The sources are (1) Entrance fee for newly-elected canons (£13 6*s.* 8*d.* each). (2) Endowments for the fabric fund. (3) Fees charged to pilgrims for showing the relics, or touching their linen with the relics. (4) Freewill offerings before the relics. (5) Contents of boxes placed in all churches of diocese. (6) Ditto of boxes in churches of Troyes. (7) From collectors who carried relics about. This job was now farmed out to a layman, on a three years' lease, for £20 a year. (8) Money paid for anniversary Masses and services for the dead. (9) Payments in corn for the same anniversaries, etc. (10) Subscriptions from diocesan Chapters. (11) Hiring out of palls for funerals. (12) Legacies of money, clothes, etc. (13) Offerings at the Mass of the Holy Ghost every Monday. (14) From three gilds which had their services in the cathedral. (15) Extraordinary receipts, from certain New Year's Masses, fines for trespasses on church lands, etc. (16) Friars' sermons in aid of the fabric. For instance, the Lector of the

Franciscans preached in 1372, and they gave him bread and wine to cost of 6s. 10d. Later on in the same year a Dominican preached for them. (17) About 1382, the Cathedral obtained bulls of indulgences from Pope Clement, for which they laid out £6. (18) In 1385 the Bishop laid the first stone of the pulpitum and paid £5 ; a canon gave 5s. for laying the second stone ; another £2 for a vault for his coffin under the pulpitum.

(c) Quicherat analyses similarly the accounts of St.-Ouen at Rouen, under nine different heads (ibid., p. 222 ; A.D. 1321).

(d) When Chapter XVII was already printed, Miss K. Wood-Legh drew my attention to four entries in the *Calendars of Papal Letters*, which showed how parish endowments were appropriated —and, as most of us would feel, unfairly appropriated—to the fabric of some church of which, in some cases, parishioners can never have heard. In 1306 the brethren of Sempringham obtained papal licence thus to swallow up the parish revenues of Thurstanton and Norton Disny " to rebuild their monastery." In 1320 the canons of Hereford, impoverished for the moment by their building expenses and by what they had paid to the papal court for the canonization of their bishop, St. Thomas de Cantilupe, were allowed to appropriate Scenigfeld. In 1343, St. Peter's at Northampton, with two dependent chapelries, was appropriated to the hospital of St. Katharine by the Tower, which " has begun to build a fair church." In 1363, St. Thomas of Salisbury was appropriated to the Cathedral repairs for six years. (*C.P.L.*, I, p. 462 ; II, pp. 14, 196 ; III, p. 88 ; IV, p. 89.)

By way of comparison, readers may be interested to see what has been done by different Masters and Fellows of one of the smaller Cambridge Colleges (St. Catharine's) for the building and the educational endowment of their own house. It will be seen that they do not suffer by comparison with the Middle Ages. HUGH GARNETT, Fellow of the College, besides other gifts, gave in 1526 his lands, messuages, and moveable goods. EDMUND HOUND, Master, left in 1577 a legacy of £100. THOMAS BUCK, Fellow of the College, gave much help towards the completion, in the year 1630, of the building thence called after his own name. JOHN EACHARD, Master, devoted his private fortune to the rebuilding of the College. By his own gifts and by the gifts of others he provided over £10,000 for the new buildings. JOHN SLADER and DANIEL MILLS, Fellows of the College, gave towards the rebuilding the former £200, the latter £160. PETER FISHER, JAMES CALAMY, OFSPRING BLACKHALL, Bishop of Exeter, and

JOHN JEFFERY, Archdeacon of Norwich, all formerly Fellows of the College, gave much help towards the new buildings; as did also all the Fellows of the College then existing, by resigning much of the profits of their Fellowships. SIR WILLIAM DAWES, Baronet, Master of the House and Archbishop of York, gave three years' profits of the Mastership towards building the Chapel. He gave further, in the year 1714, £100 to release an annuity payable by the College, and made annual payments up to the time of his death towards other annuities. JOHN ADDEN-BROOKE, M.D., formerly Fellow of the College, the Founder of Addenbrooke's Hospital in this town, left a legacy of £110. JOHN LENG, Bishop of Norwich, formerly Fellow of the College, left by will £20, having before benefited the College by the resignation of much of the profits of his Fellowship. Dr. CROSS and Dr. HUBBARD, Masters, gave, the former a tenement and gardens adjoining the College, the latter a legacy of £40. THOMAS SHERLOCK, Master and then Bishop of London, gave lands and tenements to increase the stipend of the Master's Sizar and to found a Librarians' Scholarship. He gave also his library of books and £620 towards fitting up the Library. JOSEPH PROCTOR, Master, gave during his lifetime £1,000 and also purchased land to increase the revenues of the Mastership. He died intestate, but his nephew and heir-at-law, FRANCIS PROCTOR, Fellow of the College, made over the property which Dr. PROCTOR had intended to bequeath. CHARLES WILLIAM BURRELL, Fellow of the College, gave certain lands during his lifetime to increase the dividends of the Fellows, and also gave £1,000 in cash. At his death in 1843 he left to the College £8,000, the greater part of his private property. EDMUND YORKE, for fifty-three years Fellow of the College, at his death in 1873 left £4,000 for the educational purposes of the College. THOMAS WORTLEY DRURY, Bishop of Ripon, Master, founded an Exhibition for students desiring Holy Orders and did much for the adornment of the Chapel.

APPENDIX 28.—(CHAP. XVII, p. 361)

ETON INDULGENCES

(Sir H. Maxwell Lyte. *Hist. of Eton College*, 1911, p. 9.)

"HIS [Henry VI's] envoys in Italy were instructed to apply for Papal Indulgences, which would attract strangers to Eton, and make its name famous throughout England. They succeeded in obtaining a bull granting to all penitents who should thenceforth visit the Collegiate Church of Eton at the feast of the Assumption in August, Indulgences equal to those which could be obtained on the 1st of that month at the church of St. Peter ad Vincula at Rome. All those who wished to partake of these privileges were ordered to contribute towards the maintenance of the College, and expected to offer prayers for the Founder. A year, however, had not quite elapsed from the date of this bull, before Eugenius the Fourth was induced to enlarge its provisions, by making the Indulgence plenary instead of partial, although limited to the lifetime of Henry the Sixth. Nevertheless, he warily introduced a clause enacting that three-quarters of the offerings of the penitents should be devoted towards the defence of Christendom against the Turks, an object in which he naturally felt more interest than he could feel in the prosperity of a new college in a distant land. The Bishop of Bath, the Chancellor of England, was entrusted with only one key of the alms-box at Eton, the other being committed to the Pope's collector. Chester and Caunton must have represented that these changes did not effect all that was desired by their royal master, for another bull was issued in favour of Eton a few weeks later. The Provost was thereby authorized to hear the confessions of all members of the College, either personally or by deputy, and, if desirable, to release them from excommunications, suspensions and interdicts, and even to absolve them once in cases specially reserved for the consideration of the Holy See. Inasmuch as the penances were in some cases to be continued by the heirs of deceased penitents, it is evident that they must have ordinarily consisted of monetary payments. The Pope, however, tried to guard against persons committing deliberate sin in the expectation of an easy absolution, by making certain fasts a certain part of the penance. Soon after the receipt of the Bulls of Indulgence, Archbishop Chicheley wrote to the Bishop of Exeter, ordering him to publish them in his diocese, and describing them as more ample than any hitherto issued by any Pope. The King, too, had his tents repaired ' on account of the Indulgence to be had,' at his College of Eton, perhaps with a view to providing shelter to visitors. It would appear that the payment made to the Roman Court ' for one Indulgence ' amounted to more than £158. The acceptance or publication of papal bulls was strictly illegal in England at this period under the Statute of Provisors, and offenders were liable to suffer forfeiture of their property, and indefinite imprisonment of their persons. Henry the Sixth therefore took care to provide against such a contingency in the case of the members of his new College, by issuing to them a pardon for all bulls already received, and a general licence to receive others in future. In May 1443, a third agent was despatched to Italy, in the person of Dr. Vincent Clement, a papal chaplain, for whom Henry the Sixth had, with some difficulty, obtained a degree at the University of Oxford."

APPENDIX 29.—(Chap. XVIII, p. 374)

DIVES AND PAUPER ON IDOLATRY

THE statement in my text is sufficiently startling to need a documentary voucher here, especially as the incident is typical of the treatment of this and similar subjects in books which are widely read.

Cardinal Gasquet, in a volume called *Monastic Life in the Middle Ages* (Bell and Sons, 1922), reprinted an earlier essay on "How our Fathers were taught." He there undertakes to disprove the idea that the Reformers had real religious justification for their destruction of images and whitewashing of walls; and he quotes largely from the dialogue of *Dives and Pauper*, which was probably written by a Franciscan friar about A.D. 1400, and which is certainly one of our best authorities for this and similar subjects. But this is a very rare book; and, since the Cardinal nowhere gives a single reference to section or chapter which might help the reader to check his quotations, any unfortunate student who wished to follow the matter up might waste many hours in the search. Under cover of this silence, the Cardinal treats *Dives and Pauper* by a method which can be exposed only by printing here nearly a page from his book (p. 75). He there writes: "One of the boasted reforms of the early English Protestants was that they had put a stop to the adoration which was paid to the cross and in particular had forbidden the retention in the service of Good Friday of any semblance of the old practice of honouring it by what was known as 'creeping' to it; that is approaching it with bended knee. It was claimed that by allowing this customary reverence, the Church had given occasion for the growth of serious superstition among the common people, amounting in reality to practical idolatry. In view of this it is interesting to see how Pauper deals with this question :—

'[On Good Friday],' says Dives, 'especially in Holy Church, men creep to the cross and worship the cross.—That is so [replies the teacher], but not in the way that thou meanest. The cross that we creep to and worship so highly at that time is Christ Himself, who died on the cross on that day and for our sake ... But He is that cross, as all doctors say, to whom we pray and say "*Ave crux spes unica*—Hail thou cross, our only hope."—But [rejoins Dives] on Palm Sunday, at the procession, the priest draweth up the veil before the Rood and falleth down to the ground with all the people, saying thrice thus : "*Ave Rex noster*—Hail, be Thou our King!" In this he worships the image as king!—Pauper : Absit! God forbid! He speaks not to the image that the carpenter hath made and the painter painted, unless the priest be a fool, for the stock and stone was never king. He speaketh to Him that died on the cross for us all—to Him that is King of all things ... For this reason are crosses placed by the wayside, to remind folk to think of Him who died on the cross, and worship Him above all things. And for this same reason is the cross borne before a procession, that all who follow after it or meet it should worship Him who died upon a cross as their King, their Head, their Lord, and their Leader to heaven.'"

So far writes and quotes Cardinal Gasquet ; and certainly, to any incautious reader who fails to weigh these words from *Dives and Pauper* again and again, and to note their inconclusiveness, they do give superficial colour to his contention that there was no danger of idolatry, and that the Reformers' iconoclasm had no religious justification. But when we look at the original, and realize the significance of the omission which is represented by those three unemphatic dots, we find that a whole column has been left out, so that the passage thus suppressed is actually longer than the passages which Cardinal Gasquet has thought fit to print. And, stranger still, that omitted column flatly negatives the apology which the Cardinal has painfully constructed from those mutilated remnants which he has put before his readers! For, in that column, the good friar expresses his regret that some of the Church services do in fact lend themselves to most regrettable misunderstandings as to worship of the cross. The official language, he writes, " blindeth much folk in their redynge.[1] For they mean that all the prayers that Holy Church maketh to the Cross, that she maketh them to the tree that Christ died on, or else to the cross in the church, as in that anthem, *O crux splendidior*. And so for lewdness they be deceived, and worship

---

[1] I.e. *interpretation*. The elementary medieval dictionary called *Promptorium Parvulorum* gives " Redynge =*Interpretacio*." *Mean*, of course, is used for *think* in the English of that date. So *tree* is commonly used for *wood*, and *lewd* for *illiterate*.

creatures as God Himself" (Com. I, ch. 4, ed. Berthelet f. 15b). Moreover, the author recognizes the seriousness of such mistaken devotions; for he writes: "Therefore they who make their prayers and their praises before images and say their *Pater noster* and their *Ave Maria* and other prayers and praises commonly used by Holy Church, or any other such, if they do it to the image and speak to the image they do open idolatry. Also they are not excused even if they understand not what they say, for their lights and their other wits, and their inner wit also, showeth well that there ought that no such prayer, praise, or worship should be offered to such images, for they can neither hear them, nor see them, nor help them in their needs." This passage Cardinal Gasquet quotes on p. 77 in support of his contention that there was no serious danger of idolatry; whereas, when we restore that crucial column which he has taken the liberty of suppressing, this farther quotation adds emphasis to the already acknowledged danger.

APPENDIX 30.—(CHAP. XX, p. 407)

ART AND PURITANISM

I HAVE dealt more fully with this subject in *From St. Francis to Dante*, and in vol. I of *Five Centuries of Religion* (see indexes under *Puritanism*). I had not then the advantage of reading Mr. Joseph Crouch's *Puritanism and Art* (Cassell, 1910), a book which justifies its sub-title : *An Enquiry into a Popular Fallacy*. The author is not a medievalist, but his occasional inaccuracies in this field supply an indirect testimonial to his honest attempt to see both sides ; they are quite as often, and perhaps oftener, " to his own hurt " than not. He shows how far even pre-Reformation art had lost touch with the people (p. 79), and how the objections of the early Reformers rested not on aesthetic indifference, but on serious doctrinal differences (chapter V, esp. pp. 106–7, 126–8). He emphasizes the vandalism of Laud, who regarded art, as the Puritans did, rather from the theological than the aesthetic point of view (p. 158) ; he shows how Mary I, like her doctrinal antagonists, regarded the theatre more from the political and social than from the artistic point of view (272 ; cf. 281) ; how little the post-Reformation Roman Church has done for the best art (301) ; and, on the other hand, how much has been done for religious art of their own accord by great Protestants like Dürer (305 ff.), Rembrandt (320 ff.), and the English landscapists, of whom so many came from the same district as Cromwell's Ironsides (336 ff.). No student can neglect this book who really wishes to see both sides of the question.

APPENDIX 31.—(Chap. XX, p. 418)

ARCHITECTURE AND NATURAL SCENERY

(a) Ruskin, *Seven Lamps*, Bk. III, §§ 23, 24.

" THE relative majesty of buildings depends more on the weight and vigour of their masses than on any other attribute of their design ; mass of everything, of bulk, of light, of darkness, of colour, not mere sum of any of these, but breadth of them ; not broken light, nor scattered darkness, nor divided weight, but solid stone, broad sunshine, starless shade. . . . It matters not how clumsy, how common the means are, that get weight and shadow—sloping roof, jutting porch, projecting balcony, hollow niche, mossy gargoyle, frowning parapet ; get but gloom and simplicity, and all good things will follow in their place and time ; do but design with the owl's eyes first, and you will gain the falcon's afterwards. . . . We have other sources of power, in the imagery of our iron coasts and azure hills ; of power more pure nor less serene than that of the hermit spirit which once lighted with white lines of cloisters the glades of the Alpine pine, and raised into ordered spires the wild rocks of the Norman sea ; which gave to the temple gate the depth and darkness of Elijah's Horeb cave ; and lifted, out of the populous city, grey cliffs of lonely stone, into the midst of sailing birds and silent air."

(b) Der Jüngere Titurel. (Sulpiz Boisserée, *Ueber die Beschreibung des Tempels u.s.w.*, 1835 ; cf. Blanca Röthlisberger, *Die Architektur des Graltempels u.s.w.*, Bern, 1917.)

This poem, written by Albrecht von Scharffenberg in about 1270, is a continuation of Wolfram von Eschenbach's unfinished *Parsifal*. Early in the poem, Albrecht describes how King Titurel built a temple for the Holy Grail. The Grail had here the talismanic power of fulfilling every wish of its possessor with regard to the temple ; thus the King dreamed his building into actuality, and we have a perfect edifice without a single human workman. This conception gives full licence to the poet ; he may give the freest possible rein to his imagination ; and, from one point of view, this adds special significance to his elaborate picture of the Graal-Temple.

The German poet, like Chaucer, shows frequent disregard of the actual artistic traditions of his own day ; and it is note-worthy that so many of his imaginations turn towards the direct imitation of nature. This temple of the Holy Grail, resembling in general construction a late Romanesque church, is designed in many details to transport us straight to the forest or the sea-shore. The matters upon which dogmatic symbolism would lay most stress are passed over rapidly. There are angels, and apostles, and the Crucifix, and the Virgin, and the Last Judg-ment ; the figures are so impressive that " rude folk would think them alive " ; but all this is briefly told (strophes 7, 8, 100 in Boisserée). The portals, again, are set with precious stones, and golden letters rehearsing the occult virtues of each stone ; but this is by no means peculiar to Christianity (94). Outside, were two long friezes of sculpture, that showed fighting Templar Knights and dwarves and sea-monsters interwoven with vines (49, 50) ; this work moves the poet to admiration : " I tell you truly, if my neighbour would scan that marvellous carving from end to end, he might well stand there until his housewife had finished her dinner." But here, again, is nothing which differs, artistically, from what might have been carved on a Walhalla. The poet's highest efforts are spent upon the choir arcade and the organ at the west end of the temple. In the choir, above the stalls and the carved screens of precious wood, rise the great arches on pillars of bronze ; from each capital there grows a vine, which climbs to the crown of the arch and thence descends, intertwining with its sister-vine from the neighbouring pillar ; both together " hung down a good fathom and a half over the stalls. Beneath, it was set with marvellous flowers, with roses sprouting white on trees and twigs ; white lilies, again, with their green leaves and stems ; there could the earnest gazer see the counterfeit colours of all precious flowers, the blossom of every herb that grows, of all high and noble herbs ; of all such could a man see some counterfeit trembling there in beauty, with hue and form that matched them well, stem and leaf and flower and tendril, and all in a thicket of gold. The vines were of solid gold, yet green-enamelled, for counterfeiting of the vine and for gladdening of men's eyes, and for the shade that it gave from many a wondrous gleam, so that all the walls of this choir were almost draped in emerald. The branches hung so thick that, when any breeze stirred, then men heard them tinkle gently in sweet harmony, even as though a thousand falcons should hover in a flock, with all their golden bells ringing together. Over these vines hung many a cloud of angels, as though they were fresh from Paradise; and when the vine branches began their melody, then the angels moved like living souls."

So, again, with the organ-loft at the west end (97-100). There was wrought " a tree of red, red gold, with leaf and branch and twig, whereon there sat, as had been devised, a throng of fowls on every hand, of the best that men praise for their sweetest strains; and, when the organ-bellows blew, then sang each after his own song. One sang high and another low, even as the keys moved them; the wind, by cunning work, rustled hither and thither in the tree; well knew the organ-master which of the fowls he would impel; well knew he the key that moved each to sing. Four angels stood firm on the top of the topmost branches, each with a golden horn in hand; mighty was the blast they blew, and with their other hand they beckoned, as who should cry, ' Awake, up, dead men all!' There stood the Last Doom, not painted, but cast [in bronze]; clear was the warning that came from the rueful faces of the sinners, so that the sour should go ever with the sweet, and man, in his hours of joy, should bethink him of that day of mourning."

Most original of all, perhaps, is the pavement of this Grail-Temple (101-103). The building was founded on a rock of onyx; and " here below on this onyx were graven and carved fishes and figures of every sort of sea-monster, each in his proper form; they moved even as though they were wild creatures. For pipes from without ran in all round, and the pavement was of crystal clear, under which they flickered in these gusts even as though they lived in the waves; the bellows that breathed this life into them were moved by far-off windmills. Thus did the pavement delight men's eyes and show as a sea with wallowing waves, yet covered all with ice, so clear that there-through men saw a whole world of fishes and beasts and monsters of the deep, with restless stress and storm."

We have, in this last episode, a living commentary on many of Villard's problems that might otherwise seem trivial to us. In their pleasant hours of evening speculation over the wine-pot or on the tavern bench, these medieval workmen threw out many hints which might bear indirectly, if not quite directly, most excellent fruit. This living sea under the crystal floor was indeed possible only in the romance of Titurel, where the Grail itself has the virtues of Aladdin's lamp, and where Albrecht can say here, as the Bible tells us of Solomon's temple, that all these marvels were wrought without sound of axe and hammer. But in the actual mason's or carpenter's shop, where axe and hammer were loud enough, two at least of Albrecht's Grail-wonders were sometimes wrought. That fantasy of the angel and dove, which came down from the vault at the moment of consecration in the Mass (16), was realized, for instance, at King's Lynn, and at Hull after the Lynn model; and Villard (plate 43) devises a similar mechanism for the reading-desk, which it is likely enough he not only planned, but executed somewhere; when the deacon reads the Gospel, the eagle on whose wings the book reposes will turn his head to listen. Again, the vocal birds on the organ have their actual exemplars elsewhere. In vol. 18 of *Annales archéologiques* (p. 90), X. Barbier de Montault figures a drawing made by Dom Martin Gerbert, of St. Blasien, from a MS. which by its style seems German of the twelfth century. The inscription reads " Arbor fusilis de qua in Alexandri gestis legitur quod in imis inspiratur et per ora avium dulces et diversas emittit voces "— " A tree of cast metal, whereof we read in the Deeds of Alexander that it takes its breath from below, and gives forth divers sweet sounds through birds' beaks." And Barbier quotes two historical examples. The Greek emperor Theophilus (829–842) ordered two great golden organs, set with precious stones, in which the sounds came through birds ; again, one of his later successors, Constantine Porphyrogenitus (911–959) had a similar golden organ-tree with birds fixed into one side of his throne. It is quite possible that later legend attributed one of these two marvellous imperial mechanisms to the great Alexander.

ORGAN-TREE (12TH CENTURY).

APPENDIX 32.—(Chap. XXIV, p. 473)

STANDARDIZATION BY ACT OF PARLIAMENT

STATUTE of 17 Ed. IV, Chapter 4.   The King in Parliament commands : "That every such plain tile to be made shall contain in length ten inches and a half, in breadth six inches and a quarter of an inch, and in thickness half an inch and half a quarter at the least. [Roof tiles and crest-tiles to measure 13in. × ⅜in. 'with convenient deepness according'; gutter-tiles and cover-tiles to be 10½in. 'with convenient thickness, breadth and deepness according.'] And if any person or persons set to sale to any person or persons any such tile above specified, made or to be made contrary to the said ordinance, then the seller thereof shall forfeit to the buyer of the same the double value of the same tile, and besides that, shall make fine and ransom to the King at His will." Justices of the peace are to have full power of enquiry, and to inflict a fine regulated normally at 5s. per thousand bricks, 6s. 8d. for every hundred roof-tile, and 2s. per hundred corner-tile or gutter-tile, sold in contravention of this statute.

APPENDIX 33.—(CHAP. XXIV, p. 477)

MONTALEMBERT ON VANDALISM

(*Collected Works*, vol. VI, pp. 1 ff., a letter to Victor Hugo, published in the *Revue des Deux Mondes*, March 1, 1833.)

WITHIN the last few years, thanks in a great measure to Victor Hugo's own writings, " the happiest reaction has shown itself everywhere in favour of historical truth and of respect for ancient creations. France alone has remained outside and behind this movement," even behind Italy, " where the paganism of the Renaissance made most progress and struck deepest root." " In England, for more than a century, men have been restoring and building all their churches on the medieval model. . . . The King of Prussia, an intolerant Protestant sovereign, has laid upon the whole Grand Duchy of the Lower Rhine a special tax, named *Cathedral-tax*, wholly devoted to the upkeep and the gradual completion of the Catholic Cathedral of Cologne, the metropolis of Catholic art and Gothic architecture . . . . So it is only in France that vandalism reigns alone and unrestrained. After spending two centuries, and thirty years again, in dishonouring our ancient buildings with base and grotesque additions, vandalism now takes the terrorist attitude and wallows in destruction . . . . It is like a conquered land in which barbarous invaders are seeking to efface the very last traces of the generations which have dwelt in it . . . . Men cannot even respect the ruins they have themselves made." In England and Germany, owners maintain the old castles with real pride ; but, in France " the old lord puts them up for sale to the highest bidder ; the new citizen buys it . . . and both conspire together to dishonour the old stones."

In France antiquity is respected only on condition that it shall not be Christian. " You cannot melt the divans of the provinces to pity, or the *savants* of the empire, except by invoking the respect due to paganism. If you can make them believe that a church in the ante-Gothic style was dedicated to some Roman god, they will promise you protection, untie their purse-strings, and even cut their pens to honour your discovery with a dissertation.   There would be no end to the enumeration of all the Romanesque churches which are tolerated only in virtue of this ingenious creed.   I will only quote the cathedral of Angoulême, whose curious façade has been spared only because it has been gravely proved that the bas-relief of the God Almighty, which figures there among the symbols of the four evangelists, was a representation of Jupiter."

Montalembert proceeds to arrange a list of Vandals in order of merit—i.e., in proportion to their degree of hatred for " old-fashioned stuff."   This list runs (p. 17) : "A. *Destructive Vandals* (1) the Government, (2) Mayors and Town Councils, (3) Owners, (4) [Church] Fabric Committees and the Parish Clergy, (5) (far behind the other four) Revolt. B. *Restoring Vandals* (1) Clergy and Fabric Committees, (2) Government, (3) Town Councils, (4) Owners. As for Revolt, it may at least be said for it that it never restores."   After spending 23 pages on instances of destruction by the first three categories, he devotes ten more to No. 4, the Clergy (p. 44).

" They seem to have said to each other [since the Restoration of the Monarchy], ' Now the evil days will end ; a new era of prosperity and brilliance will dawn for Catholicism in France ; so let us put our churches in holiday trim. We must make the poor old creatures young again ; we must lend all the freshness of youth to these ancient monuments of an ancient creed ; then we shall struggle better against all the new religions that swarm around us. Up, then ! let us dress them in red and blue and green and white ; white above all, for that is the cheapest, and then it is the Bourbon colour too ! Whitewash, scrape, paint, plaster the rouge on their faces, let us deck all this old stuff with the dazzling adornments of modern taste ! That will be as good a way as any other to prove that religion belongs to all ages and to all generations ! . . . Very rarely can a parish priest resist the temptation of cheaply renovating his church, and thus marking his own administration. He generally gives way, in spite of the opposition of the country-folk, among whom I have often found the most laudable dislike of these novelties . . . At St. Marcellin [a town in the Rhône valley] the principal church, very remarkable for its venerable age, has been adorned with an unhappy painting of the Last Judgment, in the centre of which reigns a God Almighty wearing a red wig, with the artist's signature in full, and this perfectly apposite inscription : *How terrible is this place !* " At Avignon, a chapel once used by the Popes " has been daubed with the most ludicrous paintings . . . It is doubtless to escape from the dangers of competition that this same brush has effaced the very last traces of a priceless fresco attributed to Simone Memmi of Siena, the friend of Petrarch and Laura, wherein he had painted the two lovers under the features of St. George and the maiden whom he is delivering from the dragon. The white place is still shown [to visitors]." At Beaumont there is " a new confessional, surmounted with two keys like an inn-sign, and for which I was seeking some comparison in my mind when a peasant who happened to be there hit the nail exactly : ' That looks for all the world like a booth at the fair ! ' You may imagine how much the dignity of the sacrament gains from such a comparison."

The reader will recognize here a good deal of the rhetoric, and doubtless even of the exaggerations, which make Montalembert's *Monks of the West* one of the most popular histories even to the present day. But the pertinent consideration here is that, in both these writings, he feels the inspiration of a religious champion. Addressing Victor Hugo directly again, he concludes this long article : " We, as sons of ancient Catholicism, stand here in the midst of our title-deeds of nobility ; we have the right to love them and to be proud of them it is our duty to fight to the last for them. That is why we call upon men in the name of ancient worship, as you call upon them in the name of art and fatherland, to repeat that cry of indignation and shame which was torn from the Popes of the great centuries by the devastation of Italy : *Let us drive these Barbarians forth !* "

APPENDIX 34.—(CHAP. XXIV, p. 478)

PUGIN'S RELIGION

From J. C. Colquhoun. *Scattered Leaves of Biography.*
London, Macintosh. 1864. Pp. 348–358.

" BUT, so far from these views being supplied to him through
Romanism, they placed him in more vehement collision
with the Romish Church and its priesthood than with the Church
he had deserted. The clergy of the Anglican Church, men of
letters and cultivation, were the first to adopt the new ideas,
and to sympathise with the restored principles of art . . . In
later days, after a longer experience, he discovered that, while
the condemned Protestant Church was purifying art, and
restoring her churches after true models, his own Church was
hopelessly given over to the vilest taste and the meanest trickery
or worship and art. The debased Italian style, to which, both
abroad and at home, the Romish ecclesiastics clung, was an
abomination which Pugin condemned with the full force of his
intrepid pen. He denounced the Romish chapels as vulgar
theatres for tawdry display. ' I once had a peep,' he says,
' into Moorfields Chapel. I saw nothing that reminded me of
the ancient religion ; from the fabric down to the vestments of
the celebrants, everything seemed strange and new ; the singing,
after the solemn chants of Westminster, sounded execrable,
and I returned perplexed and disappointed.' . . . In France
Pugin found everything execrable. In Rome he had to fly in
order to save his faith ; for the music of the Roman churches
was the music of the opera, and tripping songs were substituted
' for the song of Simeon, the hymn of St. Ambrose, and the
canticle of the Virgin.' He fared no better in the cathedral of
Cologne. . . . It is evident that, as Pugin advanced in experience
and in judgment, he became more and more dissatisfied with his
position in the Church of Rome, and conscious of the mistake
he had made in joining it. In the last work he wrote, which
he left unfinished, he traced the Reformation to one of its

QQ

undoubted causes—the vices and venality of Romish ecclesiastics
—the worldliness of the Pope and Cardinals. These evils, and
the abuses of monasteries, were described by him with a pen as
bold as Luther's ; and he shows that most of the desecration of
the buildings of that day was effected by the clergy of his own
communion. Such a man, with such independence of mind,
was a very awkward convert for the Church of Rome. They
dared not quarrel with him ; they could not renounce him—
they were compelled to humour him, and, as far as they could,
to restrain his pen. Whether they would long have been able
to do this, may be doubted. He increased in determination as
he became older. His insight into their malpractices, and his
disgust at their meanness, grew with his years. See how he
speaks of their legacy-hunting. He paints the hunting of bishops
and priests after legacies, wrung from the fears or superstitions
of the faithful, and he describes the result of this, and the indignation of the relatives of the deceased, when they found
themselves robbed and deprived of their expectations. ' The
lawyers offer their services ; it is a case for a jury ; family
interests should be protected. Proceedings are begun ; then,
to prevent scandal and to stop expense, half the property is
made over in a compromise. After this ensue rival suits between
rival bishops, and the bequest, begun in fraud, perishes in
litigation.' . . .' I should view any legal exactment, that will
induce men to be more liberal during their lives and less relying
on testamentary bequests, as a great practical blessing.' . . .
It may be taken as a proof of the extreme excitement of the brain,
which precedes the nervous system giving way, that, in addition
to his labours as an architect and to the writings upon architecture which he published, Pugin had begun, early in 1851,
a theological work. Early in that year he announced it to his
friend, Mr. Minton, and it is plain, even from the title of the
book, ' An Apology for the Church of England,' that his opinions
had undergone material change. He no longer attributed to
the Reformation the dilapidation of ecclesiastical buildings,
and the decay of taste ; and he no longer expected from the
ecclesiastics of the Romish Church the sympathy and encouragement on which he had once relied. He is reported to have said,
' The rest of my life must be one of penitence, to seek forgive-
ness for the wrong I have done to the Anglican Church.' But
we do not dwell on the hasty expressions of an excited and
diseased mind."

APPENDIX 35.—(CHAP. XXV, p. 498)

VARIETIES OF CHRISTIAN SPIRIT

The Nineteenth Century and After, January 1901, p. 173 (The Right Rev. J. C. Hedley, D.D., Bishop of Newport).

" THE visibility of the Church, and the external Ministry of the sacramental system, is, as we hold, part of Christ's ordinance. And it is apparently intended for a grand moral purpose. It is intended to deepen, to regulate, and to intensify interior religion. If we believe our Lord's word, the essence of the Christian spirit is a certain childlike docility. It is a simple fact that a man cannot be childlike unless he has practised himself in submitting to another man, and in conforming himself to an external ordinance which he has not established for himself."

Ibid., February 1901, p. 306 (Herbert Paul).

" 'It is a simple fact,' says Bishop Hedley, 'that a man cannot be childlike unless he has practised himself in submitting to another man, and in conforming himself to an external ordinance which he has not established for himself.' I always distrust a man when he talks about 'simple facts.' So few facts are simple. To me this simple fact is a simple fiction refuted every day by the Society of Friends, who have the moral (not the intellectual) simplicity of children without priests or forms. They are contented with the worship of Him to whom we all pray that He will forgive us our trespasses as we forgive them that trespass against us."

INDEX OF NAMES AND PLACES

(Excluding Names of Authors in the footnotes)

Pommeraye, Dom, 219
Pont de l'Arche, 553
Poole, Dr. R. L., 256 n.
Poppi, San Torello of, 211 ff.
Pordenone, Odoric of, 253
Porphyrogenitus, Constantine, 587
Porter, A. Kingsley, 26, 48, 173-4,
   214 n. ; on freemasons, 123 n.
Portugal, 288, 468
Postel, Guillaume, 163
Pougeoise, Sir Jehan, 352
Poussin, 391
Prato, 357
Pre-Raphaelites, 244
Previté-Orton, Mr. C. W., 122 n.
Priam, 456
Princeton University, 268
Prior Park, 413 n.
Prittlewell Priory, 156-7
Provençal, 203
Prussia, King of, 590
Psalmist, The, 573
Puccini, Biagio, 445
Pugin, 478, App. 34 ; P.-Ruskin
   school, 413 n.
Purbeck, Isle of, 204, 519, 545
Puy, le, 242
Pygmalion, 457

Q

Quatuor Coronati, 13-15
Queenborough Castle, 79
Quicherat, 104, 176, 291 n., 365,
   458, 547, 575
Quincy-le-Vicomte, 161
Quivil, Bp., 203

R

Rabanus, *see* Mainz
Rackham, 519
Ramé, 23
Ramsell, 192
Ramsey, 342, 507
Ranner, John, 353
Ranworth, 149
Raphael, 420, 570; Pre-Raphaelites,
   244

Ratger, *see* St. Gall
Ratpert, 55 n.
Raunds, 178
Ravenna, 428
Raymundo, 181
Reading, 353-4
Rebecca, 261
Redon, 512
Regensburg, Berthold of, 84, 308-9,
   313, 357, 484 ; Cathedral of,
   173 ; masons at, 126, 134, 136,
   171
Reichenau, 509
Reims, Cathedral, 9, 101-2, 178,
   260, 262-3, 292, 296, 314, 318,
   383 n., 418, 560, 563 ; Annun-
   ciation-group at, 208, 419;
   Malchus-group at, 448 ff. ;
   mason's marks at, 147 n., 158 ff. ;
   Council of, 59 ; friars in, 353 ;
   St.-Nicaise-de-, 106 n., 140 ;
   St.-Remi-de-, 302, 451
Remagen, 267
Rembrandt, 391, 483, 583
Renan, 106, 108-9, 118, 412, 523
Reynard the Fox, 208, 266
Rheinfeldur, 499
Rhine, The, 213, 267, 345, 352 n. ;
   Lower, 539, 590 ; Upper, 499
Rhineland, 499; glass importa-
   tion from, 473
Rhone, R., 591
Richard I, 324
— II, 344
Richowe, Richard, 537 ff.
Rienzo, 129, 424
Rigaldi, *see* Rouen, Abps. of
Rigware, Thomas, 187
Rimini, 428, 431
Ringmore, 21, 289
Ripon, 577
Robertson, Joseph, 567
Rodrigo, *see* Zamora
Roger, *see* Helmershausen, Theo-
   philus
Rogers, Thorold, 197, 535
Roland, legend of, **267**